DATE DUE

DEMCO 38-296

BIOGRAPHICAL DICTIONARY OF BRITISH PRIME MINISTERS

The *Biographical Dictionary of British Prime Ministers* is a wide-ranging, comprehensive guide to the political lives of Britain's prime ministers, from Sir Robert Walpole to Tony Blair. Written by some of the leading scholars in British history and politics, this authoritative dictionary provides essential information about each premiership, including facts and analytical debate on seminal issues and events in British history. Each entry has been written to a consistent style and contains:

- brief biographical information outlining career history and significant dates and events
- a brief summary of the significance and peculiarities of each prime minister followed by a more descriptive and interpretative account of his or her political life and impact on British politics
- references and further reading

The *Biographical Dictionary of British Prime Ministers* addresses many of the key themes which have influenced parliamentary politics in Great Britain in the past three hundred years, such as the historical and cultural context of each premiership; party management and reform; intra-party intellectual and ideological debate and, where relevant, the evolution of the office of the prime minister in connection to the role of monarchy and the impact of mass politics.

Robert Eccleshall is Professor and Head of the Department of Politics at Queen's University, Belfast. **Graham Walker** is Reader in Politics at the same department.

BIOGRAPHICAL DICTIONARY OF BRITISH PRIME MINISTERS

Edited by
Robert Eccleshall
and
Graham Walker

London and New York

First published 1998
by Routledge
11 New Fetter Lane, London EC4P 4EE

Simultaneously published in the USA and Canada
by Routledge
29 West 35th Street, New York, NY 10001

© 1998 Robert Eccleshall and Graham Walker

Typeset in Galliard by RefineCatch Limited, Bungay, Suffolk
Printed and bound in Great Britain by MPG Books Ltd, Bodmin

British Library Cataloguing in Publication Data
A catalogue record for this book is available from the British Library

Library of Congress Cataloging-in-Publication Data
Biographical dictionary of British prime ministers / edited by Robert
    Eccleshall and Graham Walker.
        p.   cm.
    Includes bibliographical references and index.
    (alk. paper)
    1. Prime ministers – Great Britain – Biography – Dictionaries.
    2. Great Britain – Politics and government – Dictionaries.
    I. Eccleshall, Robert.   II. Walker, Graham S.
    DA28.4.B56   1998
    941'.0099 – dc21   98–11039
                                          CIP
ISBN 0–415–10830–6 (hbk)
ISBN 0–415–18721–4 (pbk)

CONTENTS

CONTRIBUTORS

Dr Eugenio Biagini
Robinson College
Cambridge

Dr Stuart Ball
Department of History
University of Leicester

Professor Jeremy Black
Department of History
University of Exeter

Dr Marjorie Bloy
Rotherham College of Arts and
    Technology

Dr Brian Brivati
School of Humanities
Kingston University
Kingston-upon-Thames

Professor Stephen Brooke
Department of History
Dalhousie University
Halifax
Nova Scotia

Professor Kenneth Brown
Department of Economic and
    Social History
Queen's University of Belfast

Professor Muriel Chamberlain
Department of History
University of Wales
Swansea

Dr Valerie Cromwell
History of Parliament
London

Dr Eveline Cruickshanks
Institute of Historical Research
University of London

Dr Stephen Driver
School of Sociology and Social
    Policy
Roehampton Institute
London

Professor Robert Eccleshall
Department of Politics
Queen's University of Belfast

Dr Richard English
Department of Politics
Queen's University of Belfast

Professor Eric Evans
Department of History
University of Lancaster

Dr Michael Fry
Historian and journalist based in
  Edinburgh

Professor Andrew Gamble
Department of Politics
University of Sheffield

Dr Keith Grieves
School of Teacher Training
Kingston University
Kingston-upon-Thames

Dr Andrew Hanham
History of Parliament
London

Professor Christopher Harvie
Department of British and Irish
  Studies
University of Tübingen

Dr Brian Hill
Department of History
University of East Anglia

Dr Boyd Hilton
Trinity College
Cambridge

Dr Ian Hutchinson
Department of History
University of Stirling

Dr Alvin Jackson
School of Modern History
Queen's University of Belfast

Professor Peter Jupp
School of Modern History
Queen's University of Belfast

Dr Michael Kenny
Department of Politics
University of Sheffield

Professor Philip Lawson
  (deceased)
(formerly at) University of
  Alberta
Edmonton

Dr Luke Martell
School of Social Sciences
University of Sussex

Professor Arthur Marwick
Department of History
Open University

Dr Jennifer Mori
Department of History
University of Toronto

Professor Philip Norton
Department of Politics
University of Hull

Dr Jonathan Parry
Pembroke College
Cambridge

Professor George Peden
Department of History
University of Stirling

Dr Marie Peters
Department of History
University of Canterbury
New Zealand

Professor Martin Pugh
Department of History
University of Newcastle

Professor James Sack
Department of History
University of Illinois
Chicago

Professor Karl Schweizer
Department of History
New Jersey Institute of
Technology

Professor Geoffrey Searle
School of English and American
    Studies
University of East Anglia
Norwich

Professor Peter Stansky
Department of History
Stanford University
California

Dr Duncan Tanner
Department of History
University of Wales
Bangor

Dr Stephen Taylor
Department of History
University of Reading

**Emeritus Professor Peter
    Thomas**
(formerly of) Department of
    History
University of Wales
Aberystwyth

Dr Andrew Thorpe
Department of History
University of Exeter

Professor Philip Wainwright
Department of History
Stanford University
California

Dr Graham Walker
Department of Politics
Queen's University of Belfast

Dr John Walton
Department of History
University of Lancaster

Dr David Wilkinson
History of Parliament
London

PREFACE

This volume, as its title suggests, consists of portraits of each occupant of the highest office in British politics since the first half of the eighteenth century. It is scholarly in approach: the assessments of the individual prime ministers are informed by a knowledge of academic findings in the field, particularly works of history but also of the social sciences and literature. Political memoirs and diaries have also been expertly mined for what they might contribute to the critical objective. Prime ministers are placed firmly, and we hope illuminatingly, in the context of their time; scholarly debates around cognate themes such as the development of party, the role of the monarch, the impact of mass democracy, and the ideological foundations of policies and programmes are alluded to where appropriate. Contributors have been chosen with a view to the new insights they might bring to their subjects, and to their command of the broader political, social and economic context. As editors we believe the volume represents a fair reflection of scholarly progress in the realm of British political history and, indeed, contemporary history. It may also be viewed as a contribution to the study of questions of leadership in British politics and society, rightly identified by a prominent British historian as a somewhat neglected theme (Clarke 1991: 1–7).

While scholarly standards have been a guiding principle, we have tried, no less rigorously, to ensure clarity and readability. We want this volume to give pleasure as well as to provoke thought; to entertain as well as to enlighten. Again, our contributors have been chosen for their abilities in this regard. We hope that readers will find complex issues to have been clarified without being oversimplified or distorted. We hope that they will appreciate and be stimulated by the range of writing styles and critical approaches which mark these appraisals.

The book is not primarily an example of the kind of scholarly contribution usually categorized as 'political science', although as editors we happen to be located in a Politics department and there are contributors here who would class themselves as political scientists. The nature of the volume precludes systematic investigation of issues pertaining to the office of prime minister and the changing role of the premier in relation to other elements of executive government and to the wider political culture of the country. Nevertheless, much may be gleaned from these pages by the student of politics on the prime ministerial careers which form part of the empirical basis of the scholarly debates about the exercise of political power in modern Britain.

Similarly, insights into the evolution of the office can be fashioned from these pages. Controversy, of course, still surrounds the question of who actually was the first prime minister, and will survive this collection. However, Stephen Taylor's discussion of this question in his appraisal of Sir Robert Walpole not only supplies powerful arguments for following convention in the choice of Walpole as the starting-point for the book (see Van Thal 1974), but also provides a guide to the means of defining the role of the office in the unreformed system of the time.

Coming up to date, the volume may also be said to be a vital point of reference for those engaged in, or concerned to comprehend, the debate over prime ministerial power which has been joined since the 1960s. The most significant contributions to this debate, involving political and academic figures such as Richard Crossman, John MacKintosh and G.W. Jones, have been well summarized by several scholars (Barber 1991: 122–37; Madgwick 1991: 234–57; Rhodes and Dunleavy 1995: 11–37, 322–5), but new variations on the theme (for example Foley 1993) suggest that deliberations in this field are taking on a greater degree of sophistication. In addition, the premiership of Margaret Thatcher has in many ways provided an ideal focus for competing perspectives, a testing ground for the theories of growth in prime ministerial power and the employment of the 'presidential' analogy on the one hand, and those arguments which stress the enduring importance of constraints on premiers on the other. The extended analysis of Thatcher's career in this book is in a way an acknowledgement of her centrality to both the ideological and governmental developments which have profoundly affected British politics and society.

Yet political science models, while often illuminating, cannot explain those aspects of prime ministerial behaviour which derive from individual personality traits and the quality of temperaments under pressure. As political circumstances and fortunes fluctuate so the strengths and weaknesses of prime ministerial personalities and their particular approaches to the office will be revealed. This volume illustrates the great variety of governing styles – from the strong conviction-based, perhaps authoritarian, leadership of Thatcher and Gladstone, through the blend of a dominant personality and fidelity to the principle of cabinet government represented by Churchill, to the more low-key chairmanship of Baldwin and Attlee. Moreover, the collection offers much in the way of character studies: there is, for instance, critical commentary on the personal features that have lowered the reputation of such premiers as Rosebery, Eden and Heath.

At the time of writing, the United Kingdom appears to be at the threshold of an era of wide-ranging constitutional reform. It is possible that the context provided by the 'unwritten constitution' and the importance of precedents and conventions to political practices – the context in which the records of the prime ministers in this volume have to be judged – will be profoundly altered. The United Kingdom looks set to be reshaped in the form of devolution for Scotland and Wales, and possibly by an evolving structure of British–Irish relations. On the other hand, speculation about the possible establishment of a prime minister's department reflects the extent to which the system of government has become increasingly centralized. It is for these reasons that we commissioned a last-minute entry on Blair, inevitably different in scope from the other contributions, whose government – committed to a wide-ranging modernizing agenda but also determined to eliminate obstacles, inside the Labour party and beyond, to its project – was elected only a few months before the manuscript went to press.

It remains to be seen whether, perhaps in a short space of time, studies of prime ministers will have to be conducted within very different scholarly frames of reference. However, there is little doubt that the endeavour will remain a fascinating one. It is hoped that readers – scholarly or lay – will find much to fascinate them here.

References and further reading

Barber, J. (1991) *The Prime Minister since 1945*, Oxford: Blackwell.

Clarke, P. (1991) *A Question of Leadership: Gladstone to Thatcher*, London: Hamish Hamilton.

Foley, M. (1993) *The Rise of the British Presidency*, Manchester: Manchester University Press.

Madgwick, P. (1991) *British Government: The Central Executive Territory*, London: Philip Allan.

Rhodes, R.A.W. and Dunleavy, P. (eds) (1995) *Prime Minister, Cabinet and Core Executive*, London: Macmillan.

Van Thal, H. (ed.) (1974) *The Prime Ministers*, vol. 1, London: Allen & Unwin.

Robert Walpole, First Earl of Orford

Born 26 August 1676, first surviving son of Robert Walpole and Mary Burwell. Educated at Eton, King's College, Cambridge, and Lincoln's Inn. Married (1) 1700 Catherine Shorter; (2) date not known, but before 3 March 1738 Maria Skerrett. MP for Castle Rising 1701–2, King's Lynn 1702–17 January 1712 (expelled from the Commons), 11 February–6 March 1712 (election declared void) and 1713–42. One of the Council of the Lord High Admiral 1705–8; Secretary at War 1708–10; Treasurer of the Navy 1710–11; Paymaster of the Forces 1714–15 and 1720–1; First Lord of the Treasury and Chancellor of the Exchequer 1715–17 and 1721–42. Created Knight of the Bath 1725, Knight of the Garter 1726, Earl of Orford 1742. Died 18 March 1745.

Robert Walpole is one of the most remarkable figures of modern British politics. He is commonly regarded not only as the first prime minister, but also as the longest serving holder of that office, his twenty-one years far exceeding the tenure of any of his successors. He was the dominant figure of the early Hanoverian period. Contemporaries referred to him as the 'Great Man' and, unlike any other prime minister, he has given his name to the period: it is the Robinocracy.

Looking at Walpole from the perspective of the early modern period, he appears as part of a long line of dominating ministers, in the tradition of Wolsey, Burghley and Buckingham. Like many of his predecessors Walpole made a personal fortune while in office and founded a noble dynasty. No subsequent prime minister was to do the same; none left behind them a country house on the scale of Houghton. In this sense Walpole marks the end of a line rather than the beginning of one. But Walpole has also long been seen as the first British prime minister. In what way, if any, was he different from his predecessors?

Walpole was certainly not the first person to be referred to by contemporaries as prime minister. Even if we ignore references to 'chief minister' or 'premier-minister', contemporary usage gives us two earlier candidates for the title of the first prime minister – the Earl of Godolphin and Robert Harley. Harley in particular was frequently described as 'prime minister' by both supporters and opponents. Nor should too much significance be attached to the fact that Walpole occupied the post of First Lord of the Treasury, which only subsequently came to be associated with the prime ministership. Indeed, George I had got rid of the post of Lord Treasurer, placing the treasury in commission and thereby creating the position of First Lord, partly because he did not want to give any one minister the pre-eminence associated with the lord treasurership.

Can we then still regard Walpole as the first prime minister? The answer to this question is not clear-cut. Contemporaries were familiar with the concept of a prime minister before Walpole rose to power, and in many respects his role was anticipated by some of his predecessors. Nevertheless, he does mark a new departure. To understand in what way, we need to look more closely at the characteristics of a prime minister in the first half of the eighteenth century.

One of the best definitions of a prime minister is provided by Clayton Roberts: 'He monopolized the counsels of the King, he closely superintended the administration, he ruthlessly controlled patronage, and he led the predominant party in parliament' (Roberts 1966: 402). This definition might be criticized, not least because it assumes a high degree of party identity. But for the first half of the eighteenth century – the period when the concept of a prime minister became generally recognized and accepted – there did exist a fairly well-defined party structure (Hill 1976; Colley 1982; but cf. Speck 1981). Moreover, by emphasizing the role of prime ministers in managing parliament for the King, Roberts highlights what distinguishes them from all first ministers (except perhaps Danby) in the pre-Revolutionary period.

Judging by these criteria, how strong a case can be made for Godolphin and Harley? For Godolphin it fails, because he shared his court influence with the Duke of Marlborough and was never a party leader. But for Harley it is persuasive, and many historians would accept Roberts's claim that Harley was the first prime minister. Nonetheless, there is a significant difference between Harley and Walpole. Even after the Tory landslide in the 1710 elections, Harley did not regard himself as the party's leader. By instinct he was a non-party manager, attempting to create a broad coalition to support the Queen's business in parliament. Walpole, by contrast, was a committed party man. He was not only the King's minister, but also the leader of the Whig party. The emergence of a prime minister in the modern sense thus owed much to the Hanoverian succession. George I had distrusted the Tories ever since their betrayal of Hanover at the Utrecht peace negotiations. He was further alienated from them by their abuse of his German advisers and the flight of two of their leaders, Bolingbroke and Ormonde, to the Jacobite court in exile. Consequently, George I, in stark contrast to both William and Anne who had preferred non-party governments, was prepared to entrust himself to the Whigs. Had the leaders of Whig government of 1717–21, Stanhope and Sunderland, lived longer, either of them, rather than Walpole, would almost certainly be appearing as the first entry in this volume.

Walpole himself repudiated the description 'prime minister', but it is important not to attribute too much significance to this. He used the phrase in the French sense of a minister who usurps the powers of the Crown itself. Nor was 'prime minister' simply a term of abuse used by opponents. By the 1730s it was being used with unparalleled frequency by supporters as well as opponents and even appeared in the title of a pro-ministerial pamphlet as early as 1731.

But when did Walpole become prime minister? Since there was no such office, whether formally or informally, this is a difficult question to answer and one which has been the subject of much debate. Traditionally his premiership is dated from his appointment as First Lord of the Treasury in 1721. Eveline Cruickshanks has suggested 1720, the year in which he rejoined the ministry, on the grounds that the Chancellor of the Exchequer, John Aislabie, was merely a figurehead (Cruickshanks 1984: 23). In fact, a date of 1723, or even later, is much more plausible.

To explain both how and when Walpole became prime minister it is necessary to go back to 1714, when he and Lord Townshend, his brother-in-law and close political ally, were two of the beneficiaries of the accession of George I. At this time they were only part of a much broader Whig ministry. Townshend, the senior of the two and a leading aristocratic Whig in the Lords, was made secretary of state, while Walpole, who had emerged as one of the leading Whig debaters in the Commons during Anne's last years, received the lucrative but junior post of Paymaster-General. In 1715 Walpole became First Lord of the Treasury and Chancellor of the Exchequer, but this did not mark their dominance of the ministry. The older Whig leaders of Anne's reign, the former Junto, were being removed by death and illness, but Townshend and Walpole had rivals in their own generation, notably in Stanhope and Sunderland. In the resulting factional struggle Stanhope and Sunderland emerged triumphant. Townshend was first relegated to the lord lieutenancy of Ireland and then, in 1717, dismissed. Walpole resigned and followed his brother-in-law into opposition together with a small group of allies. The schism in the Whig party was followed by a split at court, as the Prince of Wales quarrelled with his father. For the next three years Walpole and Townshend, the Prince of Wales and the Tories co-operated in opposition, putting the ministry under constant pressure and subjecting it to some striking, if occasional, defeats. The aim of Walpole and Townshend was clearly to force themselves back into government.

In 1720 they achieved this aim. However, while the reasons for both sides coming to terms are obscure, it is clear that Townshend and Walpole returned as junior partners. Townshend was made Lord President, Walpole found himself once again as Paymaster, and some of their followers, such as William Pulteney, were left out in the cold. The ministry was still dominated by Stanhope and Sunderland: Walpole was so far from being prime minister that he was only a junior minister outside the cabinet. Only a combination of luck and judgement enabled Townshend and Walpole to achieve dominance of the ministry over the next months and years.

Their first stroke of luck came with the bursting of the South Sea Bubble. The ensuing financial and political chaos enabled Walpole to demonstrate his abilities by guiding through parliament the legislation necessary to restore government credit. More importantly, perhaps, it removed many of their rivals. The Stanhope–Sunderland ministry was deeply implicated in the crash. Stanhope died of apoplexy after defending himself in the Lords; Craggs, Stanhope's colleague as Secretary of State, died of smallpox after his son committed suicide; Aislabie, the Chancellor of the Exchequer, was found guilty of corruption and expelled from the Commons; Sunderland survived, but only just, and was forced to resign as First Lord of the Treasury. Townshend succeeded Stanhope as Secretary of State and in April 1721 Walpole was appointed First Lord of the Treasury and Chancellor of the Exchequer. Sunderland, however, remained a powerful rival. He now occupied only a minor court post, the groom of the stole, but it gave him access to the King, whose favour he retained, and he was soon intriguing to undermine Walpole and Townshend. But fortune again intervened when Sunderland died on 19 April 1722.

J.H. Plumb dates Walpole's premiership from this point (Plumb 1956: 378). There is much to commend this view, but in many respects Walpole was still not yet prime minister. The ministry contained many of Sunderland's former allies, not least Lord Carteret, Townshend's colleague as Secretary of State. Walpole and Townshend did not yet enjoy the confidence of the King. Moreover, there was considerable suspicion of them among the Whig party in parliament. Their factional opposition to a Whig government in 1717–20 had damaged their party credentials and, among the more independently minded Whigs, Walpole was further tainted by his role in screening the corrupt during the South Sea inquiries.

The discovery in 1722 of a Jacobite conspiracy, better known as the Atterbury plot, was thus of crucial importance to the consolidation of Townshend and Walpole's power (Bennett 1975). It is now clear that Walpole manufactured evidence to secure the banishment of Bishop Atterbury in May 1723, but it is contemporary perceptions which are important. Townshend and especially Walpole were able to portray themselves as loyal ministers and zealous Whigs who had uncovered a dangerous conspiracy against the Hanoverian succession. The plot also discredited their rivals, since Sunderland and Carteret, in an attempt to gain a parliamentary advantage over their Whig rivals, had both been involved in negotiations with the Jacobites in 1721. As Arthur Onslow later noted, this episode was

> the most fortunate and the greatest circumstance of Mr Walpole's life. It fixed him with the King, and united for a time the whole body of Whigs to him, and gave him the universal credit of an able and vigilant minister.
>
> (Historical Manuscripts Commission: 513)

Arguably, therefore, Walpole's premiership should be dated from no earlier than 1723. The ministry was more secure in the support of both the King and the Whig party, while Walpole's own prominence within the ministry was increased because he was the only cabinet minister sitting in the Commons. He therefore took the lead in defending government policies across the full range of its activities, including foreign affairs. Moreover, while Walpole, unlike many historians, did not underestimate the significance of the Lords and was at times personally involved in its management (Jones 1987), the Commons was of greater importance for most regular government business. Well over one-third of government-sponsored legislation between 1715 and 1754 concerned supply (Sedgwick 1970: i, 5), and this was both Walpole's own department and Commons' business – the convention had long been established that the Lords could not amend money bills.

Nevertheless, we must be cautious about according too much prominence to Walpole – even after 1723. First, there was continued rivalry within the ministry. Carteret remained as Secretary of State until 1724, and thereafter was Lord Lieutenant of Ireland, and he had allies in figures like General Cadogan and the Earl of Macclesfield. Moreover, George I was reluctant to allow the ministry to be dominated by Walpole and Townshend. Second, it must not be forgotten that Townshend was Secretary of State. In some ways he was still Walpole's senior; he dominated foreign policy; and he exercised the predominant influence over other areas of government policy, such as religion. In addition, Townshend had won over the King's mistress, the Duchess of Kendal, and enjoyed a better relationship with his sovereign than Walpole. Consequently, if Walpole is to be called 'prime minister' from 1723, it is a description which must be heavily qualified. To many contemporaries it was a Townshend–Walpole ministry, and it is perhaps more accurate to describe it as duumvirate. Had Walpole been dismissed at the accession of George II in 1727, we would probably find it difficult to see any significant differences between him and Stanhope and Sunderland.

Walpole's dismissal is precisely what everyone, including Walpole himself, expected on the death of George I. It is ironic, therefore, that this event secured Walpole's dominance. George II's detestation of his father's ministers was well known, and for a few days it looked as if the new King would dismiss him. But once George II had decided to keep the ministers, Walpole's position within the ministry was greatly strengthened. It is true that he had to live with some uncongenial bedfellows, not least the rival who had failed to replace him, Spencer Compton, who was compensated with a peerage. But now it was Walpole, rather than Townshend, who enjoyed the greater influence at court, largely through the influence of Queen Caroline whom he had courted assiduously while Princess of Wales. The full strength of his position became apparent over the next three years, as he challenged Townshend over foreign policy and won. Walpole was increasingly worried about Townshend's bellicose attitude towards the Austro-Spanish alliance. Acting with the Duke of Newcastle, he negotiated the Treaty of Seville (1729), which detached Spain from Austria. This marginalization of Townshend in his own sphere of foreign affairs led directly to his resignation. There is, therefore, a strong case for arguing that it is only between 1727 and 1730 that Walpole emerged, by himself, as someone enjoying the predominance within parliament and the ministry which is associated with the 'office' of prime minister.

That position was, of course, very different from that of a modern prime minister. Not only was there no office of prime minister, but also Walpole did not occupy a post which made him *officio* head of the ministry. As First Lord of the Treasury he was a departmental head, as were most of his ministerial colleagues. Indeed, it was not Walpole's government. He did not appoint the cabinet. Instead, the King appointed all the leading ministers and they reported directly to him. If Walpole wanted to dismiss a minister, he had to convince the King and that was never an easy task. Throughout his time in office Walpole had to endure the presence of rivals and critics in the cabinet, and most important policy decisions were made at meetings of a small inner cabinet. It is hardly surprising, therefore, to find that there was no concept of collective cabinet responsibility. This was made very clear in January 1742, when the ministry was defeated in parliament but Walpole alone resigned.

The discussion hitherto has concentrated on the vexed questions of whether Walpole was the first prime minister, and, if so, when he achieved that position, and it has tried to illuminate something of the nature of the 'office' of prime minister in the early eighteenth century. But little has been said about Walpole's remarkable achievement of remaining for over twenty years one of the dominant figures, if not the dominant figure, in the Whig government. How, then, was Walpole able to remain in power for so long?

It has already been noted that Walpole himself expected to be dismissed on the accession of George II. This fact highlights the importance of the King and the court in eighteenth-century politics. Britain may not have been a 'court society' on the French model, as some historians have argued (Clark 1988: 121), but Walpole was the King's minister in much more than a nominal sense. His skills as a courtier were vital to his success. It must be remembered that George II, like his father, was astute enough to keep rivals and critics of Walpole within the ministry and at court. Even the prime minister could not be allowed too easy a dominance of government. Nevertheless, in the 1730s Walpole enjoyed unrivalled access to the King and Queen, with whom, according to Lord Hervey, he developed a relationship of remarkable intimacy and trust.

But the confidence of the King, by itself, was not enough. If it had been, Compton would have replaced Walpole in 1727. George II's detestation of his father's ministers was intense – he referred to Walpole as 'a great rogue' and Townshend as 'a choleric blockhead' (Hervey 1931: 29). He had never forgiven them for the terms of his reconciliation in 1720. The problem, and the objection to Compton in 1727, was that the King also wanted someone who could get his business through parliament. Walpole had an unrivalled ability to manage parliament, and this is what tipped the balance in his favour in 1727. If the point needed emphasis, he provided it by securing for George II an increased civil list of £800,000. Conversely, at the time of his resignation in 1742 Walpole still retained the confidence of the King, but was no longer able to maintain his majority in the Commons. To explain Walpole's tenure of power, we need therefore to turn to his relationship with parliament.

The opposition to Walpole explained his parliamentary dominance very simply – by corruption. They feared that so many Members of Parliament (MPs) and peers were becoming dependent on the ministry that parliament was in danger of becoming little more than a rubber stamp for government policy. This analysis, propagated most effectively in *The Craftsman*, has exercised a great influence over historians, and often patronage appears to be the key to Walpole's maintenance of his parliamentary majority. We must not, of course, overlook the importance of patronage or the role of the First Lord of the Treasury in distributing it. As the Earl of Hardwicke later remarked, MPs 'were naturally to look thither; that there must be some principal person to receive applications, and to hear the wants and the wishes and the requests of mankind, with the reasons of them' (Sedgwick 1970: i, 41). Those in receipt of government offices and pensions did form a significant part of the membership of both houses of parliament. In the Lords there were about eighty office-holders in 1721, rising to about 100 by 1742, out of a total membership of just under 200. In the Commons they accounted for between 120 and 150 of the 558 MPs. Discipline was not as rigorous as in the modern Commons, but in general office-holders were expected to support the ministry. This was as true whether they were peers or commoners. During the excise crisis of 1733 Walpole came far closer to defeat in the Lords than the Commons, and the Dukes of Montrose and Bolton, the Earls of Stair and Marchmont, and Lord Cobham were all dismissed for voting against the government.

But office-holders, by themselves, were never numerous enough to give Walpole a majority. In addition, there were important limits to the power of patronage. Some offices were granted for life, giving the ministry little control over their holders. Indeed, one of the most independent Whigs in the House, Sir Joseph Jekyll, was an office-holder as Master of the Rolls. Other recipients of government favours had a distressing tendency to view them as a reward for past services rather than as a down payment for future support. Moreover, and perhaps most seriously, the ties of patronage were weakest precisely when the ministry most needed support. In times of crisis those dependent on government favours were faced with a dilemma: should they stay loyal to the minister and risk going down with the ship if he resigned, or should they try quietly to distance themselves from him in case they had to come to terms with a new regime? The weakness of patronage was highlighted in the most serious crisis experienced by the Walpole ministry, the excise crisis of 1733. Walpole's majorities in the Commons declined until they reached the point at which he was forced to abandon the Tobacco Excise Bill, a major piece of financial legislation. Opposition strength, however, remained more or less constant throughout the crisis. Walpole's problem lay in the attitude of previously reliable ministerial supporters, who, seeing the weakness of the ministry and fearing that Walpole was on the point of being replaced, abstained or stayed away from parliament in ever greater numbers (Langford 1975).

To explain Walpole's success in parliament, therefore, we need to look beyond patronage and examine his appeal to the more independent members of the

Commons. Walpole was undoubtedly a very effective manager of patronage, but it is perhaps in his ability to appeal to the less committed that he stands out above his colleagues and rivals. First, Walpole was a party leader as well as the King's minister. He had played a leading role in the impeachment of Henry Sacheverell, the high-flying Tory clergyman who had 'preached against the Revolution', and his later imprisonment in the Tower on charges of corruption had given him the aura of a Whig martyr. His reputation was damaged by his behaviour while in opposition between 1717 and 1720 and during the South Sea crisis, but it was partly recovered by his vigorous prosecution of the Atterbury plot. Some Whigs remained suspicious of Walpole, an attitude which contributed to the 'patriot' opposition from 1725. Nonetheless, for all his failings, he was and remained a Whig, able to appeal to Whig identity. This appeal could be particularly effective when divisions among the Whigs threatened the government's majority in parliament. In the immediate aftermath of the excise crisis, when the opposition tried to press home their attack on Walpole, he rallied Whig support by appealing to party solidarity, raising the spectre of Jacobitism and portraying the ministry as the only real defence for the Hanoverian succession and Revolution principles.

Second, Walpole possessed unrivalled abilities as a parliament man. As it is difficult in retrospect to recapture the effect of an individual's presence and the power of his oratory in the Commons, the best testimony comes from contemporaries. Lord Chesterfield's account is particularly interesting because it comes from the pen of one of the leaders of the opposition to Walpole's administration. He was, according to Chesterfield,

> both the ablest parliament man, and the ablest manager of parliament, that I believe ever lived. An artful rather than an eloquent speaker, he saw as by intuition, the disposition of the House, and pressed or receded accordingly. So clear in stating the most intricate matters, especially in the finances, that while he was speaking the most ignorant thought that they understood what they really did not.
>
> (Franklin 1993: 114)

It is in this context that the significance of Walpole's decision to abandon precedent and remain in the Commons becomes clear. Not only did this decision reveal his awareness of the importance of the lower House for government business, but also, by making a symbolic public statement of this kind, Walpole further enhanced his position in the Commons. As one contemporary noted: 'Mr W. chooses to give nobility to others, rather than to accept it himself' (British Library (BL) Additional Manuscripts (Add MSS) 70400, John Wainwright to Timothy Thomas, 17 November 1723).

Third, Walpole inspired confidence by his competence as a finance minister. The calm common sense which he brought to the restoration of government finances in the aftermath of the South Sea crisis was impressive, even if his screening of the corrupt was censured. The maintenance of public credit thereafter depended on the government keeping the confidence of the great financial institutions, and in his definitive study of public finance in this period P.G.M. Dickson has concluded:

> There is no doubt that the hard, tough men who ran the City and its institutions recognized in his handling of this and subsequent financial issues a competence equal to their own, and not found at the Treasury for any length of time since the fall of Godolphin.
>
> (Dickson 1967: 198)

Moreover, Walpole combined this unrivalled grasp of financial details with the ability, noted by Chesterfield, to explain them clearly.

Finally, Walpole tried to pursue policies which would attract broad support both in parliament and in the country. Having served his parliamentary apprenticeship during the violent party strife of Anne's reign, he was well aware of the danger of controversy. But his policies were not only dictated by a concern to stay in power; cooling the embers of party strife was also seen as the best way of preserving the Hanoverian succession, which many feared might be susceptible to the challenge from the exiled Stuarts. In foreign policy war posed a particular danger, as the attempted Franco-Jacobite invasion of 1708 had proved, giving the Jacobites the opportunity to find continental allies who would mount an expedition against Britain. This threat helps to explain Walpole's support for the Anglo-French alliance of 1716, and his reluctance in the early 1730s to admit that it had disintegrated. More generally, Walpole aimed to pursue a pacific foreign policy, keeping Britain out of continental entanglements. It was, as has already been pointed out, Walpole's concern about Townshend's bellicosity which lay at the heart of the dispute which ended in Townshend's resignation. In the 1730s, too, Walpole worked hard to keep Britain out of the War of the Polish Succession.

A pacific foreign policy had further attractions, as it helped to keep taxation low, especially the land tax. The heavy burden of the land tax had been one of the more contentious issues in Anne's reign, doing much to alienate the landed gentry who saw their money going into the pockets of financiers. Walpole's fiscal policy was, therefore, intended to appease the landed interest. In only three years – 1727, 1740 and 1741 – was the land tax levied at its 'wartime' rate of four shillings in the pound. For most of the rest of the period the rate was two shillings, and in 1731–2 it was reduced to one shilling. To achieve this, expenditure had to be controlled, which meant war had to be avoided. But Walpole's financial policy was not merely passive. In some respects he was a reformer, shifting some of the tax burden from direct to indirect taxes. This was done partly by reducing the interest payments on the national debt and partly by a series of technical measures to increase the yield from indirect taxes, such as the replacement in 1724 of customs duties by excises on tea, chocolate and coffee.

A similar strategy was pursued elsewhere, most notably perhaps in the government's religious policy. Religion had been the most divisive issue in the reign of

Anne, with high church Tories campaigning for 'a return to the past when church and state had conjoined in a single authoritarian regime' (Bennett 1975: 22). The Whig party, by contrast, was identified with low churchmen and dissenters, and many Anglican clergy believed that the church could never be safe in its hands. The Stanhope–Sunderland ministry did nothing to allay such fears, pursuing a radical religious policy and attempting to repeal the Test Act. Townshend and Walpole, by contrast, did their best to defuse these religious disputes by working to prevent Whig attacks on the church. At the same time they entrusted the management of church affairs to Bishop Gibson, a committed Whig but also a high churchman, someone who could reassure the lower clergy that the church was indeed safe in Whig hands (Sykes 1926: 83–182). It is a measure of the success of this policy that religion all but disappeared as a central issue of parliamentary politics in the years after 1720.

Lord Hervey reported the jibe that Walpole's government was based on Tory principles and pursued Tory policies (Hervey 1931: 3–4). It is easy to see the basis of this accusation. For much of the period Whig government appeared to have abandoned the Grand Alliance, which had been the cornerstone of British foreign policy for the quarter-century after the Revolution of 1688, in favour of an alliance with the old enemy, France. In religion, the dissenters were denied further concessions, albeit on the ground that the time was not proper. Walpole, however, continued to see himself as a committed Whig, and with good reason. His overriding concern remained the preservation of the Hanoverian succession and the protestant monarchy, as established at the Revolution. He had, it is true, abandoned the partisanship of Anne's reign when, following his expulsion from the Commons, he was celebrated as the Whigs' 'jewel in the Tower' (History of Parliament Trust forthcoming). He had become more pragmatic, perhaps even more moderate. His political apprenticeship in Anne's reign had been a formative experience. He had surely learnt much about the arts of parliamentary management from Robert Harley, though Walpole imposed an even more rigorous discipline on office-holders. More importantly, the party strife of those years taught Walpole that peace, low taxation and the damping the fires of religious conflict were essential both for ministerial stability and for the security of the Hanoverian succession, which remained precarious for some years after 1714.

In essence, the key to Walpole's success lay in his ability to satisfy the demands of both King and parliament. Walpole himself was conscious of this; he was 'minister with the King in the House of Commons' and 'minister for the House of Commons in the Closet' (Sedgwick 1970: ii, 41). These two roles were inextricably linked. It has already been shown that one of the attractions of Walpole for George I and George II was his ability to manage parliament. Conversely, the fact that he was the King's minister and retained the confidence of the King was crucial to his support in parliament. One of the most important reasons for the weakness of Walpole's parliamentary position in 1733 was rumours that he had lost the confidence of the court and that George II was considering his dismissal.

It is important not to underestimate Walpole's abilities. One might argue that the period favoured his style of politics: nevertheless, his is an unparalleled achievement. It is equally important, however, not to exaggerate those abilities. Walpole did make mistakes. His meddling in Irish affairs repeatedly caused trouble, never more so than in the controversy over Wood's patent in 1723–5 (Hayton 1984). His domestic politics also occasionally backfired, notably in 1733 and 1736. The Tobacco Excise Bill of 1733, intended in part to appeal to the landed gentry by facilitating a reduction in the land tax, provoked an impressive alliance of opposition Whigs and Tories in parliament, tobacco merchants, and small shopkeepers and traders through the country (Langford 1975: ch. 4). The result was a massive public campaign against the Bill and the collapse of Walpole's majority in the Commons. Three years later Walpole's espousal of the Quakers' Tithe Bill, which he saw as a minor measure of relief for one group of protestant dissenters, provoked not merely the expected hostility of the Tories, but also the united opposition of the clergy, led by Gibson and the bench of bishops. On this occasion the Bill was defeated in the Lords (Taylor 1985).

The crises of 1733 and 1736 were relatively short-lived. Once the contentious legislation had been abandoned, the boil had been lanced and the ministry was able to consolidate its position once more. It was not so easy to deal with opposition attacks on foreign policy and the conduct of the war between 1738 and 1742. First, in 1738 and 1739, concerted attacks were made by the opposition both within parliament and outside on the ministry's conciliatory policy towards Spain and its reluctance to go to war in defence of British trade with the Spanish colonies in South America. Then, after war had been declared on Spain, attention shifted to the ineffectiveness of the government's military strategy, especially the failure of the expedition against Cartagena. Towards the end of 1741 it focused on Britain's failure to support Maria Theresa, the Queen of Hungary, following the outbreak of the War of the Austrian Succession. Walpole was singled out in many opposition attacks. He was particularly vulnerable because he had opposed going to war and then virtually washed his hands of it, saying to Newcastle: 'This war is yours, you have had the conduct of it, I wish you joy of it' (Yorke 1913: i, 251). Walpole was gradually losing his predominance within the ministry. Newcastle, Hardwicke and Pelham, hitherto reliable supporters, were far more committed to the war than the prime minister.

Arguably, however, the war only provided the context for Walpole's fall. In the 1741 elections the ministry more-or-less held its own in the larger, more open constituencies, which were most susceptible to the vagaries of public opinion. It was in Cornwall and Scotland that the opposition made its major gains. In Cornwall the influence of Frederick, Prince of Wales, as Duke of Cornwall, was thrown against the ministry, a consequence of the breach between the Prince and his father in 1737. In Scotland the defection of the Duke of Argyle meant that the Earl of Ilay, Walpole's Scottish manager and Argyle's brother, was unable to secure the election of the solid bloc of Scottish MPs whose allegiance the ministry had hitherto enjoyed. It is difficult to estimate the support enjoyed by the parties when parliament reassembled in December 1741, but Newcastle's calculation that the ministry had a majority of fourteen is probably as accurate as any. But fourteen was not enough. As in 1733, Walpole soon found that supporters were staying away from the House, and through December and January the ministry suffered a series of defeats. Walpole could no longer manage the Commons for the King. His resignation became inevitable, allowing the reconstruction of the ministry around his 'Old Corps' Whig followers with the admixture of some of the 'patriot' opposition.

Walpole resigned on 6 February 1742 and was created Earl of Orford. His retirement, however, was not complete. He believed his political legacy was worth preserving, and wrote to the Duke of Devonshire that 'the Whig party must be kept together' (Coxe 1797: iii, 592). For the next four years he worked behind the scenes to ensure the predominance of the Old Corps and his chosen successor, Henry Pelham. It is far from clear how much influence Walpole did exercise. But, by the time of his death in March 1745, Pelham had become First Lord of the Treasury and the Old Corps' dominance of the government was rapidly being consolidated. A few months later the event Walpole had always feared, a Jacobite rebellion, broke out in Scotland. For a few months, as Bonnie Prince Charlie's army marched south to Derby, the position of the regime appeared precarious. But, long before the Jacobites' final defeat at Culloden, the press and public had rallied to it, revealing an impressive level of support in England at least (Harris 1993: ch. 6). Walpole's legacy was secure.

How, then, should Walpole be assessed? As a man we know surprisingly little about him. The image he cultivated of a bluff country gentleman was, to some extent, a façade. He certainly came from a Norfolk gentry family, but it was a well-established one which had sent a representative to parliament as long ago as the reign of Edward VI. Walpole himself had aristocratic pretensions and tastes. He assembled one of the finest picture collections in England, the core of which was later sold to Catherine the Great. Moreover, he fully understood the relationship between image and power. Houghton House, on which work was begun in 1721, was constructed in the newly fashionable Palladian style, and was intended to eclipse the leading aristocratic houses of East Anglia and beyond.

As a politician Walpole was neither an idealist nor a great reformer. He left no legislative monuments in the manner of the great nineteenth-century prime ministers. He was rather a practical man of business and a manager. There is no doubt that circumstances, and a large share of luck, helped to raise him to the position of prime minister and then to keep him there. But it is important not to diminish his significance too much. He excelled as a politician, and contemporaries, whether they liked him or hated him, had no doubts about his stature. Not only did he dominate the political system, but also the image of the 'Great Man' pervaded the culture of the period. To Swift he was 'the Poet's Foe'; he was Palinurus in Pope's *Dunciad*, Macheath in Gay's *Beggar's Opera* and Quidam in Fielding's *Historical Register* (Downie 1984). Walpole may not have been Britain's first prime minister, but no prime minister since has imposed his, or even her, imprint on his period of office to such an extent.

References and further reading

Bennett, G.V. (1974) 'Jacobitism and the rise of Walpole', in N. McKendrick (ed.) *Historical Perspectives: Studies in English Thought and Society*, London: Europa.

—— (1975) *The Tory Crisis in Church and State 1688–1730*, Oxford: Clarendon Press.

Black, J. (1985) *British Foreign Policy in the Age of Walpole*, Edinburgh: John Donald.

Clark, J.C.D. (ed.) (1988) *The Memoirs and Speeches of James, 2nd Earl Waldegrave 1742–63*, Cambridge: Cambridge University Press.

Colley, L. (1982) *In Defiance of Oligarchy: The Tory Party 1714–60*, Cambridge: Cambridge University Press. (Seminal study demonstrating the continued existence of the Tory party through the Walpole period and beyond.)

Coxe, W. (1797) *Memoirs of the Life and Administration of Sir Robert Walpole*, 3 vols, London. (Prints many documents. Still the starting-point for serious study of Walpole.)

Cruickshanks, E. (1984) 'The political management of Sir Robert Walpole, 1720–42', in J. Black (ed.) *Britain in the Age of Walpole*, London: Macmillan.

Dickinson, H.T. (1973) *Walpole and the Whig Supremacy*, London: English Universities Press. (Still the best brief introduction.)

—— (1977) *Liberty and Property: Political Ideology in Eighteenth-Century Britain*, London: Weidenfeld & Nicolson. (Chapter 5 provides a straightforward introduction to the arguments of the opposition.)

Dickson, P.G.M. (1967) *The Financial Revolution in England: A Study in the Development of Public Credit 1688–1756*, London: Macmillan. (An outstanding study of a technical subject.)

Downie, J.A. (1984) 'Walpole, "The Poet's Foe"', in J. Black (ed.) *Britain in the Age of Walpole*, London: Macmillan.

Franklin, C. (1993) *The Earl of Chesterfield, his Character and Characters*, Aldershot: Scolar Press.

Harris, R. (1993) *A Patriot Press: National Politics and the London Press in the 1740s*, Oxford: Clarendon Press.

Hayton, D. (1984) 'Walpole and Ireland', in J. Black (ed.) *Britain in the Age of Walpole*, London: Macmillan.

Hervey, John Lord (1931) *Some Materials towards Memoirs of the Reign of King George II*, ed. R. Sedgwick, 3 vols, London: Eyre & Spottiswoode. (Lively and readable, but hardly unprejudiced, account of George II's court by one of its leading figures.)

Hill, B.W. (1976) *The Growth of Parliamentary Parties 1689–1742*, London: Allen & Unwin.

Historical Manuscripts Commission, Fourteenth Report, Appendix, Part IX, *Manuscripts of the Earl of Onslow*.

History of Parliament Trust (forthcoming) *The History of Parliament: The House of Commons, 1690–1715*, draft biography of Robert Walpole by David Hayton. (When published this will be the standard account of Walpole's early political career. I am grateful to Dr Hayton for allowing me to read a draft of this article, and to the History of Parliament Trust for permission to quote from it.)

Jones, C. (1987) 'The House of Lords and the growth of parliamentary stability, 1701–1742', in C. Jones (ed.) *Britain in the First Age of Party*, London: Hambledon Press.

Langford, P. (1975) *The Excise Crisis: Society and Politics in the Age of Walpole*, Oxford: Clarendon Press. (An outstanding study which is much broader than its title suggests.)

Plumb, J.H. (1956) *Sir Robert Walpole: The Making of a Statesman*, London: Cresset Press.

—— (1960) *Sir Robert Walpole: The King's Minister*, London: Cresset Press. (Takes the story down to 1734. This major modern biography has never been completed.)

—— (1967) *The Growth of Political Stability in England 1675–1725*, London: Macmillan. (One of the most influential works on the period which sets the context for Walpole's premiership.)

Roberts, C. (1966) *The Growth of Responsible Government in Stuart England*, Cambridge: Cambridge University Press.

Sedgwick, R. (ed.) (1970) *The House of Commons 1715–1754*, 2 vols, London: HMSO.

Speck, W.A. (1981) 'Whigs and Tories dim their glories: English political parties under the first two Georges', in J. Cannon (ed.) *The Whig Ascendancy: Colloquies on Hanoverian England*, London: Edward Arnold. (Provides a clear statement of the view that after 1714 a Whig–Tory dichotomy was replaced by a court–country one.)

Sykes, N. (1926) *Edmund Gibson, Bishop of London, 1699–1748: A Study in Politics and Religion in the Eighteenth Century*, London: Oxford University Press. (Still the essential starting-point for an understanding of Walpole's religious policy.)

Taylor, S. (1985) 'Sir Robert Walpole, the Church of England and the Quakers Tithe Bill of 1736', *Historical Journal* 28: 51–77.

Yorke, P.C. (1913) *The Life and Correspondence of Philip Yorke Earl of Hardwicke*, 3 vols, Cambridge: Cambridge University Press.

Stephen Taylor

Spencer Compton, First Earl of Wilmington

Born c. 1674, sixth but second surviving son of James Compton, third Earl of Northampton, and Mary, daughter of Baptist Noel, third Viscount Campden. Educated at St Paul's, Middle Temple and Trinity College, Oxford. Unmarried. MP for Eye 1698–1710, East Grinstead 1713–15, Sussex 1715–28. Chairman of the Committees of Privileges and Elections 1705–10; Paymaster of Queen's Pensions 1707–13; Treasurer to Prince George of Denmark 1707–8; Speaker of House of Commons 1715–27; Treasurer to Prince of Wales 1715–27; Paymaster-General 1722–30; Lord Privy Seal 1730; Lord President of the Council 1730–42; First Lord of the Treasury February 1742 until his death 2 July 1743.

Wilmington, Walpole's successor as prime minister, has been regarded as George II's favourite nonentity. Though there is some truth in this, he was a more complex and significant figure than has been realized.

Coming from a Royalist Tory family, Compton was a Whig when he was returned for Eye in Suffolk on the interest of Lord Cornwallis. A 'Lord Treasurer Whig' under Queen Anne, he was one of Godolphin's managers in parliament.

For five years he was chairman of the Elections Committee, one of the two key committees in the House with Ways and Means, and one used by the government to increase their majority by unseating political opponents. He was rewarded with the lucrative office of Paymaster of the Queen's Pensions, despite showing some independence in voting and his criticisms of Godolphin's allies, the Whig Junto. As a manager of the trial of Dr Sacheverell, the High Tory cleric, he showed uncharacteristic passion, trembling and foaming at the mouth as he denounced Sacheverell as a criminal. In the Tory backlash of the 1710 election, the managers were liable to incur insults and personal injury from enraged Tory mobs and Compton prudently stood down. Returned for East Grinstead in 1713 on the interest of the Duke of Dorset, his political links with the Sackvilles remained lifelong.

Compton, who had been a friend of Walpole in the Queen's reign, had a full share in the Whig monopoly of office which followed the Hanoverian succession. His becoming Treasurer to the Prince of Wales (the future George II) enabled him to gain the prince's ear and to form a close relationship with him. He was appointed Speaker in the 1715 and 1722 parliaments, at a salary of £1,000 a year, an office still part of the ministerial team. An experienced politician, though not a first-rate one, he was learned in parliamentary procedure and was a stickler for precedent, particularly the rulings of previous speakers. His successor, Arthur Onslow, described him as 'very able in the chair, but had not the powers of speech out of it' (Historical Manuscripts Commission: 516). During the Whig split of 1717–20, he went into opposition as head of the Prince's household, co-operating closely with Walpole. After the reconciliation between the King and the Prince, which was achieved by giving places to the Prince's followers, he obtained the immensely profitable office of Paymaster-General of the Forces, out of which he was reported to have made £100,000.

On George I's death in 1727, George II's first intention was to replace Walpole by Compton, directing all public business to him. The reasons why Compton did not become prime minister then are explained by contemporaries hostile to him. According to John Scrope, Walpole's Secretary to the Treasury, Compton was 'frighted with the greatness of the undertaking and more particularly as to what related to money matters' (Coxe 1797: i, 287). George ordered both men to prepare the King's speech for dissolving parliament, but chose Walpole's. On the matter of settling the Queen's revenue, Compton undertook to secure £60,000 a year for her, whereas Walpole offered £100,000, which sealed the alliance between Queen Caroline and Walpole. It was not thought advisable to continue Compton as Speaker and he went to the Lords as Baron Wilmington, being made an earl in 1730. He then gave up his post as Paymaster to the Army for that of Lord Privy Seal. Though he had been responsible for cutting the profits of that office from £5,000 to £4,000 a year, he had the salary restored to its original level for himself. At the end of 1730 he became President of the Council, an important ministerial post.

The first Lord Egmont left a good description of Wilmington:

His stature is something more than the middle sort and he is not corpulent though full fleshed. He is proud though affable to those who visit him, and is rare of his speech, but then positive. He maintains no debates in the House of Peers, but never swerved from voting as the Ministry would have him being very servile to his Majesty's inclinations. He has no great genius, but cannot want experience. . . . He is extremely covetous and formal in business, was never married, but has children unlawfully begotten, which he stifles the knowledge of as much as in him lies. He has no ambition, and has told me the true interest of England was to have no chief minister, but that every great office should be immediately dependent on the King and answer for itself.

(*Egmont Diary* 1923: iii, 250)

Wilmington disliked Walpole's practice of employing political tools rather than men of substance, and did what he could to prevent the dismissal of those who had opposed Walpole's excise scheme in 1733. Nor should he be underestimated for in 1740 Lord Egmont noted there were three parties at court: Walpole's and his friends; the Duke of Newcastle's and Lord Chancellor Hardwicke's; and Wilmington's with the Duke of Dorset and his friends.

In February 1742, after the fall of Walpole, Wilmington joined the Duke of Argyll against Newcastle, Hardwicke, William Pulteney and Lord Carteret in pressing for a broadly based coalition, to include some Tories and to implement the 'Country' measures which had been demanded by opposition Whigs and Tories alike. Pulteney, the obvious choice as Walpole's successor, had disqualified himself by repeatedly declaring that he did not seek office. Wilmington was asked to become First Lord of the Treasury on the understanding that he would have his burden lightened by working with Samuel Sandys, Pulteney's second-in-command, as Chancellor of the Exchequer. At a meeting on 8 February 1742 Wilmington was asked 'upon what foundation he apprehended he was capable of supporting the place of the head of the treasury, what party of Commoners he could influence?' (Ryder 1742: 9 February 1741/2). He asked for two or three days to think it over then accepted. When Lord Carteret, a brilliant speaker in the Lords and very able though something of a maverick, was appointed Secretary of State and the effective head of the government without consulting him, Wilmington threatened to resign, going to the King to tell him so. With tears in his eyes George II reproached him 'what, my Lord, will you desert me too?', to which Wilmington replied, 'he found his Majesty so resolved to narrow his bottom [i.e. against a multi-party administration] and withstand the voice of his people, that he saw his very Crown in danger' (*Egmont Diary* 1923: iii, 254). But he agreed to stay and to try and reconcile the parties within the government. He died suddenly, while the King was in Hanover, leaving his large fortune to his nephew the fifth Earl of Northampton and nothing to the Sackvilles, who had courted the legacy. The much quoted poem by Sir Charles Hanbury Williams

See you old dull important lord
Who at the long'd for money board
Sits first, but does not lead

should be his sole epitaph. His views on the role of the prime minister were no longer politically realistic, but if he lacked the wit of Hanbury Williams, Lord Hervey or Horace Walpole, his chief critics, he had, unlike them, political scruples.

References and further reading

Black, J. (1984) *Britain in the Age of Walpole*, London: Macmillan.
Coxe, W. (1797) *Memoirs of the Life and Administration of Sir Robert Walpole*, 3 vols, London.
Egmont Diary (1923), vol. 3, London: HMSO.
Historical Manuscripts Commission, Fourteenth Report, Appendix, Part IX, *Manuscripts of the Earl of Onslow*.
Holmes, G. (1967) *British Politics in the Age of Anne*, London: Macmillan.
—— (1973) *The Trial of Doctor Sacheverell*, London: Eyre Methuen.
Owen, J.B. (1957) *The Rise of the Pelhams*, London: Methuen.
Ryder, Sir Dudley (1742) manuscript diary, 2, 3, 9 February 1742. (I am obliged to Lord Harrowby for permission to quote from this manuscript.)
Sedgwick, R. (ed.) (1970) *The House of Commons 1715–54*, vol. 1, London: HMSO.

Eveline Cruickshanks

Henry Pelham

Born c. January 1695, second son of Thomas Pelham MP (created Baron Pelham of Laughton 1706) by his second wife Lady Grace Holles, daughter of Gilbert, third Earl of Clare. Educated at Westminster, Hart Hall, Oxford, and Padua University. Married 1726 Lady Katherine Manners, daughter of John, second Duke of Rutland. MP for Seaford 1717–22, Sussex 1722–54. Treasurer of the Chamber 1720–2; Lord of the Treasury 1721–4; Secretary at War 1724–30; Paymaster-General of the Forces 1730–43; First Lord of the Treasury 1743–54; Chancellor of the Exchequer 1743–54. Died 6 March 1754.

Henry Pelham is generally considered one of the most successful of eighteenth-century premiers, and his administration one of the most stable. Such generalization seems crude in view of Pelham's prolonged struggle to achieve a prime ministerial position commensurate with that enjoyed by Walpole, and his subsequent difficulties in keeping his ministry together. The stability of Pelham's administration was more apparent than real; even the early 1750s, so often seen as the plenitude of his ministry, were aggravated by political intrigue and crisis. A flair for conciliation was the key to Pelham's political durability, though to contemporaries his subtlety and constant manoeuvring often seemed perfidious or cowardly. Detractors, such as Horace Walpole, wondered whether 'he ought to have conferred greater benefits on his country', but throughout his premiership Pelham operated skilfully within complex limitations of circumstance (Hodgart 1963: 46). If his resulting achievements seem modest, it was because he was a successful pragmatist.

Pelham showed no initial promise for high office. His abilities emerged gradually through years of experience and practice, though the early opportunity he was given to enter the world of high politics and government was of undoubted advantage. Born into one of Sussex's wealthiest gentry families, his political initiation was entirely due to his elder brother Thomas, whose recently inherited fortune and zealous championship of the new Hanoverian establishment soon after coming of age earned his promotion in 1715 to the dukedom of Newcastle. At a by-election in February 1717 Newcastle brought Henry into parliament for Seaford, a Sussex coastal town where the family exercised considerable electoral sway. Henry Pelham's earliest experiences in politics were dominated by the 'schism' within the Whig party occasioned by the resignations in 1717 of Lord Townshend and Robert Walpole from the Sunderland–Stanhope ministry. He naturally followed his elder brother's lead in supporting the government, but during the process of reconciliation in 1720 a friendship emerged between himself and Walpole, and through Townshend's influence Pelham was given the royal household post of Treasurer of the Chamber. Walpole's rapport with Pelham enabled him to capitalize on Newcastle's connection with Sunderland and helped to facilitate his readmission to the ministry in June 1720. When Walpole replaced Sunderland at the head of the Treasury in April the following year amid the political backlash from the South Sea Bubble, he swiftly acknowledged Pelham's services by appointing him to the Treasury board. Pelham was still only 25, yet under Walpole's eye at the Treasury he soon showed a capacity for administrative and financial business, while in the Commons he figured as one of Walpole's devoted acolytes.

At the general election of 1722 Pelham was chosen unanimously as a knight of the shire for Sussex. It was quite exceptional for an ambitious politician to put himself at the mercy of a large county electorate rather than remain in the safer haven of a small manageable borough. But Sussex was his elder brother's chief electoral stronghold, and the Duke naturally wished Pelham to have the most prestigious seat he could offer. In 1724 Walpole appointed Pelham Secretary at War with responsibility for the day-to-day administration of the army, while his advancement in 1730 to the paymastership of the forces placed him in overall control of the army's finances. Unlike several previous paymasters, however, he never availed himself of the opportunity to use public funds for his own purposes; indeed, throughout his career he remained free of any taint of financial impropriety. Access to ducal wealth placed him above the need for corrupt gain. An income of £5,000 a year settled on him by his father had been handsomely supplemented in 1726 on his marriage to a daughter of the Duke of Rutland with a dowry fortune of £30,000.

During the 1730s Pelham emerged as a popular front-bench man to whom the arts of government were second nature. The usually caustic Lord Hervey saw him at this time as 'a gentlemanlike sort of man, of very good character, of moderate parts, in the secret of every transaction, which, added to long practice, made him at last, though not a bright speaker, often a useful one; and by the means of a general affability he had fewer enemies than commonly fall to the share of one in so high a rank' (Hervey 1931: 120).

He served Walpole devotedly. The two men shared a common viewpoint on all political issues of the day, and Pelham regarded Sir Robert as 'my oracle' (Wilkes 1964: 230). Although relations between Newcastle and Walpole soured towards the end of the decade, Pelham did not allow this state of affairs to affect his own connection with his mentor. Pelham's exact role during the final days of Walpole's administration in January 1742 is not clear. He appears to have stayed loyal until the very end, although members of Walpole's family always maintained that the King had received 'private intimations' from the Pelhams that Walpole had 'lost' the Commons and could no longer continue in office. George II's coolness towards the Pelhams in the years that followed certainly indicates that he considered them personally responsible for Walpole's downfall.

It was within no politician's power in 1742 to resuscitate the semblance of political 'stability' which had characterized Walpole's long administration. The endless round of negotiation and manoeuvring over the next four years in seach of a workable ministry has been aptly described by one historian as a 'stately minuet of Whig cliques in and out of office' (Hill 1985: 56). In the aftermath of Walpole's resignation from office in February 1742, Pelham's conciliatory gifts played an important part in the reconstruction of the ministry. The Court and Treasury party, which had formed the backbone of Walpole's parliamentary support (thenceforth known as the 'Old Corps') remained in office, but in their determination to keep the ministry on a strictly Whig footing Old Corps leaders would brook no deal with Whig opponents disposed towards the Tories. In consequence, only William Pulteney and his followers (who had turned on their former Tory allies with opportunistic spite) entered the new ministry. Pelham assumed undisputed leadership of the Commons when in July 1742 Pulteney, his closest rival for this position, went to the Lords with the earldom of Bath. The ministry was still without a clear leader, however. Wilmington, who had succeeded Walpole as First Lord of the Treasury, was little more than an ailing figurehead. Although parliament and the cabinet were dominated by the Old Corps, it was Lord Carteret, Pulteney's chief associate and now secretary of state for the north, who monopolized the King's confidence. On Wilmington's death in July 1743, Pelham became First Lord of the Treasury, almost certainly through Walpole's continuing influence with the King behind the scenes. Although the office was coveted by Lord Bath, there was no question that Pelham was a better choice as Old Corps leader in the more volatile Commons. Moreover, the appointment set him firmly on the path towards achieving the prime ministerial role which Walpole had forged for himself. By December Pelham had entrenched his position at the Treasury by securing the removal of Bath's nominees from the board, taking advantage of the Pulteneyites' weakening credibility. And, following Walpole's example, he took the office of Chancellor of the Exchequer in tandem with that of First Lord.

Though Pelham was now in complete control of the Treasury, and the acknowledged leader of the Old Corps in the Commons, no single politician as yet dominated the ministry. Quarrels broke out in the cabinet over practically every issue between the Old Corps and the former opposition grandees now in office and known as the 'New Whigs'. The chief cause of friction was Lord Carteret's pursuit of a costly war policy designed to protect the King's Hanoverian dominions from invasion. Elaborate continental alliances were underwritten by subsidies and the Hanoverian army taken into British pay. Worst of all, Carteret conducted his diplomacy in close liaison with the King but in isolation from the government, regarding Pelham as little more than 'a chief clerk' (Wilkes 1964: 49). In parliament the Old Corps spokesmen encountered increasing difficulty in justifying such policies to country gentlemen inflamed by the anti-Hanoverian rhetoric of William Pitt and his Grenvillite associates (sometimes referred to as the 'Cobhamites' after their aristocratic leader Lord Cobham). By the summer of 1744, Pelham and his supporters within the ministry were confident that Carteret's policies were so unpopular that he could be driven from office, and in November, under carefully orchestrated pressure, the King was given little alternative but to dismiss the secretary. In the consequent reshuffle Pelham's plan was to widen the base of his support to form a 'broad-bottom administration', the intention being to accommodate as many shades of parliamentary opinion as practicable. Pelham had in fact begun negotiating with opposition chiefs several months before Carteret (now Earl Granville) was ousted. While keeping control of the principal cabinet offices, he disposed many of the lesser posts from which many Pulteneyites had been removed among leading opponents, who thenceforth become known as the 'New Allies'. The new ministry included such former opposition grandees as Lord Chesterfield and the Duke of Bedford, and several of the most effective debaters on the opposition benches in the Commons, though the King refused to accept Pitt on account of his insulting attacks on Hanover. Pelham also appointed a number of Tories, but their commitment to the ministry was conditional upon too many of their old parliamentary demands. It was to prove the least satisfactory aspect of the 'broad-bottom' experiment.

From the start, however, the new ministerial 'system' was undermined by George II's continuing confidence in Granville. Relations between the King and his ministers began to deteriorate until Pelham resolved to bring the issue to a head. He was unable to risk a ministerial crisis, however, until the Jacobite invasion of September 1745 had been safely contained. By January 1746, he had won over his most angry opponents, those of Lord Cobham's connection excluded from office in 1744, by agreeing to isolate Granville and to reduce Britain's expensive continental commitments in favour of a naval war. This time Pelham could not afford to omit the King's *bête noire*, William Pitt, whose denunciations of war policy had made the ministry's position in the Commons decidedly uncomfortable. Having obtained promises of solidarity from his ministerial colleagues, Pelham saw the King on 6 February to insist on Pitt's appointment as Secretary at War. George refused, and on the 10th Pelham resigned, followed over the next day or two by most of his colleagues, leaving the King to entrust Granville and Lord Bath with the formation of a new ministry. It was soon clear, however, that they had only minimal support in the Commons, while the City was set against advancing money to a ministry led by Granville. The King had little choice but to reappoint Pelham.

The events of February 1746 enabled Pelham to finish his self-appointed task of forming an administration on 'broad-bottom' principles. It remained his abiding concern to avoid the type of 'long opposition' which for many years had confronted and eventually toppled Walpole (Sedgwick 1970: ii, 330). Wherever possible he sought to absorb opposition talent into the ministry, which was why Pitt's inclusion by 1746 had become so imperative. But Pelham was not to achieve the broadly based administration which he had envisaged, perhaps naively, in 1744. Though Pelham had personally desired it, the inclusion of Tories in the ministry had been far from popular among his Whig colleagues. To make matters worse, the recent rebellion had revived suspicions about the association of Toryism with Jacobitism, and if anything helped to stress the abiding Whig–Tory polarity in politics. Instead, Pelham's ministry-building, drawing on widely diverse Whig groups and factions, saw English Whiggery become ever more firmly entrenched as the governing ethos. With the exception of a few courtiers, Granville's remaining friends in office were all dismissed and their places taken by former Cobhamite opponents. The King this time gave in to Pelham's wish to include Pitt, and in May he was appointed Paymaster-General.

The collective desertion of the monarch instigated by the Old Corps in 1746 was an exceptional display of what ministerial unity might achieve. That such unity was achieved at this particular juncture, however, testified to Pelham's stature within the administration, even though Granville's 'secret influence' with George II had impeded Pelham's emergence after 1744 as 'prime minister'. Contemporaries were well aware that important constitutional implications lurked behind the Pelhamite initiative of 1746. It had been demonstrated to the King that if his appointed ministers were to govern in the nation's interest they needed his goodwill, and that he could not expect to operate through politicians who lacked support in parliament. Although foreign policy was the exclusive sphere of royal prerogative, parliament, and in particular the Commons, was responsible for voting the necessary funds. Pelham and his colleagues had not aimed to circumscribe the King's power. As one historian has commented, 'as in 1742, so in 1746; the Commons might directly or indirectly impose a veto on particular ministers, but they did not dictate whom the King should employ. If George chose to limit his options, that was his privilege' (Owen 1973: 124). It cannot be denied that in forcing themselves upon the King in this way, the Old Corps and their New Allies had acted from self-interested motives. Above all, it showed how determined Pelham had become to establish the same pattern of authority in his relations with the King as Walpole had, and which he regarded as the foundation for proper governance.

There was no guarantee in 1746 that the alliance between the Old Corps and the New Allies would survive. In fact, it proved the beginning of a new period of political stability and Whig consensus which lasted until Pelham's death in 1754. But the process of keeping the political situation in check required his constant attention and was often fraught with difficulty. George II's acceptance of Pelham was at first sullen, but in time he grew to appreciate Pelham's strengths, and in the key area of financial management recognized that his capabilities surpassed those of Walpole. 'With regard to money matters', the King told Newcastle in 1752, 'your brother does that, understands that, much better' (Sedgwick 1970: ii, 331). Pelham's chief political feat, undoubtedly, was in holding together a divergent and seemingly mismatched body of politicians. As such, he went a long way towards reuniting the Whigs as the natural governing party, although in practice this involved many policy disputes and much intra-cabinet quarrelling. But if he had learnt anything from Walpole's bitter experience, it was that political differences should not be prosecuted in a manner that endangered the King's service. In all his ministerial dealings he showed tolerance and conciliation, though not infrequently his actions were derided as timorous. By nature he was a man of restraint, though the pressures of power subjected him to bouts of irascibility which in the end undermined his health.

Pelham was an effective parliamentary manager. His main focus of attention was the Commons which he regarded as 'a great unwieldy body which requires great art and some cordials to keep it together', and which, like Walpole, he chose to supervise personally rather than take a peerage and operate from the Lords through a deputy (Sedgwick 1970: ii, 331). He was an effective parliamentary performer, and his plain-speaking 'good sense' appealed to the country squires on the backbenches. Critics felt that his candour gave rise to too much 'doubling plausibility', but even Horace Walpole admitted that, once established in place, 'his eloquence cleared up, and [he] shone with much greater force' (Hodgart 1963: 46). He certainly did much to achieve his objective of curbing opposition in the Commons. His chief lieutenant there was Henry Fox, an Old Corps man, while other ministerial spokesmen included several he had disengaged from opposition such as George Grenville, George Lyttleton, William Pitt and Henry Legge. With almost all the leading officers of state in the Lords, Pelham's administration epitomized eighteenth-century aristocratic government. In practical terms it also ensured that his governmental colleagues were for the most part shielded from opposition attack, while he himself took overall responsibility for policy in the Commons where the real focus of criticism was concentrated. In 1747, Pelham enhanced his mastery over the Commons when he caught would-be opponents off-guard by calling a general election a year before the present parliament was due to expire. Government supporters regarded it as 'a master-stroke of politics' (Wilkes 1964: 69). The result was a decisive victory which strengthened his hand within the cabinet. To one acquaintance he wrote, 'Our majority is . . . much greater, which I can impute to nothing . . . but a zeal for his [the King's] person and Government – a thorough detestation of Jacobitism, and confidence in his administration' (Wilkes 1964: 74). Pelham was never faced, as Walpole had been, with the problem of a numerically threatening opposition. With the end of the war in 1748 much of the ground for attack disappeared, although the real thunderousness of opposition onslaughts led by Pitt in the mid-1740s had eased after he and his Cobhamite brethren were brought in to the administration. But the noisy criticism which often came from the depleted ranks of opponents was still enough to be disconcerting. There was the ever-present possibility that the government's reserves of 'independent' Whig support might succumb to opposition argument. A serious threat was posed by the formation during 1747–8 of the 'Leicester House' party, a combination of discontented Whigs and Tories centred upon the Prince of Wales's court. Its attraction to ambitious MPs lay in the prospects of political advancement when the Prince became King. The potential for such an opposition to grow was disturbing. In 1750 Pelham despaired that the Prince 'has as much to give in present as we have, and more in reversion. This makes my task a hard one, and if it were not for that I should sleep quiet'. What was probably less apparent to Pelham, however, was the extent to which the development of the 'reversionary interest' was hidebound by basic Whig–Tory disagreements over points of policy. Upon the Prince's sudden death in March 1751, however, his party rapidly disintegrated, thereby removing all semblance of organized opposition. As the next session got under way in November, Pelham's Secretary at War, Henry Fox, could write: 'There never was such a session as this is likely to be. . . . A bird might build her nest in the Speaker's chair, or in his peruke. There won't be a debate that can disturb her' (Connors 1993: 122).

After the 1747 election there was never any question that Pelham was 'premier', though he did not affect the grand manner of a 'sole minister' or display the arrogance of power which had made Walpole so unpopular. The main business of government was shared, with a remarkable degree of informality and closeness, between a triumvirate of Pelham, his brother Newcastle and Lord Chancellor Hardwicke. Alone they constituted the 'effective cabinet', and George II was apt to regard the larger, more formal body of ministers as being merely 'for show' (Sedgwick 1970: ii, 331). The predominance of this arrangement derived from Pelham's brotherly tie with Newcastle and the Duke's long-standing friendship with Lord Hardwicke. Its most enduring ingredient was the personality of the Duke of Newcastle. The Duke's constant jealousy and self-obsession, often bordering on paranoia, all too often embittered his working relationships with ministerial colleagues, and not least with his brother. Because of his superior rank Newcastle always thought of himself as sharing power with Pelham. As Pelham consolidated his position at the helm of government, so the Duke grew more anxious that his brother was seeking to monopolize ministerial influence in the closet at his expense. 'The truth is,' Newcastle testily complained to Hardwick in September 1751, ' . . . everything passes through my brother's hands, and I am with regard to the King as much a stranger as if I was not in the ministry' (Sedgwick 1970: ii, 331). Personal friction regularly complicated the flow of ministerial business. But no one understood the underlying strength of this brotherly relationship better than Hardwicke, and it was invariably through his soothing influence on Newcastle that differences were settled.

Pelham was troubled almost constantly by disputes and wrangling among his ministerial colleagues. By far the most serious situation was the long-running battle which developed between Newcastle and his fellow Secretary of State, the Duke of Bedford. Appointed in 1748, Bedford soon proved himself a sturdy opponent of Newcastle's costly foreign policy and was used by Pelham as a counterweight to his brother. By March 1750, however, Newcastle's growing insistence on Bedford's dismissal placed Pelham in an awkward dilemma. Reluctant to make an enemy of Bedford and his substantial following in the Commons, it became plain that Newcastle could not be assuaged for much longer and that his impatience was leading towards a full-scale ministerial rupture. The recently formed alliance between Bedford and the Duke of Cumberland, the King's militaristically minded second son, was an additional complication since Pelham had been at pains to conciliate Cumberland as a useful royal ally and because of his army connection in the Commons led by Henry Fox. But by early 1751 Bedford's open opposition to ministerial policy determined Pelham to force his removal. The death of Prince Frederick in March, and the ensuing Regency Act, enabled Pelham to minimize Cumberland's political influence by restraining his powers in the event of a regency. The after-effects of Bedford's enforced resignation in June were thereby neatly contained. Newcastle secured the appointment of the amenable Lord Holdernesse as his co-secretary of state, while the King, who had been irritated by the treatment of his favourite son in the Regency Bill, was pleased to accept the Pelhams' recommendation that Lord Granville be reinstated to the ministry as Lord President of the Council. In the Commons the loss of Bedford's faction was more than compensated by the return of ex-Leicester House supporters to the Pelhamite fold. Moreover, Bedford's association with Cumberland prevented him from forming an opposition alliance with the Tories, who regarded the Duke as a power-hungry menace. There is no doubt, however, that the ministerial struggles of 1750–1 put Pelham under considerable strain since in April 1751 he endeavoured to obtain George II's permission to retire with a lucrative sinecure. But the King, who had learned to live amicably with Pelham, would not hear of it.

Given his long apprenticeship under Walpole, it was hardly surprising that Pelham's own policies and measures bore the imprint of Walpolian pragmatism, the mainspring of which was the overriding desire to uphold domestic order and stability. Pelham was a Treasury man to the core, and it was natural that fiscal considerations dominated his priorities. Once he had achieved ascendancy over the administration, Pelham's principal concern was to end Britain's involvement in the Austrian war of succession. Like Walpole, he was painfully sensitive about the corrosive effects on backbench opinion of the expense of maintaining arms.

'We Englishmen are very stout upon our own Dunghill,' he once observed, 'but when this nation is engaged in a war . . . the country must pay for it, and then who is to bear the blame' (Sayer MSS 1738). In preference to increased taxation, the war had been financed largely through heavy borrowing and in consequence the national debt had soared by more than £20 million. One item of expenditure, the payment of treaty subsidies to continental allies, was a particular source of parliamentary annoyance. Pelham retained the confidence of the money market and established an invaluable working relationship with the London MP Sir John Barnard, the most influential of City financiers and usually a vehement critic of the government. The cost of loans, nevertheless, rose sharply. There were, of course, major differences among the ministers as to how the war could be brought to a satisfactory close. For a while Newcastle was able to circumvent Pelham's wish for immediate peace in what proved to be a dismal final attempt during 1747–8 to vanquish the French in Flanders and at sea. But it was largely due to Pelham's constant goading and intervention in Newcastle's ponderous diplomacy that a further campaigning season was avoided. Britain's gains from the peace of Aix-la-Chapelle in October 1748 were but modest, and there was much opposition barracking on this score in parliament, but it enabled Pelham to turn to the much-needed task of financial retrenchment. In the post-war years, Newcastle continued to direct a foreign policy over which Pelham was forced to exercise a restraining hand. The keystone of the Duke's strategy was the maintenance of the 'old system' of alliances with the Austrians and the Dutch in opposition to France. But Newcastle's interventionist style and readiness to secure new alliances through the payment of subsidies was a major source of anguish to Pelham, by now deeply committed to the restoration of financial equilibrium at home. Though there was a soundness in Newcastle's ambitious plan to purchase princely support for the election of the Archduke Joseph as 'King of the Romans', thereby preventing any future outbreak of war over the imperial succession and securing Anglo-Austrian relations, Pelham's support for it was at best half-hearted. Newcastle was continually irritated by Pelham's campaign to reduce expenditure, always insisting that the upkeep of alliances must come first. Pelham went along with Newcastle's scheme not least because of the King's concern for the defence of Hanover. He proved correct in believing that the plan might result in Britain's being drawn into a game, and by 1752 it had to be abandoned as the electoral princes increased their monetary demands and broke promises. There can be little doubt that Pelham's resistance to the provision of subsidies on the scale required helped relegate 'old system' diplomacy and promote the establishment of ties with Europe's newest and most vigorous power, Prussia.

Historians correctly identify Pelham's financial reforms as his major achievement. Although he carried on much of Walpole's work in the management of government debt, his approach to these problems was far more comprehensive. Indeed, Pelham's work in these pastures has been recognized as marking the zenith of the 'financial revolution'. In August 1748, with peace in sight, he told Newcastle that having had 'very little comfort in the great scene of business I have long been engaged in', his one 'selfish ambition' was to reduce the national debt which in 1748 stood at £76 million (Connors 1993: 70). Over the next two years he succeeded in scaling down government expenditure from £12 million to £7 million. This was greatly facilitated by cutting the army back from 50,000 to its peacetime level of 18,850 men, and the navy from 51,550 to 8,000. His wholesale reduction in the size and cost of the government's fiscal bureaucracy was probably the most extensive undertaken by an eighteenth-century prime minister (Brewer 1989: 87, 261, n. 77). Backbenchers received encouraging signs of the direction of his peacetime policy in 1749 when he lowered the burden of direct taxation on the landed classes by reducing the land tax from four shillings in the pound to three, reducing it again to two shillings in 1752, though it still proved necessary to make compensatory increases in indirect taxes. Pelham left the haphazard structure of revenue collection as he found it. Although an administrative shake-up might well have enabled him to introduce further economies, the furore in 1733 over Walpole's excise scheme had made it compellingly obvious that any major reform entailing an increase of government officialdom ran high political risks both within parliament and in the public domain at large.

By 1748 as much as 44 per cent of government expenditure was absorbed in the payment of interest on the greatly increased national debt. It was here, in the specialist realms of Treasury finance, that Pelham made his greatest mark. At the end of 1749, taking advantage of the buoyancy of government stock, he obtained parliamentary approval for his innovative 'conversion scheme' to reduce the interest rate on the debt from 4 per cent to 3.5 per cent by 1750, and down to 3 per cent by 1757. Such an across-the-board cut in the interest rate was an unparalleled stroke of fiscal engineering. In the early stages of its implementation the scheme was a considerable gamble and highly unpopular with the monied companies, especially the Bank of England, but Pelham quickly won their backing with the assistance of such enlightened City figures as Sir John Barnard and the Jewish financier Sampson Gideon. As a result most of the holders of 4 per cent stock were persuaded to accept stock at the lower rate, enabling Pelham to cut the cost of servicing the national debt by 12 per cent in 1750. He subsequently consolidated most of the old government stocks, thus further simplifying the machinery of public borrowing.

The wisdom of Pelham's financial strategy has not gone uncriticized, however. His pursuit of a rigorous policy of retrenchment at a time of international instability has been questioned on the grounds that it left Britain militarily ill-prepared for war in 1756 (Holmes and Szechi 1993: 271). Although this may well highlight a deficiency of foresight on Pelham's part in the realm of foreign affairs, he was forced to act within immediate political constraints. To have tried to extract high military expenditure from parliament while the nation enjoyed a muchneeded peace would have seriously undermined backbench goodwill. His policies, rather like Walpole's, stemmed from his responsibility for the Treasury and an ingrained sense of caution where the Commons was concerned.

Pelham's administration is sometimes regarded as consciously adopting a reformist stance, but there is little to suggest this was so. Although a few distinct-ive pieces of ministerial legislation reached the statute book, namely the acts to reform the calendar (1751), limit the production and sale of spirits (1751) and prevent clandestine marriages (1753), their reforming scope was limited. In the usual fashion of eighteenth-century legislation, these measures addressed specific kinds of problem in an unenterprising way. Pelham had good cause to regret Hardwicke's Marriage Bill on account of the unremitting opposition it provoked from Henry Fox, his right-hand man in the Commons, who himself had eloped with a duke's daughter. An Act of 1753 permitting Jews to become naturalized by private Act of Parliament was intended by Pelham as a gesture of gratitude to the Jewish financial community for their assistance in his debt reconstruction scheme, but popular hostility forced its repeal later the same year. While some matters of wider social importance, such as the punishment of crime and the welfare of the poor, did receive much parliamentary attention under Pelham, the initiative came from backbench MPs rather than the administration. The most draconian of Pelhamite laws sought to implement a harsh policy of 'Scotch Reformation' fol-lowing the Pretender's defeat at Culloden. Passed between 1746 and 1748, these measures were a sweeping attempt to break the traditional structures of highland society, but perhaps more than anything else they represent the severity with which the Whig establishment could respond to threats to order and stability.

Pelham died in office at the age of 59 after a short illness. In the ensuing ministerial struggle for advantage, the extent to which he had contained the tensions of disagreement was made bitterly obvious. Setting aside his weaknesses and foibles, friends and enemies alike could agree without reservation that he had discharged his public duties with exemplary care and honesty. 'He lived without abusing his power', wrote Horace Walpole, 'and died poor' (Hodgart 1963: 46).

References and further reading

Barnes, D. (1961) 'Henry Pelham and the Duke of Newcastle', *Journal of British Studies* 1: 62–77.

Brewer, J. (1989) *The Sinews of Power: War, Money and the English State, 1688–1783*, London: Unwin Hyman.

Browning, R. (1975) *The Duke of Newcastle*, New Haven, CT: Yale University Press.

Connors, R.T. (1993) 'Pelham, parliament and public policy, 1746–1754', unpublished PhD thesis, University of Cambridge.

Coxe, W. (1829) *Memoirs of the Administration of the Rt. Hon. Henry Pelham*, 2 vols, London: Longman, Rees, Orme, Brown & Green.

Dickson, P. (1967) *The Financial Revolution in England 1688–1756*, London: Macmillan.

Hervey, John Lord (1931) *Some Materials towards Memoirs of the Reign of King George II*, ed. R. Sedgwick, 3 vols, London: Eyre & Spottiswoode.

Hill, B. (1985) *British Parliamentary Parties 1742–1832*, London: Allen & Unwin.

Hodgart, M. (ed.) (1963) *Horace Walpole's Memoirs and Portraits*, London: Batsford.

Holmes, G. and Szechi, D. (1993) *The Age of Oligarchy: Pre-industrial Britain 1722–1783*, London: Longman.

Langford, P. (1989) *A Polite and Commercial People: England 1727–1783*, Oxford: Oxford University Press.

Owen, J. (1957) *The Rise of the Pelhams*, London: Methuen.

—— (1973) 'George II reconsidered', in A. Whiteman, J.S. Bromley and P. Dickson (eds) *Statesman, Scholars and Merchants*, Oxford: Oxford University Press.

Sayer MSS (East Sussex Record Office (RO), Lewes), SAY 393, Pelham to John Collier, 1 April 1738.

Sedgwick, R. (1970) *The History of Parliament: The House of Commons 1715–1754*, London: HMSO.

Wilkes, J. (1964) *A Whig in Power*, New York: Northwestern University Press.

Andrew Hanham

Thomas Pelham-Holles, Duke of Newcastle

Born 21 July 1693, eldest son of Thomas, first Lord Pelham, and his second wife, Lady Grace, sister of John Holles, Duke of Newcastle. Educated at Westminster and Clare College, Cambridge. Added name of Holles in July 1711 on succeeding (as adopted heir) to the bulk of the estates of his uncle John. Succeeded father as Lord Pelham, 23 February 1712. Created Duke of Newcastle upon Tyne, 11 August 1715. Married 1717 Lady Henrietta, eldest daughter of Francis, second Earl of Godolphin. Privy Councillor 1717; Knight of the Garter 1718. Lord Chamberlain of the Household 1717–24; Secretary of State for the Southern Department 1724–48; Secretary of State for the Northern Department 1748–54; First Lord of the Treasury 1754–6 and 1757–62; Lord Privy Seal 1765–6. Died 17 November 1768.

Newcastle was the most prominent of the Old Corps Whigs, those Whigs who stayed in office throughout the reigns of George I and George II and who found the accession in 1760 of George III with his non-party views so difficult to deal with. The Old Corps came to see themselves as the natural party of government. On 5 November 1760 the fourth Duke of Devonshire, a member of the inner cabinet, told George's favourite, the Earl of Bute, that

> the Duke of Newcastle had united with him the principal nobility, the moneyed men and the interest which had brought about the [Glorious] Revolution, had set this [Hanoverian] family on the throne and supported them in it, and were not only the most considerable party but the true solid strength that might be depended on for the support of government. That therefore his Grace was undoubtedly the most necessary person for the King to cultivate.
>
> (Brown and Schweizer 1982)

George III was not to follow this advice and his destabilization of the Old Corps led directly to Newcastle's fall. That provided one clue to the minister's earlier longevity. Although both George I and George II had on occasion disliked the hegemony of the Old Corps they were dependent on them. Neither monarch was prepared to turn to the Tory opposition, which they suspected of Jacobitism, and, among the Whigs, only the Old Corps seemed able to deliver the secure control of parliament that was necessary if the government's business was to be financed.

Newcastle played a major role in ensuring that control. Unlike Sir Robert Walpole, and Henry Pelham, his younger brother, Newcastle did not sit in the Commons and he was dependent on having the co-operation of a reliable parliamentary manager there: the failure of Henry Fox to fulfil this role in 1756 led to Newcastle's fall that year. However, as a minister willing to give much time and attention, and much of his own money to patronage, Newcastle played a crucial role in maintaining Old Corps cohesion, and thus strength, in the difficult years after the fall of Walpole in 1742.

During the reign of George I Newcastle was very much a junior minister, but he prominently displayed his loyalty. When Townshend and Walpole went over to opposition in 1717, Newcastle stayed with the ministry and attached himself to Charles, third Earl of Sunderland, a leading minister who was a relative by marriage.

Newcastle did not gain a position of business until 1724 when he succeeded Carteret as a secretary of state. He was, however, very much the junior secretary until the fall of his co-secretary, Charles, third Viscount Townshend in 1730. Thereafter, Newcastle became much more important in the formulation and execution of foreign policy, especially from 1744 when Carteret, who had regained office in 1742, was forced out by the Old Corps.

From 1744 until 1754 it is arguably more appropriate to write of a duumvirate than of a prime minister. Henry Pelham was the manager of the Commons and, as First Lord of the Treasury, a crucial minister, but Newcastle, as effective Foreign Minister, most influential politician in the Lords and wielder of much government and church patronage, was definitely not subordinate to his brother. Their correspondence survives and it is clear that each was frustrated by the difficulty of managing the other: Pelham thought Newcastle's diplomatic commitments too expensive and sought to limit them.

Similarly, and more famously, the Newcastle–Pitt ministry of 1757–61 was really a duumvirate. It is clear that Pitt did not wield the degree of power that is sometimes attributed to him. It has been shown that Newcastle was concerned about more than patronage and that George II still exercised considerable power, and thus that Pitt's role in the formulation of policy was not unchallenged. The crucial importance of the financing of the war ensured that Newcastle's post as First Lord of the Treasury was a key one.

Nevertheless, the Seven Years War (1756–63) accentuated a central feature of the political system, namely that successful parliamentary management required competent leadership and acceptable policies, as well as patronage, and that, especially in periods of real and apparent crisis, such policies tended to take note of opinion 'out of doors', however manipulated, and however it was measured, and whatever the state of ministerial control of parliament. Given this situation, it was not surprising that Pitt played a central role during the Newcastle–Pitt ministry, one that does not need to be explained solely in terms of his ability or of Newcastle's indecisiveness and desire to share responsibility.

Even less was Newcastle prime minister when he was Lord Privy Seal in Rockingham's administration. The Marquess of Rockingham had been a protégé of Newcastle, but by 1765 the Duke was increasingly an elderly figure from the political past taking on a subordinate role. If Newcastle is to be seen as prime minister then the most appropriate criterion is not that of the specific office which he held. He was First Lord of the Treasury in both 1754–6 and 1757–62, but it was only in the former period that he can really be seen as prime minister. Even then he was dependent on having a colleague who could manage the Commons. Therein lay much of the instability of the period 1754–6, for it proved impossible to arrange for effective management. Henry Fox refused to accept the task in 1754 when he discovered that Newcastle intended to retain full control of all government patronage and to manage the forthcoming general election: that would have left him without the power to give substance to his management. Thus Newcastle turned to Sir Thomas Robinson, a pliable ex-diplomat with no independent political base. Robinson was not strong enough to deal with the political problems that faced the government in 1754–5 as Britain moved closer to war with France and found her allies unwilling to offer support. As a result, in November 1755, Newcastle agreed to make Fox secretary of state and Leader of the Commons.

The Newcastle ministry had done very well in the general election of 1754; yet it was to collapse in 1756. It apparently fell as a result of the popular agitation over the humiliating loss of Minorca to the French, a defeat that also led to the execution of Admiral Byng for cowardice. Such an interpretation would appear to vindicate an analysis of eighteenth-century politics that places stress on extra-parliamentary agitation.

The situation in 1756 was in fact more complex. Though Fox's inability to stand up to Pitt, of whom he was frightened in debate, was a very important factor, the likely parliamentary storm over Minorca also brought to a head the question of relations between Newcastle and Fox and thus created a crisis of parliamentary management irrespective of the activities of the opposition. Thus, the crisis of 1756 that brought down Newcastle echoed those of 1742, 1744 and 1746 in which he had played a major role: the government was divided. Under these circumstances, it was important for politicians to consider how best to create a new stable ministerial alignment, and Newcastle was unable to do this in 1756.

Fox attributed his resignation on 13 October 1756 to Newcastle's refusal to provide him with the necessary support in the Commons and to the Duke's willingness to consider replacing him with Pitt. Fox complained that he had

> no power of making a friend or intimidating an adversary; and yet to attempt
> to lead a House of Commons with less help even in debate on our side than

was known. . . . I not only would not, but could not carry on the King's affairs without the Duke of Newcastle. It is absolutely impossible to go on with him. I therefore must get out of court . . . I find my credit in the House of Commons diminishing for want of support.

These charges were symptomatic of an essential distrust in a relationship strained by deteriorating political circumstances and put under stress by the ambiguous nature of links between senior ministers in a political system that lacked a sense of stability, clear conventions for ministerial responsibility and a prime minister whose functions of directing government business and deploying ministerial patronage were clear-cut.

These were serious structural problems, but they were exacerbated by Newcastle's personality. The standard contemporary criticisms of the Duke's frenetic fussiness and limited public ability, criticisms given mordant edge by Horace Walpole, John, Lord Hervey, and James, second Earl Waldegrave, were less significant than the charge, made by both Horace Walpole and Waldegrave, that he was dominated by jealousy. 'As to his jealousy,' Waldegrave claimed, 'it would not be carried to a higher pitch, if every political friend was a favourite mistress'. Jealousy, according to Horace Walpole,

> was the great source of all his faults. He always caressed his enemies, to list them against his friends: there was no service he would not do either, till either was above being served by him: then he would suspect they did not love him enough, for the moment they had every reason to love him, he took every method to obtain their hate, by exerting all his power for their ruin.

This surely reflected a deep personal insecurity, and, indeed, Horace Walpole stated, 'fear, a ridiculous fear, was predominant in him' (Brooke 1985: i, 109). This anxiety led to his frenetic, over-anxious conduct of himself and business, and also to the concern that led him to play a major role in undermining Townshend, Walpole, Carteret and Bedford. These underminings were born of anxiety rather than ambition, though Newcastle was not without the latter. But once he was, as a pamphlet of 1755 put it, 'the *Primum Mobile* of the whole Administration', the political impact of his distrust of others took on a new trajectory. Before 1754 Newcastle had been restrained to a considerable extent, first by Walpole and then by Henry Pelham. In 1754–6, however, he sought to surround himself by weaklings, a course already anticipated in 1751 when he had the independent John, fourth Duke of Bedford, replaced as Secretary of State for the Southern Department by the more pliant Robert, fourth Earl of Holdernesse. Yet Newcastle lacked both the personality and the position to sustain the political structure that his paranoia dictated: a concentration of decision-making and power on his own person. He could not be a second Walpole. His personality was not strong enough to take and, more crucially, bear responsibility for decisions and his anxiety led to indecisiveness. Newcastle wanted strong colleagues, able to take such responsibility, and for that reason operated best successively with Henry Pelham and Pitt. Yet he wanted these colleagues clearly subordinate and could not psychologically accept his own dependence on them; he was weak but did not wish to acknowledge this weakness.

Aside from lacking the character necessary for the successful retention of high office, Newcastle also did not hold an office that would free him from, or at least lessen, his anxieties. For all his frenetic activity, and the time and personal wealth he devoted to patronage, Newcastle was only the most important member of the ministry. The King was the head of the government and played a crucial role in the complex political negotiations of 1754–7. Although willing to accept Newcastle, George II was not close to him and this was a major source of the Duke's anxiety. Similarly, Newcastle was unsure of parliament. Despite devoting so much of his time to electoral patronage and parliamentary management, Newcastle knew that it was difficult to maintain the impression of governmental control of the Commons; this, as well as his difficulty in accepting criticism, led him to devote so much time to patronage and management. His was a personal example of a more general weakness. The Old Corps political system could not cope with failure. The absence of a reliable party unity on which government could rest left politicians feeling vulnerable to attack. It was in this context that Pitt in opposition was an obvious threat, for although enjoying a measure of Tory support, he was a Whig able to exploit adverse developments in the war, and it was difficult to feel confident of political success against such a figure. This therefore exacerbated Newcastle's anxiety about his position.

Newcastle controlled neither Crown nor Commons. He sought to be a crucial intermediary; but that was an unstable basis for political control, one that was not only prey to circumstances but also too uncertain to free the Duke from his anxieties. Thus in May 1756 Newcastle pressed one of the few able men he relied on, William Murray, later first Earl of Mansfield, to stay in the Commons, claiming that 'nobody but yourself will or can support me; and . . . in this House of Commons support the King and his measures against such a formed opposition and at such a critical conjuncture'.

This was an over-reaction, but it captured Newcastle's lack of confidence over the leadership of parliament. He tried to deal with the crisis by winning over opposition, neutering hostility by accommodating it in terms of government position. After Fox resigned on 13 October 1756, Newcastle persuaded George II to permit him to offer Pitt a secretaryship of state in return for his support. Pitt, however, sought not a reconstitution of the ministry but a rejection of the government and its policies. He demanded the resignation of Newcastle, an inquiry into recent setbacks and the dismissal of foreign troops in British pay. Pitt was determined that he should not simply defend government policy, which was what Newcastle sought. He insisted that a scheme of measures be adopted that he could approve and defend.

George II rejected Pitt's terms, but Newcastle, unsuccessful in his attempt to find a Commons leader other than Fox or Pitt, told the King on 26 October that he could not engage to conduct business in the Commons and resigned the next day.

The following year Newcastle returned to office, and the process by which he did so throws light on his problems in 1756. It proved necessary for both Newcastle and Pitt to compromise. His apparent indispensability in the Commons had allowed Pitt to set Newcastle and Fox at defiance in October 1756, and, despite Pitt's unpopularity with George II, neither Newcastle nor Fox seemed to have a good chance of forming a government that could survive in the Commons without Pitt; in large measure because it would be vulnerable to devastating oratory from Pitt if anything went wrong with the handling of the war. Fox did not have the stomach for the fight, and Newcastle had no one of sufficient stature or courage to take Pitt on. There seemed to be no alternative, and Pitt knew it. His position might have looked weak, but it was stronger than anyone else's, though not strong enough for him to run a government all by himself. The approach of the parliamentary session had destroyed the Newcastle administration in October 1756, and the creation of a viable leadership in the Commons was the key issue thereafter.

Newcastle therefore found himself in a different position in the wartime political crisis of 1744–6 and 1756–7. In the former it was the Pelhams who could offer Commons management and Carteret who was weakened by his inability to do so. In 1756–7 Newcastle could not promise a pliant Commons. Without his brother, he was in a far weaker position, but this also owed much to Pitt's ability to strike a popular political resonance, accessible to Whigs and Tories within and outside parliament; a skill Carteret lacked both for personal reasons and because of the policies he actively advanced.

Whiggery had a number of strands. It was originally an opposition movement with new ideas and that provided much of its vitality. However, its potency rested on royal favour – the replacement of James II by William III and, more securely, the accession of the Hanoverians. Newcastle was very much an establishment politician, whose political career took place during long years of unbroken (although not unchallenged) Whig hegemony. He was never an MP. He had little knowledge or understanding of populist, let alone radical, dimensions to Whiggery. That cannot be presented as a measure of failure: such dimensions were neither expected of him nor were they crucial to his falls in 1756 and 1762. Yet, if most of his limitations derived from his personality, it can also be suggested that his problems reflected in part the narrowing of the Whig tradition during a period of growing change in British society and political culture.

References and further reading

Black, J. (1992) *Pitt the Elder*, Cambridge: Cambridge University Press. (A major study of Newcastle's opponent that centres on the political crisis of 1754–7 and the Newcastle–Pitt ministry.)

—— (1993) *The Politics of Britain 1688–1801*, Manchester: Manchester University Press. (Most recent study of the political system. Much discussion of Newcastle and also offers a context within which to consider the Duke's position.)

Brooke, J. (ed.) (1985) *Horace Walpole: Memoirs of King George II*, 3 vols, New Haven, CT: Yale University Press. (Bitter and witty critic of the Duke.)

Brown, P.D. and Schweizer, K.W. (eds) (1982) *The Devonshire Diary: William Cavendish, Fourth Duke of Devonshire. Memoranda on State of Affairs 1757–1762*, London: Royal Historical Society.

Browning, R. (1975) *The Duke of Newcastle*, New Haven: Yale University Press. (The only major biographical study.)

Clark, J. (ed.) (1988) *The Memoirs and Speeches of James, 2nd Earl Waldegrave 1742–1763*, Cambridge: Cambridge University Press. (A vital source for the court and high politics during the 1750s.)

Kelch, R. (1974) *Newcastle: A Duke without Money. Thomas Pelham-Holles 1693–1768*, London: Routledge & Kegan Paul. (A detailed study of the Duke's finances that reveals the extent to which they were exhausted by his political activity.)

Newcastle, Duke of, the Newcastle papers in the Additional Manuscripts Collection in the British Library, vols 32685–33083. (Much of this collection is also available on microfilm from Research Publications. The fundamental source for the Duke's career and for mid-century politics.)

Yorke, P. (1913) *The Life and Correspondence of Philip Yorke Earl of Hardwicke*, Cambridge: Cambridge University Press. (High politics from the perspective of Newcastle's closest ally, which contains much of the Duke's correspondence.)

Jeremy Black

William Cavendish, Fourth Duke of Devonshire

Born c. 1720, first son of William Cavendish, third Duke of Devonshire, and Catherine Hoskins. Married 1748 Charlotte Boyle, daughter and heir of Richard, second Earl of Burlington. Privy Councillor 1751–3; Master of the Horse 1751–5; Lord Treasurer of Ireland 1754–5 and 1761–3; Lord Lieutenant of Ireland 1755–6; Lord Lieutenant of Derbyshire 1756–64; First Lord of the Treasury 1756–7; Lord Chamberlain 1757–62. Died 2 October 1764.

Devonshire's tenure as prime minister is one of the shortest on record. He was a victim of circumstance in the political conflagration arising from the rivalry between William Pitt and the Duke of Newcastle over the conduct of the Seven Years War (1756–63). Devonshire was known to his contemporaries as a staunch Whig of the old school. He defended the Hanoverian dynasty with every fibre of his political being, and was willing to cut any deal that kept perceived enemies of the Crown from office. His devotion to George II is the reason he became a stop-gap leader of the government in the early years of the war. Until Pitt and Newcastle could settle their differences and unite the various parliamentary factions, and the country at large, to fight the war against France, Cavendish's role was to hold the line against total government collapse from November 1756 to July 1757. Indeed, as Lord Waldegrave observed at the time, when Devonshire accepted the post of leader from the King all his advisers were stating bluntly that the 'Administration would be routed at the opening of the next session of parliament' (Clark 1988: 205).

With such modest goals in mind, Devonshire was not overtaxed in meeting them over his nine months in power. His past experience in service of the King and court rendered Devonshire the perfect foil to the intense political strife generated by the squabble between Pitt and Newcastle. Devonshire was an aristocrat of the old school. Portraits show him as imperious, smug and steely-eyed. His primary duty was to the House of Hanover which had done so much to forward the power of the Cavendish family. He believed in the superiority of aristocratic government over the threatened anarchy surrounding the activities of populist figures, like Admiral Vernon or William Pitt. His character and career demonstrated 'a natural balance of judgement, prudence, patriotism, and above all a sense of service without self-seeking' (Brown and Schweizer 1982: 1). Devonshire, in other words, stood above the fray like no other premier in the pre-reform political era.

It is odd then that his short ministry should be remembered principally for sanctioning the execution of Lord Byng, on 14 March 1757, after the loss of Minorca in the previous year's campaigning. This judicial murder proved very unpopular with some in parliament and caused the resignation of several government supporters, including William Pitt. In Devonshire's strait-laced view, however, Byng was guilty of dereliction of duty and had to be held accountable. This proved the popular view as Byng 'had been hanged in Effigy in almost every Town in England' (Clark 1988: 189). The rest of the business undertaken by government under Devonshire's leadership was perfunctory wartime preparation and the procurement of supplies. This work was done to a constant hum of intrigue and negotiation, as courtiers and parliamentary leaders sought to heal the breach between Newcastle and Pitt (Clark 1982: 283–447). The reconciliation took place in early July 1757 and Devonshire resigned as First Lord, taking the office of Lord Chamberlain from the King by way of compensation. Devonshire was very happy with this outcome. He took office only on the understanding 'that he would retain the Treasury but till some new system should be completed': thus Devonshire was 'charmed with the baubles of the Chamberlain's office' (Brooke 1985: ii, 254–7).

From this point on until his death seven years later, Devonshire returned to his favoured career of serving the King personally without the rancour of party politics. In this sense Devonshire was not a modern politician at all. He attended cabinet or council meetings until his demise but saw no utility in the processes of parliamentary government assisting decision-making in the executive branch of government. He kept a diary of wartime negotiations between 1759 and 1762 which offers keen insights into diplomatic affairs of the time (Brown and Schweizer 1982). But it reveals little of the man or his motivation to be involved in politics beyond that much hackneyed and overused phrase, *noblesse oblige*. Devonshire was a durable, reliable and honourable man who served his King, and incidentally the country, when called upon for nine short months during the dark years of the Seven Years War. He died a relatively young man at 44 years of age, a tribute to a bygone age of political organization and power-broking.

References and further reading

Brooke, J. (ed.) (1985) *Horace Walpole's Memoirs of the Last Ten Years of the Reign of George II*, 3 vols, New Haven: Yale University Press.

Brown, P. and Schweizer, K. (eds) (1982) *The Devonshire Diary: William Cavendish Fourth Duke of Devonshire Memoranda on State Affairs 1759–1762*, London: Royal Historical Society.

Clark, J. (1982) *The Dynamics of Change: The Crisis of the 1750s and English Party Systems*, Cambridge: Cambridge University Press. (This study represents the most modern and detailed treatment of Devonshire's premiership and career in the 1750s.)

—— (ed.) (1988) *The Memoirs and Speeches of James 2nd Earl Waldegrave*, Cambridge: Cambridge University Press. (A very good, gossipy, contemporary account of the events surrounding Devonshire's premiership.)

Philip Lawson

John Stuart, Third Earl of Bute

Born 25 May 1713, eldest son of the second Earl of Bute and Lady Anne Campbell, daughter of the first Duke of Argyll. Educated at Eton and Leyden University. Married 1736 Mary, daughter of Edward Montague. Representative Peer for Scotland 1737–41, 1768–80. Knight of the Thistle 1738; Knight of the Garter 1762. Secretary of State for the Northern Department 1761; First Lord of the Treasury 1762–63. Died 10 March 1792.

Bute, the first Scotsman to head the Treasury, has an unenviable reputation as perhaps the most unpopular British prime minister of all time. His swift rise to power, allied to his nationality, earned him unusually intense public abuse, and during his brief ministerial career, as well as into retirement, he was maligned in the press, threatened with assassination, attacked by the mob and burned in effigy on both sides of the Atlantic (Brewer 1973). These manifestations of popular hostility had their counterpart in his condemnation after 1763 by the nation's political leaders as well as by opposition polemicists – John Almon, Horace Walpole, Burke and others – for whom he was the embodiment of 'prerogative politics': an ambitious yet mediocre courtier responsible for the divisions following the accession of George III because of his determination to extend regal power. Recent scholarship has taken a more benevolent view, raising Bute's standing as a politician and also recognizing his enlightened patronage of science and the arts.

Although Bute was elected a Scottish representative peer in April 1737, he attended the House only occasionally and evidently took no part in the debates. Losing his seat in the election of 1741, he retired to his Scottish estates where he pursued the study of agriculture, literature and botany. Soon after the outbreak of the Jacobite rebellion, he moved to London and in 1747 made the chance acquaintance of Frederick, Prince of Wales – perhaps the major turning-point in his life. He became a favourite at Leicester House, the Prince's London residence, and after Frederick's premature death in 1751 a confidant of the royal widow, Princess Augusta. This friendship subsequently led to Bute's appointment as tutor and principal adviser of the new Prince of Wales, the future George III.

In this capacity he not only directed the Prince's formal education but also gained the latter's confidence and affection, becoming in George's own words 'his dearest friend' (Bullion 1989). This relationship developed rapidly, the impressionable Prince's emotional dependence upon his mentor facilitating a ready acceptance of Bute's personal ideals and political principles, portrayed in written assignments which combined formal instructions in history, consti- tutional theory and finance with ambitious plans for governmental reform (Bul- lion 1986). Elaborated further in daily correspondence, their ideas comprise a blend of traditional Leicester House themes and 'country party' precepts: a com- posite political creed advocating an isolationist foreign policy – specifically the avoidance of expensive continental commitments – and domestically, the aboli- tion of party distinctions, the purging of corruption and the enhancement of monarchical control over policy and patronage (Sedgwick 1939). However con- ventional as opposition ideology, these ideas were taken seriously by Bute and his pupil who were determined to implement them. They represented a common vision of Britain's future, and as such influenced decisively the reconfiguration of politics during George III's early reign.

Bute first became active in the political world following the death of Henry Pelham in 1754, negotiating on behalf of Leicester House an agreement with William Pitt to oppose the Newcastle–Fox connection – an alliance based on their shared hostility to George II's pro-Hanoverian policy in the face of impending war against France. This arrangement unravelled throughout 1757, once Pitt joined forces with Newcastle – becoming secretary of state – and then reversed his stand on the German war, thereby alienating his former political allies and creating a breach that was never repaired (Brooke 1972: 60–72). Meanwhile Bute, though not in parliament, had emerged as one of the leading politicians in the kingdom. Key figures both within and outside the confines of Leicester House looked to him for patronage, asked for his intervention at the highest levels, and sought his advice on their plans for political advancement. His unquestioned dominance at the young court secured him the position of Groom of the Stole (1756) and he was widely considered a prime candidate for high office whenever his ward ascended the throne.

The long awaited moment came with the death of George II on 25 October 1760. Within two days after George III's accession, Bute was named to the Privy Council, and in March 1761 entered the ministry as secretary of state with a cabinet seat – to the manifest displeasure of Pitt and other senior ministers who scorned his inexperience and resented his standing with the King (Brown and Schweizer 1982).

From the outset Bute's rapid elevation created confusion, strife and misunderstandings not warranted by the actual train of events. Despite an inevitably altered atmosphere at court, existing arrangements continued: Newcastle remained in charge of Treasury affairs, Pitt's management of the war proceeded unchanged and the main contours of Britain's overall military–diplomatic strategy remained intact. Even Bute performed his duties as secretary of state with an efficiency and dedication that surprised many. Recent studies have shown that Bute was a competent, hardworking, conscientious minister, well versed in European affairs and quite capable of pursuing coherent policies with intelligence and resolution. He swiftly developed self-confidence once in office, winning both the respect and loyalty of his subordinates, particularly the veteran Under-Secretary Edward Weston, with whose collaboration he worked to improve the operational efficiency of the Northern Department. He also made a good impression on the foreign representatives in London – men invariably shrewd and well informed – as industrious, perceptive and capable, qualities considerably greater than his historical reputation suggests (Schweizer 1988: 6–7). This conclusion has been substantiated by work on the Anglo-French negotiations for peace during the summer of 1761, demonstrating that Bute, not Pitt, was primarily responsible for devising the proposals submitted to France and maintaining the political unity that made effective deliberation possible (Schweizer 1981: 262–75). Bute sided with Pitt on most of the issues but could not sanction his proposal for a pre-emptive strike against Spain – then joined to France in alliance – a refusal which hastened the cabinet crisis, leading to Pitt's resignation on 5 October 1761.

Unable to compromise or share power, Pitt (perhaps intentionally) defied united cabinet opinion and hence made his resignation inevitable. In the public perception, however, he was a victim of court intrigue, and the remaining ministers, Bute especially, came under bitter mob and press attack. Bute calmed partisan clamour by continuing Pitt's military policies and adopting firm measures against Spain, causing that power to become openly defiant and Britain, consequently, to declare war on 4 January 1762. Simultaneously, in response to growing war weariness, Bute secretly renewed the lapsed peace negotiations with France and, anxious about the financial implications of war with Spain, adopted a policy of retrenchment from the continent, resulting in the progressive dissolution of Britain's alliance with Prussia, its wartime partner since 1757, and an alternately greater focus on colonial commitments (Schweizer 1991). Here again, recent revisionist scholarship has been sympathetic to Bute's diplomatic programme, placing it in the context of a gradual eastward shift in the pattern of European alignments which seriously diminished Britain's continental influence after 1763, thereby precluding any innovative diplomatic strokes (Scott 1990). On many diplomatic issues Bute brought to successful completion policies initiated earlier, between 1758 and 1760, by the Pitt–Newcastle administration. In the military realm, too, Bute's leadership in retaining and supporting the essential elements of Pitt's wartime strategy yielded further triumphs, including the capture of St Lucia, Martinique and Havana, the key to Spain's West Indian possessions. This suggests that the contrast between Bute's administration and that of his immediate predecessors, certainly in foreign affairs, was less dramatic than is usually assumed – an important conclusion with wide implications for Bute's historical status.

Nevertheless, Bute's severance of the connection with Prussia, part of his over-all determination to reduce Britain's continental commitment, gave rise to deep political divisions over the general direction of government policy, culminating in Newcastle's resignation on 26 May 1762 as First Lord of the Treasury and Bute's appointment in his place. Now at the head of affairs, Bute accelerated the pending negotiations with France – negotiations that were tortuous and fraught with difficulty. On three key issues – the future of St Lucia, the possibility of a separate peace without Spain and the question of compensation for Havana – Bute encountered bitter resistance from his cabinet colleagues which required all his authority combined with royal intervention to overcome. The Duke of Bedford was then dispatched to Paris as special ambassador; he completed the deliber-ations without further incident and the preliminaries of peace were signed in November 1762.

Although the terms of peace were vehemently attacked by Pitt in parliament as grossly inadequate, most historians agree that the treaty *per se*, considered by Bute himself to be his major achievement, was an honourable, advantageous settle-ment: rich compensation for Britain's global victories and a serious blow to French power. George III called it 'a noble peace' and the consensus of political opinion agreed: the preliminaries passed both in the Lords and the Commons by decisive majorities and received formal ratification on 10 February 1763.

Since, with the exception of London and segments of the merchant com-munity, the country at large approved of the treaty, it seems clear that such opposition to the peace as existed derived from personal antagonism towards Bute by his political rivals who fanned public hostility against him (Schweizer 1974). This steadily gathered momentum until by the spring of 1763 Bute was 'the most unpopular man in England', vulgarly abused and maligned wherever he went, the target of unrelenting vilification in the press (Coats 1975: 30). Com-pounding the uproar was the unfortunate proposal at this time by Sir Francis Dashwood, Bute's Chancellor of the Exchequer, for a tax on cider, the collection and enforcement of which would have threatened personal liberty through intru-sion of inquisitorial officials. This measure was portrayed by Bute's opponents as part of an odious scheme to introduce a 'general excise', similar to what Walpole had allegedly envisaged in 1733. Despite its intense unpopularity Bute ably defended the Bill in the Lords and it received royal approval on 1 April 1763.

Eight days later, physically ill, weary of politics and politicians, and unnerved by the savage attacks against him, Bute resigned from office, declaring that 'the ground I stand on is so hollow that I am afraid not only of falling myself, but of involving my royal master in my ruin' (Pike 1968: 61). Bute was replaced as First Lord of the Treasury by his nominee, George Grenville, but though no longer a minister, he still retained the King's confidence. George III appears to have con-sulted him at all the critical junctures over the next few years: the overtures towards Pitt and the Bedford connection in August 1763, the Stamp Act, the Regency Bill and probably the negotiations with the opposition in 1767. Inevitably this gave rise to the notion of 'secret influence': the belief, prevalent for some time, that even in retirement Bute directed the wheels of government from behind the scenes, advising the King and manipulating ministries in ways that explained the incessant political crises of the 1760s (Schweizer 1988: 57–81). Successive administrations attributed their misfortunes to Bute's covert machinations and persistently demanded that George cease to consult the favourite – indeed, as with the Grenvilles, made this a condition of their continuance in office. Certainly by 1767 George III's faith in Bute had waned, and henceforth the latter's influence in matters of state declined rapidly. He was abroad for much of 1768–9, and by 1770 his sway over the King had effectively ended. Belief in the secret influence of Bute nevertheless continued long after it had any justification in fact, eventually broadening into a conspiracy theory which characterized the ideology and manoeuvres of leading opposition groups well into the age of Lord North.

Bute spent the last years of his life at Christchurch, Hampshire, where he built a villa overlooking the Needles and the Isle of Wight. There, in melancholy grandeur, he pursued his botanic studies, collected pamphlets, books and scientific instruments, and guided the fortunes of his large family to whom he was much attached. He died at his house in South Audley Street, London, from complications following an accident, and was buried at Rothesay in his ancestral island of Bute.

Personifying the changing agenda implicit in George III's accession – that of ending party distinctions and reasserting royal independence – Bute has been blamed for the political instability resulting from the new King's quest for unrestrained executive power. His reputation was not enhanced by personal reserve. Although an affectionate friend and devoted family man, in public Bute appeared cold, distant and haughty – probably more from shyness than arrogance, for he felt himself unsuited by character and background for the demands of office. Happiest in scholarly seclusion, Bute was ill at ease on the political stage. His ministerial career is the tragic story of a man called to politics in middle age assuming a position he initially feared and eventually came to detest.

Bute's tenure as prime minister was brief, unhappy and turbulent, but not without success. Although the involuntary progenitor of prolonged political conflict between the Crown and the nation's politicians, Bute showed himself generally capable of leading a ministry in time of stress and war. For all his limitations, he did implement a coherent political strategy, one that consolidated Britain's imperial achievement and projected a minimalist continental policy at a time of intensifying national concern over the financial consequences of the Seven Years War. Altogether Bute was a responsible, cautious minister who maintained his concentration on the most important issues and had a clear sense of political priorities. This accomplishment commands all the more respect when one remembers his psychological aversion to governing and the multitude of problems confronting him from the outset. The lack of support from cabinet colleagues, his own personal unpopularity, bitter factionalism within the Whig ranks, a hostile press and the need to control a complex system of government – all might well have unsettled a more experienced minister. That Bute's concern for King and country prompted him to struggle on reveals qualities of courage and dedication not invariably associated with the trade of politics. Not selfish ambition, but loyalty and sincere affection for the King, led him to shoulder the cares of administration, despite vivid premonitions of the trials which lay ahead and the sacrifices he would have to make. 'I follow one uniform system', he wrote to Henry Fox shortly before his resignation, 'and that is founded in the strictest honour, faith and duty' – no mean epitaph for any public figure (BL Add MSS 51379 f. 1601).

References and further reading

Black, J. (ed.) (1990) *British Politics and Society from Walpole to Pitt, 1742–1789*, London: Macmillan.

Brewer, J. (1972) 'The faces of Lord Bute: a visual contribution to Anglo-American political ideology', *Perspectives in American History* 6: 95–116. (An interesting account of how Reynolds' portrait, completed in 1763, became a visual symbol of the sinister political role ascribed by so many contemporaries to Bute – a role in turn contrasted with the 'patriot' virtues personified by Pitt.)

—— (1973) 'The misfortunes of Lord Bute: a case-study of eighteenth century political argument and public opinion', *Historical Journal* 16: 3–43. (Still the most complete account of Bute's ubiquitous unpopularity and the constitutional issues this raised, though his interpretation of the Bute ministry's press policy has been amended on key points by the work of Marie Peters (1980) and the present author.)

—— (1976) *Party Ideology and Popular Politics at the Accession of George III*, Cambridge: Cambridge University Press. (Analyses in detail, with much new material, the political schisms and their constitutional effects created by Bute's brief career.)

Brooke, J. (1972) *King George III*, London: Constable. (Highly critical of Bute and Pitt, blaming both in near equal measure for the political instability of George III's early reign.)

Brown, P. and Schweizer, K. (eds) (1982) *The Devonshire Diary, 1759–1762*, London: Royal Historical Society. (Perhaps more than any other contemporary source, this diary, compiled by William Cavendish, fourth Duke of Devonshire, illuminates the sentiments of the Whig political elite towards George III's accession and Bute's rise to power. Also very useful for its first-hand account of the important cabinet meetings of 1761–2 over which Bute presided.)

Bullion, J. (1986) ' "To know this is the true essential business of a King": the Prince of Wales and the study of public finance', *Albion* 18: 429–54. (Analyses Prince George's essays on public finance and related subjects, composed under Bute's directions, and shows how the ideas developed therein affected his actions as monarch.)

—— (1989) 'The Prince's mentor: a new perspective on the friendship between

George III and Lord Bute during the 1750s', *Albion* 21: 34–55. (Develops a new interpretation of the friendship between George III and Bute, one that stresses political and ideological elements as much as personal bonds and evaluates the decisive impact of these on the first decade of George III's reign.)

Coats, A. (1975) *Lord Bute: An Illustrated Life*, Aylesbury: Shire Publications. (A lightweight biographical sketch based solely on secondary sources.)

Fox Manuscripts, British Library Additional Manuscripts 51379. (Contains many important letters from Bute to Fox, 1762–3.)

McKelvey, J. (1973) *George III and Lord Bute: The Leicester House Years*, Durham, NC: North Western University Press.

Peters, M. (1980) *Pitt and Popularity: The Patriot Minister and London Opinion during the Seven Years War*, London: Oxford University Press. (Includes a perceptive discussion of how the issues concerning relations between the King and ministers, and among ministers, were highlighted by the public press debate over Bute's political career during the years 1761–3.)

Pike, R. (1968) *Britain's Prime Ministers from Walpole to Wilson*, London: Odhams. (A brief biographical account which exaggerates George III's influence over Bute.)

Schweizer, K. (1974) 'Lord Bute and anti-Scottish feeling in eighteenth century English political propaganda', *Scottish Colloquium Proceedings* 8/9: 23–33. (Argues that Bute's nationality was a decisive factor in his intense unpopularity.)

—— (1981) 'William Pitt, Lord Bute and the peace negotiations with France, May–September 1761', *Albion* 13: 262–75. (Makes the case that Bute rather than Pitt was the decisive force in the 1761 negotiations with France and that he devised a viable and coherent peace strategy.)

—— (ed.) (1988) *Lord Bute: Essays in Reinterpretation*, Leicester: Leicester University Press. (Ten essays, based on manuscript materials, re-examining neglected aspects of Bute's public and private life.)

—— (1991) *Frederick the Great, William Pitt and Lord Bute: Anglo-Prussian Relations, 1756–1763*, New York: Garland Press. (Depicts Bute as an intelligent and effective minister forced to adapt his continental policy to the exigencies of intra-alliance politics as well as compelling domestic and financial restraints.)

Scott, H. (1990) *British Foreign Policy in the Age of the American Revolution*, Oxford: Clarendon Press. (Denies that Bute's Prussian policy was responsible for Britain's prolonged diplomatic isolation after 1763.)

Sedgwick, R. (1939) *Letters from George III to Lord Bute, 1756–1766*, London: Macmillan. (A fundamental source, covering virtually every aspect of Bute's relationship with the King, but not definitive, as there are over 400 additional letters located at Mt Stuart, Isle of Bute, still unedited. These were undiscovered when Sedgwick published his edition.)

Karl Schweizer

George Grenville

Born 14 October 1712, second child of Richard Grenville and Hester Temple. Educated at Eton, Christ Church, Oxford, Inner Temple and Lincoln's Inn. Married 1749 Elizabeth Wyndham, daughter of Sir William Wyndham, third baronet. MP for Buckingham 1741–70. Lord of Admiralty 1744–7; Lord of the Treasury

1747–54; Privy Councillor 1754; Treasurer of the Navy 1754–5, 1756–7 and 1757–62; Secretary of State 1762; First Lord of the Admiralty 1762–3; First Lord of the Treasury 1763–5. Died November 1770.

George Grenville's two-year premiership had a profound effect on Britain's position as an emerging world power. After twenty-three years in parliament, Grenville knew not only the intricacies of procedure and precedents that drove parliamentary business but also the global issues of finance and imperial regulation (Smith 1852–3). He has become famous, or infamous, in Anglo-American history as the man responsible for the Stamp Act which ultimately led to the loss of the colonies. Such a judgement hardly does justice to a career that encompassed a most dynamic period in Britain's history and expansion overseas. Grenville was recognized by his contemporaries as a figure of the first rank devoted to his country's best interests. His character remained unblemished in an age of tarnished reputations. While premier he secured a party of followers that followed him unflinchingly until his death in 1770. Here was a man of integrity and loyalty who, as one admirer put it, 'would go to hell with you before he would desert you' (Lawson 1984b: 287). Few politicians or prime ministers have received such an accolade! In short, the traditional view of Grenville is too restricted, requiring breadth and depth to reveal the full perspective on his life's work.

Grenville's career in politics began in 1741 in strange circumstances. His uncle, Lord Cobham, had fallen out with Robert Walpole and used his vast wealth to organize an opposition against the long-serving premier in the late 1730s and early 1740s. This disparate group became known as 'Cobham's Cubs', consisting mostly of close relations by blood or marriage, and including, most notably, William Pitt. Grenville joined the pack in the dog days of Walpole's administration, giving up a promising law career at the behest of his domineering uncle. Grenville's initial role in the Commons was to be obedient division fodder, but over the next two decades he displayed talents in the House and office beyond this servile function.

First, Grenville proved a very effective speaker in the Commons. What he lacked in oratorical skills, Grenville more than compensated for in the depth of knowledge he always brought to bear on constitutional or procedural matters. He usually bloodied anyone foolish enough to tackle him on these points. Indeed, by 1760 his skills in the House had given him great influence over a system dominated by precedent, and he became touted as a future Speaker in the Commons. Second, Grenville showed a distinct talent for administration and the *minutiae* of office. Public business, in fact, was a sheer, if perverse, joy for him. His cousin, Thomas Pitt, wrote in awe that 'an act of parliament was in itself entertaining to him' (Lawson 1984b: vi). Grenville read everything that came across his desk. He could not be caught out on detail. He was a modern politician in the sense that he dedicated himself to service of the state and the public good for reasons of duty and ministerial salary, eschewing all other dubious perks and prerequisites of office. Certainly, no other senior politician at the time knew so much about official business pertaining to the Treasury, the navy, the empire and parliament: information gained with the experience of service in different departments of state.

A third aspect of Grenville's early career frequently overlooked is the fact that he always sought to reform arcane and redundant practices of government departments. His motives lay in a belief that the people of Britain had a right to efficient administration, serving their best interests, because nothing else could so surely secure loyalty to the Hanoverian dynasty established in 1714. Examples of this belief can be found across the span of Grenville's career at Westminster. At the Admiralty in the 1750s, he opposed the barbarism of press-ganging to man the navy and the irregular or fraudulent voucher system used to pay seamen. In 1766–7, he supported payments from the Treasury to help British subjects suffering from hunger after a series of crop failures. In every respect, then, Grenville knew the ins and outs of parliamentary government before becoming premier in 1763.

The manner in which Grenville became prime minister in April 1763 proved no less strange than his entry to the Commons twenty-two years earlier. An ambitious young monarch, George III, had come to the throne in October 1760 determined to overthrow a governmental system he believed had enslaved his grandfather, George II, and corrupted the purity of the balanced constitution made up of King, Lords and Commons. For three years, from 1760 to 1763, George III and his trusted adviser, Lord Bute, assaulted the old Whig families that had dominated national politics since 1714 in an effort to restore balance to the constitutional power of the realm. By April 1763, however, the scheme was in disarray and George and Bute decided to invoke a fall-back position. Their ally George Grenville would be brought into office as First Lord of the Treasury on the understanding that Bute would lead and direct the government from behind the scenes, and that Grenville would follow. The plan proved too clever for its own good. Contrary to what the great scholar, Sir Lewis Namier, and others have said, Grenville was willing to serve but refused to obey (Namier and Brooke 1964: 1, 537–41). It took George and Bute some time to realize this fact and by then Grenville had established himself as a fine leader in the Commons. More significantly, Grenville's vision of a balanced constitution with parliament, not the King, to the fore under strong cabinet leadership, led to serious clashes between monarch and premier. One historian has implied that Grenville was a 'grounded republican' (Brooke 1987: 188) and it is fair comment in view of the hatred George III came to harbour for his protégé. Only after a huge row over the regency in June 1765 did the King find the courage to dismiss his disobedient First Lord who showed scant respect for the King's person.

In this atmosphere poisoned by personal acrimony, it is surprising how much Grenville's administration achieved on the policy front. On taking office, Grenville found that he had inherited some intractable problems in three main areas of policy: empire, revenue and constitution. Difficulties over the first two offered the Grenville administration its most profound challenge. The Seven

Years War (1756–63) had brought Britain a smashing territorial victory over its rivals, France and Spain. But with the new acquisitions in North America, the Caribbean and India came huge financial responsibilities. The nation was reeling under a vast debt in 1763, and it fell to Grenville's government to provide relief. In this task Grenville's experience shone through as he sought to overhaul the fiscal structure of Britain and its empire (Brewer 1989: 175–6). Each would contribute its share to paying the debt. And it is in this context that the passage of the Sugar Act 1764 and Stamp Act 1765 for America can be understood. Grenville also attended to securing Indian revenues through the agency of Robert Clive's command in Bengal (Lenman and Lawson 1983: 810–23), and passed a sweeping revision of customs collection in the Atlantic empire. The effects of reform on a notoriously lax system were deeply felt but Grenville had been dismissed before the storm of protest in America reached British shores.

On the constitutional front, Grenville became involved in one of the most famous challenges to executive power, arising from the case of John Wilkes and general warrants, 1763–5. In brief, general warrants with power of arrest and confiscation had been used by ministers of the Crown through the eighteenth century to silence publishers, printers and writers hostile to government policy. John Wilkes confronted this power through publication of an article he wrote attacking the King in the *No. 45 North Briton*. The general warrant issued to suppress the *No. 45* became a constitutional test case and the parliamentary opposition took up Wilkes's cause at Westminster. It proved profitable, for in February 1764 the opposition came close to defeating the government in a division on the illegality of general warrants.

Grenville's role in the business has been generally misunderstood. He did not disagree with the opposition that ministers should be forbidden use of general warrants but believed that it was a matter for the courts, not parliament, to settle. In 1766, when in opposition himself, he sponsored a Commons resolution to this effect that passed unanimously. The last constitutional dimension to Grenville's premiership relates to his role in the development of cabinet government. As premier he saw the need for regular meetings of leading ministers to discuss the proliferation of problems and policies emanating from the legacy of the Seven Years War. This body under Grenville's leadership became known as the effective cabinet, and acknowledged its duties through handwritten notes and minutes of cabinet proceedings (Christie 1958; Lawson 1984a). Grenville's effective cabinet had all the hallmarks of a modern inner cabinet handling policy and priorities of the state.

After his dismissal in July 1765 Grenville did not fade into anonymity. He spent the final five years of his life in active parliamentary opposition, contributing to the rise of party politics and keeping a watchful eye on imperial, constitutional and revenue issues. He died with his boots on at the opening day of the parliamentary session, 13 November 1770, being eulogized later by Edmund Burke, as a man whom 'this country owes very great obligations' (Burke 1849: xi, 37).

References and further reading

Brewer, J. (1989) *The Sinews of Power: War, Money and the English State, 1688–1783*, London: Unwin Hyman. (Excellent account of state structures within which Grenville operated.)

Brooke, J. (1987) 'Review', *Parliamentary History* 6: 187–8.

Burke, E. (1849) *The Works of the Right Honourable Edmund Burke*, 12 vols, London: Everyman.

Christie, I.R. (1958) 'The cabinet during the Grenville administration 1763–65', *English Historical Review* 73: 86–92.

Lawson, P. (1984a) 'Further reflections on the Cabinet in the early years of George III's Reign', *Bulletin of the Institute of Historical Research* 57: 237–40.

—— (1984b) *George Grenville: A Political Life*, Oxford: Oxford University Press. (The only biography of Grenville available; it fully revises, within the contemporary context, accepted notions of his life and career.)

Lenman, B. and Lawson, P. (1983) 'Robert Clive, the "Black Jagir" and British politics', *Historical Journal* 26: 801–29.

Namier, Sir L. and Brooke, J. (eds) (1964) *The House of Commons 1754–1790*, 3 vols, London: HMSO.

Smith, W. (ed.) (1852–3) *The Grenville Papers: Being the Correspondence of Richard Grenville Earl Temple K.G. and the Right Hon. George Grenville their Friends and Contemporaries*, 4 vols, London: Murray. (Grenville's political career can be followed in this standard Victorian compendium of letters and diaries originally belonging to the family.)

Philip Lawson

Charles Watson-Wentworth, Second Marquess of Rockingham

Born 13 May 1730, eighth child and only surviving son of Thomas Watson-Wentworth and Lady Mary Finch. Educated at Westminster School and Cambridge University. Married 1752 Mary Bright. Viscount Higham 1739; Earl of Malton 1745; inherited the marquessate December 1750. Lord Lieutenant and Custos Rotulorum of the North and West Ridings of Yorkshire and of York 1751; elected as a Fellow of the Royal Society 1751. Took his seat in the House of Lords May 1751. Lord of the Bedchamber 1752–62; Vice-Admiral of Yorkshire 1755; Knight of the Garter 1760; Governor of Charterhouse School 1762; Prime Minister 1765–6 and 1782. Died 1 July 1782.

Rockingham has been underestimated as an eighteenth-century political figure. He inspired loyalty in his supporters and had a remarkable network of contacts; his circle of friends was wide and he was active in politics all his adult life. His first ministry is usually noted for the amount of legislation which it repealed, while his second ministry is often ignored completely. Yet Rockingham and his supporters did much to shape later eighteenth-century political life.

Rockingham has received little positive recognition for his achievements. He has been described variously as being 'totally void of all information . . . with excessive indolence; fond of talking business, but dilatory in the execution' (Walpole 1894: ii, 197), 'of small intellect, a bad and nervous speaker . . . more at home on the racecourse than in Parliament' (Turberville 1927: 322–3). He has been dismissed as 'an inept politician [who] originally had no clear ideas of importance on political issues' (Owen 1974: 180–1). Rockingham and his followers have been condemned for priding themselves on their consistency, 'which with foolish people means that once you have said a thing you must adhere to it for evermore' (Brooke 1972: 124). However, Rockingham assiduously attended the Lords and led the largest single group of parliamentary Whigs in the period 1751–82. As prime minister he found what may well have been the solution to the 'American problem' had his successors not destroyed his handiwork, and did much to alleviate political problems in Ireland. He found time also to develop agriculture and industry on his estates, to follow his passion for horseracing and to take a leading role in the politics of Yorkshire.

Rockingham had many advantages, not least of which was his great wealth: his annual income from his English and Irish estates was about £40,000. His father had instilled in him the principles of Whiggery including the restriction of royal power, economic reforms and religious toleration for all. The second Marquess's leadership in Yorkshire was to some extent inherited from his father: family relationships accounted for a number of political allies. Among his early connections were William, Duke of Cumberland, Earls Fitzwilliam and Scarborough, the Dukes of Newcastle and Devonshire, his close friend Sir George Savile and a veritable flock of Finches. In 1753 the Whig Club in York renamed itself the Rockingham Club in his honour, and from then on its 133 members gave the Marquess their wholehearted political support.

Rockingham virtually controlled political life in Yorkshire and had a sizeable following in the Commons. In 1761 he could count on the support of sixty-two MPs; in 1768 they numbered eighty-nine, and by 1774 they had increased to over one hundred. His first foray into parliamentary politics came in 1753 when he failed to have his candidate, Savile, elected for one of the Yorkshire seats; however, the Marquess learned from his mistakes and thereafter all his parliamentary candidates invariably were elected. In 1768, twenty-six of the thirty MPs returned for Yorkshire constituencies were committed supporters of the Marquess; the two county seats were held by Sir George Savile and Edwin Lascelles for twenty years.

One reason why Rockingham had such a secure hold over the county was that he paid attention to the needs of the people. His maiden speech in 1751 was on behalf of the Yorkshire woollen interest, and during the American crisis he was a vociferous spokesman for the woollen and iron merchants whose colonial trade had collapsed. At his own expense he attempted to strengthen Hull's defences against the encroachments of John Paul Jones in 1779 by commissioning Samuel Walker of Rotherham to cast six cannon for the city, thereby not only hoping to help Hull but also attempting to contribute to the local economy. He also played a prominent role in ending the activities of a coin-counterfeiting gang in the Halifax region in 1769.

The Marquess was in opposition for sixteen years, but this did not mean that he was politically inactive. In 1764 he played a major part in establishing and maintaining the parliamentary opposition against Grenville during the *North Briton* affair and even paid Wilkes a pension during 1765–6 to keep him out of the country. His successors were not so astute as the Marquess, and Wilkes returned in 1768 to encourage discontent and to create mayhem in the general election. In 1769, following the Middlesex election fiasco, the petitioning movement which demanded a dissolution of parliament was spearheaded by Rockingham and his Yorkshire supporters once the county meeting had consented to such a course of action.

In 1779 Christopher Wyvill called a Yorkshire county meeting with the intention of petitioning parliament to demand economic reform, an extension of the franchise, one hundred extra county seats in the Commons, triennial parliaments and the election only of MPs who subscribed to the foregoing points, which were embodied in a 'form of Association'. Although Rockingham deliberately kept a low profile by not attending the meeting, he was firmly in control of the proceedings – whatever Wyvill thought to the contrary. Stephen Croft, one of the leading lights of the County Association, was also one of Rockingham's political agents and a member of the Rockingham Club. He informed the Marquess of all the association's activities, consulted Rockingham over the resolutions to be proposed, and was able to carry out his instructions almost to the letter. Thirty-eight of the committee of sixty-one were Rockingham's friends: so strong was the Marquess's following that Wyvill's 'form of Association' was disregarded in the county. Neither of the Yorkshire MPs nor Lord John Cavendish, York's MP, would subscribe to the association yet all three were re-elected in 1780.

As the leading aristocrat in Yorkshire, Rockingham played an important role in the community. As Brooke notes, the first Rockingham administration 'is the only one formed around the members of the Jockey Club' (Brooke 1972: 122): certainly the Marquess was one of its founding members. He was responsible for founding the St Leger race and made substantial contributions towards the building of the grandstands at York and Doncaster racecourses. The Marquess used the occasion of the York races to conduct political business and to maintain his support among the gentry who attended in great numbers. His stables and stud at Wentworth generated work for dozens of men.

The Marquess also was an agricultural improver, personally conducting experiments in new agricultural techniques and encouraging his tenants to embark on their own improvements. The King may not have valued Rockingham as a politician, but regarded him highly as a model landowner. Even Arthur Young was fulsome in his praise for the Marquess's work at Wentworth (Young 1771: i, 278–94). Other ventures in which Rockingham was involved at Wentworth included the development of coal-mines, road and canal building and the conservation of woodlands. All this activity contributed both to Rockingham's income and the local economy, and many were grateful to the Marquess for employment.

Rockingham was by upbringing and conviction an Anglican. During the Marquess's lifetime John Wesley brought his own brand of doctrine to Anglicanism and made great inroads into the established church. Wesley preached at Wentworth church several times and was a frequent visitor to Barley Hall, near Thorpe Hesley, where Rockingham's friends, the Johnsons, lived. In 1757 Lord and Lady Rockingham attended a Methodist meeting at Barley Hall, much to the surprise of some of their friends. The Marquess may have sympathized with the Methodist cause; certainly he was not anti-Methodist because he allowed them to establish societies on his estates.

The Marquess first attracted royal attention in December 1745 during the Jacobite crisis when he rode to Carlisle to join the Duke of Cumberland's army. Cumberland was impressed by the young man's actions and they became friends, which may account for the Duke's insistence that Rockingham should head the 1765 ministry. During his second grand tour in 1748–50, Rockingham attended the Hanover court of George II daily, making himself known to the King and securing the friendship of the Duke of Newcastle, who thereafter saw himself as the Marquess's mentor.

Rockingham's tenure as a Lord of the Bedchamber ended in 1762 when he resigned after a disagreement with George III over the 'Massacre of the Pelhamite Innocents'. The King stripped Rockingham of all his Yorkshire appointments in what looks remarkably like a fit of pique, although Rockingham did reinstate himself in 1765 when he became prime minister. By December 1762 a small group of young politicians including Rockingham had met to organize an opposition club. The young Whigs began to desert Newcastle's supporters and to follow the Marquess. In 1763 Rockingham acted as a 'whip', leading forty-eight peers in a division against Bute's Cider Bill. A recognizable opposition party of some strength had begun in parliament, and apart from the two periods when he held office it was led by Rockingham, who had attracted a hard core of followers in both Houses of parliament. These men formed the best organized party in existence. The Marquess continued to oppose Bute, an act which cost Rockingham dearly in terms of national political advancement but did much to enhance his already prominent position among his followers. The 'Bute myth' expounded by Edmund Burke stems from Rockingham's personal and political dislike of the royal favourite.

Burke became the Marquess's secretary in 1765, and proved to be an excellent choice since he articulated the principles upon which Rockingham's political conduct was based and justified the existence of the Rockingham party on the grounds that 'when bad men combine, the good must associate'. Even Dunning's famous motion of 1780 follows Burke's declaration that 'the power of the Crown . . . has grown up anew . . . under the name of Influence'.

Burke's role within the Rockinghamite group should not be exaggerated: once he had joined them, he expounded almost nothing new in terms of ideology but proved to be a superb propagandist on their behalf. His theory of the 'secret cabinet', set out in *Thoughts on the Cause of the Present Discontents* (1770), is part of Rockingham's evaluation of contemporary politics based on the suspicion that

Bute still had a continuing influence on the King, for example. Burke's *Thoughts* pulled together in a single volume the ideas of Rockingham and his friends and like other Rockinghamite pamphlets, it was circulated among the key members of the group for amendment and/or approval prior to publication. This in no way detracts from Burke's writing but it does illustrate that the Marquess did have ideas of his own and did lead his party.

Burke proved invaluable to the Rockinghamites when they were drafting their petitions in 1769 and also whenever they needed a mouthpiece in the Commons. His many powerful speeches during the American debates reiterated the Marquess's arguments against the colonial conflict and they clarified Rockinghamite policy, but at no time was Burke one of the leaders of the party; nor was his opinion sought any more than that of any other man. Burke believed that the traditional Whig nobility had an important part to play in government and only ever was the servant of the aristocratic Rockinghamites. Burke became his own man in political life after 1782 when he no longer had to follow Rockingham's ideas.

That a Rockingham party existed cannot be disputed; that an eighteenth-century two-party system did is still the subject of debate. The view that two parties could be easily identified was demolished by Sir Lewis Namier (1957), although in recent years the discussion has been resurrected and continues (Colley 1982; Hill 1985). However, Langford sums up the situation when he says that by the 1760s 'Toryism no longer represented a coherent creed, let alone a party organization' (Langford 1989: 357).

After 1714 anyone labelled 'Tory' was *persona non grata* on the grounds that he or she probably supported the Stuarts, possibly was Catholic and may well have believed in the divine right of kings. By the 1760s the fears of 'toryism' were fading but anyone aspiring to political greatness called himself either 'Whig' or 'independent gentleman'. In the 1760s groups of MPs surrounded a variety of great noblemen, all calling themselves Whigs and all vying for political power in some form or other. The Rockinghamites were content to remain in opposition to a series of governments rather than take office at any price, which is remarkable; that the Marquess had so many followers who were prepared to forgo the perquisites of patronage is an indication of his personal charisma and political honesty.

After Bute's resignation in 1763, Grenville's fall from grace and the failure of negotiations with Pitt in 1765, George III asked his uncle Cumberland to form a ministry. Cumberland appointed Rockingham as First Lord and on 10 July the first Rockingham administration was born. Rockingham never had held high office and was regarded by many as having little political expertise: furthermore, he came to power in the midst of a major crisis. Since 1763 a spate of legislation culminating in the Stamp Act had been aimed at the American colonists. This had resulted in colonial disaffection and a non-importation agreement on British goods which both angered British politicians and adversely affected the British economy.

Rockingham had been collecting information about the American crisis from both sides of the Atlantic since 1764, and in 1765 he decided to repeal the

Stamp Act despite much opposition from parliament, the King and the Duke of Cumberland, who perhaps fortuitously for Rockingham died in October 1765 and thus was unable to send troops to America as he wished. Rockingham used his extensive connections successfully to organize some twenty-six merchant petitions for repeal on the grounds of domestic hardship; privately he felt that the Act was both counter-productive and unenforceable. The price he paid for repeal was the Declaratory Act although he never intended that it should be implemented: that Townshend chose to do so in 1767 was not Rockingham's responsibility.

By addressing the grievances of the colonists, initially by repealing the Stamp Act, the Marquess envisaged a secure and lasting foundation for continued Anglo-American friendship within the colonial context. Following the repeal, Rockingham planned to undertake a comprehensive and thorough revision of all colonial commercial regulations: little of his proposed legislation succeeded because of a parliamentary opposition which smacks of factionalism, and so perhaps the best hope for transatlantic reconciliation was lost. Ironically the most lucrative piece of legislation in America was Rockingham's Revenue Act 1766, which produced more than all the other revenue measures put together.

Rockingham was involved in negotiations to form a ministry in 1767 but he refused to bow to the demands of Bedford and the Grenvilles that in any matters to do with America, Britain's sovereignty must be asserted. The planned ministry was abandoned because the Marquess would not compromise his principles.

Anglo-American relations deteriorated in the period 1767–75. Rockingham was aware of the deleterious domestic effects of the colonial non-importation agreement which commenced in 1768, and did his utmost to prevent parliament from escalating the conflict. The Marquess had a subtle idea of 'sleeping sovereignty' over America which seems to have been beyond the comprehension of many of his contemporaries. He saw both Britain and America as suffering from the oppression of royal prerogative and the threat of absolutism which by then had become part of the Rockinghamite tradition. He believed that parliament had legislative supremacy over the colonies but doubted the expediency of asserting it: he preferred the traditional approach of 'salutary neglect'. Consequently, he and his party opposed most of Lord North's punitive legislation of 1774, and also objected strongly to the use of troops in America because it 'would only prevent obedience [and] every town at which they were stationed would be turned into a Boston' (Albemarle 1852: ii, 256).

Because of the extensive correspondence which he received from America Rockingham quickly perceived that the colonial problem was more far-reaching than his contemporaries believed, but his efforts to end the conflict went unheeded. His warnings that Britain would probably be defeated by the colonists were either jeered at or were ignored. Rockinghamite speeches in the Commons, at first advocating immediate conciliation with America and then by 1778 demanding that the effective independence of the colonies be recognized, were howled down in the House. Ultimately it was of no consolation to anyone that the Marquess had been right and most of the rest of parliament had been wrong in continuing the colonial war. Rockingham's first tasks as prime minister in March 1782 were to acknowledge America's independent status and to try to establish a general peace with Europe. He threatened to resign if he was opposed, and issued orders for an immediate truce to end the bloodshed in America even before negotiations were begun. He died before the settlement was finalized and his successors received the credit for his work.

Rockingham, a landowner in County Wicklow, took a keen interest in the affairs of Ireland. Unlike many landowners, he was prepared to allow Catholics to take out leases on his lands provided that they could pay the rents. He was kept informed of the declining Irish economy by Hugh Wentworth, his land agent; consequently Rockingham remitted or reduced rents to his tenants and sub-tenants. However, in 1773, when the Dublin parliament proposed a land tax of 10 per cent on absentee landlords in an attempt to pay the £1 million public debt, Rockingham was galvanized into strenuous and successful opposition on the grounds that the tax would reduce property values in Ireland and would lead eventually to the separation of the two countries. The fact that he and his friends would save about £10,000 a year between them was probably another incentive.

Sir George Savile was responsible for the Catholic Relief Act 1778, which relaxed some of the anti-Catholic penal laws but more importantly allowed Catholics to join the army without taking the Oath of Allegiance to the Anglican Church. The Act reflected the Rockinghamite policy of religious toleration and was sensible enough, given that Britain was at war with America and that France seemed likely to join in on the American side. However, it did have repercussions when, during the Gordon riots of 1780, the London homes of a number of leading Rockinghamites including Savile and Lord Mansfield were attacked in a demonstration of Protestant displeasure at concessions being made to Catholics.

During the American War volunteer units were established in Ireland to protect the country from possible invasion since the regular regiments normally stationed there had been sent to America. The Wicklow men asked permission from the Marquess to call themselves the Rockingham Volunteers and, although their request was refused, they adopted Rockingham's motto *Mea Gloria Fides* as their own. They were pleased also to accept cash contributions from the Marquess towards their expenses. The Irish Volunteers used their strength to wring a number of concessions from the government in 1780: many politicians feared an Irish revolt, and meeting the demands of the Irish may have seemed to be an easy way out of the escalating crisis and war.

In his 1782 ministry, in an attempt to stabilize Anglo-Irish relations, Rockingham repealed both the Irish Declaratory Act and Poyning's Law, giving the Dublin parliament more freedom than it had possessed for three hundred years. Irish opposition politicians promptly aligned themselves with the Marquess and his policies. A satisfactory, if temporary, solution had been found for the 'Irish Question' at last.

Rockingham's second ministry lasted for only fourteen weeks. He took office in March 1782 after the fall of Lord North, who suggested to the King that the

Rockinghams at least must be included in any new ministry, indicating the continuing strength of the party. Having attempted to arrange a 'broad-bottomed ministry', the King finally was obliged to admit that Rockingham was the only man with sufficient support in parliament to form a government. The Marquess's conditions for acceptance were stringent: he insisted that he should be at the Treasury; that the King would accept all nominations for office; that he would approve all the ministry's legislation; that he would accept American independence. Initially the King was not prepared to comply with the conditions but was obliged to accept in order to maintain the government of the nation. The ministry immediately embarked on a reform programme including the disenfranchisement of revenue officers, the removal of government contractors from the Commons and Burke's Establishment Bill. This Bill for Oeconomical Reform was a double-edged sword because it cut the cost of government and reduced the King's influence in the Commons by limiting the number of royal placemen. The measures, which had been the main platform of the Rockingham Whigs for twenty years, passed into law with little parliamentary jubilation and no royal enthusiasm. Proposals for a reform of parliament were shelved because of a split in the Rockinghamite ranks but before the rift could be repaired the Marquess died.

Rockingham's sudden and unexpected death threw his party into disarray and destroyed the cohesion which had existed between very different characters. The Marquess's contribution to political life at both national and local level should not be belittled: his consistency, high principles, honesty and genuine concern for his country set the standard for future prime ministers to emulate.

References and further reading

Albemarle, Earl of (1852) *Memoirs of the Marquis of Rockingham and his Contemporaries*, 2 vols, London: Richard Bentley. (An example of a selective political hagiography from a contemporary and friend of Rockingham.)

Bloy, M. (1986) 'Rockingham and Yorkshire', unpublished PhD thesis, University of Sheffield.

Brooke, John (1972) *King George III*, London: Constable.

Colley, L. (1982) *In Defiance of Oligarchy*, Cambridge: Cambridge University Press.

Hill, B. (1985) *British Parliamentary Parties 1742–1832*, London: Allen and Unwin. (This begins persuasively enough but appears to lose conviction by the 1760s.)

Hoffman, R. (1973) *The Marquess: A Study of Lord Rockingham 1730–82*, New York: Fordham University Press. (The only biography in existence to date, this work deals with Rockingham's personal and political life.)

Langford, P. (1973) *The First Rockingham Administration 1765–66*, London: Oxford University Press. (This is one of the few major works dealing with Rockingham's political impact on the later eighteenth century.)

—— (1989) *A Polite and Commercial People: England 1727–83*, Oxford: Oxford University Press.

Namier, L. (1957) *Structure of Politics at the Accession of George III*, 2nd edn, London: Macmillan.

O'Gorman, F. (1975) *The Rise of Party in England: The Rockingham Whigs 1760–82*,

London: Allen & Unwin. (An extremely thorough discussion of the Marquess's political life and the development of Rockingham party.)

Owen, J. (1974) *The Eighteenth Century*, London: Nelson & Sons.

Turberville, A. (1927) *The House of Lords in the Eighteenth Century*, Oxford: Clarendon Press.

Walpole, H. (1894) *Memoirs of the Reign of King George the Third*, ed. G. F. R. Barker, 4 vols, London: Lawrence & Bullen.

The *Wentworth Woodhouse Muniments*, R- series. (The major source of information for the second Marquess of Rockingham. I am grateful to Olive Countess Fitzwilliam's Wentworth Settlement Trustees and the Director of Libraries and Information Services, Central Library, Sheffield, for permission to use the papers.)

Young, A. (1771) *A Six Months Tour through the North of England*, 6 vols, London: Strahan & Nicholl.

Marjorie Bloy

William Pitt, First Earl of Chatham

Born 15 November 1708, fourth child and second son of Robert Pitt and Harriet Villiers. Educated at Eton, Trinity College, Oxford, and Utrecht. Married 1754 Lady Hester Grenville, daughter of Richard Grenville and Hester, Countess Temple. MP for Old Sarum 1735–47, Seaford 1747–54, Aldborough 1754–6, Buckingham 1756, Oakhampton 1756–7, Bath 1757–66. Groom of the Bedchamber to Prince of Wales 1737–45; Privy Councillor 1746; Vice-Treasurer for Ireland 1746; Paymaster-General 1746–55; Secretary of State for the Southern Department 1756–7 and 1757–61; Lord Privy Seal 1766–8. Created Earl of Chatham 1766. Died 11 May 1778.

In Pitt's lifetime, the term 'prime minister' was contentious and usually derogatory, indicating an unconstitutional arrogation of power from the King and other ministers. Historians usually allow the title to those contemporaries who enjoyed a threefold basis of power: the King's favour, a majority in the Commons and control of the Treasury. Pitt never combined these three advantages. Moreover, he held office of first rank for barely eight of his forty-three years in politics. Yet undoubtedly he dominated two administrations (1756–61) during the very successful Seven Years War and, at least briefly, the Chatham administration of 1766–8. He was recognized by contemporaries as (with Walpole) one of the Hanoverian eighteenth century's two 'great men' of politics. If for these reasons he can be called a 'prime minister', his claim rests on unusual and fragile foundations.

Pitt was in politics eleven years before he held any crown office and nearly twenty-two before he rose to first rank. 'Connection' – with his elder brother, as one of Lord Cobham's 'Cubs', and with the Prince of Wales – brought him into parliament and shaped his commitment to opposition to Robert Walpole, while his political ambitions developed as he realized his abilities as a speaker in the Commons. As a dissident Whig both before and after the fall of Walpole in 1742, he exploited the cross-party rhetoric of 'patriotism' which criticized supposed corruption at home and neglect of British interests abroad, first against Spain and then in wider European war. But he was not the leader of any Whig 'connection', and the offence he gave the King, especially by his vitriolic anti-Hanoverian rhetoric in 1742–4, was a major obstacle to office. So not until the final stage of the negotiations of 1744–6 – which secured Henry Pelham and his brother, the Duke of Newcastle, as the heirs of Walpole and brought most dissident Whigs into alliance with Walpole's 'Old Corps' – were the Pelhams persuaded to insist on office of second rank for Pitt.

Nearly ten years as Paymaster-General gave Pitt experience of administration and proved his usefulness as a government spokesman in the Commons. But they did not win advancement in office commensurate with his growing ambition. From 1754, however, opportunities opened for Pitt. When Henry Pelham died unexpectedly, Newcastle succeeded him as First Lord of the Treasury. He needed an effective and trusted spokesman in the Commons, especially as decisive action became necessary in 1754–5 over deteriorating relations with the French in North America and their consequences in Europe. Further room for manoeuvre was created by a rift from 1755 between the King and his grandson, George, now Prince of Wales.

In these circumstances, Pitt played his cards skilfully to secure office of first rank, powerfully aided by luck and the mistakes of others. When pressing for advancement from within the ministry had no success, he moved in 1755 to other well-recognized ploys in Whig competition for office: links with the Prince's court at Leicester House and parliamentary opposition to subsidy treaties with European allies which made renewed use of 'patriot' rhetoric. But these tactics destabilized the administration only when the prolonged outcry over the loss of Minorca to the French in June 1756 threatened trouble in parliament. And only in conjunction with the mistakes and needs of others – notably Newcastle's inability to find alternative allies to lead the Commons majority he never lost and the general wish to restore unity in the Royal Family – did Pitt's renewed and carefully defended 'patriot' reputation have some effect on the negotiations which formed, first, the brief Devonshire–Pitt administration, and then the Newcastle–Pitt coalition of July 1757.

The war with France had begun badly in America as well as the Mediterranean. More time would inevitably be necessary to mobilize resources to fight more effectively. Furthermore, the coalition was initially unpopular. Pitt had already compromised his 'patriot' policy by support for the alliance with Prussia. Soon he became its acknowledged proponent and in 1758 he supported the commitment of British troops to Germany. There were tensions with colleagues and the King over moves in domestic policy designed to sweeten these moves for his followers. Not until the major British victories of 1758–9 at Louisbourg, Quebec and Guadeloupe, together with Minden (1759) in Germany and the naval victories which turned the threat of invasion that year, could Pitt be said to be secure in office.

By then, to most contemporaries at home and abroad, Pitt was the dominant 'war minister', presiding over continuing victories. However, the extent to which Pitt exercised this role has become debatable (Middleton 1985: 19–21, 49–50, 212–18). As Secretary of State he held a leading office and there was nothing unusual in his domination over the other secretary with whom his responsibilities were shared. But, according to eighteenth-century constitutional convention, such domination did not extend to oversight of other departments, whose heads were responsible directly to the King. The secretaries transmitted the King's orders; they did not determine them. Nor did administrative machinery allow such oversight. The co-ordination of departments which war required was achieved informally through negotiation in the King's closet and in cabinet – the meeting together of the King's leading ministers. In these venues of co-ordination, the crucial role of Newcastle, both formally as First Lord of the Treasury and informally as minister with George II's confidence and a majority in parliament, is increasingly recognized. He was never a subordinate of Pitt and without his skills in management and raising money the war effort would have been crippled.

As Secretary of State, Pitt observed contemporary conventions and he was certainly no innovator in administration. Yet there are clear grounds for allowing him a political dominance in the coalition, particularly by 1759–60 (Fraser 1976: 51–4). This he achieved in cabinet by force of his personality, for which there is abundant contemporary evidence. His dominance was reinforced by his pre-eminence in the Commons. Newcastle probably did not need Pitt simply to retain his majority there; ministries survived quite easily with Pitt (and Newcastle) in opposition in the last stages of the war. But had Pitt remained in opposition throughout, he would undoubtedly have revived the bitter controversies of earlier wars and hampered the mobilization of the material and moral resources necessary for success. Instead, Pitt's public role in the Commons gave a front of unity – even party unity – to the war effort. It also enabled him to mould his image by claiming credit for successes while denying responsibility for the less palatable aspects of the war. Through the press, his admirers carried a similar message to a wider audience. The interaction of reality and carefully cultivated image combined, by 1759–60, with reconciliation with the King and great victories to create undoubted pre-eminence.

The purposes to which this pre-eminence was exercised are less clear (Peters 1993: 43–6, 49–50). Pitt quickly adapted to the realities of office by adopting and extending lines of European policy already established. Arguably, this was consistent with his earlier stands by allowing pursuit of British interests in maritime and colonial war and attempting to prevent the dissipation of victories in peace negotiations. But it was not original to Pitt. Nor, usually, did Pitt have to impose the primacy of America on unwilling colleagues. The extension of the war beyond North America owed more to his initiative, as did the dubiously successful expeditions to the French coast. But his distinctive emphasis on pushing the war to its limits came only from 1760, when circumstances had markedly changed. The traditional view that Pitt, uniquely among his colleagues, had a clear blueprint for both war and peace cannot be sustained. In any case, the conditions of global warfare in the eighteenth century hardly allowed the imposition of a grand strategy.

Pitt's claim to be 'war minister' and hence, perhaps, 'prime minister' thus rests not on office or overriding control of policy, but on the politics of royal closet, cabinet and Commons, together with vigour in administration which all acknowledged, some greater clarity of vision about the objects of war, and determination to press on when others might have compromised (Peters 1993: 52). This uniquely based pre-eminence gave Pitt an unrivalled and lasting reputation. It was, however, never uncontested even in the euphoria of 1759–60. And in October 1760 the accession of George III destabilized the coalition ministry. He no longer trusted Pitt, his erstwhile ally. The Earl of Bute, not Newcastle, now had the King's ear. Furthermore, as the difficult question of making a peace which matched the costs and victories of war arose, the King and Bute sympathized with the swing of opinion against continuing the war. The cabinet held together through the eventually unsuccessful negotiations with France in 1761, despite Pitt's increasingly uncompromising views. But his colleagues would not follow him in declaring immediate war against Spain after the collusion of the Bourbon monarchs in the Family Compact was revealed. In October, Pitt resigned. Undoubtedly there was a genuine policy difference, but it seems that in large part Pitt's growing intransigence over both war and peace was provoked by the loss of that informal dominance he had so skilfully built up.

Pitt's resignation, accompanied by a well-deserved pension for himself and a barony for his wife, provoked public controversy in which his right as supposed 'prime minister' to dominate other ministers and 'dictate' to the King was thoroughly but inconclusively debated (Peters 1988). Aspects of the debate dented his reputation as a 'patriot' but his status as the great war minister was virtually untouched. However, this reputation brought little tangible political support, while Pitt's cavalier treatment of his political allies meant that he now had no strength from 'connection'. The impotence of reputation and oratory alone was soon shown when, in December 1762, the peace preliminaries negotiated by Bute passed smoothly through the Commons in face of trenchant criticism from Pitt.

In the fractured politics of the new reign, Pitt's reputation, skilfully exploited, could have allowed him to dominate any ministry or opposition he chose to join. Instead – partly because of chronic ill-health – he adopted the role ostensibly of the great statesman, in fact that of the spoiler. He spurned concerted opposition as much as any negotiation for office not conducted directly with the King. When approached directly, in August 1763 and June 1765, he demanded terms which precluded success. These tactics were justified by the catch phrase, attractive in principle if hardly practised in contemporary politics, of 'measures not men'. In contrast to his earlier tactics in opposition, Pitt's attitude now had the advantage of eventually building a rapprochement with George III. This, more than anything else, at length brought Pitt to office again in July 1766 in a position of apparently impregnable strength. He had the complete confidence of the

King and virtual *carte blanche* on both 'men' and 'measures' when all potential opposition groups were bitterly divided over both.

However, royal favour and a divided opposition alone could not ensure an effective administration. The men Pitt chose as ministers were linked by nothing except a sometimes reluctant willingness to serve under him. Strangely, he decided to lead them in the non-executive office of Lord Privy Seal, and from the Lords as Earl of Chatham – a move which not only handicapped political management but also seemed to many to abandon his honourable status as 'the Great Commoner'. High expectations of the administration were more substantially damaged by its handling of grave issues of policy. Immediate difficulties in foreign policy were gratuitously created by Chatham's unrealistic attempts to recreate the wartime alliance with Prussia and to bring in Russia when both powers were now more preoccupied with eastern than western Europe. Issues regarding India and America, the long-term legacy of successful war, were aggravated by Chatham's handling of them. He decided to proceed by open confrontation with the East India Company to try to acquire from its greatly increased influence in India some financial benefit for the state. Both here, and over America, where his mistake was rather one of omission than decisive action, Chatham showed no realization of intractable problems behind immediate issues (Peters 1994: 397–402).

These shortcomings were no greater than those of other post-war ministries. Chatham's most glaring failures were personal ones. He gave little attention to the management of the Commons. His colleagues were neither fully informed nor consulted over major issues but were expected rather to act as minions of the great man. The administration was already falling apart before Chatham succumbed, in February–March 1767, to illness – his worst yet and now clearly psychosomatic.

Chatham returned to politics in mid-1769, just as the crisis over the election of the arch-demagogue, John Wilkes, as MP for Middlesex was coming to its height. Chatham's reappearance triggered the collapse of the Grafton administration but failed to carry him into office. Indeed, the disillusionment of the King after Chatham's collapse in 1767 was so great that he never again had a realistic chance of office. In another period of intense activity in 1770–1, Chatham attempted a new combination of earlier techniques of forcing his claim. But co-operation with others in opposition in parliament soon collapsed over differences of policy, exacerbated again by Chatham's arrogance. He made a more direct appeal than ever before to extra-parliamentary opinion, particularly in the City of London, but Wilkes had taken the issues and methods of extra-parliamentary politics in directions that Chatham could not comfortably follow. The chief obstacle to Chatham's success, however, now and for the rest of his life, was the King's discovery of an effective 'prime minister' in Lord North.

By the end of 1771, Chatham had returned to rural seclusion. He reappeared in 1774–5 and 1777–8 to speak out for reconciliation in the growing crisis over the American colonies with more sympathy for the Americans than any other leading politician, but no greater grasp of imperial problems or political realities.

In March 1778, following defeat at Saratoga and the Franco-American alliance, the King reluctantly sanctioned an approach to Chatham to strengthen the administration, but it predictably foundered on Chatham's dictatorial demands. On 7 April, in the midst of a passionate protest over any thought of American independence, Chatham collapsed in the Lords, dying a month later.

Chatham's undeniable strength was his oratory, always stronger in emotive power than rational substance. This gave him his status as the Great Commoner (but not by itself majority support) and, with success in war, helped him to build from above a reputation 'out of doors' far greater than any other contemporary politician. This reputation was cultivated by the cross-party 'country' or 'patriot' rhetoric dominant in opposition until the late 1750s. This rhetorical appeal never fully overcame Whig–Tory ideological differences in opposition. However, Pitt's tactical use of Tory attraction to it, by eventually bringing the Tories to some degree of support of the wartime coalition, contributed to the breakdown of old party identities by the late 1750s (Peters 1984). For this the coalition was celebrated in the press. By conviction Pitt himself was always a Whig, a believer in 'liberty' and the 'great Revolution principles', coupled with a somewhat old-fashioned emphasis on Protestantism but also with the growing authoritarianism typical of the later eighteenth century. His Whiggism certainly eased his initial path to office but, by the 1760s, Whig ideological appeal could no longer be used, as Walpole had used it, to cement a hold on power, and Pitt never so exploited it. Nor, after his first years in politics, did Pitt adhere to party in the sense of connection and he never had more than a handful of personal supporters. Distaste for 'connection' strengthened his patriot appeal but weakened him politically, most obviously in the Chatham administration.

In the 1750s, Chatham won political pre-eminence by deploying a subtle mix of the 'high' politics of closet, cabinet and parliament with extra-parliamentary reputation. Success allowed him to articulate with unique panache the mood of rising national confidence and triumph over the Bourbons and to be in this sense, then and later, the spokesman for a growing sense of empire (Peters 1993: 43, 52–55; 1994: 417). Many contemporaries, impressed also by his sense of presence, were convinced of his superior abilities. It is, however, hard to disentangle the threads of reality and myth, especially in a career so dogged by ill-health and compromised by personal failings. The grasp of policy with which Chatham has been credited dissolves on close examination. Except in belated recognition of the importance of the King, his later career shows none of his earlier political skill. His inadequacy to the demands of the post-war years for a greater attention to policy and its implementation suggests that he never moved beyond a highly personalized view of politics. He thought in terms of being, in Horace Walpole's words, 'the most illustrious man of the first country in Europe' (Walpole 1985: iii, 2). To the end he believed, it seems, that he had only to intervene vigorously for all difficulties to be solved, as apparently had happened in the Seven Years War. Time had passed him by.

References and further reading

Ayling, S. (1976) *The Elder Pitt Earl of Chatham*, London: Collins. (A creditable and readable attempt at a modern biography.)

Black, J. (1992) *The Elder Pitt*, Cambridge: Cambridge University Press. (An up-to-date scholarly study, with new material especially on Pitt's career to 1756.)

Brooke, J. (1956) *The Chatham Administration*, London: Macmillan. (Indispensable, strong on high politics, perceptive but very light on policy.)

Fraser, E. (1976) 'The Pitt–Newcastle coalition and the conduct of the Seven Years War 1757–1760', unpublished DPhil thesis, University of Oxford. (Strong on the politics of Pitt's wartime dominance; with Middleton (1985) and Peters (1980), helps to provide the thorough account of the wartime coalition still not written.)

Middleton, R. (1985) *The Bells of Victory: The Pitt–Newcastle Ministry and the Conduct of the Seven Years War, 1757–1762*, Cambridge: Cambridge University Press. (The best account of wartime policy-making and administration but misses the full force of Pitt's political role.)

Namier, L. and Brooke, J. (eds) (1964) *The House of Commons 1754–1790*, 3 vols, London: HMSO. (With Sedgwick (1971) provides the best brief account of Pitt's political career.)

Peters, M. (1980) *Pitt and Popularity: The Patriot Minister and Popular Opinion during the Seven Years War*, Oxford: Clarendon Press. (Charts the vagaries of Pitt's reputation and their political impact.)

—— (1984) ' "Names and cant": party labels in English political propaganda c. 1755–1765', *Parliamentary History* 3: 103–27. (Discusses, *inter alia*, the impact of Pitt's tactics and the wartime coalition on party identity.)

—— (1988) 'Pitt as a foil to Bute: the public debate over ministerial responsibility and the powers of the Crown', in K. Schweizer (ed.) *Lord Bute: Essays in Re-interpretation*, Leicester: Leicester University Press. (Explores the debate of 1761–2 over what rights as 'prime minister' Pitt's wartime dominance gave him.)

—— (1993) 'The myth of William Pitt, Earl of Chatham, great imperialist. Part I: Pitt and imperial expansion', *Journal of Imperial and Commonwealth History* 21: 31–74.

—— (1994) 'The myth of William Pitt, Earl of Chatham, great imperialist. Part II: Chatham and imperial reorganization', *Journal of Imperial and Commonwealth History* 22: 393–431. (These two articles reach sceptical conclusions from a thorough reassessment of Pitt's role in imperial policy, while acknowledging his articulation of national aspirations.)

—— (forthcoming) *William Pitt Earl of Chatham*, London: Longman. (Offers a revisionist account of Pitt's political career while taking account of his contemporary standing.)

Sedgwick, R. (ed.) (1971) *The House of Commons 1715–1754*, 2 vols, London: HMSO.

Taylor, W. and Pringle, J. (eds) (1838–40), *Correspondence of William Pitt, Earl of Chatham*, 4 vols, London: John Murray. (A small selection of the Chatham papers in the Public Record Office, which in fact offer little direct evidence from Pitt himself.)

Walpole, H. (1985) *Memoirs of King George II*, ed. J Brooke, 3 vols, New Haven: Yale University Press. (With Walpole's voluminous correspondence and other memoirs, one of the best sources for contemporary views of Pitt.)

Williams, B. (1913) *The Life of William Pitt Earl of Chatham*, 2 vols, London: Longmans, Green. (Still the best comprehensive biography, though shaped by the 'great man' approach.)

Marie Peters

Augustus Henry Fitzroy, Third Duke of Grafton

Born 9 October 1735, second son of Lord Augustus Fitzroy and Elizabeth Cosby. Educated at Hackney School and Peterhouse, Cambridge. Married (1) 1756 Anne Liddell, daughter of Lord Ravensworth (separated 1764, divorced 1769); (2) 1769 Elizabeth Wrottesley. MP for Bury St Edmunds in 1756–57. Lord of the Bedchamber to Prince George 1756–7; Succeeded to dukedom in 1757 on the death of his grandfather. Lord Lieutenant of Suffolk 1757–63. Secretary of State for the Northern Department 1765–6; First Lord of the Treasury in Chatham's ministry in 1766; de facto Prime Minister 1767–8 and in his own right 1768–70; Knight of the Garter 1769; Lord Privy Seal 1771–5 and 1782. Died March 1811.

Grafton's political career centred around his admiration of Pitt the Elder which coloured many of his actions. Grafton appeared to be indecisive and he allowed others to assume responsibilities which should have been his own. He had little interest in aspiring to political supremacy; he presided over deteriorating relations with America. His involvement in the 1768 Middlesex election fiasco resulted in demands for his resignation. He was the butt of the *Junius Letters* and was a political lightweight.

Grafton was descended from Charles II and Barbara Villiers, and seems to have inherited Charles II's looks – Grafton was known as 'Black Harry' – and his enthusiasm for horses and women. Grafton's first noticeable entry into politics came in 1762 when the Duke of Newcastle's 'young friends' met at Grafton's London home to organize a formal opposition against Bute's peace preliminaries to end the Seven Years War. Consequently Grafton became a victim of the 'massacre of the Pelhamite Innocents', being deprived of his lord lieutenancy of Suffolk.

By 1764 Grafton's political career was overshadowed by his private life. He had left his wife to live with Anne Parsons, alias Mrs Houghton. The keeping of a mistress was not particularly scandalous but Grafton outraged his contemporaries by taking her openly into high society. He also felt publicly shamed by his wife's elopement with the Earl of Upper Ossory, whom she married in 1769. Early in 1769 Grafton's divorce was granted; at the end of the year he married Elizabeth Wrottesley. It is perhaps somewhat unfortunate that personal difficulties distracted the Duke from his public duties.

After lengthy discussions with Pitt, Grafton accepted office as Secretary of State for the Northern Department under Rockingham in 1765 on what Grafton thought was an understanding that negotiations would take place for Pitt to enter the ministry. When this did not materialize, mainly because Rockingham saw no need to include Pitt, Grafton resigned and played no part in the remainder of Rockingham's government. He subsequently accepted the post of First Lord of the Treasury in Pitt's – now the Earl of Chatham's – ministry.

Chatham, who had lost his reputation as the 'Great Commoner' on accepting his peerage, proved to be a dictatorial and secretive master and Grafton became an almost silent minister, soon giving up all pretence of knowing what Chatham's policies might be. Chatham then withdrew from parliament on the grounds of ill-health, leaving Grafton as *de facto* prime minister, an office for which he was ill-prepared and inexperienced. In May 1767 Grafton was unable to prevent Townshend from proposing the American Duties Bill in the Commons. Townshend died shortly after this legislation had been passed and Grafton was bequeathed a legacy of colonial discontent. Following only a three-vote victory on American affairs in the Lords, Grafton threatened to resign since he felt unable to continue with such a small majority. However, Chatham graciously granted Grafton an interview for the first time in weeks and persuaded him to stay in office.

The Townshend Duties led to riots and violence in America and in 1768 to a second non-importation agreement which again adversely affected the British economy. By this time the colonists also were questioning their relationship with Britain, but Grafton's ministry did not take any decision which might have allevi-ated the situation. He must, therefore, shoulder some of the responsibility for the eventual loss of the American colonies.

In 1767 the King hoped to broaden parliamentary support for Chatham's increasingly unstable government and commissioned Grafton to negotiate with Rockingham, Bedford and Grenville for them to join the ministry. The Duke did not clarify the exact nature of the negotiations and the proposed reorganization disintegrated over the differing views on America held by these peers, with the exception that the Bedfords accepted some offices. The ministry continued under the nominal leadership of Chatham although Grafton was the mainstay of the government. He then had to deal with the French annexation of Corsica. From Britain's viewpoint any extension of Bourbon power in the Mediterranean was dangerous but nothing was done by Secretary of State Weymouth to prevent the transfer of Corsican sovereignty from Genoa to France in 1768, although the dispatch of a naval squadron would have deterred the French. Ironically, through government inactivity the most famous Corsican was, by a whisker, a French citizen: Napoleon was born on 15 August 1769.

In 1768 a general election was required by law. This marked the reappearance of John Wilkes and the beginning of the Middlesex election crisis. The whole affair was mishandled and Wilkes's election was declared void four times. Ultim-ately Luttrell was proclaimed victorious despite receiving 847 fewer votes than Wilkes. This allowed Wilkes to become the hero of the reformers under the slogan 'Wilkes and Liberty'. At this point Chatham recovered sufficiently to appear in parliament and denounce the activities of his own ministers; he then resigned and Grafton became prime minister in his own right, primarily from a sense of duty to the King.

The Duke had to deal with a number of difficulties in his two-year ministry. His decision on the Middlesex election led to the 1769 Petitioning Movement, so-called because it produced petitions for the dissolution of parliament which were signed by a quarter of the electorate in the hope that the government would resign. Grafton chose to disregard the petitions as irrelevant to the conduct of government. The Wilkes affair also led to Horne Tooke's establishment of the Society for the Supporters of the Bill of Rights (SSBR), the main object of which was to support Wilkes financially but which also proved to be an important development in the methods used by subsequent extra-parliamentary pressure groups. The SSBR campaigned for the extension of the franchise and shorter parliaments by paying travelling speakers, holding public meetings and using the press to publicize its demands.

In an attempt to pacify Ireland, which was experiencing economic and political difficulties, the Lord Lieutenant was ordered hereafter to reside in Dublin which was a positive step, and Grafton also passed the Octennial Act: until then there had been general elections in Ireland only on the death of the monarch. Now the Irish had more control over their parliament and Grattan's Patriot party began to break free from the control of the 'Undertakers', setting the stage for future conflict. The Act was Grafton's reciprocation for Ireland's increased military contribution in raising troops to deal with the escalating tensions in America.

The year 1768 saw poor harvests with consequent food shortages and inflated prices. High unemployment and a severe winter provoked riots among the Spitalfields silk-weavers and East End coal-heavers. Merchant seamen in Hull, Tyneside and London went on strike for increased wages which consequently reduced the essential trade of the country. These problems only added to Grafton's burdens.

From November 1768 the *Junius* letters in the *Public Advertiser* made Grafton the target of fierce political satire and held up the prime minister for popular hatred. To add insult to injury Chatham suddenly recovered from his current illness, returned to parliament and attacked the new ministry, formed mainly because of his own resignation. Grafton had difficulty in passing a money bill through parliament and then faced the threatened resignation of Hillsborough, Secretary for American Affairs, who was determined to join the Rockinghamites.

The ministry continued until the beginning of the new session in January 1770 when further troubles afflicted Grafton. Chatham opposed the government's address to the Crown; Lord Chancellor Camden attacked his own colleagues and was dismissed; Granby resigned in protest and Yorke committed suicide. This all proved to be too much for the Duke, who retired from high politics, although he did accept the office of Lord Privy Seal under both North and Rockingham.

Grafton's later years were spent in opposing domestic repression during the French Wars, seeking peace with France and in pursuing religious enlightenment which ultimately took him into the ranks of the Unitarians. He died at the age of 76 in relative obscurity.

References and further reading

Anson, Sir W. (1898) *Autobiography and Political Correspondence of Augustus Henry Fitzroy, Third Duke of Grafton*, London: John Murray. (This is the only full-scale work on Grafton. As an edited autobiography it is perhaps not surprising that it is almost totally complimentary.)

Grafton's political life is covered in most of the general texts and specific biographies dealing with this period.

Marjorie Bloy

Frederick North, styled Lord North 1752–90, Second Earl of Guilford

Born 13 April 1732, first son of Francis, first Earl of Guilford, by his first wife Lady Lucy Montagu, daughter of George, first Earl of Halifax. Educated at Eton and Trinity College, Oxford. Married 1756 Anne, daughter of George Speke. MP for Banbury 1754–90. Lord of the Treasury 1759–65; Joint Paymaster-General 1766–7; Chancellor of the Exchequer 1767–82; First Lord of the Treasury 1770–82; Home Secretary 1783. Privy Councillor 1766; Knight of the Garter 1772. Chancellor of the University of Oxford 1773–92. Lord Warden of the Cinque Ports 1778–92. Succeeded father as second Earl of Guilford 4 August 1790. Died 5 August 1792.

'The worst prime minister since Lord North' was for long a political cliché. Specialist scholarship in recent decades has to a large extent rehabilitated North's reputation. Although the stigma of being premier when the American colonies were lost will always be with him, North is now seen not only as a successful politician, managing King and parliament with consummate skill, but also as a prime minister whose policy initiatives were in many respects innovative and successful.

'There is now no prime minister. There is only an agent for government in the House of Commons. We are governed by the cabinet, but there is no one head there, as in Sir Robert Walpole's time.' This contemporary opinion, voiced in 1775 by the Tory Dr Samuel Johnson, received a Whig gloss from his modern editor. 'Lord North was merely the King's agent. The King was really his own minister at this time' (Hill and Powell 1934–50: ii, 355). That legend, that Lord North was merely a puppet prime minister while George III in reality ruled Britain himself, is a contemporary and historiographical myth long since demolished by historians. Lord North was no royal favourite like Bute. For some time before his appointment in 1770 his fellow politicians saw him as a future prime minister. His parliamentary skills and financial expertise marked him out for that post. North had proved himself in many heated debates during the 1760s, and was already the main prop of government, as both Leader of the Commons and Chancellor of the Exchequer for over two years, when in January 1770 George III identified him as the only man able to hold off the parliamentary opposition onslaught that threatened the King's right to choose his premiers. The explanation for this circumstance lay in the contemporary political scene.

There was then no party system: recent attempts to resurrect the old idea of a Whig–Tory alignment at this time, even extending to the claim that North headed a Tory party of government, have foundered on the rocks of historical evidence (Christie 1986). Those old party terms were employed by contemporaries to denote attitudes of mind, not political organizations. The analysis of mid-eighteenth-century politics by Sir Lewis Namier in 1929 (Namier 1929; revised 1957) has been confirmed by subsequent detailed studies of that period. MPs can be classified for convenience into three broad categories. 'The party of the Crown' comprised actual and potential holders of public and court offices, from motives of personal advantage and a belief in a duty to support the King's government. They numbered perhaps around 150 out of the total of 558 MPs, such assessments varying according to definitions and periods. Second, there were the politicians, about 100 altogether, usually mustered in groups around leading figures, though some did plough a lone furrow, like North himself. At any point in time some of these politicians would constitute the ministry and others head the opposition. Since the court party and the ministerial politicians would not provide a majority in the Commons, the key to political power lay in that mass of MPs who were 'independent', a designation or claim covering infinite varieties of behaviour. Some would vote regularly for government and others invariably against it, respectively following the old 'court' and 'country' traditions of political behaviour. But the majority were open to persuasion, and any ministry needed the support of a substantial proportion of such MPs to ensure its survival, let alone the successful enactment of policies.

Herein lay the explanation of the advantage that North enjoyed of being an MP when all his possible rivals for power were peers. In the nineteenth century the discipline of party made it possible for successful prime ministers to sit in the Lords: but in the eighteenth century that was patently not possible. Historians who contend that there was no need for successful prime ministers then to be in the Commons are confusing convention with political reality. Although only six of the first fourteen prime ministers between 1721 and 1806 were commoners, they served in that post for sixty-nine of those eighty-five years: ministries headed by peers were short-lived, averaging two years each. The long ministries of Walpole and Pelham had accustomed MPs to having the acknowledged head of government in their midst. They were now unwilling to be led by the subordinate of a peer, an attitude reinforced by institutional jealousy of the upper House by men conscious that the lower House was becoming the centre of political power. The tactical advantage of 'the Minister' being in the Commons was so evident to North's predecessor, the Duke of Grafton, that, so the press reported, he gave the King that reason for his resignation.

As he found the great strength of the increasing minority was in the lower House, he thought it most material as well as advisable, to nominate a premier there, in the scene of action, as he found, by daily experience, that that was the fittest place for a prime minister, and that there was no doing anything without it as in the case of Walpole, Pelham and Pitt.

(*London Evening Post*, 27 January 1770)

The office of prime minister, as created by Walpole, could not indeed be fully exercised by a peer. There were other considerations, quite apart from the transcendental practical need for the premier to be the Leader of the Commons. The prime minister was the eye and ear of government there as well as its voice, and acted as link between Crown and Commons, conveying impressions and opinions from one centre of power to the other in a way that no peer could have done. Finance, moreover, was the main business of government, and the office of Chancellor of the Exchequer appertained to the Commons. The premier, if a commoner, invariably held this post, which in itself entailed a heavy burden of work: regular attendance, twice weekly, at the Treasury Board for routine matters; deciding on both government expenditure and the taxes and loans to meet it; and the need to explain and defend all of this in the Commons. Being First Lord of the Treasury, the premier's official title and function, was itself an onerous task. The most important department of state was the fount of much government patronage, the dispensation of which was both an administrative chore and a delicate political problem. North kept lists of requests and recommendations, and deployed his charm to assuage disappointment, causing hilarious delight in the Commons in 1772 when he explained 'that when he only nodded, or squeezed the hand, or did not absolutely promise, he always meant No' (*London Evening Post*, 25 February 1772). His other key functions as premier were his excellent personal relationship with the King, the management of parliament as Leader of the Commons, and the chairmanship of the cabinet, responsible for deciding policy; these roles were even more unofficial than the post of prime minister, but they formed the essence of his political leadership. Deferential and charming, North proved congenial in the royal closet. George III bestowed the Garter on him in 1772, a rare honour for a commoner, and paid his personal debts in 1777. The King was never to part willingly with North, for he knew how well he conducted the business of government in both Westminster and Whitehall.

Parliamentary duties took up much of his time. As the official spokesman for government, designated in debate by other MPs simply as 'the Minister', North had to be in his place on the Treasury Bench in the Commons every day of public business during the parliamentary session. During his first five sessions as prime minister he made some 800 speeches and interventions in debate, and a guess-estimate would therefore be that he spoke some 2,000 times in the Commons when premier. He was perforce the leading administration speaker on all important subjects. Government legislation had to be justified in both principles and details, as when he made seventy-two speeches on the Quebec Act 1774. As important as his major proposals of policy and defences of ministerial decisions, often in speeches of an hour or two, was North's role in the cut and thrust of debate. North fulfilled the part admirably. Imperturbable good humour, symbolized by his notorious propensity to fall asleep during debate, was allied to a ready wit. Nor did he ever make the mistake of inflicting formal orations on his audience, relying on an excellent memory, perhaps a few notes, and extempore language, even for his budget speeches. Clarity, essential in such an assembly, was perhaps his chief parliamentary virtue, gentle humour his best weapon. The younger Pitt, an inveterate opponent both when North and he himself were premiers, was later to say that he had never heard any other debater with the same 'lively good-humoured wit'. George III commented in 1801 that no current politician could deploy 'that easy natural flow of genuine good-natured wit which distinguished Lord North and forced a smile from those against whom it was exercised' (Bickley 1928: i, 149, 326). Political opponents did not become personal enemies. No other prime minister has been more generally and genuinely popular in the Commons.

Posterity, however, judges prime ministers by achievements in office, not by contemporary popularity. In this respect North has often been criticized on two implicitly contradictory grounds: that he did not decide policy himself; and that he was a failure in many ways, notably over the loss of America. The comment of Dr Johnson was not, as his editor assumed, the charge that North was a dummy prime minister; and there can be no doubt that, as with other premiers, George III left the business of government to North, albeit with the benefit of royal opinions on many matters of policy. The accusation was that North was not master of his cabinet. But the system of government that operated under North was more characteristic of the period than the existence of a dominant premier. It is misleading to compare North only with such strong ministers as Walpole and the two Pitts. During the 1760s Bute, Grenville and Grafton were all overruled in their own cabinets on important matters of policy: decisions there were collective, often compromised and sometimes taken by a vote. Contemporaries always made much of the indecision of North, but some colleagues who knew him well had more favourable opinions. Charles Cornwall, who served six years with him at the Treasury Board, ended a candid character assessment with this proviso: 'When forced to engage, he shows himself exceedingly capable'. Lord Hillsborough, a cabinet colleague of North for seven years, observed that 'in important affairs [he was] not governed by others' (Hutchinson 1883–6: i, 404, 444). To say that North took time to make up his mind is a fairer assessment than to portray him as a ditherer. The important measures of the North ministry were essentially the policies of the prime minister himself, and it is fitting that he should be judged on their success and failure.

It has long been accepted that as Chancellor of the Exchequer North displayed considerable financial competence; but the extent to which he was innovative has often been overlooked. During the years of peace he bowed to a popular shibboleth, fear of the size of the national debt, by achieving a substantial reduction: in 1774 he informed the Commons that since 1763 it had been cut from £136 million to £126 million, without the imposition of any new taxes. In part this had been due simply to increased customs duties, but North had converted an existing national lottery, designed to encourage the raising of government loans by allowing subscribers priority in the purchase of the much coveted tickets, into one that produced a direct revenue for the Exchequer as well. The American War severely tested North's financial skills, for annual spending rose to over £20 million, whereas peacetime revenue had been around £8 million. The new taxes North introduced were avowedly, as far as possible, on property and luxuries. Under the influence of Adam Smith, an advocate of direct taxation, he introduced a house tax in 1778. But the war had to be financed primarily by borrowing; although North mitigated the burden of this method by use of annuities and lottery tickets, his wartime loan operations increased the funded debt by £75 million in raising £57 million by issuing low-interest discounted stock. North argued that the burden of the national debt lay in the annual interest, not the nominal capital, and was the first prime minister to state that it would never be paid off.

As if raising money and other problems of wartime were not enough to occupy his attention, North in his role as Chancellor of the Exchequer sought to tackle what his long experience at the Treasury had made him all too aware of, the costly inefficiency of that department. In 1776 the Treasury decided that henceforth competence not seniority would be the criterion for promotion. In 1777 North ordered the Customs, Excise and Stamp Boards to prepare schemes for consolidation of revenues, such as were to be implemented a decade later by Pitt the Younger. That premier was also indebted to North for the Commission on Public Accounts, established in 1780, for its reports provided much of the information for his own reforms. Altogether North had a most creditable record as a finance minister. His clear presentation of the national accounts on budget days; his institution of a revenue lottery; his belief in direct taxation; his frank avowal that the national debt was a permanent institution; his appreciation of the need to reform the revenue departments and the measures he himself initiated to that end, which were indicative of how much more he would have done but for the American War: all these initiatives mark him out as both a capable and a far-sighted Chancellor of the Exchequer.

Finance was not an issue of high politics. Here, quite apart from foreign policy, in which North was not directly concerned, his cabinet was confronted by an extraordinary variety of imperial problems: control of a ruling settler minority in Ireland; the government of a conquered native people in India; pacification of a conquered alien settler majority in Canada; and the political aspirations of Britain's own colonists on the eastern coast of North America.

Attention to North's Irish policy has tended to focus on the problems arising out of the American War, and thereby to overlook the most important decision he made concerning Ireland, as soon as he became prime minister. The Irish problem at this time was not that of the subdued Catholic majority, but the behaviour of the ruling Protestant Ascendancy. Before the accession of George III management of Ireland had been delegated by frequently non-resident Lord Lieutenants to leading Irish magnates, the 'Undertakers'. Fears that in consequence control of

Ireland was slipping from British hands led to a cabinet decision in 1765 that this system should be replaced by a resident Lord Lieutenant. But political vacillations and distractions prevented the implementation of this crucial change until in February 1770, less than a month after North became prime minister, his cabinet assured the current Lord Lieutenant of full support for this plan. From then until the Union of 1800 successive Lord Lieutenants directly managed the Irish parliament by a mixture of persuasion and patronage. North has seldom received credit for the resolute manner in which he initiated this new system in the earlier 1770s. But the disadvantage of this change, that the British government was now in direct conflict with Irish politicians, became apparent when an Irish crisis developed in the closing years of his ministry. The American War brought economic depression to Ireland, cutting off trade to America and Europe, and led to Irish demands for an end to commercial restrictions long imposed by Britain to prevent Irish competition. Lord North sympathized with Ireland, but was prevented in 1778 and 1779 from taking any effective measures by the vehement opposition of British manufacturers and merchants. It is curious, and unfair, that his failure to act then should be the main reason for the general charge of indecision levied against him by both contemporaries and historians: North knew what had to be done, but was unable to act until circumstances changed. That was when an Irish trade boycott of British goods in 1779 had undermined the hostility of English vested interests. Then, aware that Irish discontent was developing into disorder, North moved swiftly and granted the bulk of the Irish demands by early 1780. But the delay had generated an Irish political consciousness, voicing resentment at Ireland's subordination to England: this new problem was bequeathed to North's successors, for it came to a head at the time of his fall from office early in 1782.

In India Britain's success in the Seven Years War had led to the anomaly that its East India Company, a trading organization, now controlled the populous territory of Bengal; while the return home of numerous wealthy Company servants led to widespread suspicions of malpractices in India. Such considerations, however, were not held to justify government interference in breach of the Company's chartered rights; but the intervention of the North ministry was made possible by the Company's financial weakness in 1772. A deficit had occurred because rising costs of military defence and payment of high dividends were accompanied by declining income, notably a fall in the sale of tea whence the Company derived 90 per cent of its commercial revenue. When the Company appealed to the ministry for help, North was disposed to agree to the requests for a loan and for customs concessions over tea exports. He was willing to allow the Company to retain Bengal, despite his own personal opinion that all territory acquired by conquest belonged to the state. But the price he exacted for help was some reform of the Company's London organization and, more significantly, the nomination by the ministry of a Governor-General and Council to rule Bengal. This was the first government intervention in the rule of India, a bold step that invoked contemporary comparison with Oliver Cromwell. North's policy of

1773, indeed, was intended only as an interim measure, with a full review of the Indian problem being planned for 1780 when the Company's charter was due for renewal: but by then the American War and its repercussions engrossed ministerial attention, and nothing more was done about India.

Britain's triumph in the Seven Years War posed another problem that it fell to North to resolve, through the acquisition of the French colony of Quebec. Here the rehabilitation of North's reputation must be put into reverse, ironically so in that even his severest critics always rated the Quebec Act the sole redeeming feature of his ministry. The Act has long been acclaimed for its generous provisions, allowing the French majority the free exercise of their Roman Catholic religion, including the levying of tithes, and the retention of their own civil laws: for both provisions faced vociferous contemporary prejudices. These ideas, however, were common currency among leading British politicians. They had been formulated by the ministries of the 1760s, and North's role was simply their enactment. His personal contribution to the measure was twofold: the decision that the colony should be governed by a nominated council, since an elected assembly would have been composed of Catholics, an idea abhorrent to British opinion; and the extension of the boundary southwards to the Ohio River, an alteration that contributed to the discontent in the older British colonies. Both decisions, although justifiable in 1774, have exposed North to the hindsight criticisms of posterity.

More pertinent is the present-day realization that the Quebec Act was not what it had always been deemed, a statesmanlike measure that saved Canada for the British Empire. Its timing in 1774 was coincidental rather than deliberate, and, far from being an act of political wisdom, it alienated the great majority of the Canadian people. The measure had been devised in consultation with the *noblesse*, the small group of French landowners. For the peasantry it confirmed the burdens of church tithes and feudal dues which they had hoped to escape, while the small British Protestant minority was outraged at the provisions. Both of these segments of the Canadian community welcomed the 1775 American invasion, and Canada was retained for Britain not through the loyalty of the population but by a military reconquest in 1776.

North's record as prime minister, his successes and failures in other respects, is overshadowed by the responsibility of his administration for the American Revolution. He remains in historical memory as 'the minister who lost America', and the most sympathetic modern analyses do not altogether exonerate him from responsibility. Although not the foolish hardliner of legend, he cannot avoid his share of blame for the outbreak of the American War. Nevertheless, it should be remembered that he inherited an American problem in 1770. The Stamp Act crisis of the mid-1760s had raised suspicions and issues of principle in both Britain and its colonies. The decision of Charles Townshend in 1767 to resume the search for an American revenue by devising new import duties had revived the conflict of opinion, as Americans now unequivocally denied the right of parliament to tax them; the more so as Townshend intended to use this revenue for the payment of British salaries to colonial officials, thereby usurping that role from the colonial assemblies. North had been one of the cabinet majority that on 1 May 1769 voted to retain the tea duty while repealing the others. That was not a decision to abandon an American revenue, as long assumed by historians. The tea duty had brought in about three-quarters of the new tax revenue, and was kept not merely as a symbol of parliament's right of taxation, but also to provide finance for Townshend's plan.

North enacted and implemented this policy, and it was a short-term success. The American trade boycott, initiated in protest at the taxation, collapsed during 1770, and North, by 1772, was paying a number of colonial officials from the tea duty revenue: for although most colonists bought smuggled foreign tea instead of British taxed tea, enough of the latter was purchased to provide a small income. Then the final colonial crisis was inadvertently precipitated by an arrangement made between the North ministry and the East India Company in 1773 which would enable the Company's taxed tea to undersell smuggled tea in the colonies. This was perceived by Americans as a British attempt to force the issue of taxation, and widespread colonial resistance culminated in the violence of the Boston Tea Party on 16 December 1773. The response of the North ministry was the 'Intolerable Acts' of 1774, that closed Boston Harbour and generally sought to impose tighter control on the colony of Massachussetts of which Boston was the capital. The confrontation escalated into crisis when the Continental Congress, meeting in Philadelphia that autumn, denied the right of parliament to legislate for America at all.

At this moment Lord North took a policy initiative for which he has seldom been given full credit. It was a solo attempt to avert the civil war evidently threatening between Britain and its colonies. Despite the opposition of many of his colleagues and supporters he offered conciliation, albeit with the simultaneous dispatch of more army and navy units to America and after legislation to prevent colonial trade and fishing until British control had been restored. His conciliatory propositions of February 1775 offered to renounce taxation of any individual colony which agreed to pay its costs of civil government and defence. This proposal, conceding no rights to the colonists and regarded in America as deliberately divisive, would probably have been unsuccessful even if fighting had not commenced in April 1775 before news of it arrived. Formal rejection by Congress in July 1775 did not deter North from offering it again in the Peace Commission sent to America in 1776, and North's intention was to enforce that arrangement on the colonies if Britain had won the war. North had shrewdly perceived that a return to the status quo was unrealistic, and his proposal was as far as British opinion would allow him to go. All suggestions, both contemporary and retrospective, that a more conciliatory American policy should have been essayed in 1775 ignore political reality.

The war was, of course, not won but lost. This failure has strengthened the historical condemnation of North, as the prime minister seemingly responsible for Britain's only military defeat in modern times. An analysis of the causes of this disaster lies beyond the scope of this essay, for North himself had little direct responsibility for the conduct of the war. Strategy was in the hands of American Secretary Lord George Germain and of Lord Sandwich at the Admiralty. North's main contributions were the provisions of adequate finance, a task successfully performed, and defence of the ministry in parliament. If he should incur blame, it would be for lack of positive leadership; but the political weaknesses of the ministry were not a significant cause of the British failure in the war. Yet, like Walpole in 1742, North had to pay the political price of military failure by resignation on 20 March 1782. In his letter to the King he explained the reason for this step. 'The parliament have altered their sentiments, and . . . their sentiments whether just or erroneous must ultimately prevail' (Fortescue 1928: v, 395).

It now seems absurd that North could ever have been deemed a royal favourite rather than a parliamentary politician. During a debate of 1783 he proudly reminded MPs that his career had been centred on the Commons.

> I was not, when I was honoured with office, a minister of chance, or a creature of whom parliament had no experience, I was found among you when I was so honoured. I had long been known to you. In consequence I obtained your support; when that support was withdrawn, I ceased to be a minister. I was the creature of parliament in my rise; when I fell, I was its victim.
>
> (Cobbett 1806–20: xxiii, 852)

North was only 49 years of age when he resigned, and many contemporaries assumed that his parliamentary skills, his favour with George III, and the lack of any other choice, would soon see him the King's minister again. It was not to be, primarily because of the meteoric rise of Pitt the Younger, partly due to the rapid deterioration in North's health. Early in 1783 North formed an alliance with his old Commons rival Charles James Fox to oppose the peace terms negotiated by Lord Shelburne's ministry, and was briefly Home Secretary for nine months when their coalition ministry imposed itself on an unwilling King. Thereafter North, though prominent in parliament until his death, was not a candidate for high office.

References and further reading

Bickley, F. (ed.) (1928) *The Diaries of Sylvester Douglas, Lord Glenbervie*, 2 vols, London: Constable.

Binney, J. (1958) *British Public Finance and Administration 1774–92*, Oxford: Clarendon Press.

Bowen, H. (1991) *Revenue and Reform: The Indian Problem in British Politics 1757–1773*, Cambridge: Cambridge University Press.

Brooke, J. (1972) *King George III*, London: Constable. (On North's relationship with his sovereign.)

Cannon, J. (1970) *Lord North: The Noble Lord in the Blue Ribbon*, London: Historical Association. (An early revisionist sketch.)

—— (1974) 'Lord North', in H. van Thal (ed.) *The Prime Ministers*, 2 vols, London: Allen & Unwin. (About the man rather than his policies.)

Christie, I. (1958a) *The End of North's Ministry 1780–1782*, London: Macmillan.

—— (1958b) 'Party in politics in the age of Lord North's administration', *Parliamentary History* 6: 47–68.

—— (1986) 'George III and the historians: thirty years on', *History* 71: 205–21.

Cobbett, W. (1806–20) *Parliamentary History of England from 1066–1803*, 36 vols, London.

Fortescue, Sir John (ed.) (1928) *The Correspondence of King George the Third*, 6 vols, London: Macmillan.

Hill, G. and Powell, L. (eds) (1934–50) *Boswell's Life of Johnson*, 6 vols, Oxford: Oxford University Press.

Hutchinson, P.O. (ed.) (1883–6) *The Diary and Letters of his Excellency Thomas Hutchinson Esq.*, 2 vols, London: Sampson Low.

London Evening Post (1770, 1772).

Namier, L. (1929) *The Structure of Politics at the Accession of George III*, 2 vols, London: Macmillan.

Pemberton, W. (1938) *Lord North*, London: Longmans. (Readable but now dated.)

Thomas, P. (1976) *Lord North*, London: Allen Lane. (A brief, revisionist survey.)

—— (1991) *Tea Party to Independence 1773–1776*, Oxford: Clarendon Press. (A reinterpretation of American and Canadian policies.)

Valentine, A. (1967) *Lord North*, 2 vols, Norman, OK: University of Oklahoma Press. (A massive study, but its value as a source of information is reduced by many errors.)

Peter Thomas

William Petty, Second Earl of Shelburne

Born 2 May 1737, eldest son of John, first Earl of Shelburne, and Mary Fitzmaurice. Educated by a private tutor and at Christ Church, Oxford. Succeeded father as second Earl of Shelburne and second Baron Wycombe 1761. Created Marquess of Lansdowne 1784. Married (1) 1765 Lady Sophia Carteret, daughter of John, second Earl Granville; (2) Lady Louisa Fitzpatrick, daughter of John, first Earl of Upper Ossory. Lieutenant 1757; Colonel 1760; Major-General 1765; General 1783. MP for Chipping Wycombe 1760–1; First Lord of Trade 1763; Secretary of State for the Southern Department 1766–8; Secretary of State for Home Affairs 1782; First Lord of the Treasury 1782–3. Knight of the Garter 1782. Died 7 May 1805.

Shelburne's brief period as prime minister revealed how a personally unpopular first minister, who lacked the support of a party and had to win parliamentary support for contentious measures, could not prevail. The circumstances would have tried any ministry. The War of American Independence was the most unsuccessful war Britain had waged since Charles I's humiliating conflicts with France and Spain in the 1620s. The process of compromise inherent in peace negotiations could be contentious at the end even of a successful war, as the controversies surrounding the peace treaties of Utrecht (1713), Aix-la-Chapelle (1748) and Paris (1763) had indicated. In February 1783 Shelburne had to persuade parliament to accept peace preliminaries that were genuinely unpopular, especially the lack of any guarantees for the Loyalists and for British debts. He was defeated twice – on 17 and 21 February – and on 24 February submitted his resignation.

Although it was to be another month before George III accepted the resignation, this was the end of the ministerial career of the most intellectual of eighteenth-century British politicians. Yet Shelburne did not fall because of the unpopularity of his peace terms: his was a defeat of men not measures. The Commons defeats represented the rejection of the 'universally disliked' Shelburne (BL Add MSS 35528 f. 27). In addition, however, a major reason for Shelburne's fall was that the other two competing groups of politicians, the largest parties in the House by far, led by Fox and North, were aiming to secure office, and were prepared to do so regardless of any claim by the King to choose his ministers.

Thus to stress Shelburne's unpopularity is to paint in one aspect only of the crisis. Yet it was also a major factor. Why was Shelburne so unpopular? He was a talented man open to new ideas, both those of British intellectuals whom he supported, such as Jeremy Bentham, Richard Price and Joseph Priestley, and those of the French *philosophes*, especially his friend Abbé Morellet. On many issues, particularly administrative and electoral reform, the government of Ireland, relations with the American colonies and foreign policy, Shelburne was far-sighted. In 1786, for example, he stressed the need for major change in Ireland, particularly the commutation of tithe payments to the clergy of the Anglican Church of Ireland and the ending of abuses by the latter:

> the Church of England runs the risk of falling in Ireland and if great care is not taken all property and government will be endangered at the same time. . . . Force never has effected good on either side, and on which ever side it is exerted, carries with it something abhorrent to our manners and Government. Preventive wisdom is certainly the greatest qualification which Government can have . . . the circumstances of Ireland and England are so very different, in regard to religion, that they must necessarily require a different system in that respect.
> (Shelburne to Silver Oliver MP, 26 July 1786, Bowood, Shelburne papers, Box 59)

Yet, to contemporaries, Shelburne was Malagrida (a Portuguese Jesuit) or the 'Jesuit of Berkeley Square', where he lived. He was thus termed because Jesuits were believed to be synonymous with deceit. Shelburne had a justified reputation for arrogance: he could be aloof and cutting. He also responded to the difficulties of politics by failing to consult with colleagues. Shelburne associated his own views with national interests, a frequent failing among politicians, and believed that secrecy, not consultation, was the best way to achieve Britain's goals. He informed the Foreign Secretary, Lord Grantham, that he had told the Spanish envoy that we could never think of anything which was not fundamentally agreeable to parliament, but that there was a great deal of difference between coming to parliament for a yes or no, and Parliament's meeting while things were depending, and more or less public. Such was the case of the Gibraltar article. Such I am sure will be that of the rest of the articles, if not immediately concluded. . . . The Mediterranean merchants will cry up Minorca . . . the same reasoning which has proved applicable to parliament applies in some degree to Council, which for the sake of all concerned had better be to say yes or no.

(Bedford County Record Office, Lucas papers 30/14/306/1)

This was not the language of a man who trusted his ministerial colleagues. Shelburne was evasive and seemed to contemporaries to be inconsistent: this contributed to his reputation for cynicism and opportunism. Furthermore, Shelburne had no real support within parliament. He was an opponent of party or, in his words, faction, a view he took from Pitt the Elder. This was an important theme in eighteenth-century political thought, one that looked back to Boling-broke and the 'Country' opposition to Walpole; a theme that linked Shelburne and George III. Indeed, Shelburne's views on the matter helped to ensure that although his interest in reform and his somewhat radical views were unwelcome to the King, nevertheless, he was acceptable as a first minister, certainly more so than any Rockinghamite. Thus, Shelburne came into office after the fall of the North ministry in large part because he could be relied upon not to work with Rockingham. They had important policy differences, for example over Shelburne's support for parliamentary reform, and in 1782 not least over the crucial peace negotiations; and George III was confident that Shelburne would not join with Rockingham in putting pressure on him.

When Rockingham unexpectedly died, the King chose Shelburne as first minis-ter, rather than the new leader of the Rockinghamites, the Duke of Portland. This led to a resignation of prominent Rockinghamites, especially Charles James Fox, but the King's determination to defend his prerogative of choosing his own min-isters was generally accepted. Shelburne defended the King's right to choose his ministers and his rejection of Foxite ideas regarding the choice of prime ministers and collective responsibility within the cabinet (Cobbett 1806–20: xxiii, 191). However, Shelburne was more like Pitt the Elder, to whom George III had similarly turned in 1766, than like Pitt the Younger, to whom he was to turn in December 1783. Although Pitt the Elder and Shelburne differed over policies, not least over Shelburne's interest in reform, they were alike both in their hostility to party and in their inability to work successfully with others: the two aspects were psychologically related.

At the outset of his political career, Shelburne had been a King's friend, close to Bute and Henry Fox: an unpopular and distrusted position. His varied political career thereafter reflected the difficulties of forming a lasting ministry, and also his own intellectual development and political shifts, especially over reform and

America. Shelburne's own political views were finally to separate him from the bulk of the political nation. In 1788 Sir James Harris wrote that the francophile Shelburne, now Marquess of Lansdowne, had 'principles and opinions' that should not be communicated 'to a foreigner let him be ever so well disposed as can be'. Three years later Lansdowne praised the French National Assembly for determining that the right of making peace and war came from the nation, not the Crown, and he urged the British government to follow the example of trusting the people. In 1793 he protested against the war with France, and thereafter pressed both for peace and against moves to limit the rights of domestic radicals. His last parliamentary speech, on 23 May 1803, was in favour of conciliation with France.

These positions were unpopular, and contributed to the widespread mistrust of Shelburne. The interest in new ideas, the philosophization of politics that Shelburne had sponsored, seemed dangerous in a world made more conservative by the French Revolution. In 1787 he had written to Morellet, 'that it is the Public which decides upon measures with us' (7 August 1787, Beinecke, Osborn Files, Lansdowne). In May 1798 he had pressed the Lords for parliamentary reform 'while it could be done gradually, and not to delay its necessity till it would burst all bounds' (Cobbett 1806–20: xxxiii, 761–2). Yet in this period 'the public' did not favour his politics. Although he supported what were by the standards of his age 'radical' causes, they were potentially undercut by the most radical, his interest in a measure of democratization. A similar contrast helped to give a violent edge to the French Revolution.

Shelburne can thus appear inconsistent, even naive, in his political attitudes in his latter years. However, he also revealed a degree of flexibility, in particular over Ireland and peace with France, that was in fact to be eventually matched by ministers. More generally, Shelburne had a capacity for change and reflection that contrasted with most of his contemporaries. His originality was a combination of traditionalism regarding the powers of the Crown and party with very radical notions in other areas. At the outset of his career he had gained credit from his conduct at the battle of Minden (1759), and had come into parliament for a pocket borough without even having to attend the election. At the age of 23 he became a colonel and aide-de-camp to George III. Yet for Disraeli he was 'the first great minister who comprehended the rising importance of the middle class' (Disraeli 1905: 25), the man who understood pressures for reform. Shelburne's ability and willingness to reflect upon and respond to a changing world was impressive: if he could not understand people and failed to manage measures, he nevertheless had a strong interest in humankind. Shelburne's was not a politics of selfishness.

References and further reading
I would like to thank Ian Christie, John Derry and Bob Eccleshall for commenting on earlier drafts.

Black, J.M. (1993) *The Politics of Britain 1688–1800*, Manchester: Manchester University Press. (Most recent discussion of the political system.)

Brown, P. (1967) *The Chathamites*, London: Macmillan. (Locates Shelburne in terms of the influence of Pitt the Elder.)

Cannon, J. (1969) *The Fox–North Coalition*, Cambridge: Cambridge University Press. (Central for Shelburne's fall.)

Cobbett, W. (ed.) (1806–20) *The Parliamentary History of England . . . from 1066 . . . to 1803*, 36 vols, London: T.C. Hansard.

Disraeli, B. (1905) *Sybil: Or the Two Nations*, London: John Lane.

Fitzmaurice, Lord E. (1875–6) *Life of William, Earl of Shelburne*, London: Macmillan. (Extensive quotations from Shelburne's papers and correspondence.)

Norris, J. (1963) *Shelburne and Reform*, London: Macmillan. (Studies Shelburne as a reformer and as a 'magnificent failure'.)

O'Gorman, F. (1974) 'The Earl of Shelburne', in H. van Thal (ed.) *The Prime Ministers*, London: Allen & Unwin. (Judicious assessment of reasons for failure.)

Ritcheson, C. (1982) 'The Earl of Shelburne and peace with America 1782–1783: vision and reality', *International History Review* 5: 322–45. (Presents Shelburne as skilful, and discusses the European sources of his ideas.)

Scott, H. (1990) *British Foreign Policy in the Age of the American Revolution*, Oxford: Oxford University Press. (Best study of foreign policy in this period.)

Shelburne, Earl of, the Shelburne papers in Bowood House, Wiltshire. (The leading collection of the Earl's papers.)

—— the Shelburne papers in the William L. Clements Library, Ann Arbor, Michigan. (Important collection of Shelburne material.)

Stuart, C. (1981) 'Lord Shelburne', in H. Lloyd-Jones, V. Pearl and B. Worden (eds) *History and Imagination: Essays in Honour of H.R. Trevor-Roper*, London: Duckworth. (A brief, largely sympathetic study.)

Jeremy Black

William Henry Cavendish-Bentinck, Third Duke of Portland

Born 14 April 1738, first son of William Bentinck, second Duke of Portland, and Lady Margaret Cavendish Harley. Educated at Westminster and Christ Church, Oxford. Married 1766 Lady Dorothy Cavendish, daughter of the Duke of Devonshire. MP for Weobly 1761–2. Succeeded his father as third Duke 1762. Lord Chamberlain 1765–6; Lord Lieutenant of Ireland 1782; First Lord of the Treasury 1783; Home Secretary 1794–1801; Lord President of the Council 1801–5; First Lord of the Treasury 1807–9. Died 30 October 1809.

Portland was not a successful prime minister. His two periods as First Lord of the Treasury, in 1783 and 1807–9, were unhappy, short-lived and controversial. There are strong grounds for denying that he ever was a 'prime minister' in any meaningful sense. In contrast to his dismal performance as prime minister, his political career, when viewed as a whole, was marked with considerable success.

For nearly fifty years he was never far from the forefront of politics, either in administration or opposition. Portland's career not only demonstrates the importance of the Whig aristocracy in shaping political alignments, but reveals the ideological and structural fluctuations in party politics. In 1783 Portland presided over a Whig ministry, formed out of a coalition of Foxites and Northites. In 1807, however, his principal colleagues were politicians who, from the nineteenth-century perspective, must be deemed Tories. The explanation for Portland's unique distinction of having been at the head of both a Whig and a Tory ministry lies in the fragmentation of party allegiances in the years following the French Revolution. Portland, therefore, is most often remembered for breaking with Fox and leading the conservative Whigs into coalition with Pitt in 1794.

Portland became a Duke in 1762 at the tender age of 24, and was swiftly recruited into the circle of opposition peers headed by the Duke of Newcastle. As a protégé of Newcastle, he became Lord Chamberlain in the first Rockingham ministry in 1765. He was not required to resign on the changeover to the Chatham ministry in July 1766, but did so in November at Rockingham's behest. Portland's resignation signified his desire to be a politician rather than a mere courtier. He became thoroughly converted to Rockingham's high-minded and exclusive political style. The Rockinghamites promoted themselves as the true and only Whigs, focusing their discontent on the power of the Crown and the supposed system of secret influence that was preventing aristocratic Whigs from fulfilling their self-ordained role as the country's natural leaders.

The Rockingham party was dominated by powerful aristocrats who used their electoral influence to create a core of parliamentary support in the Commons. Portland was an ambitious player in the expensive game of electoral politics, and in 1768 became involved in a famous dispute with Sir James Lowther. The speed with which the ministry came to the aid of Lowther, who just happened to be Bute's son-in-law, proved (to minds already jaundiced) the calculated hostility of the Crown towards the Whig aristocracy. Portland's sufferings gave rise to a national debate on the rights of property and the powers of the Crown. This high profile as a Whig martyr, in conjunction with a consistently loyal support of Rockingham, transformed Portland into one of the leading peers in the opposition. This rise to prominence took place without any evidence of parliamentary ability on his part. He rarely spoke in the Lords and confined his activities to the details of political correspondence and party management. The Rockingham party became the largest of the opposition groupings, evincing a degree of ideological coherence, aided by careful deployment of patronage, and cemented by genuine personal respect for Rockingham.

After nearly sixteen years in opposition, Portland was appointed Lord Lieutenant of Ireland in the second Rockingham ministry in 1782. He soon became convinced that Irish demands for legislative independence could not be resisted. In exchange for sweeping concessions, Portland hoped to secure a redefinition of the Anglo-Irish relationship, but these efforts failed; whether he might have achieved better success in the longer term remains a matter of speculation, since he resigned in July 1782 following Rockingham's death. The Rockingham ministry had been destabilized throughout its brief existence by the machinations of Shelburne and George III. The promotion of Shelburne to the Treasury after Rockingham's death precipitated a crisis. Charles Fox, who was already exasperated with Shelburne's behaviour, contended that the preponderance of the Rockinghamites within the cabinet gave them a right to nominate the First Lord of the Treasury – thereby challenging the King's prerogative of choosing his own ministers. Fox and some of his colleagues chose to resign rather than serve under Shelburne. At a subsequent party meeting, the mantle of party leadership was offered to Portland, who had not yet returned from Ireland. As a landed aristocrat of impeccable Whig credentials with a record of loyalty and service to the party, Portland was an eminently suitable replacement for Rockingham. Charles Fox might appear to have been the more obvious candidate for the leadership, but the personal hostility of George III provided one practical reason for making an anodyne selection. Equally significant, however, was the Rockinghamite perception that Fox was unacceptable as the official representative of an avowedly aristocratic party.

Parliamentary politics were now in a state of flux. If the former Rockinghamites, under the leadership of Fox in the Commons, were to combine with their old enemies the Northites, then Shelburne would be unable to command a working majority. A pragmatic coalition was forged between Fox and North, which succeeded in defeating the ministry and forcing Shelburne's resignation in February 1783. The Fox–North coalition was not an unholy alliance. The ending of the American War and the completion of the economical reform programme had removed two issues which had formerly divided Rockinghamites and Northites. Portland considered the arrangement as entirely justified and defended the criteria by which offices were apportioned within the coalition. The lion's share of efficient offices went to the former Rockinghamites, whereas the Northites were compensated with a greater share of the lesser places. The real problem for the coalition lay not in the division of the spoils, but in overcoming the resistance of George III. From the King's perspective the situation had degenerated considerably since the crisis following Rockingham's death. At that time he had successfully resisted the claim that a majority within the cabinet gave the Rockinghamites the right to nominate the new head of the ministry. The demands of the Fox–North coalition were considerably greater. That Portland was to assume the Treasury was taken as an essential starting-point. In addition, the Duke insisted on face-to-face negotiations with the King, at which he stipulated that the entire cabinet be approved before entering into any discussions about lesser offices. This, in contemporary parlance, was 'storming the Closet' with a vengeance. The King finally acquiesced in April 1783, but he intended to dismiss Portland as soon as possible.

Portland was at the head of the ministry, occupying the office customarily associated with the premiership, but his authority was severely compromised. As a peer he could exert no direct influence over the Commons and was ineligible for the important additional post of Chancellor of the Exchequer. Some contemporaries simply viewed Fox as 'the Minister'. As Foreign Secretary and Leader of the Commons, his power was certainly considerable; what Fox lacked was the confidence of George III. This was a deficiency that Portland might have made good, since his later career demonstrates that he was capable of developing a good working relationship with the King. In 1783, however, all his efforts were rebuffed. George III signalled his dissatisfaction with the coalition by refusing to grant any British peerages. He also created difficulties over a financial settlement for the Prince of Wales and attempted to precipitate a change of ministry. This did not take place because the King, as yet, was unable to negotiate any viable alternative and Portland decided that compromise was preferable to resignation. Matters had reached an uneasy stalemate by the time of the parliamentary recess in the summer of 1783. During this interval, Edmund Burke drafted a scheme to remedy long-standing problems with the East India Company. This India Bill was successfully introduced into the Commons in November, passing through all stages without difficulty or any hint of royal disapproval. The King chose instead to use his influence to defeat the measure in the Lords. He authorized Lord Temple to declare that anyone voting for the Bill would henceforth be considered as a personal enemy. Portland had no hope of combating such underhand tactics. He had never been a good debater and his parliamentary performance prior to this unprecedented crisis was at best second-rate. After bungling the management of the first important debate, he lost key divisions on 15 and 17 December. Those peers and bishops who defeated the India Bill did so partly out of self-interest, but also because of a growing conviction that it was an objectionable measure. In the proposed arrangement, the power of appointing commissioners for overseeing Indian affairs was to be vested initially with parliament rather than entrusted to the King. From the Whig perspective this was a justifiable precaution against increasing the influence of the Crown. A more cynical view was taken by opponents, who saw that considerable patronage would thereby be placed at the disposal of the coalition.

The King, in a preconcerted arrangement, dismissed the coalition and called on Pitt to form a minority ministry, which held out against repeated defeats until a dissolution the following year. The losses suffered by the Fox–North coalition at the general election of 1784 were considerable and can be attributed to a combination of governmental electoral influence and a swing in public opinion. Portland, surprisingly, emerged from the crisis of 1782–4 with his political status greatly enhanced and it would be unfair to dismiss him as Fox's mere cipher. Portland acted in accordance with his own interpretation of the Rockinghamite creed and was not simply obedient to the whims of Fox. The crisis of 1782–4, moreover, set the pattern of politics for a decade, and Portland, just as much as Fox, became identified with those decisive events. Although the parliamentary duels between Pitt and Fox became legendary, the party which supported Fox cannot be simply described as Foxite. Contemporaries often referred to themselves as attached to 'the Duke of Portland's interest'. This was more than a figure of speech. The political importance of Portland increased considerably in the period after 1784. His financial difficulties, which had been acute, were alleviated by the death of his mother in 1785. He could now afford to resume occupation of his splendid London residence, Burlington House, which he had vacated in the interests of economy. Burlington House provided an ideal venue for party meetings and became a centre for organizational activity. By the time of the Regency Crisis of 1788–9, there was no doubt that Portland had confirmed his indispensability to any Whig ministry which the Prince of Wales might sanction. The recovery of George III blasted Whig hopes, but the party did not crumble under the disappointment. Portland worked hard in preparation for the general election of 1790 and presided over a relatively sophisticated level of party organization. His diligence contrasted sharply with Fox's intermittent bouts of activity and indolence. The emergence of an identifiable Portland party in the troubled 1790s must be attributed, at least in part, to the Duke's proven commitment to party organization.

The disintegration of the Whig party was a complex process, sometimes simply summarized as a Burkean reaction to the horrors of the French Revolution. In fact, the direct influence of Burke's opinions on Portland was minimal. The Duke privately castigated Burke for the divisive effect of his actions and long maintained a pointed silence on controversial topics. Portland's aim was to avoid for as long as possible any formal separation from Fox. He clung to this strategy, despite increasing alarm among conservative Whigs at Fox's reformist sympathies. The gradual process of fragmentation creates difficulties for defining political loyalties in the period 1792–4, but depending on when the calculation is made, between forty-seven and sixty-two members could be numbered as Portland Whigs. This head-counting does not fully explain the importance of Portland because the loyalty of aristocratic grandees, such as Lord Fitzwilliam, was of considerable significance in its own right. Political alignments were further complicated by the formation of a 'Third Party' in February 1793: a group of thirty-eight MPs that included twenty-eight former members of the Whig party. The leader of this squadron, William Windham, became dissatisfied with its halfway status and by the end of the year was looking for a rapprochement with Portland. The Duke, meanwhile, was becoming increasingly alarmed at the military situation and consequently dissatisfied with Fox's negative attitude towards the war. At odds with Fox on both domestic and foreign policy, Portland was driven reluctantly to recognize that a formal separation could no longer be avoided. In January 1794, at an eve-of-session meeting, Portland announced not only that he had broken with Fox, but also that he intended to give wholehearted support to the government over the war-effort. After a period of transition, Portland led the conservative Whigs into coalition with Pitt in July, taking for himself the office of Home Secretary. The Portland Whigs had not simply drifted towards a reactionary government, but had actively sought 'to make it reactionary by joining it' (Pares 1953: 194).

It is an oft-cited truism that a crisis of confidence in a ruling elite facilitates revolution. Portland's conduct exemplifies the refusal of the British elite to doubt its ability to rule. He devoted himself to combating all threats to the established order. To this end he condoned the use of surveillance, repression, and military force. He also adopted a hard-line approach to the distress caused by the serious food shortages which occurred during his period in office. In 1795, he refused to countenance the concessions to Irish Catholics which were advocated by Fitzwilliam, the Lord Lieutenant. This caused a permanent rift between Portland and Fitzwilliam, thereby destroying a crucial relationship within aristocratic Whiggery. Following the Irish rebellion of 1798, Portland became convinced of the political, military and diplomatic advantages of a legislative union, and sanctioned the illegal use of British secret service money in Ireland in order to smooth the passage of the measure after its initial rejection by the Irish parliament in 1799. The rights of Irish Catholics figured little in his calculations. Although he had been prepared to concede the theoretical possibility of Catholic emancipation in a post-union parliament, he decided against resigning with Pitt over this issue in 1801 (Wilkinson 1995, 1997a).

The once sizeable Portland party in the Commons had by this stage dwindled almost to nothing. Elevations to the peerage, retirements, deaths and defections had all taken their toll. Portland now owed his political importance principally to the confidence of the King. His position as an elder statesman within the cabinet was terminated by Pitt's death and the formation of the 'Ministry of All the Talents' in 1806 – a coalition that also excluded a number of former Pittites, including George Canning, Spencer Perceval, Lords Castlereagh and Hawkesbury (the future Lord Liverpool). After a period of indecisive manoeuvring these disgruntled politicians chose Portland as their nominal leader. It would be an oversimplification to describe this group as a fully fledged Tory party. They saw themselves as Pittites rather than Tories, the latter term still having negative connotations. Subsequent events, however, reveal this political realignment as embryonic Toryism. Certainly, Portland's Whig credentials counted for little with his new associates: he was chosen on account of his stalwart service to Pitt. A further consideration was that, by agreeing to act under the aegis of Portland, personal rivalry within the group might be kept in check.

Portland, therefore, entered the final stage of his career in paradoxical circumstances. In March 1807, the King clashed with his ministers over a limited measure of Catholic relief, and called on Portland to save him: a situation which, if compared to the events of 1783, amounted to a reversal of roles for the Duke. Unwisely, he accepted the offer to become First Lord of the Treasury. He was not fit for this task. In the past few years he had suffered serious ill-health, and would do so again while in office. There are even less grounds for calling him a prime minister during this period than in 1783. He is recorded as only having set foot in the Lords on fifteen occasions and did not speak there once. The co-ordinating hand of a prime minister was notable by its absence and most of the business of the Treasury was delegated to Perceval as Chancellor of the Exchequer. The contrast in style and ability between Portland and the late-lamented Pitt was keenly felt. Pitt had supervised policy to the extent that he became, in Perceval's telling phrase, 'the government in all departments', whereas the Portland ministry was 'constituted with so many of equal or nearly equal pretensions' that no minister was pre-eminent:

> It is not because the Duke of Portland is at our head that the government is a government of departments: it is because the government is and must be essentially a government of departments that the Duke of Portland is at our head.
>
> (Walpole 1874: 2, 16)

This arrangement seemed to work tolerably well for the first eighteen months of the ministry's existence, but bad news from the war in Portugal and Spain gave rise to disagreements within the cabinet. Canning first objected to the manner in which the Convention of Cintra was accepted, and then disapproved of Castlereagh's defence of Sir John Moore's posthumous reputation after Corunna. Parliamentary criticism from the opposition inevitably followed these military reverses. Further embarrassment was caused in January 1809 by sensational accusations of corruption against the Duke of York. Although this storm was weathered, minor problems persisted: Castlereagh, for example, was accused of having abused government patronage. Canning became increasingly dissatisfied with the government's performance and approached Portland privately, threatening resignation if nothing was done.

Between March and September 1809 a complicated series of negotiations took place. A plan emerged whereby Canning was to be placated by the removal of Castlereagh from the War Department and his replacement by Lord Wellesley. Portland and George III insisted that this arrangement should be kept as secret as possible. The objective was to retain the services of both Canning and Castlereagh. Gradually, other members of the government were let into the secret, but not Castlereagh himself. The timing of any disclosure was complicated by concurrent preparations for a large-scale military expedition to Walcheren. It would have been impolitic to inform Castlereagh of his fate while he was organizing the expedition; and then, after it had sailed in July, circumstances contrived to create a further delay. Lord Camden, who had offered to surrender his office of Lord President to Castlereagh, was deputed to break the news. Since Camden was also Castlereagh's uncle, this channel of communication seemed only natural. When Camden balked at the prospect, Portland duly promised to perform the unpleasant task. The Duke failed to carry out his intention because he suffered a life-threatening seizure in August. Although Portland survived, it became imperative to decide upon a successor. Canning's subsequent behaviour may be explained as an attempt to obtain the premiership for himself: an interpretation confirmed by his unguarded assertion that the prime minister must be a member of the Commons. This, in effect, created a two-cornered contest between

Canning and Perceval. Matters were brought to a head when the failure of the Walcheren expedition became known on 2 September. Canning now insisted on the implementation of the promise to remove Castlereagh. Perceval, conversely, suggested that Castlereagh need know nothing of what had been happening if his transfer was made part of a reshuffle including Portland's own retirement. Should Castlereagh be humiliated, however, Perceval and his friends threatened to resign as well. Since Perceval had already declared his willingness to serve under a prime minister selected from the Lords, the pretensions of Canning were placed in an unflattering light. Faced with an impossible situation, Portland tendered his own resignation on 6 September. Canning therefore relinquished his claim for Castlereagh's removal, but refused to attend a cabinet meeting the following day. Castlereagh could no longer be kept in the dark; and, after discovering the full extent of the campaign against him, he challenged Canning to a duel. Meanwhile, Perceval emerged as the only viable prime minister, formally succeeding Portland on 4 October. The Duke died within the month. 'A perfectly amiable man, with an honourable mind', noted one contemporary diarist, adding laconically, 'his death is now not likely to create any sensation whatever in the state of parties' (Harcourt 1860: ii, 428).

References and further reading
Cannon, J. (1969) *The Fox–North Coalition: Crisis of the Constitution 1782–84*, Cambridge: Cambridge University Press.
Ginter, D. (ed.) (1967) *Whig Organization in the General Election of 1790: Selections from the Blair Adam Papers*, Berkeley, CA: University of California Press.
Gray, D. (1963) *Spencer Perceval: The Evangelical Prime Minister 1762–1812*, Manchester: Manchester University Press.
Harcourt, L. (ed.) (1860) *The Diaries and Correspondence of the Right Hon. George Rose*, 2 vols, London.
Kelly, J. (1992) *Prelude to Union: Anglo-Irish Politics in the 1780s*, Cork: Cork University Press.
Mitchell, L. (1971) *Charles James Fox and the Disintegration of the Whig Party 1782–94*, London: Oxford University Press.
O'Gorman, F. (1969) *The Whig Party and the French Revolution*, London: Macmillan.
—— (1975) *The Rise of Party in England: The Rockingham Whigs 1760–82*, London: Allen & Unwin.
Pares, R. (1953) *King George III and the Politicians*, Oxford: Clarendon Press.
Smith, E. (1975) *Whig Principles and Party Politics: Earl Fitzwilliam and the Whig Party 1748–1833*, Manchester: Manchester University Press.
Turberville, A. (1938–9) *A History of Welbeck Abbey and its Owners*, 2 vols, London: Faber & Faber. (The second volume contains a biography of Portland. Now outdated in its political analysis, but still useful as a source of information, particularly on family history.)
Walpole, S. (1874) *The Life of the Right Hon. Spencer Perceval*, 2 vols, London.
Wilkinson, D. (1995) 'The Fitzwilliam episode, 1795: a re-interpretation of the role of the Duke of Portland', *Irish Historical Studies* 39: 315–39.

—— (1997a) 'How did they pass the union? Secret Service expenditure in Ireland, 1799–1804', *History* 82: 223–51.

—— (1997b) 'The political career of William Henry Cavendish-Bentinck, third Duke of Portland, 1738–1809', unpublished doctoral thesis, University of Wales, Aberystwyth.

David Wilkinson

William Pitt 'the Younger'

Born 28 May 1759, third child of William Pitt, first Earl of Chatham, and Lady Hester Grenville. Educated privately (Revd. Edward Wilson) and at Pembroke Hall, Cambridge. Unmarried. MP for Appleby-in-Westmoreland 1781–4, Cambridge University 1784–1806. Chancellor of the Exchequer 1782–83; First Lord of the Treasury and Chancellor of the Exchequer 1783–1801, 1804–6. Died 23 January 1806.

Pitt was the second longest serving prime minister in British history: he was also the youngest, having first taken office at the age of 24. Pitt's reputation as an enlightened minister sympathetic to fiscal, administrative, constitutional and humanitarian reform was established in the 1780s, a decade of diplomatic and economic recovery from the humiliations of the American War of Independence. With the advent of the French Revolution, he seemed to abandon the liberalism of his youth. In 1793 Britain went to war against revolutionary France, an expensive and exhausting military conflict that was accompanied by the repression of a popular democratic reform movement at home. In pursuing these policies Pitt became during the 1790s the figurehead of a conservative, loyal state. His 1801 resignation shortly preceded the formal cessation of hostilities. In 1804 he returned to lead the country once more to war against France but died two years later, a victim of suspected cancer.

Few British prime ministers are as difficult to place in intellectual terms as Pitt the Younger. The achievements of the 1780s, the 'years of acclaim', would appear to identify him as a Whig but when the enlightened tolerance of youth gave way to the defensive caution of middle age it seems more appropriate to classify Pitt as a 'Tory' (Clark 1985: 340–4). He was canonized as a founding father of the British Conservative party by early nineteenth-century Tories (Sack 1993: 85–90), a development he would have regarded with horror, for he always called himself an 'independent Whig' (Derry 1990: 33; O'Gorman 1989: 27).

Pitt's contemporaries accepted this self-assigned political identity throughout the 1780s. He was regarded as a champion of ambitious legislative programmes, particularly in the realms of finance and administration. The Commutation Act 1784, Consolidated Fund Act 1787 and Sinking Fund Act 1786 not only rationalized the collection and administration of revenue, but established Pitt's reputation as an enemy of corruption and inefficiency (Ehrman 1969: 278–9). This was 'economical reform' in its strict sense, an attempt to reduce the abuse of executive and administrative power by servants of the state. These achievements deserve less praise than they have received (Rose 1911a: 179–94) for Pitt did not believe that parliament's supervisory authority extended to the inner councils and structures of the bureaucracy (Breihan 1984: 77–81). He was also reluctant to antagonize vested interests in both private and public sectors (Ehrman 1969: 300). Pitt did not strike against antiquated official procedures with the crusading zeal that characterized his early mentor, the Earl of Shelburne, and did not succeed in modernizing accounting practices at the Treasury, or entirely replacing fees, sinecures and pensions with salaries.

Limited though Pitt's vision was, his public commitment to fiscal and administrative retrenchment was instrumental in making *laissez-faire* economic theory fashionable during the late eighteenth century. Pitt's reputation as a reformer was more important than his policies (Breihan 1984: 82–3) both in terms of maintaining a climate of intellectual tolerance within the parliament of the 1780s and as an inspiration to the administrators of the post-Napoleonic War period. The Liverpool ministry was to resurrect many of Pitt's early reforms during the 1820s (Derry 1990: 189–91). Pitt's progressive outlook and oratorical talents secured him comfortable majorities in an independent Commons willing to listen to moderate, if not radical, schemes of reform. Pitt had first taken office in December 1783 as a nominee of the King, at which time he had only a handful of personal supporters. In November 1783 Charles James Fox, then government leader in the Commons, had introduced an East India Bill that proposed to vest the vast reserves of East India Company patronage in Fox's hands. A horrified George III had stopped the progress of the Bill by a personal appeal to the Lords, following which Fox and his partner, Lord North, tendered their resignations. Pitt took office as the defender of the King's right to exercise a mediatorial and corrective influence upon an imbalance in the constitution; in this case between Crown and Commons (Ehrman 1969: 136). After five months of minority government, parliament and the nation came to share Pitt's outlook and returned him to power with a comfortable majority. Following the launch of Pitt's official reform policies in 1785 the Foxite Whigs, who had led the 'liberal' opposition in parliament since 1778, found themselves deprived of both platform and supporters.

Fox always believed that Pitt was the toady of the Crown. Pitt, a lifelong enemy of faction and party, saw Fox from 1791 onwards as a disruptive troublemaker. Pitt never had more than sixty personal followers in the Commons, and in the 1780s far fewer. Throughout his first decade in office, Pitt and Fox could be found supporting the same reform measures, most notably the abolition of the slave trade, to which Pitt remained committed throughout his career, and parliamentary reform, which he seemingly deserted after the defeat of his 1785 Bill (Rose 1911a: 205; Ehrman 1969: 228). Unlike Fox, however, Pitt consistently opposed the repeal of the Test and Corporation Acts, a resistance to measures of religious toleration that seems to presage the conservatism of the 1790s (Clark 1985: 341–2).

Pitt's 1785 Reform Bill was no clarion call for the extension of the franchise but his commitment to its 'economical reform' features remained strong throughout the 1780s. Pitt's main interest in reform lay in the reduction of bribery and corruption at elections and the reassertion of property, not influence, as the exclusive arbiter of parliamentary representation. The admission of copyholders to the county franchise and the redistribution of borough seats to new urban constituencies reflected a synthesis of ideas stemming from a tactical alliance between Pitt and the Revd Christopher Wyvill's Yorkshire Association (Ehrman 1969: 73–6, 223–6). These proposals were not on Pitt's original 1782 reform agenda. Wyvill's recommendations were not, however, inconsistent with Pitt's theory of political rights. As an advocate of virtual representation Pitt was no democrat, but believed that the composition of the Commons was obliged to reflect socio-economic developments. The origins of parliament, he claimed in 1783, dated from the reign of Edward I, at which time the representation of the country had been established in principle as a flexible mechanism (Cobbett 1806–20: xxv, 431–8). The composition of the Commons could be modified in perpetuity to reflect demographic, social and economic change. This justified the abolition of rotten boroughs and the redistribution of Commons seats. When Pitt was betrayed by the extra-parliamentary reform organizations which ought to have sent petitions in support of the 1785 Bill to parliament, he abandoned Wyvill's suffrage amendment proposals and the county association movement. He continued to support electoral reform, in favour of which he voted in 1786, 1787, 1788 and 1790.

Of borough reform Pitt had said in 1785 that 'sooner or later something would be effected' (BL Add MSS 35382 f. 302, P. Yorke to Lord Hardwicke, 22 March). This was his attitude to the repeal of the Test and Corporation Acts. The original decision to oppose repeal in 1787 was not automatic, for Pitt demanded an episcopal vote on the issue, and even after a negative verdict was returned he remained undecided until swayed by the opposition of George III (Ehrman 1983: 65–6). Pitt's case against repeal was based on expediency rather than principle. The maintenance of the church–state partnership was, he asserted, 'necessary' as a bulwark against potential politico-religious activism. The ultimate determinant of his resistance to repeal was the hostility of the established church. As he told the young George Canning in 1794, the church was 'too numerous and powerful a party in the country' to offend although repeal was 'a matter of little importance' (W. Yorkshire RO, ff. 74–5, Canning Diary, 24–25 May). Pitt was, however, an advocate of reform in the church. From 1788 to 1791 he lobbied the Anglican establishment to endorse Mitford's Catholic Relief Bill, which proposed to admit English Catholics to certain public offices upon the swearing of an oath of allegiance rather than a sacramental test (Ehrman 1983: 81–4). Test amendment was acceptable; test repeal was not. In 1791 and 1799 he also urged the commutation of tithes upon an unwilling episcopate.

Pitt does not emerge from the debates of the 1780s as a Tory (Sack 1993: 83–4). His final placement within the British political spectrum hinges on the abrupt change of direction undergone during the early 1790s. In 1792, when British supporters of the French Revolution began to mobilize in popular political societies to agitate for democratic parliamentary reform, the Pitt ministry, hitherto neutral towards the Revolution, moved against its British sympathizers. In May 1792 a royal proclamation against seditious writings warned the nation's magistrates that radical publications like Thomas Paine's *Rights of Man* could drive the populace to riot. In December two-thirds of the militia in selected counties were embodied on the grounds that the nation was threatened by insurrection. In 1793 the British government went to war against revolutionary France and began to persecute the native popular radical movement. Pitt, in the eyes of the British public, had embarked upon a holy crusade against the intellectual, social and military forces of revolution.

By 1791 the global repercussions of the French Revolution were becoming a major issue in British high politics. The fears of Edmund Burke, author of the *Reflections on the Revolution in France* (1790), were shared by the 'conservative' Whigs who, under the leadership of the Duke of Portland, joined the Pitt ministry in 1794. Fox and the 'radical' Whigs, who thought that the Revolution represented the triumph of liberty over royal absolutism, remained committed to the battle against prerogative and the defence of civil liberties. Both Whig groups questioned the strength of Pitt's opposition to the Revolution at home and abroad: to the Foxites 'Tory' scaremongering gave Pitt a justification for the exploitation of executive and judicial power; for Burke and his friends Britain's 'ideological' war was dominated by a sordid interest in trade and colonial conquest. Both groups of Whigs were quick to spot the ambivalent features of the Pitt ministry's official war policy: most notably a reluctance to impose any pre-determined system of government on post-war France. The intellectual inconsistencies in this public image of the war were deliberate. 'Indemnification for the past and security for the future' (Cobbett 1806–20, xxx: 1016–17) was a platform broad enough to appeal to every political group of the 1790s: alarmists, doctrinaire conservatives, pragmatists and some liberals. Pitt was appealing to a broad-based cross-section of public opinion, but what emerged from the independent parliament of the 1790s was a new high political consensus with an identifiably conservative slant. In less socially exclusive realms of government public relations – newspapers, pamphlets and political tracts – the ministry's image from 1793 onwards was overtly Tory (Sack 1993: 12–13). Pitt, nevertheless, was reluctant to impose a doctrinal uniformity upon the government's policy statements. Having attempted to do so in 1794, he found himself deserted by William Wilberforce, one of his dearest friends, and a group of anti-war MPs. By the end of 1795, when the British government announced that it was prepared to make peace with the Directory, the war had lost much of its ideological tone.

Pitt's personal attitudes towards France ruled out the conduct of foreign or domestic policy on ideological grounds. The Revolution had paralysed France in Europe (Black 1994: 154–5). In 1787 and 1790 the British government capitalized on French impotence to score notable victories: the former against France in the United Provinces and the latter against Spain in the Pacific North-West (Nootka Sound). Pitt's attitudes towards France before the Revolution were no different from those of any Englishman of his generation. His 'free trade' treaties, the most famous of which was the 1786 Eden Treaty with France, did not herald a new era of liberal international commerce but were framed to protect the already advantageous situation of British merchant houses in Europe (Ehrman 1969: 511–12). In 1784 Pitt told his Foreign Secretary, the Marquess of Carmarthen, that he favoured in principle the creation of an alliance system to counterbalance the House of Bourbon. Its disappearance from the European stage was no great loss. Pitt regarded the Revolution as a long overdue exercise in fiscal, administrative and constitutional reform. Unlike all conservative theorists, he was capable of dissociating the early events of the Revolution from those of the 1790s; in 1795 Pitt said of what amounted to a draft of Burke's *Thoughts on a Regicide Peace* that 'like other writings from the same pen, there is much to admire and nothing to agree with' (Bath and Wells 1861: 320).

Pitt, who repudiated both the natural rights claims of democrats and the universal social fears of conservatives, was unwilling to condemn the entire French experience as a socio-political evil. His view of the Revolution as a unique historical 'event' also led him to deny that it was an object of international appeal. The Commons was told on the eve of war that England's situation was analogous to 'the temperate zone on the surface of the globe' (Cobbett 1806–20: xxx, 243–4). Montesquieu's *L'Esprit des lois* had been invoked to praise the conditions of climate and geography that had created a specific political, social and economic order. Britain would not succumb to the Revolution because it was not *ancien régime* France. Democratic popular radicalism could have no real home in England 'unless it is studiously and industriously brought into this country'. Pitt knew throughout the 1790s that Britain was loyal (O'Gorman 1989: 35). His conviction, however, that the Revolution was acknowledged by all native social groups as an inappropriate model for political change resulted in an inability to recognize the independent identity of the British reform movement. It also dictated Pitt's practical and ideological response to the problem of civil disobedience during the 1790s.

Tory concepts of social progress dictated the rejection of natural rights theory and the upholding of the inegalitarian moral foundations on which Britain's hierarchical society was based (Schofield 1986: 601–11). The Whig vision, though similar in its emphasis upon the achievements of a wealth founded on an unequal distribution of property, concentrated not on the continuity of historical values, but upon a defence of Britain's polite and commercial society couched in contemporary terms (Claeys 1990: 62). Britain's mixed constitution of monarchy, aristocracy and democracy, claimed Pitt in 1792, by the regulating effect of its internal checks and balances 'produces the exertion of genius and labour, the extent and solidity of credit, the circulation and increase of capital: which forms and upholds the national character' (Cobbett 1806–20: xxix, 834–45). This interpretation of British constitutional theory and practice fits into a utilitarian political outlook that, neither Benthamite nor Paleian, assigned value to historical development in terms of its tendency to contribute to the common good. Civil liberty he defined as the absence of constraint, a right and security to be defended by law. Although Britain's social and political stability was *potentially* jeopardized by the activities of native reformers, repressive measures were introduced during the 1790s only when the government had strong reason to believe that armed reinforcement of the radicals was imminent, from either the lower orders or France itself.

For much of the 1790s the Pitt ministry concentrated on deterrence rather than repression. The popular political societies were not outlawed until 1799. The Seditious Meetings Act and the Treasonable Practices Act (Two Acts) of 1795 were passed to forestall radical attempts to exploit the all too real socio-economic grievances of a starving nation. The suspension of *habeas corpus* in May 1794 followed six months of preparation for a French invasion which, though illusory, was widely feared. The 1797 acts prohibiting the administering of unlawful oaths and the inciting of the armed forces to mutiny followed naval mutiny at the Nore in which some, if not all, of the mutineers had been members of the United Irishmen. In 1799, prior to the passage of the Corresponding Societies Act, the Secret Committee of the Commons reported that French sponsorship lay at the root of sedition, treason and civil disobedience throughout Britain. By 1798 this was certainly true of Ireland, the United Englishmen and the London Corresponding Society – all of which were under government surveillance (Dickinson 1985: 52).

Illusion was more important than reality in determining the official response to sedition and treason. Extreme as Pitt's response to popular radicalism appears in hindsight – and tempting though it would be to believe that he exploited the domestic situation to silence the critics of an unsuccessful war with France (O'Gorman 1989: 35) – the government had reason to believe that subversive elements were active within the British reform movement. The cost of an effective police force lay beyond the resources of an eighteenth-century state which relied, not on the strict enforcement of injunctions and statutes, but on the psychological powers of deterrence imposed by the passage and limited application of punitive legislation. The British government, subject throughout the 1790s and 1800s to the mounting financial, administrative and manpower demands of war, partially overcame its infrastructural deficiencies by formal and informal appeals to voluntary 'patriotic' sentiment on an unprecedented scale. Britons were asked to join loyalist associations in 1792, to enlist in volunteer corps of militia from 1794, to change their dietary habits in 1795–6 and 1799–1800, to contribute to a loyalty loan in 1796 and to start paying income tax in 1799. While these requests were not often explicit, they constituted what the Foxites called a 'loyalty test' by virtue of their incorporation within proclamations or enactments of parliament (O'Gorman 1989: 32). This resulted in the identification of Pitt and his government as the forces that had reconstituted the 'nation' as a conservative state. Direct compulsion via legislative instruments was nevertheless the last resort of a ministry that preferred not to redefine its authority in statutory terms.

Pitt's reputation rested on selective memories of the dead man rather than an overall analysis of his policies. The 1794 coalition with the Portland Whigs did not result in the ideological reconstruction of the ministry on 'Tory' lines, particularly in the realms of military and diplomatic policy. Pitt had gone to war to rescue the United Provinces and Austrian Netherlands from French attack and occupation. Although resistance to French expansion in western Europe was a traditional British diplomatic principle which, at a deeper level, constituted a defence of the old diplomatic order, the overthrow of the First Republic was not demanded as a precondition of peace nor, to the chagrin of Burke, was the restoration of the *ancien régime* French monarchy. The first coalition vowed not to make peace with France until it had renounced its policies of interference in the domestic politics of other countries, but more important by far was the establishment of enlarged buffer zones on the French periphery. In 1793 Perpignan was to go to Spain, Alsace-Lorraine to the German princes of the Holy Roman Empire, French Flanders to Austria and parts of what is now Belgium to the United Provinces. The British commitment to the expulsion of the French from the Low Countries was impressive, if unsuccessful, in Pitt's lifetime. The reconquest of French-occupied Europe constituted the military remit of the 1799 second coalition and 1805 third coalition. In 1798–9 North Italy was added to the list of prospective security zones, and in 1805 Pitt proposed to Tsar Alexander I that Britain and Russia act as guarantors for the comprehensive redrawing of borders in the Low Countries, Rhineland and North Italy. This was to be the cornerstone of the 1815 Vienna Peace Settlement.

As an eleventh-hour entrant to the French revolutionary wars the British government found its views difficult to impose upon its allies. Pitt, convinced that a pre-revolutionary legacy of debt and disunity had crippled the republic at birth, maintained throughout the 1790s that sustained allied military pressure would precipitate the eventual collapse of the French war effort. This attitude was responsible, not only for Pitt's legendary optimism in the face of repeated disasters in the European theatre, but also for his consistent underestimation of enemy resources and manpower, not to mention the placement of blame for the setbacks of the war upon allied disunity alone.

Unpredictable though Pitt found the regimes of revolutionary France, he was prepared to honour the 'general will' (Cobbett 1806–20: xxx, 281) of the enemy with regard to its forms of domestic government. On a personal level, he felt that the establishment of a constitutional monarchy in France would facilitate the reconciliation of dissident social groups in the old and new regimes. Pitt always saw the Revolution in terms of power relationships rather than abstract social and intellectual principles: in 1795–6, persuaded that political correctness was giving way to pragmatism, he assumed that the Directory would, in return for the restoration of French West Indian colonies, evacuate the Netherlands and United Provinces. In 1797 Lord Malmesbury found the French disinclined to dismember their 'one and indivisible' republic at Lille, after which the Anglo-French conflict became an explicit war of attrition. After the collapse of the second coalition in 1800–1, the British government was no longer in any position to bargain for favourable terms. Almost all Britain's overseas conquests were restored to France and its satellites, Spain and the United Provinces. In 1802 the Peace of Amiens was signed by the Addington ministry, for Pitt had left office in 1801 following George III's refusal to sanction the grant of Catholic emancipation to Ireland which Pitt and his colleagues had been promising Irish Catholics since 1799.

The King's opposition to religious toleration was so strong that Pitt was inviting a political confrontation by insisting upon the abolition of the sacramental test for Catholic admission to the united parliament. By 1800 Pitt was in poor health and his failure to prepare the King for the introduction of an Emancipation Bill suggests that the years of war had taken their toll on his strength of will (Harvey 1978: 117–19; Mackesy 1984: 172–5). Pitt left office with little reluctance. It must, however, be remembered that the principal aim of his Irish policy had always been the reconciliation of Ireland to British rule. The origins of the union are difficult to date; in 1792 Pitt claimed that it had been 'long in my mind' after which a degree of Catholic emancipation 'could not then be dangerous' to the Protestant interest (Rose 1911b: 390). In 1792 and 1793 limited Catholic Relief was given to Ireland over the vociferous protests of the Protestant Ascendancy to prevent an alliance between Catholic and Presbyterian reformers inspired by the French Revolution. Under the 1793 legislation Catholics were permitted to vote but not stand for election to the Dublin parliament. When Lord Fitzwilliam, the Portland Whig champion of full Catholic emancipation, was appointed Lord Lieutenant in December 1794, union as an abstract proposal was under ministerial consideration. Fitzwilliam was recalled primarily because he had dismissed leading members of the Dublin administration without clearance from London (Ehrman 1983: 426–7, 431–8). Catholic emancipation had not been ruled out, though its precipitate endorsement by Fitzwilliam had been deplored. A legislative union came to be seen in London as an imperial necessity following the emergence of the United Irishmen as a revolutionary Home Rule movement, two French military expeditions to Ireland and the 1798 Irish insurrection. This was not the case in Dublin where the Union proposals, having been rejected in 1799, were approved in 1800 after months of heated Irish debate and some government bribery. The Act of Union was intended to create a political forum where Irish grievances could be aired with relative freedom from sectarian influence. Emancipation was a vital part of that package.

The formation of the Addington ministry witnessed the fragmentation of old Pittite political consensus (Harvey 1978: 121–5). Lord Grenville, the ex-Foreign Secretary, and some of the Portland Whigs went into opposition, there to remain until the formation of the 'Ministry of All the Talents' (1806–7). Pitt remained active behind the scenes as an adviser to Addington but when Britain began to prepare for the renewal of hostilities against Napoleon in 1803, the national clamour for Pitt's return was too strong to be resisted. In 1804 he again took over direction of the British war effort for the next two years. He had promised an ailing George III that Catholic emancipation would not be revived for the rest of his reign. The cumulative pressures of overwork and ill-health proved to be insurmountable and Pitt died in 1806. His reputation as 'the Incorruptible' minister was borne out by a refusal to enrich himself at the expense of the state and his personal debts, which amounted to £40,000, were paid by a grateful nation. His canonization as the saint of Britain's revolutionary war effort had begun before his death; in 1804 he had been lauded by Canning as 'the Pilot who weathered the Storm'.

References and further reading
Bath and Wells, Bishop of (1861–2) *The Journal and Correspondence of William, Lord Auckland*, 4 vols, London.
Black, J. (1994) *British Foreign Policy in an Age of Revolutions, 1783–1793*, Cambridge: Cambridge University Press. (Exhaustive. Discusses the first decade of Pitt's foreign policy in the context of foreign and domestic events.)
Breihan, J. (1984) 'William Pitt and the Commission on Fees, 1785–1801', *Historical Journal* 27: 59–81. (Explains Pitt's limited commitment to fiscal and administrative reform in terms of Blackstonian constitutional theory.)
Claeys, G. (1990) 'The French Revolution debate and British political thought', *History of Political Thought* 11: 59–80. (Rescues loyalist propaganda and thought from the clutches of conservative political theory.)
Clark, J. (1985) *English Society 1688–1832*, Cambridge: Cambridge University Press. (Polemical, thought-provoking and widely criticized. Attributes to Pitt a degree of interest in Anglican politico-theological debate which is entertaining, if unsupportable.)
Cobbett, W. (ed.) (1806–20) *The Parliamentary History of England, . . . from 1066 . . . to the Year 1803*, 36 vols, London: T.C. Hansard.
Derry, J. (1990) *Politics in the Age of Fox, Pitt and Liverpool: Continuity and Transformation*, London: Macmillan. (A-level introductory guide to British politics in the late eighteenth and early nineteenth centuries.)
Dickinson, H. (1985) *British Radicalism and the French Revolution, 1789–1815*, Oxford: Blackwell. (Concise short guide to radical and conservative movements in Britain during the revolutionary era.)
Duffy, M. (1989) 'British diplomacy and the French Wars 1789–1815', in H. Dickinson (ed.) *Britain and the French Revolution 1789–1815*, London: Macmillan.
Ehrman, J. (1969) *William Pitt: The Years of Acclaim*, London: Constable. (Meticulously researched, encyclopaedic in content and utterly unreadable. Remains, however, the indispensable biography of Pitt. Volume 1 of a triple decker.)
—— (1983) *William Pitt: The Reluctant Transition*, London: Constable. (Much like volume 1 but puzzlingly silent on Pitt's attitudes to popular radicalism, the post-war future of Europe and the management of parliament during the 1790s.)
—— (1996) *The Younger Pitt: The Consuming Struggle*, London: Constable.
Emsley, C. (1985) 'Repression, "terror" and the rule of law in England during the French Revolution', *English Historical Review* 100: 801–23. (Places Pitt's 'Reign of Terror' in its true light as a campaign of limited law enforcement.)
Harvey, A. (1978) *Britain in the Early Nineteenth Century*, London: Batsford.
Mackesy, P. (1984) *War without Victory: The Downfall of Pitt, 1799–1802*, Oxford:

Oxford University Press. (Attributes the 1801 resignation to the cumulative impact of inter-ministerial conflict, the collapse of the second coalition and the poor state of Pitt's health.)

Mori, J. (1995) *William Pitt and the French Revolution, 1785–1795*, Keele: Keele University Press. (Still resembles the doctoral thesis it once was but firmly places Pitt in the Whig political tradition, if not the Whig pantheon.)

O'Gorman, F. (1989) 'Pitt and the "Tory" reaction to the French Revolution 1789–1815', in H. Dickinson (ed.) *Britain and the French Revolution 1789–1815*, London: Macmillan. (Explains Pitt's domestic policies of the 1790s as a combination of genuine fear and political caution.)

Rose, J. (1911a) *William Pitt and National Revival*, London: G. Bell. (First half of a two-volume biography, this remains a classic, though dated, account of Pitt's first seven years in office.)

—— (1911b) *William Pitt and the Great War*, London: G. Bell. (Volume 2, which has yet in some parts to be superseded by Ehrman.)

Sack, J. (1993) *From Jacobite to Conservative: Reaction and Orthodoxy in Britain, c.1760–1832*, Cambridge: Cambridge University Press. (Very good on the Tory 'christianization' of Pitt in the early nineteenth century, and succeeds in divorcing the saint from the man.)

Schofield, T.P. (1986) 'Conservative political thought in Britain in response to the French Revolution', *Historical Journal* 29: 601–22.

Jennifer Mori

Henry Addington, First Viscount Sidmouth

Born 30 May 1757, first son of Anthony Addington and Mary Hiley. Educated at Winchester, Brasenose College, Oxford, and Lincoln's Inn. Married (1) 1781 Ursula Mary, daughter of Leonard Hammond; (2) 1823 Mary Anne, daughter of Lord Stowell. MP for Devizes 1784–1805. Speaker of the House of Commons 1789–1801; Prime Minister and Chancellor of the Exchequer 1801–4; Lord President of the Council 1805; Lord Privy Seal 1805–6; Lord President of the Council 1806–7 and 1812; Home Secretary 1812–22; Minister without Portfolio 1822–4. Left Commons 1805, ennobled the same year. Died 15 February 1844.

For more than a century after his death, Addington's reputation as a prime minister was held in low esteem for two main reasons. First, he seemed intellectually and politically lightweight by comparison with such contemporaries as Pitt and Fox, a view encapsulated in Canning's famous doggerel: 'Pitt is to Addington/As London is to Paddington'. And second, his administration began by making peace with France in 1802 but collapsed when it was judged incapable of waging the war that had resumed in 1803. In fact, it was not until the publication of Philip Ziegler's biography in 1965 that his prime ministership began to be seen in a more favourable light.

His qualifications for the office he acquired in March 1801 certainly appear to have been weak. As critics never failed to point out, he was not a member of the landed classes, his father being a doctor and his family having no claim to bear arms. He was therefore Britain's first prime minister from the professional classes, a fact that led him to be referred to sneeringly as 'The Doctor'. In addition, he had no previous experience of cabinet office and no party of supporters. For the previous eleven years he had been Speaker of the Commons and before that a backbencher. What made this deficiency all the more striking was the fact that he became prime minister at one of the most critical junctures of the war. The second allied coalition had collapsed, leaving Britain facing Bonaparte's France virtually alone. The union with Ireland was in place but the concession of equality of political rights to Catholics, which many in Ireland expected to follow, had just been ruled out by the King. It was this that had led to Pitt's resignation. Some feared that another rebellion in Ireland, similar to that of 1798, was likely to take place. It was in these circumstances that Addington, an anti-Catholic but a politician with no family connections within the elite, with no experience of office and no personal supporters, acceded to the King's request to form an administration.

On closer inspection Addington's circumstances and prospects were not as unusual or bleak as they might seem. Being of professional origins was not an advantage but he had been educated alongside members of the traditional elite at Oxford and Lincoln's Inn. Further, this was a period when high politics were particularly open to promising newcomers from beyond the pale – such as two future prime ministers, George Canning and Spencer Perceval. Like Addington, both sprang to prominence under Pitt's tutelage in the 1790s. Nor was he devoid of political strengths. It was generally felt that he had been a successful Speaker and this, combined with his moderate conservatism on issues such as the slave trade and the war as well as his more forthright opposition to Catholic relief, had endeared him to the independent country gentlemen in the Commons, without whose support no government could survive. In addition, while he lacked cabinet experience, he was far from uninformed on the inner workings of Pitt's government. On the contrary, he had been a confidant of the prime minister on a variety of matters, particularly financial policy. Finally, although the issues of war, the Irish Question, and the economy required urgent policy decisions, the prospects for his political survival were far from hopeless. In fact, he had four strong advantages. The first was the support of the King, to whose request to form an administration he had acceded and whose adherents in parliament were still a potent force in politics. The second was the support of Pitt who, although he could not carry all his former colleagues with him, pledged co-operation and advice. The third was the support of the country gentlemen, and the fourth was the fact that the only formed opposition consisted of the demoralized and much diminished Whig party, then numbering less than one-eighth of the Commons. Addington's prospects in the first union parliament were therefore relatively bright.

His prime ministership was dominated by two issues: war policy and the proliferation of parties caused by the collapse of Pitt's hegemony. The question of Ireland, the issue which had brought Addington to power, was put to one side as both the King and his prime minister were now opposed to Catholic relief.

With regard to the war the key to Addington's overall strategy was his belief that the combination of a lack of effective allies and a weakened economy necessitated a period of recuperation before the struggle could be resumed with any hope of success. He therefore focused his attention on three related policies: peace negotiations; improvements to national finances; and national defence. In the case of a peace, he made its desirability a subject of his first speech as prime minister on 25 March 1801, and regarded its fulfilment exactly a year later in the Treaty of Amiens as a major achievement. In some respects it was. It gave Britain a respite and received overwhelming support in parliament. On the other hand, it was hardly a diplomatic victory. All conquests were returned, with the exception of Ceylon and Trinidad, and the respite was brief as the war was resumed in May 1803 when the government refused to accede to Bonaparte's latest demand – the British evacuation of Malta. The analogies with Munich in 1938 are clear enough.

However, Addington's chief hope of the peace was that it would enable him to prepare the economy for war, a task he made his own. Like Pitt, he was both First Lord of the Treasury and Chancellor of the Exchequer. In these he met with considerable success. Regarded by some authorities as at least as skilled in financial matters as Pitt, he was responsible for four budgets with the following principal features. The first was the introduction of the equivalent of the modern budget statement. Hitherto, accounts of past performance and future prospects were scattered during a session. Addington gathered them together and delivered a review of the past and a prognosis for the future in one speech. The second was the abandonment of Pitt's income tax and the raising of a huge loan to defray the mortgage on it, the interest on the loan being raised by a series of pledged taxes. This replaced the self-assessed system of income tax which, somewhat predictably, had never raised its anticipated revenue. The third, and most important feature, was the establishment of an innovative income tax in 1803 to meet the costs of the renewed war. The novelty lay in the fact that the tax was based on the principle of deducting it at source. This was the foundation of a system of taxation that has survived to the present day and proved much more efficient than the system it replaced.

Addington's other priority was national defence. His lack of faith in a war policy based on continental alliances and a land war, and his preference for a far flung naval strategy, led him to devise measures to enlarge the regular army with a trained reserve as circumstances required; and to establish a home guard to repel an anticipated invasion. At the time the measures were strongly criticized for undermining the regulars and being ineffective. However, the historiographical consensus is that they provided 30,000 trained reserves and more than 300,000 volunteers, some of whom would have proved an effective force if they had been needed.

Nevertheless, it was the government's defence measures that brought about its downfall. Since forming his administration, Addington's continuance in office had depended partly on Pittite support and partly on the Whig opposition not being enlarged. At first all had gone well. Although he was obliged to cobble together a none too impressive executive from a mixture of those who stayed in office and his own friends and relations, only Lord Grenville and Canning of the major figures in Pitt's administration went into opposition, and then as part of relatively small groups. Pitt, for his part, abided by his agreement to lend the government his support.

However, following a general election in 1802 which made little difference to the strength of parties, his position became increasingly difficult. The first major setback took place in the winter of 1803–4 when Fox put an end to Addington's efforts to entice members of the Whig party into the government and came to an agreement with the Grenvillites, thereby making their combined forces the largest party in the Commons. The second and fatal blow came in April 1804 when Pitt, who had felt increasingly neglected and slighted by his former protégé, also went into opposition on the grounds that the renewal of the war required more dynamic foreign and domestic policies, particularly with regard to the military. Although Addington still had the King on his side, he was now opposed by the parties of Pitt, Fox and Grenville as well as the 'flying squadrons' of Canning and the Prince of Wales. He therefore decided to resign rather than resist, a course of action that he calculated would preclude the King being forced into a corner on the composition of the next government. In that calculation he was undoubtedly correct. Thus, having become prime minister at the King's request, he resigned in order to protect the King's prerogative of having a free hand in the choice of ministers.

Lord Sidmouth, as Addington became in 1805, continued to play an important role in parliamentary politics for a further twenty years, initially because of the votes of the group of followers that he had assembled when prime minister. This was the principal reason why first Pitt, and then Grenville, invited him into their cabinets, although a sense of duty was the main reason why he accepted. However, neither experience was a fruitful one, Sidmouth resigning on both occasions as a result of differences of policy – in the case of the Grenville government, because of his opposition to any concessions to Catholic claims. For the following five years he and his dwindling party were a factor considered in ministry-making but it was only in 1812 that he became part of the rehabilitation of Pitt's old hegemony that started under Perceval and was completed by Lord Liverpool in 1822.

Sidmouth himself regarded his prime ministership as a painful experience but it was not without merit. He had come to the rescue of the King at a critical moment and when the monarchy was a much greater object of public veneration than used to be thought. Moreover, he achieved some of his objectives. A respite from the war was secured, albeit a brief one; the national finances were put on a better footing than Pitt had been able to manage; and a home guard was raised in an impressive display of patriotism that affected virtually every part of Britain. What he lacked was the guile and charisma to subdue the great guns of the previous administration.

References and further reading

Belfield, E.M.G. (1959) *The Annals of the Addington Family*, published privately by Warren and Son, Winchester: The Wykeham Press. (An unsuccessful attempt to breathe life into the subject.)

Pellew, G. (1847) *The Life and Correspondence of the Right Honble. Henry Addington, First Viscount Sidmouth*, 3 vols, London: John Murray. (A soundly based attempt to rehabilitate Addington's reputation but marred by errors in the transcription of some of the original manuscripts.)

Thorne, R.G. (1986) 'Henry Addington', in R.G. Thorne, *The History of Parliament: The Commons 1790–1820*, vol. 3, London: Secker & Warburg. (This is the definitive account of his parliamentary career, being based on all the available published and unpublished material at the time that it went to press.)

Ziegler, P. (1965) *Addington*, London: Collins. (An excellent biography based on a thorough knowledge of the Addington papers as well as some unpublished theses on aspects of his career.)

Peter Jupp

William Wyndham Grenville, First Baron Grenville

Born 24 October 1759, third son and seventh surviving child of George Grenville (Prime Minister 1763–5) and Elizabeth Wyndham. Educated at Eton and Christ Church, Oxford. Married 1792 the Hon. Anne Pitt, daughter of Thomas Pitt, first Baron Camelford. MP for Buckingham 1782–4, Buckinghamshire 1784–90. Created Baron Grenville 1790. Chief Secretary for Ireland 1782–3; Paymaster-General 1783–9; Board of Control 1784–90 (President 1790–3); Board of Trade 1784–6 (Vice-President 1786–9); Speaker of the Commons 1789; Home Secretary 1789–91; Foreign Secretary 1791–1801; Prime Minister 1806–7; Chancellor of the University of Oxford 1810–34. Died 12 January 1834.

In 1862, the fourteenth Earl of Derby, thrice a Conservative prime minister, reminisced with his eldest son on the three leading political characters of his youth, Pitt the Younger, Charles James Fox and Lord Grenville. He reflected that Pitt's reputation was ever-increasing while Fox, though wrong in his support for the French Revolution, had at least fought for principles. Grenville, on the other hand, 'had less principle than either of them: with him the leading idea was the importance of his family connection, and to this he was always ready to sacrifice the public interest' (Vincent 1978: 184–5). Derby's assessment of Grenville's patriotism, though perhaps unduly harsh, was nonetheless a fairly common critique. More than any other prime minister in British history (with the possible exception of Lord Grey), Grenville has been identified in the public mind with the wealth and jobbery of his wider family circle. To be a 'Grenvillite' in nineteenth-century British politics always suggested a somewhat shady experience.

Lewis Namier might have had the Grenville faction in mind when he revolutionized the study of pre-1832 British history by suggesting that much of high parliamentary politics represented not ideological struggles between Whigs and

Tories but factional conflict in the pursuit of sinecures, pensions, and court jobs (Namier 1985). There were no two more assiduous seekers after public emoluments and honours than Grenville's eldest brother George (1753–1813), created first Marquess of Buckingham in 1784, and his nephew Richard (1776–1839), created first Duke of Buckingham and Chandos in 1822. From their palatial estate at Stowe, in Buckinghamshire, these senior Grenvilles oversaw a political empire of parliamentary boroughs, annual rent rolls in excess of £60,000, and, during the lifetime of the first Marquess, the lucrative tellership of the Exchequer, worth £23,000 in 1808. The Stowe Grenvilles were nothing if not generous in their pursuit of public money for their assorted children, brothers, nephews and friends. Of the first Marquess's two brothers, Thomas (1755–1846) was for life Chief Justice of Eyre, south of Trent, at £2,316 per annum and Lord Grenville himself was Auditor of the Exchequer, at £4,000 per annum. The rest of the Grenville family were not politicians of the first rank and their grasping for public money, though embarrassing, was not of great political moment. Grenville was of foreign secretarial and prime ministerial calibre, however, and his family's receptivity to abnormal grants of public money hurt his own reputation and that of his followers. When First Lord of the Treasury in 1806, for example, Grenville was placed in the awkward position of auditing his own accounts. On 27 January 1806 the *Courier* newspaper no doubt reflected public opinion when, at the commencement of Grenville's premiership, it described the Grenville family as 'gorged with places and pensions'. It was a charge Grenville was to bear his entire political life.

What made the attacks upon Grenville's probity the more painful was the fact that by certain standards of his age he was one of the soberest, most painstaking, conventionally moral of statesmen. Not for him the alcoholism of a Pitt or the libertinism of a Fox. Grenville was the prototype of a dutiful, earnest, religious politician in the age of the hedonistic Regency. His chief intellectual interests were Greek scholarship and political economy, while for exercise he took up gardening at Dropmore, his home in Buckinghamshire, and Boconnoc, his estate in Cornwall. Grenville had an enviable ability to see through to the core of intricate financial or political questions. Few of his leading contemporaries had a better grasp of the intersection of foreign policy and imperial issues with financial and economic ones. As a politician he lacked one ingredient usually necessary for ultimate success: a sense of *camaraderie*. He was stiff, formal and, as George III thought, obstinate. Grenville was quite aware that he was no leader of men. He was more at ease discussing political economy with Francis Horner than sustaining his followers with drink and entertainment.

As head of a coalition including his own faction, the Foxite Whigs, and the followers of Henry Addington, Grenville was prime minister for only thirteen months. Neither George III nor the professional administrative class which had grown up under the long ministry of Pitt the Younger had much confidence in the staying power of his diffuse government. The one abiding achievement of the administration, and on which the prime minister worked closely with Fox and

Wilberforce, was the abolition of the slave trade. In foreign affairs there was probably little room for much creative diplomacy – bounded as the ministry was by Austerlitz and Friedland – and the government certainly failed to distinguish itself in its South American or Mediterranean expeditions. The ministry's fall from power in March 1807 involved a refusal by the leading cabinet figures to promise George III never again to raise the Catholic question – an issue which had been percolating in early 1807 due to a ministerial desire to allow Roman Catholics the higher positions in the United Kingdom military.

Grenville's importance in British history derives less from his ephemeral premiership than from his foreign ministry in the 1790s and his leadership of the Grenvillite party after 1801, as well as that of the 'Whig' coalition between 1804 and 1817. As Foreign Secretary Grenville was a 'Europe-man'. He sat in a cabinet composed of able and strong-willed individuals such as Henry Dundas, Secretary of War, William Windham, Secretary at War, and Pitt himself, the prime minister. Dundas exemplified the old 'blue water' school, favouring naval and military expeditions to the West Indies, Spanish South America or French-held Egypt. Windham was inclined towards restoring the Bourbons and invading France. Grenville, in the first and second coalitions, was determined to defeat French atheism, republicanism and aggression on the Rhine and the Elbe, and in Switzerland, the Netherlands, Savoy and Naples. While in the short term his European views were a failure, he never retracted them. His strongly argued opposition to Britain's participation as a major force in the Peninsular War (1809–13) was partially based on his view that events in Spain and Portugal were a distraction from the main theatre of combat. Grenville saw the defeat of Napoleon in eastern and central Europe in 1813 and 1814 as a vindication of his own policies of the 1790s.

Grenville was arguably as important in the development of the nineteenth-century British party system as was Joseph Chamberlain of the twentieth. When William Pitt (and Lord Grenville) resigned in 1801 over the issue of Catholic emancipation, the new prime minister, Henry Addington, not only took a generally anti-Catholic line in Ireland but quickly negotiated the Peace of Amiens with Bonaparte. Both Grenville and his brother, the Marquess of Buckingham (whose wife was a Roman Catholic), opposed Addington's Catholic and European lines. In this they were joined by other prominent members of Pitt's former administration such as Windham, Earl Spencer, late of the Admiralty, and Earl Fitzwilliam, Pitt's controversial Irish Lord Lieutenant of 1795. Windham, Spencer and Fitzwilliam, as well as Grenville's own brother Thomas, were four of the leading members of the 'Portland Whigs' – those conservative Whigs who, under Edmund Burke's inspiration, had left their ancestral political ties in 1793 and 1794 to join Pitt's war administration. This loss greatly weakened the main body of the Foxite Whig opposition. In 1804 Lord Grenville led these Portland Whigs into a Grenville–Foxite coalition whose chief cement was their common support for Catholic emancipation. This political alignment facilitated the by no means historically determined return of many great aristocratic families to the Whig party. By the time the Grenville family reunited with the Tory descendants of Pitt between 1817 and 1822, the Portland Whigs were firmly ensconced in the bosom of mother whiggery. Grenville was also important in providing the main body of the Whigs with their only major experience in national public office between 1783 and 1830. It is difficult to believe that George III would ever have called Charles James Fox, Charles Grey or Lord Holland to his councils without the healing presence of Lord Grenville as prime minister in 1806–7.

References and further reading

Beckett, J. (1994) *The Rise and Fall of the Grenvilles: Dukes of Buckingham and Chandos, 1710–1921*, Manchester: Manchester University Press. (Especially strong on the family's complicated financial conundrum in the nineteenth century.)

Harvey, A. (1978) *Britain in the Early Nineteenth Century*, London: Batsford.

Historical Manuscripts Commission *Fortescue* (1892–1927), 1–X. (Contains ten volumes of the correspondence of Lord Grenville.)

Jupp, P. (1985) *Lord Grenville*, Oxford: Oxford University Press. (The standard biography which stands comparison with the best of modern British political biographies.)

Namier, L. (1985) *The Structure of Politics at the Accession of George III*, London: Macmillan.

Sack, J. (1979) *The Grenvillites, 1801–1829: Party Politics and Factionalism in the Age of Pitt and Liverpool*, Urbana, IL: University of Illinois Press.

Vincent, J. (ed.) (1978) *Disraeli, Derby and the Conservative Party: The Political Journals of Lord Stanley, 1849–69*, New York: Barnes & Noble.

James Sack

Spencer Perceval

Born 1 November 1762, second son of John Perceval, second Earl of Egmont, and Catherine Compton. Educated at Harrow, Trinity College, Cambridge, and Lincoln's Inn. Married 1790 Jane Wilson, daughter of Sir Thomas Spencer Wilson. MP for Northampton 1796–1812. Commissioner of Bankrupts 1790; Surveyor of the Meltings and Clerk of the Irons, Tower of London 1791; Counsel to the Admiralty 1794–1801; King's Counsel 1796; Solicitor to the Ordnance 1798; Solicitor-General 1801–2; Attorney-General 1802–6; Chancellor of the Duchy of Lancaster 1807–12; Chancellor of the Exchequer and Leader of the Commons 1807–9; First Lord of the Treasury and Chancellor of the Exchequer 1809–12. Died 11 May 1812.

Perceval is famous for two things: for being the first Evangelical prime minister, and for being assassinated. Although it is to be hoped that his last claim to fame remains unique, current thinking is that he was by no means unusual in his Evangelicalism and that he deserves to be remembered most for being the Younger Pitt's successor as leader of the Tory party and for policies that successfully supported the war effort at a critical stage in its history.

The structure of politics in which his career developed has also been the subject of revision. The consensus now is that it was exceptionally fluid and that he became prime minister in the midst of a transition from the limited monarchy of the 1760s to the parliamentary government of the 1840s. Royal power, in fact, was still substantial. George III's support to a government was crucial to its existence and he was accustomed to exercising his veto over men and measures. Moreover, widespread deference to royal power was a factor in delaying the development of the office of prime minister and the institution of the cabinet. Thus, although both had become accepted facts of political life as a result of the increasing scope of central government and the practicalities of managing global war, neither was fully institutionalized due to the threat they posed to the exercise of the royal prerogative. Further, although the number of 'King's Friends' in parliament was on the decline, the influence of the Crown was still a factor in parliamentary politics. It was a major source of disagreement, for example, between the two parties who dominated the parliamentary agenda – the Pittites and the Whigs. Indeed, the former were dubbed Tories by the latter because of their deference to the Crown on constitutional issues. The issue accounts to some degree for the impermanent nature of party organization, particularly on the Tory side, as some believed that a too powerful party system could present a threat to the free exercise of the royal prerogative. In fact, the two parties accounted for no more than half the MPs in the Commons, the rest being either members of personal factions or independents, the last of whom usually supported the party in power provided that it had the blessing of the King.

Perceval became prime minister principally as a result of good fortune, hard work, his skill as a debater, and a personality and policies that appealed to the King and a broad spectrum of Pittites and independent MPs. It owed far less to personal ambition, in which he was notably lacking.

Good fortune was bestowed by his family. His first posts during Pitt's first government, leading to his becoming Counsel to the Admiralty in 1794, were due mainly to the influence of his elder brother, Lord Arden, who was a junior minister. Moreover, his election to parliament in that year was at the request of his cousin, Lord Compton, who controlled a major electoral interest in Northampton. However, it was a characteristic of Perceval's career that he made the best of any duties that were placed in his way. He was a diligent and distinguished student at Harrow and Cambridge, and sufficiently interested in public affairs to have published a pamphlet on the dangers of the French Revolution. The success of his first major speech in 1798 established him as one of the most skilled debaters among the up and coming Pittites, and his ability secured him his senior legal posts under Addington and in the period 1801 to 1806. Following Pitt's death in January 1806, Perceval strengthened his reputation by playing a prominent part in debate against Grenville's government, and when it collapsed in March of the following year he was regarded, along with the more prominent figures of Canning, Castlereagh and Lord Hawkesbury, as one of those from whom Pitt's eventual successor would be chosen. The stop-gap successor and prime minister, Portland, therefore offered him the Chancellorship of the Exchequer with the lead in the Commons – the last, possibly, because of the difficulties of choosing between the competing claims of the other three. Perceval initially declined on the grounds of his preference for the more lucrative Attorney-Generalship and his dislike of what he described as the 'financial and other labours' of the posts (Gray 1963: 95) but eventually accepted them when Portland included the Chancellorship of the Duchy of Lancaster in order to increase the income.

But Perceval's personality and views also played their part in his success. Small in stature and dressed habitually in black – he was known as 'Little P' – he exuded a moral probity and earnestness as a result of a commitment to Evangelicalism formed at Cambridge. This influenced his private as well as his public life. He brought it to his marriage by the habit of daily prayers with his numerous family, and in general tried to live the life of a Christian gentleman by campaigning against the vices of the day and giving large sums of his own money to good causes. In the words of a contemporary, William Roberts, he was 'Christianity personified' (Gray 1963: 16). Evangelicalism was also the bedrock of his politics. Thus throughout his career he sought to strengthen the Church of England by measures to reduce non-residence, to improve clerical stipends, and to build churches in expanding towns. It was also one of the sources of his implacable opposition to Catholic emancipation which, he said, would fail to appease Catholic Ireland and would weaken the Church of England. However, there was also a touch of millenarianism and simple bigotry in Perceval's anti-Catholicism.

Evangelicalism contributed to his other views, most notably his support for the abolition of slavery and the regulation of child labour, but it coexisted with a Burkean conservatism stimulated by the French Revolution and fostered by the spread of radicalism in Britain. He therefore became a fervent supporter of the war against France, and although prepared to countenance some reform of the political system in the shape of reductions in ministerial patronage he was firmly opposed to any alteration in the franchise and the distribution of parliamentary seats. On the other hand, like many other Pittites, he was a pragmatist when it came to matters that did not impinge directly on the pillars of the state. As Portland's Chancellor of the Exchequer, for example, when one of the main issues was how to pay for a prolonged war effort against Bonaparte's continental hegemony, he produced budgets that eschewed innovations and resorted with some success to retrenchment in civil expenditure and the raising of loans at favourable rates.

Despite his qualifications for the prime ministership – his impeccable character, his skill in debate, the broad appeal of his conservatism and humanitarianism among the Pittites and, above all, his modest success as Chancellor and Leader of the House – Perceval succeeded Portland in 1809 with reluctance and after a lengthy period of high-political manoeuvring. The crux of the problem was the competing claims of Canning, Castlereagh and Hawkesbury (now Lord Liverpool). It was resolved in Perceval's favour largely because Canning and Castlereagh were at loggerheads over war policy, and to a lesser extent because Liverpool was now in the Lords when it was widely felt that the next prime minister should be in the Commons in view of the numerical strength of the Whig opposition. Perceval himself, although unwilling to serve under Canning, had suggested alternatives but in the end his colleagues recommended him to the King on 30 September 1809. The King, who shared Perceval's anti-Catholic views, accepted the recommendation eagerly and Perceval duly complied on 2 October despite the fact that he was obliged to continue as his own Chancellor as a result of there being no one else willing to accept the post. He would not be found 'wanting in exertion, in industry, in zeal and in duty', he told the King, but 'in talent and power, he feels his great defects for such a station in such arduous times' (Aspinall 1962–70: v, 386).

Perceval's gloom was justified, for few prime ministers can have had such a difficult first year in office. As a result of recriminations over his succession and differences over policy, he was unable to command the support of some leading Pittites, most notably Canning. In addition, he faced such a formidable opposition in the 1810 session, particularly on the subjects of the disastrous military expedition to Walcheren and the composition of a select committee to review the national finances, that his government was defeated in the Commons in six major divisions. Finally, the King, who was a major source of support for the government among independent MPs, lost his sanity in October 1810. This necessitated the Regency of the Prince of Wales, who was regarded as a patron of the Whigs.

That Perceval survived these vicissitudes and emerged in the spring of 1812 as one who, in the words of Lord Liverpool, had 'acquired an authority beyond any minister in my recollection except Mr Pitt' (Gray 1963: 426), was to a large degree fortuitous. On the critical issue of the Walcheren expedition, the government survived in 1810 as a result of the resignation of the commander, Lord Chatham, and the fact that the waverers and independents in the Commons preferred the government to the opposition. As for the Regency, Perceval was fortunate on two counts. Thus, although he introduced the same Regency Bill as Pitt had done in 1788 and which had then engendered the Prince's wrath because of its limitations on his power, the opposition bungled the campaign against it. Moreover, with the Regency established in February 1811 and the Prince provided with the opportunity to change his ministers in favour of the Whigs, he astonished the political world by declining it, largely as a result of his fear of what the King would do should he recover his sanity and find his old enemies in office. What was even more surprising, given the stark contrast in their characters, was that the Prince subsequently grew to admire his prime minister and thereby reattached the not inconsiderable royal interest to his government.

But his emergence as a powerful prime minister was also due to his abilities as a tactician and an administrator. In the case of his own party, for example, he skilfully reattached two powerful dissidents in Lords Castlereagh and Sidmouth and managed to engineer the resignation of a dangerous loose cannon in the shape of his Foreign Secretary, Lord Wellesley. Moreover, while remaining a reluctant Chancellor, his budgetary policy achieved the enviable objective of finding fresh resources for the war without raising new taxes. Thus, although he toyed on this occasion with such novelties as raiding Pitt's hallowed Sinking Fund and actually implemented one in a successful method of obtaining specie for the troops at the front, he fell back on the tried and trusted policies he had pursued under Portland: further retrenchment in government departments and loans raised on terms that limited long-term debt. The result was that Perceval's government was able to give crucial financial support to what proved to be Britain's most decisive contribution to the war effort – the Peninsular campaign.

With regard to domestic issues Perceval's conservatism did not weaken his position. In 1810 he confronted the leader of a resurgent London radicalism, Sir Francis Burdett, and had him committed to the Tower for, in effect, accusing the government of abusing the privileges of the Commons and of restricting the liberty of the press. Although this led to one of the most serious confrontations seen in London between government and radical forces, Perceval stood by Burdett's imprisonment and appeared to be vindicated in his opinion that metropolitan conservatism would predominate over radicalism when Burdett's release in June passed off without any significant demonstration in his favour.

He displayed a similar firmness on the Catholic question. Thus in response to the Whigs' idea of a royal veto on episcopal appointments to accompany political emancipation and the Irish Catholic leaders' decision to greet the Regency by holding a convention in Dublin to put pressure on parliament, he published a pamphlet against the veto and concession. Moreover, he was assisted by the Regent, who undermined the point of the convention by suddenly proclaiming his own allegiance to the Protestant constitution.

Perceval was therefore at the height of his power when he was assassinated in 1812 by a merchant with an uncontrollable grudge against the government. It was that unique event in the history of the office for which Perceval is chiefly remembered. His career, however, was not devoid of success and significance. On the probity of his private and public life and his skill as a debater – second only to Pitt and Fox in the view of one observer – contemporaries and historians are agreed. With regard to his policies, on the other hand, there has been a reassessment in his favour since the publication of Denis Gray's biography in 1963. Hitherto, Whig historiography followed the Whig politicians of the day and condemned him for his Evangelicalism, for his opposition to Catholic relief and parliamentary reform, and for his enthusiastic support for the war against both revolutionary and imperial France. In recent years, however, Perceval's views and policies have been placed firmly in a contemporary context. Thus Evangelicalism is now regarded as a broader and more popular *corpus* of ideas than hitherto. Moreover, opposition to Catholic relief and support for the constitutional status quo are no longer regarded as the beliefs of a privileged minority. Above all, the war against France is now seen as a continuous official and popular commitment that was a good deal stronger than the peace movement. Perceval may have been the first Evangelical prime minister but his policies were probably broadly in tune with the views of the majority of English people. It is here, however, that the case for Perceval must rest. Pittism – the body of ideas and practices associated with

Pitt – required a reappraisal if it was to survive in the context of the momentous changes taking place in Britain's economy and society. Perceval had neither the ambition nor the imagination to tackle this. His philosophy was rooted in the alarmism of the 1790s and his knowledge of the world reached little further than London and its suburbs.

References and further reading

Aspinall, A. (ed.) (1962–70) *The Later Correspondence of George III*, 5 vols, Cambridge: Cambridge University Press.

Gray, D. (1963) *Spencer Perceval: The Evangelical Prime Minister 1762–1812*, Manchester: Manchester University Press. (The definitive study and one of the best biographies of any prime minister.)

Thorne, R.G. (1986) 'Perceval, Hon. Spencer', in R.G. Thorne, *The House of Commons 1790–1820*, vol. 4, London: Secker & Warburg. (Adds information on Perceval's parliamentary career but is based on Gray's account.)

Walpole, S. (1874) *The Life of the Rt. Hon. Spencer Perceval*, 2 vols, London: Hurst & Blackett. (A conventional nineteenth-century 'Life' written by a conservative politician who happened to be Perceval's grandson. He printed some of Perceval's papers, although they are not always transcribed accurately.)

Peter Jupp

Robert Banks Jenkinson, Second Earl of Liverpool

Born 7 June 1770, only son of Charles Jenkinson, later first Earl of Liverpool, and Amelia Watts, although his father had a son and a daughter by subsequent marriage to Catherine Bisshopp. Educated at Charterhouse and Christ Church, Oxford. Married (1) 1795 Lady Theodosia Louisa, daughter of the fourth Earl of Bristol (died 1821); (2) 1822 Mary Chester, daughter of Revd. Charles Chester and granddaughter of the Earl of Dartmouth. MP for Rye 1790–1803. Acquired the courtesy title Lord Hawkesbury on his father's ennoblement in 1796 and transferred from the Commons to the Lords in November 1803 when created Baron Hawkesbury. Member of the Board of Control for India 1793–6; Master of the Mint 1799–1801; Foreign Secretary 1801–4 and 1809; Home Secretary 1804–6 and 1807–9; Secretary for War and the Colonies 1809–12; Prime Minister 1812–27. Became Earl of Liverpool on father's death 1808. Died 4 December 1828.

Liverpool was prime minister for almost fifteen years. When he reached the premiership he had already enjoyed experience of most of the high offices of state. No prime minister since Liverpool has held the office for so long and, of his predecessors, only Robert Walpole and the Pitt the Younger can claim longer tenure. Both of them are universally recognized as among the greatest of British prime ministers; Liverpool is not. It is interesting to speculate why. It is doubtless too facile to state that Disraeli's famous jibe, in his novel *Coningsby*, about the 'Arch Mediocrity' whose highest attribute was his 'meagre diligence', just stuck. Contemporaries were not lavish in their praise. He was widely regarded as a fussy, somewhat nervous and detail-driven man to whom grand projects and bold schemes were alien.

Liverpool's father, Charles Jenkinson, was from a well-established but unremarkable gentry family and enjoyed a considerable political career. He held a number of government posts from the 1760s, most notably Secretary at War and President of the Board of Trade. He was a loyal servant of George III and played an important role in developing those reliable 'King's Friends' who provided the King's ministers with majorities in the Commons and who attracted the virulent hostility of the Whig opposition. Like his son, Charles Jenkinson was solid and competent, much more effective as an administrator than as a political leader. It was characteristic of his caution that, when launching his son on a parliamentary career in 1790, he earmarked not one 'managed' borough for him but two, Appleby and Rye. The young Robert Jenkinson chose to sit for the latter (Gash 1984: 17).

While on a brief tour of Europe, just before entering parliament, Jenkinson visited Paris. Here, in July 1789, he became an eyewitness to the popular unrest which led to the fall of the Bastille and the early stages of the French Revolution. The experience marked him. As a representative of the landed classes, Liverpool remained convinced that extension of voting rights would lead to confusion and destabilization, if not outright revolution. Like most contemporaries from his background, the French Revolution confirmed his strong preference for government in the hands of 'property and intelligence' rather than 'mere numbers'.

Jenkinson made no immediate impression on the Commons. Like his father, he was considered a loyal supporter of Pitt. His first speech, supporting government's foreign policy towards Russia over the Ochakov affair, was not delivered until 27 March 1792. It drew little attention. We may discount one contemporary wit's account that Liverpool's face during parliamentary debates was 'as if he had been on the wrack three times and saw the wheel preparing for a fourth' (Petrie 1954: 15), but he never took easily to parliamentary performance. In this, as much else, he offered a sharp contrast to his exact contemporary and later rival George Canning. Nevertheless, he soon gained a reputation for meticulous preparation, knowledge of his subject and for being, in general, 'a safe pair of hands'.

Throughout the 1790s, he remained loyal to Pitt, an easy choice on both ideological and family grounds since his father – who was created first Earl of Liverpool in 1796 – was President of the Board of Trade for virtually all of the period. He was, however, much less convinced than Pitt of the need to offer concessions to Roman Catholics and this led to startling promotion in 1801. Pitt's resignation was forced on the Catholic issue by George III, but, along with his father and the Duke of Portland, Hawkesbury offered his support to the incoming prime minister, Henry Addington. He was rewarded with the foreign secretaryship. In this capacity, he began negotiations for peace with the French which were concluded as the Peace of Amiens in 1802. Though the peace was initially popular, and helped to consolidate support for Addington's ministry at a general election held the same year, it was always fragile. Certain that a resumption of war could not be long delayed, Hawkesbury convinced the cabinet that

Malta, which the British were to have quit under the terms of the peace treaty, should remain a British garrison.

When resumed, the war did not go well for the British and, as invasion scares mounted during 1803, Addington's government lost support in parliament. When he resigned in 1804, to be replaced by Pitt, Hawkesbury's own position came under scrutiny. Pitt seems to have shared the general view that he had been 'unimpressive in the post' (Ehrman 1996: 671) and moved him to the Home Office. His friendship with Canning, however, became strained. Canning seems to have been jealous that he, who had been at least as valuable to Pitt during the 1790s and who had shared his scruples over the Catholic issue in 1801, remained outside the cabinet while Hawkesbury, now also a peer, remained in it. Canning indulged in 'light and sometimes wounding patronage' of Hawkesbury and nurtured 'a suspicion ... of rivalry for Pitt's affection' (Ehrman 1996: 718). Hawkesbury used his growing personal skills during the last Pitt government first to ensure that his breach with Canning did not become permanent and, second, to repair the old disagreement between Pitt and Addington. Addington, as Viscount Sidmouth, returned to government for a few months in 1805 as Lord President of the Council.

After Pitt's death at the beginning of 1806, Hawkesbury became a key figure in the group which resolved to stay together as 'Pitt's friends' (Ehrman 1996: 840). They refused to join the 'Ministry of All the Talents' (1806–7), making it considerably 'under-talented'. This group, which also included Castlereagh, Canning and Perceval, was dismissed by the aristocratic Whig Lord Holland as mere 'clerks and secretaries' (Harvey 1978: 171). In reality, although personal rivalries frequently soured relations, they provided the basis of a politically anti-reformist and administratively competent group which valued land as the most important form of property, respected royal authority and which looked for support in parliament from independent country gentlemen. Though party politics are confused in this period, it offered what would soon be recognized as the party of 'Tory' appeal. It is no accident that Liverpool's ministry eventually became the first since the Hanoverian succession in 1714 to acknowledge that it was 'a Tory government'.

Hawkesbury and the Pitt group were not out of office for long. After the Talents ministry collapsed, Hawkesbury, who had conducted many of the preliminary negotiations with the King for Portland to head the new government, returned to the home secretaryship in 1807. A general election, in which support for the King's anti-Catholic stance was an important element, strengthened the parliamentary position of the new government and gave Hawkesbury an opportunity to confirm his opposition to Catholic emancipation. He served Portland as Home Secretary and his successor Spencer Perceval as Secretary for War and the Colonies. In this latter capacity he persuaded parliament in 1809 to abandon the British expedition to Walcheren. He oversaw administration of the forces in support of Wellington's campaigns in the Peninsula and, in 1811, reorganized military recruitment in order to maintain an effective fighting force there. Wellington, however, frequently complained that government efforts were insufficient or otherwise ineffective. It cannot be argued that Liverpool's tenure of the office was an unequivocal success, despite his grip on the administrative responsibilities it entailed.

Spencer Perceval's assassination in May 1812 presented the Prince Regent with a quandary. Perceval's government had a secure parliamentary majority and there was no need for a radical overhaul of personnel. George was, however, far from convinced that Liverpool had the requisite leadership qualities. Additionally, like his father, he always retained a personal preference for broadly based coalition governments. It took a month, and refusals by others, for George to confirm Liverpool as Perceval's successor. An important factor in the process was the Regent's increasing realization that most of the remaining Pittites saw Liverpool as their obvious leader.

Nevertheless, Liverpool's government was neither stable nor secure in its early years. Negotiations to bring Canning into the cabinet in the summer of 1812 had foundered on Castlereagh's unwillingness to accommodate his old enemy's preferences over office. For a time, opposition politicians entertained what they considered a realistic prospect of bringing the government down. In November 1812, for example, Grenville was encouraged that Marquess Wellesley was preparing 'a very good and very violent attack on Liverpool and Co.' while 'Report says, that Canning is grown more hostile to the Government, which is likely enough, since the opinion of their weakness is so much increased' (Buckingham 1856: i, 416–17).

Liverpool also lacked debating talent in the Commons at this time and Canning's belated return to office as President of the Board of Control in 1816 afforded important stiffening. The Duke of Wellington's acceptance of office as Master-General of the Ordnance in 1819 did not help Liverpool much during debates in the Lords but the presence of the victor of Waterloo on the government benches substantially increased its authority. By 1821, when the Grenvillites finally ended their always fragile alliance with the Whigs and their leader in the Commons, Charles Williams-Wynn, accepted minor office, Liverpool's parliamentary position was impregnable and Whig hopes of a return to office, which had flickered on frequent occasions since 1812, were finally extinguished. During 1822–7, indeed, with Canning, Peel and Huskisson all presenting government policy with skill and authority, Liverpool's ministry won all the important arguments in the lower House as well as the votes.

Liverpool's main economic objectives were reduction of debt and trade liberalization. In this, as most else, he was following the lead of Pitt during the peacetime phase of his mentor's government. In 1813, he responded to a petition from cotton-weavers for a continuation of the employment regulations to protect them against wage-reductions as large numbers of new operatives entered the industry. Such protection he deemed unacceptable:

> The wisest principle of proceeding, with respect to commerce and manufactures, was . . . *laissez faire* – This principle was particularly necessary to be

kept in respect of the machinery and mechanical inventions of the country, which . . . had raised this kingdom to its high rank among the commercial nations of the world.

(Daunton 1995: 277)

In a speech on 26 May 1820, he went beyond Pitt, becoming the first prime minister formally to accept the logic of Adam Smith's arguments when he committed his government to a systematic policy of tariff reductions with the eventual objective of free trade (Gash 1979: 106).

While Liverpool advocated trade liberalization in respect of workers and commerce, he was clear that the landed interest deserved to receive continued protection. In defence of the highly controversial Corn Law of 1815, which restricted the import of foreign corn until the domestic price had reached 80 shillings (£4) per quarter, he told the Lords that the main object was to render 'ourselves as independent as possible of foreign supply. . . . The important point to attain was a steady and moderate price' (Evans 1989: 101).

Government economic policy was frequently blown off course in the early years. Most importantly, in 1816, Liverpool failed to persuade parliament to retain the income tax in peacetime. This tax had been introduced by Pitt the Younger as a wartime expedient in 1799 and it had proved a substantial revenue-earner. Liverpool saw it as a valuable contribution to reducing the dangerously high level of debt which the war had produced. The Commons would have none of it, rejecting the proposal by almost forty votes. In the wake of this defeat, the government also gave up its attempt to restore the lucrative malt tax. During the next three years, it was forced to resort to a fiscally unhealthy combination of increased borrowing and a spread of indirect taxes which bore disproportionately upon the poor. Adverse economic circumstances and widespread unemployment also contributed to the severe disturbances which afflicted Liverpool's government. The discharge of almost 400,000 ex-servicemen compounded the problem as they glutted the labour market and squeezed wages downwards. The cost of poverty relief through the old poor laws increased dramatically. By 1818, its total cost stood at £8 million, almost four times as much as when the Younger Pitt came into office only thirty-five years earlier.

The government faced many forms of discontent. From 1811–16, Luddite machine-breaking activity broke out in the East Midlands, South Yorkshire and Lancashire in defence of the wage levels of skilled artisans whose livelihoods were threatened by new machinery. In 1816, widespread rural disturbances broke out in East Anglia, encompassing rick-burning and attacks on millers, a usual target because of their reputation for profiteering. Rural labourers, traditionally the most docile members of the workforce, demanded 'bread or blood'. The movement for parliamentary reform also revived. Liverpool's new Corn Law was a special target of criticism as legislation intended to benefit the few by bringing high bread prices to the many. Large demonstrations were held in many parts of the country, not infrequently spilling over into violence, as happened at Spa

Fields (London) in December 1816. In March 1817, a group of distressed Lancashire handloom weavers were forcibly prevented by the local yeomanry from marching south to present a petition to the Prince Regent – the 'March of the Blanketeers' – and an attempted rebellion in Derbyshire three months later led to the execution of three of its leaders. Government attempts to defend its position in sympathetic newspapers were ineffectual in the face of radical journalism of very high quality. Newspapers such as Cobbett's *Political Register*, T.J. Wooler's *Black Dwarf* and William Hone's *Reformists' Register* educated their readers to believe that the true cause of their misery was excessive taxation and corrupt 'misgovernment'.

Liverpool responded much as Pitt had done in the 1790s. He asserted that the main responsibility of government was public order and the defence of property. Accordingly, he set up a parliamentary Committee of Secrecy in 1817 to investigate clandestine activity, suspended the Habeas Corpus Amendment Act, thus allowing radical suspects to be held indefinitely without trial, and passed legislation which banned 'seditious' meetings. All of these measures were strongly supported in parliament, and popular with most property owners outside. His government made modest gains at the general election of 1818.

Liverpool's most serious challenge from the radicals came in 1819–20 when renewed distress brought further, and even more threatening, protest meetings in London, Birmingham, Leeds and Manchester, among other places. The entire cabinet survived an assassination attempt in the 'Cato Street Conspiracy'. His government's reputation outside parliament probably suffered most damage from an event over which it had no direct control – the 'Peterloo Massacre' on 16 August 1819. The decision to break up a pro-reform crowd, assembled to hear a speech by the famous Henry 'Orator' Hunt, was taken by a confused, frightened Manchester yeomanry. It resulted in eleven deaths and provided the radicals with those valuable innocent martyrs which the government had been anxious to deny them. Liverpool's private frustrations were apparent in a letter to George Canning. In it he argued that, while the action of the Manchester magistrates may have been 'justifiable', it was certainly not 'prudent'. Since Liverpool could hardly condemn the yeomanry, and thus risk alienating property owners nationwide, he agreed that 'there remained no alternative but to support' the magistrates, but the decision was taken reluctantly (Gash 1979: 96).

The government incurred further odium by passing the 'Six Acts' in the wake of Peterloo which, among other things, gave magistrates additional powers to prevent reform meetings and search for arms. The government had to endure further attacks in 1820–1, both from the radical press and from an ungrateful monarch, over the latter's ill-fated attempt to divorce his wife.

Liverpool's relationship with the Prince Regent – from 1820 George IV – was frequently strained. He had not been the Regent's first choice. When government majorities dipped alarmingly in the wake of defeats on taxation in 1816, Liverpool sent a memorandum to the Prince Regent in which he said – with only limited exaggeration – that 'the Government certainly hangs by a thread' (Gash 1984:

127). George came back from Brighton to bolster his government on this occasion but he did so reluctantly. Tensions had already flared over the Regent's lavish expenditure on Brighton Pavilion and his embarrassingly profligate lifestyle at a time when the government was trying hard to restrain public expenditure. The irascible and self-regarding monarch also felt that Liverpool served him badly in the matter of his divorce from Queen Caroline. Shortly before becoming King, George had informed his government that he would prefer matters to be settled by what he called private 'arrangement' rather than by adversarial proceedings. When the cabinet informed him that the concealment implied by such a manoeuvre was not practical or desirable, he sulked. In 1820, Liverpool and George had an angry meeting over the cabinet's recommendation that the Queen be merely deprived of her title. It was concerned that divorce proceedings would not only divide the nation but, very probably, fail to gain a majority in the Commons. Relations became so bad that ministers expected news of their imminent dismissal (Gash 1984: 151).

George also resented Liverpool's entirely practical advice in 1823 that parliament would never sanction the expenditure of £450,000 for the conversion of the Queen's house 'into a palace for the habitual town residence and court of the Sovereign' (Aspinall 1963–71: viii, 430–1). When, in 1823, Liverpool rejected the King's request to have Sir William Knighton, his confidential adviser and Keeper of the Privy Seal, made a Privy Councillor, his anger boiled over. He wrote a sulphurous, secret letter to the Duke of Wellington – a senior member, be it remembered, of Liverpool's government – on 17 July. In it he said that the response was

> Lord Liverpool's *usual* absurd, weak, and disgusting conduct. Depend upon it, that Lord Liverpool, if he lives till Doom's Day, will never be corrected, or made fit for the high office to which I rais'd Him, and I should consider it a mercy to be spar'd the irritations to which he continually subjects me.
>
> (Aspinall 1963–71: viii, 447)

By 1823, however, Liverpool knew well enough that he could afford to ignore royal bluster. For most of the 1820s, his government enjoyed success as trade revived and the crippling debts of the first seven or eight years were eliminated. Whereas Liverpool's government ran at an average deficit of £4.2 million in the years 1816–20, its income was exceeded by expenditure to the extent of around £3.3 million in the years 1821–6 (Evans 1996: 411–12). Since the more tranquil later years occurred after a fundamental reshaping of his government in 1822–3, some have seen this as a distinct second period of 'Liberal Toryism' (Brock 1967) contrasting with the repression of Liverpool's earlier years. The idea is superficially attractive. New cabinet appointees such as Robinson, Huskisson and Peel are strongly associated with fiscal and administrative reforms, whereas Canning at the Foreign Office appeared to follow policies more favourable to nationalism than Castlereagh.

Any idea that Liverpool underwent any kind of 'conversion' to reform in 1822 or 1823 should, however, be firmly resisted. He was advocating the return of cash-payments and a deflationary money policy as early as August 1818 (Hilton 1977: 39). His so-called 'new men' were actually long-serving junior ministers now moved up. Canning and Robinson had been in Liverpool's cabinet since 1816 and 1818 respectively, while both Peel and Huskisson had been converts to economic *laissez-faire* before they entered the cabinet. 'Old men' could be reformist too. Nicholas Vansittart, Liverpool's first Chancellor of the Exchequer who remained in government after the reshuffle, produced a final budget in 1822 which yielded nothing to his successor, Robinson, in fiscal rectitude and in the priority given to low taxation and a balanced budget. In truth, the circumstances changed, not Liverpool. And he trod warily anyway. His ministers

> had inherited a mass of legislative restrictions on freedom of economic activity ... and these their conservatism suggested ought to be repealed only gradually and in a measured, orderly fashion. There was to be no sudden flurry of pen strokes in honour of the memory of Adam Smith.
>
> (Gordon 1979: 3)

His career affords yet another parallel with Pitt's, though on this occasion in reverse. Pitt gave priority to financial innovation and administrative reform during the early years of his long ministry, before war required him both to borrow and to repress 'French principles' in the form of radical societies. Liverpool inherited both war and debt and necessarily shelved his Pittite, reformist principles until economic circumstances both contributed to the retreat of radicalism and made it practicable to budget for surplus.

In one sense, however, Liverpool contrasts with Pitt. The latter toyed with parliamentary reform at least until the mid-1780s; Liverpool always firmly resisted it. Liverpool's Tory party supported the unreformed political system as the best guarantor of the primacy of property. The radical press which berated him so persistently, and in some respects so unfairly, at least had him absolutely right on political reform. Under Liverpool, opposition to political reform and support for the Church of England became the two most obvious defining characteristics of Toryism.

Church of England Toryism was, however, deeply divided over how to deal with Roman Catholicism. The last years of Liverpool's government were wracked with internal dispute about the Catholic question. The cabinet was split between a 'Liberal' wing, comprising Canning, Huskisson and the Grenvillites, who favoured Catholic emancipation as the best means of quieting Ireland and making the recent union stick, and a 'Protestant' element, in which Peel, Bathurst and the Lord Chancellor, Eldon, were prominent. Liverpool, temperamentally a 'Protestant', shuffled somewhat uneasily between the factions using his conciliatory skills, his now huge experience and the authority of his office to stop the issue coming to the boil: 'Mediating constantly between the two sections of the administration, defending Canning's views to the illiberal group, Liverpool became a major bond of unity' (Mitchell 1967: 193). The cabinet agreed not to raise the Catholic issue at the delayed 1826 general election, where it became, nevertheless, the most contentious popular question on the hustings.

Had he survived, it would have been interesting to see whether Liverpool would have been any more successful in holding back the forces of internal division than his successors proved to be. From late 1826, however, he was under medical supervision for a recurrence of high blood pressure. On 17 February 1827, he succumbed to the massive stroke which ended his career. His resignation from office was delayed for several weeks, not least because both the Tories and an ungrateful monarch recognized the importance of his presence for political stability and he was not officially succeeded by George Canning until 10 April. He lingered long, and his last twenty-two months were lived out in pitifully diminished circumstances. Towards the end, he became unconscious for long periods before slipping quietly to his death in December 1828.

As prime minister, Liverpool cannot stand comparison with such nineteenth-century luminaries as Peel, Gladstone, Disraeli or even Salisbury. It is worth considering why, despite obvious shortcomings, he survived for so long. The first reason is the nature of politics before the Reform Act 1832. General elections were not usually frequent and hardly ever genuine tests of public opinion. Once administrations established themselves they were likely to stick, even if – like North's from 1770 to 1782 – they were not notably successful. Between 1714 and 1832, the general pattern was one of long-serving ministries, punctuated by briefer periods of instability, such as those in the 1760s and during 1782–4. Liverpool's government might thus be seen as the last of the long eighteenth-century ministries.

Liverpool was fortunate in that the first years of his government (1812–15) saw the decisive turn of fortune in the long wars against France. He was stabilized by military success. He also faced a Whig opposition lacking confidence, cohesion and unity (Mitchell 1967). Royal support, or at least acquiescence, also remained important. Monarchs could dismiss ministries with parliamentary majorities, and William IV was to do so as late as 1834. Liverpool could generally rely on George IV not to turn him out. Even when the King was at his most petulant and irascible, as during the Queen Caroline divorce fiasco, the self-indulgent but never quite self-destructive monarch calculated that the Tories were a better bet than the Whigs. Liverpool's ministries also contained some extremely experienced and able politicians. Canning, Goderich and Peel would succeed him to the highest office; Castlereagh and Huskisson, both of whose careers suffered premature and violent ends by suicide and railway accident respectively, might have done so. Liverpool's governments in the 1820s also gained credit for effective financial management and for dextrous administrative reform.

Liverpool's own political skills are also a relevant factor. He was no inspiring leader but his skills were appreciated in a less public forum. He developed into an effective chairman of cabinet. His leadership there helped to consolidate its collective constitutional identity. It became far less likely that the monarch could dismiss the prime minister and install a replacement from within the cabinet. His experience and understanding of human nature also made him an effective conciliator. This skill was important. Some of his colleagues, notably Canning, Huskisson and Peel, were prickly men. When personal vanity combined with genuine ideological difference, as over the Catholic question in the 1820s, a combustible mixture was created which took all of Liverpool's experience to contain. Perhaps the true measure of Liverpool's modest merits as prime minister is the sorry history of the Tory party after he left office. In less than four years, it had shattered into at least three feuding factions and the Whigs had come back into office where, with one brief break, they were to remain for eleven years.

Liverpool, then, was no 'arch mediocrity' and it is a pity that no full-length biography has been produced in recent years to provide a secure revaluation. It is highly unlikely, however, that any such reinterpretation would raise Liverpool's reputation to that of a Peel or a Gladstone. The likeliest judgement would be similar to that offered by John Ehrman, who noted that Liverpool deserved respect for an 'authority which he managed to sustain, with unassuming skill, over some fifteen challenging years' (Ehrman 1996: 842).

Liverpool was a consolidator, not an innovator. The Younger Pitt was his mentor and his long ministry was founded on Pittite principles: consolidation of the interests of property against the threat of revolution first; efficient administration second. Reaction to the French Revolution consolidated the majority of property owners firmly behind defence of order and existing institutions for at least a generation. During the massive disturbances of 1815–20, Liverpool could count on huge majorities in both Houses for his firm measures against the radicals. When the radical threat receded during the more prosperous years of the 1820s, his government continued measures of administrative reform whose intellectual origins can be discerned in the peacetime Pitt government of 1783–93. The Liverpool government thus survived partly because of his experience and his conciliatory abilities but mainly because its conservative objectives so closely matched those of fearful property owners heavily represented in the unreformed Commons. Liverpool's was the first ministry since the Hanoverian succession to acknowledge the label 'Tory'. It was also the last long-lived ministry of the old political world.

References and further reading

Aspinall, A. (1963–71) *Correspondence of George, Prince of Wales*, 8 vols, London: Cassell.

Brock, W.R. (1967) *Lord Liverpool and Liberal Toryism, 1820–27*, 2nd edn, London: Cass. (Originally published in 1941, the book deals with the last years of the ministry. Its title offers a view about the government's later period as a 'liberal' one, which few now support.)

Buckingham, Duke of (1856) *Memoirs of the Court of England during the Regency, 1811–20,* 2 vols, London: Hurst & Blackett.

Cookson, J.E. (1975) *Lord Liverpool's Administration, 1815–22*, Edinburgh: Scottish Academic Press. (A very sound study of the so-called 'repressive' phrase of Liverpool's government.)

Daunton, M. (1995) *Progress and Poverty: An Economic and Social History of Britain 1700–1850*, Oxford: Oxford University Press.

Ehrman, J. (1996) *The Younger Pitt: The Consuming Struggle*, London: Constable. (The third and final volume of a mighty biography. Invaluable for Liverpool's early career and his relationship with Pitt.)

Evans, E. (1989) *Britain before the Reform Act: Politics and Society 1815–1832*, London: Longman. (A survey of the period with documents on the policy of Liverpool's government.)

—— (1996) *The Forging of the Modern State: Early Industrial Britain, 1783–1870*, 2nd edn, London: Longman.

Gash, N. (1979) *Aristocracy and People: Britain 1815–1865*, London: Arnold. (A valuable textbook for British political history and written during the early stages of his preparation of material for his biography of Liverpool.)

—— (1984) *Lord Liverpool*, London: Weidenfeld & Nicolson. (The most modern, though relatively brief, biography which is an attempt at rehabilitation.)

Gordon, B. (1976) *Political Economy in Parliament 1819–1823*, London: Macmillan.

—— (1979) *Economic Doctrine and Tory Liberalism 1824–1830*, London: Macmillan.

Harvey, A. (1978) *Britain in the Early Nineteenth Century*, London: Batsford. (A useful survey of the high politics of the period.)

Hilton, B. (1977) *Corn, Cash, Commerce: The Economic Policies of the Tory Governments 1815–30*, Oxford: Oxford University Press. (A detailed study of Liverpool's economic policies.)

Mitchell, A. (1967) *The Whigs in Opposition, 1815–30*, Oxford: Clarendon Press. (Explains why the Whigs were unable to mount a more convincing challenge to the Liverpool government.)

Petrie, C. (1954) *Lord Liverpool and his Times*, London: Barrie. (Sees Liverpool's virtues and attempts a rehabilitation but its political analysis is now seriously outdated.)

White, R. (1968) *Waterloo to Peterloo*, Harmondsworth: Penguin.

Yonge, C. (1868) *The Life and Adminstration of Robert Banks, second Earl of Liverpool*, 3 vols, London. (Includes extensive material from Liverpool's private correspondence.)

Eric Evans

George Canning

Born 11 April 1770, son of George Canning and Mary Ann Costello. Educated at Eton and Christ Church, Oxford. Married 1800 Joan, daughter of General John Scott of Balcomie. MP for Newtown 1793–6 and 1806–12, Wendover 1796–1802, Tralee 1802–6, Liverpool 1812–27. Under-Secretary at the Foreign Office 1795–9; Commissioner of the Board of Control for India 1799–1800; Joint Paymaster-General 1800–1; Treasurer of the Navy 1804–6; Foreign Secretary 1807–9; Ambassador to Portugal 1814–16; President of the Board of Control for India

1816–20; Foreign Secretary 1822–7; Prime Minister April 1827. Died in office 8 August 1827.

Canning's story may be the saddest in the history of the premiership. He was a man of humble origins who rose to the top of the aristocratic *ancien régime*, but whose brilliant gifts never found full expression in its mediocre twilight. He consciously aimed for the highest office, yet was constantly thwarted by his own impetuous character and by his colleagues' suspicions. After a career of dramatic twists and turns, he reached his goal only within four months of his death. He might have been at his dextrous best in guiding the country through the crisis which was to issue only five years later in the first Reform Act, and managing it in a manner more profitable to the Tory party. But he did not get this chance to alter the course of British political history. His only permanent contributions were lesser ones.

He had connections in Scotland through his marriage, to a kinswoman of the Dundases, and late in life he became a friend of Sir Walter Scott. To him Canning confessed that he felt himself an Irishman. Though born in London, his blood was certainly Irish. On his father's side it was Anglo-Irish, out of a line settled at Garvagh in County Londonderry. His mother was presumably of native Irish stock. After her husband's early death she made a sort of living from the stage, or rather survived in irregular liaisons with actors. Her young son George would have faced a wandering, poverty-stricken existence had his more prosperous relatives not plucked him from it and sent him to Eton. But his Irishness survived his education. It would always come out in his mordant wit, his malicious glee in political intrigue, his constant gambles (a good many of them lost), his unquenchable eloquence, his general recklessness. A man who in 1809 could fight a duel with a colleague, Lord Castlereagh, who could be rumoured a lover of the Princess of Wales, who by turns gratuitously resigned office and showed almost indecent ambition to get it back, had without doubt much of the devil-may-care in him.

Even so, all this scarcely justifies reclaiming him for Ireland, as Conor Cruse O'Brien has tried to do with Edmund Burke, Canning's philosophical mentor. But he early showed a continuing benevolent interest in the land of his fathers. When he first talked about a job in government to his political patron, William Pitt the Younger, he asked for the Chief Secretaryship, and he sat for the Irish borough of Tralee in the parliament of 1802. Above all he retained, like Burke, a lifelong commitment to Catholic emancipation, which was to exert a decisive effect at the climax of his career. If, as was the custom of his age, he habitually referred to his country as England, not Britain or any variant thereof, he was in a sense, and with the special exception of Lord Bute, the least English of all the leaders of the *ancien régime*. And he, more than any other single man, undermined it.

To that extent, the English landed oligarchy was quite right to suspect him as a man from beyond the pale. He operated at his best on a broader stage than in the hallowed halls of Westminster. He was one of the few politicians in the unreformed system who could count himself a success in the country at large. He represented for the greater part of his career the brash and burgeoning city of Liverpool. By the standards of the time it was a popular constituency, and many of his speeches attested to his ability to persuade a popular audience. His first election, in 1812, which pitted him against Henry Brougham, the best Whig orator, was a classic of effective campaigning. Canning certainly felt a need to explain and gather public support for policy, especially in his studied appeals to the commercial interest. Foreigners, too, he could read like a book, and often outwit, whereas he never seemed to realize how much distrust he aroused on his own side.

Above all he knew what had to be done in Ireland, something that escaped most Englishmen. It was his commitment to Catholic emancipation that in 1827 led him in effect to dissolve the system of broad-bottom government on which ministries had been formed in the half century since Pitt first took power. The system, if sometimes honoured more in the breach than the observance, assumed that all public men of goodwill and ability would rally round the King's government, leaving opposition to the merely fractious and disaffected. This might have been a recipe for strife-torn and unstable administrations, and sometimes was. But it also produced two periods of notable stability, under Pitt himself till 1801, then in 1812–27 under Lord Liverpool. While broad-bottom government lasted, it formed an effective pragmatic argument against constitutional change. At least to its defenders, it combined continuity with flexibility, keeping the ruling class in power but allowing new talents and forces to be accommodated. The fresh liberal directions taken by Liverpool's government during the 1820s, in economic and foreign policy, seemed proof enough of the point.

Canning himself personified such policies. He had resigned in 1820 over the King's divorce. But Liverpool felt anxious to have him back, if only because he was too able to be safely left out, as the most thorough political professional of his day, the master equally of the parliamentary arts and of the administrative grind. He had served at the Foreign Office before, and so made the perfect candidate when it became vacant on Castlereagh's death in 1822. Canning had in fact already given up hope of further preferment at home and settled for the Governor-Generalship of India. But Liverpool manoeuvred him in, and during this second term as Foreign Secretary he did his finest work. The department itself he put into something like its modern shape, clearing away the aristocratic nonchalance of an earlier era and imposing centralized control from his own desk over an increasingly professional diplomatic service. He was also a major innovator in policy. He recognized the independence of the South American republics from Spain. He intervened in Portugal on the liberal side. He gave diplomatic support to the Greeks in their struggle for liberation. Nevertheless, he sustained Turkey against Russia.

If a general line could be found amid this opportunism, it was to clip the wings of the European autocracies. For this he was criticized by the high Tories around the Duke of Wellington, as a danger to the international settlement at the end of the Napoleonic Wars. But he was concerned not so much with ideology as with the need to hold the world open to a trading nation and its rising commercial class. In that sense, he represented on the inside of Tory government the interests of outsiders.

He was meanwhile treated as heir apparent. When a stroke forced Liverpool to retire early in 1827, George IV, after some hesitation, gave Canning the King's commission. His formation of a government all but foundered on Catholic emancipation. The divided outgoing cabinet had treated it as an 'open question', agreeing to disagree and not seeking to formulate a policy in advance of opinion in parliament or the country. In consequence, nothing was done. Now, with Canning resolved to grasp this nettle, the high Tories refused to join him. He had to construct his ministry from a mere rump of his former colleagues and from the more conservative Whigs. The coalition did not look durable, though he died before it could really be tested.

The episode was marked by deep personal animosity, but high principles were at stake. They concerned Britain's nature as a confessional state with a protestant constitution, depriving Catholics of civil rights. It may seem odd that, in the confusion of a period when party labels were fluid and often regarded with distaste, Canning laid claim to the title of Tory. Whatever he meant, it cannot have been simple defence of the *ancien régime*. Yet he often spoke of the glories of the constitution. He rejected sweeping rationalist reform, seeking in vain to perfect the state on abstract principles. A mixed system, between absolutism and democracy, was in his view good for Britain: it could continue to work and ought to be retained. But he also agreed with Burke and Pitt that it must be adapted to present dangers and changing circumstances, with a view to preserving its essential character. The task of the statesman was to weigh those criteria and act on them. In the conditions he faced, he decided it was time to lay the confessional state to rest. Irish Catholics in particular had a legitimate grievance, and there was no other means to bring them within the workings of the constitution. The improvement it would make to people's lives, thereby securing their loyalty, outweighed the abstract principle involved. In that sense, he did adhere to the standard doctrines of British conservatism.

Not least among the cruel ironies in Canning's life was that the necessary legislation had to be left to his high Tory successors. The main direct result of his own exertions was to unleash the rampant factionalism which the broad bottom had held in bounds. The argument for reform then became unassailable, and the old Tory party was rendered incapable of holding off rapid progress towards it.

References and further reading

Dixon, P. (1976) *Canning: Politician and Statesman*, London: Weidenfeld & Nicolson. (Straightforward political history with little speculation on motives, but stressing Canning's moderation and debt to Burke.)

Hinde, W. (1973) *George Canning*, London: Collins. (Detailed, careful and thoughtful study, with career linked to biography, and sound but not startling conclusions on the politics.)

Petrie, C. (1946) *George Canning*, 2nd edn, London: Eyre & Spottiswoode. (Does not quite manage the balancing act of stressing at the same time Canning's Irishness and his Toryism.)

Rolo, P.J.V. (1965) *George Canning*, London: Macmillan. (Three biographical studies on the man, the politician and the statesman, not always well distinguished, but a cogent presentation of Canning as a Tory.)

Stapleton, E. (ed.) (1909) *Some Official Correspondence of George Canning*, 2 vols, London: Longmans. (Key documents on his later politics.)

Temperley, H. (1925) *The Foreign Policy of Canning 1822–1827*, London: Frank Cass. (Classic diplomatic history based on exhaustive archival work, with the statesman, and the nation, as hero.)

Michael Fry

Frederick John Robinson, First Viscount Goderich, First Earl of Ripon

Born 10 October 1782, second son of Lord Grantham and Lady Mary Yorke. Educated at Harrow and St John's College, Cambridge. Married 1813 Lady Sarah Hobart, daughter of the Earl of Buckinghamshire. MP for Carlow 1806–7, Ripon 1807–27. Under-Secretary for War and Colonies 1809; Lord of the Admiralty 1810–12; Vice-President of the Board of Trade 1812–18; President of the Board of Trade 1818–23; Chancellor of the Exchequer 1823–7; Prime Minister 1827–8; Secretary of State for War and Colonies 1830–3; Lord Privy Seal 1833–4; President of the Board of Trade 1841–3; President of the Board of Control for India 1843–6. Ennobled as Viscount 1827, as Earl 1833. Died 28 January 1859.

'Who was Lord Ripon? What did he do?' asked his obituarist in *The Times*. The answer then, as now, was that he has to be counted among the most obscure and inglorious figures ever to have held the highest office. It was thrust on him in an attempt to avoid more difficult decisions amid the developing terminal crisis of the *ancien régime* before 1832. The crisis would defeat much abler men than him, and he was simply overwhelmed by it.

By background Frederick Robinson was a conventional member of the English ruling class. His first job came accordingly through patronage. In 1804 a kinsman on his mother's side, the Earl of Hardwicke, then Lord Lieutenant of Ireland, made him his private secretary. It was for an Irish borough that Robinson first entered parliament at the general election of 1806. When the fall of the 'Ministry of All the Talents' brought another election early the next year, Robinson translated to Ripon, the seat he would represent for the rest of his career in the Commons. He had, as a well-liked young man, made friends in Ireland, notably Lord Castlereagh, to whom he now attached himself. He did so despite their disagreement over Catholic emancipation, on which Robinson was a consistent liberal, perhaps because of this early Irish experience. In 1809 he became Under-Secretary at the War Office under Castlereagh, but almost immediately resigned with him, as a result of his notorious duel with George Canning. When Castlereagh went to Paris to conduct the negotiations ending the Napoleonic Wars, Robinson again joined his suite.

Meanwhile, Robinson's career gained some independent impetus, but in the sphere of economic policy. He was to serve at the Board of Trade for eleven years, as Vice-President until 1818, then as President with a seat in the cabinet until 1823. Here too his views tended to the liberal side. But as only a subordinate member of a government moving forward with pragmatic caution from the old mercantilism, he had to tread warily in applying the novel doctrines of political economy. In particular, he could not afford to annoy the agricultural interest, and as a consequence his policy often contained contradictions.

Robinson saw the advantage for a commercial nation in opening foreign markets. Even while the struggle against France went on, he disliked the protectionist measures thought necessary to counter the Continental system. Oddly, given modern conceptions, he ruled that trade should be allowed to continue between Britain and the United States during the War of 1812–14. Later he entered into a commercial convention with the Americans, which restored the access to Great Britain, though not to the rest of the British empire, that they had enjoyed before 1783.

Robinson's liberalization of colonial trading regulations was not unbounded. The centrepiece of inherited policy was the Corn Laws. Although Robinson later claimed to have always been against them in principle, in 1815 he piloted through one of the most notorious, setting a minimum internal selling price for corn which all but the landowners thought too high. It was a great enough grievance to the poor to provoke riots in London, during which a mob wrecked Robinson's house. Even when he reached more senior positions, however, he would not break ranks and reopen the question.

But a progressive reputation was what won him further promotion from the prime minister, Lord Liverpool, as he tried to extend the government's political base after overcoming the initial economic and social upheavals of peacetime. Robinson at length rose to be Chancellor of the Exchequer. By high Tories he was often pilloried, along with George Canning at the Foreign Office and William Huskisson at the Board of Trade, as one of a liberal fifth column in the cabinet. It may actually have helped him to be attacked at the same time by economic radicals such as Joseph Hume and David Ricardo. In the event, his performance at the Treasury gave few grounds for complaint to anyone not ideologically motivated.

It was his good fortune that decisive recovery from the terrible depression after 1815 now at last took place. He could nevertheless claim credit for sustaining it, yet meeting the need universally accepted at the time to start eliminating the huge national debt left over from the wars. He was one of the first to understand that an economic upturn would make the revenue buoyant, letting him cut taxes and still run a surplus on the public accounts. This was precisely the strategy he outlined in the speech presenting his first budget in 1823, when he abolished assessed taxes, such as the notorious one on windows. The policy worked, and in the two following budgets he was able to reduce tariffs. He spoke of the economy in terms so glowing that William Cobbett, not otherwise an admirer, gave him his sobriquet of Prosperity Robinson. This was the climax of his career. By the end of 1825, rising inflation brought on a banking crisis and a temporary halt to expansion.

Though the premiership still lay before Robinson, his political decline dated from this point. At first he wanted to leave politics himself after Liverpool had a stroke and resigned in the spring of 1827. But Canning, working desperately to succeed and casting about for support, urged Robinson to stay on. He concurred with the new prime minister on the main lines of policy to be pursued, Catholic emancipation and resistance to parliamentary reform, so saw no reason not to serve. He refused to retract when many of his former colleagues took the opposite view. He received a peerage and the leadership of the Lords, suddenly one of the hardest ministerial jobs because opposition to Canning was there at its fiercest. Viscount Goderich, as he now was, could not master it. In particular, he failed to stop the Duke of Wellington emasculating a Corn Bill, the government's one major measure before Canning died in August.

George IV summoned Goderich to form a new ministry the very next day. He hoped that none of the furiously competing factions would take exception to a compromise figure. Canning had led a coalition of moderate Tories and conservative Whigs, which though possibly a formula for success in time had begun shakily. Ideally, Goderich would have wanted to reconstitute a broad-bottom government, but found little room for manoeuvre. The King objected to his proposal to include two more Whigs, Lords Holland and Wellesley. The Whigs were anyway up in arms at the appointment as Chancellor of the Exchequer of John Herries, who commended himself to the monarch as a Tory returning to the fold, but annoyed them as an opponent of Catholic emancipation. Goderich managed to cobble together a cabinet in September, yet before the end of 1827 it was already falling apart. He gave up just after the new year. George IV, realizing that the strain of high office was just too much for him, at once accepted the resignation. The King kindly lent Goderich a hankie when he blubbed as he handed over his seals.

He was offered no post by his high Tory successors, Wellington and Peel. He actually joined Grey's Whig administration as Secretary of State for War in 1830, and supported the Reform Act 1832. He was little trusted in this unfamiliar company, however. Grey forced on him the inferior post of Lord Privy Seal in 1833, though giving him a step up in the peerage. But the next year saw the new Earl of Ripon in the ranks of the 'Derby dilly', the group of ex-Tories round Lord Stanley who deserted the Whigs and eventually returned to their former allegiance. Ripon occupied further posts in Peel's cabinets after 1841. Like the prime minister, he became convinced that the Corn Laws had now to be repealed. After the fresh Tory split on that question in 1846, he took little further part in public life.

Ripon's political armoury lacked two essentials, powers of leadership and persuasion. He was at least a hard-working and skilful administrator, effective enough so long as pragmatic measures could be carried through on their merits, but quite out of his depth when times were turbulent and reforms had to be fought for.

References and further reading
Jones, W. (1967) *Prosperity Robinson: The Life of Viscount Goderich 1782–1859*, London: Macmillan. (This is the only study, which says all that needs to be said.)

Michael Fry

Arthur Wellesley, First Duke of Wellington

Born 29 April 1769, sixth child of Garret Wellesley, Lord Mornington, and Anne Hill. Educated at Brown's Preparatory School, Chelsea, and Eton. Ensign in the 73rd Foot 1787; Lieutenant in the 76th Foot 1787; Aide-De-Camp to the Lord Lieutenant of Ireland 1787–93; Captain 1791; Major 1793; Lieutenant-Colonel 1793; Colonel 1796; Major-General 1802; Lieutenant-General 1808; General 1811; Field Marshal 1813; Commander-in-Chief of the Army 1827–8 and 1842–52. MP for Trim (Irish parliament) 1790–5, Rye 1806–7, Mitchell 1807, Newport 1807–9. Governor of Mysore 1799. Chief Secretary for Ireland 1807–9. Knight Commander of the Order of the Bath 1804. Viscount Wellington of Talavera 1809; Earl of Wellington 1812; Marquess of Wellington 1812; Duke 1814. Master-General of the Ordnance 1819–27; Prime Minister 1828–30 and 1834; Foreign Secretary 1834–5; Minister without Portfolio 1841–6. Died 14 September 1852.

Wellington, whose Anglo-Irish family left Dublin for London when he was a child, secured through his military adventures a heroic place in British memory. His international prestige as the conqueror of Napoleon had sealed an impressive hold on the early nineteenth-century national imagination and, after Waterloo, it was understandable that he should be sought out for use in government. Wellington is unique in modern British history as the only professional soldier to have become head of the government, although he did bring to the office a measure of administrative experience: in India from 1797 to 1805, with over 50,000 soldiers under his orders at one time, his responsibilities had extended to those of civil administrator and diplomat. Yet while he brought reputation and certain administrative competence, Wellington's undoubted military ability was not matched by comparable political skills. At heart a soldier rather than a politician, he displayed the soldier's frequent disinclination towards politics and was reluctant to join the cabinet. He became Master-General of the Ordnance – an appropriately military post – in Liverpool's cabinet, but his early ministerial career was comparatively inconspicuous. In the last three years of the Liverpool administration, however, he emerged as a leading figure in an anti-Canning, anti-Catholic faction within the government.

Wellington became prime minister following the brief administrations of Canning and Goderich because George IV preferred him to either Grey or Peel. Indeed, the notion of Wellington as prime minister had been aired for some time, especially after Liverpool's stroke. Canning's administration had demonstrated that he lacked the support of a substantial number of Liverpool's old cabinet, and had also seen Wellington clearly emerge as Canning's most formidable opponent. Agreeing to become prime minister in January 1828, he was reluctant to resign as Commander-in-Chief of the forces and did so only when pressed by his cabinet colleagues. But during his prime ministership Wellington's opponents at times suggested that the government had tendencies towards the militaristic. He was certainly a believer in firm government and a rigid upholder of law. But it should also be remembered that his accession to the prime ministership was not his first political experience. He had been a member of the Irish Commons in the 1790s and Chief Secretary for Ireland during the following decade, and exhibited both administrative ability and commitment. But he was used to being obeyed rather than contradicted, and the authoritarianism understandable in a military leader was perhaps less well suited to a prime minister. Keen to establish strong government and on the exhibition of firmness, Wellington was intolerant of criticism and opposition and this was unfortunate given the circumstances of his tenure of office. For Wellington's ministry represented a reunion of the old Liverpool party, with divisions running deep within it. In fact, the cabinet was markedly divided. He had decided to include four leading Canningites: William Huskisson (Secretary for War and the Colonies), Charles Grant (President of the Board of Trade), the Earl of Dudley (Foreign Secretary) and Palmerston (Secretary at War).

The mixture of views in the cabinet was extremely ominous: harmony over either foreign or domestic policies was difficult to achieve. Wellington found himself in a minority over important issues, including foreign policy and the Corn Bill, and was not on good terms with Palmerston or Grant. Huskisson resigned over the redistribution of disfranchised seats (and, contrary to his expectations, was not asked to reconsider) and his resignation was followed by that of the other cabinet Canningites in May 1828. Wellington's lack of delicacy in dealing with Huskisson and the other Canningites reflected his inability to cope with such divisions. He lacked tact. He was egotistical and comparatively inexperienced. Ill suited in some ways to the role of prime minister, he acted characteristically within it: as a strong, decisive man frequently behaving without appropriate delicacy or nuance.

There were other areas in which Wellington's lack of political finesse was all too apparent. In the economic realm his social conservatism blocked imaginative proposals such as the modified income tax included in the draft budget of 1830. He was a poor public speaker (Thomas Carlyle considering him to have been the worst he had heard), did not manage people particularly well and showed an indifference to public opinion on key questions. As might be expected, the eventual fall of Wellington's government arose not from a single cause. The combination of relevant factors included the Canningite break, the disaffection of the ultra-Tories over Catholic emancipation, the lack of economic movement, the lack of parliamentary reform, the personal ill-suitedness of Wellington to the demands of the position, and ultimately the crucial lack of support in parliament. One key feature concerned the issue of parliamentary reform. Reform had much support, but opposition to it was something of a settled principle with Wellington. Indeed, removal of (the perceivedly reactionary and increasingly unpopular) Wellington from office came to look like a necessary precondition for the achievement of reform. In November 1830 Wellington's declaration against parliamentary reform proved disastrous. He stated not only that he had no intention of introducing reform, but also that he would oppose any such scheme which might be proposed by others. He aimed in this declaration to put an end to the then prevalent discussion of the issue. Later that month he was, in fact, out of office, the ministers having lost control of the House.

Wellington's hostility to reform had been intensified by events in France and by the fear that reform might produce more radical change ('Beginning Reform is beginning Revolution'). His attitude towards political change and the threat of unrest was also key to understanding another crucial issue of Wellington's prime ministership: Catholic emancipation. The King had expected Wellington to share his desire to let this matter rest. But the Duke had for many years been in favour of concession on this issue, and Catholic emancipation was to prove the supreme achievement of his government. In May 1828 the Commons had carried Francis Burdett's resolution stressing the expediency of considering the laws concerning Catholics. When, in July 1828, the Irish nationalist leader Daniel O'Connell was elected MP for Clare (defeating the Protestant Vesey Fitzgerald, the Duke's choice as successor to Grant at the Board of Trade), Wellington recognized that an Irish solution was urgently needed. As things stood a Catholic could be elected to, but could not take up, a seat in the Commons. And, as things stood, O'Connell's movement for emancipation threatened serious unrest in Ireland should some solution not be found. Wellington fundamentally disliked popular movements (and they were especially dangerous perhaps in Ireland). Around the time of the 1819 'Peterloo Massacre' he had felt that a tough line was required to ensure that revolution was avoided. But despite his opposition to agitators, demagogues and the popular movements which followed them – and despite his essential lack of sympathy with the notion of Catholic relief itself – he had come to the decision that emancipation was necessary.

In the early 1790s, as a member of the Irish parliament, he had supported a government bill giving Catholics the franchise, but had opposed an amendment admitting them to parliament. Yet, contrary to the impression sometimes given, he had indeed been quite prepared to consider Catholic relief well before 1828. His change of attitude in the crisis situation of 1828 was between different kinds of settlement, not between rejection and acceptance of the idea of settlement itself. It is important to register his precise attitude: keen to satisfy Irish Catholics without imperilling the union, he held that it was essential to any settlement that the Catholic church be brought under state control. Tied to this was the belief, which he firmly held, that the political supremacy of Great Britain over Ireland should be maintained. Having decided that urgent movement was required, Wellington worked between August and December 1828 towards the goal of emancipation and struggled to persuade George IV to come round to this way of thinking. In April 1829 Catholic emancipation was achieved, Wellington having finally persuaded the King to give his consent to the Roman Catholic Relief Act.

This was a momentous development in the politics of Britain and Ireland. In 1823 O'Connell had founded the Catholic Association to pursue the attainment of full political rights for Catholics. Charisma, oratory and organizational skills combined to make him a formidable figure, and he effectively introduced mass politics into Ireland. He preferred to work within the existing system wherever possible, but it was his use of force – 'moral, agitatory, intimidatory force' (MacDonagh 1991: 269) – which had carried the day and brought change within a parliamentary context. Catholic emancipation enabled Catholics to enter parliament and also to hold most public offices. But its respective implications in Britain and Ireland were of a very different order. Emancipation marked an important step in Britain towards the secularizing of the state; in Ireland it established the foundations upon which sturdy sectarian politics would be built, and confessional allegiance was long to determine political attachment after this period. Emancipation also had consequences for Wellington. He alienated the ultra-Tories who felt that he had committed apostasy over the Catholic question. Indeed, he had to dismiss the Attorney-General, Charles Wetherell. Thus while the breach with the Canningites lost him support on one side, Catholic emancipation lost him significant sympathy on the other.

While Wellington is rightly seen as an opponent of parliamentary reform – and one whose opposition occasioned much hostility – his government had therefore introduced highly significant political change. Less important, but also worthy of notice, was the introduction of two reforms during the government's first months in office: repeal of the Test and Corporation Acts (by which all members of corporations had to receive communion in the Church of England) and the passing of a Corn Bill which moved in the direction of free trade. Other achievements included the establishment of a London police force. The Metropolitan Police Bill was introduced by Peel in the Commons and Wellington in the Lords in 1829. Wellington had long believed in the need for a London police force – as Chief Secretary for Ireland he had reorganized the Dublin police – and, while the measure was really Peel's, the prime minister's support was significant. The bill was passed in June, and by November Wellington was congratulating Peel for the 'entire success' of the new force: 'It is impossible to see any thing more respectable'.

In late 1834 Wellington refused the premiership, but acted as caretaker prime minister for Peel. This was followed by a brief period as Foreign Secretary in Peel's 1834–5 administration. During the years 1835–41 Wellington was leader of the opposition in the Lords, and on Peel's reassumption of the prime ministership in the latter year he entered the cabinet as Minister without Portfolio.

Wellington came to be represented by some Victorians as the embodiment of Englishness: the myth of Wellington celebrated his supposed common sense, his loyalty to the state, his hard work, courage, sense of duty and justice; 'his reputation as the man of honour, the embodiment of power without ambition, courage without ostentation, loyalty without greed, care without distasteful public shows of emotion, had become and remained the essence of how the English liked to see themselves' (Pears 1993: 233). It might also be suggested that Wellington appropriately embodied Linda Colley's three-layered foundation of Britishness: profits, Protestantism and the prosecution of war (Colley 1992). Wellington accumulated vast financial rewards from his career; in his dealings over Catholic relief he was profoundly concerned that securities be provided for the Irish Protestant church; and his military achievements were legendary and played their part in establishing British power in the nineteenth-century world.

There were ironies here, Catholic emancipation being the most conspicuous among them. For Wellington perceived himself as the defender of an old constitution which was sound; yet he actually played a part in its destruction. He was a Dublin-born believer in the rightness of British supremacy in Ireland, yet he passed the measure which signalled the beginning of Catholic nationalist dominance on the neighbouring island. And he was a politician who did not greatly like, or suit, politics. Wellington's personality remains striking and his myth resilient in popular memory. Frank, decisive, quick and hard-working; vain, stern, direct and downright; abrupt with people and extremely outspoken; well-organized and attentive to detail; keen to keep his emotions firmly under control, he enjoyed discussing his military campaigns more than his emotions and he exhibited impressive self-control and *sangfroid*. He remains something of a popular hero despite, rather than because of, his brief and increasingly unpopular period as prime minister.

References and further reading
Colley, L. (1992) *Britons: Forging the Nation 1707–1837*, London: Pimlico. (Wide-ranging and provocative study of the foundations of Britishness.)
Gash, N. (ed.) (1990) *Wellington: Studies in the Military and Political Career of the First Duke of Wellington*, Manchester: Manchester University Press. (Collection of scholarly essays dealing with a wide range of subjects relating to Wellington's career.)
Hibbert, C. (1997) *Wellington: A Personal History*, London: HarperCollins. (Popular biography which focuses on the private man as well as the public figure.)
Longford, E. (1971) *Wellington: The Years of the Sword*, London: Panther.
—— (1972) *Wellington: Pillar of State*, London: Panther. (Detailed, two-volume study.)
MacDonagh, O. (1991) *O'Connell: The Life of Daniel O'Connell 1775–1847*, London: Weidenfeld & Nicolson. (The most authoritative treatment of the Irish nationalist leader.)

Pears, I. (1993) 'The gentleman and the hero: Wellington and Napoleon in the nineteenth century', in R. Porter (ed.) *Myths of the English*, Cambridge: Polity. (Analysis of the Wellington myth in English memory.)

Wellington, second Duke of (ed.) (1867–80) *Despatches, Correspondence and Memoranda of Field Marshal Arthur Wellesley, Duke of Wellington, 1819–32*, 8 vols, London: John Murray.

Richard English

Charles Grey, Second Earl Grey of Howick

Born 13 March 1764, first surviving son of General Charles Grey, later Earl Grey, and Elizabeth Grey. Educated at Eton and Trinity College, Cambridge (no degree). Grand tour. Married 1794 Mary Elizabeth Ponsonby, daughter of Henry Ponsonby, later Baron Ponsonby of Imokilly. MP for Northumberland 1786–1807, Appleby 1807 and Tavistock 1807. First Lord of the Admiralty 1806; Foreign Secretary 1806–7; First Lord of the Treasury 1830–4. Styled Lord Howick on father's elevation to peerage 1806. Succeeded as second Earl Grey 14 November 1807. Knight of the Garter 1831. Died 17 July 1845.

Two things which strike the observer of Grey's long political career are that he was very rarely in office and that his later reputation has been closely, almost exclusively, associated with the passing of the first Reform Act in 1832. He was only once in office, in 1806–7, before he became prime minister in 1830 but led the Whig party in opposition for a quarter of a century. The reason for the imbalance between office-holding and opposition was the exclusion of the Whig party from government by the combined efforts of George III, George IV and the Pittite-cum-Tory party. Grey's most difficult task was holding his party together through the years of adversity after the death in 1806 of his predecessor as leader, Charles James Fox, making possible the great ministry which carried the Reform Act, the abolition of slavery, an important Factory Act and the notorious Poor Law Amendment Act.

Much criticism has been levelled at Grey's achievement as a parliamentary reformer. Contemporary radicals saw his leadership of the party as deleterious to the more sweeping reformist causes they favoured. It is certainly true that the aristocratic Grey was not a radical reformer, but his devotion from the 1790s to major revision of borough representation signalled a commitment which continued, if dormant, during the long period of opposition when he had to co-ordinate deeply conservative Whigs with radicals and Irish MPs. If he sometimes played down reform at this time it was mainly because it was unattainable and divisive of his party. The charge that Grey was not interested in secret ballot and manhood suffrage was true, but these measures did not command a national consensus of support until long afterwards. Orator Hunt's observation that the Reform Bill did little for working men does not diminish the magnitude of Grey's achievement in getting it through parliament at all, against the combined reluctance of the Tories, the monarchy and many of his own party. He was a genuine reformer for his class and his day.

Grey was born at Fallodon in Northumberland of a landed family and later made his home at the other family seat, Howick. He was returned in a by-election for that county in 1786, with the backing of the powerful Percy family, and was generally assumed to be a supporter of the Younger Pitt's government. But Grey's inclination in fact centred on the Foxite Whigs, opponents of the royal influence to which Pitt had apparently succumbed since his appointment in 1783. Grey fell under the spell of the opposition leader Charles Fox, and remained a Foxite Whig by conviction for the rest of his career.

Support for Fox in his great duel with Pitt involved criticism of active monarchy, dislike of tyrannies abroad and the desire for constitutional liberties and personal freedom under the law, avowed principles of the Whig party since the Revolution of 1688. Grey joined in the impeachment of Warren Hastings for alleged misgovernment in India, assisting its chief instigator Edmund Burke from 1788 as a manager of the prosecution on behalf of the Commons. But Grey and Fox soon lost faith in this cause, and Grey then made parliamentary reform his main interest despite the reluctance of a leader who was constrained by the responsibility of holding together a heterogeneous party, much as Grey himself was to be later.

Discord was opened within the opposition Whig ranks by the Regency Crisis of 1788–99 when George III had the longest bout of mental and physical illness he had yet suffered. Burke came to differ from his colleagues in stubbornly pressing the claims of the Prince of Wales to unrestricted Regency as of right. Fox and Grey withdrew from the 'claim of right' which they had first supported, seeing it as deleterious to the party in the realm of public opinion. The quarrel with Burke sowed the seeds of the later party schism over Fox's approval of the French Revolution.

Grey went ahead of Fox by bringing reform proposals in the Commons. In 1792 he formed, along with Richard Brinsley Sheridan and other like-minded Whigs, the Association of the Friends of the People, a body devoted to obtaining the support of the nation for moderate reform. The Friends' subsidiary purpose was to counter Burke, who was gaining ground with many of the Whig party in his denunciations of Revolution abroad and reform at home. Grey's motion for reform a year later obliged Fox to declare himself, despite verbal equivocations, by voting with the reformers. But Grey's forty-one votes indicated that his views appealed to only a small minority of the party amid war fever and fear of revolution in Britain.

The final desertion of the opposition by those Whigs who disliked Fox's stand over French affairs was joined by the Duke of Portland, the party's leader in the Lords, as well as by Burke. The juncture of these more conservative Whigs with Pitt's governmental party proved to be the basis of a renewed Tory party by the end of George III's reign. From 1794 political life was divided on more clearly ideological lines than at any time since the American war in the 1770s. Fox and

Grey led a denuded party of about sixty members in the Commons who were now virtually all committed to reforms of one kind or another, though not necessarily to parliamentary reform. Grey's sense that not all his colleagues were with him on this issue may have contributed to his several refusals, at about this time, of Fox's suggestions that he should take over the Commons leadership of the opposition Whig party.

Pitt's revised ministry, with Portland as Home Secretary, opposed all reforms. Even the abolition of the slave trade, called for by Pitt's friend William Wilberforce, was abandoned in the emergency of war with France. Both Pittites and Portlandites chastised reformers as 'Jacobins', suppressing organizations like the London Corresponding Society which called for reforms such as mass suffrage. Grey wrote of his unsuccessful attempts to arouse national opposition to the repressive Seditious Meetings and Treasonable Practices Bills: 'We have determined here to use every effort to oppose them, and to obtain the opinion of the People upon this last question respecting their remaining rights' (11 November 1795: Grey MSS, Box 7, File 10). His motion for opening a peace negotiation with France obtained only fifty votes, and he again failed in 1797 in attempting to obtain a censure of government mismanagement of the naval mutiny at Spithead. His new and detailed proposals in the same year for parliamentary reform envisaged new single-member constituencies, more seats for the counties and major cities and a uniform franchise based on tax-paying householders in the boroughs. The scheme went well beyond the later Act of 1832 in some respects and achieved the support, even in inauspicious times, of ninety-one members of parliament.

In 1801 Pitt, followed by most of the abler members of his ministry, resigned after the King refused to agree to the cabinet's scheme for Catholic emancipation, which was designed to accompany the new union of British and Irish parliaments. George III's choice of Addington as prime minister led to the latter's offer of a share of office for the opposition on the common ground of desire for peace. But Grey, in Fox's absence, demanded leading measures of reform by any ministry in which his party had a share. Even the repeal of the Treasonable Practices and Seditious Meetings Acts, offered by the minister as an inducement, was not enough to tempt Grey unless accompanied by more positive reforms. After the collapse in 1803 of the Peace of Amiens obtained by Addington two dozen important recruits came to the opposition Whigs, led by Pitt's associate and former Foreign Secretary Lord Grenville who deplored his leader's failure to oppose Addington's ministry. This accession brought the effective strength of opposition party in the Commons up to about 150 including sympathetic new Irish members who had joined the parliament at Westminster after the union.

Grey voiced considerable unease about alliance with these former Pittites, a development which was greatly to hamper him in later years. But Fox's policy of taking help where he could get it was useful at the time, and Grenville gave a new and authoritative lead to the opposition in the Lords. But the Grenvilles also brought a conservative caution to the Whigs' counsels and influenced them against parliamentary reform for over a decade, slewing the thrust of reformist endeavour towards Grenville's preoccupation with Catholic emancipation.

The Foxites' formation of the 'Ministry of All the Talents' in 1806 added in the longer term to Grey's distrust of alliances of expedience. Grenville's concern for emancipation, together with the inclusion of Addington for the sake of the numbers he brought, led to disaster within a year on the lines of Fox's attempt at coalition with Lord North in 1783. But the ministry gave Grey his first and only opportunity of office before he became prime minister nearly a quarter of a century later. As First Lord of the Admiralty he raised the pay of the navy, a long-overdue measure, and bore responsibility for national defence at the height of war with Napoleon. With Grenville as prime minister, by Fox's acquiescence, the ministry carried through only one major reform, the abolition of the slave trade for which William Wilberforce had so long campaigned in vain. The death of Fox a few months after that of Pitt brought Grey a few months of different valuable experience as Foreign Secretary and a hard but wasted negotiation for peace with Bonaparte. In the course of this he lost his pacific inclinations and gave the Commons his opinion that until the government of France changed its principles and character there was no hope of peace.

Grey's most valuable experience in this ministry came in court politics. Grenville's concern for emancipation was unpopular with King and country alike. The proposal was in fact a very restricted one, but George III's refusal to accept it followed closely the pattern of his reaction to Pitt's far more sweeping proposals six years earlier: a demand that the matter should never be raised again in his lifetime. The ministry resigned, following the precedent laid down by Pitt in 1801. Grey was left with a strong and lasting dislike of royal interference in politics. On Fox's death Grey had succeeded to the leadership of the party by acclaim. But the Whigs were unpopular at the polls when a new 'Pittite' ministry under Portland called a snap election. Grey himself had to retreat from his prestigious county seat for Northumberland and get himself returned for a closed borough. In the ensuing opposition he began to fall out with Fox's friend the Prince of Wales, who was no friend to Catholic emancipation. The Prince nurtured a grievance against all those who did not support his domestic campaign against his wife, Princess Caroline, and Grey scarcely bothered to conciliate him in this matter.

Grey's elevation to the Lords in succession to his father took place in 1807 and brought new problems. Though still overall party leader the new Lord Grey was much hampered by the increasing demands of radicals, like his brother-in-law Samuel Whitbread and Sir Francis Burdett, in the lower House. This increasingly vociferous band of men refused to let wartime exigencies interfere with their campaign for widespread reforms. Grey accordingly sponsored the appointment as party leader in the Commons of his wife's relation George Ponsonby, an Irish Whig who had made his reputation in the former Dublin parliament. This proved to be a costly mistake; Ponsonby was acceptable to the Whigs but proved to be quite unable to cultivate any unity with the increasingly effective radicals.

The temporary disgrace of the ministers Canning and Castlereagh, for duelling, led to a new ministerial approach to Grey for limited entry to the government. He rejected the overture firmly, despite Grenville's initial willingness to negotiate: Grey's view was that 'nothing but a complete change of system can afford the country a chance of safety' (Hill 1985: 192). His insistence on the Whigs' taking office only as a party, not piecemeal, thereafter became inveterate. One of his greatest problems in the years of the party's association with Grenville was to restrain the latter's zeal for coalition and keep the Whigs intact to take office as a whole party when an opportunity arose.

That opportunity was long in coming. The short-lived ministries of Portland and Perceval were followed by Liverpool's from 1812. The Prince's celebrated abandonment of the opposition Whigs, as soon as he acquired the title of Prince Regent in 1811 through the King's incapacity, served to prolong their exclusion from office for the rest of the Regent's life. To his distaste for Catholic emancipation was added a dislike, again all too reminiscent of his father, of being dictated to by the Whigs.

When the Napoleonic War came to an end Grey was not able at first to take full political advantage of the widespread distress and disturbances caused by depression and wheat prices forced up by new Corn Laws. Suspension of the Habeas Corpus Act actually found support from some of the opposition, notably Grenville and William Lamb, later Lord Melbourne. But their drift away from the Whigs relieved Grey of the need to restrain his party from outright opposition on all fronts. His advice to his followers was 'to debate and *to divide* constantly; without any regard to numbers' (A. Mitchell 1967: 112). This new fighting spirit reflected also, after Waterloo, the end of wartime constraints on attacking the government.

Opposition numbers were slightly reduced after the Grenvillite defections, but better results were achieved when party leadership in the Commons passed, after Ponsonby's death in 1817, to George Tierney and later to several younger spokesmen acting in combination, including Lord John Russell, Lord Althorp and Henry Brougham. A boost was given to the opposition when four of the royal dukes, George III's sons, chose a time of national stringency to ask for public funds for marriage or other reputedly more dissolute purposes. Even government backbenchers recoiled, helping the Whigs to reject some of the more excessive claims and gain some popular support.

The scandal of the 'Peterloo Massacre' in 1819, with its overtones of militarism and repression, brought Grey and the aristocratic Whigs into the front line with radicals in defence of traditional British libertarian and constitutional principles. In the debates on the ministry's subsequent repressive 'Six Acts', Grey was at his best, following a carefully chosen line between the two extremes of his radical and conservative followers by opposing measures against freedom of the press and public meetings but supporting those against quasi-military drilling and armed insurrection. The Whigs' stand was a moderate and acceptable one, and the accession of the Regent as George IV in 1820 brought them further popularity for their opposition to an Act of Pains and Penalties against Queen Caroline, introduced at the new monarch's instigation. Grey spoke eloquently and carried no fewer than 95 votes against the ministry's 123 in the heavily ministerial House of Lords. It was a triumph of the first order when the Bill was dropped, and Grey's prestige was greatly enhanced. The Whigs' capture of widespread public support on this issue was a step forward in their consolidation in the country, though they still had to capture the restricted electorate.

When the new King blamed the ministry for the consequences of his own malicious prosecution of Caroline, approaching Grey to form a ministry, he was met by a cool refusal unless some reform and the partial repeal of the 1819 legislation were conceded. George again turned to Liverpool, and in the election of 1820 the Whigs could not make substantial headway, despite their recent successes. The problem they still had to surmount was Tory control in most of the small closed boroughs. The failure convinced Grey and other leading men that if the Whigs could not win an election in the favourable conditions which then prevailed they would never win without prior reform of the borough seats. Grey himself made up his mind, in private at least, as to what measure of parliamentary reform was needed. The increasingly strong statements he made in letters to Fox's nephew Lord Holland show him deciding that nibbling at the edges of the problem would not do, and that at least a hundred seats must be removed from the smaller boroughs (Trevelyan 1920: App. A). The Whigs' most zealous recent recruit, Lord John Russell, made one attempt on these lines in 1822, but his Bill was easily rejected.

Liverpool's ministry in its last phase brought in a series of legal and economic reforms, not least in an attempt to 'dish the Whigs'. This strategy had some success, and Grey often retired to the country in despair of making any progress. Much of the younger Whigs' thinking now centred upon supporting the 'Liberal Tory' wing of the ministry under Canning, in an effort to split the Tory party. Grey, however, was not very hopeful of such an outcome and did not see his colleagues' tactics as propitious for parliamentary reform, which Canning currently opposed. From 1826 Grey permitted Lord Lansdowne, the chief exponent of supporting the Canningites, to take over leadership of the Whig party. When Liverpool resigned in 1727 through ill-health and was succeeded in swift succession by Canning and, after his death, by the Canningite Lord Goderich, both ministers allowed the Lansdowne Whigs only minor offices in return for their support against ultra- and anti-Catholic Tories, and many other Whigs followed Grey in holding themselves aloof.

The King soon tired of the Canningite experiment, turning instead to Wellington and Peel to lead the Tories. The end of Lansdowne's support for the moderate Tories permitted a reconciliation in the Whig party and the return of Grey to the party leadership. His policy was shown to be the right one in the long run, for when Canning's former followers joined the Whigs it was as the subsidiary element and not as a nominally superior one to be shored up. Though Grey nursed some grievance against Lansdowne for supporting the two short Canningite ministries, the wounds were soon healed and Grey became a more active leader as a result of his temporary withdrawal.

The first fruit of Whig reunity was the repeal of the Test and Corporation Acts in a measure brought by Russell from the opposition benches and supported by the Canningites. With this achieved, Catholic emancipation too could no longer be held back. Wellington saw no alternative to conceding it, and in doing so mortally offended the ultra-Tories with fatal consequencies to the ministry. George IV died in 1830 and was succeeded by his more amenable brother, the Duke of Clarence, as William IV. Grey became more optimistic than for many years, especially when the popular Althorp at last succumbed to party pressure and accepted the duties of sole Whig leader in the Commons.

Although the general election which followed George IV's death was not fought by the Whig party specifically on parliamentary reform this issue dominated many constituencies. A well-publicized campaign by Brougham in Yorkshire attracted much attention and served to focus the efforts of other Whigs on borough reform now that the religious reforms had been obtained. The fall of Wellington's ministry came swiftly, with the ultra-Tories voting against the prime minister. The King sent for Grey to form the first Whig ministry for twenty-three years. In the new cabinet the Whigs held eight seats and Canning's former followers four. Four future prime ministers were to serve in this cabinet: Melbourne, Russell, Derby and Palmerston.

The country was clamouring for reform. Grey appointed a committee including his Radical nephew Lord Durham and Lord John Russell to devise a bill. The prime minister's brief was definite: they were to produce a measure large enough to satisfy public opinion and 'to afford sure ground of resistance to further innovation' (Cannon 1973: 204). The committee's response, slightly amended by the cabinet, was sweeping rather than extremist. Sixty-one boroughs were to lose both seats and a further forty-seven only one. Most of the redistributed seats were to go to the large-franchise English counties, to large unrepresented cities and to London. The borough franchise would at last be made uniform, based on households rated at £10 a year. But the Radicals' desire for secret ballot and manhood suffrage, or at least complete household qualification, was rejected.

The fight to get the resultant Reform Bill passed in both Houses was herculean, and Grey must be given most of the credit for its success. He is found constantly stressing the national mood, conciliating the doubters of his own party, obtaining an unequivocal Whig majority in a new appeal to the polls and threatening the Lords with massive new creations of Whig peers to pass the bill. Grey was aided by a sincere conviction that there was no alternative to reform if civil strife were to be avoided. His social position, personal integrity and innate conservatism carried conviction with waverers in both Houses. After defeat in the Lords, Grey and his colleagues offered their resignation to the King without hesitation, making it clear that the choice was between yet another general election, certain in the reformist mood of the nation to be another Whig landslide, and creation of sufficient new peers to pass the bill. Receiving the required promise from William, the ministry was able to carry the measure in 1832 without resort to further creations; the threat to debase the currency of the Lords alarmed peers more than did the proposed reform of the lower House.

Grey's refusal to sponsor parliamentary reform openly in the years before 1830, until public opinion was unequivocal and most of the Whig party were in agreement, was a major contribution to his final achievement. The Reform Act as finally passed was far more sweeping than any which could have been obtained earlier and probably represents the maximum that could have been achieved in 1832. To obtain its passage Grey had to make concessions to his more cautious Whig followers, particularly in offering a small reduction in the number of seats transferred, and in accepting the Tory Lord Chandos's amendment which enfranchised tenants in the county constituencies to the considerable advantage of landowners.

After the Reform Act Grey showed many signs of his exertions, but his ministry did more before he finally withdrew from office. The abolition of slavery, finishing the Whigs' earlier work of illegalizing the slave trade, places them on a par with William Wilberforce, whose lifelong campaign for these measures was ignored by his own party. Ashley's Factory Act was notable for, among other provisions, establishing an inspectorate to oversee its subsequent enforcement. The new Poor Law, however, was eventually to be seen as a disastrous mistake; Grey and his colleagues did not foresee the worst effects of the abolition of out-relief for the poor, any more than those who had passed the South Sea Act a century earlier foresaw the horrors of the slave trade. Grey fell somewhat ignominiously in 1834 after quarrels in the cabinet over a proposed appropriation of Irish Church revenues for lay uses, a measure close to Russell's heart.

Grey at his best, in the more positive aspects of opposition and during the Reform Bill debates, was unsurpassed as an effective parliamentarian, despite the lamented handicap of being in the Lords for most of his career. He left office angered by his colleagues' disunity over the Irish Question, but was himself too tired or lethargic to deal successfully with this. He later came increasingly to despise what he saw as the drifting ministry of his successor, Lord Melbourne. By the 1840s Grey became an admirer of the Conservative prime minister Peel, a pragmatic politician not unlike himself who saw the need to adjust to the times. Grey himself died in 1845. His achievements were a temporary party unity, the most anyone could have obtained, and the climactic reforms of 1830–4.

References and further reading
Brock, M. (1973) *The Great Reform Act*, London: Hutchinson.
Cannon, J. (1973) *Parliamentary Reform 1640–1832*, Cambridge: Cambridge University Press. (Sets reform in the longer context and is particularly helpful for its critique of D.C. Moore's controversial views.)
Derry, J. (1992) *Charles, Earl Grey: Aristocratic Reformer*, Oxford: Blackwell. (A very readable biography but thin on Grey's many years as leader in opposition.)
Grey MSS, Department of Palaeography and Diplomatic History, University of Durham.

Hill, B. (1985) *British Parliamentary Parties 1742–1832*, London: Unwin Hyman. (A documented treatment of parties during most of Grey's career.)

Mitchell, A. (1967) *The Whigs in Opposition 1815–1830*, Oxford: Clarendon Press. (A seminal study of early nineteenth-century politics by one who subsequently made politics his profession.)

Mitchell, L.G. (1971) *Charles James Fox and the Disintegration of the Whig Party*, Oxford: Oxford University Press. (A useful account, more historical than biographical in its approach.)

O'Gorman, F. (1967) *The Whig Party and the French Revolution*, London: Macmillan. (Good on party organization in the 1780s, though underestimating the importance of party developments in the late seventeenth and early eighteenth centuries.)

Roberts, M. (1939) *The Whig Party 1807–1812*, London: Macmillan (repr. Cass 1965). (An older monograph, still very useful as a supplement to other more recent works on the Whigs by A. Mitchell (1967), L.G. Mitchell (1971) and F. O'Gorman (1967).)

Sack, J. (1993) *From Jacobite to Conservative: Reaction and Orthodoxy in Britain, c. 1760–1832*, Cambridge: Cambridge University Press. (Much detail though confused by author's use of descriptions like right-wing, admittedly known little, if at all, at the time, rather than the contemporary if occasionally ambiguous term Tory.)

Smith, E. (1990) *Lord Grey 1764–1845*, Oxford: Clarendon Press. (A modern political biography in loving detail.)

Trevelyan, G.M. (1920) *Lord Grey of the Reform Bill*, London: Longmans. (A classic biography in the Whig tradition, still worth reading for its author's shrewd insights and family knowledge of the early nineteenth century.)

Brian Hill

William Lamb, Second Viscount Melbourne

Born 15 March 1779, second son of Peniston Lamb and Elizabeth Milbanke. Educated at Eton and Trinity College, Cambridge. Married 1805 Lady Caroline Ponsonby, daughter of the third Earl of Bessborough (separated 1825). MP for Leominster 1806–7, Portarlington 1807–12, Northampton 1816–19, Hertfordshire 1819–26, Newport (Isle of Wight) 1827, Bletchingley 1827–9. Succeeded 1829 to the Viscountcy of Melbourne, with seat in the Lords, on the death of his father. Chief Secretary for Ireland 1827–8; Home Secretary 1830–40; Prime Minister 1834 and 1835–41. Died 24 November 1848.

Melbourne was an intelligent and colourful figure with a wide range of interests, including literature, theology and art. He often gave the impression of less than total dedication to the serious business of politics. While, unlike his near-contemporary Peel, he was not the kind of administrative professional who mastered every brief and closed every loophole, he was a more serious politician than he liked to pretend and was always highly astute. Succeeding to the prime ministership after the resignation of Grey, he was anxious to ensure that the Whigs retained office after their long period in the wilderness before 1830. He is perhaps best remembered for his fraught and unhappy marriage to the neurotic, Byron-obsessed Lady Caroline Lamb and his later tutelage of Queen Victoria in the arts of constitutional monarchy when she came to the throne at the age of 18 in 1837. His reputation as prime minister has long suffered by comparison with that of Peel, whom he both preceded and succeeded in office, but his ministry passed several substantial reforms which helped to stabilize aristocratic government in an increasingly industrial age.

Lamb entered the Commons as a Whig and spent many years on the back-benches, despite overtures from party leaders who recognized his talents. He was never a strong supporter of the leading Whig causes of the day, parliamentary reform and Catholic emancipation. He asserted in 1815 that he supported what he called

> The Whig principles of the [Glorious] revolution. . . . the irresponsibility of the crown, the consequent responsibility of ministers, and the preservation of the dignity of parliament as constituted by law and custom. With the heap of modern additions, interpolations, facts and fictions, I have nothing to do.
>
> (Ziegler 1982: 70)

He frequently supported the Liverpool government in its attacks on extra-parliamentary radicalism. By the early 1820s, it was difficult to determine whether he should more properly be described as a 'conservative Whig' or a 'liberal Tory'. His admiration for George Canning increasingly inclined him in the latter direction and he was happy to accept his first ministerial post, as Chief Secretary for Ireland, when Canning formed his brief coalition government in 1827. His tenure of office was uneventful, although he forged a relationship of trust with the Catholic leader, Daniel O'Connell, which was to be of value during the 1830s.

After Canning's death Lamb was soon associated with the 'liberal Tory' group led by William Huskisson, and it was no surprise that, along with Huskisson and Palmerston, he left Wellington's government in May 1828. Few of the 'Huskissonites' would ever return to the Tory fold. Out of office for almost three years Melbourne (as he had now become) returned as Home Secretary in Grey's Whig government formed in November 1830. He thereby committed himself to support for parliamentary reform. This was ironic, since Melbourne was one of the least enthusiastic reformers in the government. As Home Secretary he was responsible for public order and therefore susceptible to the practical argument that reform was the securest guarantor against extensive disorder, even revolution. But his heart was never in it. As he told the Lords in October 1831:

> If ever there was an individual . . . more anxious than another that the affairs of the country might have gone on without our being forced to incur the hazard and responsibility which must result from so great and fundamental a change in the House of Commons, I am that person.
>
> (Ziegler 1982: 142)

He had nothing to do with drafting the Reform Bill and he used both his influence and his charm to stop the factions within government from tearing themselves apart on an issue the practical details of which hardly concerned him.

As Home Secretary, Melbourne was little inclined to take the side of the underdog. He came to office soon after the 'Swing Riots' of agricultural labourers had broken out. He immediately advertised a reward of £500 to be paid to anyone who brought rioters to justice (Marshall 1975: 83). He was similarly firm over trade unionism. He confided to Lord Lyttleton in March 1834 his fear that 'they [the unions] may inflict serious evil upon the commerce and prosperity of the country'. He was clear that they must on all occasions obey the law, and supported the prosecution of the Tolpuddle Martyrs on this ground: 'I trust that the convictions which have lately taken place in Dorsetshire will have some effect in proving to them the illegality of their combinations' (Ziegler 1982: 159–60).

Melbourne became prime minister in July 1834 on Grey's resignation for two reasons: he had the support of the King, in whose company he was frequently to be found, and he would cause less resentment among his colleagues than anyone else. 'Melbourne is the only man to be prime minister', said Lord Durham, 'because he is the only one of whom none of us would be jealous' (Ziegler 1982: 169). The reasons for his selection said much both about his personality and his essential conservatism. Among other reasons, William IV liked him because he trusted Melbourne's instincts.

That said, it may seem ironic that only four months later Melbourne became the last prime minister to be dismissed on the personal decision of the monarch, rather than for losing support in parliament or at a general election. The King's decision turned on religion. When the dependable Althorp moved to the Lords on his father's death, Melbourne proposed making Lord John Russell leader of the Commons. This the King could not accept because Russell was associated with support for appropriating church revenues for wider secular purposes. William IV, like his father, regarded such tampering with the rights of the church as a breach of his coronation oath and, arguing that Melbourne's government was anyway split on the issue, dismissed it (Newbould 1990: 157–9).

Melbourne was not out of office for long. Peel was unable to fashion majorities in the Commons and, after a general election produced insufficient Tory gains, Melbourne met with leading Radical MPs and with Daniel O'Connell in April 1835 to agree how to force the Tories out. This 'Lichfield House Compact' was immediately successful and some historians have seen it as 'the point of origin of the Victorian Liberal party' (Gash 1979: 161). We should be chary of accepting this. Party allegiances, especially among backbenchers, were not especially strong and the 'compact' anyway later gave Melbourne considerable trouble. In the short term, however, he was triumphant. He resumed office with a ministry very much of his own choosing, rather than one bequeathed to him by Grey; he stayed there for six years. A number of reforms issued forth, none more important than the Municipal Corporations Act 1835 which replaced 178 local closed boroughs – many Tory dominated – with a network of elected borough corporations. These corporations had powers to raise rates and the annual elections saw vigorous contests between local elites. In northern industrial towns, in particular, non-conformists increased their power and influence very substantially.

The King, whose gamble had failed, now had to accept his *bête noire*, Lord John Russell, as Home Secretary. Nevertheless, the Whig leadership probably suffered from being perceived by an overwhelmingly propertied electorate as too influenced by the Irish, by various radical extremists and by the urban non-conformists. Certainly, the Tory opposition made further gains in the general election of 1837, necessitated by the death of William IV.

Also, many of the more sober 'administrative' reforms, such as the Tithe Commutation Act 1836 and Civil Registration of Births, Marriages and Deaths 1837, were passed with discreet Tory support. The government could also count on Tory votes for measures designed to head off the threat from Chartism in 1838–9. Similarly, some of the more 'dangerous measures', beloved of radicals, such as the secret ballot and the removal of bishops from the Lords, were voted down by the leaderships of both parties (Newbould 1990: 214–17; Jenkins 1994: 30).

Melbourne's relationship with Queen Victoria was one of close friendship and mutual regard. As a conventional Whig, Melbourne believed in the subordination of monarchy to parliament and he advised the Queen of his interpretation of a complex constitutional position. Victoria's father, the Duke of Kent, had been close to the Whigs and Melbourne well knew the importance of having the support of the monarchy. The aversion of George IV, both as King and previously as Prince Regent, to the Whigs had contributed to the length of their period in opposition from 1807 to 1830 and Melbourne was shrewd enough to see the political advantages, as well as the personal pleasure, to be derived from educating the young Queen.

Before Victoria married Prince Albert in 1840, Melbourne was in almost constant attendance at Court. Bizarre though it might seem, he took on the post of private secretary to the Queen, while also prime minister. The *Dictionary of National Biography* called this an act of 'admirable self-denial' (DNB: xxii, 1273) but it was more politically calculating than that. When his ministry seemed likely to fall in May 1839, and Melbourne advised the Queen to send for Peel, he knew that her dependence upon him was likely to work to his political advantage. As anticipated, the Queen found Peel cold and distant. She refused to dismiss any of her Whig-supporting ladies of the bedchamber when Peel asked her to do so. In the circumstances, Peel declared that he could not continue his plans for forming a minority Conservative government. As the Queen told the Duke of Wellington, she looked upon Melbourne 'as a friend and almost a father' (Ziegler 1982: 292). Melbourne resumed office, telling the Lords that he 'would not abandon my sovereign in a situation of difficulty and distress' (Ziegler 1982: 297). The Whigs stayed in power for a further two years.

A strong case exists for seeing the last years of Melbourne's second ministry as a long diminuendo. A sympathetic observer, the Whig Lord Holland, was noting as early as 1838:

It is impossible not to see that the Ministers are losing strength and reputation. Resting on the popular support of a variety of parties, they must yield to pressure from without of any one of them, and the vacillating policy which is the consequence of their position must necessarily lower them in public Estimation. In the Lords they have few speakers on their side, and even in the Commons they are frequently out spoken.

(Kriegel 1977: 385)

During these years, the government deficit mounted alarmingly. Successive Chancellors of the Exchequer, Thomas Spring Rice and Francis Baring, showed no sign of being able to control it. By 1840, it was projected to reach almost £3 million and lack of clear government strategy gave Peel numerous opportunities to exploit its embarrassment. Finally, Baring proposed to reduce tariffs on timber and sugar and to introduce a lower tariff on corn in the hope that lower duties would stimulate trade and increase government revenue. The government lost a vote on the proposal to reduce duties on imported sugar in May 1841. Peel proposed a no-confidence motion on 4 June which the government lost by a single vote, precipitating a general election. Peel, campaigning as the leader of the party of protection, completed the Tories' revival with a substantial victory, based on the English counties and small boroughs.

Melbourne continued to lead the Whig opposition from the Lords until he suffered a stroke in 1842. He wrote to the Queen that he had succumbed to 'a very awkward and severe illness and cannot deny that he is much annoyed and disheartened by this attack coming upon him as it did, at a moment when he thought his health better' (Ziegler 1982: 353–4). He did not participate actively again in politics.

It is too easy to dismiss Melbourne as a prime ministerial anachronism, an eighteenth-century landowning politician at odds with an increasingly industrial world. The fact that Peel wreaked such debating havoc on the government benches in the years 1838–41 tends only to feed the illusion, as does Greville's famous anecdote about the insouciant way in which Melbourne was supposed to have accepted the prime ministership. In a private conversation with the King's private secretary, Melbourne is supposed to have

'thought it a damned bore, and he was in many minds what he should do – be minister or no'. Young replied: 'Why dammit, such a position never was occupied by any Greek or Roman, and, if it lasts only two months, it is well worthwhile to have been Prime Minister of England'. 'By God, that's true' said Melbourne, 'I'll go'.

(Mandler 1990: 105)

Less well known is Greville's assessment of Melbourne's survival strategy as a politician.

Melbourne is a gentleman, liberal and straightforward, with no meanness, and incapable of selfish trickery and intrigue, but he is habitually careless and *insouciant*, loves ease, and hates contests and squabbles, and though he would never tell a lie, he has probably not that stern and rigid regard for truth which would make him run any risk rather than that of concealing anything or suffering a false impression to be formed or conveyed with respect to any matter he might be concerned in.

(Greville 1874: iii, 170–1)

This later assessment gives a sharper insight into the paradox of an old-style aristocrat who was nevertheless a substantial political figure. On all the major issues, Melbourne had clear objectives which he followed in a professional manner. He led a party of reform but tempered its impulse so that both land-owners and aristocratic values retained their full influence in a rapidly changing world. His administration's reforms are far from contemptible and have tended to be undervalued alongside Peel's radical reconstruction of government eco-nomic and fiscal policy in the 1840s. Many contemporaries, however, recog-nized their importance. Among them were both Gladstone and Disraeli, who agreed about very little. Gladstone said that 'Melbourne's Government had witnessed the enactment of many important laws, useful in their general char-acter and well suited to the condition of the public mind'. Disraeli praised them as 'generally moderate, well-matured and statesmanlike schemes' (Newbould 1990: 267).

Melbourne also played a not insignificant part in ensuring that leadership of the Whig–Liberal party, at a time of rapid change, remained in the hands of landowning gentlemen. It was aristocratic Whiggery, moderated by patriotism and government expertise, which provided leadership for the Liberals in the substantial shapes of Palmerston and Gladstone until the last years of the nine-teenth century. Melbourne's part in facilitating this orderly, and fundamentally conservative, transition should not be underestimated.

Reading and further references
Gash, N. (1979) *Aristocracy and People: Britain 1815–65*, London: Arnold. (A useful political history textbook.)
Greville, G. (1874) *Journals of the Reigns of George IV and William IV*, 3 vols, London: Longman. (Very high-class gossip, spiced with much insight, by an intelligent insider.)
Jenkins, T. (1994) *The Liberal Ascendancy, 1830–1886*, London: Macmillan.
Kriegel, A. (ed.) (1977) *The Holland House Diaries, 1831–40*, London: Routledge. (The diaries of Lord Holland, a leading Whig who was not blind to the increasing weakness of the Melbourne government.)
Mandler, P. (1990) *Aristocratic Government in the Age of Reform*, Oxford: Clarendon Press. (A new interpretation of high politics, stressing its essential conservative nature before 1850.)
Marshall, D. (1975) *Lord Melbourne*, London: Weidenfeld & Nicolson.

Newbould, I. (1990) *Whiggery and Reform, 1830–41: The Politics of Government*, London: Macmillan. (The most impressive of several recent studies which attempt to rehabilitate the Whigs.)

Ziegler, P. (1982) *Melbourne*, New York: Athenaeum. (The fullest biography though not particularly strong in linking Melbourne to his times.)

Eric Evans

Robert Peel

Born 5 February 1788, third child of Sir Robert Peel and Ellen Yates. Educated at Harrow and Christ Church, Oxford. Married 1820 Julia Floyd, daughter of General Sir John Floyd. MP for Cashel 1809–12, Chippenham 1812–17, Oxford University 1817–29, Westbury 1829–30, Tamworth 1830–50. Under-Secretary of State for War and Colonies 1810–12; Chief Secretary to the Lord Lieutenant of Ireland 1812–18; Home Secretary 1822–7 and 1828–30; Prime Minister 1834–5 and 1841–6. Succeeded his father as second baronet 1830. Died 2 July 1850.

'His place as the founder of modern Conservatism is unchallengable' (Gash 1972: 709). 'Arguably the greatest peacetime Prime Minister in British history' (Read 1987: ix). Both judgements reflect a twentieth-century estimation of Peel's worth, and would have astonished his contemporaries. Both contain a smidgen of truth, but both are fundamentally misleading. Peel did not found modern Conservatism, even though it was under his leadership that the governing Pittite coalition adopted the title 'Conservative'. Following his fall in 1846, this party went into the political wilderness for over twenty years, and when the Conservative cause was eventually revived under Disraeli and Salisbury it was along lines which were wholly antithetical to those of Peel. Indeed Peel's legacy, in terms both of personnel and of political ideology, was inherited by the Liberal party under Gladstone rather than by the Conservatives. However, with the downfall of the Liberal party after the First World War, the Conservative party absorbed a good deal of its free-market ideology, becoming in effect 'Peelite' for the first time. This paradox explains why some historians have been misled into supposing that Peel had founded modern Conservatism. As for the judgement that Peel was 'the greatest peacetime Prime Minister', he was certainly a dominant one, commandeering cabinet 'colleagues' and civil servants as no other had done since Walpole. He also earned a reputation for economic competence, being helped in this respect by the commercial upturn which coincided with his second ministry (1841–6). Yet the two achievements on which he might lay claim to greatness in the eyes of posterity – Catholic emancipation and the repeal of the Corn Laws – were regarded at the time as crushing admissions of failure. Those who abhorred such policies saw only that he had twice abandoned his election pledges and split his party. Those who supported such policies condemned him for having previously opposed them. They argued that Peel's reputation and exceptional parliamentary skills had given heart to the 'reactionaries', and had thereby ensured that, when emancipation and repeal did at last eventuate, it was in an atmosphere of popular clamour and recrimination.

Peel's grandfather was a Lancastrian yeoman turned calico printer who died in 1795 worth about £140,000. Peel's father – 'the first "cotton king" to sit in parliament' (Thorne 1986: 741) – became squire of Drayton Manor in Staffordshire. As MP for Tamworth (1790–1820) he was responsible for promoting bills to regulate the employment of children in cotton mills, a tenderly philanthropic streak which his hard-nosed son did not inherit. Despite considerable wealth and squirearchical pretensions, their manufacturing background meant that the Peels were horny-handed provincials, not even part of the commercial, financial and professional elite which had inter-married and mingled with the landed aristocracy for centuries. This 'outsider' status was to colour Peel's personality. He never achieved the easeful grace in Tory-aristocratic circles enjoyed by Canning, the actress's son. He was to compensate for his social unease by cultivating artistic and scientific pursuits and by adopting a superior moral tone: no politician ever referred more profligately to the dictates of 'his conscience'.

At Harrow he seemed prematurely mature: a contemporary, Lord Byron, described himself as being 'always in scrapes, Peel never'. At Christ Church, where he took a brilliant double-first *viva-voce*, Peel developed a certain stardom. Far from socially assimilating, however, he emerged from public school and varsity with his carapace harder. Politically he had become attached (as fervently, perhaps, as only an outsider can be) to established institutions, and particularly to the Protestant constitution in church and state. To use a word which was contemptuously bandied about by their opponents but not yet adopted by themselves, he was one of the stern and unbending 'Tories'. Such was his prestige that within two months of becoming MP for a close borough in 1810 he was given junior office, and in 1812 at the age of 24 he became Chief Secretary of Ireland. In this post he displayed his abundant appetite and talent for administration, and became the undisputed champion of those MPs who resisted the Catholics' demands to be allowed to sit in parliament. By the time of his retirement from Ireland in 1818 there was talk of 'Mr Peel's party', most members of which were considerably older and less talented than himself (as he was later tactlessly to point out).

It is not clear why Peel – an official man if ever there was one – resigned in 1818. Some said he was piqued by Frederick Robinson's recent promotion to be President of the Board of Trade. Whatever the reason, it meant that as a backbencher Peel was eligible for the chairmanship of the secret committee of the Commons appointed in 1819 to consider whether and when the Bank of England should resume cash payments. This was undoubtedly a key event in Peel's career. He knew nothing about the subject at first, and relied heavily on the expertise of William Huskisson, but he read methodically and came to the firm view that the bullionists – i.e. those who wished to return to the gold standard immediately – were right and the anti-bullionists wrong. This involved recanting earlier pronouncements and marked his immersion in liberal, free-market political economy. All his later social and economic policies stemmed from his decision in favour of the gold standard, which he was to defend with an anxious passion against ultra-Tory and radical critics for the remainder of his career. He took the decision on doctrinaire rather than practical grounds, but the doctrine he espoused owed less to Ricardo than to Edward Copleston, an Oxford cleric who believed that cash payments would stabilize the economy by discouraging excessive speculation. Copleston also argued that one could expect the poor to 'stand-on-their-own-feet' – i.e. without welfare handouts – only if one could be sure that their poverty was a consequence of their own misbehaviour, and that one could be sure of that only if the money supply were to be rendered as 'neutral' (and therefore blameless) as possible (Hilton 1978: 31–66; 1988: 107–8, 222–5).

Like most manufacturers at the time – though many were to change their minds later – Peel's father opposed the decision made in 1819 to resume cash payments. Expressing regret at the course his son proposed to adopt, he informed parliament that thirty years before, when his son was being christened at the font, he had dedicated the baby's life to the service of his country, so that he might follow in the steps of 'the immortal Mr Pitt'. This was trumpery paternal moonshine – apart from anything else Pitt had hardly become recognized as one of the immortals by 1788 – and it must surely have embarrassed Peel, but the significant point is that it was mainly taken seriously on the government backbenches in a packed Commons. What this shows is that these backbenchers, only too conscious of a 'march-of-mind' liberalism abroad in the land, were desperate to find a successor to that pilot who had weathered the storm and who had been prematurely taken from them. It meant that Peel was invested with political longings which he did not share, and it placed him in such a false position as to dog the rest of his career.

The falsity of the position is evident from a question which Peel asked a friend in the following year:

> Do not you think that the tone of England – of that great compound of folly, weakness, prejudice, wrong feeling, right feeling, obstinacy, and newspaper paragraphs, which is called public opinion – is more liberal – to use an odious but intelligible phase – than the policy of the Government? Do not you think . . . that [public opinion] is growing too large for the channels that it has been accustomed to run through?
>
> (Croker 1885: i, 170)

These pregnant questions reveal not only some contempt for the general public but also Peel's conviction that that public must be appeased. With hindsight it is clear that this champion of 'Tory' and 'establishment' values was desperate to be a 'liberal'. He was in the wrong party.

During the later stages of Liverpool's period in office, however, it seemed that

Peel's desire to be a 'liberal' might be accommodated within the ruling Pittite party. During 1821–3 Liverpool carried out a major reconstruction of his ministry, which included appointing Peel Home Secretary in January 1822. Together with Canning, Huskisson and Robinson, Peel came to be perceived – quite rightly – as embodying a distinctly 'liberal' wing of the governing party, a group usually described by historians as 'liberal Tories' (since the word 'Tory' gradually came to be applied to the party as a whole during the 1820s). As in Ireland, Peel's flair for executive government asserted itself, and he quickly made a mark second only to that of Canning. His most celebrated work as Home Secretary was the consolidation of aspects of the criminal code, followed by the introduction of the metropolitan police force in 1829. The latter measure was a straightforward recognition of the inadequacy of the old magistracy to keep law and order in Britain's rapidly expanding towns. The motivation for his legal reforms was more complex. Peel himself described them as a 'mitigation of the severity of the criminal law', and many historians have therefore credited him with having been the first politician to dismantle Britain's notorious 'bloody code'. More recent research has demonstrated that serious reductions in the numbers of convicts hanged began only after the Whigs came to power in 1830 (Beales 1974: 879–80). Peel's real intention seems to have been to make the legal system more certain and predictable by repealing capital statutes which had mainly fallen into desuetude, rather than to make it more merciful. He had absorbed the prominent evangelical attitude to the magnitude of human sinfulness, and held a sternly deterrent view of the value of retributive punishment. Part of his duties as Home Secretary was to guide the Privy Council in hearing appeals against capital convictions, and it is evident that his influence was rarely wielded on the side of 'mercy' in marginal cases. While it may be a little unfair to call him a 'great hangman' (Gatrell 1994: 566), he was certainly no humanitarian like James Mackintosh or the prison reformers Fry and Howard, and he was keen to institute a graded series of secondary punishments – transportation, solitary confinement, the treadmill, whipping (public or private – once, twice or thrice) – for certain less serious crimes, rather than have petty criminals acquitted on capital charges by soft-hearted juries and allowed to go scot-free.

The first crisis in Peel's career came in 1827 when he and five other of Liverpool's ministers refused to serve under Canning. His stated reason was that he could not serve under a prime minister who was known to favour Catholic emancipation, even though Canning promised to let that issue remain an 'open' one. The difficulty was that in all other respects Peel's 'liberal Tory' stance was very close to Canning's, and – although this was not widely known – he had already privately acknowledged the need for conceding the Catholic claims, albeit on terms. It was widely suspected that Peel refused to serve Canning because he himself wanted to be prime minister and hoped that Canning would fail; this suspicion of bad faith dogged him for the rest of his life. When Canning unexpectedly died a few months later Peel was in a dilemma: though privately aware of the need for emancipation, in public he had justified his decision to abandon Canning and split the party by arguing that emancipation had at all costs to be prevented. Nemesis was swift. January 1828 saw him back at the Home Office in Wellington's new government, while six months later the election of a Catholic, Daniel O'Connell, for County Clare brought the emancipation issue to a head. Desperately Peel sought to resign, arguing that he was too strongly pledged to the Protestant constitution to take any personal part in emancipation, but Wellington would not let him. It therefore fell to Peel as leader of the government in the Commons to introduce the measure in 1829. With its passage Peel could claim responsibility for the most dramatic constitutional adjustment since the 'glorious revolution' of 1688, and one moreover which led directly to the fall of the old regime and a panoply of further reforms. Peel could take little pride in this achievement, however, for his reward was to be denounced as a 'Judas' by all those backbench Tories who had hitherto regarded him as their champion. Worst of all, having been forced to stand for re-election in his Oxford University constituency, he was beaten humiliatingly by an ultra-Tory and forced to find refuge in a close borough.

Most historians have described Catholic emancipation as a pragmatic decision taken in order to avoid civil war in Ireland following the Clare election (Eastwood 1992: 29–30). In fact, Peel had (as he wrote at the time) 'not the slightest apprehension of the result of civil commotion' (Peel 1856: i, 293) – at least not in the short term – and what frightened him about the Clare election was that it was so orderly. Moreover, his four stated reasons for emancipation all in different ways signalled his acceptance of liberal doctrine. First, he cited the movement of English public opinion in favour of emancipation, opinion which it was impossible to 'roll back'. Second, he accepted that the attempt to govern Ireland through the disinterested agency of Protestant magistrates and police authorities had failed because there were too few Protestants. It followed that if Catholics were not to be kept down administratively, then they must be reconciled to British rule, and that in turn required that Catholics be granted equality of civil rights. Third, Peel argued that Ireland's only salvation lay in embracing English-style market economics, which required that the predominantly Catholic population had to be encouraged into becoming middle-class capitalists. Finally, he argued that the doctrine of competition applied as much to religion as to economics: Catholicism had prospered in Ireland because it was persecuted, while Protestantism had suffered because it was protected. Only if there were to be a 'free trade in creeds' could the true faith be expected to vanquish the papal antichrist (Hilton 1993: 71–8).

Catholic emancipation made the ultra-wing of the Tory party incandescent with bitterness and rage, and led directly to the fall of Wellington's government in November 1830. Peel was genuinely relieved, being sick of all the contumely. A haughty, proud man, and highly emotional under his frigid exterior – O'Connell famously said that his smile was like the gleam on the silver plate of a coffin lid – Peel now grew to hate his backbenchers, and continued to do so for the rest of his career.

How can those, who spend their time in hunting and shooting and eating and drinking, know what were the motives of those who are responsible for the public security, who have access to the best information, and have no other object under Heaven but to provide against danger, and consult the general interests of all classes!

he spat contemptuously. Opposition did not bring much respite from intra-party strife, however. For a start, Peel's tactics in the Reform Bill debates of 1831-2 were condemned by many on his own side. Willing to accept a moderate instalment of parliamentary reform, and anxious at all costs to distance himself from the ultra-Tories, Peel was disconcerted to find that the Whig bill was much more extreme than expected. By the time he had galvanized his forces in opposition, however, public opinion had rallied in favour of reform, which meant that it would have been too dangerous to abort the measure. Peel's relations with Wellington, still party leader, were also sour at this time. A turning-point came, however, with the King's dismissal of the Whigs in November 1834. Wellington refused to take office again, and so Peel led a minority government which lasted just one hundred days before being blown away by the fourth general election in six years. At the time it seemed that he had succeeded only in uniting the disparate wings of the Whig–Liberal–Radical–Irish coalition against him, but in retrospect it can be seen that his ministry had done very much more. The Reform Act, once carried, seemed so extreme that a large part of the political nation longed for a period of conservation and consolidation. Peel caught this mood, not least with his famous Tamworth manifesto of 1834, an election address whose sentiments were vacuous, but which merely by its existence helped to rally the forces of resistance to change. Meanwhile, thanks in particular to F.R. Bonham, the Conservative party was organized into an efficient electoral unit (Gash 1982). Bonham and Peel both saw the need to 'register' the newly enfranchised voters as Conservatives, and particularly those well-to-do tenants-at-will who had been the beneficiaries of the Chandos clause of 1831. From the disastrous nadir of 1832, when it won only 175 seats, the Conservative party recorded 98 gains in the election of 1835 and another 40 in 1837. Peel was by this time utterly dominant in Commons debates, so much so that he might even be thought to have earned Disraeli's accolade of being the greatest parliamentarian that ever lived. He held the Melbourne government in the palm of his hand, protecting it time and again from defeat at the hands of its own Radical rebels, and then deciding when to strike and bring it down. The first strike came in 1839, but Peel did not form a government on that occasion, ostensibly because Queen Victoria refused to accede to his demand for changes among the ladies of the bedchamber, in reality because Peel did not yet feel that he could win a general election and had no wish to repeat his experience in the minority government of 1834–5. The second strike came in 1841, followed by a general election which gave the Conservative party a majority of 76.

It used to be thought that Peel set out to broaden his party's appeal by

attracting the new £10 householder vote – predominantly the industrial and trading, middle-class, urban vote – and that the election victory of 1841 marked the
success of that policy (Gash 1972). In fact, Peel tried to do no such thing, dismiss-
ing the £10 householders as a 'vulgar privileged pedlary'. Even supposing that he
had tried to do this, the 1841 election would not have been a triumph, since it was
overwhelmingly won in the counties and small country boroughs, not in the
industrial towns. It was a victory for three types of Tory extremist, all of whom
Peel despised and tried desperately to distance himself from. The first of these
were the ultra-Protestant Tories of the Orange lodges. The second were the ultra-
protectionists, alarmed by the Melbourne government's decision to fight the
1841 election on a proposal to reduce the Corn Laws. The third were paternalists
like Lord Shaftesbury and Benjamin Disraeli, who longed for a caring, welfare-
orientated backlash against economic *laissez-faire*, and who called for the enforced
reduction of factory hours and for an end to the harsh new Poor Law which the
Whigs had introduced in 1834. Now Peel strongly opposed the regulation of
hours of work and warmly supported the new Poor Law. So far from being a
personal triumph, it is possible to regard the Conservative surge of the late 1830s
and victory in 1841 as a case of abject 'failure' on Peel's part (Newbould 1983).

At any rate, the seeds of party dissension were present from the start of Peel's
'great' ministry. Few other governments can have followed so coherent a set of
policies, but then few can have been so dominated by a single person. And as in
the Liverpool, Canning and Wellington governments – of which Peel's was in
many respects a continuation – the issues of corn, cash and Catholics dominated.
In Ireland emancipation had clearly failed to reconcile a majority of people to the
union with Britain as Peel had hoped. One of his reasons for disliking Catholicism
was his belief that the Irish peasantry would follow like sheep wherever their
priests led them, but at least this promised a solution to the Irish problem. If the
clergy could be detached from O'Connell's nationalist party by a programme of
concessions to the Catholic Church, then the mass of the population would
follow. The culmination of this programme was his decision to increase the parliamentary grant to the Catholic college of Maynooth in 1845. The measure was
carried but split the Conservative party, and gave the discontented backbencher
Disraeli an opportunity to cover Peel with bitter and brilliant sarcasm.

The 1842 and 1845 budgets – which unconventionally were introduced by the
prime minister and not the Chancellor of the Exchequer – continued the work of
cutting import and export duties begun by Huskisson and Robinson in the
1820s. To make good the revenue sacrificed, Peel introduced and then renewed
an income tax – the first in peacetime – of about 3d in the pound on incomes
above £150. It was meant to be temporary, but so far there has been no sign that
this is so. The Bank Charter Act 1844 took steps towards the centralization of
note issue in the Bank of England, which Peel thought was necessary to ensure
that Britain remained on the gold standard. This can be seen as the high point of
Peel's evangelical, hair-shirt economics. His intentions were severely deflationary,
since if the Act had worked as planned it would have squeezed investment by

limiting the money supply to the amount of gold deposited in the vaults of the Bank. In the event the Act did not work as intended, partly because it was twice suspended, partly because of an unexpected increase in the amount of gold deposited after 1850, and it probably proved beneficial in helping to moderate the mid-Victorian boom of the 1850s and 1860s. Meanwhile, Peel continued to set his face against welfare payments and industrial regulation, thereby offending many of his own backbenchers once again.

There seems little doubt that Peel was complicit in Huskisson's project of the 1820s for an eventual free trade in corn. Their motives were quite different from those of younger free traders such as Cobden and Bright of the Anti-Corn Law League, who regarded free trade as the key to export-led economic growth. For Peel, Corn Law repeal was mainly essential in order to ensure the provision of food supplies to a rapidly growing population. Second, it was needed in order to stabilize the monetary system, especially once the Act of 1844 had rendered the gold standard vulnerable to wild fluctuations in such an important staple commodity. The Corn Laws were also a symbol of landlord monopoly and a restraint on trade; as such they threatened the jobs of all those employed in the export industries and rendered them susceptible to the blandishments of the People's Charter. Moreover, like all restraints on economic activity, the Corn Laws interfered with what Peel liked to call the 'dispensations of providence'. He did not suppose for a moment that repeal would banish distress, but he did argue that under free trade any distress which occurred could be seen to be God's wilful retribution on the individuals concerned, rather than being 'caused by laws of man regulating in the hour of scarcity the supply of food'. This moral, even religious aspect of Peel's policies must not be underestimated.

Given all this, the repeal of the Corn Laws was for Peel a question of when, not if. He dared not show his true hand before the 1841 election for fear of splitting his party, and during the campaign itself he spoke with a distinctly double tongue. In 1842, having been elected, he reduced the Corn Laws significantly, and probably planned a series of further reductions over the following decade, a painless extinction or 'euthanasia', as the Home Secretary Sir James Graham called it. However, by the summer of 1845 if not before, Peel had come to the conclusion that the Laws would have to go quickly, that is before the next election. Maybe the success of the Anti-Corn Law League convinced him that unless he disposed of the issue the Whigs would sweep to power on the issue of the people's food. His opportunity came in the autumn of 1845 when the potato crop failed in Ireland, marking the onset of a tragic famine in which over 1 million people died. Corn Law repeal would do nothing to help the Irish, but symbolically the famine provided just the pretext Peel was looking for. When ultra-Tories screamed blue murder, he could say how wicked it was while people were starving to preserve a monopoly which raised the price and prevented the free flow of grain.

Having failed to carry a united cabinet on repeal, Peel resigned. However, the Whig leader Lord John Russell was apparently unable to form a government, and in Disraeli's famous phrase he 'handed back with courtesy the poisoned chalice'.

Peel did not flinch. The difference between 1829 and 1846 was that in 1846 he revelled in his martyrdom. Assailed by many of his followers, and lacerated by Disraeli's brilliant invective, Peel nevertheless floated on waves of righteous self-esteem. Repeal was carried by 339–242 on second reading thanks to the votes of the opposition Whigs, but more than two-thirds of Tory MPs voted against. In June these disaffected Tories rebelled again on a Coercion Bill for Ireland, the sort of measure which they would normally have supported automatically, and Peel resigned forthwith. It is impossible to know whether, during the next four years, he seriously contemplated another comeback, another Tamworth manifesto. His band of Peelites – about ninety were elected in 1847 – remained staunchly loyal, and on 28 June 1850 he made what was arguably his finest parliamentary speech. It was in favour of international peace and justice, and against what he saw as Palmerston's diplomatic bullying over the Don Pacifico incident. On the following afternoon Peel was thrown from his horse and, being in too much pain to be carried upstairs, he died on the dining-room table four days later. This dramatic death, coinciding as it did with the beginning of an economic boom and an unfamiliar sense of national pride and well-being, combined to invest his memory with a warm glow. He was widely and popularly mourned as the man who had broken the landlords' monopoly and brought the people cheap bread, and was commemorated in statues and in celebration mugs and plates throughout the country (Read 1987: 287–312). This posthumous (and, it must be said, incongruous) adulation paved the way for Gladstone, his most devoted disciple, who carried forward Peel's liberal principles of peace, retrenchment and free trade. If it is impossible to understand Peel's reputation in establishment circles during the early 1820s without realizing that he was seen as a surrogate Pitt, then it is impossible to understand Gladstone's popular reputation in the early 1860s without realizing that in turn he was a surrogate Peel.

References and further reading

Beales, D. (1974) 'Peel, Russell, and reform', *Historical Journal* 17: 873–82.

Croker, J. (1885) *The Croker Papers: The Correspondence and Diaries of John Wilson Croker*, ed. L.J. Jennings, 2nd rev. edn, London: John Murray.

Eastwood, D. (1992) 'Peel and the Tory party reconsidered', *History Today* 42: 27–33.

Gash, N. (1961) *Mr Secretary Peel: The Life of Sir Robert Peel to 1830*, London: Longman.

—— (1972) *Sir Robert Peel: The Life of Sir Robert after 1830*, London: Longman. (These two volumes constitute the standard biography. The first is excellent, the second too reverential and weak on some important issues such as economic and religious policy.)

—— (1982) 'The organization of the Conservative Party, 1832–1846', *Parliamentary History* 1: 137–59; 2: 131–52.

Gatrell, V.A.C. (1994) *The Hanging Tree: Execution and the English People 1770–1868*, Oxford: Oxford University Press. (Passionate and brilliant account of how the 'bloody code' was gradually abandoned; contains a fierce diatribe against Peel, who is depicted as a cruel Home Secretary.)

Hilton, B. (1978) *Corn, Cash, Commerce: The Economic Policies of the Tory Governments 1815–1830*, Oxford: Oxford University Press.

—— (1979) 'Peel: a reappraisal', *Historical Journal* 22: 585–614. (Questions the traditional view of Peel as a fundamentally pragmatic politician.)

—— (1988) *The Age of Atonement: The Influence of Evangelicalism on Social and Economic Thought ca.1785–1865*, Oxford: Clarendon Press.

—— (1993) 'The ripening of Robert Peel', in M. Bentley (ed.) *Public and Private Doctrine: Essays in British History Presented to Maurice Cowling*, Cambridge: Cambridge University Press. (Claims that Peel genuinely changed his mind on the Catholic question and explains why.)

Newbould, I. (1983) 'Peel and the Conservative party 1832–41: a study in failure', *English Historical Review* 98: 529–57.

Parker, C. (1891–9) *Sir Robert Peel from his Private Papers*, 3 vols, London: John Murray. (Contains the most extensive selection of Peel's correspondence, though a high degree of editorial licence makes it necessary to treat this volume with caution.)

Peel, R. (1856) *Memoirs*, ed. Lord Mahon and E. Cardwell, 2 vols, London: John Murray. (Peel's defence of his actions over Catholic emancipation and Corn Law repeal, with many original documents.)

Read, D. (1987) *Peel and the Victorians*, Oxford: Blackwell. (Interesting on Peel's posthumous popular reputation.)

Thorne, R.G. (1986) 'Robert Peel I' and 'Robert Peel II', in R.G. Thorne, *The House of Commons 1790–1820*, vol. 1, London: Secker & Warburg. (Excellent account of Peel's career to 1820.)

Boyd Hilton

Lord John Russell, First Earl Russell

Born 18 August 1792, third son of John, sixth Duke of Bedford and the Hon. Georgiana Byng. Educated at home and at Westminster, Mr Smith's school at Woodnesboro', and Edinburgh University. Married (1) 1835 Adelaide (died 1838), daughter of Thomas Lister; (2) 1841 Frances Elliot, daughter of the second Earl of Minto. MP for Tavistock 1813–17 and 1818–20, Huntingdonshire 1820–6, Bandon 1826–30, Tavistock 1830–1, Devon 1831–2, South Devon 1832–5, Stroud 1835–41, City of London 1841–61. Paymaster of the Forces 1830–4; Home Secretary 1835–9 and Colonial Secretary 1839–41, while Leader of the Commons; Prime Minister 1846–52; Foreign Secretary 1852–3; Minister without Portfolio 1853–4. Lord President of the Council 1854–5, while Leader of the Commons; Colonial Secretary 1855; Foreign Secretary 1859–65; Prime Minister 1865–6. Ennobled 1861. Died 28 May 1878.

Russell was prime minister twice, but neither tenure was considered either at the time or by posterity to have been particularly successful. Paradoxically, however, Russell's significance as a party leader and political reformer is enormous. He was leader of the Liberal party in the Commons for over twenty years, and leader of the government in that House for over fourteen – longer than anyone else in British history since the Great Reform Act 1832. His conception of the role of party, leadership and principle in politics was clear and unwavering – perhaps excessively so. It was of critical importance to the development of nineteenth-century liberalism and the coherence of the Liberal party.

Russell's principles were founded on the whiggism of his father's hero, Charles James Fox. He was brought up to believe that public-spirited aristocratic families such as the Russells had a duty to provide political leadership aimed at protecting and promoting the civil and religious liberties of the people. He never lost these beliefs, but he developed them in ways suited to the nineteenth century. His major interest, as a young Whig MP in opposition in the 1820s, was in parliamentary reform. When the Whigs came into power in 1830, he and Lord Durham were the most important members of the 'Committee of Four' charged with drawing up the Great Reform Bill, and he introduced it into the Commons in March 1831. The resulting Act of 1832 was designed to abolish most of the nomination boroughs which had sustained Tory rule, and make the Commons represent a much wider range of interests. Russell had no doubt that reform was compatible with leadership by aristocrats, as long as they were assiduous and flexible in responding to the needs of a large, varied electorate. But Whig aristocratic exclusiveness was no longer viable if power was to be retained. 'I always thought that the Whig party, as a party, would be destroyed by the Reform Bill', Russell wrote in 1837 (Walpole 1889: i, 285). What was now needed was a cause able to unite most 'Reform' MPs – those MPs, many from large towns, who were willing to uphold the principle of responsiveness to public grievances. The problem of leading this heterogeneous force soon became Russell's problem, because he rose so quickly that he became leader of the reformers in the Commons from 1834, and the principal influence on domestic policy during the Melbourne government of 1835–41. Gladstone later wrote of Russell that the 'great and beneficial acts' of that government were 'almost wholly his' (Gladstone 1890: 54). Indeed it was Russell's political agenda that did most to create a coherent 'Liberal party' out of the amorphous 'Reform' coalition by the late 1830s.

His agenda owed a lot to his views on history and religion. He was convinced that public morals and manners had played a major role in the fall of great states of the past, such as Rome. The duty of the statesman was to try to guide morals for good – though not by repressing freedom, for liberty of discussion was the greatest engine of human progress. Russell asserted the state's duty to nurture beneficial values. 'It is upon law and government, that the prosperity and morality, the power and intelligence, of every nation depend' (Parry 1993: 10). In particular Russell was anxious to see the spread of a tolerant form of Christianity, founded on the message of Christ to love God and one's neighbour. He felt that access to the basic Christian message was the best way of awakening the moral senses and developing the energies of the population, diminishing the ignorance, sensuality, criminality and vice which afflicted large portions of the community. As a good

Foxite, he felt 'the injustice of subjecting to the penalties of the criminal law persons who had never been taught their duty to God and man' (Russell 1875: 374). This attitude dictated his lenient policy to Chartism as Home Secretary from 1835 to 1839. It also led him to apply the power of the state in new ways, partly in a conscious response to the Chartists' dissatisfaction. An Act of 1839 established government responsibility for elementary education by setting up a committee of the Privy Council to superintend the annual grant to schools (begun in 1833), and an inspectorate to monitor their teaching. His reform of the criminal law swept away most of the survivals from the bloody code of the eighteenth century, reducing the number of offences carrying the death penalty from 33 to 16; from 1841, in practice, executions took place only for murder and high treason. And the Prison Acts of 1835 and 1839 established a prison inspectorate, enforced classification of prisoners and a disciplinary code, and encouraged localities to build prisons capable of operating a regime of systematic reformation.

Russell's other contribution to the Liberal agenda in the 1830s was to pay attention to Dissenting and Irish grievances. Again this developed a Foxite concern – with the rights of religious minorities. In the 1820s Russell had been prominent in the Whig campaign against the statutes which prevented Dissenters and Catholics from holding political office; and he played the main role in the repeal of the Test and Corporation Acts in 1828. He was sure that the Irish could be civilized if offered good government by dutiful property-owners. So he would not tolerate a coercive Irish policy unless legitimate Catholic grievances were also addressed. In 1834, he was responsible for a shift in the government's Irish policy which altered its basis of support, with far-reaching political consequences. He announced his approval of the principle that the surplus revenues of the Anglican Church in Ireland should be appropriated to general educational uses. Appropriation was a great symbol for Irish Catholics and British Dissenters, because it signalled that a government could redistribute the resources of an established church if they were surplus to the requirements of the population. It pleased many other reforming MPs because it asserted parliament's right to remodel a powerful corporation in the interests of the nation rather than a small group, yet would allocate the surplus to a national moral purpose – a joint bible-reading education for Protestants and Catholics. But it was deemed revolutionary by many Conservatives and some former government supporters, because it made the Church and other property vulnerable to any populist parliamentary manoeuvre. Four cabinet ministers resigned in protest at the shift in government policy.

The King, appalled, unwisely removed his ministers in November 1834. A few months later, the bulk of the reformers returned to power. Appropriation was now their unifying principle, the ministry's centre of gravity on religious policy shifted leftwards, and the name 'Liberal party' was increasingly adopted. The Melbourne government of 1835–41 reformed the Irish police force and magistracy and made several other gestures to Catholic sentiment, which contributed to a decline in disorder and in the potency of the repeal movement. And it was more sympathetic to Dissenting grievances on church rates, marriage and university education than any previous ministry. (In addition, in 1839 and 1841, and again in 1845, Russell shifted the party's policy on tariffs; without these moves, Corn Law repeal could never have become practical politics, though the credit for it eventually went to Peel.)

So Russell's leadership of the Commons helped to push the Liberal party in several novel directions, most connected in one way or another with moral reform. His leadership was once described as 'creating a moral atmosphere in which bad laws could not easily survive' (Reddaway 1926: 158). His parliamentary manner reflected his own religious simplicity – what the *Daily News* (4 December 1872) called his 'innocent morality'. Bagehot later wrote that he 'perhaps alone . . . has succeeded . . . in the oratory of conviction' (Bagehot 1907: 30). Ready for any debate, resolute in adversity, fearlessly plucky, yet courteously good-tempered in deference to a gentlemanly assembly, Russell won golden plaudits for his leadership. Sydney Smith considered that Russell was 'beyond all comparison the ablest man in [Melbourne's] Administration; and . . . the Government could not exist a moment without him' (Walpole 1889: i, 303). Russell believed that the leader of a progressive country and of a heterogeneous group of free-thinking MPs could succeed in winning parliamentary support only by 'character' – by the purity and public-spiritedness of his behaviour. His detractors accused him of vanity, and they were right; but his vanity was on account of his name, his anxiety to play the part in directing national affairs which was Russell's honour and duty.

Russell's leadership style was founded on his own fidelity to principle. Throughout his career, he expected Liberal MPs to follow him as long as he was faithful to noble liberal ideals. He believed in leading from the front, in laying down the paths of righteousness. So his style was very different from that of Melbourne and Palmerston, the two Liberal prime ministers under whom Russell served. They sought to govern more in accordance with consensus opinion in the Commons. This was a less elevated approach to leadership, though more pragmatic and often more successful. It had the merit of appearing to flatter MPs and the ill-defined 'public opinion' which they claimed to represent. Russell was more emotional. When confronted with a lack of popular sympathy for Irish Catholic grievances in 1844, he snapped: 'If the people were wrong they ought to be put right' (Parry 1993: 133). Acutely conscious of the weight of superstition, intolerance, complacency, apathy and narrow-mindedness in the world, he believed that consensual government often meant bad government. Russell's training taught him that great statesmen gained honourable fame by their determination in devising remedies for popular grievances.

Russell, then, had a great name, great talents and great ideals. He rallied old Foxite Whigs, parliamentary reformers, Dissenters and Irish Catholics with a potency that no politician of his time could match. He had a striking moral presence in the Commons and an overpowering sense of public duty. On Melbourne's retirement, he was obviously the leading Liberal and destined for the premiership – which he attained in 1846. Yet his career – particularly from the 1840s – has received an indifferent press. Why is this?

One problem was that his bold leadership initiatives were often coolly received. When they did not come off, he laid himself open to the charge that he was out of touch with public or parliamentary opinion. He was peculiarly susceptible to this allegation because his social life seemed heavily reliant on an extended family clique. Always delicate, Russell had not endured the socializing experience of a public-school education. He preferred the peace and intellectual stimulation of literary talk to hot, noisy, energetic but empty-headed London society. His protective, unworldly and cloyingly religious second wife encouraged him to shrink from metropolitan political salons as well as reinforcing his high conception of the Russells' destiny in political life. In 1847, Queen Victoria allowed them to live in Pembroke Lodge in Richmond Park; they treated this as a country residence, and aimed to sleep there half the week even during the parliamentary session. Russell's shyness compounded this remoteness; together with his sense of family dignity it made him appear cold, proud, angular, abrupt and taciturn. It also made him unpredictable. On many occasions his penchant for taking abrupt initiatives can be explained, not by considered boldness, but by his unhappiness at his own vacillation and weakness. To this cause can be traced his three great errors of the early 1850s: his Durham Letter of 1850, his dismissal of his Foreign Secretary, Palmerston, in December 1851, and his resignation from the Aberdeen coalition government in January 1855.

Russell's personality traits damaged him far more after 1846 than before, for one reason above all, which is the key to explaining his comparative failure as prime minister in 1846–52 and 1865–6, and his demotion from the Liberal leadership in Palmerston's favour between 1855 and 1865. Russell offered bold, issue-based leadership; but the Liberal party did not have a working majority between 1846 and 1857, and thereafter, when it did, so many of its MPs voiced Palmerston's rather than Russell's sentiments that the party was hardly more sympathetic than before to Russell's agenda. The majority which had given him freedom of manoeuvre in the 1830s had disappeared. This cramped his style; it also engendered frustration which issued in petulant gestures.

Russell did not become prime minister in 1846 because the Liberals won an election. Indeed he must take some of the blame for the loss, in 1841, of the majority which had sustained them through the 1830s; this was caused by the erosion of propertied Anglican county and small-borough support, largely because of the Liberals' supposed radicalism on church and Irish questions. In 1846, Russell benefited from Peel's ejection as prime minister after the split in his party over the Corn Laws. This split left the Protectionists and the Liberals as the two largest parties, with initially about a hundred Peelite supporters of free trade holding the balance. Though the Liberals gained nearly forty seats at the 1847 election, they had a merely nominal majority over the two wings of the old Conservative party. Their total, furthermore, included a hundred vociferous and troublesome Irish and radical MPs. The Peelites would not guarantee to support Russell except on free trade, while many radicals demanded, as the price of their support, moves towards parliamentary reform, retrenchment and the abolition of state endowment of religious institions and teaching. A number of Russell's cabinet colleagues were hostile to radical pressure and preferred to seek a close alliance with Peel on the principles of administrative efficiency rather than legislative excitement, arguing that this better reflected the conservative sentiments of the country. Yet Russell itched to respond to the immense social problems of the 1840s demonstrated by the Irish famine, the revival of Chartism and the Irish repeal movement, and the publicity given to inner-city squalor by official reports. He badly wanted the state to promote moral, social and educational reform.

In these difficult circumstances, his achievement in holding power for six years was considerable. Helped by his attractive parliamentary image, Peel's informal support, and the momentum given to him by a couple of issues on which he could rely on a majority (principally free trade; hence the repeal of the Navigation Acts in 1849), he was able to do something towards his preferred agenda. For example, in 1846–7 he presided over a crucial change in the distribution of the state educational grant, in order to encourage schoolmasters to improve themselves and to offer a more meaningful and uplifting teaching. This, and a couple of later changes, caused the annual grant to rise from £75,000 in 1845 to £1.3 million in 1862. The Public Health Act 1848 was the first major piece of compulsory health legislation; it established local boards of health with wide powers to impose effective sewerage and drainage and to make other sanitary improvements. Russell's reform of the Church of England aimed to make it more tolerant and better able to promote education, morality and social peace. Aware of the need to combat infidelity in populous areas which the church had failed to reach, his government established a new see at Manchester in 1847. In search of a more intellectually flexible religious leadership, he systematically promoted learned and liberal men to bishoprics and deaneries. In 1850, Royal Commissions dominated by liberal-minded clerics and Fellows were appointed to review the structure and teaching of Oxford and Cambridge universities.

Even in these fields, though, expectations were not realized. Russell was never able to break down the hostility of Tory and radical ratepayers to the more systematic extension of state influence over education, to which he envisaged the 1846–7 changes as a prelude. Similarly, ratepayer pressure led London MPs to agitate successfully to get the metropolis excluded from the Public Health Act 1848, while in other towns there was great hostility to the General Board of Health which the Act set up to monitor local conscientiousness in sanitary matters. Meanwhile, Russell's church policy, especially his appointment of the heterodox Oxford Professor R.D. Hampden to be Bishop of Hereford, inflamed High Church insecurity, which was building up for other reasons into a campaign for more ecclesiastical freedom from state interference. This response then led Russell to stigmatize Tractarian High Churchmen as Roman Catholics in his emotional but counter-productive and impolitic Durham Letter of late 1850. It was counter-productive because the furore mobilized High Churchmen further, so that they soon succeeded in their campaign to revive convocation as the church's own discussion forum. And it was impolitic because Russell's objects in writing the Letter – the attack on Tractarianism, and the purely symbolic restatement of the state's sovereignty in ecclesiastical matters in reaction to the announcement of the pope's establishment of a Catholic hierarchy – did not coincide with the popular reaction to the pope's action. Fuelled by Bonfire Night hysteria, 5 per cent of the English population petitioned for the repeal of the papal enactment. Russell, who had spent much of his career preaching tolerance to Catholicism, could and would not satisfy this feeling; in effect, his Ecclesiastical Titles Act 1851 merely reasserted the state's nominal sovereignty. So he left fervent Protestants with the impression that he was not a trustworthy defender of English values, while his Letter antagonized Irish MPs whose support he badly needed.

This was a sad end to Russell's attempt to give Ireland good government – an attempt which had been derailed by the Irish famine even before he took office. He had hoped to reconcile the powerful Catholic clergy to the government, and reduce their dependence on the peasantry, by offering them state financial support. And he had sought economic modernization, in order to eliminate the gross inefficiency in agricultural organization which left the country so pauperized, vulnerable to famine and discontented. But the terrible famine of 1845–7 raised the spectre of mass starvation. The Treasury extended aid to the existing landlords, and then liberalized the Poor Law in 1847, in an attempt to stabilize the countryside. While this extra aid could not be generous enough to prevent severe suffering, it made it impossible to proceed very far with economic restructuring. Then the return of Irish political agitation in late 1847 severely embarrassed Russell. He was reluctant to resort to coercion, but the cabinet agreed to suspend *habeas corpus* when faced with a fully fledged repeal movement in 1848. Russell's response was to urge a programme of remedial measures to win the affection of the people. The Irish electorate was greatly increased by an Act of 1850, and in 1849 something was done towards encouraging a transfer of estate ownership to landlords who might sink capital into improving the land and consolidating tenancies. But most of Russell's ideas, including his plan to subsidize the priests, had to be abandoned owing to lukewarmness in the cabinet and party. This reverse severely dented his authority.

Russell was criticized more generally for not projecting the image of command which Peel had conveyed. Lacking a real majority, his government seemed always to be withdrawing and revising its proposals in line with factional criticism, whether on the sugar duties, the navigation laws, hours of factory labour or public health legislation. This apparent weakness was most awkward in the taxation field. Government financial policy was handicapped by its reliance on the income tax – in the absence of tariffs – and yet the need to keep defence expenditure high in the fraught international circumstances of the late 1840s. Unfortunately, radicals stridently criticized official extravagance, as did the Chartists, and urged tax and spending reductions in order to revive the economy and secure social harmony. Protectionists, meanwhile, were unsympathetic to income tax in order to demonstrate the need to restore tariffs. Yet economic depression had reduced revenues. In 1848, the government had to present no fewer than four budgetary statements before its proposals were accepted. The 1851 budget was also badly mauled.

It was partly in order to respond to radical and Chartist criticism of the government that Russell decided to take up the parliamentary reform issue again. He wanted to rally liberal forces in and outside parliament behind a bold invigorating cause. He sought to reassure the respectable working classes about the responsiveness of Liberal government. And he hoped to arrest the ugly class division between land and trade caused by the emergence of a Protectionist landed interest party. The initiative would also assert his own vision of the future of Liberalism in opposition to the Peelite approach – legislative conservatism and mere fiscal expertise. But Russell's supporters were deeply divided on the desirability of further Reform. Many radicals pressed hard for it, and in fact the government resigned briefly in 1851 after being defeated on Locke King's proposal to equalize the English county and borough franchises. But the consensus in the cabinet and among the Peelites was that reform was unnecessary and destabilizing. Russell tried to persuade the cabinet to take up reform in 1849, but he could not get it to allow him to bring in a Bill before 1852. Then, the lack of party enthusiasm was one cause of the government's resignation. The immediate reason for it was defeat on a Militia Bill, which the recently dismissed Palmerston used as his 'tit-for-tat' with Russell. But the underlying explanation was a consensus in parliament that Russell's government had lost all momentum and authority – a view which he seems to have shared.

In the aftermath of the government's fall, Palmerston and the Peelites both sought to gain control of the direction of the anti-Protectionist forces in parliament. Both did so by suggesting that Russell was a less effective leader of those forces than they were. One way of arguing this, particularly favoured by the Peelites, was to point to his apparent lack of administrative command. But the best way of undermining Russell was to portray his circle as exclusively aristocratic and patronage-seeking, dependent on a few grasping family networks, and therefore incapable of offering classless and efficient rule. This was a severe embarrassment in the climate of the 1850s. Russell was undoubtedly damaged by his cold personal manner and his anxiety to show that aristocrats could offer national leadership (in 1846 he had appointed eight peers – including his father-in-law – and an heir to an earldom to a cabinet of sixteen). His dismissal of Palmerston in 1851 had played into the hands of these critics by suggesting that he was a Court stooge who was willing to abort Palmerston's liberal and populist foreign policy.

But this was not the main reason why Russell was now superseded as the leading politician on the anti-conservative side of politics. Rather, it was because so many MPs found him too radical – on parliamentary reform, on state interference with ratepayer autonomy on social questions, and in his activist approach to legislation. Since the political situation forced Liberals and Peelites to attempt to work together, it was generally agreed that Russell was too partisan to head such a coalition; the Peelite Aberdeen was appointed prime minister instead, in

December 1852. Yet Russell was still the leader of the largest element in that coalition; he was committed to further constitutional and educational reform; and he was very sensitive about his demotion from the premiership. The next seven years were very painful for him. Every time he asserted his position, he damaged the coalition, yet almost always damaged his own character more. He ended up overthrowing Aberdeen in 1855 and Palmerston, the new prime minister, in 1857 and 1858, but not advancing his own position. Parliamentary and education reform made insignificant progress. Britain was sucked into a terrible war in 1854, and Russell's private and public criticism of the coalition's mismanagement of it, though patriotic, looked selfish and, on the occasion of his two resignations of 1855, arguably treacherous. Even so, when the coalition returned to power in 1859 on more secure foundations, he might well have become prime minister, had parliamentary reform dominated the political agenda – as it did briefly in 1858–9. Unfortunately, the Italian question intruded, and Palmerston was appointed instead. Russell accepted the foreign secretaryship, taking great pride in promoting the cause of Italian liberty over the following eighteen months. Though Palmerston allowed Russell to bring in another Reform Bill in 1860, it received a lukewarm reception and was withdrawn. Russell accepted defeat. Aware that he lacked the opportunity, free time and, increasingly, stamina to resist Palmerston's dominance in the Commons, he took a peerage in 1861 when he was left a modicum of Irish property in his brother's will.

Russell's second premiership, on Palmerston's death in October 1865, lasted just nine months. Past commitments required him to put parliamentary reform at the head of his programme; so did the prospects for social reform, which would be small without the galvanizing impetus of a reformed parliament. Yet the party which he inherited from Palmerston contained many fainthearted reformers, who protested at his radical appointments (ironically, given the earlier criticism of his aristocratic leanings) and at his refusal to refer the reform question to the scrapheap of a ponderous Royal Commission. In the 1866 session, Russell was often justifiably pessimistic about the chances of his Bill, in the face of right-wing liberal hostility. In April he commented that he felt he had 'done my duty' – to the past and the future – simply by introducing it. When the government was finally defeated on it in June, he resigned. In 1867, he proposed parliamentary resolutions urging radical reform of the Irish Church and the British educational system. Then, having done his best to lay down a programme for the next liberal government, he told Gladstone in December that he was retiring as party leader. He never held office again.

Russell's career is open to misinterpretation because of his personal and familial vanity, his preference for aristocratic colleagues, and his habit of justifying his actions by reference to the principles of past generations of Whigs. These tendencies allowed contemporaries to portray him as a less innovative leader than he was. In fact he was responsible – sometimes single-handedly – for maintaining momentum behind the great causes of early and mid-Victorian Liberalism: parliamentary, religious, Irish, social and educational reform. Historians, taking his successor Gladstone as the norm for a Liberal leader, have criticized his neglect of the arts of popularity and his deliberate superciliousness towards the press, which did him real damage by inflaming the vanity of the great *Times* editor John Delane against him. But Russell believed that the arousal of popular sympathy for Liberal candidates was essentially a matter for local, not national politicians. His job was to guide those returned as MPs to support constructive, libertarian and moral causes. His success in doing this in the 1830s and 1840s entitles him to one of the two or three most prominent places in the Liberal pantheon. Though his personal failings help to explain why his triumphs were not greater or longer-lasting, it was mainly the conservatism of the reformed parliament which let him down thereafter. Even so, he did as much to create the Liberal agenda of 1868–74 as Gladstone – who should have the last word. Reading Russell's biography in 1889, he commented that it 'takes two volumes – Palmerston's occupies five. But Lord John's place in British history is five times as great' (Fitzmaurice 1905: i, 93).

References and further reading

Bagehot, W. (1907 edn) *Biographical Studies*, ed. R.H. Hutton, London: Longmans.

Brent, R. (1987) *Liberal Anglican Politics: Whiggery, Religion and Reform, 1830–41*, Oxford: Clarendon Press. (Excellent analysis of the politics of religion in the 1830s, and of Russell's contribution. Good on his religious and historical thought.)

Chadwick, O. (1966) *The Victorian Church*, vol. 1, London: A. and C. Black. (Includes an important long chapter on the crisis in the church coinciding with, and partly provoked by, Russell's first premiership.)

Fitzmaurice, Lord E. (1905) *The Life of Granville George Leveson Gower, Second Earl Granville, 1815–1891*, 2 vols, London: Longmans.

Gladstone, W.E. (1890) 'The Melbourne government: its acts and persons', *Nineteenth Century* 27: 38–55.

Gooch, G.P. (ed.) (1925) *The Later Correspondence of Lord John Russell, 1840–1878*, 2 vols, London: Longmans.

MacCarthy, D. and Russell, A. (1910) *Lady John Russell: A Memoir with Selections from her Diaries and Correspondence*, London: Methuen.

Mandler, P. (1990) *Aristocratic Government in the Age of Reform: Whigs and Liberals, 1830–1852*, Oxford: Clarendon Press. (An enjoyable and bold treatment of conflict within the Liberal party on domestic issues; takes Russell refreshingly seriously as a social reformer.)

Newbould, I. (1990) *Whiggery and Reform, 1830–41: The Politics of Government*, London: Macmillan. (A careful, full-length modern account of the governments of the 1830s.)

Parry, J. (1993) *The Rise and Fall of Liberal Government in Victorian Britain*, New Haven, CT: Yale University Press. (A rare modern overview of the development of nineteenth-century parliamentary liberalism. Places Russell's contribution higher than does the run of previous historiography.)

—— (1996) 'Past and future in the later career of Lord John Russell', in T. Blanning and D. Cannadine (eds) *History and biography: essays in honour of Derek Beales*, Cambridge: Cambridge University Press.

Prest, J. (1972) *Lord John Russell*, London: Macmillan. (The only post-war biography: it provides new depth on many issues, but is weak on Russell's political outlook, copious writings and later career, and is not designed to rescue his reputation from its long decline.)

Reddaway, W. (1926) 'Lord John Russell', in F. Hearnshaw (ed.) *The Political Principles of Some Notable Prime Ministers of the Nineteenth Century*, London: Macmillan.

Russell, John, Earl (1875) *Recollections and Suggestions*, London: Longmans. (Russell's own memoirs, but written when his powers of memory and argument were fading. A partial and disorganized treatment.)

Russell, R. (ed.) (1913) *Early Correspondence of Lord John Russell, 1805–40*, 2 vols, London: T. Fisher Unwin.

Smith, F. (1966) *The Making of the Second Reform Bill*, Cambridge: Cambridge University Press. (The fullest and clearest account of its subject.)

Walpole, S. (1889) *The Life of Lord John Russell*, 2 vols, London: Longmans. (The definitive Victorian double-decker.)

Jonathan Parry

Edward George Geoffrey Smith Stanley, Fourteenth Earl of Derby

Born 29 March 1799, eldest child of Edward Smith Stanley, thirteenth Earl of Derby, and of Charlotte Margaret Hornby. Educated at Eton and Christ Church, Oxford. Married 1825 Emma Caroline, second daughter of Edward Bootle Wilbraham, later the first Lord Skelmersdale. MP for Stockbridge 1822–6, Preston 1826–30, Windsor 1831–2, North Lancashire 1832–44. Under-Secretary of State for the Colonies 1827; Chief Secretary for Ireland 1830–3; Secretary of State for the Colonies 1833–4 and 1841–4. Ennobled in father's barony of Stanley 1844; succeeded to earldom 1851. Prime Minister February – December 1852, 1858–9 and 1866–8. Died 23 October 1869.

Writers on the formative years of the modern Conservative party in the nineteenth century have tended to debate the relative importance of its leaders, Peel and Disraeli, as determinants of the party's philosophy and as founders of modern conservatism, with barely a nod in the direction of Derby. Yet he was three times a Conservative prime minister, albeit briefly on each occasion. In his last premiership, moreover, he presided over the passing of the second electoral Reform Act in 1867 – that 'leap in the dark' which trebled the size of the British electorate. In the Lords from October 1844, he led the Conservative party in both Houses of parliament through long periods of frustrating opposition. When Disraeli unveiled a statue of him in Parliament Square in July 1874, he allegedly summed up Derby's career with 'He abolished slavery, he educated Ireland, he reformed parliament'. Perhaps the key to Derby's somewhat low-key image as a Conservative leader lies in his having secured the first two of these three political objectives as a Whig cabinet minister.

Edward Stanley (henceforward given as 'Derby') was born heir to one of the oldest earldoms (1485) and to one of the greatest landed estates in Britain. On succession to the earldom, he is thought to have inherited a debt of half a million pounds. His descendant, the eighteenth earl, was to leave over £43 million at his death in November 1994. On Derby's death in 1869, however, he was like his father to leave a mound of debt, around £680,000, to his son, who guessed he would need fourteen years and considerable domestic economies to clear it (Vincent 1978: 344). These substantial debts appear to have arisen from wildly unbusinesslike estate management as well as from extensive racing expenditure. Although none of his horses won any of the great classic races, Derby was not entirely unsuccessful as a racehorse owner: until his stud was sold in 1863 he may have won as much as £92,000 in stakes. He was also a considerable and forward-thinking philanthropist, being renowned in the 1850s for his schemes of social welfare for the cottagers on his north-east of England estate – with contributions from employee and employer intended to ensure that no one went to the work-house or had to seek charity (Vincent 1978: 380–1). He headed the Lancashire Relief Association. At Knowsley, he received the same medical attention as his cottagers. Dr Gorst, his local doctor, was paid £300 a year to attend the poor gratis. Derby was also generous to the poor in his London parish through the rector of St James's, Piccadilly.

In 1822 Derby was elected a Whig MP, and though it was two years before he made his maiden speech his oratorical skills were thereafter quickly recognized: in the Commons he was known as the 'Darling of Debate'. In his prime, he was often described as 'dashing'. By 1827 he was in office and his evident administrative skills led to rapid ministerial promotion. Yet the development of his later political career was not to be easy. From the 1850s he was badly affected by what was assumed to be gout, which was often particularly bad at crucial political moments. Given his great wealth and recurrent ill-health, his willingness to lead his party for long periods in opposition is somewhat surprising – particularly as he volunteered to be elevated to the Lords in 1844 in advance of his father's death, a move which suggested to his contemporaries a gradual withdrawal from the political limelight.

For the first twenty years of his parliamentary career, Derby's political allegiance reflected the fluidity of contemporary party sympathies and structures: sometimes he characterized himself as a Whig liberal, at others as 'an old consti-tutional Whig'. He could certainly be described in this period as a conservative reformer. He came to ministerial office in a period of great political volatility. With other Whigs, he found himself able to support George Canning and accepted from him the under-secretaryship for the colonies, thereby cutting his teeth on problems of colonial administration. Having refused to serve under Wellington in 1828, he became a member of Grey's government in 1830 as Chief Secretary for Ireland and had clearly established himself by then as a major figure in the Commons. He soon seemed destined to become the next leader of the House, having shown himself as the government's principal and most effective spokesman on Irish matters. While the Commons were preoccupied with the passing of parliamentary reform, Derby was constructing a new policy for Ireland in the crucial early years following Catholic emancipation in 1829. The most significant of the Irish legislation he steered through parliament was the Education Act 1831, which established an Irish board of national education and gave children of all religious denominations opportunity to attend government-assisted schools. Having thus proved his capacity as an administrator, he was promoted to Secretary of State for the Colonies and embarked at once on busi-nesslike groundwork for the abolition of slavery, which was achieved in August 1833. Before that Bill came into force, however, he had with others left the government over Russell's proposed appropriation of Irish church lands for lay purposes. Derby feared the pressure of militant radicalism and dissenting religion – which seemed to have flourished in the wake of electoral reform – and with his defection the Whigs lost one of their ablest ministers and certainly their best debater. Disraeli was never to forget a curious conversation he had in 1834 with Lord Melbourne, who had discouraged him from hoping to become prime minister:

> No chance of that in our time. It is all arranged and settled. . . . Nobody can compete with Stanley. . . . If you are going to enter politics and mean to stick to it, I dare say you will do very well, for you have the ability and enterprise; and if you are careful how you steer, no doubt you will get into some port at last. But you must put all those foolish notions out of your head; they won't do at all. Stanley will be the next prime minister, you will see.
>
> (Torrens 1890: 275)

Disraeli was to serve three times under Derby as prime minister. Derby was never to rejoin the Whigs, though Palmerston kept up contacts with him and at times hinted at the possibility of ministerial office – in rather the same way as Derby himself occasionally approached Gladstone in the 1850s. Aberdeen also made a number of ministerial offers to him, largely in the hope of circumventing Palmerston.

For some years Derby was to speak and vote as an independent member, but, although Peel failed in 1835 to persuade him and other former colleagues of Grey to join his ministry, he began to move towards the Conservative party. His rest-lessness reflected the fluidity of party structure in the 1820s and 1830s. For a brief period in 1834 he had toyed with the idea of collaborating with Graham to create a separate, more whiggish grouping soon nicknamed the 'Derby Dilly', but by July 1835 he had been sufficiently impressed by signs of Peel's progressive Tory policies to sit with his supporters in the Commons. The support of such a talented MP was eventually rewarded by the offer of the Colonial Office again in 1841, this time at the hands of Peel, now prime minister, triumphant after a clear election victory. Derby settled back into his old office and in 1834 supported the Canadian Corn Bill, which was unpopular with the Conservative party's protectionist wing. It was his brilliant speech which saved Peel after Disraeli had achieved a successful vote against him on colonial duties in 1844. His defence in the Commons of the government's Irish policy also proved invaluable. Strong debating skills were also needed by the government in the Lords, and Derby asked to be elevated early on the grounds of his deteriorating health: he was also to a certain extent discouraged by his somewhat difficult relationship with Peel. Peel agreed reluctantly to his request. In the Lords, Derby's shifting views became apparent when he argued against immediate free trade, though he eventually agreed to the suspension of the Corn Laws because of the Irish famine. He became increasingly unhappy with Peel's commercial policy and its implications for the landed interest, and his break with him came with Peel's declaration in favour of the complete and immediate repeal of the Corn Laws. Derby had no intention of pursuing the kind of policy which he had felt to be unacceptable as a Whig over a decade earlier.

Although initially somewhat suspicious of the disaffected wing of the party, Derby was to lead the new protectionist Conservative party which emerged after the split with Peel and his supporters over the repeal of the Corn Laws. Both Derby and Peel later regretted their separation in 1845. Derby was particularly saddened to have parted from Graham, his closest political ally from Canningite days, whose career had closely followed Derby's political moves and who had gradually acquired a substantial administrative reputation. Peel did his best to keep the talented remains of his party together after the defections, and the 1847 election indicated the weakness of the protectionist powerbase. Stanley's leadership of the breakaway protectionist party remained unchallenged, but his absence from the Commons proved a serious disadvantage until Disraeli finally emerged as its leader there in 1849 and Peel died in 1850. It was becoming clear that the new party under Derby would no longer press for the reintroduction of protection despite constant sniping from the agricultural interest. Disraeli began work on a scheme for agricultural relief. In the main, for the next decade and a half, the persistence of whiggish administrations supported by the remaining able Peelites ensured the neutralization of pressures from a lively group of radical members and the consequent marginalization of the protectionists. A reunion of the protectionists with the Peelites was not unthinkable, especially in the Lords. On the resignation in February 1851 of the Whig government, after a defeat in a Commons division on parliamentary reform at the hands of its radical supporters, Derby was given the opportunity to form a government. But his approach to Gladstone was rebuffed and the attempt failed. The Duke of Wellington spread around his opinion of the current state of the parties as expressed to the Queen:

> There are two sections of the Conservative party: on one side officers without men, on the other men without officers. He had thought the best thing they could do was to unite and form an army, but since personal differences prevented this, nothing remained except to recall their predecessors.
>
> (Vincent 1978: 52)

It was to be again the inherent weakness of the Whig government, dependent as it was on disparate elements, which in February 1852 provided Derby – having by now succeeded his father – with his second, this time successful, chance to form a protectionist administration. Its ineffectiveness as a minority government was neutralized temporarily by divisions among the Whigs and their radical supporters. By the summer Derby had been forced to concede a dissolution and, though left in a minority by the July election, soldiered on until defeated in December on the budget. It was by now clear that the policy of protection had been abandoned. Several attempts to mobilize support from Palmerston or from the remaining Peelites had failed. This volatile and complex balance of political forces continued till Palmerston was installed as prime minister in 1859. On the defeat in February 1858 of the Whig government on Palmerston's Conspiracy to Murder Bill – provoked by the Orsini plot against the French emperor – Derby was presented with another opportunity to form a government, but again in a minority in the Commons. Derby as Leader of the Commons and Chancellor of the Exchequer worked hard to co-ordinate support and, despite lack of success in the 1859 election, the government did not resign until narrowly defeated over its policy to Italy in June. Its introduction of a moderate bill to equalize the county and borough franchises indicated that Derby's attitude to electoral reform had substantially shifted from his somewhat diehard youthful resistance. The error of judgement on the part of both Disraeli and Derby, which had produced a narrow defeat rather than a small majority, may partly be explained by Derby's increasing ill-health. Malmesbury, his Foreign Secretary and particular victim of the defeat, believed that Derby 'wished to resign, worn out by repeated attacks of gout and the toil of office, and was indifferent to continuing the struggle' (Malmesbury 1884: ii, 189). Derby certainly withdrew from active participation in the Lords, which became, wrote Lord Campbell, 'quite dull, without mighty divisions and interesting "party logomachy"' (Hardcastle 1881: ii, 446). But as long as he could get to pre-session meetings and maintain a general surveillance of developments, Derby felt it reasonable to remain leader.

The new Palmerston government of 1859 was to survive until 1865, largely as a result of the informal agreement by Derby that his party would support the government as long as it pursued acceptable conservative policies. This it did. In this way the radicals were outflanked and greater political stability was established, if of a somewhat conservative nature. The agreement seems to have been renewed yearly, and inevitably proved frustrating for Conservative peers with political ambitions as well as for Disraeli and his supporters in the Commons. In these years, Derby showed within and outside parliament concern for national social welfare which reflected his attitudes to his own tenants. His support for the poor who were to be evicted by the constructors of metropolitan railways, and his work for the Lancashire cotton operatives who were made redundant by the interruption of cotton supplies from America as a result of the Civil War, derived from his own personal concern as well as from a fear of the rioting which economic distress might provoke. By 1864 Palmerston's great age was clearly affecting the strength of his leadership and Derby was amusing himself by drafting lists of possible Conservative cabinets. Depressed by the increased majority which Palmerston achieved in the 1865 general election, he came to think a future Conservative majority unattainable. All was transformed by the death of Palmerston in October 1865.

The assumption of power by Russell with a more radical cabinet led to greater ideological polarization. And yet, ironically, it was the Conservative government under Derby which was to achieve major legislation for extensive electoral reform. Derby came to power for a third time in 1866 with the support of the anti-reforming Whigs on a wrecking amendment to Russell's government's Reform Bill. These Whigs were soon to be disillusioned when the Conservatives, out of office for nearly eight years, moved towards electoral reform within six months of again forming a minority government. Derby retained the leadership despite his steadily deteriorating health and the changing nature of the party. In his ministerial statement on taking office, he indicated how far he had travelled – 'Nothing, certainly, would give me greater pleasure than to see a very considerable portion of the class now excluded admitted to the franchise' – but cautioned that he would not introduce a Bill without good chance of its passing both Houses.

In the event Derby's deteriorating health meant that Disraeli had to carry most of the responsibility for difficult political management in the months preceding the passing of the second Reform Act in 1867. Yet his involvement at crucial stages in the tortuous parliamentary manoeuvrings which led from some highly complex resolutions to a relatively simple Bill was crucial in bringing wide support from the party in the Lords and the Commons behind the government's changing proposals. His backing at an early stage for household suffrage was vital, though he was uneasy with the constant twists and turns the proposals took as they passed through the Commons. In thanking the Lords after the Bill's passing, he acknowledged the risk of its uncertain future effects – 'a great experiment and "taking a leap in the dark"' – while trusting in 'the sound sense of my fellow-countrymen'. All ratepaying householders could now vote, as could £10 lodgers in the boroughs and £12 occupiers in the counties. It was Derby's last and greatest achievement.

References and further reading

Cowling, M. (1967) *1867: Disraeli, Gladstone and Revolution: The Passing of the Second Reform Act*, Cambridge: Cambridge University Press. (An exemplar of the 1960s 'High Politics' school. Excellent on the associated wheeling and dealing.)

Hardcastle, Hon. Mrs (1881) *Life of John, Lord Campbell*, 2 vols, London: John Murray.

Jones, W. (1956) *Lord Derby and Victorian Conservatism*, Oxford: Blackwell.

Malmesbury, Earl of (1884) *Memoirs of an Ex-Minister*, 2 vols, London: Longman.

Smith, F. (1966) *The Making of the Second Reform Bill*, Cambridge: Cambridge University Press. (The clearest account of the complex manoeuvrings and parliamentary procedure.)

Stewart, R. (1971) *The Politics of Protection: Lord Derby and the Protectionist Party, 1841–52*, Cambridge: Cambridge University Press.

Torrens, W. (ed.) (1890) *Memoirs of Viscount Melbourne*, London: Ward Lock.

Vincent, J.R. (ed.) (1978) *Disraeli, Derby and the Conservative Party: Journals of Lord Stanley, 1849–1869*, New York: Barnes & Noble. (Crucial diary by his son who was also heavily involved in political events between 1850 and 1869.)

Valerie Cromwell

George Gordon (later Hamilton-Gordon), Fourth Earl of Aberdeen

Born Edinburgh 28 January 1784, eldest child of George, Lord Haddo, and Charlotte Baird. Educated at Harrow and St John's College, Cambridge. Married (1) 1805 Lady Catherine Hamilton (died 1812), eldest daughter of the First Marquess of Abercorn; (2) 1815 Lady Hamilton (née Harriet Douglas) (died 1833), the widow of the Marquess of Abercorn's heir. Succeeded to the Scottish title of Earl of Aberdeen on the death of his grandfather in 1801. Travelled extensively in the Near East 1803–4. Elected a Representative Peer for Scotland 1806, 1807 and 1812. British Ambassador to Austria 1813–14. In 1815 created Viscount Gordon in the United Kingdom peerage. Chancellor of the Duchy of Lancaster 1828; Secretary of State for Foreign Affairs 1828–30; Secretary of State for War and the Colonies 1834–5; Secretary of State for Foreign Affairs 1841–6; Prime Minister 1852–5. Knight of the Thistle 1808; Knight of the Garter 1855. Died London 14 December 1860.

As prime minister when Britain entered the Crimean War in 1854, Aberdeen's reputation has been blighted by the lack of military success. He had bitter enemies, including Disraeli, and came to be regarded as a weak, inefficient and cold man. His whole career is often read backwards with this reputation in mind, overlooking the fact that he was the trusted colleague and friend of Wellington and Peel, both good judges of men, and among politicians was regarded as a safe pair of hands – in contrast to the unpredictable Palmerston. The charge of coldness is not surprising. He was always unable to project himself to the public. This was his great weakness in his contests with Palmerston. The private man was very different. As a young man he had been an adventurous traveller and a member of a brilliant group at Bentley Priory. Personal tragedies made him draw into himself but he remained a devoted family man, warmly regarded by an inner circle of friends and well-liked by the tenants on his Scottish estates.

Aberdeen's entry into English politics owed much to chance. The Gordons of Haddo had not previously played a major role in Westminster politics – though his grandfather, the third Earl, had some thwarted ambitions to do so. But when, in April 1791, George's father died in a riding accident, his mother quarrelled with his grandfather and took her seven young children to England. There she sought the protection of Henry Dundas, later Lord Melville. She died in 1795 but the children remained in England and, through Dundas, came to the attention of William Pitt the Younger, then prime minister. At the age of 14 George, now Lord Haddo, exercised his right under Scottish law to choose his own 'curators' or guardians and named Pitt and Dundas. Pitt remained Aberdeen's hero to the end of his long life and firmly implanted in him the idea that he must pursue a political career.

When the third Earl died in 1801, his successor was dismayed to discover the neglected condition of his estates. But Aberdeen was not yet of age (21 in those days) and there was little he could do immediately. Instead, he took advantage of the Peace of Amiens to embark on the grand tour in the company of two slightly older friends, Hudson Gurney of the banking family and the Reverend George Whittington. Whittington was writing a remarkable history of the development of Gothic architecture, which Aberdeen completed after his friend's untimely death in 1807. Aberdeen was not content with the conventional grand tour but accompanied a fellow Scotsman, William Drummond, to Constantinople, where Drummond was to succeed Lord Elgin as British Ambassador. Tiring of Constantinople, he embarked on an exploration of the Ottoman empire, through Asia Minor, looking for the site of Troy, and then through Greece. It was then a dangerous undertaking, and what evidence survives suggests that his archaeological excavations were unusually sophisticated for the time. It was from this period of his life that he gained the soubriquet 'Athenian Aberdeen', bestowed sarcastically by his cousin, the poet Lord Byron, in his *English Bards and Scotch Reviewers*. On his return he contributed articles to the *Edinburgh Review* and wrote an introduction to William Wilkins's new edition of Vitruvius' *De Architectura*. From 1812 until 1846 he was President of the Society of Antiquities and, when out of office, a very active one.

He was now of age and set about reforming his neglected estates according to all the best contemporary models; yet he also had an active social life in London, frequenting Devonshire House, Holland House and, above all, Bentley Priory (their differing politics plainly counting for little). At Bentley Priory he fell deeply in love with Catherine Hamilton. It was an idyllic marriage but, after three daughters, Catherine gave birth to a son who lived only an hour. Catherine had contracted tuberculosis, and her death in 1812 shattered Aberdeen, who wore mourning for the rest of his life. He spent years nursing, in a way extraordinary for a nineteenth-century father, his three daughters, who had all inherited the condition. In 1815 he entered into what was essentially a marriage of convenience with the widowed Lady Hamilton. Aberdeen became the guardian and surrogate father of Lord Abercorn's infant grandson and heir, and administered the Abercorn estates in Ireland as well as his own Scottish estates. The marriage produced four sons, who survived, and one more daughter, who died. Harriet herself died in 1833. He was, as Princess Lieven once remarked, the most unfortunate of men and the more deeply scarred because he could not bring himself to speak of his tragedies.

His public life too had been dogged by misfortune. In 1806 William Pitt unexpectedly died, ending his hopes of political patronage. Pitt had promised him a United Kingdom peerage – his Scottish peerage did not automatically carry a seat in the Lords. Instead, Aberdeen had to fight an election to become one of the sixteen Scottish representative peers. Although he did remarkably well, being the only candidate not on the King's List (that is, not supported by the government) to be elected in 1806, he hated electioneering and the desire to establish a case for a United Kingdom peerage was a factor in his accepting the Embassy to Austria in 1813. He never became at ease in speaking in parliament, but played an active part on committees and kept a watchful eye on Scottish questions. The offer of the Vienna Embassy in 1813 was not as surprising as some historians have supposed. He was already an established politician, and though only 29 it was a young man's world: Metternich, the Austrian chancellor, was only 33.

Aberdeen caught up with the Court of the Austrian Emperor, Francis I, at Teplitz (Teplice) on 3 September 1813, and wrote to his sister-in-law, Maria Hamilton, that 'the whole road from Prague to this place was covered with waggons full of wounded, dead and dying. The shock, and disgust, and pity produced by such scenes are beyond what I could have supposed possible at a distance.' This revulsion was reinforced by what he saw after the battle of Leipzig, even though that was an Allied victory. Apart from Wellington, Aberdeen was the only nineteenth-century British prime minister to have seen a battlefield, and a sense of the horror of war never left him.

His first diplomatic assignment to help to create and finance a grand coalition against Napoleon, which would not fall apart as all the previous coalitions had done, was difficult enough. The monarchs of Europe were on campaign, creating something like a permanent summit conference in which Britain was very under-represented. Aberdeen's two fellow ambassadors, Lord Cathcart – who was accredited to Russia – and Lord Stewart – to Prussia – were soldiers, and the three men got on badly together. In the end Lord Castlereagh, the Foreign Secretary, had to come out to represent Britain. Nevertheless, Aberdeen's achievements should not be underestimated. Britain had been isolated from continental affairs from 1809 until Napoleon's invasion of Russia in 1812. Castlereagh still feared, with good reason, that Russia, Austria and Prussia would make a 'Continental Peace' with Napoleon that ignored British interests. Aberdeen formed a friendship with Metternich and re-established Britain in the counsels of Europe. Although Castlereagh was satisfied with his performance and anxious that he should accompany him to the Congress of Vienna, Aberdeen wished to return home.

He secured his United Kingdom peerage, remarried and concentrated on his private life, including the care of his delicate daughters – though he still spoke fairly regularly in the Lords. He may have been invited to take office when Liverpool's government was reconstituted in 1822, but he did not accept it until Wellington became prime minister in 1828. He initially became Chancellor of the Duchy of Lancaster, with the understanding that he would assist Lord Dudley at the Foreign Office. Dudley was known to be incompetent but could not be removed until the Canningites resigned from the government in May, when Aberdeen became Foreign Secretary.

The two great issues were the war of Greek independence against the Ottoman empire and the civil war in Portugal. Wellington and Aberdeen worked closely together. On Portugal Aberdeen agreed with Wellington's judgement that what they were witnessing was simply a civil war between 'two brothers of the House of Braganza', Pedro and Miguel, whose politics did not greatly differ, and that it did not therefore much matter to Britain who won – unlike Palmerston who believed that Pedro represented the cause of Portuguese liberalism and must be supported. On Greece Aberdeen and Wellington disagreed, though Aberdeen had to conform his policy to that of the prime minister. Wellington, with his background of service in India, was mainly impressed by the dangers which would follow the collapse of the Ottoman empire and the probable increase of Russian power in the Eastern Mediterranean, and wished to keep Greek gains to a minimum. Aberdeen, with his first-hand knowledge of Greece, was much more sympathetic to the Greek cause. Just before Wellington's ministry fell, the restored Bourbons were overthrown in France. Wellington and Aberdeen were agreed that the new government of Louis Philippe must be recognized to ensure French stability. They also summoned the London Conference to adjudicate on Belgium's revolt against the Dutch rule imposed by the Congress of Vienna, although it was left to Aberdeen's successor, Palmerston, to carry on the intricate negotiations for the next nine years.

Aberdeen returned to office as Secretary of State for War and the Colonies in Peel's brief administration of 1834–5. He professed himself bored by the office, particularly the patronage aspects, but ran it with his usual competence. His next period in office, as Peel's Foreign Secretary from 1841 to 1846, was certainly the time of his most solid achievements, and in political circles his reputation stood much higher than that of Palmerston. Palmerston had left the country teetering on the brink of war with both France and the United States, reviving memories of the coalition of 1779. Palmerston was convinced that his policies would have triumphed everywhere, but his optimism was not universally shared. The quarrel with France had centred on the Eastern Question and the issues which provoked it had mostly been resolved before Palmerston left office, although bad feeling remained. The quarrels with America – mainly about the Canadian border and the actions of British warships in intercepting slaving ships, which were prone to hoist the American flag illegally – were still acute. Aberdeen sent Lord Ashburton on a special mission to Washington which succeeded in resolving most of the issues. Palmerston launched an unsuccessful campaign to condemn Aberdeen for surrendering British interests. In fact, on the 'North East Boundary', between Maine and New Brunswick, Britain probably got a very good bargain. This was less true of the Oregon boundary, west of the Rocky Mountains, which was not resolved until 1846. Here Britain probably had the better historic claim but American settlers were already entering the area. Having restored relations with the United States to something like normal, Aberdeen pursued a policy of co-operation with France which came to be dubbed the *entente cordiale* – the phrase was actually coined at Haddo House in the autumn of 1843. Understanding with France was traditionally a Whig rather than a Tory policy and even Peel had reservations, but Aberdeen was convinced that his close personal relations with the French prime minister and Foreign Secretary, François Guizot, were important for the stability of both Europe and France. Queen Victoria enthusiastically co-operated and a number of royal visits were exchanged. At times the *entente* came under severe strain, particularly in 1844 when the French, pursuing Algerian rebels, bombarded Tangier, which was the supply base for Gibraltar, and the French annexed Tahiti, where Britain had missionary and other interests, and imprisoned the British Consul. Peel co-operated with Aberdeen in calming the public excitement, which could have brought the two countries to the verge of war. By this time, however, Peel was listening to Wellington, who believed that there was a real threat from France and that Britain must look to its own defences. Peel and Aberdeen vigorously debated the truth or otherwise of the old adage, 'If you wish for peace, prepare for war', but Peel refused to accept Aberdeen's resignation on the grounds that he was indispensable as Foreign Secretary.

Peel's ministry finally fell on the Corn Law question in 1846. Aberdeen had steadily supported Peel and, together with most other cabinet ministers and leaders of the party, remained loyal to him, forming the group known as the Peelites – though the majority of the party supported Lord Stanley (later Lord Derby) and were for a time known as the Protectionists. Peel was clear that he had no intention of taking office again, and Stanley made a number of attempts to reunite the two wings of the party. He particularly targeted Aberdeen, who was not unresponsive, because he had no other potential Foreign Secretary. Aberdeen was partly influenced by his anxiety at the policy of Palmerston, who had once again succeeded him.

The French *entente* quickly broke down. During the great upheavals of 1848–9 Aberdeen leaned to the conservative side. His own views were not extreme but he came to have a profound distrust of what he saw as Palmerston's irresponsible rhetorical support for the liberal side, which he believed was simply playing to the gallery of radical opinion at home. He came near to a breach with Peel, who would not publicly condemn Palmerston because he wished to keep Russell's free trade government safely in office. The showdown came over the ridiculous Don Pacifico affair, when Palmerston allowed the British fleet to blockade Athens in support of Pacifico's dubious claims. Stanley and Aberdeen co-operated in a set-piece attack in the Lords on the whole of Palmerston's policy. This time Peel supported them in the Commons but the next day suffered the fatal fall from his horse. Aberdeen was now the acknowledged leader of the Peelites and had to act for the whole group, not just for himself.

Although the 1852 election reduced the Peelites in the Commons to about thirty, neither the Whigs nor the Protectionists could form a majority government without them, and political negotiations went on continuously. Aberdeen, along with the Duke of Newcastle, played a crucial role in the discussions between the Whigs and the Peelites in the summer of 1852. It is clear from the surviving correspondence that they had in mind the formation of a genuinely new party by the fusion of two great traditions. Aberdeen wanted to call the party 'Liberal Conservative' but Russell jibbed at abandoning the old name of Whig. Nevertheless, in a real sense, those negotiations laid the foundations of the Liberal party of the late nineteenth century. Their belief that this was a genuine fusion of the two traditions helps to explain why, when the coalition was finally formed under Aberdeen in December 1852, offices were divided almost equally between Whigs and Peelites rather than in proportion to parliamentary strength.

Aberdeen's coalition, a real 'Ministry of All the Talents', should have been one of the great reforming governments of the century (Conacher 1968). In Gladstone as Chancellor of the Exchequer they had a great financier. Even Palmerston had come in to the unaccustomed role of Home Secretary. They were prepared to tackle parliamentary reform after the notoriously corrupt 1852 election, and also education, penal reform, issues that would now be called environmental – such as clean air and clean water for London – legal reforms and the admission of Jews to parliament. Almost all these projects were aborted by the Crimean War. The first session was largely taken up with Gladstone's budget, which was designed to begin an overhaul of the British fiscal system. Aberdeen would also have persisted with parliamentary reform, despite the outbreak of the Crimean War, arguing that in wartime above all one must have the support of the people. It was Russell who lost his nerve and determined to postpone the measure.

It was apparent even to contemporaries that if either Aberdeen or Palmerston's policy had been consistently pursued, the Crimean War might well have been avoided. As it was the British government continually gave contradictory signals. There is no evidence that Tsar Nicholas wished to seize Constantinople, still less to provoke a European war. Russian policy was still guided, as it had been since 1829, by the belief that a moribund Ottoman empire provided the best protection for their southern flank. When the Aberdeen coalition was formed Aberdeen and Palmerston were agreed that there was a danger of war, but that it came from France, where the great Napoleon's nephew Louis Napoleon, later Napoleon III, had recently come to power. It was in fact Napoleon who first disturbed the peace of the Ottoman empire by pressing the claims of the Latin clergy. Austria then employed some strong-arm tactics over Bosnia. The Tsar, not to be outdone, sent the tactless Prince Menshikov to assert the claims of the Orthodox Church. When the Turks resisted, the Russians occupied Moldavia and Wallachia (roughly the modern Romania). Britain had no doubt that the Turks had every right to go to war to defend their territory, but begged them not to do so while there was still a hope of international negotiations succeeding. The Tsar for his part agreed not to escalate the situation further while the negotiations went on. It was this which made the British government take so seriously the 'massacre of Sinope', when a Russian fleet sank a Turkish squadron. The encounter was apparently accidental, but initially looked like a deliberate Russian descent on the Turkish Black Sea coast. Even Aberdeen lost faith in the Tsar's good intentions and agreed to join the French in sending warships into the Black Sea and demanding that the

Russian fleet return to its Sebastopol base. The Russians declined, and Britain and France finally declared war at the end of March 1854.

Aberdeen should, of course, have resigned. He did not do so, believing that negotiations could restore peace without much actual fighting and that he had the best track record in difficult negotiations. Militarily, the war was disastrous in its early stages. This was due partly to the long neglect of the army and its support services, partly to bad luck such as the storm which wrecked the vital supply fleet in November 1854, as well as to bad strategy. The obvious point of attack would have been the occupied provinces of Moldavia and Wallachia but the Russians had pre-empted that by giving them into the neutral keeping of Austria. Britain therefore embarked on the risky strategy of invading the Crimea to capture Sebastopol too late in the season. At one point it was rumoured that Sebastopol had fallen. When the report turned out to be false, public anger exploded. The Crimean War was the first war fought with full press coverage and no effective censorship – in that it resembled the Vietnam War. Aberdeen's government was now profoundly unpopular, and he resigned following a defeat in the Commons in February 1855. Palmerston succeeded him as prime minister, and Aberdeen asked his Peelite followers to stay in the government which, for a short time, they did.

There is no doubt that Aberdeen felt responsible for the Crimean War but it was not at first a crushing sense of guilt. He continued to advise the Foreign Secretary, Lord Clarendon, and even considered coming back as prime minister during a new political crisis in 1858. There is the well-known story, related by his son, of how he refused to rebuild a church on his Scottish estates and wrote out over and over again the passage from *Chronicles* in which King David tells his son, Solomon, that the Lord has forbidden him to build the Temple because he has 'shed blood', but this belongs to the last months of his life before his death in December 1860 when his health and, to some extent, his mind had failed.

Aberdeen was convinced that history would vindicate him. He left all his voluminous papers carefully arranged, and instructed his youngest son, Arthur, to publish them; but, fearing that Arthur, still comparatively young and inexperienced, might commit indiscretions, he gave a final oversight to two old political friends, Sir James Graham and William Gladstone. Graham died fairly soon after Aberdeen. Gladstone served his friend and mentor, whom he professed to revere, extremely ill. Fearing revelations that would embarrass him, such as his previous opposition to parliamentary reform, Gladstone contrived to prevent the publication. Until recently, Aberdeen's story has remained untold.

References and further reading
Aberdeen, Earl of (1809) *An Inquiry into the Principles of Beauty in Grecian Architecture; with an Historical View of the Rise and Progress of the Art in Greece,* London: John Murray. (An essay on aesthetics in which he challenged some of the views of Edmund Burke.)
—— (1938–9) *Correspondence of Lord Aberdeen and Princess Lieven,* ed. E. Jones

Parry, 2 vols, 3rd ser., nos 60, 62, London: Camden Society. (Well-edited publication of Aberdeen's correspondence with the arch intriguer.)

Balfour, F. (1922) *Life of George Hamilton Gordon, Fourth Earl of Aberdeen*, 2 vols, London: Hodder & Stoughton. (Disastrously inept attempt at biography. Publishes some letters but often inaccurately.)

Chamberlain, M. (1983) *Lord Aberdeen: A Political Biography*, London: Longman. (First biography by a professional historian.)

Conacher, J. (1968) *The Aberdeen Coalition 1852–1855*, Cambridge: Cambridge University Press. (The first historian to recognize the importance of the Aberdeen government.)

—— (1987) *Britain and the Crimea, 1855–56: Problems of War and Peace*, New York: St Martin's Press.

Iremonger, L. (1978) *Lord Aberdeen*, London: Collins. (The first modern rehabilitation, concentrating mainly on his private life.)

Mount, F. (1994) *Umbrella: A Novel*, London: Heinemann. (A *jeu d'esprit* on 'the most shadowy of Queen Victoria's Prime Ministers'.)

Stanmore, Lord (Sir Arthur Gordon) (1893) *The Earl of Aberdeen*, London: Sampson Low. (A short memoir by Aberdeen's youngest son, who also acted as his private secretary. Indispensable for its first-hand information.)

Whittington, G. (1809) *An Historical Survey of the Ecclesiastical Antiquities of France* (with a Preface and Notes by the Earl of Aberdeen), London: J. Taylor.

Muriel Chamberlain

Henry John Temple, Third Viscount Palmerston

Born London 20 October 1784, second but eldest surviving child of Henry Temple, second Viscount Palmerston, and Mary Mee. Educated at Harrow, Edinburgh University and St John's College, Cambridge. Married 1839 Emily (née Lamb), sister of Lord Melbourne and widow of Lord Cowper. Succeeded his father as third Viscount Palmerston 1802 (an Irish peerage not carrying a seat in the Lords). MP for Newport, Isle of Wight 1807–11, Cambridge University 1811–31, Bletchingley 1831, South Hampshire 1832–5, Tiverton 1835–65. Junior Lord of the Admiralty 1807–9; Secretary at War 1809–28 (entered Cabinet 1827); Secretary of State for Foreign Affairs 1830–4, 1835–41 and 1846–51; Home Secretary 1852–5; Prime Minister 1855–8 and 1859–65. Died 18 October 1865.

Legend said that Lord Palmerston was descended from Leofric, the eleventh-century Earl of Mercia, and his wife, Lady Godiva. It seems an appropriate pedigree for one of the most colourful characters of the nineteenth century. The popular picture of Palmerston is probably still that of Philip Guedalla's 1926 biography with its famous judgement that, with the death of Palmerston, the last candle of the eighteenth century went out. With his cheerfully amoral private life, Palmerston was no Victorian – though he has been rightly judged a Regency buck rather than a true man of the eighteenth century (Taylor 1934). But, in another sense, Palmerston seemed to be the epitome of Victorian England, a confident

John Bullish figure at the height of the British empire, giving the law to Europe. There have been many careful studies of Palmerston's diplomacy – those of Sir Charles Webster (1951) and H.C.F. Bell (1936) being the best traditional studies – but only with the publication of Jasper Ridley's book in 1970 did truly modern reassessments of Palmerston the man begin.

Legend aside, the Temples were a Warwickshire gentry family whose political rise began under the Tudors and who acquired estates in Ireland. Their title came from Palmerston, near Dublin. Their main estates were in County Sligo. The third Viscount was not so neglectful as his father, who rarely visited the estates, but his occasional enthusiasm for reform was constantly interrupted by public office. One collateral ancestor, William Temple, had been a famous diplomat under William III but the Temples had not been one of the great political families. Palmerston's father had been an MP but more interested in travel, astronomy, the arts and social life than in politics. He may have hoped that Harry (as he was known to his family) and his brother, William, would go into the diplomatic service, and gave them a grounding in languages. The third Viscount was always a very competent linguist. His father's zeal for travel provided the family with an unpleasant experience when they were briefly caught up in the French Revolution in 1792, which may have left his son with an abiding hatred and fear of the 'underclass'.

After Harrow Palmerston went to the University of Edinburgh. The Scottish universities then had a much higher reputation than the English ones, and many leading families sent their sons there for a serious education before going to Oxford or Cambridge to acquire social polish and contacts. In Edinburgh Palmerston came under the influence of Dugald Stewart, a disciple of Adam Smith, and was converted to the virtues of free trade, on which he was prone to lecture foreign statesmen for the rest of his life.

Palmerston unsuccessfully contested the Cambridge University seat in 1806, but entered the Commons the following year for the rotten borough of Newport in the Isle of Wight. He had already been given a minor government office as Junior Lord of the Admiralty. In 1809 he was offered the post of Chancellor of the Exchequer. It was a less important office then than now but it was still an extraordinary offer to an untried man. Palmerston declined it. It may have been that he did not wish to tie his fortunes too closely to that of an unstable government or he may have felt unwilling to commit himself to a demanding job, preferring to emulate his father's dilettante lifestyle. But he acted partly on the advice of his experienced mentor, Lord Malmesbury, and the explanation may be that Palmerston was already an ambitious man and did not want to ruin his prospects by failing in an office that was beyond him.

Certainly his friends and family expected great things of him, and that makes the next twenty years of Palmerston's life very difficult to explain. Instead, he accepted the post of Secretary at War and remained there until 1828. Guedalla was amused by Palmerston's judgement, in the middle of the Napoleonic Wars, that the office was 'better suited to a beginner', but it was a fairly junior office with limited responsibilities. The Secretary at War (unlike the more senior

Secretary of State for War) was primarily concerned with relations between the army and the Commons, which meant mainly finance. Palmerston had to introduce the Army Estimates, which he did competently but with no great flair. He emerges from this period as a competent bureaucrat, quite unlike the later rumbustious Palmerston (Bourne 1982). This was probably not a happy period in Palmerston's life. He was in financial difficulties. He had many mistresses and earned the nickname 'Cupid', but he was in love only with Lord Melbourne's sister and she was married to Lord Cowper. It was an open secret that Palmerston was the father of Lady Cowper's younger children but he could not marry her until 1839, after Cowper's death.

When Canning formed his ministry in 1827 Palmerston, though retaining the office of Secretary at War, entered the cabinet. It is said (perhaps correctly, although there is little real evidence) that this gave him access to cabinet papers, including foreign dispatches, and for the first time aroused his interest in foreign affairs. He made an important foreign policy speech, attacking Wellington's government, in June 1829, but most people were surprised when Grey offered him the Foreign Office in November 1830. With his background (on both sides of his family) in the City of London and his known interest in political economy, the obvious office for Palmerston had always seemed to be the Chancellorship of the Exchequer – which, indeed, he was offered on a number of occasions throughout his career – or possibly the lord lieutenancy of Ireland. Palmerston was one of those Canningites who had left Wellington's Tory government and joined Grey and the Whigs in the political upheavals of the late 1820s. Palmerston had always supported Catholic emancipation, but his support for parliamentary reform was lukewarm and he was relieved that the Great Reform Act 1832 was less revolutionary in its effects than some had anticipated.

Grey appointed Palmerston Foreign Secretary only when more obvious candidates, like Lord Holland, had declined it but, in any case, Grey meant to keep a firm hold on foreign policy himself. The Whig party was traditionally pro-French but the 1830s were a testing time. Wellington's government had already recognized Louis Philippe's government, after the overthrow of the Bourbons in 1830, but the strategically important question of Belgium remained unresolved. The Allies in the Vienna settlement of 1815 had placed Belgium under the Dutch King to provide a strong border for France but the Belgians, alleging discrimination, had risen against the Dutch in 1830. The British government did not believe it to be practical politics to revive the union of Holland and Belgium but were determined to keep Belgium out of French hands. A conference met in London from 1830 to 1839, which finally achieved international recognition for Belgium as a permanently neutral state. (It was Germany's breach of this treaty which was the immediate reason for Britain entering the First World War.) His handling of the Belgian question has usually been counted as one of Palmerston's major successes, although Grey may have had a good deal of input into the earlier stages.

After Melbourne replaced Grey in 1834, Palmerston had more independence.

He brought the same hard work and efficiency that he had displayed in the War Office, and few cabinet colleagues dared to challenge the later Palmerston on foreign affairs. Belgium was not the only crisis of the decade. Civil wars occurred in both Spain and Portugal. The British public was still very interested in the Iberian Peninsula because of the Duke of Wellington's campaigns during the Napoleonic Wars, and it was generally accepted that France must not be allowed to become too powerful there. Palmerston supported what he chose to define as the 'liberal' side in each case – the party of Queen Isabella in Spain and of Queen Maria in Portugal – and tied France's hands by a famous treaty, the Quadruple Alliance, in 1834 which also provided a useful counterbalance to the conservative Holy Alliance of Russia, Austria and Prussia.

It has always been an open question how far Palmerston was really guided by ideological considerations in his conduct of European diplomacy. He probably had a genuine preference for constitutional states, because he shared the contemporary English view that Britain was a 'free' country, more advanced politically than continental despotisms, and also because constitutional states tended to have strong middle classes, which made good trading partners for Britain. But his actions were pragmatic and, despite the rhetoric, usually cautious. Palmerston came near to the truth when he declared his conviction that Britain had 'no eternal allies, only eternal interests.' As Foreign Secretary it was always his duty to put British interests first.

The other great crisis occurred in the Near East. The Ottoman (Turkish) empire always seemed on the point of collapse. In 1833 the powerful ruler of Egypt, Mehemet Ali, rose against his suzerain, the Sultan in Constantinople, nominally to claim Syria – which he had been promised under an earlier agreement – but possibly in an attempt to seize the whole empire. The British distrusted Mehemet Ali, who was known to be under French influence. The Sultan appealed for British help. Palmerston would have responded but his cabinet colleagues disliked open-ended commitments. In despair the Sultan turned to Russia in the Treaty of Unkiar Skelessi, 'as a drowning man clutches a serpent'. In 1839 the Sultan, Mahmud, knowing he was dying, sought a final showdown with Mehemet Ali. Palmerston, believing that the French were backing Mehemet, made common cause with the three Eastern powers in a convention in July 1840. Mehemet was forced to retreat. The French felt seriously aggrieved and had the sympathy of the pro-French majority in Palmerston's own party. As a result of the quarrel the quintuple treaty between the European Great Powers to suppress the Slave Trade – a cause close to Palmerston's heart – was not ratified.

The suppression of the slave trade also caused a serious quarrel with the United States. Slave ships of nations with whom Britain had 'right of search' treaties sometimes made good their escape by flying the flag of the United States with whom Britain had no treaty. Palmerston complained that it was monstrous that they should get away by 'hoisting a piece of bunting'. It was reported in the States that Palmerston had called the American flag 'a piece of bunting'. Combined with quarrels about the disputed American–Canadian border, Britain and the United

States, as well as Britain and France, were on such bad terms when Palmerston left office in 1841 that war did not seem far away. Britain was already at war in Afghanistan and with China. The war with China, although nicknamed the Opium War, really related to a whole range of British grievances that China would not open what they regarded as normal diplomatic and trading relations. Palmerston was convinced that he could have resolved all these crises to Britain's advantage and took his loss of office very badly, the more so because he was succeeded by the conciliatory Earl of Aberdeen, an old rival, whom he saw as weak and irresolute.

Few people saw the situation through Palmerston's eyes in 1841, and his attempts to discredit Aberdeen – for example over the settlement with the United States – misfired very badly. When Peel first offered his resignation over the Corn Law crisis in 1845, there were many who did not want Palmerston back at the Foreign Office and he had to do some hasty fence mending both in London and on the continent before he could resume the office in Lord John Russell's administration in 1846.

The *entente*, which Aberdeen had painstakingly constructed with France, broke down in a quarrel over the marriage of the Queen of Spain and her younger sister. The French had to turn to conservative Austria for an ally and Palmerston believed that this had been so unpopular with the French people that it played a part in the downfall of Louis Philippe and his prime minister, François Guizot, in 1848.

The 1848 revolution in France, preceded by earlier disturbances in Italy, triggered the great revolutionary year which convulsed not only France and Italy but also Germany and the whole Austrian empire. Only Russia and Britain did not succumb to revolution. Even in Britain Chartist agitation and disaffection in Ireland (the great famine had occurred two years earlier) seemed to threaten upheaval. So far as Britain was concerned Palmerston showed himself to be a hard-line right winger. He was particularly tough on the Chartists and, as an Irish landlord, disclaimed any responsibility for the poverty of his tenants, although he did ship some of them to Canada.

It is the more surprising that he gained the reputation among European conservatives of being a dangerous radical, supporting revolutionary causes. In fact, his policy was cautious and always determined by his judgement of British interests. He did have some sympathy for Italian aspirations believing that Austria's influence in the peninsula, whether in Lombardy and Venetia which it ruled directly, or further south in the states with which it had treaty relations, was generally pernicious. He also believed that it would be better for the balance of Europe if Austria confined itself to Germany, where it had a legitimate role, and the Danube, where it would be a useful counterweight to Russia. At the same time he was well aware that the Vienna settlement had made Austria the dominant power in Italy in order to keep the French out. The problem, as A.J.P. Taylor (1934) once expressed it, was 'to get the Austrians out without letting the French in'. To achieve this Palmerston was prepared to switch tactics several times. In

1848 he joined France in an offer of joint mediation – the old tactic of controlling a rival through an alliance. But the Italian nationalist movement was falling apart. The radical republicans like Mazzini had little in common with the supporters of monarchist Piedmont, and the Pope, Pius IX, turned away from his earlier liberalism to denounce the whole movement. By the summer of 1849 the status quo had been largely restored. Palmerston did not show any particular sympathy for German nationalism but he did feel some sympathy for the Poles and Hungarians. He was narrowly dissuaded from meeting the Hungarian nationalist leader, Louis Kossuth, and he tendered a very lukewarm apology to the Austrian government when an Austrian general, Haynau, who had been responsible for brutal repression, was beaten up in London.

The court was seriously worried by his attitude, and the breach between Palmerston and Victoria and Albert was never really healed. He had given hostages to fortune. The Pope had successfully appealed for support to the new French government of Louis Napoleon, the nephew of the great Napoleon, and he, anxious to gain the approval of the clerical party, had sent troops to Rome – the last outcome Britain wanted. It could be argued that the British fleet, under Sir William Parker, had, with Palmerston's approval, encouraged the Sicilian rebels but had then left them to their fate. Parker's fleet had certainly entered the Dardanelles in breach of the international convention of 1841 to stiffen the Sultan's resistance to handing over Polish and Hungarian rebels to the Russians and Austrians. Parker's fleet finally became embroiled in the fiasco of the Don Pacifico incident. Pacifico was a Portuguese Jew with some claims to British citizenship who sought exaggerated compensation for the destruction of his property in what had undoubtedly been a very nasty anti-Semitic incident in Athens in 1847. Palmerston had his own grievances against Greece, which had defaulted on loan repayments, and seized the chance to blockade Piraeus, the port of Athens, ignoring Russia and France, Britain's fellow guarantors of Greek independence. His domestic opponents decided he had gone too far and the conservative Lord Stanley and the Peelite Lord Aberdeen led a successful attack on his whole foreign policy in the Lords. Palmerston was now fighting for his political life in a major set-piece debate in the Commons in June 1850. He carried off one of the greatest triumphs of his life in a four-hour speech in which he made the Don Pacifico incident – in reality the weakest point in his case – the centre piece of his defence. Just as a Roman citizen had been able like St Paul to say 'Civis Romanus sum' ('I am a Roman citizen') and appeal to Rome for justice, so every British citizen must be able to look to England for protection. He won his vote of confidence.

The Commons loved it. So even more did the country. How had Palmerston, the diffident bureaucrat of his early years, transformed himself into the national hero? Unlike his great rival, Aberdeen, who always believed diplomacy to be a matter for the professional, Palmerston perceived that the world had changed. With a wider electorate, one must appeal to public opinion. British public opinion could also be useful weapon in bargaining with other powers. Palmerston had always cultivated good relations with the press, giving favoured newspapers information and even writing unsigned contributions himself. He now took the battle to the hustings. The breakthrough may have come in the 1847 general election campaign, when Palmerston engaged in a great debate on foreign policy in his own constituency of Tiverton with the Chartist leader, George Julian Harney, which was widely reported. From that time Palmerston seems to have understood the possibilities of manipulating public opinion. His actual conduct throughout the revolutionary years of 1848–9 was cautious. His rhetoric, in particular his support for Italian nationalism, was not.

Conservative Europe, like British public opinion, was deceived but Palmerston overstepped the mark by alarming not only the court but also his political colleagues. His break with the prime minister, Russell, came over policy towards France. The British government had viewed the establishment of the second French Republic, after the fall of Louis Philippe, with alarm. Would it be as dangerous for European stability as the First Republic of 1792? They had mixed feelings about the emergence of Louis Napoleon. He seemed to represent a return to conservatism but he had won in the name of Bonaparte. Would he feel compelled to emulate the military feats of his uncle? In December 1851 Bonaparte carried out a species of *coup d'état*, dissolving the National Assembly and extending his own term as President. Without the agreement of his colleagues, Palmerston told the French Ambassador that he approved of the action. Russell asked for his resignation. Palmerston was extremely angry and kept among his private papers press cuttings and the many letters he received from private individuals protesting at his removal. He soon had his revenge. Russell's government was not strong without him and he secured its defeat on the Militia Bill.

During the next few years Palmerston was a political freelance, still further complicating the confused politics of those years. At one point he seemed about to make common cause with Disraeli in opposition to further parliamentary reform. In December 1852, to most people's surprise, he joined Aberdeen's Whig–Peelite coalition government in the unaccustomed role of Home Secretary. Few doubted that he had been included because it would be too dangerous to leave him out. He was a good Home Secretary. During the first year of the ministry, before it was overtaken by the Crimean War, he piloted through important penal legislation, including the Penal Service Act which substituted imprisonment for transportation and a Youthful Offenders Act to allow the transfer of juveniles from prison to reform schools, some modest extension of the Factory Acts and some public health legislation including an important 'Clean Air' Act for London. But on the further extension of the franchise he was adamant. He feared the lower classes. Can it be expected, he asked, that men who murder their children for £9 to spend on drink will not sell their vote for whatever they can get for it? He resigned for a short time in December 1853 over the franchise issue and so was absent from the most crucial cabinet decision in the run up to the Crimean War.

Neither Aberdeen nor Palmerston expected a threat from Russia in 1852. The country they feared was France. But Russia was extremely unpopular with the

British public for the role it had played in 1848, especially the suppression of the revolution in Hungary. Palmerston eventually seemed to come to share that Russophobia, welcoming war as a chance to free Finland and Poland, and perhaps, to return the Crimea to Turkey, arguing, rather improbably, that Turkey was now a more enlightened and reformed country than Russia. At the outset neither Palmerston nor Aberdeen really believed that Russia wished to disturb the peace and partition the Ottoman empire, despite Tsar Nicholas's suggestions of contingency plans for its collapse. Both knew that he had been provoked by French moves in the region but, whereas Aberdeen wished to keep the temperature low and settle everything by negotiation, Palmerston wanted to signal very clearly to the Tsar, by British fleet movements, the boundaries he must not cross. As early as October 1853, he wished to see an Anglo-French fleet in the Black Sea with orders to intercept Russian warships. The British cabinet only agreed to this in December after the 'massacre of Sinope', when a Russian fleet sank a Turkish squadron.

War was declared on 28 March. It went badly. Almost from the beginning there were demands that Palmerston should become Secretary of State for War. It is now known that the disastrous decision to attack Sebastopol was largely Palmerston's own strategy. He wisely took charge of all the cabinet memoranda on the subject but they survive among his private papers, docketed by Palmerston himself 'Memoranda of Cabinet Ministers on my memorandum as to measures to be adopted against Russia'. In January 1855 the ministry was defeated on a vote of confidence. The country now wanted Palmerston and, in the end, a reluctant Queen sent for him.

With one short break in 1858–9, Palmerston was to be prime minister until his death in 1865. His first task was to win the war. Some reforms had already been put in train and Palmerston had personally backed Florence Nightingale in her attempts to reform the medical services, whose shortcomings had been so devastatingly revealed by *The Times*. Sebastopol eventually fell in September 1855 but the end of the war was brought about more by negotiations among the Great Powers than by military action. The peace settlement, the Treaty of Paris of 1856, disappointed the British public, although it did something to curb Russia by insisting on the neutralization of the Black Sea, which meant the disbandment of the Russian Black Sea fleet.

As a peacetime prime minister Palmerston was curiously inert. He continued to oppose parliamentary reform and the question was virtually adjourned until after his death. More surprisingly for such an energetic former Home Secretary, he saw no need for further practical reforms, telling an amazed G.J. Goschen: 'We cannot go on adding to the Statute Book *ad infinitum*' (Elliott 1911: i, 165). Almost the only measure of importance which was passed (until Gladstone's budgets of the 1860s, with which Palmerston himself did not much sympathize) was the Matrimonial Causes Act 1857 which, for the first time, allowed divorce through the civil courts.

Foreign affairs continued to occupy the central place in Palmerston's thoughts.

The Crimean War was succeeded by a war with Persia and by the Indian Mutiny. The Indian rising may have been encouraged by their observation of the ill-success of British troops in the Crimea. It was only suppressed with the help of troops on their way to fight a new war, the 'Arrow war', with China. The 'Arrow' was a ship which may well have been engaged in piratical activities but which claimed protection because of its British registration.

Richard Cobden led a remarkable cross-party coalition to condemn what he saw as Palmerston's bullying and immoral policy. Palmerston could not repeat his Don Pacifico triumph in parliament and lost a vote of confidence. But, when he went to the country, popular reaction was quite different. It was a one-issue election. Were you for or against Palmerston? He gained a majority of eighty-five, and Cobden and some of his chief supporters lost their seats. Ironically, Palmerston lost office the following year, 1858, when he was judged to have bowed too easily to French pressure and proposed to amend British legislation, following an assassination attempt on Napoleon III (the Orsini Plot), alleged to have been hatched in Britain. Even Palmerston could not always control the new jingoistic public opinion he had created.

He returned to office the following year at the head of a new coalition which included both Lord John Russell and William Gladstone, and which is tradition-ally regarded as the first 'Liberal' government. It is arguable that this was essen-tially a revival of the coalition formed in 1852, but it did have an additional element – the common policy on Italy, which had persuaded Gladstone to join Palmerston rather than Derby. The Italian question had flared up again in 1859 with Napoleon III's pact with Piedmont and the subsequent Franco-Austrian War. As in 1848–9 Palmerston was not able to do very much. France played a far more important role than Britain in the Italian unification, which was almost completed in 1860, but Palmerston satisfied British opinion by saying the right thing and despatching a British fleet, which exercised mainly a watching brief.

The 1860s saw the outbreak of the American Civil War. Palmerston's own sym-pathies, like those of most upper-class Englishmen, leaned towards the South. (It must be remembered that, at the outset, it was not a clear contest between slavery and anti-slavery.) The most dangerous moment came when a Northern warship intercepted a British mailsteamer, the *Trent*, and removed two Southerners. The Prince Consort, in his last political act before his premature death, toned down a belligerent British dispatch, but Palmerston kept up the pressure through the press and by sending troop reinforcements to Canada. In fact, the North was in the wrong and climbed down but – as it became apparent that the North was likely to win – Palmerston, ever pragmatic, behaved with scrupulous neutrality. Ironically, Palmerston's reputation was damaged in his last years by an act for which his Foreign Secretary, Lord John Russell, was more responsible than he was. Russell publicly implied that Britain would support Denmark in its quarrel with Prussia over the Duchies of Schleswig and Holstein, by force if necessary. The Prussian Chancellor, Otto von Bismarck, soon showed this to be mere bluff. Palmerston had always been a great bluffer. He once said that any country would give up three out of four causes rather than go to war but you must never let your opponent know which three. But he generally knew when bluff would not serve. He did not live to see German unification, but in a letter shortly before his death he prophesied the rise of Russia to what would later be called superpower status and the need for a strong Germany to restrain it. He died, still in office, with his dispatch box beside his bed and a half-completed letter in front of him.

References and further reading

Bell, H.C.F. (1936) *Lord Palmerston*, 2 vols, London: Longmans, Green. (A very solid work, focusing on the diplomacy, using the official records and some contemporary private papers but without access to the bulk of Palmerston's own papers.)

Bourne, K. (1982) *Palmerston: The Early Years, 1784–1841*, London: Allen Lane. (The first truly comprehensive study, using the whole range of both official and private papers but unfortunately going only to 1841.)

Bullen, R. (1974) *Palmerston, Guizot and the Collapse of the Entente Cordiale*, London: Athlone. (A study of an important diplomatic event.)

Bulwer, H. and Ashley, E. (1871–6) *Life of Viscount Palmerston*, 5 vols, London: Bentley. (The official life, incorporating many private letters. Bulwer, as a diplomat who had served under him, and Ashley, as his step-grandson, were also able to provide first-hand information.)

Chamberlain, M. (1987) *Lord Palmerston*, Cardiff: University of Wales Press. (An interpretative essay with some use of the private as well as the official papers.)

Elliott, A. (1911) *Life of George Joachim Goschen, First Viscount Goschen, 1831–1907*, London: Longmans, Green.

Guedalla, P. (1926) *Palmerston*, London: Ernest Benn. (Donald Southgate called this 'a work of art rather than a biography', but it remains most people's picture of Palmerston.)

Ridley, J. (1970) *Lord Palmerston*, London Constable. (A very interesting study – the first really modern assessment of Palmerston.)

Southgate, D. (1966) '*The Most English Minister . . .': The Policies and Politics of Palmerston*, London: Macmillan. (A fighting defence.)

Taylor, A. (1934) *The Italian Problem in European Diplomacy, 1847–1849*, Manchester: Manchester University Press. (An in-depth study of one of the most crucial episodes in Palmerston's career.)

Webster, C. (1951) *The Foreign Policy of Palmerston, 1830–1841*, 2 vols, London: G. Bell & Son. (The classic account by the doyen of diplomatic historians but covering only one decade.)

Muriel Chamberlain

Benjamin Disraeli, First Earl of Beaconsfield

Born 21 December 1804, second child of Isaac D'Israeli and Maria (Miriam) Basevi. Educated at Mr Potticary's School, Blackheath, at Higham Hall, Epping Forest, and at home. Married 1839 Mary Anne Wyndham Lewis. MP for Maidstone 1837–41, Shrewsbury 1841–7, Buckinghamshire 1847–76. Chancellor of the

Exchequer 1852, 1858–9 and 1866–8; Prime Minister 1868 and 1874–80. Ennobled 1876. Died 19 April 1881.

Disraeli has been described as 'the greatest leader of the opposition modern Britain has known' (Vincent 1990: 6). Vincent goes on to point out that he 'led his party in opposition for longer than anyone else'; and as Tory leader he had an unrivalled record of general election defeats, punctuated only by the victory of 1874 which ushered in the six-year term with a secure majority on which much of the Disraeli legend is founded. His period in office, and his contribution to legislation, pale into insignificance beside the achievements of his arch-rival Gladstone, or indeed those of his predecessor, Peel, whose career as prime minister Disraeli played such a prominent and controversial part in curtailing. But, in the long term, his name has passed into common political parlance in association with ideas of 'One Nation' and 'Tory democracy', which have exercised totemic power in the enduring popular appeal and propaganda of the Conservative party. He has been identified with a Conservative commitment to social reform and to a recognition of the responsibilities of the propertied towards the less fortunate; for many years his name was invoked as part of a definition of Conservative identity which linked the celebration of his and other social reforms with the preservation of national institutions and the upholding of empire (Bellairs 1977: 17). His was the birthday that members of the Primrose League, which organized the party's working-class support (especially in urban areas), commemorated by wearing buttonholes of his favourite flower, and the title of his earldom, Beaconsfield, was a popular label for local lodges of this formidably successful organization (Pugh 1985).

Disraeli's after-life has been at least as important to his party as his own career; and at the end of the Thatcher regimes, after more than a decade of government by a brand of conservatism which comprehensively disowned his legacy, it was still possible to find a rump of about fifty Conservative MPs who wore the badge of 'One Nation'. All this makes Vincent's efforts to emphasize the similarities between Thatcher and Disraeli ring pretty hollow, even though the latter's acceptance of the financial orthodoxies of his time can be made to look proto-Thatcherite if we sweep away all historical context (Vincent 1990: 120). Vincent is right to remind us that Disraeli and Thatcher 'originated in, and continued to identify with, groups outside gentry Conservatism'; but he omits to mention here Disraeli's identification with the aristocracy – which elsewhere he dismisses tendentiously as merely aesthetic (Vincent 1990: 119) – and Disraeli's suspicion of the provincial middle classes, from which Thatcher's father, Alderman Roberts, sprang, would not bode well for warm mutual endorsement.

Part of Disraeli's appeal has lain in his identity as an apparent outsider, an exotic hothouse bloom in a Conservative garden dominated by hardy native perennials. Historians differ as to how surprising his rise was: Vincent plays it down, presenting Disraeli as 'the talented heir to a Chiltern estate', while Ian Machin follows a more orthodox line in emphasizing that 'no other Briton in the nineteenth century had to rise so far in order to attain the premiership' (Vincent 1990: 117; Machin 1995: 2). Disraeli's very comfortably-off father, a literary man who inherited a stockbroking fortune, was capable of becoming, in effect, acting squire of Bradenham in Buckinghamshire in the late 1820s, forging Disraeli's first links with the county he was to represent for so long; but Isaac D'Israeli rented the house rather than buying or inheriting the estate, and Vincent is wrong to suggest that Disraeli might have inherited it (Blake 1969: 255).

Disraeli came from London's literary *haute bourgeoisie* rather than from the landed background which might have been expected of a future Tory premier: high society was not part of his inheritance, and he had to work in various ways to gain acceptance. His path would have been eased by a conventional education, as assumed by the ruling class of his time, but he went neither to public school (although the money was available to send his younger brothers to Winchester) nor to university, and his European and Mediterranean tours did not make up for the lack of that shared frame of reference and experience which was almost universal among nineteenth-century British prime ministers. Disraeli shared with Wellington the distinction of being the only such office-holder who had not been to university (Machin 1995: 2). In order to become noticed, moreover, Disraeli had turned to literary endeavours which were to embarrass him in later life, and even the 'Young England' novels of the 1840s that contributed to his enduring political myth were not the weighty stuff which normally bolstered prime ministerial reputations. Not only his early novels and epic poems, but also his salon career as 'Disraeli the adventurer', languid, ringletted and flirtatious, had to be lived down as he forged an identity as a serious politician. The extra-marital affairs and libellous commentaries of these formative years left a lasting legacy of raffishness and disrepute. Rumours about the relationship between Disraeli, his mistress Henrietta Sykes and his first political patron, the Earl of Lyndhurst, gave rise to damaging gossip in Buckinghamshire after the trio visited Bradenham in 1835, and it was alleged that Disraeli was trading her favours for his own political advancement. Disraeli was to pass from being the protégé of older men to having younger favourites of his own, and Bruce Coleman may be right to endorse Sarah Bradford's (1982) hints that there was something equivocal about his own sexuality (Coleman 1995: 501). Blake was remarkably dismissive in writing off Disraeli's protestations of love for Lord Henry Lennox in 1852 as 'the hyperbole of the time' (Blake 1969: 327). More than twenty years later Disraeli was to 'astonish . . . his colleagues in the Cabinet by the high position in the public service for which he thought Henry Lennox was suitable' (Shannon 1992: 193). He was indulgent towards Lennox's various misbehaviours in office, which distracted his cabinet from more important matters, while recognizing that his fondness for dubious company made him unsuitable for a Dublin post and that aspects of his involvement in an obviously fraudulent company promotion were deplorable. There was ample scope for Disraeli's private life to get in the way of his political advancement, including his sometimes turbulent marriage to a woman twelve years his senior whose financial resources helped to service his serious debts. One of the most impressive aspects of his rise to power is that he managed to put the various sources of gossip and innuendo behind him.

Disraeli also had his Jewishness to contend with. He was baptized into the Church of England at 12 years of age, under somewhat fortuitous circumstances, and as an established politician was a regular worshipper and Easter communicant – so there was no legal obstacle to his political career (Blake 1969: 503). But his racial origins stayed with him, and he encountered anti-Semitic jibes, prejudice and opposition throughout his career – from the earliest of his election campaigns in the 1830s to the controversy over the Eastern Question which dominated the latter years of his 1874–80 ministry. Cartoons in *Punch* and elsewhere presented him in alien, oriental guise, as a charlatan or fakir or old-clothes merchant. Wohl (1995) has laid great emphasis on representations of Disraeli in the Liberal press of the later 1870s, which accused him of purveying an un-English, even Judaic (and perhaps traitorous) foreign policy, of being a wandering Jew with no fixed national loyalties, of being slippery and untrustworthy and of possessing similar traits ascribed to 'orientals'. Such prejudices were certainly not absent from his own party, and a colleague as friendly as the fifteenth Earl of Derby could regard him as in key respects a foreigner in his outlook. His enemy, the third Marquess of Salisbury, went further in 1868, calling him a 'Jew adventurer' (Steele 1989: 189). Disraeli took ostentatious pride in his own ancestry, claiming a spurious descent from an international Jewish aristocracy; his attempts in the middle of the century to claim a special status for his ancestors' religion did not go unnoticed and were, no doubt, remembered. His enemies claimed that his Eastern policy in 1876–8 was an attempt to realize the romantic plot of his philosemitic novel *Tancred*, a view that Salisbury, his colleague in the Berlin Congress of 1878 which brought 'peace with honour', clearly did not share. But race was a central and complex ingredient in Disraeli's philosophical and emotional make-up, with emphasis on the cultural superiority of the Jews and the distinctiveness of their legacy to Christianity (Vincent 1990: 27–45). As perceived by others, however, Disraeli's Jewishness was yet another obstacle to be overcome.

When we consider the disadvantages, inherited and self-generated, under which Disraeli's political aspirations laboured, his rise to the leadership of an aristocratic party devoted to upholding traditional institutions and (increasingly, under his own tutelage) to a strong version of English national identity was a surprising development. It was far from being plain sailing, and his ascent of the 'greasy pole' (as he himself put it) could have been thwarted at many points, not least in the later stages of his career. His emergence as leader in the Commons of what was left of the Conservative party, after the split which followed Peel's repeal of the Corn Laws in 1846, was grudgingly accepted and always vulnerable. Disraeli's attacks on Peel during 1845–6, first on the proposed increase in the grant to the Irish Catholic seminary at Maynooth, then on the Corn Laws themselves, played a large part in nourishing that sense of betrayal which brought the bucolic backbenchers to rebel against their leader; but his oratory was readily ascribed to pique and personal ambition rather than to principle, and his manner and demeanour were alien to the country squires whose forces he had rallied. So his finest political hour hitherto was also, in a sense, something to be lived down. He was, indeed, never really committed to agricultural protection as a cause (Stewart 1978: 233; but cf. Machin 1995: 71–2). It took three years, and some intricate manoeuvring on the part of those who would have preferred to marginalize him, before Disraeli became the accepted leader of the Conservatives in the Commons; he still owed overall allegiance to Lord Stanley, soon to become the fourteenth Earl of Derby, who offered suitable aristocratic overlordship from the Lords. Moreover, his continuing ascendancy was always under threat from the possible return of some or all of the seceded followers of Peel, especially after the latter's untimely death in 1850. Disraeli benefited from the lack of alternative talent in the post-1846 Conservative party; but the loss of the Peelites consigned his party to minority status and near-permanent opposition. From time to time overtures were made to leading exiles, culminating in a magisterial rebuke from Gladstone when Disraeli himself tried to recruit him to a vacancy in the minority administration of 1858–9. This episode underlined that Disraeli's position was itself an obstacle to the return of the Peelites, which in turn gave him power in his own party under conditions that gave it no hope of forming a majority government. The gaining of an intermediate goal had made higher ones more difficult to attain.

As Disraeli mastered the black arts of near-permanent opposition, seeking to destabilize governments which themselves depended on the reconciliation of potentially warring factions, he also had to look to his own position. He featured prominently in the Tory administration of 1852 as Chancellor of Exchequer – an exalted introduction to government – and devoted much ingenuity to presenting a budget which sought to find room for tax relief for agricultural interests, but fell foul of the Peelite financial intellects on the opposite benches, as he strove to put together an early budget with inadequate information and under pressure to raise the military estimates. At the same time he was conscious of a groundswell of distrust and unrest among colleagues who were nevertheless unable to manage without him, and such problems persisted: by the mid-1850s 'there can be no doubt that Disraeli was highly unpopular . . . with a large section of the party' (Blake 1969: 368). He depended on Derby's goodwill, and had hardly any personal following. In 1860 Disraeli threatened to resign as leader of the Conservatives in the Commons in face of what Derby called a 'cabal' against him, and he was attacked in the *Quarterly Review* by Lord Robert Cecil, the future third Marquess of Salisbury, for opportunistic, spoiling opposition, the abandonment of principle and a willingness to use radicals to win important votes. The Jewish issue reared its head again (Blake 1969: 426–7).

Even Disraeli's great triumph in navigating the Reform Act 1867 through parliament, after orchestrating the demise of the Liberals' own reform attempt, was not greeted with universal acclaim from colleagues. A group on the party's right wing resuscitated complaints about the reform attempt of 1859, with added venom now that a much more radical-seeming measure had been passed.

Criticisms of Disraeli's willingness to conciliate radical opinion to get his measures through resurfaced, and again the future third Marquess of Salisbury was prominent (Machin 1995: 97, 113). Shannon has even suggested that discontent was sufficient to threaten Disraeli's ascent to the party leadership, and therefore to the post of prime minister, on Derby's enforced retirement through ill-health in February 1868. He sees a 'benign conspiracy between Derby and the Queen' to 'smuggle Disraeli into the leadership' before opposition to him could crystallize (Shannon 1992: 31). This is a minority view: no one else sees anything sinister in the three-day pause between Derby's resignation and the royal summons to Disraeli, and although there is disagreement about the extent of Disraeli's current popularity with his peers, there is consensus that he was seen to be Derby's only possible successor (Blake 1969: 486; Machin 1995: 114).

Even when – to his own surprise – Disraeli became prime minister, his position was not secure. His quiescence in the vigorous early years of Gladstone's ministry was partly due to poor health – success had come to him late in life – and partly to recognition that the arts of political manoeuvre which had kept him busy in previous periods of opposition were no longer viable: this was because of the clearer definition of parties following Palmerston's death in 1865 and the second Reform Act. He used the time to write a best-selling novel, *Lothair*, which kept his name in the public eye; but there was much speculation about his impending retirement, and the real possibility that his enemy Salisbury might become leader of the party in the Lords made this seem more likely. In 1872 a meeting of party grandees at Burghley, Lord Exeter's country seat, registered discontent at Disraeli's leadership and expressed a preference for the new Earl of Derby. Perhaps aroused by rumours of this meeting, perhaps by intimations of a sea-change in the political prospects, Disraeli then reactivated himself, reaching out to new constituencies with great public speeches at Manchester and the Crystal Palace, and articulating aspirations about empire and social reform which were to fuel the posthumous legend. But even after the Conservative electoral triumph of 1874, which set him in the saddle for six years with a substantial majority, Disraeli had compromises to make, especially in dealing with Derby's heir, the fifteenth Earl, who was widely seen in the party as his successor – especially if failing powers brought a premature end to the premiership. The 1874 cabinet was not as Disraeli had envisaged before the event: it included Salisbury and his ally Carnarvon, after the former had been persuaded to set aside his intense dislike of Disraeli; and Derby was above all responsible for R.A. Cross's promotion to the Home Office, from which this Lancashire banker, a middle-class novelty in a Conservative cabinet, successfully pushed the social reforms whose details left Disraeli cold, but of whose propaganda value he was enthusiastically aware. It 'was not the cabinet Disraeli wanted, nor one he could find easy to manage, still less dominate' (Vincent 1994: 13–14). Bouts of illness and weakness curtailed Disraeli's power to dominate still further, and it would be dangerous to overestimate his practical contribution to the work of 'his' ministry.

At very least, however, Disraeli provided an environment in which a distinctive ethos, and to some extent a distinctive programme, was able to flourish. He made a difference. In looking more closely at the ideas he stood for and the policies he advanced, we need to identify themes which ran through his career and place them in the wider setting of the development of the political system and the Conservative party.

At one extreme in the spectrum of interpretations stand those who emphasize the theme of 'Disraeli the adventurer', going with those contemporary critics who regarded him as merely a power-seeking opportunist. Machin's view is a recent example:

> The most consistent strand in Disraeli's career was his determination to gain and keep political power. There was no similar consistency in the principles or policies he adopted when he was striving to win power or keep it. He was entirely pragmatic in the way he took up and discarded policies as seemed suitable to his salient quest.
>
> (Machin 1995: 5)

Others emphasize Disraeli's concern to advance the fortunes of his party, with which (especially after 1846) his personal career was completely bound up. Following Blake's magisterial biography, they highlight Disraeli's efforts to extend conservatism's appeal beyond the landed and agricultural interests and the Church of England without compromising its inherited identity: a path which Peel had already been following, and some suggest that Disraeli, after a decent interval, merely took up the same approach. A 'party for the sake of party' interpretation of what motivated Disraeli is also compatible with a perceived lack of principle; and this view has been widely held. But were there other purposes, beyond the pursuit of power through party, which might have motivated Disraeli?

The most obvious sustained theme in Disraeli's career is the defence of the power and privileges of the aristocracy. This runs through from the 1830s to the 1870s, being articulated in his polemical *Vindication of the English Constitution* in 1835, and finding echoes in his speeches ever afterwards. Disraeli held that the Conservative party should sustain a natural harmony of interests between the different layers of an ordered, hierarchical society, presided over by a responsible, humane, caring aristocracy which recognized a duty to govern in the interests of the nation as a whole rather than just in its own interests as a class. This recognition that property and power confer duties as well as rights is at the core of Disraelian conservatism. Disraeli saw the constitution which expressed this ideal as organic, living, handed down through the generations, as opposed to the artificial, mechanistic, foreign systems he associated with Benthamites and Whigs. The latter are depicted in the *Vindication* as a clique or cabal within the aristocracy, who represent only their own grubby self-interest cloaked in alien nostrums about political rights.

As part of his hierarchical vision of society and government, Disraeli was also a staunch defender of the powers and responsibilities of traditional local government against the threat of centralizing tendencies which might lead to continental-style despotism. Such local government was, of course, to be over-seen by the propertied and especially the landowning classes: the ideal, clearly, was the county, ruled (except in Lancashire) by suitably connected members of the aristocracy and gentry, giving their time (as the convention went) out of a sense of duty to take on governing responsibilities on behalf of the community as a whole. Just as the democracy of numbers was absent from this view of politics and society, so was any real embracing of equality of opportunity: despite his own ascent from what to aristocrats looked like obscurity, Disraeli was deeply attached to a patronage and clientage model of social relations, which retained its practical power through his lifetime and beyond (Bourne 1986). This was how Disraeli himself had risen, of course, and in so far as he believed in an open aristocracy this was how it was supposed to work, through what has been called 'sponsored mobility' (Stone 1969). A corollary of all this was Disraeli's rejection of what he saw as the Whig view that people were motivated only by narrow economic self-interest (although at times, as in the 1852 budget, he might behave as if he thought this to be so). What he wanted was to sustain aristocratic government on what he saw as traditional lines, through established institutions, by an open (but not too open) aristocracy which governed responsibly, redressed legitimate griev-ances, relieved distress, and allowed the restless and ambitious to seek advance-ment with some hope of success. The key problem was to reconcile this Tory vision of how the constitution *ought* to work with the rapidly changing economy and society in which Disraeli moved, in an era of industrial, commercial and communications revolutions and massive urbanization. How was Toryism to fulfil its mission of sustaining the aristocratic constitution under such conditions (Walton 1990: 9–23)?

Blake rightly highlighted Disraeli's concern to perpetuate the landed aris-tocracy and its institutions, making much of his letter to Lord Stanley about the party leadership on Boxing Day 1848:

> The office of leader of the Conservative party in the H. of C. at the present day, is to uphold the aristocratic settlement of this country. That is the only question at stake, however manifold may be the forms which it assumes in public discussion, and however various the knowledge and the labor which it requires.
>
> (Monypenny and Buckle 1910–20: iii, 125)

Blake regards this as 'the key to Disraeli's policy for the rest of his life', and as representing his 'profoundest conviction' (Blake 1969: 278–84). We might also highlight his belief, expressed in 1846, that the 'territorial constitution' – which based power in the localities on the owners of landed property who also paid taxes and sustained the machinery of necessary government – provided 'the only barrier against that centralizing system which has taken root in other countries' (Blake 1969: 281). Similar ideas can be found in the *Vindication*, when Disraeli's opposition to the New Poor Law must have fuelled them; and they help to explain his opposition to the Public Health Act 1848. *Pace* Vincent, nothing more alien to Thatcherism can readily be imagined.

All this was perfectly compatible with the prevailing dominance of *laissez-faire* ideas, which spanned Disraeli's career and which it would have been political suicide to attack head-on, as Ruskin found when *Unto this last* encountered uncomprehending outrage and derision. As Vincent comments: 'Disraeli could not, and probably did not want to, challenge the Victorian economic consensus. He was not the manor-house pink of later collectivist myth' (Vincent 1990: 47). Rather, he was concerned to persuade the ruling class to do its duty voluntarily, in such a spirit that mutual respect and support between rich and poor would sustain the social order without need for state intervention. The aristocracy should justify its privileges by its deeds.

Disraeli's career can certainly be interpreted in these terms; we should remember that his 'Two Nations' critique of existing practices in the 1840s was neither original nor unusual in the context of the time. The first two novels of the 'Young England' trilogy, and the romantic medievalism of the 'Young England' ginger group which Disraeli led in the early 1840s, carry on in the spirit of the political writings of the mid-1830s. His opposition to the repeal of the Corn Laws, however opportunist, was also a defence of what landed society perceived to be an economic bulwark. His ingenious 1852 budget sought to find ways of easing the financial lot of agricultural landowners and farmers. The second Reform Act itself was designed to increase the political strength of landed society – and thereby of the Conservative party, of course – by redistributing seats to the counties and taking urban influences out of them. The discovery of urban and working-class Toryism in the aftermath of reform came as a pleasant surprise. And by the time of his ministry with a majority, Disraeli was in some respects more aristocratic than Derby himself: even more suspicious of middle-class men even when, like R.A. Cross, they had a great deal to offer. In 1877 Derby, perceiving middle-class opposition to war with Russia, commented that 'unfortunately the Premier neither understands nor likes the middle class', and a little earlier he reported Disraeli's remark that, 'The middle classes would always be against a war: but unfortunately the middle classes did not now govern' (Vincent 1994: 413, 457). Apropos the preferment of the bookstall magnate W.H. Smith to the cabinet, perceived as a social novelty, Derby again commented that Disraeli had 'an odd dislike of middle-class men, though they are the strength of our party' (Vincent 1994: 416).

This made it more difficult, at the margins (these things were not said publicly), to broaden conservatism's social base; but it reflected Disraeli's enduring prime concern. He had had to be set up as a landed gentleman at Hughenden with money from the Duke of Portland's family to aspire to a county constituency and leadership of the Commons in the first place; but he fully internalized aristocratic values, despite a habit of irony which was sometimes detectable. He moved with the times to the extent of resisting what he knew to be the lost cause of a return to agricultural protection in 1879, when agricultural depression revived the issue; but his sense of having held the line was expressed in his prediction in 1880 that 'the politics of this country will probably for the next few years consist in an assault upon the constitutional position of the landed interest', both in government and property (Cannadine 1990: 448, 35). Cannadine's charting of the 'decline and fall of the British aristocracy' effectively begins with Disraeli's death; and this may be only partly coincidence.

The other pillars of the aristocratic constitution, apart from landed property, were the Crown and the Church of England. Disraeli cultivated a cordial relationship with Queen Victoria during his years as prime minister, winning her over with gossipy portrayals of government business and using his talent for emotional friendship: which is not to say that there was no genuine mutual regard. Early suspicions, verging on hostility, had to be overcome on the Queen's part, in the aftermath of Disraeli's attacks on Peel, but a display of ostentatious sympathy on the death of Prince Albert, coupled with conspicuous support for measures to commemorate him, enabled Disraeli to win her over. He was careful to manage her susceptibilities, while being managed himself from time to time. He had to give ground, for example, in securing the passage of the Royal Titles Act 1876, which gave the Queen the title of Empress of India (though not for display in Europe). Disraeli was in favour of this in principle, but the timing owed everything to royal pressure, and there was opposition within the cabinet as well as in parliament. At this point Disraeli described the Queen to Lord Derby as 'very mad': a far cry from his habitual flattery (Vincent 1994: 290). But he was able to do business with the Queen, helping to persuade her to show herself more to her subjects and to emerge from the self-imposed seclusion which had followed Albert's death, during which republican sentiments had begun to gain ground. The Queen's experience and contacts made her a force to be reckoned with in foreign policy, and Disraeli was sometimes accused of encouraging her prejudices in an arbitrary direction. At the margins his party certainly reaped advantages from his closeness to the Queen in the 1870s. Wooing the Queen with fine words was one thing, however; boosting the royal prerogative was another, and where it counted the Queen's power remained shadowy rather than substantial.

The Queen did exercise some influence over the religious side of politics. The Conservative party saw itself as the Church of England's bulwark against the rival pretensions of Roman Catholicism and Protestant nonconformity, and against a rising tide of apathy and secularism. Disraeli subscribed to the view that the church was a great traditional institution which bound the nation together and helped to maintain social stability. He had no strong doctrinal or theological convictions or interests himself, apart from his fascination with the relationship between Judaism and Christianity, which he kept out of the public arena after the publication of *Tancred* and the debate on Jewish political emancipation in 1847, when his views had annoyed Tory backbenchers. He had flirted with a romantic attachment to an idealized medieval Catholicism in the early 1840s, but went over to the 'No Popery' agitators when he saw the hostility to Rome within his own party in 1851. Henceforth he was always ready to play the anti-Catholic card. At times, as in the 1868 election, he may have done this too strongly and too crudely, gaining the support of ultra-Protestants of the Orange Order (an important group in urban Lancashire) but alienating more moderate opinion elsewhere. In any case, the argument for disestablishing the Irish Church, which brought out this Protestant fervour in response, was strong enough to deny Disraeli the hoped-for political reward (Shannon 1992: 52–4). Disraeli enjoyed exercising the church patronage which came his way as prime minister, trying to use it against the extremes of High and Broad Church; but it was here that the Queen was able to intervene effectively, using her superior grasp of the issues to affect important outcomes. She was also able to embarrass Disraeli in 1874, at the outset of his ministry, by backing Archbishop Tait's bill to restrain 'Popish' practices in Church of England services and inducing him to lend it government support, thereby alienating High Church sympathizers in the cabinet. But generally, as with Sandon's Education Act 1876, Disraeli's policy went along with protecting and, where possible, enhancing the influence of the Church of England. He was particularly eager to follow this path in the early 1860s, when he successfully resisted a series of attempts to abolish church-rates, the local taxation which was supposed to provide for the upkeep of church buildings. This opposition to attacks on the church by urban dissenters of the sort Disraeli particularly disliked served the additional purpose of differentiating the Conservatives from Palmerston's government, which had stolen most of the party's clothes during his ministry of 1859–65. It was, indeed, to be Palmerston's death which opened out Disraeli's opportunity by enabling him to put clear blue water between the Conservatives and Gladstone's redefined Liberals (Blake 1969: 535). Under the new circumstances Disraeli lost his 'churchiness', which always sat rather oddly except in terms of the Church of England's role as social stabilizer. Ultimately, as Vincent's reading of *Tancred* suggests, 'Disraeli's message is that religion or ideology is socially necessary, or a means of social control' (Vincent 1990: 99).

The attachments to empire and social reform which dominate the Disraelian legend were much later in coming to the fore. Disraeli had never discounted the importance of overseas possessions, but more for the power they would give the nation on the world stage than as ends in themselves. He was particularly anxious about the protection of India and the routes thereto, and he had an almost obsessive suspicion of Russian plans to destabilize British interests there. This helps to explain his eagerness to gain control of the Suez Canal when a majority shareholding came on the market, although it seems that his own role in the transaction was less heroic and romantic than used to be thought: this was itself part of the legend (Vincent 1994: 21). Soon after this coup of 1875 Disraeli found himself supporting the Turks, with whose culture he felt a lasting affinity, against Russian pressure and Gladstonian denunciation of their ways of bringing subject provinces to heel. The Russophobe war fever of 1877–8 uncovered a vein of working-class support for assertive nationalism in foreign policy, although it is not clear how far this was orchestrated by agitators and how far its real popularity extended. But it now seems clear that Disraeli's 'triumph' at the Berlin Congress of 1878 was more a matter of public relations than of solid negotiated achievement on his own part, and the settlement did not prove lasting. In more aggressive vein, the colonial wars and annexations of Disraeli's years in office seem to have arisen from extensions of the logic of inherited policies, or from decisions taken on the spot without reference to the cabinet. Disraeli's hands-off approach to the ministers concerned makes it difficult to regard wars in Afghanistan and southern Africa as his responsibility, despite Gladstone's suggestions to the contrary, although he sometimes adopted a rhetorical line which might have been thought to encourage adventure in distant subordinates. Too much has probably been made of the short passages of imperial rhetoric in the speeches at Manchester and the Crystal Palace in 1872, and of Gladstone's denunciations of government policy as he saw it (or chose to present it) in the later 1870s. Those who suggest that Disraeli merely took up the Palmerstonian foreign policy which came naturally to himself and to his party carry most conviction (Shannon 1992: 268–72).

Subsequent propaganda also inflated the importance of social reform in Disraeli's 1874–80 ministry. Paul Smith put this into perspective in an enduring reappraisal (Smith 1967). The 'social reform' measures were inherited from the previous government; or pushed (as in the case of housing and trade union legislation) by Cross, who was not a natural ally of Disraeli; or derived from the talent for agitation of a single MP, Samuel Plimsoll. They were seen as low profile and almost as a poor use of parliamentary time by contemporaries, and their economic orthodoxy was impeccable: even the trade union legislation, which Disraeli endorsed enthusiastically after having fallen asleep during cabinet discussions, echoed previous Liberal intentions, although the consequences of an amplified right of peaceful picketing may not have been anticipated. Initiatives, hedged around with restrictions, were left to local government rather than prescribed from the centre, and little of practical value resulted from the housing, food adulteration or river pollution legislation as it stood. The burden on the exchequer was minimal, and dismissive contemporary attitudes to this kind of legislation rendered it uncontroversial in the form adopted here. Disraeli made room for it, and (importantly) soon spotted the propaganda value that could be squeezed from it; but the programme was entirely compatible with Disraeli's major pledge not to harass the electorate with unnecessary, divisive or expensive legislation. As Shannon puts it: 'Never did a political party make, unwittingly, a more profitable investment for the future in half a dozen items of low-key legislation' (Shannon 1992: 212).

All this suggests that Disraeli's main role as Tory leader was to shore up the aristocratic constitution in church and state to the best of his ability, working within the established framework of economic orthodoxies. He had little interest in or knowledge of the middle or working classes, and this is reflected in his failure to sustain the cultivation of local party organization. He was capable of harnessing the propaganda value of diplomatic coups and 'social reform' legislation, especially by expressing what looked like big ideas in evocative language; it was this aspect of him, above all, that was picked up by his party after his death, when it became increasingly important to attract the loyalty of a popular constituency which Disraeli had never really understood. Nor had he talked of 'One Nation': this was a later extrapolation from his derivative commentary on the 'Two Nations', rich and poor (Norman and Saxon?), in his novels of the 1840s. Disraeli's main importance in the long run has been to the spin-doctors of his party, and only in the past few years has this aspect of him been largely abandoned.

References and further reading

Bellairs, C. (1977) *Conservative and Industrial Reform: A Record of Conservative Legislation between 1800 and 1974*, London: Conservative Political Centre.

Blake, Robert (1969) *Disraeli*, London: Methuen. (Still indispensable: meticulously researched, beautifully written. Underlying assumptions are those of the Macmillan era of Toryism.)

Bourne, J. (1986) *Patronage and Society in Nineteenth-Century England*, London: Arnold. (Provides an important context for some of Disraeli's assumptions.)

Bradford, S. (1982) *Disraeli*, London: Weidenfeld & Nicolson. (A large biography with new research material, especially on Disraeli's private life and finance.)

Cannadine, D. (1990) *The Decline and Fall of the British Aristocracy*, New Haven: Yale University Press.

Coleman, B. (1988) *Conservatism and the Conservative Party in Nineteenth-Century Britain*, London: Arnold. (Clear-eyed, critical, anything but an in-house history.)

—— (1995) 'Review of S. Weintraub, *Disraeli: A Biography* and Benjamin Disraeli, *Letters, Vol. 5: 1848–1851*', *History* 80: 501.

Machin, I. (1995) *Disraeli*, London: Longman. (Adopts a chronological approach and treats Disraeli's quest for personal power and advancement as its dominant theme.)

Monypenny, W.F. and Buckle, G.E. (eds) (1910–20) *The Life of Benjamin Disraeli, Earl of Beaconsfield*, 6 vols, London: John Murray. (This six-volume biography is still essential for the primary sources it reproduces.)

Pugh, M. (1985) *The Tories and the People 1880–1935*, Oxford: Oxford University Press. (The most up-to-date academic treatment of the Primrose League.)

Shannon, R. (1992) *The Age of Disraeli 1868–81: The Rise of Tory Democracy*, London: Longman. (Lively, assertive, sometimes dismissive. Shannon seems to prefer Salisbury to Disraeli.)

Smith, P. (1967) *Disraelian Conservatism and Social Reform*, London: Routledge. (An enduring reinterpretation.)

—— (1987) 'Disraeli's politics', *Transactions of the Royal Historical Society* 37: 65–85.

Steele, T. (1989) 'From gentleman to superman: Alfred Orage and aristocratic socialism', in C. Shaw and M. Chase (eds) *The Imagined Past*, Manchester: Manchester University Press.

Stewart, R. (1978) *The Foundation of the Conservative Party, 1830–67*, London: Longman. (Good on Disraeli's rise and the years of opposition and minority government.)

Stone, L. (1969) 'Literacy and education in England, 1640–1900', *Past and Present* 42: 73–4.

Vincent, J. (1990) *Disraeli*, Oxford: Oxford University Press. (More on Disraeli as thinker than politician. Wayward and interestingly original by turns.)

—— (ed.) (1994) *A Selection from the Diaries of Edward Henry Stanley, 15th Earl of Derby (1826–93) Between September 1869 and March 1878*, London: Royal Historical Society. (Novel insights into the workings of Disraeli's cabinet, with a helpful introduction.)

Walton, J. (1990) *Disraeli*, London: Routledge. (A brief thematic treatment, citing more pre-1990 publications than are listed here.)

Wohl, A. (1995) '"Dizzi-Ben-Dizzi": Disraeli as alien', *Journal of British Studies* 34: 375–411. (Stresses enduring anti-Semitism.)

John Walton

William Ewart Gladstone

Born 29 December 1809, fourth child of Sir John Gladstone and Anne Mackenzie Robertson. Educated at Eton and Christ Church, Oxford. Married 1839 Catherine Glynne, eldest daughter of Sir Stephen Glynne of Hawarden. MP for Newark 1832– 45, Oxford University 1847–65, South Lancashire 1865–8, Greenwich 1868–80, Midlothian 1880–95. Junior Lord of the Treasury 1834; Under-Secretary for War and the Colonies 1835; Vice-President of the Board of Trade 1841–3; President of the Board of Trade 1843–5; Colonial Secretary 1845–6; Chancellor of the Exchequer 1852–5; Lord High Commissioner Extraordinary for Ionian Islands 1858–9; Chancellor of the Exchequer 1859–66, 1873–4 and 1880–2; Lord Privy Seal 1886 and 1892–4; Prime Minister 1868–74, 1880–5, 1886 and 1892–4. Died 19 May 1898.

' "Truth, justice, order, peace, honour, duty, liberty, piety", these are the objects before me in my daily prayers with reference to my public function, which for the present commands (and I fear damages) every other: but this is the best part of me. All the rest is summed up in "miserere"' (Matthew 1986: 168). This reflection from Gladstone's diaries captures his self-perception on approaching the apex of his powers and career, and also the motivations and some of the tensions which made his life so fascinating and unique. His political life covered the period of Britain's greatest power and international influence, from the days of the Duke of Wellington, who defeated Napoleon in 1815, to those of Asquith, who led Britain in the First World War: both were at one time Gladstone's colleagues in office. His name was to become synonymous with liberalism, not only in Britain, but throughout the British empire and Western Europe. He was admired and emulated by Canadian, New Zealand and Australian statesmen, as well as by Irish and Indian national spokesmen. Italian and German liberals emulated him, while Bismarck execrated him as the personification of a way of conducting Europe's affairs radically opposed to the one he envisaged himself. The Liberal party which Gladstone helped to create, and then led until 1894, became a sociological model for European political commentators, including the Italian Marco Minghetti, the Russian Moisei Ostrogorski and the German Max Weber, for whom Gladstone represented the 'ideal type' of a new kind of democratic statesman.

Gladstone was born in Liverpool of a family of merchant princes. Both his parents were first-generation Scots immigrants. Though his father was steeped in the traditions of Scottish Presbyterianism, his mother was Episcopalian, and William grew up in a wholly Anglican context. His early religious experiences were shaped by the influence of Evangelicalism, embodied by Hannah More, one of his mother's friends (Jagger 1991: 6–7), and by his elder sister, Anne Mackenzie Gladstone, who died unmarried and 'sainted' at the age of 26. To their example – if not to their teaching – the statesman remained always faithful. Gladstone was converted in 1818 or 1819, according to his mother, but he himself preferred to describe his own spiritual experience as a gradual process of change rather than a sudden conversion. During his time at Eton and Oxford he continued Evangelical practices, such as the daily study of the Bible, and throughout his life was committed to the doctrinal pillars of Anglicanism, including the *Thirty-nine Articles* and the *Prayer Book* (Jagger 1991: 137). However, he gradually moved away from most beliefs associated with Evangelicalism – the turning-point being his acceptance of baptismal regeneration in 1828 – and showed sympathy for the Oxford Movement, which from 1833 was to play a major role in the revival of the High Church. His attitude to the sacraments as God's means of conveying grace, and to the 'real presence' in the elements of Communion, beside his emphasis on apostolic succession and the sacrality of the ordained ministry, placed him very close to many Tractarians. But though several adherents of the movement eventually transferred to the Roman Catholic Church, Gladstone always remained faithful to the Anglican confession.

Allied to his theological views was his conception of the relationship between state and church. In his book *The State in its Relation with the Church* (1838) Gladstone tried to justify the principle of an ecclesiastical establishment, arguing that the defence of Anglican Christianity was one of the primary duties of the state. Unable to contemplate the use of force for the imposition of religious conformity, young Gladstone struggled to combine his organicist vision with toleration and freedom of conscience.

At Eton and at Christ Church, Oxford, where his naturalization as a member of the aristocratic elite was completed, Gladstone excelled in both classics and mathematics, gaining a double first in 1831. Classical literature was to remain one of his lifelong interests, and his command of both Greek and Latin was extraordinary even by the standards of the time. At Oxford he was introduced to Joseph Butler's *Analogy of Religion* (1736) with its emphasis on the careful collection and weighing of evidence as the necessary preliminary to action – a methodology that Gladstone adopted himself and later applied to his own political practice (Bebbington 1991: 237). It was also at Oxford that he first read Edmund Burke's works (Morley 1903: i, 203), on which he continued to meditate for the rest of his life, especially at such crucial times as the Irish Home Rule crisis. From Burke,

Gladstone derived a historicist approach to constitutional conservation through change and reform, and this was to inform his attitude to both domestic politics and the empire.

But his most important formative experience was the practical schooling received in Peel's government of 1841–6. Resisting Gladstone's request for the Irish department, Peel posted him to the 'technical' Board of Trade, which provided, as Peel hoped, an effective antidote to Gladstone's Anglican idealism. Full immersion in the details of administrative reform at the Board of Trade, first as vice-president and then from 1843 as president with a seat in the cabinet, helped Gladstone to discover his vocation: within a few months he mastered the intricacies of the British system of trade tariffs (including the Corn Laws) as well as political economy, which had not been part of his syllabus at Oxford. The growth of his interest in this field, as well as the quasi-religious attitude with which he approached it, can be seen from the fact that by 1845 time spent on departmental 'business' was counted with study and devotion as time spent in a 'Godly way' (Matthew 1986: 67). A further consequence of this experience was Gladstone's gradual conversion to the repeal of the Corn Laws, the issue which was to split the Conservative party in 1846. As his acquaintance with the commercial needs of the expanding industrial economy grew, Gladstone looked beyond the question of the Corn Laws and became a supporter of a gradual move towards a general free trade. It was an important step towards liberalism, supplemented by his later experience as Colonial Secretary. In this latter capacity he was involved in the framing of new constitutions for Canada and New Zealand, and – true to his Burkean convictions – he became a strong advocate of colonial self-government. More surprisingly, given his views in 1838 of the relationship between state and church, he took a hand in dismantling the confessional state by supporting measures such as ecclesiastical reform in Canada and by voting for state funding of Roman Catholic education in Ireland – despite having resigned from the Board of Trade over the latter issue in January 1845 (Butler 1982: 76–123).

By the time the Peel government fell in 1846, Gladstone had discarded most of his initial 'stern and unbending' Toryism: he had adopted free trade, developed a new emphasis on representative government, and abandoned his dogmatic views of church establishment. Appropriately for a man of strong High Anglican convictions, his move towards liberalism did not take the form of a sudden conversion, but of a gradual evolution.

Though his initial disillusionment with Toryism came over the question of free trade, the final break had to do more with Italian than British politics. Like most other upper-class Victorians, Gladstone visited Italy several times between 1838 and 1851, and studied its culture and history. Classics provided a good introduction to Italian studies, but it was Dante and the Italian Romantics which fired Gladstone's emotions and intellect. Dante became an important component of his High Anglican idea of a non-Roman and anti-papal Catholic church, stretching back across the centuries into Apostolic times (Chadwick 1985: 73–86). The Italian Romantics, particularly the Catholic liberals Silvio Pellico and Alessandro

Manzoni, whom Gladstone met, typified the continuity of the Dante tradition into modern times. They stood for a strongly Christ-centred spirituality which could be viewed as closer to Protestant sensitivity than to traditional Catholic religiosity: a perception which, in the case of Manzoni, was justified by his Jansenistic background and involvement with Swiss Protestantism.

The political effects of this literary experience were completed by direct exposure to the repressive machinery of the Neapolitan government, one of the pillars of the Vienna Treaty settlement in Italy. In 1850–1, while Gladstone and his family were holidaying in Naples, he had the opportunity to follow the trial of Baron Carlo Poerio, an eminent Neapolitan liberal. When the latter was 'condemned by a travesty of justice to the living death of the Neapolitan prisons' (Battiscombe 1956: 86), Gladstone managed to visit him there. On returning home he published two *Letters to the Earl of Aberdeen* (April and July 1851) in which he denounced the Neapolitan police-state as 'the negation of God erected into a system of Government'. However reactionary Bourbon rule was, Gladstone's initiative was not acceptable to either European or British conservatives, but was welcomed by liberals.

The break with the Conservative party was completed when, after refusing to join Derby's Conservative administration, Gladstone, in a celebrated speech in December 1852, demolished the budget proposed by the Tory Chancellor of the Exchequer, Benjamin Disraeli. Humiliated in the House, the Conservatives were defeated at the ensuing general election, and Gladstone was invited to join Aberdeen's coalition government as Chancellor of the Exchequer. His 1853 budget was the first of a series which provided Victorian Britain with a 'social contract'.

According to Schumpeter's (1954) classical analysis, Gladstonian finance was based on three principles: retrenchment and rationalization of state expenditure; a system of taxation which would interfere as little as possible with industrial and commercial operations; and the production of budgets balanced with surpluses to allow for fiscal reforms and the reduction of the national debt (Schumpeter 1954: 403–5). This scheme, however, does not account for Gladstone's sensitivity to the political importance of the distribution of taxation, and tends to confuse attempts to minimize central government's expenditure with a 'minimalist' approach *tout-court*. In fact, Gladstone's financial strictures were compatible with non-expensive forms of state intervention such as factory legislation, and also with an expanding role for local government whose responsibility and budget continued to grow throughout his parliamentary career. Thus, while *laissez-faire* and retrenchment were preached at Numbers 10 and 11 Downing Street, the organization of social services was carried out by 'municipal socialists' in town councils and local school boards under the supervision of central government inspectors and with the help of the loans and 'grants in aid' which Gladstonian surpluses made available. At all levels the principles of *laissez-faire* were applied in a pragmatic way and with due attention to what economists called the 'exceptions' to the principles themselves. These included an open mind towards the nationalization of 'natural monopolies' like the telegraphs (1868) and the railways, which Gladstone considered a practical and desirable option (Matthew 1986: 119; Biagini 1992: 103–4).

Thus, though he was to become the main architect of the British version of *laissez-faire*, Gladstone retained a pragmatic approach to economics. In fact, his financial strategies owed more to his religious convictions than to economic dogma: if conversion to free trade had been guided by empirical observation, the zeal with which from 1853 Gladstone pursued its establishment was a religious one, being sustained by his will to 'make atonement' (Hilton 1988: 340–72) for the suffering of the poor – particularly the Irish in the 1845–7 famine.

His concern for the poor was one of the earliest sources of his popularity among the working classes and gained him the nickname of the 'People's William'. It was also instrumental in bringing about the 'politicisation of the Chancellorship' (Matthew 1986: 113). This involved a degree of independence from the prime minister, and the cultivation of public opinion through 'big bills and big budgets', duly disseminated by the national press through detailed reports of his elaborate speeches.

It was his work on the public revenue side which brought him greatest credit, generating psychological expectations of balance, social equity and political justice. His budgets coupled a symbolic component with a degree of material relief. In choosing which taxes and duties to abolish Gladstone followed criteria more complex than the mere encouraging of popular consumption: his main focus was employment, which he sought to increase by fiscal incentives to internal and international trade. This approach constituted the only long-term employment policy devised by financiers and requested by popular radicals as well until the end of the century (Biagini 1992: 104–5).

One of the means whereby Peel and Gladstone had been able to stabilize the revenue and relieve social tensions had been the income tax, which Peel had introduced in 1842 to compensate for reductions in indirect taxation. Under Gladstone the income tax had become one of the engines of the new free trade fiscal system. By lowering the exemption rate to incomes of £100, he had turned it into 'the dividing line . . . between the educated and the labouring part of the community' (Matthew 1986: 127), which also corresponded, within certain limits, to the dividing line between those who had the franchise under the 1832 Act and those who did not. But when the 'educated' classes did not respond to his calls for retrenchment, as shown by their support for Palmerston's foreign policy in 1858–63, Gladstone began to consider parliamentary reform: he expected that the enfranchisement of the 'moral and responsible working man' – Nonconformist, thrifty and free trader – would provide the route to greater public economy. His expectations were fulfilled to some extent after the electoral reform of 1867, when Gladstone formed his first administration (Biagini 1991: 134–47). Indeed, by February 1874 he felt able to propose a new series of fiscal 'boons', including the repeal of the income tax.

The latter is one of the most controversial aspects of Gladstone's career, often seen as an attempt to bribe the middle-class electorate at the expense of the workers. However, the proposed repeal of the income tax was part of a broad programme of fiscal reconstruction which involved local as well as central taxation. Income-tax reform was not a repeal of all taxes on income, let alone on property, but it aimed at relieving the lower and the professional middle classes – which had been taxed out of all proportion to their means – by redistributing part of the burden onto land, and part onto real property, raised by local taxation. This was in tune with the development of local government responsibility for social reform (following the Education Act 1870) and involved reforming both the rating system and local government. It was one of the most ambitious plans for social and political reform Gladstone ever conceived. Some of its aspects, those concerning local government, were carried out only in 1888–93.

Gladstone's tactical mistake in 1874 was to call an election without the preparation provided by a long electoral campaign, essential for stirring up popular support and increasing the voters' turnout. This was because his programme had an anti-imperialist edge which, he feared, would have broken up the party if publicly explored. Trusting in his personal popularity and the achievements of his government, he hoped that a snap election would provide him with a new majority and the authority to impose a 'fiscal constitution' on those government departments which were expensive – War, Admiralty and Colonial Office. Despite gaining a majority of the popular vote, the Liberals obtained a minority in the House due to the archaic distribution of seats which did not reflect the balance of either population or electorate. As the Liberal party turned upon itself and recriminations raged, Gladstone responded by resigning his leadership, though he retained his seat in parliament. It was a semi-retirement which marked a watershed in his career: from the executive politician of the Peelite tradition to the charismatic leader of a new and more democratic age.

One of the unexpected by-products of Gladstone's successes as Chancellor of the Exchequer was a new relationship with 'the people'. The first foreshadowing of this phenomenon was his visit to Newcastle upon Tyne in 1862 when thousands of miners, shipwrights, factory workers and artisans – men, women and children – turned out to welcome 'the People's Chancellor'. From then on Gladstone and working-class radicals entered an alliance which perhaps began as 'a parallel movement of fairly distinct forces' (Feuchtwanger 1975: 116) but soon became a full symbiosis. He had developed a specifically Christian interpretation of the moral obligations of the aristocracy towards the poor. He retained an evangelical conviction that the labourers, in their humility and simplicity, were closer to God than the wealthy and complacent upper classes. Nevertheless, he expected the landed gentry to lead and carry out their responsibilities with Peelite self-denial. When aristocratic support for a Peelite 'politics of atonement' dwindled, Gladstone voiced his disappointment and criticism with increasing vehemence, culminating in the famous 1894 speech against the House of Lords.

Important steps in this trajectory were the electoral reforms of 1867 and 1884. With Palmerston's death in 1865, the 1832 electoral dispensation lost its most powerful defender. By then, as we have seen, Gladstone had already conceived of further electoral reform as a means to greater financial probity. In 1866 he and the new party leader, Russell, proposed a Reform Bill which aimed at enfranchising the better-off urban artisans. The bill itself was far too moderate to excite public opinion, but, surprisingly, it awoke strong opposition in the Commons. When it became clear that it would be rejected, it was taken up enthusiastically by the trade unions and other working-class organizations in the country. Their emotional response – and the role of 'passion' rather than rational argument – was to become a typical feature of Gladstonian popular Liberalism, which was remarkable for involving not only radicals but also innumerable common people without a developed political consciousness. In 1866–7 they were incensed by the anti-reformers' claim that the working classes were politically 'unfit' for, and morally unworthy of, the vote. The collective identity of Victorian urban artisans was based on values such as 'self-respect', 'independence' and patriotism, which were more widespread and deeply rooted than any ideology of democratic rights. By questioning these values, the anti-reformers played into the hands of the radicals, and generated a wave of popular indignation which provided the Bill with the support it required (Biagini 1992: 257–75).

Gladstone displayed a remarkable sensitivity towards the moods and susceptibilities of the masses, and built his political credibility on the popular outcry about electoral reform. By resigning, the Liberal government called the bluff of the anti-reformers and left them to face the consequences of their political miscalculations. A minority Conservative government led by Derby and Disraeli felt bound to propose an alternative Reform Bill. Moderate in its original form, this Bill was soon taken over by the parliamentary left as the government lost control of the debate. Eventually it was passed in July 1867 with the aid of Liberal votes, against the advice of many Tory backbenchers, and with a series of important amendments introduced by left-wing Liberal MPs. The outcome of this unusual event was a far more democratic measure than most politicians, including Gladstone, would have found acceptable in 1866. The most important changes took place in the 'boroughs', where the new household franchise conferred the vote on all resident ratepayers, irrespective of property qualifications. This produced a dramatic change in the electorate both in terms of numbers (the borough electorate was doubled) and of social composition (manual workers became the single largest group in many boroughs). A new principle – that of household suffrage – was firmly established, and would provide the framework for the late-Victorian 'constitution' when in 1884 Gladstone extended it to the county constituencies.

Though the new electoral dispensation was not Gladstone's doing, he flourished under its aegis. He developed a style that marked a new departure in British political leadership. He managed to combine his formidable experience and competence as a cabinet minister and party leader with communication skills and charisma of quite a novel type, linked to the mass media. The popular 'penny' press and the railways provided a national audience for his electoral campaigns, which increasingly resembled American presidential primaries. He became a master of the then newly discovered power of populist rhetoric combined with the mass press. Whereas in the past great orators had been able to exercise a direct influence only on their immediate hearers, Gladstone always spoke for two audiences: the one physically present at the 'mass meeting', and the nationwide readership of the daily and weekly press (Matthew 1987). Hundreds of thousands of people all over the country read verbatim accounts of Gladstone's speeches only hours after their original deliverance.

Another aspect of Gladstone's success was his empathy with the religious spirit of the age. He combined High Anglican populism with the rhetoric of the Calvinist work-ethic. A strong Churchman, he could speak convincingly as the conscience of the most evangelical of the Dissenters, who were the backbone of the Liberal party. It was this religious spirit that in 1876 brought Gladstone back to the forefront of national politics on the wave of a nonconformist-led campaign to stop the massacre of Christian peasants by Turkish troops in Bulgaria, then struggling for independence. In this context Gladstone developed the charismatic style subsequently celebrated by Max Weber. The climax of his popularity was reached during the famous 'Midlothian campaigns' from 1879 to 1880. These led in April 1880 to Gladstone's election to that Scottish constituency and to the nationwide defeat of the Conservative party. Though historians debate the extent to which the 'Midlothian campaigns' were actually effective in winning the election, contemporaries had little doubt that Gladstone was the chief architect of the Liberal victory and the only man who could form a cabinet. Despite the hostility of the Queen, who disliked Gladstone at least as much as she liked Disraeli (Jenkins 1995: 332–52), the 'People's William' was asked to form his second government in 1880.

Gladstone's second term in office was more turbulent and less notable than the first one, but he managed to retain full popular support. But his success in mustering the working-class electorate paid a political price. As the party moved steadily towards the left, especially on franchise and land reform, the Whig landed aristocracy – the traditional front bench – felt positively alienated. Thus the Duke of Argyll resigned over the 1881 Irish Land Bill, which he found hardly compatible with property rights. Other grandees would soon follow suit: Gladstone's diaries for 1880–6 reveal his continuous struggle to preserve as many of them as possible, but most Whigs could give only reluctant support to policies which were increasingly too 'democratic' for their tastes.

The crisis came, quite predictably, over Irish issues in 1886, when Gladstone adopted home rule. The resignation of Lord Hartington and the secession of many Whigs was an inevitable outcome of the radicalization of the Liberal party, especially at a stage when the Conservative party was attractively moderate and beginning to tackle the issue of populist imperialism, which – in the age of the 'Scramble for Africa' – exerted a powerful emotional appeal on the lower-middle-class electorate.

Though Gladstone was still a patrician who believed in the aristocratic principle, he became a leader of democrats, their Grand Old Man, an icon for those who loathed the landed aristocracy. This outcome was curious, but not difficult to explain. In principle, Gladstone pursued stability, not change. In practice he realized that stability could be achieved only by establishing a greater degree of social justice and equity, qualities which required political and economic reforms. Thus, import duties had to be abolished in order to liberate the balancing tendencies within the market; taxation had to be equalized and redistributed in order to stimulate productivity and employment; the franchise had to be lowered in order to liberate the forces of stability and progress embodied by working-class householders; Ireland had to be given a separate parliament in order to empower the natural sense of responsibility possessed by both Irish politicians and electors, and to lighten the burdens of the imperial parliament. In all these instances the aim was the 'restoration' of a self-acting mechanism which would require no further external intervention and reform. However, the cumulative effect of all these 'restorative' measures was to turn Gladstone – in practice though not in theory – into a conservative radical, or rather a radical liberal.

Like most other aspects of Gladstone's personality and politics, his attitudes to foreign relations were shaped by his Christian faith. In foreign policy his 'tutor' had been Lord Aberdeen, under whom Gladstone had served at the Colonial Office. This pious Scottish nobleman shared Gladstone's conviction that foreign policy should exemplify Christian values, and encouraged his preference for peace, conciliation and concession (Bebbington 1991: 109). Humanitarianism and the avoidance of the horrors of war, whenever diplomacy could operate, were the two guiding principles. In this spirit Gladstone opposed the bullying of Greece over the Don Pacifico incident in 1850, and more generally the 'jingoistic' style of British foreign policy during Palmerston's long tenure of office. He was not a pacifist, however, and under certain circumstances was ready to sanction the use of force. So in 1859–60, after an initial period of perplexity, he supported the unification of Italy, though it involved war, revolution and the end of the Vienna Congress settlement. Generally, however, the approach he advocated was one which allowed for peaceful change and the enforcement of international treaties; it was exemplified by his response to the international crises of 1870–1. At that time he protested against the German annexation of Alsace-Lorraine against the will of its inhabitants; he convinced the Russians to come to the negotiating table rather than unilaterally to break the Black Sea clauses of the 1856 Paris Treaty; finally he managed to settle by international arbitration the Anglo-American dispute over the losses inflicted to US shipping by British-built Confederate cruisers during the American Civil War.

As already noted, his fame as a Liberal leader was to reach a new height in 1876, when he took the lead in the crusade to stop 'Bulgarian Atrocities'. Gladstone's Christian faith played a particularly important role in shaping the course of actions adopted during the Eastern crisis, because as a High Churchman he recognized the Eastern Orthodox Church as a legitimate 'national' branch of the universal Church of Christ; and also because of the parallel he drew between the unity of Christendom and the Concert of Europe. If there ought to be co-operation, reciprocal support and 'joint action' among the various national branches of the Church, the same ought to be the case among the governments which these churches sought to guide (Matthew 1995: 7–30). In 1876, as Gladstone's Christian sense of the 'unity of Europe' bred what has been appropriately described as his 'cosmopolitan patriotism' (Hammond 1938: 698–9), his High Church reasoning coincided with the Evangelical humanitarianism of the Nonconformists. The old alliance between the 'People's William' and the earnest Dissenter was thus renewed on issues of foreign policy.

Gladstone's campaign against the methods and strategies adopted by Disraeli continued and was indeed intensified between 1877 and 1880, when he focused on a new series of blunders committed by the Tory administration and their colonial proconsuls. He focused on the difficult and expensive wars in South Africa against the Zulus and in Afghanistan, as well as on the new expansion in the Mediterranean. The latter involved the occupation of Cyprus and the purchase of shares in the Suez Canal, which he feared would be the prelude to an ever-growing British involvement in North Africa.

In Midlothian, in 1879, he outlined an alternative foreign policy, based on six principles which would 'form a landmark in the history of Liberal internationalism' (Bebbington 1991: 179). These included a commitment to the preservation of the peace, to strengthening the Concert of Europe as the arbiter and arena for the peaceful solution of international conflicts, and respect for the people's right of self-determination. Yet, in Gladstone's formulation, these principles were not supposed to have universal application: on the whole they were limited to 'the Christian nations of the world' (Matthew 1995: 123). Moreover, though his dislike for imperialism was genuine, there was no hint of pacifism in them, but only a resolute attempt to promote peace and regulate and restrain the use of force by subjecting it to international authority.

The implications of his qualified anti-imperialism were seen after his return to power in April 1880, when his Liberal government became involved in a series of expensive colonial conflicts, including the first Boer War in 1881, the invasion of Egypt in 1882, and the Sudan campaign of 1884–5, which far exceeded any of Disraeli's 'misdeeds'. As a consequence, the credibility of the Liberal rhetoric about imperial and foreign policy, as well as the very existence of a 'Concert' of Europe were fatally undermined: from 1882 Britain and France were at loggerheads while Russia resumed its expansion in Afghanistan, and most European countries embarked on the 'Scramble for Africa'. A philosophy based on national interest and 'countervailing antagonisms', and energetically propounded by the German Chancellor Bismarck, was to inspire the new rules of the international game in the run up to 1914. How can we explain such a failure?

It was not just a question of inconsistency and duplicity, though this thesis has been restated (Harrison 1995). The Liberal government reacted in different ways to different imperial challenges. Gladstone saw the empire as a voluntary association of peoples under British stewardship, a vision which anticipated the modern idea of the British Commonwealth. Yet he missed an opportunity for a magnanimous application of his new policy in the case of the Boers in South Africa. Something like 'home rule for Transvaal' came within Gladstone's electoral promises in 1879–80: however, in 1880–1, being engrossed with the Irish Question and the impending Egyptian crisis, his government failed to respond to Kruger's demands, while the colonial authorities in Cape Town mismanaged the situation, as so often in the past. The Boers took up arms and inflicted a series of embarrassing defeats on the British army. Faced with the alternative of enforcing large-scale repression or conceding something like independence, Gladstone opted for the latter course, even at the cost of implying that he was capitulating to the Boers. This move 'from coercion to conciliation' (Schreuder 1969: 160) was the prelude to a similar change in Irish policy from 1886.

In India too there was an important move towards a more liberal regime with the appointment of Lord Ripon as Viceroy. The establishment of forms of representative government at the provincial level, the repeal of the restrictive Vernacular Press Act, and the passing of the Ilbert Act, which gave Indian magistrates jurisdiction over Europeans, were highly controversial among the British community in India. Gladstone, however, firmly supported Ripon all the way along. This was the context in which the first Indian National Congress (1883–5) was established as an organization basically inspired by the ideals of Gladstonian Liberalism.

Rather different was the outcome of Liberal policy in Egypt. British involvement in the Suez Canal Company (of which Gladstone himself was a shareholder), together with Anglo-French financial control of the country and the imposition of a Khedive generated growing discontent and spurred on the formation of a nationalist movement spearheaded by Egyptian army officers. Gladstone initially regarded this movement as a further instance of 'a people rightly struggling to be free', but in the course of 1882 local British officials, fiercely hostile to the nationalists, managed to convince him that the situation was degenerating into anarchy and military despotism. When most Liberal ministers demanded the forcible restoration of the status quo, Gladstone was reluctant to act, and his old Quaker colleague John Bright resigned from the government in disgust. However, once embarked upon a policy of intervention, Gladstone characteristically pursued it without vacillation or misgiving. Militarily successful, the operation turned into a veritable Pandora's Box of troubles for the Liberal government: on the one hand, the British found that their 'police' operation had to be prolonged indefinitely in order to fill the power and legitimacy vacuum that their intervention had created; on the other, they realized that Egypt came with Egyptian commitments, particularly in the Sudan.

There too, according to Gladstone, was a 'people rightly struggling to be free', though their struggle was inspired by revivalist Islam – hardly a liberal creed – and their mores involved slavery and the upkeep of the slave trade. Yet Gladstone was committed to total withdrawal from the Sudan, and General Gordon was chosen to implement the government's policy. A romantic imperialist of deep religious convictions, Gordon decided that a withdrawal would be either wrong or unfeasible. This was a major act of insubordination and amounted to forcing a radical change of British policy in the region; it was also militarily unrealistic, and

Gordon was soon besieged in Khartoum by overwhelming Sudanese forces. Yet, by defying the government on an issue of great public concern, Gordon created a political situation which eventually forced Gladstone to send an expeditionary force to his rescue. The British troops reached Khartoum in February 1885, two days after the city had fallen and Gordon had been killed. Militarily insignificant as it was, the news of Gordon's death generated an enormous political backlash against Gladstone in Britain. Yet, on the wave of success in home politics with the passing of electoral reform in 1884–5 – the single greatest step towards democracy in Victorian Britain – the government managed to recover credibility. Another colonial crisis, this time on the Indian frontier, was handled with much greater ability and success: as a result a war with the Russian empire was averted and the status quo consolidated.

It is difficult to make sense of Gladstone's foreign and imperial policy if we do not bear in mind that, though he wanted peace, he believed only in a peace based on order and international treaties. Afghanistan and the Transvaal had been evacuated only after the signing of treaties, and these could be concluded because in each case there was a stable government with which the British could enter into agreement. By contrast, in 1881–2 Egypt seemed devoid of any degree of stability and Gladstone managed to convince himself that the nationalist leader Arabi was not a patriot, but a military adventurer. He first tried to restore 'order' by means of an international congress, with Turkish military intervention, and then with a multinational European expeditionary force. Unilateral British action was resorted to only when all the other options appeared to be unworkable. Significantly, the settlement that Gladstone had in mind for Egypt – 'home rule' under Turkish suzerainty – was the same as he had proposed for Bulgaria in 1876–8, implemented for the Transvaal in 1881, and proposed for Ireland in 1886–94.

Of all the imperial crises, the ones associated with Ireland were by far the most difficult to solve. When he was invited to form his first government in 1868 it seems that Gladstone uttered the famous sentence: 'My mission is to pacify Ireland'. He had a three-stage plan: first, to disestablish the Anglican Church with a view to producing religious equality; second, to reform the land legislation in order to improve the lot of the tenant farmers; third, to improve the system of Irish education. This strategy was based on the assumption that the Irish problem was not one of national independence, but mainly a social and religious issue. Such a view was at the time shared by both British and European observers, including J.S. Mill, de Tocqueville, Cavour and Mazzini (Mansergh 1940: 56–82). There was no home rule party in parliament and Fenianism was mainly an imported movement. The disestablishment and partial disendowment of the Church of Ireland was carried out in 1869, and in 1870 parliament passed a much amended Land Act which, though failing to achieve Gladstone's aims, nevertheless set an important precedent in that the 'sanctity' of land property rights was for the first time challenged and social concerns were given priority. University education proved impossible to deal with, partly because British Liberal views were at odds with Catholic ideas: it was on this issue that the government was defeated in 1873.

With the onset of the agricultural depression in the second half of the 1870s, the extent to which Ireland had not been 'pacified' became evident, as evictions and 'outrages' provided the background to the rise of Parnell's Nationalist party. During his second and third governments Gladstone's reform programme was intensified. He tried, consecutively, three policies, which were also designed to have a cumulative effect in achieving the stabilization of the country: further, increasingly radical, land reform in 1881 and 1886; full political equality, in terms of electoral rights and legislation, between Britain and Ireland in 1884–5; and between 1886 and 1894 legislative autonomy with a parliament in Dublin subordinated to the 'imperial parliament' at Westminster.

Land reform could be carried out in two different ways: either by establishing the 'three F's' – fixity of tenure, fair rent, freedom of sale for tenant farmers; or by buying out the landlords from public expenditure and providing loans for the creation of homestead farms, whose tenants would become proprietors after the repayment of a terminable annuity. The latter approach was more difficult and complicated, and required, in Gladstone's view, the establishment of forms of representative government which would be able to act as intermediaries between the British Treasury and the farmers. Something like the 'three F's' was therefore the guiding principle of the Land Act 1881. Its main features were the introduction of a system of virtual co-proprietorship (farmers could be evicted only for non-payment of rent) and the legal adjudication of rents through special land courts to which tenants could appeal. Furthermore, in order to bring to an end agrarian 'outrages' and give a fair trial to the new Land Act, this measure was accompanied by a Coercion Bill which gave special powers to the constabulary and the magistracy. Parnell himself was arrested under the new legislation.

The combination of concession and repression seemed to have the desired effect: the Land League lost its grip on the farmers, who flocked to the land courts to have their rents reduced. One of the most important consequences of the Act was to convert the Irish nationalist movement from revolution to constitutional reform. The change was ratified by the 'Kilmainham treaty', when Parnell was released from prison in exchange for promising to support public order. In a sense, Gladstone was transplanting a form of 'popular liberalism' among the Irish farmers. Nevertheless, however 'constitutionalized', Irish popular nationalists were still primarily nationalists, and it was difficult to co-operate with them without accepting, at least in part, home rule. As the agricultural crisis deepened and 'outrages' continued (in May 1882 the Irish Secretary, the husband of one of Gladstone's nieces, was murdered in Dublin) Gladstone himself began to contemplate forms of self-government for Ireland.

However, the next step in Gladstone's strategy was electoral reform: with the Franchise Act 1884 and the Redistribution of Seats Act 1885 for the first time the whole of the United Kingdom was brought under the same electoral system. Household franchise with a residence qualification cut across class and ethnic lines, though not age and gender ones. Gladstone intended that the bill would be followed by a comprehensive reform of local government, with the establishment in Ireland of a Central Board which would control the Irish executive. But the government was defeated on the 1885 budget and resigned. At the ensuing general election Ireland, with the exclusion of north-east Ulster, voted for Parnell's Nationalist party with large majorities in most constituencies.

It has been established beyond doubt that Gladstone's 'conversion' to home rule was not a sudden event, but a gradual change which began in 1880–1 (Matthew 1995: 188–9, 199–200) and unravelled itself in a typically Burkean, historicist way. In 1885 this change was quickened by the electoral result in Ireland – practically a referendum in favour of home rule – and by the fact that Parnell's demands looked both viable and temperate, and substantially similar to Gladstone's own ideas, which he was developing along the lines of the precedent of the Canada Act 1867.

His proposed Home Rule Bill came with a sweeping Land Bill: the former involved the creation of an Irish legislature and a responsible Irish executive; the latter the purchase of land with funds advanced by the Treasury, which the Irish government would repay in annuities. The cost to the British government was likely to be in the region of £120 million. Both plans were technically feasible and politically moderate, and were acceptable to the Irish. However, the Tories denounced the proposals as destructive of both the United Kingdom and the empire, and the Liberal party split: most of the Whigs (including Gladstone's heir-apparent, Lord Hartington) and some of the radicals (led by Joseph Chamberlain) voted with the Conservatives. The Liberal schism was further deepened at the following general election of June 1886, which resulted in a victory for the anti-home rule coalition. While Unionist Liberals and Conservatives went on to form a government from 1886 to 1892, Gladstone and his new ally Parnell proceeded to reorganize their forces. By 1890 there seemed to be excellent prospects for a Liberal–home rule victory in the next general election, but the Parnell divorce scandal split the Irish party and discredited the Gladstonian alliance. By the time the general election was called, in 1892, the Gladstonian–Nationalist coalition emerged with a majority of only forty MPs. This was sufficient to push a second Home Rule Bill through the Commons, but it was certain that the Lords would reject it. When this happened, Gladstone advised the dissolution of parliament and a general election on the issue of the of the Lords' right to veto legislation. His colleagues, however, refused to support him, and Gladstone resigned and retired from public life. Despite his advice to appoint Lord Spencer as his successor, the Queen chose Rosebery, who in 1895 led the party to a disastrous electoral defeat.

During the last three years of his life Gladstone was at last able to enjoy that retirement for which, as his diaries show, he had been longing for over twenty years. He sought refuge in the 'Temple of Peace', his study in the family country residence of Hawarden Castle in Flintshire. Here he had spent most of the time when not in London since his marriage to Catherine Glynne, whose family owned the castle and estate. His days were spent reading extensively in five languages and writing articles and books on topics ranging from finance and Christian apologetics to Ireland and the classics. Tree-felling, his famous physical recreation which had become charged with political symbolism (Biagini 1992: 395–405), was accompanied by vigorous tree-planting.

Family life, and women in general, were extremely important to Gladstone. Though the statesman was by no means a 'feminist', the Gladstone women were rather unconventionally active in the public sphere. Catherine, whom he met at Hawarden in 1836, courted in Italy in 1838 and married in 1839, was a beautiful, lively and well-connected aristocrat. The statesman's companion for sixty years in a generally happy marriage, she was strong-minded and independent. Endowed with a very practical intelligence and piety, and a contagious sense of humour which was to become one of the leading features of the Gladstone ménage, she was totally loyal and supportive, and played an important role in resisting her husband's desire for retirement at crucial stages in his career. She was the first woman to sit on a statesman's platform at mass meetings and the first President of the Women's Liberal Federation; yet she shared her husband's hostility to the early suffragist movement. By the 1880s she had become a political icon and her effigy found its way next to that of her husband on commemorative plates and knick-knacks.

Though there are no direct references in Gladstone's diaries or his correspondence, William and Catherine probably enjoyed a rather active sexual life (with nine pregnancies in fourteen years). Yet it was not sufficient for a man of William's energy. His famous rescue work among prostitutes, though motivated by a genuine Christian concern, was also a way of letting off steam during political crises and frequent abstention due to distance, pregnancy or menstruation (Matthew 1986: 89–91). Gladstone courted temptation, but it is unlikely that he ever succumbed to it, though his diaries record recurrent emotional stress accompanied by repentance and self-scourging. When in London, Catherine co-operated with William in his potentially embarrassing work among prostitutes, who were regularly invited to their home. While she took much personal care of those whom they 'rescued', her letters to William show few misgivings apart from concern about the danger of physical assault to which he exposed himself while walking the London East End (Battiscombe 1956: 96–7).

In a different category from that of 'rescue' work was Gladstone's relationship with a number of other women, notably the reformed courtesan Laura Thistlewayte. For over ten years from when they met in 1864, theirs was a very close friendship and, though Laura was 'not Gladstone's mistress in the physical sense', she did fulfil 'the other functions of that office' (Matthew 1986: 242). His links with Thistlewayte, as well as other female friendships, reflected Gladstone's need for a more intimate intellectual and psychological companionship than Catherine was able to provide.

Later the Gladstone daughters, especially Mary and Helen, provided important intellectual support for the ageing statesman. Mary became a protagonist of late-Gladstonian Liberalism as one of Gladstone's private secretaries from 1879 to 1886. Helen – one of the first women students at Cambridge, eventually becoming vice-principal of Newnham College – took over from her sister following the latter's marriage in 1886. After the death of both her parents she resumed her academic work, and in 1901 became Warden of the Women's University Settlement in Southwark (Jalland 1985: 97–122). Of his sons, Herbert was the only one to have an illustrious political career, as the Liberal Chief Whip who engineered the 'Lib-Lab' victory of January 1906.

Gladstone has been described as 'the quintessential statesman of [Victoria's] reign, its epitome and, almost as much as herself, its symbol' (Jenkins 1995: 631). His greatest achievements were the consolidation of the Victorian 'social contract' and the updating of Liberalism. The former helped Britain to avoid the upheavals caused by periodical revolutions which tormented neighbouring countries. The latter enabled the Liberals, uniquely in Europe, to absorb and contain pressures as different as those from collectivist social reformers or ethnic nationalists. The Liberals entered the twentieth century as the strongest and most dynamic force in the British 'Left', strengthened rather than weakened by Celtic revivalism, and without fear of socialist competition.

Gladstone's greatest failure was the collapse of the Concert of Europe in 1870–1 and again in the early 1880s, following British unilateral intervention in Egypt. The impotence of Britain in the ensuing Bismarckian settlement, based on permanent military alliances and the assumption of Russo-German and Franco-German hostility, was to become the key to the tragedies of the following century. However, despite its immediate failure, 'the essential Gladstonian plan of the collective guarantee of the common interests' (Medlicott 1956: 315) was to be revived after 1918 by the League of Nations, and, more successfully, after 1945 by the United Nations. Moreover, Gladstone's ideas, including his desire to open up diplomacy to popular scrutiny, were to exercise great influence on Liberal and Labour reformers, including 'Woodrow Wilson and many American Liberals, and the pacifist movement from the late nineteenth century onwards' (Medlicott 1956: 315).

The rejection of home rule, which is often referred to as his major defeat, was also the defeat of a new concept of a 'United' Kingdom inclusive of Ireland. The British people voted twice in Gladstone's time to reject his proposed constitutional experiment. The latter had offered the last chance to preserve the political unity of the British Isles, though on the basis of a new constitutional model, which reflected Canadian federalism as much as the British tradition. Given that the Thatcher and Major governments of the 1990s rigidly adhered to the old notion of parliament's indivisible sovereignty (even to the extent of jeopardizing Britain's influence in the European Union, and exasperating the Scots and Welsh communities), Gladstone's defeat a century earlier is hardly surprising, and should not be ascribed only to his mistakes.

References and further reading
Battiscombe, E. (1956) *Mrs Gladstone: The Portrait of a Marriage*, London: Constable.

Bebbington, D. (1991) *William Ewart Gladstone: Faith and Politics in Victorian Britain*, Grand Rapids, MI: Erdmans. (The best study of Gladstone's complex spiritual life.)

Biagini, E. (1991) 'Popular Liberals, Gladstonian finance and the debate on taxation, 1860–1874', in E. Biagini and A. Reid (eds) *Currents of Radicalism: Popular Radicalism, Organized Labour and Party Politics in Britain, 1850–1914*, Cambridge: Cambridge University Press.

—— (1992) *Liberty, Retrenchment and Reform: Popular Liberalism in the Age of Gladstone 1860–1880*, Cambridge: Cambridge University Press. (On working-class support for Gladstone, focusing on the importance of free trade and Gladstone's charismatic leadership.)

Butler, P. (1982) *Gladstone: Church, State and Tractarianism: A Study of his Religious Ideas and Attitudes, 1809–1859*, Oxford: Clarendon Press.

Chadwick, O. (1985) 'Young Gladstone and Italy', in P.J. Jagger (ed.), *Gladstone, Politics and Religion*, New York: St Martin's Press.

Clarke, P. (1978) *Liberals and Social Democrats*, Cambridge: Cambridge University Press.

Feuchtwanger, E. (1975) *Gladstone*, London: Allen Lane.

Hammond, J. (1936) 'Gladstone and the League of Nations mind', in J. Thomas and A. Toynbee (eds) *Essays in Honour of Gilbert Murray*, London: Allen & Unwin.

—— (1938) *Gladstone and the Irish Nation*, London: Longmans, Green. (A classic study, discussing the broader context of Gladstone's attitudes to empire and democracy.)

Harrison, R. (1995) *Gladstone's Imperialism in Egypt*, Westport, CT: Greenwood Press.

Hilton, B. (1988) *The Age of Atonement: The Influence of Evangelicalism on Social and Economic Thought 1785–1865*, Oxford: Oxford University Press. (An influential analysis of the religious background to free trade, with an important section on Gladstone.)

Jagger, P. (1991) *Gladstone: The Making of a Christian Politician*, Allison Park, PA: Pickwick.

Jalland, P. (1985) 'Gladstone's daughters', in B.L. Kinzer (ed.) *The Gladstonian Turn of Mind: Essays Presented to J.B. Conacher*, Toronto and London: Toronto University Press.

Jenkins, R. (1995) *Gladstone*, London: Macmillan. (Perhaps the best one-volume biography, and certainly the most elegantly written.)

Mansergh, N. (1940) *The Irish Question 1840–1921*, London: Allen & Unwin.

Matthew, H. (1987) 'Rhetoric and politics in Great Britain 1860–1950', in P.J. Waller (ed.) *Politics and Social Change in Modern Britain: Essays Presented to A.F. Thompson*, Brighton: Harvester. (A pioneering work on Gladstone's communication style and techniques.)

—— (1986) *Gladstone 1809–1875*, Oxford: Clarendon Press.

—— (1995) *Gladstone 1875–1898*, Oxford: Clarendon Press. (Together with the *Gladstone Diaries* (Oxford: Clarendon Press, 14 vols, most of which are edited by Matthew) these two volumes have set new standards; in terms of originality and influence Matthew's masterly scholarship can be compared only to that of Morley (1903).)

Medlicott, W. (1956) *Bismarck, Gladstone and the Concert of Europe*, London: Athlone.

Morley, J. (1903) *Life of William Ewart Gladstone in Three Volumes*, London: Macmillan. (More than a classic, still the best biography of Gladstone.)

Saab, A. (1991) *Reluctant Icon: Gladstone, Bulgaria and the Working Classes, 1856–1878*, Cambridge, MA: Harvard University Press. (Excellent, sympathetic interpretation of his motivations in joining the 'Bulgaria Agitation' in 1876, with important quantitative analysis of popular support.)

Schreuder, D.M. (1969) *Gladstone and Kruger: Liberal Government and Colonial Home Rule, 1880–85*, London: Routledge & Kegan Paul.

Schumpeter, J. (1954) *History of Economic Analysis*, London: Allen & Unwin.

Shannon, R. (1963) *Gladstone and the Bulgarian Agitation 1876*, London: Nelson. (For long the standard study, his assessment has now been challenged by Saab (1991).)

Eugenio Biagini

Robert Arthur Talbot Gascoyne-Cecil, Third Marquess of Salisbury

Born 3 February 1830, second son of the second Marquess of Salisbury and Frances Gascoyne. Educated at Eton and Christ Church, Oxford. Married 1857 Georgina Alderton. Known as Lord Robert Cecil until 1865 when, following the death of his elder brother, he became Viscount Cranborne. Succeeded his father as Marquess in 1868. MP for Stamford 1853–68. Secretary of State for India 1866–7 and 1874–8; Foreign Secretary 1878–80, 1885–6, 1887–92 and 1895–1900; Prime Minister 1885–6, 1886–92 and 1895–1902. Died 22 August 1903.

In a career stretching from 1853 to 1902 Salisbury dominated his party for twenty years, served as prime minister four times and played a major role in shaping British imperial and foreign policy. Yet he has never loomed as large in historical writing as this record would lead one to expect. Whereas biographers continue to be attracted to both his predecessor, Disraeli, and his successor, Balfour, they have largely avoided Salisbury. As a result his importance, especially in domestic politics, has not been recognized.

In part this reflects a lack of appreciation for him within his own party. Traditionally Conservatives regarded Disraeli as the prime author of their party's modern revival. By comparison Salisbury appeared a negative and passive figure; he did not lend his name to any readily identifiable policy, idea or philosophy; above all he took a condescending view of his party which he regarded as somewhat less objectionable than the Liberals. Only since the 1970s have some right-wing Conservatives rediscovered the merits of Lord Salisbury. At the same time historians have also begun to readjust their perspective on conservatism generally. It has been recognized that too much emphasis has been placed on the progressive leaders and on the Conservatives' capacity for adaptation and modernization, and not enough on reactionary figures and on resistance to change. Salisbury's career is a corrective in that it reminds us that anti-reformism was more typical in Victorian conservatism than Disraelianism, and also that a traditionalist approach to politics could be an asset rather than a liability.

In many ways Salisbury seems a more natural leader for nineteenth-century conservatives than a Peel or a Disraeli. His combination of aristocratic title and landed status with intellect and administrative capacity was all too rare in the depleted ranks of the post-1846 parliamentary party. However, few expected him to reach the top in politics. From boyhood his moodiness and nervousness combined with academic ability and an aversion to sports made him a withdrawn and even isolated figure. He hated Eton so deeply that even when prime minister he refused to accept invitations to return as a guest of honour. At the age of 22 he regarded himself as unfit for all the careers open to younger sons of peers: politics, the church and the Bar. He rejected his father's offer of a colonelcy in the militia: 'Your proposition gave me a stomach-ache all this morning' (Kennedy 1953: 27). However, as a young man he derived comfort from his intense religious feelings; indeed Salisbury's Christianity left its mark on his politics in the form of a reverence for tradition, a submission to authority as a necessary condition of liberty, and a sense of the sheer inadequacy of the human intellect in the face of the vast and intractable problems of society.

All of this suggests that Salisbury was temperamentally unsuited to the role of a party leader and prime minister. Yet in spite of his misgivings he agreed to enter parliament as MP for Stamford in 1853, a suitably undemanding position which left him plenty of time for writing articles for the *Saturday Review* and the *Quarterly Review* from which he obtained some much-needed income. His writing shows that unlike many of his contemporaries Salisbury failed to appreciate the significance of the growing prosperity and responsible behaviour of the working classes. On the contrary, Chartism, the European revolutions and the Paris Commune provoked a shrill and nervous reaction in him. Reform, he argued, led to democracy which was tantamount to rule by the mob. Inevitably, when the economy deteriorated the poor would pressurize government into confiscating property. This situation would lead to some form of absolute rule which was just as unstable as democracy.

By contrast Salisbury argued that the British system of constitutional government worked by preserving a balance between class interests, industry and agriculture, and between the majority and the minority. This was achieved by a division of powers between the centre and the localities, between the executive and the legislature and between the Commons and the Lords. Any reform was almost bound to be damaging, and Salisbury pointed to the example of the United States as proof of this. The popular element there had the effect of concentrating power in the legislature which became vulnerable to shifts in public opinion; this deterred able men from entering politics, led to rule by mediocrities, and made power conditional upon offering material bribes to masses of voters. He felt that the larger urban constituencies in England already exhibited similar signs of degeneracy.

Of course, in the 1860s none of this marked Salisbury as unusually reactionary; the endemic corruption in traditional borough elections was widely seen as a conclusive argument against major extensions of the franchise. But Salisbury was, as yet, an undergraduate politician; he took his ideas utterly seriously and all his worst fears were realized when the minority Tory government introduced a Parliamentary Reform Bill in February 1867. He chose to blame this not on Derby but Disraeli, whom he regarded as unprincipled and ostentatious, an upstart and a Jew. In fact, he owed his recent promotion as Secretary of State for India to Disraeli's influence, but in no time at all he had resigned. 'It seems like treachery,' Disraeli wrote to the prime minister (Kennedy 1953: 56). In an article on 'The Conservative Surrender' in the October 1867 issue of the *Quarterly Review* Salisbury proceeded to vent his anger on the Tory leaders for betraying their principles and endangering property:

> to give the power of taxation to those from whom no taxes are exacted . . . is to adopt in the management of empire principles which would not be entertained for a moment in any other department of human affairs.

As a result Salisbury found himself out of office after a mere eight months; even worse, his revolt wholly failed to prevent reform because so few Tories were prepared to follow him. Surprisingly this mistake did not wreck his career. In fact it pushed him into the front ranks of the Conservatives, partly because by 1868 many MPs had concluded that the Reform Act had been a mistake. Moreover, Disraeli proved to be tolerant of his bitter attacks, perhaps recalling his own role in the 1840s, and offering him his former post. Salisbury's principles made refusal inevitable.

However, during the next six years he matured. His father's death in 1868 forced him to go to the Lords. The huge volume of radical reform enacted by Gladstone naturally made him feel grateful for the Conservative victory at the 1874 election; and in time he became more appreciative of Disraeli's success in refashioning conservatism as the national party. He nonetheless retreated to the safety of Hatfield after the election where he received the offer of the India Office. To accept still seemed humiliating, but, on balance, to spend more years in the wilderness was worse.

When Disraeli died in 1881 it was widely assumed that Sir Stafford Northcote, the Tory leader in the Commons, would become the next Conservative prime minister; Salisbury, though now Leader in the Lords, seemed both remote and extremist. Contemporary misgivings about his suitability were not without foundation. He suffered from a lifelong aversion to cultivating his parliamentary followers, relied heavily on his Chief Whip and his nephew, Arthur Balfour, to keep in touch, and withdrew to the tranquillity of Hatfield whenever he could. 'Why should I spend my evenings being trampled on by the Conservative Party?' he complained (Marsh 1978: 151).

However, Salisbury's reputation is somewhat misleading. In time he managed to adapt to novel conditions, and he would hardly have survived so long as leader had he not displayed some skill in management. Whereas Disraeli had taken little interest in the mundane aspects of party organization, Salisbury consulted regularly with his Chief Agent, R.W.E. Middleton, and applied himself to electoral issues with good effect. Though scarcely an inspiring orator he undertook a heavy burden of public speaking during the 1880s, made 'stumping' visits to the major towns and delivered annual addresses to the National Union and the Primrose League, invariably without notes. He showed more appreciation than Disraeli of the need to reward his followers. Indeed, his fastidious attitude towards the more vulgar arts of politics was wholly at odds with the extensive sale of honours to Conservative supporters under his leadership from 1886 onwards. Moreover, Salisbury showed a firm grasp of long-term political strategy. Greatly encouraged by the growing divergence between the right and left wings of liberalism under Gladstone's leadership, he was anxious to assist a breakaway by the Whigs and the absorption of middle-class voters into the Conservative fold.

This objective was accomplished by stages between 1881 and 1895. In the aftermath of Gladstone's victory in 1880 Salisbury's rise was greatly facilitated by the activities of Lord Randolph Churchill and the Fourth Party in undermining Northcote in the Commons. When Churchill extended his campaign by demanding more powers and funds for the National Union at the expense of the party leadership, it was Salisbury who eventually negotiated a compromise in 1884. This involved no significant concession on Salisbury's part, for he saw the National Union as a potential threat, a fear soon to be justified by its troublesome habit of adopting protectionist policy resolutions at annual conference. But Salisbury had shrewdly recognized that Lord Randolph was not trying to become a Tory Chamberlain; he could be detached from the cause of the party organization by means of a promise of a cabinet post in the next Conservative government.

Salisbury also appreciated that Churchill had pioneered a more acceptable form of popular organization for Conservatives in the shape of the Primrose League. Its devotion to *traditional* Tory causes – the Anglican Establishment, religious education, private property, monarchy and empire – not only seemed safer than domestic reform but actually won votes. Thus Salisbury granted official recognition to the Primrose League and even consented, rather improbably, to become its Grand Master. Using remarkably 'Disraelian' language he contrasted the League with the National Union: 'The Primrose League is freer. It is more elastic. It brings classes more together, and I think its greatest achievement of all is that it has brought the influence of women to bear on politics' (speech at Edinburgh, 29 November 1886). As a result Salisbury followed Disraeli in extending his personal support to women's enfranchisement, albeit on a limited basis. For the politician who had stormed out of the cabinet over the Reform Bill in 1867 this seems an extraordinary turnaround. But it reflected Salisbury's growing appreciation of the underlying strength of conservatism in the country and of the scope for exploiting it.

The controversy over the National Union was closely followed by the dilemma presented by Liberals' franchise reform in 1884–5. The proposal to extend the household and lodger qualifications to the counties was a direct threat to Tory seats, and the Lords responded initially by rejecting the Bill. Salisbury knew that he would have to back down, however, because the peers' resistance simply encouraged the radicals to launch a campaign against the hereditary principle on which the upper chamber rested. The two sides reached a compromise on the basis that the peers would pass the franchise reforms in return for a redistribution of the constituencies. This involved a novel move to single-member seats which Salisbury believed would promote his party's representation by separating the Conservative minority in the towns and by preserving landowner influence in the counties. Subsequent elections were to show how shrewd his calculation had been; for the shift of middle-class voters created many Conservative strongholds in the new residential suburbs, commercial seats and seaside resorts which now enjoyed their own representation. This was to be the basis of the party's strength for a century to come.

The final building block in Salisbury's new Conservative party involved the Liberal–Unionist split with Gladstone over Irish home rule. Although he was essentially the fortunate beneficiary of the Liberals' internal difficulties, Salisbury nonetheless manoeuvred adroitly to maximize the gains. Though he regarded the departure of the Whigs from the Liberal party as inevitable, he saw the risks in involving them in his own party. If mavericks such as Churchill were given the chance to team up with Hartington and Chamberlain, his own leadership might be threatened.

Thus Salisbury adopted a two-part strategy. First, he co-operated with Gladstone to polarize the parties over home rule by delivering some extreme speeches in which he suggested that the Irish were as fit for self-government as the Hottentots or the Hindus. Then, having accelerated the withdrawal of the Whigs, he endeavoured to maintain them as a separate Liberal Unionist party; this was accomplished by securing the support of local Conservative Associations for their candidates at the 1886 general election. Wisely he avoided bringing the Liberal Unionists into his new cabinet. The dramatic resignation of the new Chancellor and Leader of the Commons, Lord Randolph Churchill, might have destroyed the government. But Churchill was isolated and Salisbury gladly disposed of his troublesome minister. He strengthened his position by offering the Exchequer to a very right-wing ex-Liberal, George Goschen; and he enacted a few domestic reforms to check any drift back to Gladstone by the Chamberlainites. Not until 1895 did Salisbury judge it to be safe to incorporate the leading Liberal Unionists in his cabinet, thereby beginning the process which led to their complete amalgamation with the Conservative party in the Edwardian period.

Though flexible in his methods Salisbury never really lost his ideological hostility to interventionism in domestic politics: 'I fear these social questions are destined to break up our party – but why incur the danger before the necessity has arrived?' (Williams 1988: 430). Whenever legislation became bogged down in disagreements between Conservatives, Chamberlainites and Liberal Unionists he took a cynical pleasure in thwarting the reformers. But he appreciated the need for certain concessions to make Chamberlain's co-operation respectable. Hence the introduction of free elementary education in 1891 and the bills for the creation of allotments in 1887 and smallholdings in 1892. Salisbury's dilemmas were most acute in tackling the question of county government in 1888. By establishing some form of elected county councils the Conservatives effectively prevented a more radical innovation by Gladstone. The bill antagonized Tory landowners such as Sir Michael Hicks-Beach, however, who resented the infringement of the powers of the country gentlemen. Salisbury – in effect playing Disraeli's role – appeased them by creating an electorate more narrowly based on property than the parliamentary one, and by diluting the elective element with nominated aldermen.

Reform was not entirely a matter of tactical manoeuvres on Salisbury's part. He showed some sympathy over social issues, but believed that self-help was the best policy. Even in the case of housing, where his interest was most fully engaged, he preferred to stick to traditional permissive legislation. Ireland was the chief exception. Salisbury left Gladstone's Land Act 1881 intact in spite of its effects in reducing the value of property in Ireland. In addition, the government financed the purchase of Irish estates and their resale on generous terms to small tenant farmers. Though unpalatable this policy seemed a necessary price to pay for maintaining the union.

After 1895 the inclusion of Chamberlain in the government put Salisbury under further pressure over social reform. But he shrank from the costs of such innovations as old age pensions, and condemned legislative attempts to restrict the working day as interference with the freedom of employers and workers to settle their own conditions. Increasingly, Salisbury's philosophy had become classical liberalism tempered by political expediency. He disapproved of the income tax as inquisitorial and potentially fatal to the rights of private property. He believed that no class should be taxed for the benefit of another, and that indirect taxes on consumption were the least objectionable way of financing state services. During the 1890s this approach became increasingly unrealistic in the face of the pressures created by naval rebuilding and imperial conflicts. Eventually the war in South Africa forced Salisbury's government to double the income tax, suspend the Sinking Fund, borrow heavily and impose new duties on basic food items. This finally destroyed the basis of Conservative thinking on financial policy. By 1901 Chamberlain had concluded that there could be no return to traditional retrenchment and low taxation. Thus, when Salisbury finally retired in August 1902 he was leaving his government on the verge of a disastrous split between the advocates of protectionism and traditional Gladstonian finance.

Salisbury's prolonged service at the Foreign Office is of obvious importance in the context of Britain's retreat from isolation; but it also throws light on his elevation to the premiership. In March 1878 his willingness to replace Derby, who had resigned over dislike of Disraeli's belligerent policy in the Middle East, was interpreted as proof of unsuspected ambition, for Salisbury's views on the Eastern Question differed sharply from those of the prime minister; he showed great hostility to the Turks and believed it a mistake to base British policy on the assumption that the Ottoman empire could be propped up indefinitely. Yet he managed to work cordially with Disraeli for two years. Although the Congress of Berlin was seen as a Disraelian triumph in that it curtailed Russian gains, it also bore Salisbury's influence: the Turks had to promise better treatment of the Christians, they lost territory in Europe and received from Britain a guarantee of their Asiatic territory only, which was never treated very seriously.

Salisbury's later policy was dominated by his consciousness of Britain's weakness both as a military power in Europe and as a naval power in the East. He attempted to maintain British interests by limiting the costs of empire and by fostering co-operation with Germany and the Triple Alliance. This meant that private interests should bear the strain of expansion where possible; thus in 1888 he granted a charter to the British East Africa Company with a view to safeguarding the sources of the Nile on which the security of Egypt was thought to depend. This, of course, antagonized rivals, especially the French. Salisbury had once defined British policy as 'to float lazily downstream, occasionally putting out a diplomatic boathook to avoid collisions' (Gascogne Cecil 1921–32: 2, 130). But the question now arose whether something more deliberate was required. Salisbury endeavoured to obtain the benefits of a formal alliance with the Triple Alliance powers without the obligations involved in a binding treaty. Thus he thought that the Mediterranean Agreements of 1887 with Italy and Austria had effectively won German backing for the maintenance of the status quo in return for mere diplomatic support on Britain's port. He liked to claim that the British parliamentary system precluded permanent commitments to foreign powers, but this was merely a convenient excuse. The real objection was that a binding pledge could be costly and would probably accelerate a war with France and Russia.

Salisbury undoubtedly regarded Germany's goodwill in colonial questions as essential, especially in view of French hostility over Egypt and Russian expansionism in Asia. In 1890 this resulted in a major redistribution of territory in which Britain gained Zanzibar, Kenya and Uganda while handing over Heligoland and a large stretch of East Africa to the Germans. At home Salisbury was criticized for missing the chance of linking Britain's Southern African colonies with its East African possessions; but he had little patience with the sentimental expansionists. Much African land was of no intrinsic value, and he believed that Britain had enjoyed the best of the deal.

However, after 1890, when Bismarck fell from power, relations with Germany began to deteriorate and Salisbury came under increasing criticism from colleagues who regarded Britain's semi-detached position as dangerous. The problem became acute in the Far East where Britain failed to prevent the Russians and the Germans acquiring leases on Chinese territory. The task of safeguarding British trade in the Yangtse Valley by upholding an open door policy seemed to be beyond its powers. As a result Salisbury faced pressure from Joseph Chamberlain to negotiate an Anglo-German Alliance. Despite the prime minister's misgivings talks did take place in the late 1890s on the basis that Germany would help to restrain Russia in the Far East in return for British naval support against France. Salisbury was by no means displeased at the eventual failure of these negotiations. But he seemed unable to resolve the underlying problem; Britain badly needed some means of relieving itself of obligations it could not maintain single-handed. It is significant that as soon as Salisbury gave up as Foreign Secretary in 1900, under pressure from both the cabinet and his family, his successor, Lord Lansdowne, successfully negotiated an alliance with Japan. By the turn of the century Salisbury was drifting rather than controlling foreign policy.

From a twentieth-century perspective Salisbury's premiership seems remarkable in two respects: he remained a member of the Lords, and he combined the Foreign Secretaryship with the prime ministership. This latter practice, emulated only by Ramsay MacDonald in 1924, attracted criticism from Gladstone, who believed that the wide responsibilities of the prime minister were more than enough for any individual. Salisbury's behaviour can be explained in several ways. Essentially he enjoyed the work of the Foreign Office more than any other department of government. Moreover, he believed that as Foreign Secretary with the authority of a prime minister he would be able to overrule the Treasury which weakened national policy by its obsessive retrenchment policies. Unhappily for Salisbury this theory broke down in the face of a rigid retrenchment-minded Chancellor, Sir Michael Hicks-Beach, with results that became apparent in the war of 1899–1902. Finally, Salisbury spent less time on the details of legislation than, say, Gladstone, and, in view of his party's huge majority in the upper House, could afford to indulge himself by retreating to Hatfield for long periods.

Of course, the absence of the prime minister from the Commons had its drawbacks. Disraeli's departure for the Lords in 1876 had been widely recognized as having weakened his government in the Commons. At first Salisbury sought to meet the danger by using the oratorical skills of Lord Randolph Churchill as Leader of the House and Chancellor. This, however, rapidly blew up in his face when Churchill resigned in 1886. In some desperation Salisbury drafted in W.H. Smith as Leader of the House and, later, promoted his nephew Arthur Balfour to this role which became, in effect, a deputy prime ministership. Given the close relations between the prime minister and both Smith and Balfour this worked well. But in any case the task of managing the Commons had become easier since 1886 when the home rule crisis polarized opinion. This accelerated the existing trend towards tighter party discipline such that by the 1890s nine out of ten Tory MPs could be relied upon to follow the whip in over 90 per cent of all divisions.

In the upper House the events of 1886 had given the Conservatives a huge majority; but this only made the hereditary element a tempting target for attack by the radicals. Salisbury developed a typically bold defence of the peers' role by challenging the authority of the elected majority in the Commons. He claimed that the peers had a right to reject measures for which the government had not obtained a mandate. However, this was so transparently a rationale to justify the rejection of liberal legislation that even Salisbury seems to have felt uncomfortable about defending the privileges of hereditary peers. In 1888 he attempted to put the upper Chamber on a firmer footing by introducing a bill to create fifty life peers chosen from judges, officers, civil servants, diplomats and ex-colonial governors. The Bill was nevertheless withdrawn.

The cabinet expanded considerably under Salisbury; by 1900 it comprised twenty-two members in contrast to twelve to fourteen typical of the mid-Victorian period. This arose partly from the creation of new departments including the Scottish Office (1885), the Board of Agriculture (1889) and the Board of Education (1899), and the inclusion of three Irish ministers, the Chief Secretary, the Lord Lieutenant and the Lord Chancellor for Ireland. Moreover, after 1895 Salisbury led, in effect, a coalition government with the Liberal Unionists and thus found it necessary to reward senior figures by expanding the cabinet.

Salisbury ranks among the more relaxed premiers in his handling of his ministers. On the whole he avoided interfering in their departmental affairs, and in cabinet he behaved as no more than the first among equals. He readily allowed the cabinet to vote and accepted decisions that went against him. This may help to explain why his four governments suffered only one resignation on principle, that of Churchill, and why Chamberlain and Devonshire (the former Lord Hartington) managed to work more happily than they had done under Gladstone and were to do under Balfour. No doubt Salisbury's approach was simply natural for a prime minister whose general strategy was to do as little as possible; as long as he remained in control of foreign policy he could afford to take a relaxed view of cabinet discussions. However, the defects of this attitude eventually became apparent in the casual way in which he allowed Chamberlain and Lord Milner to drag the country into the South African War in 1899. Moreover, once the war had broken out Salisbury showed himself to be far too detached to be a successful war minister. He was extremely lucky that the mood of patriotism in the country saved his government at the general election of 1900, and was wise to have left office in 1902 before the full consequences of the war had begun to destroy his party.

With the exception of Liverpool, Salisbury retained the premiership for longer than any other nineteenth-century statesman. His claim to be a prime minister of the first rank rests upon this record, his three election victories in 1886, 1895 and 1900, and, above all, on successfully managing the absorption of the Liberal Unionists, the Whigs and much of middle-class England and Scotland into the late-Victorian Conservative party. However, the culmination of his foreign and imperial policy in the disasters of the Boer War and the sheer speed with which the Conservative government unravelled within a year of his departure detracts from his reputation; it suggests that in many ways he had been lucky as much as skilful.

References and further reading

Blake, R. and Cecil, H. (eds) (1987) *Salisbury: The Man and his Policies*, London: Macmillan. (Includes some original essays especially on economics, foreign policy, India and religion.)

Gascoyne-Cecil, Lady Gwendolen (1921–32) *Life of Robert, Marquess of Salisbury*, 4 vols, London: Hodder & Stoughton. (Sympathetic but still useful for an understanding of Salisbury's personality.)

Grenville, J. (1964) *Lord Salisbury and Foreign Policy*, London: Athlone.

Kennedy, A. (1953) *Salisbury, 1830–1903: Portrait of a Statesman*, London: John Murray.

Lowe, C. (1967) *The Reluctant Imperialists: British Foreign Policy, 1878–1902*, 2 vols, London: Macmillan.

Marsh, P. (1978) *The Discipline of Popular Government: Lord Salisbury's Domestic Statecraft 1881–1902*, Hassocks: Harvester Press. (A perceptive analysis which reveals Salisbury's skill in limiting the activities of his own governments.)

Pinto-Duschinsky, M. (1967) *The Political Thought of Lord Salisbury, 1854–68*, London: Constable. (Though useful it does have the effect of emphasizing the negative approach of the young Salisbury at the expense of the flexibility of the mature statesman.)

Smith, P. (ed.) (1972) *Lord Salisbury on Politics*, Cambridge: Cambridge University Press.

Taylor, R. (1975) *Lord Salisbury*, London: Allen Lane.

Williams, R.H. (ed.) (1988) *The Salisbury–Balfour Correspondence 1869–92*, Hertford: Hertfordshire Record Society. (Valuable for showing the extent to which Salisbury relied on his nephew for information about the party he led.)

Martin Pugh

Archibald Philip Primrose, Fifth Earl of Rosebery

Born 7 May 1847, third child of Archibald, Lord Dalmeny, and Lady Wilhelmina Stanhope. Educated at Eton and Christ Church, Oxford. Entered Lords 1868. Married 1878 Hannah de Rothschild (died 1890). Under-Secretary of State for Home Affairs 1881–3; First Commissioner of Works and Lord Privy Seal 1885; Foreign Secretary 1886 and 1892–4; Prime Minister 1894–5. Died 21 May 1929.

If contemporaries puzzled over Rosebery's place in British politics, historians have been no less impressed by the enigmatic quality of his private and public lives. An air of privileged detachment, verging on unreality, accompanied Rosebery throughout his relatively brief spell in the political limelight and the still significant years of his retreat to the wings. As Liberal prime minister for fifteen months in 1894–5 he provided an unhappy spectacle; as political lodestar, orator and statesman between 1880 and 1905 he was in the mould of his original leader, Gladstone.

Liberals of all shades felt let down by Rosebery's failure to live up to his gifts. The journalist A.G. Gardiner's astringent assessment in 1908 concluded that Rosebery lacked 'character', and invoked the observation of his tutor at Eton that he desired 'the palm without the dust'. Biographers, ranging from the dutiful (Marquess of Crewe 1930) and the scholarly (Rhodes James 1963) to the irreverent (Raymond 1923) reveal a man deeply imbued with a sense of failure, although this should perhaps be viewed in the context of the Calvinism of 'seventeenth century Scotland' vintage which John Buchan believed was at the heart of Rosebery's outlook (Buchan 1930).

It appeared that Rosebery enjoyed the luxury of walking away from the political maelstrom and returning, or signalling a return, when it suited him. Yet his motives may not have been straightforwardly self-indulgent. He was undoubtedly a figure who lived for various pleasures, chief among them the racehorses for which he chose to have his studies at Oxford terminated rather than give up. Rosebery was born into landed affluence and grew considerably wealthier, first on becoming fifth Earl of Rosebery in 1868, and then on his marriage to Hannah Rothschild, heir to the family fortune, in 1878. He gambled, collected works of art and rare books, and entertained lavishly at his various country estates in Scotland and England. His attachment to Lord Drumlanrig, son of the wretched Marquess of Queensbury, has led to speculation that the public pillorying of Oscar Wilde in 1895 served conveniently to divert attention from similar scandals surrounding Rosebery who was then prime minister (Ellman 1988: 402; Parris 1995: 67–74).

On the other hand, Martel has suggested persuasively that awareness of pleasurable distractions produced intense self-doubt regarding his capacity to overcome temptation and perform public duties effectively (Martel 1986: 3–8). Rosebery's reticence, inconstancy and hesitancy, for which he has been roundly condemned, sprang from genuine inner turmoil; in public office he often felt frustrated yet out of the political world he pondered the emptiness of a life of frivolity. His troubled thoughts were reflected in frequent mood swings, unpredictable behaviour and insomnia, the latter of which became a chronic condition after the death of his wife in 1890. Rosebery truly admired, and wrote Carlylean biographical studies and sketches of, some of history's 'Great Men' – Cromwell, Frederick the Great, Pitt, Chatham, Napoleon. They possessed the leadership qualities he entirely lacked: ruthless single-mindedness, decisiveness and stamina. On the surface a sybarite, and with the temperament of an artist rather than a politician, Rosebery nonetheless fitted quite snugly into the prevailing context of Victorian religiosity and moralizing strictures (Rhodes James 1963: 217–19).

Rosebery made his maiden speech in the Lords in 1871, by which time his Whig background and mildly radical leanings had confirmed him as a Liberal. Intellectually precocious and already a polished speaker, he struck contemporaries as destined for greatness. In the period of Disraeli's Tory government between 1874 and 1880 Rosebery made significant critical interventions on foreign affairs, the policy area which was most to absorb his energies and abilities throughout his career. Having duly impressed Gladstone, Rosebery cultivated his credentials as 'the coming man' still further in 1880 by stage-managing and financing his party leader's triumphant Midlothian election campaign. This episode soon became legendary: it came to be viewed as the prime example of how to work the new mass electorate and, more dubiously, an indication of the 'democratization' of

British political culture. Rather incongruously in the light of this, Midlothian was also notable for the rowdy popular acclaim accorded in Scotland to the aristocrat Rosebery; by this time he had opportunistically modelled himself as the champion of Scottish interests and the personification of Scotland's more egalitarian values.

Within the framework of competing interests and pressure groups that constituted Gladstone's Liberal party (Hamer 1972; Vincent 1972), Rosebery pressed the case for more efficient management of Scottish affairs and, more specifically, the creation of a Minister of State for Scotland. In this he was stoutly supported by the Scottish press led by the *Scotsman* editor Charles Cooper, the first of several prominent editors who were virtually to put themselves and their papers at Rosebery's disposal at different points in his career. In 1881 Gladstone brought Rosebery into his new government as an under-secretary at the Home Office with special responsibilities for Scottish business. Rosebery seems to have held out the hope of a speedy elevation to the cabinet as spokesman for Scotland but nothing so path-breaking attended his efforts and he resigned, peeved, in 1883. Two years later he was called to the much more prestigious rank of Lord Privy Seal and turned his sights away from Scotland. Nevertheless, his tireless advocacy must be held chiefly responsible for the all-party agreement which resulted in the creation of the Scottish Office and Secretary (initially without cabinet rank) in 1885. As prime minister in 1894 Rosebery was also responsible for the establishment in the Commons of a Scottish Grand Committee.

If cross-party consensus was achievable in relation to Scotland, the Irish Question by contrast convulsed British politics in the years 1885–6. Gladstone's conversion to Irish home rule and the subsequent bill put before parliament in April 1886 split the Liberal party – with many Whiggish MPs and peers, and a coterie of Chamberlainite radicals, breaking away. Rosebery, for all his Whig-grandee trappings, stayed loyal to Gladstone, exulting indeed in the issue's cathartic effects and its capacity to 'concentrate' the party's diverse energies (Hamer 1972: 124–6). However, he was no enthusiast for the issue *per se* in the manner of Gladstone himself or the new Irish secretary John Morley. Rosebery viewed its potential benefits in the wider context of the development of autonomy throughout the United Kingdom (including of course Scotland) and the empire. By the time of the home rule controversy Rosebery had become greatly enamoured of the idea of imperial federation; he had toured Australasia in 1883–4 extolling the virtues of a socially progressive 'Commonwealth', and in 1884 had declared his support for the newly formed Imperial Federation League (Rhodes James 1963: 152–89). The imperial theme was to be paramount in his future political career.

Although excluded from Gladstone's counsels in the process of ministry-formation in 1886 (Cooke and Vincent 1974: 131–3), Rosebery was awarded the considerable prize of the Foreign Office. He appreciated the delicious intricacies and fine points of diplomacy. It was a rarefied world in which Rosebery felt at home. It gave him the opportunity to detach himself to a great extent from the fractiousness of humdrum party politics. It was a political role which could be personalized beyond probably any other, and in the short six-month period of his tenure before the government fell with its Irish Bill, Rosebery made a substantial impact (Martel 1986: 51–3). He appeared to continue the policy of his predecessor Lord Salisbury towards the turbulent Balkan region, and in particular the emergence of Bulgarian nationalism. Indeed, Rosebery claimed that continuity in foreign policy should be a governing principle, something which indicated his coolness towards the party system as it then operated. Rosebery maintained Britain's diplomatic 'free hand' in relation to the great European powers. He made it clear that he believed that no foreign engagements should be undertaken without sufficient resources, and that imperial interests should determine policy considerations elsewhere (Martel 1986: 14–23). The brevity of his spell in office helped prevent Rosebery's empire-orientated foreign policy philosophy from coming too damagingly into collision with the Cobdenite 'Little England' sentiment in the Liberal party, but this was merely a struggle postponed (Shannon 1976: 243–4).

Out of power, the Liberals continued to be beset by the turbulence of the 'Irish preoccupation' and of special interest crusades around such causes as Welsh Disestablishment and temperance. Rosebery kept sufficiently in the limelight to enhance his future leadership credentials while denying any such intention. His chairmanship in 1889–90 of the newly created London County Council boosted his image in radical circles; in this capacity he worked closely with social reformers, including Fabians, and his attitude on slum-landlordism had the effect of deflecting attention from his own privileged lifestyle. In tandem he trumpeted the cause of the reform of the Lords, conscious perhaps of the difficulties that would be involved in being chosen to lead a party and a government from the upper House. Lady Rosebery's death in 1890 brought a tragic cessation of all such political activity and it seemed for a time that Rosebery would be impervious to the many pleas for his return. In the event he was reluctantly persuaded to resume duties at the Foreign Office when the Liberals next formed a government in August 1892.

Rosebery dreaded the prospect of the intense infighting which would naturally bedevil the party, returned to government as it was with the vital backing of the Irish Nationalists and on the basis of the bizarrely compendious 'Newcastle Programme'. It was a state of affairs from which Rosebery would strive to remain aloof, but his conduct of foreign policy was always likely to be carefully monitored by Gladstone and other senior colleagues such as the quarrelsome Harcourt and the high-minded Morley who, like Rosebery, were obvious candidates to succeed the leader (Stansky 1964).

Rosebery's approach was duly the subject of intra-party strife, first over the issue of Uganda, then in relation to Egyptian controversies. On the former Rosebery faced down the protests of those who considered his imperialist priorities more appropriate to the Tories than the Liberals, while his opposition to the Gladstonian desire to evacuate Egypt and improve relations with France was grounded resolutely in the belief that the latter was Britain's main antagonist and required to be contained by means of an 'informal' British link to the Triple Alliance of Germany, Italy and Austria. Overall, Rosebery's policy was geared to the consolidation of territory rather than expansion (Martel 1986: 120–1), and to limiting French and Russian expansion in the Far East and the Mediterranean.

By the beginning of 1894 it looked likely that Gladstone, having had his second Irish Home Rule Bill thrown out by the Lords, would resign as prime minister. The succession quickly crystallized into a choice between Rosebery and Harcourt, with the views of Morley an important factor in the situation. There followed a short period of frantic manoeuvring (Rhodes James 1963: 294–328; Stansky 1964: 19–91), most notably that carried out on his father's behalf by Lewis 'Loulou' Harcourt. However, Loulou overreached himself and if anything alienated support. Rosebery commanded the backing of most of the party's younger talent and the Liberal press, not to mention the Queen. Rosebery felt settled in the Foreign Office and claimed not to want the premiership, but he seems to have found the intrigue too good to resist and there was also the unappetizing prospect of having to serve under Harcourt (Rhodes James 1963: 498–512). Either way the days of Rosebery's tenure at the Foreign Office appeared numbered. The summit of politics beckoned to him in circumstances which served only to exacerbate his doubts and expose his lack of conviction.

Rosebery was invited to form a government by the Queen on 3 March 1894, and duly kissed hands on 5 March. Harcourt and Morley were both piqued and attempted to extract terms from Rosebery on which they would serve. Harcourt could not prevail upon Rosebery to have a veto on his choice of Foreign Secretary (another peer, Lord Kimberley), but was under the impression that he had secured a degree of autonomy in the Commons which amounted to virtually a joint premiership. Some contemporaries thus understood it and some historians have taken the same view (Rhodes James 1963: 332; Shannon 1976: 245). Rosebery, on the other hand, was under no such impression and seemed more perturbed by having to appease Morley (Rhodes James 1963: 334–5). More to the point was the ominous tone set from the start regarding Rosebery's premiership, and in particular his relationship with his Chancellor, Harcourt, in the Commons.

Within days of taking office Rosebery severely tested his colleagues' confidence in his leadership by making ill-judged remarks on Irish home rule now being dependent on the will of England, 'the predominant partner' in the kingdom. He had long been unenthusiastic about Irish home rule, something he had publicly signalled in 1893 to the annoyance of Gladstone. On becoming premier Rosebery clearly wished to move on from 'the Irish preoccupation' and find some other way of uniting the party's disparate energies. Before long, indeed, he was to attempt to transcend such sectionalism by identifying reform of the Lords as such a 'concentrating' issue (Hamer 1972: 196–207). But Rosebery's method of shelving the Irish question was tactless; he upset the Irish Nationalists (by now split into 'Parnellite' and 'Anti-Parnellite' factions) and offended the 'Celtic consciousness' of the Liberal party in seeming to bow to the primacy of English national opinion. The offending speech had to be quickly followed by another in Edinburgh in an attempt to heal wounds, but this only brought damaging castigation from political opponents such as Chamberlain.

Rosebery's credibility as leader was further undermined by what has been generally viewed as the most significant event of his premiership: Harcourt's 'Death Duties' budget of 1894. This was a far-reaching measure in relation to questions of property, privilege and landownership, and Harcourt's successful negotiation of it through parliament was toasted by radical opinion (Brooks 1986: 13–42). It was too radical for Rosebery, who feared that it would result in a 'horizontal division of parties' around questions of class interest. In Harcourt's view such a division was inevitable and the Liberals could only jeopardize their future strength by protecting the propertied. As Harcourt's star waxed, Rosebery was cast in the part of 'a rich man who disliked being taxed' (Marquess of Crewe 1931: ii, 468). This was somewhat unfair, given Rosebery's generally progressive approach to social questions, but the budget did highlight very vividly the dilemma for the Liberals in pursuing such a reformist course while attempting to retain its Gladstonian capacity to draw cross-class support. Rosebery was much more in tune than many of his colleagues with the growth of a mass popular culture around sport and leisure: his horses won the Derby in 1894 and 1895 and he became a patron of football clubs. Rosebery felt that important issues, such as reforms in the powers of the Lords, could be addressed without the loss to the Liberals of the wealth and intellectual energies of such men of his class who remained in the party. However, the campaign against the Lords was handled as maladroitly as Irish home rule; Rosebery was insufficiently specific about what he wanted and contrived only to alarm the Queen and confuse his party. Public opinion on the Lords, moreover, was dormant at this juncture (Brooks 1986: 44–59). In the face of another demoralizing episode, Rosebery took to complaining about lack of co-operation from his cabinet colleagues, especially Harcourt.

In foreign affairs Rosebery worked closely with Kimberley and communicated matters economically to Harcourt and other colleagues. Trouble was never far away and the government duly rode into a storm over the conduct of diplomacy relating to French designs on the Nile. A British–Belgian treaty which attempted to block French access through the Congo drew a fierce diplomatic response from the French and, in this instance, their German backers, and had to be withdrawn. All this ensured a furious backlash from Rosebery's colleagues who had largely been kept in the dark during the whole affair. Relations with France continued to be the central concern of foreign policy and a matter of perpetual friction in cabinet. The declaration, in March 1895, by Foreign Office minister and Rosebery acolyte, Sir Edward Grey, that Britain would regard as 'an unfriendly act' any French incursion into the Nile Valley, was a prime example of a potentially far-reaching diplomatic stroke taken with a minimum of consultation. Rosebery faced down the internal revolts over foreign policy issues but towards the end of his premiership it was clear that his diplomatic paradigm was coming apart, with Russian relations as well as French under severe strain and Britain's tenuous links to the Triple Alliance increasingly less acceptable to the Germans. Britain's position in international politics had become decidedly more circumscribed (Martel 1986: 242–51, 257).

By mid-1895 Rosebery's lame government seemed simply to want to be put out of its misery. It had run into the legislative sands on questions such as Welsh Disestablishment and crofters' rights in Scotland and had suffered by-election reverses. A defeat in the Commons resulting from the issue of army supplies prompted Rosebery to resign, but the Tories refused to take the initiative and dissolved. The general election in July found the Liberal leaders campaigning on different things and the party duly suffered the heaviest electoral reverse (as a party of government) in its history. The Unionist majority of 152 reflected in particular the decline of the Liberals in England; now more than ever the Liberals appeared a party of the 'Celtic Fringe'.

Rosebery's premiership thus concluded as ignominiously as it had begun and proceeded, yet the difficulties of dealing with Gladstone's legacy, of holding together a naturally fissiparous party, and of leading from the Lords should not be forgotten. Historians have been generally damning in their assessments but there has been acknowledgement of Rosebery's prescience on the matter of giving priority to reform of the upper House (Brooks 1986: 263), and Rosebery's young followers, such as the influential Haldane, were far from disillusioned: they would continue to show great faith in him in some dramatic political interventions to come.

Rosebery remained party leader after the election. He joined in the Liberal chorus of condemnation of the Jameson Raid in South Africa, although there is evidence which possibly suggests that he had known about Cecil Rhodes's plans (Rhodes James 1963: 494–7). On the other great foreign issue of the day, the Armenian problem, Rosebery's apparent reluctance to condemn the behaviour of the Turks contrasted starkly with the outrage expressed by his party and, in a significant foray out of retirement, Gladstone. An exasperated Rosebery responded by resigning the leadership in October 1896. Gladstone's intervention may have been the catalyst, but the issue was wider: Rosebery had come to view the task of being an effective party leader as incompatible with his desire to lead public opinion on empire and foreign-policy questions and, perhaps, to reshape Liberalism in the process (Stansky 1964: 212–22; Hamer 1972: 246–62). There is no doubt that if his ultimate aim was to return to the top of the political tree, he would have wanted to do so as leader of a party truly united around his own priorities and purposes.

In the event, it was the context of the Boer War between 1899 and 1902 that brought Rosebery back into the political limelight. The war provided a clear opportunity for Rosebery to elevate the cause of empire above the run of party squabbles and to inspire the coterie of supporters behind him who had become known as the 'Liberal Imperialists'. From the advent of Irish home rule as the issue which stimulated thinking about Imperial Federation, Rosebery had gathered important, and in the main young, Liberals to the cause of a progressive conception of empire and of imperial responsibilities (Matthew 1973). By the end of the century these men – Haldane, Grey, Asquith and others – looked set to provide Rosebery with the base from which to attempt to recapture the Liberal leadership, and replace the apparently stolid Henry Campbell-Bannerman who had taken over from Harcourt in 1898. The possibilities of political realignment and the defection of the Gladstonian radical wing of the Liberal party seemed to Rosebery to be encouragingly likely.

For a short time the Liberal imperialists rode the patriotic tide, particularly in Scotland where, in the 1900 general election, they stood between the Liberal party and a much more crushing setback. In November 1900 Rosebery used the medium of his Glasgow University Rectorial address to emphasize the need for future generations to be better fitted to meet the demands of empire: he thus connected significantly two major themes of the day – empire and 'National Efficiency' – and appeared to echo the same clarion call as Joseph Chamberlain and Lord Milner, the latter being in many ways the definitive imperial statesman of the time. 'Efficiency' for Rosebery and the Liberal imperialists meant a reformed educational system which gave greater priority to science, technical training, business studies and modern languages, and better standards of government and administration, drawing on experts and businessmen rather than muddling through on the 'gentleman amateur' principle (Matthew 1973: 228–35; Searle 1995: 53–8). Social reform was also central to the Liberal imperialist outlook, but the influence of Sidney Webb and the Fabians on Rosebery was evident in his preference for reform through the efforts of an educated elite rather than a more conventional radical policy programme.

Opposition to Liberal imperialist designs came predictably from the radical and pro-Boer wing of the Liberal party, but Campbell-Bannerman too proved a more than able strategist in holding the centre ground and exhibiting leadership qualities in contrast to Rosebery's Olympian posturing. The high-water mark of jingoism had already passed by the time Rosebery made his much-quoted Chesterfield speech of December 1901 urging Liberals to 'clean the slate' of 'obsolete policies' (chief of them Irish home rule) and march to the beat of what he yet regarded as the popular imperial mood in the country. The deceptive chorus of acclaim for his oratory emboldened Rosebery to establish the Liberal League early in 1902, but the ending of the South African War in May of that year rapidly marginalized it as a vehicle for change in the Liberal party. The pressures towards Liberal unity around Campbell-Bannerman steadily increased, and the eruption of political controversy around Chamberlain's adoption of tariff reform in 1903 made them irresistible. Even Rosebery had to throw his weight behind the classic Liberal cause of free trade.

By this time also any possibility of a new departure in British politics along the lines of a coalition or a new centre party had gone. In 1902 the influential Liberal newspaper editor J.L. Garvin canvassed the prospect of Rosebery ('the seer') and Chamberlain ('the executor') coming together to transcend petty rivalries; and Rosebery's disdain for the party system was by this time well established (Grainger 1986: 206–18). Nevertheless, there were still sufficient, petty or otherwise, differences between the Roseberyites and Chamberlain to render this possibility stillborn even before the tariff reform controversy, and Rosebery's gnomic behaviour only drove away potential allies and disheartened his acolytes

(Searle 1995: 58–63). By 1905 the most substantial of the latter such as Asquith and Grey had made their peace with Campbell-Bannerman and prepared themselves for service in a new Liberal government. Rosebery faded from political view and never again appeared as a credible rallying point for party dissentients or a national 'saviour' ready to lead a rescue and reconstruction mission.

Rosebery lived on until 1929, but the lights had gone out in 1917 when his son Neil was killed in the war and in the following year when he suffered a stroke which left him paralysed. He died a rather sad and haughty figure, largely forgotten in a new era of class-based party politics and imperial decline.

References and further reading

Brooks, D. (ed.) (1986) *The Destruction of Lord Rosebery: From the Diary of Sir Edward Hamilton, 1894–95*, London: Historian's Press. (An indispensable source for Rosebery's premiership. Hamilton was a senior civil servant close to Rosebery, Gladstone and other leading Liberals.)

Buchan, J. (1930) *Lord Rosebery 1847–1929*, London: Proceedings of the British Academy XVI.

Cooke, A. and Vincent, J. (1974) *The Governing Passion*, Brighton: Harvester.

Crewe, Marquess of (1930) *Lord Rosebery*, London: John Murray.

Ellman, R. (1988) *Oscar Wilde*, Harmondsworth: Penguin.

Gardiner, A. (1909) *Prophets, Priests and Kings*, London: Dent. (The most incisive short essay on Rosebery's career and character.)

Grainger, J. (1986) *Patriotisms*, London: Routledge & Kegan Paul.

Hamer, D. (1972) *Liberal Politics in the Age of Gladstone and Rosebery*, Oxford: Oxford University Press. (A substantial scholarly contribution which is strong on the wider context of Liberal Party politics.)

Martel, G. (1986) *Imperial Diplomacy: Rosebery and the Failure of Foreign Policy*, Kingston and Montreal: McGill-Queen's University Press. (A penetrating assessment of Rosebery in relation to foreign affairs.)

Matthew, H. (1973) *The Liberal Imperialists*, Oxford: Oxford University Press. (Still the most comprehensive treatment of the subject.)

Parris, M. (1995) *Great Parliamentary Scandals*, London: Robson Books.

Raymond, E. (1923) *The Man of Promise, Lord Rosebery*, London: T. Fisher Unwin.

Rhodes James, R. (1963) *Rosebery*, London: Weidenfeld & Nicolson. (The most satisfactory of the Rosebery biographies.)

Searle, G.E. (1995) *Country before Party: Coalition and the Idea of 'National Government' in Modern Britain, 1885–1987*, London: Longman.

Shannon, R. (1976) *The Crisis of Imperialism 1865–1915*, London: Paladin. (Densely detailed and grippingly narrated.)

Stansky, P. (1964) *Ambitions and Strategies: The Struggle for the Leadership of the Liberal Party in the 1890s*, Oxford: Clarendon Press.

Vincent, J. (1972) *The Formation of the British Liberal Party 1857–68*, Harmondsworth: Penguin.

Rosebery Papers.

A voluminous collection is held in the National Library of Scotland. Of particular interest is the mainly political correspondence (MS10001–216). In the collection Acc. 8365 there are notes made in preparation for some of Rosebery's published works. Apart from the biographies Rosebery published, note should also be made of his *Miscellanies Literary and Historical*, a volume edited by John Buchan and published by the London firm of Hodder & Stoughton in 1921.

Graham Walker

Arthur James Balfour, First Earl of Balfour

Born 25 July 1848, eldest son of James Maitland Balfour and Lady Blanche Cecil, daughter of the second Marquess of Salisbury. Educated at Eton and Trinity College, Cambridge. Unmarried. MP for Hertford 1874–85, Manchester East 1885–1906, City of London 1906–22. President of Local Government Board 1885–6; Secretary for Scotland 1886–7; Chief Secretary for Ireland 1887–91; First Lord of the Treasury and Leader of the Commons 1891–2 and 1895–1902; Prime Minister 1902–5; First Lord of the Admiralty 1915–16; Foreign Secretary 1916–19; Lord President of the Council 1919–22 and 1925–9. Left Commons and ennobled 1922. Died 19 March 1930.

Balfour, prime minister from July 1902 to December 1905, is in many respects the odd-man-out among modern premiers. Usually the premiership comes as the culmination of a politician's career, after which all is anti-climax or oblivion. Balfour's premiership, on the other hand, seems in retrospect to be merely an episode, and not necessarily the most important single episode, in a long life of public service. For though his record as prime minister was chequered and ended in humiliating electoral rejection, he quickly recovered from these setbacks. Nor did his political career end after he had been forced from the leadership of his party six years later. Indeed, Balfour was still a cabinet member in early 1929, nearly a quarter of a century after finally leaving 10 Downing Street.

Balfour's early political achievements owed much to family circumstance. He was born in 1848 at Whittingehame, East Lothian, the eldest son of James Maitland Balfour, a Scottish landowner. Through his mother he was closely tied to the Salisbury dynasty, being the nephew of the third Marquess, who was three times prime minister – a factor of great significance in Balfour's own career.

Balfour received his education at institutions appropriate to someone of his class. However, at university he opted to study the 'moral sciences' (philosophy) rather than classics, the subject favoured by most aristocratic youths. Shortly afterwards, in 1874, Balfour entered parliament, helped by the Cecil influence emanating from nearby Hatfield House. But it was only in the early 1880s, with his adhesion to the 'Fourth Party' (the other members being Lord Randolph Churchill, Drummond Woolff and John Gorst), that Balfour came to wider public attention. The 'Fourth Party' was a group of rebellious Conservative backbenchers who set out to rile Gladstone and his Liberal ministry, in the process showing up the pedestrian qualities of Sir Stafford Northcote, their leader in the

Commons. However, once Churchill had launched a personal bid for power, Balfour transferred his allegiance to Lord Salisbury, the leader in the Lords – a move which helped his uncle secure the premiership when Gladstone's ministry finally collapsed in June 1885. Balfour's reward was to be made President of the Local Government Board. In July 1886, following the short-lived interlude of Gladstone's third (home rule) ministry, he became Secretary of State for Scotland, entering the cabinet four months later.

Balfour had insufficient time to establish himself in either of these posts before he enjoyed a singular stroke of fortune. In March 1887 the Chief Secretary for Ireland, Sir Michael Hicks-Beach, resigned office, broken in health and spirits by the challenge being mounted to the British authorities by the defiant Irish Nationalists. Balfour's appointment as his successor was greeted by the Irish with derision, but the languid dilettante, whom they called 'Pretty Fanny', soon earned their grudging respect (and hatred) as 'Bloody Balfour', a minister whose courage, coolness, ruthlessness and willingness to stand by the officers of the Crown when attacked (as in the Mitchelstown Incident) did much to restore the self-confidence of the loyalist community.

Then in October 1891 the popular minister W.H. Smith suddenly died, and Balfour, who only five years earlier had been virtually unknown, took Smith's place as First Lord of the Treasury and Leader of the Commons: in the late nineteenth century there were periodic departures from the custom of combining the offices of prime minister and First Lord of the Treasury. He held this position until the end of Salisbury's government in 1892 and resumed it when his uncle returned to power in 1895. Balfour was now effectively joint Leader of the Conservative party, and, not being tied down by specific departmental responsibilities, enjoyed the freedom to take charge of a wide range of government business. In two areas of policy he made a significant contribution, Ireland and foreign policy. Now that the British government's authority in Ireland had been restored, he felt confident enough, aided by his brother Gerald, the new Irish Secretary, to introduce a series of reforming measures, which included the Irish Local Government Act 1898 and a series of land purchase schemes, culminating in the Wyndham Irish Land Act 1903. All this testifies to Balfour's lifelong belief that, since Irish nationalism was a symptom of that country's economic and social backwardness, the Irish Catholic population would accept its place within the Union once its material circumstances had improved – a perspective which no doubt came naturally to an upper-class Scotsman happily integrated into the British establishment.

Balfour also made his mark in foreign affairs. Diverging for once from the line being pursued by Salisbury, he found himself co-operating with younger politicians of his own generation in the search for new alliances that might shore up Britain's increasingly vulnerable position as a great power. However, nothing substantial came of these ventures, and Britain was still isolated when the Second Boer War broke out in October 1899.

Initially the war was a disaster for the British forces, and Balfour, as a prominent minister, shared in the government's resulting unpopularity, causing particular annoyance by the seemingly flippant manner in which he publicly responded to criticism. However, such was the state of division within the Liberal opposition that the Conservatives and their Liberal Unionist allies were able to secure a renewed term of office when parliament was dissolved in October 1900.

In the summer of 1902 the Boer armies unconditionally surrendered, and this provided the occasion for the ageing Salisbury to retire. He was succeeded as premier by Balfour, who had no serious rivals since the two other leading cabinet 'heavyweights', the Duke of Devonshire and Joseph Chamberlain, were both Liberal Unionists, which made them unacceptable to their dominant Conservative partners.

Unfortunately, Balfour entered Downing Street at an unpropitious moment. Wisdom of hindsight suggests that, with the Irish home rule issue temporarily dormant, Unionism was faltering for want of a clear mission. Moreover, many leading ministers, worn out by their long years in office, were becoming increasingly accident-prone. It was an inheritance which might well have undermined *any* prime minister.

Nevertheless it is ironic that Balfour quickly ran into difficulties as a result of one of his most creative initiatives: the Education Act 1902. This measure swept away the old school boards in England and Wales, and concentrated responsibility for elementary and secondary education in the hands of the newly created local education authorities (LEAs), an important step in the rationalization of the educational system. But the provision compelling the LEAs to provide rate aid to the mainly Anglican voluntary schools aroused nonconformity to paroxysms of anger. The ensuing uproar helped reunite and reinvigorate the Liberal opposition. It also unsettled and offended the Colonial Secretary, Joseph Chamberlain, a Unitarian heavily reliant upon dissenters' votes in his native Birmingham. This circumstance may in turn have contributed to Chamberlain's decision to launch the disruptive tariff reform campaign in May 1903.

Chamberlain succeeded in mobilizing a large sector of the Liberal Unionist and Conservative parties at both national and constituency levels when he unfolded a programme which, he claimed, would unite the empire through a system of imperial preferences, raise money for social reform, and protect home industries from 'unfair' foreign competition. But this challenge to the sanctities of free trade swiftly provoked the 'Unionist Free-Fooders' into forming organizations of their own. It was perhaps inevitable that Balfour should incur the abuse of both factions as he attempted to steer a middle path.

Balfour's ploy was to devise a fiscal compromise which envisaged the possible adoption of tariffs, but defined their main purpose as being the strengthening of the hands of the British government in its negotiations with protectionist foreign countries. Balfour elaborated on this idea in his pamphlet, *Insular Free Trade*, and in a series of public speeches. But persuading his party of the viability of this 'solution' did not prove easy. True, in the autumn of 1903 Balfour enjoyed a minor triumph when he managed to rid his administration of some of its fiscal fanatics – encouraging Chamberlain to leave the government, while simultaneously pushing into resignation the intransigent free traders, including his Chancellor of the Exchequer, C.T. Ritchie. However, Balfour's ingenious but abortive attempt to retain the services of the influential Duke of Devonshire merely contributed to his reputation for untrustworthiness. And although it was undoubtedly Balfour's tactical guile which held the Unionist ministry together for the following two years, a heavy price was exacted for this achievement. Manoeuvres like the one executed in March 1905, when Balfour used a procedural device to evade an opposition motion framed so as to expose Unionist divisions on the fiscal question, could readily be construed, by fellow Unionists as well as by political opponents, as the behaviour of someone who lacked 'settled convictions' – one of Balfour's own phrases, which critics wrenched out of context and regularly used against him.

From the autumn of 1903 onwards Balfour gave the impression of being a prime minister under siege. In addition to the damaging fiscal divisions, the government suffered one mishap after another, sometimes resulting in painful quarrels between the prime minister and long-standing friends such as George Wyndham, the Irish Secretary, and Lord Curzon, the Governor-General of India. The administration was especially damaged by its failure to satisfy the clamour for military reform that had broken out in the wake of the recent Boer War setbacks.

However, it would be a mistake to suppose that nothing positive came out of Balfour's three-and-a-half year premiership. As well as the Education Act 1902 and the Wyndham Irish Land Act 1903, Balfour was deeply involved in important measures to reform the navy, set up an army general staff and reorganize the Committee of Imperial Defence. The latter reform, which involved the creation of a forum where politicians, aided by a permanent secretariat, could meet military and naval experts on an equal footing, was an important step in the modernization of the machinery of government, prefiguring Lloyd George's decision to attach a secretariat to his war cabinet in 1916. Meanwhile the Foreign Secretary, Lord Lansdowne, ended British 'isolation', first with the Anglo-Japanese Alliance, and later with the Anglo-French Entente. Nor was Balfour what would normally be considered a weak prime minister. On the contrary, after the departure of Chamberlain and Devonshire he dominated his cabinet to perhaps an excessive degree, and such was his prowess as a parliamentary debater that the very survival of the ministry was put in jeopardy by his periodic bouts of influenza.

All the same, by the end of 1905 the Unionist ministry had reached the end of the road. In December, in a last desperate throw, Balfour tried to wrong-foot his opponents by resigning office instead of dissolving parliament. His hope was that divisions within the Liberal ranks would make it difficult for them to form an effective administration of their own and that this would damage their party electorally. However, after a week of uncertainty the Liberal leader, Campbell-Bannerman, succeeded in putting together an impressive ministerial team, and in the general election that shortly followed the Unionists were reduced to a mere 157 seats. Balfour himself was rejected by his constituents, one of only two twentieth-century premiers (the other being Ramsay MacDonald) to suffer this indignity; another dozen of his front-bench colleagues also failed to secure re-election.

However, in a by-election in February 1906 Balfour returned to the Commons, and later in the year his troubled relationship with his fractious and disheartened party was partly eased when Chamberlain suffered a severe stroke. Balfour then successfully rallied the opposition by drawing attention to Germany's serious challenge to British naval supremacy. He also appropriated some of the rhetoric of tariff reform, but turned it to his own purpose by presenting the tariff as a mechanism for raising fresh sources of revenue. Although by temperament better suited to government than to opposition, Balfour deserves some credit for the restoration of his party's fortunes after 1906: in the two general elections of 1910 the Unionists were returned to Westminster in almost equal numbers to the Liberals. But, supported by Labour and the Irish Nationalists, the Liberals remained in office.

Balfour's last chance of re-entering 10 Downing Street came and went in 1910 in the course of the constitutional crisis precipitated by the Lords' defeat of the 'People's Budget' – a fateful move which Balfour himself had sanctioned. Balfour was ready to form a minority government to rescue the King from the invidious responsibility of threatening a mass creation of peers so that the Parliament Bill, curbing the powers of the Lords, could become law. But Edward VII's private secretary, Lord Knollys, one of Balfour's former friends, withheld this information from the new monarch, George V. Balfour was furious when he later heard of Knollys's 'deception'.

In the summer of 1911 the Liberals emerged triumphant from the constitutional crisis, after Balfour had ordered his followers in the Lords to abstain over the Parliament Bill – a humiliation which in turn sparked off a rebellion within the Unionist party, orchestrated by the journalist, Leopold Maxse, coiner of the slogan 'BMG' (Balfour Must Go). In November Balfour duly stepped down as leader, to be replaced by Andrew Bonar Law, whose pugnacious style now better suited the mood of a party demoralized by three successive election defeats and yearning to be led by a 'winner'.

But Balfour, still only 64 years old, had no thought of retiring from public life. Enjoying his new status as 'elder statesman', he sat at Asquith's request on the Committee of Imperial Defence, where his experience and intelligence were highly valued. Hence, it was no surprise when, on the formation of the first wartime coalition in May 1915, Balfour became First Lord of the Admiralty. Balfour did not shine in this office: he came under particular criticism for his handling of the press releases after the indecisive Battle of Jutland in June 1916. But Asquith stood by Balfour, and therefore had an unpleasant surprise when, during the ministerial crisis of December 1916, Balfour abandoned the prime minister and joined Lloyd George, who went on to form his own administration in which Balfour served as Foreign Secretary.

There had been a certain sympathy between Balfour and Lloyd George going back to the pre-war years: significantly, Balfour had been tempted by Lloyd George's secret proposal to establish a coalition government in 1910. After December 1916, also, the two men worked well together. This was in part because Balfour was usually prepared to play second fiddle to Lloyd George, allowing the premier, for example, to dominate the British delegation during the peace negotiations at Versailles in 1919. However, the controversial 'Balfour Declaration' of November 1917, in which the Jews were promised a 'national homeland', was very much the Foreign Secretary's personal initiative.

In October 1919 Balfour exchanged the Foreign Office for the post of Lord President of the Council, but he continued to do important work for Lloyd George's coalition government, notably his negotiation of the Washington Naval Treaty with the United States and Japan in 1922, in recognition of which the King conferred on him the Order of the Garter, followed in May by the earldom to which, as a former premier, he was traditionally entitled. Indeed, Balfour, the one-time party leader, had by now become converted to the desirability of permanent 'national government'. This led to a spell in the wilderness when Lloyd George's coalition collapsed in October 1922.

In April 1925 Balfour returned to office, Baldwin appointing him Lord President for a second time. Here he made two important contributions. First, at the Imperial Conference of 1926 he came up with the formula which was later to define the relationship between the United Kingdom and the Dominion States. Second, he actively promoted scientific research through the recently founded Medical Research Council (MRC) and the Department of Scientific and Industrial Research (DSIR). Balfour finally left office after the Conservative defeat in the general election of June 1929.

Balfour's importance in the political life of late-Victorian and early-twentieth-century Britain is not in doubt, but historians, like contemporaries, are divided over his character and achievements. What kind of person was he? As a young man, the centre of a chic social coterie called 'the Souls', Balfour had dazzled nearly all who met him with his intelligence and charm. But he seems never to have entirely recovered from the unexpected death, through typhoid fever, of his fiancée, May Lyttelton, in 1875. Balfour remained a bachelor, and though he continued to be surrounded by adoring female friends, the most important of whom was Mary Elcho, this once affectionate man acquired a chilling self-control; sadly, the 'court' over which 'Prince Arthur' had once presided gradually disintegrated as its social leader became estranged from most of his one-time friends.

As a public figure Balfour seems equally elusive. Lloyd George, in an uncharitable moment, once dismissed him as 'just like the scent on a pocket handkerchief', while others have questioned whether a man who had so many interests outside politics could have been entirely in earnest as a statesman. It is certainly the case that Balfour devoted large amounts of time to golf and tennis, and had a deep love of music (Handel being one of his lifelong favourites). He wrote two books on philosophy, *A Defence of Philosophic Doubt* and *The Foundations of Belief*, and he could debate scientific issues with professional scientists. Balfour, in many ways, was the archetypal intellectual in politics, a man whose elegant memoranda reveal a 'donnish' intelligence and fastidiousness.

Many contemporary intellectuals responded sympathetically to these traits. For example, during the Edwardian years Balfour was on friendly terms with the Fabian leadership, a circumstance which partly explains why Beatrice Webb was appointed a member of the royal commission on the poor laws in 1905. H.G. Wells was particularly impressed by Balfour's far-sighted views on science; in his novel, *The New Machiavelli* (1911), he portrays Balfour, thinly disguised as 'Evesham', as a great visionary statesman. But were the Fabians simply succumbing, as so many others did, to what Asquith once called Balfour's 'superficial charm'?

Detachment and intellectual curiosity are not usually thought to be the primary virtues required of a party leader, and Maxse was therefore not alone in suspecting that to Balfour politics was merely another game. Others saw him as a dialectician incapable of decisive action. This complaint is in some ways unfair, since, when his mind was made up, Balfour could act quickly, even brutally. Nevertheless, despite his skill in negotiations and in Commons debates, as a party leader Balfour was hardly a success. He is one of only four twentieth-century prime ministers never to have won a general election. Balfour affected to despise the press, had none of Chamberlain's magnetism as a platform speaker, and lacked the common touch necessary for widespread popularity. His habit of communicating with the outside political world via his indispensable secretary, Jack Sandars, further accentuated his aura of aloofness. At the same time Balfour left many of his less intelligent backbenchers with the feeling that he despised them or was laughing at them (an impression which he also made on Edward VII).

What ideological assumptions did Balfour bring to the premiership? At one level he was a traditionalist who believed that his primary duty was to hold the Conservative party together at almost any cost. This in turn reflected his conviction that the stability of civilization rested on the survival of the established church, the Lords, and landed privilege, which only a strong Conservative party could protect. Birth and social connections combined to make Balfour one of the last of the aristocratic Conservative leaders – in sharp contrast to his immediate successors, Bonar Law, Austen Chamberlain, Baldwin and Neville Chamberlain, all quintessentially middle-class figures. Even in his own heyday, contemporaries, contemptuous of what they called the 'Hotel Cecil', complained of nepotism and social cliquishness. Balfour, it seems, was the first prime minister to be addressed in cabinet by his first name, and his administration often gave others the impression of being a family house party, albeit one where friends and relatives were on somewhat tetchy terms with one another. Balfour managed his party in a similarly personal way through Sandars and his Chief Whip, Acland-Hood, leaving fundamental organizational reforms to his successor.

Yet there is another side to Balfour's character: a sensitive awareness of the significance of the enormous social and political changes which were happening throughout the course of his career. Balfour had first been elected to parliament for what was effectively a nomination borough: he lived long enough to serve in an administration which enacted adult suffrage. Similarly, Balfour came into public life at a time of significant imperial expansion, only to see the empire develop into the commonwealth and leadership in world affairs pass from Europe to America.

What marked Balfour off from many contemporaries was his realization that, if he was to preserve anything of the social order into which he had been born, he would have to persuade his own class to modernize itself and adapt. Indeed, in some respects – for example, his commitment to state-aid for science – he was well ahead of his age, helped perhaps by his relatives' involvement in scientific research. Equally far-sighted was his support of a limited enfranchisement of women at a time when most of his colleagues opposed votes for women on principle.

Balfour was the most flexible of Conservative leaders, quick to see the need for change in an evolving world. The experience of the First World War, for example, convinced him of the indispensability of a figure like Lloyd George in steering the country into an era of mass democracy and it also made him question the continuing usefulness of traditional two-party politics. Moreover, while the 'diehards' tried to maintain the empire unchanged, Balfour, himself an imperialist of sorts, came to see that British power needed underpinning by new alliances. He helped negotiate the transition from empire to commonwealth; he was a lifelong devotee of the special relationship with the United States; and he quickly grasped the importance of Zionism.

Even in Ireland Balfour's impact was not entirely negative: his claim to have shaped the Irish Free State through his earlier social and economic reforms has some justification. But his most important legacies are the Education Act 1902 and the reorganization of the Committee of Imperial Defence, both these measures being central to the wider Edwardian movement to promote 'National Efficiency'. Balfour's main significance, then, is as a modernizing aristocrat, with a keen appreciation of the importance of expertise. No doubt his beliefs were an unstable compound. But in his day Balfour helped steer the country through a period of bewildering change.

References and further reading
Dugdale, B. (1936) *Arthur James Balfour, First Earl of Balfour*, 2 vols, London: Hutchinson. (The author was Balfour's niece, and as such the repository of many confidences. Still worth reading.)
Dutton, D. (1992) '*His Majesty's Loyal Opposition': The Unionist Party in Opposition 1905–1915*, Liverpool: Liverpool University Press.
Egremont, M. (1980) *Balfour*, London: Collins. (An attractively written biography, perhaps the most convincing portrait of Balfour as a man, but also shrewd about his politics.)
Gollin, A. (1965) *Balfour's Burden: Arthur Balfour and Imperial Preference*, London: Anthony Blond. (Narrowly focused on Balfour's handling of the cabinet crisis of the autumn of 1903.)

Mackay, R. (1985) *Balfour: Intellectual Statesman*, Oxford: Oxford University Press. (Heavily dominated by Balfour's contribution to foreign policy and strategic planning.)

Ramsden, J. (1978) *The Age of Balfour and Baldwin*, London: Longman. (Part of a multi-volume history of the Conservative party. Unsurprisingly, Balfour emerges poorly when considered in this context.)

Ridley, J. and Clayre, P. (eds) (1992) *The Letters of Arthur Balfour and Lady Elcho 1885–1917*, London: Hamilton. (Throws interesting light on Balfour's personal and social life.)

Searle, G. (1971) *The Quest for National Efficiency, 1899–1914*, Oxford: Blackwell. Reissued (1990) London: Ashfield Press. (Emphasizes Balfour's role as a 'modernizer'.)

Shannon, C. (1988) *Arthur J. Balfour and Ireland, 1874–1922*, Washington, DC: Catholic University of America Press.

Williams, R. (1987) 'Arthur James Balfour, Sir John Fisher and the politics of naval reform, 1904–10', *Historical Research* 60 (1): 80–99. (Emphasizes Balfour's commitment to cross-bench co-operation in matters of naval reform.)

Zebel, S. (1973) *Balfour: A Political Biography*, Cambridge: Cambridge University Press. (Particularly good at unravelling the complex fiscal controversy.)

Geoffrey Searle

Henry Campbell-Bannerman

Born 7 September 1836, second son of James (later Lord Provost Sir James) Campbell and Janet Bannerman. In 1868 changed surname to Campbell-Bannerman on inheriting an uncle's estate in Kent. Educated at Glasgow High School and the Universities of Glasgow (non-graduating) and Cambridge. Married 1860 Charlotte (died 1906), daughter of Major-General Sir Charles and Lady Charlotte Bruce. MP for Stirling District Burghs 1868–1908. Financial Secretary, War Office, 1871–4 and 1880–2; Parliamentary and Financial Secretary, Admiralty, 1882–4; Chief Secretary for Ireland 1884–5; Secretary for War 1886, 1892–4; Leader of the Liberal party, 1899–1908; Prime Minister 1905–8. Knight Grand Cross of the Order of the Bath 1894. Resigned as Prime Minister 3 April 1908. Died 22 April 1908.

Campbell-Bannerman's twenty-eight months' tenure of the premiership has frequently been portrayed as relatively undistinguished. Few significant reforms were enacted. Several major bills were shredded in the Lords, including ones on plural voting, English and Scottish land reform, and licensing reform. Other measures were rejected as much by the party's supporters in the country as by Unionist peers – notably the Education Bills of 1906 and 1907. When bills were passed, they were either somewhat technical, such as a Patents Act, or the fruits of cross-party consensus, such as the Trade Disputes Act. Campbell-Bannerman had no apparent scheme to circumvent the Lords' veto. Moreover, there was little stimulus given by him to the social reform programme which was to characterize the party under his successor. The decision to launch old age pensions was indeed taken, but this was essentially the creation of Asquith and the social reform elements in the ministry. Campbell-Bannerman's interest in this question lay more in the pruning of defence expenditure – a classic Gladstonian viewpoint – than in providing pensions. In his relations with the cabinet he seemed lackadaisical and reactive. Some insiders commented critically on the diffuse debates and ill-focused methods of handling business in his cabinet. He has been blamed for not reining in Grey's foreign policy. The decision in 1906 to initiate conversations on defence interests with the French was not brought before the full cabinet, and Campbell-Bannerman was either implicated in a conspiracy to conceal or was unaware of the consequences of these diplomatic overtures. Either way, his competence is severely questioned. Part of the problem was his nature: genial but rather unenergetic, he was not a thruster. Also, he was elderly: at over 69 he was (and remains) the oldest first-time premier since 1832. He was seriously ill, and had several heart attacks while in office. The death in 1906 of his wife, to whom he was closely attached, was a severe blow to his spirit, and reduced his dynamism still further.

Damning though this indictment may appear, it is nevertheless possible to construct a more favourable interpretation of Campbell-Bannerman's incumbency, particularly for some long-term aspects of the premiership which his tenure initiated or epitomized, and also because he laid the necessary basis for the more effective Asquith government which followed.

He was part of that remarkable half-century in which the Scottish connection dominated holders of the post of prime minister. Between 1880 and 1935 five of the ten premiers were Scotsmen, and another two represented Scottish constituencies and had close Scottish family ties. Between 1832 and 1880, only one of the nine prime ministers was Scottish; and since 1935, again only one of the ten has been Scottish. In this way, Campbell-Bannerman symbolized the full integration of Scotland into the Union, and the confident acceptance by the majority of his fellow Scots of their secure role in the British state. The two national identities fused easily: he was quite proud of his Scottishness, yet felt no less British.

Campbell-Bannerman was also the first prime minister to have direct experience of business, and not to come from a landed, Anglican background. He worked in the family's highly successful retail firm from the age of 22 (becoming a partner within two years) until he entered parliament. Campbell-Bannerman did own an estate in Scotland, but this was acquired during his adulthood rather than being an inherited badge of elite status. His devout Presbyterianism precluded sympathy with aristocratic privilege. Thus he can be regarded as setting the trend in terms of the social background of the majority of twentieth-century premiers, where the landed interest has been in retreat.

A further novel aspect of his premiership was that he was the first holder of the office to project himself as distinctly non-metropolitan. Although very wealthy and the owner of a substantial Scottish estate, he was by upbringing and instinct never part of high society in the way of his predecessors. He and his wife were not glittering social figures; his closest political intimates, T.R. Buchanan, Robert Reid, John Sinclair, were mostly outside or on the very fringes of fashionable society. In offering a more provincial image, he opened a path followed by the majority of twentieth-century premiers – apart perhaps from only Churchill, Eden, Macmillan and Home.

Partly as an outcome, Campbell-Bannerman introduced another new element into the premiership. He was not, in contrast to his predecessors, a grandee, condescending to communicate *de haut en bas* with the party rank-and-file in the constituencies. A large part of the affection in which he was held by Liberal party supporters arose from his 'ordinariness', so that they felt he was really very close to them in outlook. This came about, to some extent, because of his long-standing and strong impulse to preserve the unity of the party and his instinctive loyalty to the cause. This was seen to perfection during the Boer War, when he was perceived as articulating the innate wishes of the grass roots to find a common ground which would maintain unity. This relationship with the membership was new: Balfour famously said that he would as soon take political advice from his valet as from the National Union of Conservative Associations; Rosebery's aloofness was a frequent source of complaint. Campbell-Bannerman's successors frequently adopted the mantle of an average party supporter in a bid to win internal support: Baldwin and Thatcher for the Tories, Attlee, Wilson and Callaghan for Labour.

Campbell-Bannerman also established a different approach to running a reforming party in government from his predecessors. He was not a dynamic leader who played a starring and active part in the government. This approach was adopted by Gladstone, MacDonald, Rosebery and Wilson. Campbell-Bannerman was a manager and a facilitator for brighter figures to shine. His role was to steady the exuberant ministers and mediate between conflicts, mostly acting as a final check, rather than an instigator. The administrations of Attlee and Callaghan were to be characterized by a similar style. His style of relaxed supervision was vital in allowing talented departmental ministers to function in a self-directed manner, so perhaps inspiring greater creativity than tighter oversight might have permitted. Lloyd George, for example, was given his head at the Board of Trade, where he flourished. He produced a stream of useful, if uncontroversial, legislation. This enabled him to escape his previous reputation as a hotheaded rabble-rouser by displaying a high degree of administrative competence. When his combative utterances about the Lords drew the wrath of the King on two occasions, Campbell-Bannerman unstintingly backed his minister. In this way he inspired trust from his ministers, while his readiness to defend them from external criticism also indicates that his light touch was not the product of indolence.

His inclination not to meddle much in ministerial business contributed to the rise of departmental autonomy. This trend was most clearly seen in foreign policy, where he left Grey to pursue an essentially bipartisan line, continuing along the position laid down by the previous Unionist government. It is not clear whether Campbell-Bannerman failed to make Grey's initiation of closer links with France more widely known to cabinet because of a sense of his lack of expertise in diplomacy (Robbins 1971: 145–9). However, his actions elsewhere, when he wished to tilt government policy in a direction which he preferred, suggest otherwise. Three instances show this: the constitutional legislation for the Boer republics of South Africa; plans to reform the Lords; and trade union legislation.

Smuts recounts how Campbell-Bannerman was fully persuaded by the Boer delegation of the importance of putting the government of their provinces on a broad, expansive footing, rather than the restrictive degree of democratic participation proposed by his own departmental ministers. Then, almost alone in cabinet, the prime minister swung opinion, which had been heavily against, over to his position (Wilson 1973: 476–530). This episode also reaffirmed the image of Campbell-Bannerman as a man of unwavering principle, his support for Boer self-government being the logical consequence of the stance he expounded during the Boer War of 1899–1902.

In dealing with the obstacle to legislation presented by the Lords' veto, Campbell-Bannerman adopted a policy of avoiding head-on collisions until public sympathy was pronouncedly on the Liberals' side. Though unglamorous, this was a skilful line, and came to fruition in 1909–11. His political shrewdness was seen in his rejection of a cabinet committee's scheme to reform the Lords. He recognized that the proposals were unwieldy and inconsistent. Instead he pushed through his own option, which became substantially the basis of the Parliament Act 1911 (Wilson 1973: 554–630). Here he deployed greater political *nous* than Asquith, who had initially endorsed the Ripon Committee's approach.

His handling of the Trade Disputes Act is revealing. On the floor of the Commons, without consulting his colleagues, he overturned his own ministers' measure, instead accepting a Labour backbencher's bill. This latter was much more favourable to trade union rights, and created consternation among legal experts (McCord 1993: 256–9).

His attitude to the emergent Labour party was significant in shaping relations between the two anti-Conservative parties in the period down at least until 1914. He entertained no qualms or foreboding about recognizing Labour's claim to a separate existence. He was one of the leading actors in the creation of the Liberal–Labour electoral pact of 1903, being consulted by his negotiator, the Chief Whip Herbert Gladstone, at each stage in the talks. The arrangement, which ensured electoral co-operation between the two parties, was in keeping with Campbell-Bannerman's sympathetic response to the demands of Labour. He had been relaxed about the intervention of Labour candidates in by-elections between 1900 and 1906. His stance during the Boer War probably facilitated this rapport with Labour. In government, his appointment of the first working man (John Burns) to a cabinet position is consistent with his general stance on this matter, as was his crucial role in the shaping of the Trade Disputes Act, as discussed above.

Probably Campbell-Bannerman's greatest achievement precedes his term of office as prime minister. He managed to hold the Liberal party together through the strains imposed by the Boer War, when there was a three-way rift, between the

Liberal Imperialists, the pro-Boers, and the middle group, who tried to steer between these two polarities. Campbell-Bannerman strove successfully to keep all three sections within the party. Yet after the war he stressed the need for reconciliation. Asquith, the leading Liberal Imperialist MP, was given charge by Campbell-Bannerman of the Liberals' onslaught from 1903 on the Unionists' flirtation with Tariff Reform, thereby restoring a sense of common purpose. Campbell-Bannerman's outflanking of the Liberal Imperialist plot in 1905 (the Relugas pact) to remove him from the leadership of the government in the Commons by elevating him to a nominal position in the Lords was not followed by a vendetta on his part. All three of the conspirators (Asquith, Grey and Haldane) were given senior posts, and they received the prime minister's full backing for their policies on departmental matters (Wilson 1973: 423–58). Nor should his role in the 1906 general election be underestimated. His Albert Hall speech on 21 December 1905 was widely credited with putting the Unionists on the defensive for the rest of the campaign, while simultaneously emphasizing the connections between free trade and foreign policy, economic recovery and social reform (Russell 1973: 101–3). His tour of constituencies in the north-west of England in early January 1906 may well have been a contributory factor in the remarkable gains made by the Liberals in that area.

The make-up of his administration confirmed Campbell-Bannerman's striving for harmony and co-operation between sections of Liberalism. Besides a full quota of Liberal Imperialists, there was a good representation of the Gladstonian tradition (Morley, Ripon, Herbert Gladstone, and the prime minister himself); along with a fair number of Whigs (Elgin, Crewe) and a judicious sprinkling of radicals (Lloyd George, John Burns, Churchill). In this context, Campbell-Bannerman was essential as a balancing presence within a party slowly recovering from the internal feuding of the later 1890s and early 1900s. He acted to check the overweening influence of any particular faction, and so created a sense of unity and shared purpose which was utilized by Asquith to inaugurate a period of radical reform.

References and further reading

Gilbert, B. (1987) *David Lloyd George, a Political Life: The Architect of Change, 1863–1912*, London: Batsford. (Gives a view of the administration from the standpoint of the most radical member of Campbell-Bannerman's cabinet.)

Harris, J. and Hazlehurst, C. (1970) 'Campbell-Bannerman as prime minister', *History* 55: 360–83. (Stresses his personal qualities, but notes his failings as a head of government.)

McCord, N. (1993) 'Taff Vale revisited', *History* 78: 243–60. (Critical of the loose wording of the 1906 Act and of the measure's efficacy.)

Robbins, K. (1971) *Sir Edward Grey: A Biography of Lord Grey of Falloden*, London: Cassell. (Helpful on the prime minister's involvement in foreign policy.)

Rowlands, P. (1968) *The Last Liberal Governments: The Promised Land, 1905–10*, London: Barrie & Rockliff. (A very solid and factual treatment of all aspects of the Campbell-Bannerman premiership.)

Russell, A. (1973) *Liberal Landslide: The General Election of 1906*, Newtown Abbott: David & Charles. (A close study of the election, with attention paid to Campbell-Bannerman's role in the campaign.)

Wilson, J. (1973) *CB: a Life of Sir Henry Campbell-Bannerman*, London: Constable. (A full biography, well grounded on the subject manuscripts, but not by a professional historian. Stronger on character than interpretation.)

Iain Hutchinson

Herbert Henry Asquith, Earl of Oxford and Asquith

Born 12 September 1852, second child of Joseph and Emily Asquith. Educated at Huddersfield College, Fulneck School, City of London School and Balliol College, Oxford. Married (1) 1877 Helen Melland (died 1891); (2) 1894 Margot Tennant. MP for East Fife 1886–1918, Paisley 1920–4. Home Secretary 1892–5; Chancellor of the Exchequer 1905–8; Prime Minister 1908–16. Left Commons 1924, ennobled 1925. Died 15 February 1928.

Despite his previously brief experience of political office, Asquith's premiership was the longest for almost a century and the last Liberal one. Under him 'new Liberalism' culminated in a spate of reforms, providing the modern basis of taxation and paving the way for the later creation of the welfare state. He effectively set the future pattern of parliamentary government by constraining the powers of the upper House. The introduction of payment for MPs and legalization of the political levy both influenced the subsequent shape of party politics, allegedly allowing the Labour party to replace the Liberal party at Westminster. Asquith was unable to resolve the Irish Question, but he held both his party and the country together when the First World War broke out. Ultimately, however, his political style was deemed inappropriate to the needs of total war. His resignation in 1916 epitomized internal divisions within the Liberal party, and neither it nor he were ever again to assume office.

Asquith shared few of the social advantages enjoyed by his contemporaries in late-nineteenth-century Liberal politics. At the age of 8 he lost his father, a minor employer in the woollen trade. Effective family life perished with him. After early schooling in Yorkshire Herbert and his brother William went into lodgings in order to attend the City of London School as day boys, while their semi-invalided mother settled in Sussex. At school Asquith revealed the grasp of diction, the precision of language and the logical faculty that were to make him into one of the most effective parliamentary orators of his day, and which caused Benjamin Jowett to predict a significant future for him.

Although Asquith's arrival at Balliol as a classical scholar in 1869 coincided with Jowett's election as Master, he was intellectually and politically closer to T.H. Green. Asquith spent his spare time arguing the orthodox advanced Liberal case before the Oxford Union of which he ultimately became president. A first class degree in Greats, followed by a college fellowship in 1874, appeared to open the door for an academic career, but Asquith was intent upon the law as a more promising entrée to the world of politics on which his heart was set.

A junior barrister supplementing his income by journalism, Asquith became first secretary of the Eighty Club, a group of young radicals with imperialist tendencies. He came to the attention of Gladstone when, as devil to the Treasury counsel, he prepared a brief on the significance of the parliamentary oath. Encouraged by R.B. Haldane, the only man with whom he ever developed an intimate friendship, Asquith successfully contested East Fife in the election of 1886. Both his legal and his political prospects improved enormously in 1889 when he clinically exposed the criminal neglect with which the manager of *The Times* had published libellous material about C.S. Parnell, leader of the Irish party.

Gladstone was sufficiently impressed to offer Asquith the post of Home Secretary in August 1892, a 'signal tribute to your character, abilities and eloquence' (Jenkins 1964: 60). As a minister he was noted for his administrative efficiency and self-confidence. He never doubted that he was right to authorize the use of troops at Featherstone in 1893, even though the ensuing deaths of two striking miners often came back to haunt his public life. More constructive was his Factory and Workshops Act, which extended the factory inspectorate and established women inspectors for first time. When Gladstone resigned in 1894 he told Asquith that while they faced great problems in the future, 'I know no one more likely to face them, . . . with a manly strength, . . . with a determined integrity of mind' (Jenkins 1964: 71).

Barely a year later Gladstone's successor, Rosebery, resigned first as premier and then as party leader. Asquith developed a close working relationship with his replacement, Campbell-Bannerman. Although it was threatened briefly by Asquith's imperial sympathies at the time of the Boer War, Asquith always opposed any moves which in his view would weaken the party. His opposition (on practical rather than sectarian grounds) to the controversial Education Bill of 1902 did much to re-establish Liberal unity and his own prominence. So, too, did his relentless attack on Joseph Chamberlain's campaign for tariff reform and imperial preference which he demolished with a devastating combination of logic, facts and economics, none of which figured overmuch in Chamberlain's own presentations. Asquith's criticisms derived added weight from his Liberal imperialist credentials.

When Balfour finally resigned at the end of 1905 Campbell-Bannerman decided to form an administration before holding an election. The prospect of the Exchequer was sufficient to break Asquith's commitment to the Relugas pact, by which he, Grey and Haldane had all agreed not to serve unless Sir Henry went to the Lords. In fact, all three accepted cabinet posts and the Liberals enjoyed a sweeping electoral success. As Chancellor, Asquith introduced compulsory returns on all categories of income, instituted inquiries into the feasibility of graduated taxation and differentiation between earned and unearned income, and overcame Treasury opposition to supertax. His third budget announced the introduction of old age pensions, the first step towards developing a welfare state.

Even without these innovations Asquith was the obvious successor when the ailing Campbell-Bannerman resigned in April 1908. Apart from his outstanding parliamentary ability he was, after John Morley, the senior man in the cabinet and had led the House during Campbell-Bannerman's absences. He assumed office at a critical stage in the government's fortunes. The enthusiasm of 1906 had begun to ebb, cracks were appearing in Liberal unity, by-elections had been lost, the economy was turning down, and something of a legislative logjam had developed as the Lords had rejected important measures. Campbell-Bannerman had successfully welded diverse Liberal interests together and Asquith made only a few marginal changes of cabinet personnel in a 'momentary display of inelegant butchery' (Hazlehurst 1970: 505). Where he improved on his predecessor was in encouraging a more coherent programme to develop, and if he exercised executive authority indirectly and discreetly, he was far more than just the passive recipient of others' ideas (Koss 1976: 100). This was particularly evident in the sphere of social reform, where Asquith, less of a radical than has sometimes been suggested, skilfully brought together the ideas of his cabinet's new Liberal and non-Progressive members (Tanner 1990: 46). The legislation establishing pensions was passed in 1908. It was followed by labour exchanges, trade boards and unemployment insurance. Essentially *ad hoc* responses to specific social evils, these measures collectively constituted a fundamental break with past efforts to deal with poverty, rejecting the long-standing assumption that it was the fault of the individual and bringing systematic state intervention to bear in the labour market for the first time. Health insurance in 1911 was more of an ambulance wagon than a major attempt to eliminate the cause of illness, but it, too, set the pattern for the next generation.

This legislation inevitably involved some consideration of new ways of raising revenue, especially as there was also pressure to increase naval expenditure in the light of German competition. Building on Asquith's own previous budgets, Lloyd George introduced in 1909 a controversial Finance Bill. It proposed to shift the emphasis from indirect to direct taxation related to the capacity to pay, and also entailed some limited redistribution from the rich to the poor, mainly through the land and other wealth taxes. It was so radical that it brought to a head the long-simmering dispute with the Lords. Greatly diminished in the Commons after 1906, the Unionists had utilized the upper chamber to obstruct government bills. Asquith resisted demands to challenge the peers immediately, suspecting that the electorate would be more influenced by the unpopularity of the defeated measures than by the constitutional principle raised in their rejection by the Lords. There is nothing to suggest either that he deliberately encouraged confrontation with the Lords via the 1909 budget. It probably never occurred to him that the peers would defy constitutional precedent by rejecting a Money Bill but once they did, he took over as the government's chief protagonist. Briefly, after the general election of January 1910, which left him dependent upon the support of the Irish and Labour parties, his confidence wavered, and the phrase he coined at this time, 'wait and see', was afterwards used against him quite unfairly in different circumstances. The budget was finally approved at the end of April 1910 but the government's intention to deal with the constitutional issue was frustrated by the sudden death of Edward VII. Asquith felt bound to avoid pressing the new King for an immediate dissolution and promises that sufficient new peers would be created in order to force through reforms in the powers of the upper House. Accordingly, therefore, he initiated constitutional talks. They foundered partly because the Unionists feared that any diminution in the Lords' powers would prevent them from resisting home rule. Albeit somewhat reluctantly, therefore, George V gave Asquith the guarantees he sought, but only on condition that he first call another election. Held in December 1910, this merely confirmed the January verdict. When the unrepentant peers massacred the Parliament Bill in committee, Asquith called on the King to deliver his promise. Knowing that if they did not give way their numbers would be suddenly and hugely inflated, the bitterly divided peers caved in and narrowly passed the bill restricting their powers.

The constitutional crisis was perhaps Asquith's finest hour, even though it absorbed two years and entailed the sacrifice of the great Liberal majority of 1906. The parliamentary battleground was one in which Asquith excelled and he generally handled the situation firmly and sensitively. Not only had he preserved reasonably good relations with the Crown, but in curbing the Lords' powers he had also prepared the way for Irish home rule.

Its imminence, however, provoked considerable unrest both in Ulster and on the part of extreme Unionists. In conjunction with upsurges of industrial and suffragette militancy, the Ulster *impasse* subsequently prompted the suggestion that Asquith's peacetime record should be 'subjected to the severest scrutiny' (Hazlehurst 1970: 531). But he was a firm believer in parliamentary supremacy and the appeal of reason. Like his mentor Gladstone, he did not mistake popular agitation for public opinion. Thus he never fully came to terms with the demand for women's suffrage because he had tried to keep the passion out of what was an intrinsically passionate issue. He was similarly baffled by Ireland where rationality seldom ruled, remarking to Venetia Stanley in 1914 on 'the folly of thinking that we can ever understand, let alone govern them' (Jenkins 1964: 322). Essentially a patient man, he took the view that since under the terms of the Parliament Act the Lords could reject a Commons Bill only twice, the first two Home Rule Bills were merely dummy runs. Push would not come to shove until the third circuit. But Asquith has been rightly criticized for failing to appreciate that the Ulster Protestants would present a major stumbling block and, in effect, he allowed them to force concessions from his government, intensifying Nationalist suspicion of his good faith. He erred in thinking that the passage of time would bring the Ulstermen and their Unionist supporters to their senses. In the event, however, the implementation of the third bill in 1914 was postponed by the outbreak of war.

As Europe spiralled towards conflict following the assassination of the

Archduke Franz Ferdinand and the Austrian ultimatum to Serbia, Asquith's cabinet was deeply divided about its response. Here, however, his preference for delay paid off. He bought valuable time by refusing to make an immediate declaration of Britain's intentions. Once it became clear that Germany would not respect Belgian neutrality, the peace party virtually evaporated. Only four ministers opposed British intervention to the point of resignation, and two of them quickly changed their minds when pressed by the prime minister. Asquith thus carried a united cabinet into the war, losing only John Morley and John Burns.

A large war council was established, including outsiders such as Arthur Balfour as well as the chiefs of staff and Lord Kitchener as War Minister. The latter was a politically astute appointment in that the Conservatives could not attack him as they would have done a Liberal. But the war council was established as a formal committee of the cabinet to whose veto it was thus subject, and the civilians did not abdicate conduct of the war to the soldiers. The politicians were primarily responsible for instigating the opening of campaigns in the Dardanelles and Salonika. Lloyd George soon fell out with Kitchener whose powers were progressively reduced and it was over his head again that the war council appointed a committee to investigate claims that military success was being frustrated by a lack of shells.

Both the shell scandal and the general lack of military progress served to fuel dissatisfaction with the government's conduct of the war. Conservatives, inherently distrustful of Liberals who had been so committed to peace before 1914, were particularly frustrated because their leader, Bonar Law, was reluctant to attack the government openly. Jenkins suggests that for his part Asquith was so distracted by the break-up of his long-standing friendship with Venetia Stanley that he uncharacteristically allowed a scheme for coalition government to be foisted upon him (Jenkins 1964: 363). Certainly when this possibility was raised the whole thing was settled in less than fifteen minutes (Lloyd George 1938: 136). But Asquith always kept his private and public lives apart and coalition appealed for very practical reasons. Not only would it would nullify Conservative criticism but also it would strengthen his position against those of his own party who were either against the war or who demanded that it be fought on pure Liberal principles. Furthermore, he constructed the new cabinet with some skill. He was unable (or unwilling) to save Haldane, who fell victim to Tory press allegations of pro-German sympathies, but he retained other old allies like Grey while elevating supporters like McKenna. He exploited Conservative rivalries by giving Balfour the Admiralty and putting Bonar Law in a minor office. Neither the promotion of McKenna nor the retention (after some initial hesitation) of Kitchener appealed to Lloyd George, the new Minister of Munitions. The coalition had enormous potential for internal dissension, making even more crucial Asquith's own role as the calming central influence and mediator.

It has been suggested that if the war had ended in 1915 Asquith would have been hailed as a national saviour (Cassar 1994: 235). The country had been taken into the conflict without financial panic, political schism or civilian unrest.

Appropriate economic measures had been implemented, the navy had driven the German merchant fleet from the sea, and the British Expeditionary Force had been landed in France in time to stop the apparently irresistible German advance on the channel. But while Asquith can take credit for some of these achievements, none of them brought military victory any nearer. Neither did the formation of the coalition, even though it solved an immediate political problem. Criticism of the costly military stalemate continued to mount. Asquith had few positive ideas to offer. Liberalism was proving impossible to reconcile with total war, and even modest measures like the Defence of the Realm Act had been attacked by party purists. This inner tension came to a head in 1916, first when McKenna introduced a protectionist budget, and then, more seriously still, over the issue of military conscription, which was widely mooted as the only way to feed the army's insatiable appetite for manpower. The very notion was anathema to hard-core Liberals but Asquith overestimated the strength of feeling in the country against it. As always, he searched for a middle way, asking anxiously 'Shall I be able to devise and build a bridge?'(Jenkins 1964: 386). He was not, and because he himself accepted universal conscription only when Lloyd George drove him into a corner by threatening resignation, it appeared that his primary concern had been his party and his personal position, not the national interest. 'What he is really aiming at all through', claimed C.P. Scott, 'is not to do the best possible for the army, but to keep his party together and himself in power' (Wilson 1970: 166). Lloyd George had long been critical of Asquith's handling of the war, claiming that

> He came to Cabinet meetings with no policy which he had decided to recommend, listened to what others said, summed it up ably and then as often as not postponed the decision. It was a futile method of carrying on a war.
>
> (Lloyd George 1938: 243)

During 1916 Asquith's failing credibility suffered two further blows. First, the government's failure to anticipate the Easter rising in Dublin was exacerbated by its brutal suppression. Second, Asquith's decision to take over the War Office when Kitchener was drowned inevitably implicated him in the botched battle of the Somme, which claimed his own son, Raymond, among its thousands of casualties. By the end of the year, Lloyd George was scathing, complaining that Asquith was 'absolutely hopeless. He cannot make up his mind about anything, and seems to have lost all will-power' (Taylor 1971: 127).

As an obvious candidate for the succession Lloyd George was hardly a disinterested commentator, but his opinions were born out of genuine frustration. He wanted the war effort to be run by a small war council, independent of the cabinet. Asquith was not unsympathetic to this but he was adamant that it must be chaired by the prime minister who 'cannot be relegated to the position of an arbiter in the background or a referee to the Cabinet' (Jenkins 1964: 430). After some attempts at accommodation, Asquith resigned, possibly with the intention of seeking a fresh mandate from the King (Beaverbrook 1960: 464), or more probably because he realized that his position was no longer tenable (Wilson 1966: 105).

The circumstances which brought about Asquith's fall have often been interpreted as the outcome of a plot jointly engineered by the Tory press and Lloyd George who replaced him. Although the two had never been particularly close, politically they had formed a powerful peacetime partnership (Koss 1976: 113). Asquith had promoted Lloyd George, supported him during the budget crisis, and used his conciliatory skills to resolve industrial problems. He had been privately critical of the Chancellor's involvement in the Marconi scandal but, once convinced that he had done nothing illegal, defended him publicly. But perhaps Asquith never quite trusted him. He had put Charles Hobhouse at the Treasury in 1908, partly as a safe pair of hands but partly to report back to him behind Lloyd George's back, and there is no doubt that the coalition chancellor, McKenna, did his best to turn Asquith against Lloyd George. While Lloyd George appears to have had no particular wish for the premiership, telling Frances Stevenson that Asquith could be left to run ' "his show", i.e. the Cabinet', he was determined to have control of the war effort (Taylor 1971: 127). He must have known that his proposals were unacceptable to Asquith and his own self belief was thus sullied by the political opportunism which did not scruple to take advantage of his chief's difficulties.

Certainly in later life Asquith comforted himself with the thought that Lloyd George had stabbed him in the back, and his own official biographers agreed, attributing the subsequent disintegration of the Liberal party to wartime quarrelling among the leaders brought about by Lloyd George's ambition (Spender and Asquith 1932: ii, 250–1). On the other hand, it could be argued that the seeds of party decline were sown well before 1914 in pre-war measures for which Asquith, as leader, must bear some responsibility. The decision to secure Labour party support for the National Insurance Bill by introducing payment for members of parliament subsequently made it much easier for that party to put up candidates. So, too, did the Trade Union Bill of 1913 which boosted Labour's potential funds by reversing the Osborne decision of 1909 and legalizing the political levy. It has also been suggested that Asquith did not give sufficient attention to the maintenance of the Liberal party machine before 1914 (Emy 1973: 285). In his defence, it can be countered that only the creation of a mass electorate in 1918 made the impact of this neglect and the gratuitous boosts to Labour finance of such importance.

Whatever the cause of the Liberal party's collapse – and it is worth remembering that its vote continued to increase throughout the 1920s – Asquith's own reputation was in tatters by the end of the war. Criticized by some for failing to adhere to Liberal principles he was simultaneously assailed by those who believed that consensual, patient, logical and responsive approaches to politics could never achieve victory in a war that demanded swift decisions, incisive leadership, active involvement and passionate commitment. Out of office, he adopted a tolerant

attitude towards his successor but by refusing to join Lloyd George's government he seemed to be disguising personal pique as political principle (Koss 1976:
235). In the election of 1918 the constituency which he had represented for
thirty-two years rejected him as decisively as the country rejected the rump of his
party.

Although he won a by-election early in 1920, Asquith appeared tired and
uninterested, prompting J.L. Hammond to complain in 1921 that neither he nor
Sir Edward Grey gave the impression 'that they mean business'(Clarke 1978:
214). He led only a handful of Liberals in the Commons and attempts at reconciliation with Lloyd George were at best lukewarm. Asquith's whole political
demeanour appeared old fashioned in the world of slogans, rhetoric and emotion
characteristic of the mass democracy created by the Franchise Act 1918.

A.G. Gardiner's verdict that Asquith was a consummate political engineer,
rather than a seer, is only partially justified (Gardiner 1916: 87). It is true that he
had no long-term social or economic vision for the country as a whole but his
characteristic patience and receptivity did afford full rein to the many positive
policies of his most able colleagues, particularly in the sphere of social reform.
Both in peace and war, furthermore, he had a clear view of constitutional propri-
ety, as indicated by his handling of the 1909–11 crisis and by his determined
defence of the prime ministerial prerogative against Crown attempts to influence
policy on Ireland and industrial relations. In the end, it could be argued, he fell
from power because he insisted that ultimate control should reside in the hands of
the prime minister and his cabinet. Despite the unwarranted claim that Asquith's
political technique was to overcome one crisis by creating another, few would
challenge Gardiner's verdict on Asquith's political skills (McKenna 1921: 107).
He was well able to hold together a divided cabinet, whether over the naval
estimates in 1909 or the war issue in 1914. He was also capable of subtle disposi-
tions of office, as the structure of the 1908 cabinet and the coalition government
both indicated. Perhaps his particular skills and abilities were better suited to the
more leisurely world of Edwardian politics. His initial handling of the war was
perhaps more successful than is commonly acknowledged, but ultimately he
proved unable to make the huge mental adjustments necessary to secure victory
in a conflict of unprecedented dimensions. Like the generals, his reputation
perished, though less deservedly so, on the battlefields of the First World War.

References and further reading
Asquith, M. (1920) *Autobiography*, London: Butterworth.
Beaverbrook, Lord (1960) *Politicians and the War*, London: Oldbourne.
Brock, M. and Brock, E. (eds) (1982) *H.H. Asquith: Letters to Venetia Stanley*,
    Oxford: Oxford University Press. (Revealing political gossip among the
    protestations of love.)
Cassar, G.H. (1994) *Asquith as War Leader*, London: Hambledon Press. (Acknow-
    ledges Asquith's defects as a war leader but suggests that in the unprecedented
    circumstances of total war his accomplishments were substantial and impressive.)

Clarke, P. (1978) *Liberals and Social Democrats*, Cambridge: Cambridge University Press.

Douglas, R. (1971) *The History of the Liberal Party 1895–1971*, London: Sidgwick & Jackson. (Draws attention to pre-war Liberal blunders, although Herbert Gladstone, rather than Asquith, is identified as the chief culprit.)

Emy, H. (1973) *Liberals, Radicals and Social Politics 1892–1914*, Cambridge: Cambridge University Press.

Gardiner, A. (1916) *The Pillars of Society*, London: Dent.

Hazlehurst, C. (1970) 'Asquith as prime minister', *English Historical Review* 85: 502–31. (Unusually critical of Asquith's peacetime record.)

Jalland, P. (1980) *The Liberals and Ireland: The Ulster Question in British Politics to 1914*, Brighton: Harvester. (Argues that the failure of Asquith's Irish policy between 1911 and 1914 was a major factor in the party's subsequent decline.)

Jenkins, R. (1964) *Asquith*, London: Collins. (An elegant and sympathetic portrait which contrives to be equally fair to Lloyd George.)

Koss, S. (1976) *Asquith*, London: Allen Lane. (Drawing on previously unused private papers, this is the first major biography not written under the aegis of the Asquith family and thus provides a more objective assessment.)

Lloyd George, D. (1938) *War Memoirs of David Lloyd George*, London: Odhams. (Self-justification though not as prejudiced as might be expected.)

McKenna, S. (1921) *While I Remember*, London: Butterworth.

Oxford and Asquith, Earl of (1928) *Memories and Reflections*, London: Cassell.

Phillipps, V. (n.d.) *My Days and Ways*, London: privately published. (Affectionate portrait by a sometime private secretary and Liberal whip.)

Spender, J. and Asquith, C. (1932) *Life of Lord Oxford and Asquith*, London: Hutchinson. (The official biography, with dated interpretations of central events.)

Tanner, D. (1990) *Political Change and the Labour Party, 1900–1918*, Cambridge: Cambridge University Press.

Taylor, A.J.P. (ed.) (1971) *Lloyd George: A Diary by Frances Stevenson*, New York: Harper & Row. (Provides clear evidence of Lloyd George's mounting frustration with Asquith.)

Wilson, T. (1966) *The Downfall of the Liberal Party 1914–1935*, London: Collins. (Excellent analysis of the events surrounding Asquith's fall.)

—— (ed.) (1970) *The Political Diaries of C.P. Scott, 1911–1928*, London: Collins. (Strongly influenced by Scott's susceptibility to Lloyd George's flattery and Asquith's relative indifference to the press.)

Kenneth Brown

David Lloyd George, First Earl of Dwyfor

Born 17 January 1863, second child of William George and Elizabeth Lloyd. Educated at Llanystumdwy National School. Married (1) 1888 Margaret Owen (died 1941); (2) 1943 Frances Stevenson (died 1972). MP for Caernarfon Borough 1890–1945. President of the Board of Trade 1905–8; Chancellor of the Exchequer 1908–15; Minister of Munitions 1915–16; Secretary of State for War 1916; Prime Minister 1916–22. Left Commons and ennobled 1945. Died 26 March 1945.

In both peace and war David Lloyd George was the central figure of British parliamentary life in the first quarter of the twentieth century. This achievement was the more remarkable in that he was a Welsh 'outsider' in a world dominated by the networked products of fee-paying English education. Although he had been born in Manchester, Lloyd George was brought up in rural north Wales, an environment which conditioned in him firm opposition to Anglicanism, land privileges and squirearchical control. His early political life took shape during the reawakening of Welsh national identity and cultural self-confidence in the last quarter of the nineteenth century; this was the backdrop to his by-election victory in Caernarfon Borough in 1890, a parliamentary seat he held for fifty-five years. In the Commons in the early years of his career his commitment was first to Welsh causes and second to the Liberal party. A reputation as a 'maverick', which was to accompany Lloyd George throughout his political life, was forged in these early days out of an 'undisciplined' backbench record and a high profile, and politically risky, opposition to the Boer War. Nevertheless, as the premier representative of an almost entirely Liberal Wales in 1906, he secured ministerial office. Thereafter his horizon widened well beyond distinctively Welsh causes, although his limited experience of urban and industrial conditions disadvantaged him in relation to matters of labour unrest and employer–worker conflict in the large industries such as coal-mining.

Lloyd George seemed to embody the vital radical nonconformist dimension of British politics. In reality, however, his religious attitudes were complex: although deeply influenced by a strict Baptist tradition – he was elected president of the Welsh Baptist Union in 1908 – Lloyd George increasingly entertained doubts about his faith. His intimate association with Free Church institutions did not survive the traumas occasioned by the First World War and its aftermath. Even in the Edwardian period he had been prepared to compromise the nonconformist position on the role of churches in education.

After 1906 Lloyd George's early 'old' liberal and nonconformist political commitments were gradually superseded by an enthusiasm for the enlarging possibilities of state action. Despite his public hostility to the Education Act 1902, Lloyd George supported the notion of a systematic state-driven solution to the anomalies of provision under competing rate-aided and voluntary principles. At the Board of Trade regulation of private enterprise was massively increased, and Lloyd George's personal attachment to a state pensions scheme was apparent as soon as he went to the Treasury. Although his 'People's Budget' of 1909 appeared to be a classic hallmark of a 'Radical Government', his radicalizing fiscal scheme was accompanied increasingly by a pragmatic managerial approach which denied the importance of party unity and the separate traditions of the two major parties of government. By 1910 he equated old Liberalism with stagnation and, hence, political failure.

Lloyd George relished the end of the Lords veto in 1911 which he described as 'the dream of Liberalism for generations realised at last'. But in 1910, as one general election was quickly followed by another, he had been more intent on forming a coalition government to solve the constitutional crisis for which he was prepared to concede universal military service, naval rearmament and tariff retaliation. The Sea Lords were only slightly less irksome – and much more powerful – than the dukes. Consequently, Lloyd George developed a personal identification with the instrumentality of state power as a balance in the national interest between opposing social and political forces, whether in industrial disputes, health insurance or Franco-German relations. He was eager to establish cross-party alliances in the pursuit of 'National Efficiency', and this distance from party organization – coupled with a disregard for precedent, admiration of social imperialism and willingness to extend state activity in the national interest – suggest the development of a centrist politician in the mould of Joseph Chamberlain. They shared the view that party management should follow policy formation, rather than determine political programmes. In addition, the Marconi scandal brought confirmation of Lloyd George's 'outsider' status, not least by confirming the slender financial basis of his parliamentary life.

If any one person can be described as the architect of victory in the British war effort 1914–18 it was Lloyd George, and had he taken Bonar Law's advice and retired in December 1918 he might still be regarded primarily as a great war minister. On 20 December 1916 Lloyd George, as the newly appointed prime minister, was depicted in *Punch* as the 'New Conductor' of the '1917 Overture'. The cartoon forcefully suggested that great changes could be expected in the executive management of the war effort which would amount to the transformation of the methods and qualities of British political leadership. A.J.P. Taylor later drew the celebrated conclusion that the changes in the structure of government initiated by Lloyd George in December 1916 amounted to 'a revolution, British style', and John Grigg highlighted the dynamic, resourceful and innovative aspects of his political leadership (Taylor 1965: 109; Grigg 1985a: 7). These contributions to the historiography of Lloyd George have provided the context for much revisionist discussion of his rise to the premiership and subsequent achievements.

The expectation of dynamic leadership, which in actuality proved more apparent than real, stemmed from the rhetorical urgency with which Lloyd George left the Treasury – whose significance diminished as 'business as usual' faltered – to create the Ministry of Munitions. He became its first minister in May 1915 and immediately tackled the shell crisis. The implementation of the National Insurance Act before the war had provided evidence of Lloyd George's willingness to employ experts to staff the extending role of the state. In 1915 his search for 'great improvisers' with managerial experience of large-scale enterprise to take responsibility for specific production problems, apply solutions and monitor new output levels, was well publicized as a bold ministerial response to the unforeseen scale and peculiarities of the European war. Egotistical business entrepreneurs and managers responded to impassioned torrents of Celtic eloquence, provided their own staff, and connected Whitehall to the unexpected imperatives of an artillery war by 'racing against time' in the construction of National Filling Factories.

In his captivating way, Lloyd George presented this experimental new ministry as a patriotic expression of consensual relations between capital and labour. As Secretary of State for War after July 1916 he quickly contravened the expectation that military dilemmas should be resolved by regular army officers. He transferred his munitions organizers into uniform to rectify the 'civilian' problems of dock work and transport which faced the British armies in France by the autumn months of 1916. Advocates of change, dismayed by 'dilly and dally', were enthralled by this spurning of customary military procedures. The anxious Liberal peer, Lord Buckmaster, noted that Lloyd George 'cares nothing for precedents and knows no principles but he has fire in his belly'; and according to Lord Esher, observer and critic *par excellence* of Asquith's failure to plan a war economy, his 'administrative plan of selecting a Man to carry out a difficult task that baffles committees and groups of men, should be applied immediately to the greatest and most difficult problem with which he is faced' (Lloyd George MSS, F/41/5/2 Lord Esher to Lord Murray of Elibank, 28 November 1916). Throughout the crisis which led to Asquith's tactical resignation on 5 December 1916, Lloyd George remained conciliatory. But his intention to control the war effort as head of the small War Committee was widely supported by adherents of 'National Organization' who looked forward to the more efficient management of the nation's manpower and material resources. The expectation of great change which stemmed from his munitions crusade and (unsteady) adherence to compulsory national service was further reflected in his distance from many Liberal backbench MPs, who looked on his rise to the premiership with dismay.

Initially, there was little indication of a more dynamic war effort. Neville Chamberlain, Lloyd George's Director of National Service, appealed for volunteers instead of introducing conscription. Furthermore, the strategic presuppositions of British operational plans on the Western Front were not reviewed in advance of the opening battles of the third Ypres campaign. Nor did the reconstituted War cabinet decisively intervene after initial objectives proved, yet again, to be too ambitious. After August 1917 the medical re-examination of discharged men for military service fuelled such fierce 'Asquithite mischief' that Lloyd George developed an exaggerated fear for the survival of his government. Only after the Passchendaele offensive ground to a halt did Lloyd George publicly acknowledge the need for him to become the trustee of manpower. In December 1917 his belated review of priority areas of the war effort was assisted by the national disappointment in British high command which was widely expressed after the final phase of the battle of Cambrai. A timely reconsideration of the 'large army first' principle ensued. After many months of continuity with Asquithian practice the War cabinet recognized that although an 'unbroken line' needed to be maintained on the Western Front, unchecked demands for men for military service would endanger the wider national contributions to an increasingly Allied war effort. The unchanging expectations of the Derby–Haig–Robertson triumvirate of 'westerners' posed a political dilemma as awkward as those which were encountered in parliament.

On these issues Lloyd George received much support from the social imperialist Lord Milner whose vision of domestic harmony, national defence and an active state was not dissimilar from the range of ideas which interested the prime minister. In 1918 the two co-operated in a more authoritative War cabinet in the knowledge that there could be no more Passchendaeles (Woodward 1983: 305). After an initial reinforcement of the line the process of responding to the German spring offensive quickly brought renewed effort to food production, coal output and the mercantile marine. This process was informed, but not determined, by greater government awareness of a war-weary, more homogeneous working class whose representatives demanded equality of sacrifice. In his quest for 'all out' war, Lloyd George became aware that 'fair play' was the dominant feature of the moral economy on the home front. He first announced British war aims to the Trades Union Congress on 5 January 1918. Lloyd George responded to inequalities of food distribution and sought to extend the capital levy.

Although Lloyd George took seriously Home Office reports on morale and the scale of sacrifice evident in all communities, his insistence on the vigorous prosecution of the war remained undimmed and he was fortified in this commitment by his coterie of 'leading hustlers' who became businessmen-in-government in 1917. The new ministries formed by Lloyd George co-opted expertise from the 'interests' which they were created to regulate (Turner 1988: 204–5). They remained outside experts, however, and the demand of employers for a Ministry of Industry to co-ordinate reconstruction went unappeased (Turner 1992: 351–3). Businessmen remained in government after 1918 as individuals with particular loyalties to Lloyd George, but their temporary availability did not foreshadow the permanent enlargement of the state. In war their personal allegiance to Lloyd George provided him with a compensatory source of authority, given that Asquith retained the leadership of the Liberal party. Much attention has been devoted to the search for causes of the demarcation between Lloyd George's supporters and critics in the First World War. Gradually Liberal MPs divided according to whether they believed Lloyd George should lead the nation into peacetime as the only suitably decisive political leader, or because they bitterly resented the abandonment of liberal principles in pursuit of military victory. Lloyd George's reputation as a valiant, committed and selfless war leader was evident to Liberal MPs who supported the government in the Maurice debate in May 1918, but the significance of the decision as an 'acid test' of loyalty to the prime minister was far from clear to many who did not vote.

More significance should be attached to the limitations imposed by the fact that only 150 Liberal candidates were 'couponed' for the general election, which unexpectedly arose in conditions of peace. The abeyance of party strife between coalition Liberals and the Conservative party reflected the enormity of Lloyd George's achievement as 'The Man Who Won the War', but obscured considerable uncertainty on future policy priorities beyond securing permanent peace in Europe and the defeat of the Labour party. Triumphalist election oratory in

December 1918 did not provide a foundation for the pursuit of reformist schemes.

Lloyd George reached the 'zenith of his career' in 1919 (Wrigley 1992: 94). He spent much of the first six months of 1919 in Paris where his dextrous diplomacy moderated French demands of a debilitated Germany, while he simultaneously voiced belligerent statements regarding reparations and war guilt to appease searchers of the spoils of war. The pressures of peace-making were all consuming, as illustrated by the texts of telegrams between the prime minister in Paris and anxious ministers in supply departments, who endeavoured to stem the ebbing interventionist tide. Initially, the availability of Sir Eric Geddes and other businessmen made the peacetime Liberal–Conservative alliance less obviously unequal. The diverse collection of temporary ministers, Lloyd George Liberals and maverick Unionists, who believed in a 'neutral' extended state which would harmonize the interests of capital and labour, appeared to provide the prime minister with the means of promoting economic prosperity and maintaining social stability. But though impressive feats of diplomacy were evident at the Paris Peace Conference, the onset of Treasury control swiftly dismantled these domestic grand schemes.

In 1919 Sir Eric Geddes, first Minister of Transport, looked forward to the development of a state-subsidized integrated transport network. However, the railway industry was restored to private enterprise in 1921 after a brief period of nationalization. 'Homes for Heroes' was the *raison d'être* of the Housing and Town Planning Act 1919, but without the regulated supply and pricing of new materials and construction of new roads the Treasury house-building subsidy was a blunt 'pump priming' instrument of state welfarism. The creation of the Forestry Commission was a small fragment of the scheme to regenerate the rural economy. Instead, the disestablishment of the Church of Wales, limited land settlement schemes for ex-servicemen, and the extension of pensions and national health insurance, suggested continuities with unfinished business from the pre-war era. The interest charges on war debts and the sanctity of private ownership allowed no delay to fiscal retrenchment, and corporatists were quickly disabused of their schemes. At home the first year of Lloyd George's peacetime premiership was far from 'prime-ministerial' (Morgan 1970: 144–5).

During 1920–1 his main assets – war record, crusading zeal and aloofness from party structures – wore thin. His political relationships with Milner, Christopher Addison, Winston Churchill and Geddes declined. Lloyd George's anti-socialism was expressed in a responsiveness to 'diehard' and anti-waste campaigns. A measure of this trend was the failure of negotiations for a Centre party in 1920 (Pugh 1988: 129–57; 1991: 25–8). The idea of fusion won little support from more confident backbench Conservative opinion, especially as by-elections indicated that coalition Liberals could not survive the general election. A Centre party implied support from Labour politicians, but after 1916 Lloyd George described the needs of the 'under dog' in an increasingly out-of-touch fashion.

Sympathetic observers of Lloyd George's pre-war career noted that his deviation from Edwardian Liberalism was nowhere more apparent than in the coercive policies applied in Ireland. His dual policy of military conscription alongside – but planned to be implemented in advance of – home rule, and his appointment of Field Marshal Lord French of Ypres as Viceroy of Ireland, suggested a 'careless devolution of responsibility' (Ward 1974: 107). Later the reprisals of the Black and Tans so appalled Asquithian and left opinion that the record of the British military presence in southern Ireland overshadowed subsequent achievements. After the cease-fire in July 1921 negotiations for the Irish Free State found Lloyd George's consummate skills in opportunism, ingenuity, resilience and obfuscation employed, as at Paris, beyond public view.

At the Paris Peace Conference and in Anglo-Irish relations, Lloyd George's aim was to maintain the territorial integrity of the British empire. In neither instance did he acknowledge significant decline in Britain's 'policing' role as a great power. To the end of his premiership his ambitious quest for world peace on British terms echoed his close attention to Anglo-American relations, particularly in the naval sphere, in the last year of the war. His exaggerated belief in Britain as an honest broker, and over-confidence in his powers of establishing the comity of nations, were revealed by the duration and irrelevance of the Genoa conference in May 1922. The Rapallo agreement exposed Lloyd George's pretensions as the arbiter of European security issues; and much sought after success in the international arena, to buttress his support among Conservative leaders at home, proved elusive.

Coalition government did not lead to permanent political realignment. Fundamental disagreement on the state's role in the reconstruction of the economy had long pointed the way towards the revival of conservatism, and Lloyd George's emphasis on social harmony became largely rhetorical. But for all its failures, according to Kenneth Morgan, 'the Lloyd George Coalition of 1918–22, alone of peacetime British governments this century, tried to harness political consensus for positive ends' (Morgan 1979: 375). On this account the achievements which were secured would have been unattainable had diehard Unionists or Asquithian Liberals held power, but the question remains as to how earnestly Lloyd George strove for political consensus in pursuit of social progress after the plans for reconstruction were reduced to piecemeal innovation.

The realization gradually dawned that the 'return to normalcy' was the predominant political quest of 'high politics', and that Lloyd George's usefulness to the Conservative party as the 'man of the people' had waned. In the more certain political context of 1922 Lloyd George's energy, disdain for conventional politics, and implacable executive individualism were to no avail. Consequently, his quest for political survival contributed heavily to the tarnished idea of coalition government in the inter-war years. Ramsay MacDonald and Stanley Baldwin remembered the events of 1920–2 as reason enough for his exclusion from National governments in 1931 and 1935. Neville Chamberlain's resolute hostility towards Lloyd George originated in the trauma of his resignation from the National Service Department in 1917.

On 19 October 1922 Lloyd George resigned as prime minister and started the long elusive search for an anti-socialist centre party with a progressive bias. As prime minister he had encountered the complex interplay of long-established political parties in transition, party-less statesmen anxious for survival, unforeseen cultural and economic consequences of mass attritional war, and the extension of the electorate. It becomes ever more evident that the problems which Lloyd George confronted, whether from ex-servicemen's organizations, rank-and-file movements or militant nationalism, represented forces 'from below' and ideologies of class for which radical politicians schooled in late-Victorian individualism and national identity were unprepared.

Nonetheless, after October 1922 Lloyd George adopted an energetic approach to the translation of 'advanced' liberal ideas into election pledges which would demonstrate that the parliamentary party was far from moribund. His land inquiry of 1925, and commitment in 1928 to reduce unemployment in 'Britain's Industrial Future', were notable examples of an often strenuous campaign to remain significant in British political life by offering the electorate an alternative anti-socialist focus. The General Strike provided a further opportunity for Liberal schism, and Lloyd George finally obtained leadership of the party on Asquith's resignation in October 1926. In 1931 hospitalization ensured that he played no part in the formation of the National government, and at the general election his political isolation was finally transparent. The hope of obtaining enough Liberal MPs to hold the parliamentary balance received a final setback as his grasp on the few remaining rural districts and towns loyal to Liberalism loosened in the face of the MacDonald – Baldwin axis. He aspired to the sort of position which Joseph Chamberlain had attained after 1886. Instead, he suffered a descent into the political wilderness, punctuated by reminders of his creativity in addressing the evolving 'condition of England' question.

Lloyd George found solace in a few friends and complicated domestic arrangements. At a weekend party in 1924 he reflected with Arthur Lee and Sir Eric Geddes on whether, with their innovative talents free of party discipline, they would be called on again to rally the nation in crisis. At Criccieth his wife Margaret actively electioneered and participated in constituency functions. In London and after 1922 at Churt, near Hindhead, Surrey, his 'second love' Frances Stevenson provided a refuge from 'the constant wear and tear' of political life (Morgan 1973: 196). His tiredness and relentless fascination with politics was neatly encapsulated in the *Punch* cartoon 'A Temporary Retirement' of 15 March 1922, in which while walking in the Welsh hills he was depicted resting, having taken off his crown. The caption read: 'It's a relief to get this thing off for a bit; but after a time I expect I should feel the draught'. Out of office he grew more fatalistic. He contextualized his man of action approach to political life through references to a mixture of poetic and biblical truths, Welsh songs and sermons, a biographical knowledge of past 'doers' such as Oliver Cromwell, Disraeli and Lord Randolph Churchill, reflections on the war, golf and extended holidays.

As the battle of the memoirs unfolded in the mid- and late 1920s, Lloyd George organized a remarkable autobiographical project which began in earnest in 1932. By 1938 six volumes of his *War Memoirs* had emerged containing one million words. Like so many aspects of his political life, the *War Memoirs* were inspirational, defiant, breathless, grandiose and perfidious as he aspired to the position of the greatest war minister since Lord Chatham. Conservative reviewers found the discussion of the British establishment and its institutions injudicious, which served as a reminder of Lloyd George's social and cultural distance from the dominant influences on parliamentary life. Similarly, its self-propagandizing assertion of the author's centrality in all war-related matters found few equals, excepting Churchill's autobiography *The World Crisis 1911–18*. In 1936 Thomas Jones recorded Margot Asquith's pride in her mother's saying, 'I always knew that L[loyd] G[eorge] had won the war but until I read his *Memoirs* I did not know that he had won it single-handed' (Jones 1954: 169).

In this participant history, character portraits, dramatic events and heroic feats of civilian organization were woven into a Lloyd George-centric version of the war. The uncomplicated structure of the memoirs, his access to cabinet papers and to Sir Maurice Hankey as the great verifier of decision-making at the highest level, and his forthright expression of reflections, allowed Lloyd George access to politics by other means in the years before the Second World War. The essential purpose of the *War Memoirs* was to remind readers that he was the only cabinet minister who held office throughout the war years, and also that no other politician had a vision of how the war could be won. The reputations of Lord Grey and Field Marshal Lord Haig were demolished as Lloyd George's 'great man' rendition of history presented his leadership in epic proportions (Lloyd George 1936: ii, 2032–43).

In a war of nameless attritional character Lloyd George unduly emphasized the actions of 'Great Men'. He assumed that the course of events was always determined by the condition of 'high politics' and the conversations of 'brasshats' and 'frockcoats', rather than the resilience of an embattled home opinion and the quiet stoicism of countless uniformed men and women. He wrote of what he knew, and Lord Beaverbrook's ownership of the Lloyd George papers during the 1950s perpetuated the view that the war effort was 'managed' by incisive prime-ministerial interventions, whether investigating convoys or subordinating Haig to French strategic plans. Consequently, it was for his vitality, decisiveness, optimism and problem-solving ability that Lloyd George wished to be judged by posterity, rather than for his attachment to any constant factor in politics such as party, programme or place. His adaptability brought political advantages for as long as agenda-setting was the prerogative of Westminster–Whitehall or determined in a theatre of war. But after 1918, in the context of a ruined Liberal party organization and the arrival of Labour as a governing party, Lloyd George's political high tide had ebbed: the main preoccupations of 'high politics' were redefined to his cost.

References and further reading

Cline, P. (1970) 'Reopening the case of the Lloyd George Coalition and the postwar economic transition 1918–1919', *Journal of British Studies* 10: 162–75.

Egerton, G. (1988) 'The Lloyd George *War Memoirs*: a study in the politics of memory', *Journal of Modern History* 60: 55–94.

Grigg, J. (1985a) 'Lloyd George and ministerial leadership in the Great War', in P. Liddle (ed.) *Home Fires and Foreign Fields: British Social and Military Experience in the First World War*, London: Brassey's.

—— (1985b) *Lloyd George: From Peace to War 1912–1916*, London: Methuen. (Based on the themes that Lloyd George knew that words could rally a nation in crisis and that although he saved the situation, his defects contributed to a decline in the standards of British politics. Commends his crusading qualities and lack of pomposity.)

Jones, T. (1954) *A Diary with Letters 1931–1950*, Oxford: Oxford University Press.

Lloyd George, D. Unpublished papers, together with those of Frances Stevenson, available in the House of Lords Record Office.

—— (1936) *War Memoirs*, 2 vols, London: Odhams.

Morgan, K. (1970) 'Lloyd George's premiership: a study in "Prime Ministerial Government"', *Historical Journal* 13: 135–57. (Highlights Lloyd George's personal ascendancy in the years 1916–22, and draws attention to the semi-presidential nature of policy-making and governing structures.)

—— (ed.) (1973) *Lloyd George Family Letters, 1885–1936*, Oxford: Clarendon Press and Cardiff: University of Wales Press.

—— (1979) *Consensus and Disunity: The Lloyd George Coalition Government 1918–1922*, Oxford: Oxford University Press. (Commends Lloyd George's 'middle way' and vision of social harmony and international conciliation in the immediate post-war years.)

Pugh, M. (1988) *Lloyd George*, London: Longman.

—— (1991) 'Left in the centre? Lloyd George and the centrist tradition in British politics', in J. Loades (ed.) *The Life and Times of David Lloyd George*, Bangor: Headstart History. (Other essays in this work include K. Morgan, 'Lloyd George and Welsh Liberalism', G. Machin, 'Lloyd George and nonconformity' and C. Wrigley, 'Lloyd George and the Labour movement after 1922'.)

Taylor, A.J.P. (1965) *English History 1914–45*, London: Pelican.

—— (ed.) (1971) *Lloyd George: A Diary by Frances Stevenson*, London: Hutchinson.

Turner, J. (1988) '"Experts and interests": David Lloyd George and the dilemmas of the expanding state 1906–19', in R. Macleod (ed.) *Government and Expertise: Specialists, Administrators and Professionals 1860–1919*, Cambridge: Cambridge University Press.

—— (1992) *British Politics and the Great War: Coalition and Conflict 1915–1918*, New Haven, CT and London: Yale University Press. (A study of considerable substance which discusses the involvement of non-governmental institutions to administer the enlarging functions of the wartime state, arguing that this development did not entail the implementation of a broader corporatist vision.)

Ward, A. (1974) 'Lloyd George and the 1918 Irish conscription crisis', *Historical Journal* 17: 107–29. (Suggests that he was poorly informed on this issue and that the British government did not handle Ireland with skill or understanding in 1918.)

Woodward, D. (1983) *Lloyd George and the Generals*, London: Associated University Press. (Packed with material on key themes in civil–military relations 1916–18.

Emphasizes personalities rather than structures and suggests that Lloyd George failed to have a decisive impact on the military conduct of the war.)
Wrigley, C. (1992) *Lloyd George*, Oxford: Blackwell.

Keith Grieves

Andrew Bonar Law

Born 16 September 1858, fourth child of Revd James Law and Elizabeth Kidston. Educated Gilbertfield School, Hamilton, and Glasgow High School. Married 1891 Annie Pitcairn (died 1909). MP (Unionist) for Blackfriars, Glasgow 1900–6, Dulwich, Camberwell 1906–10, Bootle 1911–18, Glasgow Central 1918–23. Parliamentary Secretary at the Board of Trade 1902–6; Leader of the Opposition in the Commons 1911–15; Secretary of State for the Colonies 1915–16; Chancellor of the Exchequer 1916–18; Lord Privy Seal 1918–21; Prime Minister 1922–3. Died 30 October 1923.

Bonar Law was underestimated by Liberal contemporaries, and – with few exceptions – has been treated by scholars with condescension and a lack of subtlety. The pithy taunts of H.H. Asquith, who described him as 'meekly ambitious' and as 'the unknown Prime Minister', continue to echo through and influence scholarly evaluation of Bonar Law's attainments (Chamberlain 1935: 224; Blake 1955: 531). Yet Lord Riddell, an intimate of many Edwardian political leaders, felt that Liberal criticism arose precisely because Bonar Law was a brutally effective Conservative leader (Riddell 1934: 100). Lloyd George, in a subtly argued assessment, hinted that Asquith's famously dismissive attitude reflected more directly on his own, rather than Bonar Law's, limitations (Lloyd George 1933: 1024–5). And there were other contemporary verdicts. Thomas Jones, who was well qualified to judge, remarked that Bonar Law 'was supreme as leader of the Commons, and his ascendancy has been compared with that of Walpole in the eighteenth century and of Peel in the nineteenth' (Jones 1937: 491). Stanley Baldwin, no friend to the second coalition, referred to the alliance between Bonar Law and Lloyd George as the 'most perfect partnership in political history' (Lloyd George 1933: 1021). Among other Conservatives – even those (like Austen Chamberlain) who had suffered from Bonar Law's leadership, or those (like F.E. Smith) not otherwise noted for their political charity – there was a unity of affection and respect.

Bonar Law's family and professional background were decisive, if indirect, political influences. He was the first man of colonial birth and upbringing to become prime minister: he was born at Kingston, New Brunswick, Canada. He was the first man of an Ulster Protestant background both to lead the Conservative party and to form a Conservative government (though other figures such as Disraeli's Lord Chancellor, Earl Cairns, had come near to the first rank of the party): Bonar Law's father, Revd James Law, hailed from near Portrush in north Antrim, and retired there in 1877 (Bonar Law was a frequent visitor in the years 1877 to

1882). Bonar Law was also the first man from a thoroughly humble background to climb the 'greasy pole' of Tory politics: his father's New Brunswick manse was characterized by material, if not intellectual, poverty, and he left in 1870 to join his mother's prosperous family connection in Glasgow and Helensburgh. He was not the first middle-class Conservative leader, but he did represent a new generation of middle-class Conservative in the Edwardian House of Commons – a generation impatient with the intellectual and social snobbery of Balfour as well as with his utter inability to win elections (Ridley 1985). At the age of 16 Bonar Law joined a merchant bank owned by his cousins, the Kidston brothers. At the age of 27 with the assistance of the brothers, he was able to buy a partnership in the iron firm of William Jacks. He remained active in this company until his election to the Commons in 1900.

Bonar Law declared, famously, that the two issues which motivated him in politics were tariff reform and Ulster Unionism. Tariff reform was the cause which brought Bonar Law to national prominence. His enthusiasm had a number of sources. He was a businessman, and the legislative protection of British commercial and industrial interests seemed likely to promote the interests of his class. He was also a Canadian by birth, and the system of imperial tariff preference envisaged by Joseph Chamberlain seemed likely to promote closer ties within the British empire. His impoverished background in the Presbyterian manse encouraged in Bonar Law a Christian paternalism which found expression in a concern for the social conditions of the labouring poor (although it should be emphasized that as Unionist leader he did not think it possible for his party to compete with the Liberals by acting as a proactive agency for social reform) (Green 1995: 294). Nevertheless, tariff reform seemed to represent a means of financing welfare legislation without the despoliation of the middle and upper classes. Tariff reform was for Bonar Law the greatest possible social reform, promising material benefits and political tranquillity; tariff reform was, for Bonar Law and other enthusiasts, a means of averting revolution (a prospect which preoccupied many Edwardian Tories).

Bonar Law's unremarkable maiden speech in February 1901 was in defence of Joseph Chamberlain and Cecil Rhodes; but the speech which first attracted widespread attention was delivered on 22 April 1902, in praise of Sir Michael Hicks-Beach's duty on corn. This led to his first ministerial appointment, to the parliamentary secretaryship at the Board of Trade – a junior position, but one of some strategic significance given the internal party debate over tariff reform, and one which gave Bonar Law an ideal position from which to argue for preference. A short speech on the Sugar Bounty Convention won the enthusiastic support of Chamberlain; and when – in May 1903 – Chamberlain launched his campaign for imperial preference Bonar Law swiftly emerged as a fluent and informed disciple. The Unionist electoral cataclysm of January 1906 claimed many ministerial victims, including Bonar Law. It was a reflection of the respect which his parliamentary skills had already earned that he was swiftly allocated a safe constituency – Dulwich – and he was returned for this division in May 1906. A combination of a diminished Unionist parliamentary party and the retirement, in the summer of

1906, of Chamberlain, brought Bonar Law to the first rank of national politics. With Chamberlain's son, Austen, he was the leading spokesman for a cause which now, with only 157 Unionist MPs, dominated the parliamentary party. Between 1906 and 1910 he consolidated this position, converting his parliamentary reputation into a national prominence.

Bonar Law's success with the tariff reform question eventually brought him the leadership of the Unionist party. The skill with which he defined his position deserves some attention. Bonar Law contrived to win favour with the most extreme supporters of the protectionist cause – the 'confederates' – and yet to remain acceptable to other elements within the party. He was an outspoken tariff reformer at a time when the cause was coming to dominate the internal politics of the party; yet in December 1910 he had been willing to resign from his safe seat in Dulwich in order to contest a much more marginal and difficult constituency – Manchester North West – in the Unionist free trade heartland of Lancashire. In March 1911 he was returned for Bootle, also in Lancashire. He was therefore an advanced tariff reformer sitting for a constituency where Unionist free-food sentiment ran high. Despite his public reputation as a protectionist firebrand, he was in reality highly pragmatic. He accepted increasingly that tariff reform was an electoral liability for the Unionist party, and – though in principle a 'whole-hogger' (a thoroughgoing tariff reformer) – he accepted the more tentative Balfourian strategy of submitting the issue to a public referendum. Unlike many whole-hoggers he did not advocate sustained resistance to the Parliament Act 1911. This mix of pragmatism and conviction was made credible by the general perception – shared even by Liberals – that Bonar Law was a man of selfless integrity: this mix made possible his election to the Unionist leadership in November 1911, for Bonar Law had the necessary credentials to unite the party after a period of intense division. He seemed capable of offering a decisive lead (where Arthur Balfour had apparently been capable only of sophistry); he shared the dominant tariff reform conviction of the party (but not to the fanatical degree of his leadership rival Austen Chamberlain); and he combined fire with tact and patience (unlike another rival, the choleric squire Walter Long).

The fate of the tariff reform question under Bonar Law may be briefly mentioned. The referendum pledge (which was widely seen as a means of avoiding an active tariff reform policy) was abandoned at a meeting of the shadow cabinet in April 1912. The same meeting reaffirmed that a food tax was a necessary component of tariff reform. The decisions were made public in November 1912. But this in turn sparked a revolt among the free food Unionists, particularly in Lancashire, where opinion was represented and directed by the seventeenth Earl of Derby. Many other Unionists, unmoved by either the protectionist or the free food case, feared electoral disaster if the newly abrasive attitude of the leadership were sustained. Faced with the prospect of a party schism – always a powerful threat – Bonar Law accepted that any duties on food would have to be submitted independently to the electorate. This climb-down effectively meant the end of tariff reform as a major focus of Unionist concern (Sykes 1979: 284).

For most Edwardian Conservatives, tariff reform was intimately connected to the defence of the Union: tariff reform and Unionism were the twin props of an imperial strategy designed to divert electoral attention from the temptations of the New Liberalism. Many prominent Ulster Unionist MPs, including Edward Saunderson, Edward Carson and James Craig, were in favour of tariff reform, some – Craig, for example – being enthusiastic whole-hoggers (Jackson 1989: 291–3). For Bonar Law, given his Ulster Protestant ancestry, this connection between Unionism and tariff reform was all the more compelling. Aside from the important issues of sentiment and conviction – and Bonar Law, like his predecessor, Salisbury, was unquestionably a convinced advocate of the Unionist cause – there were party political advantages in a brazenly loyalist stand. After his election as leader Bonar Law used Ulster Unionism both as a means of unifying a still highly fissile Unionist party and as a means of consolidating his own, still vulnerable, leadership. The very vigorous defence of Ulster Unionism which Bonar Law sustained between his election as leader in November 1911 and the party truce of July 1914 was partly a matter of what Thomas Jones called 'primitive passion', but it was also a considered, if risky, party political strategy (Jones 1937: 491; Smith 1993: 177–8). Bonar Law systematically endorsed Ulster Unionist resistance, both indirectly – through his presence at the Balmoral demonstration of 9 April 1912, where there was military-style drilling – and in plain, direct language (such as his famous Blenheim pledge of 29 July 1912 when he could 'imagine no length of resistance to which Ulster can go in which I should not be prepared to support them'). His consistently bitter parliamentary language, his determined attitude with trimmers – even with George V – were both a natural expression of frustrated principle, as well as a conscious strategy designed to win a dissolution of parliament and an election. But it should also be emphasized that, though contemporary Liberals affected to be appalled by Bonar Law's militancy, his language stood full square in the tradition of English Unionist menace (Jackson 1989: 117).

Bonar Law, like Carson (whose strategic initiatives he followed), fostered a number of more ambivalent attitudes behind this front. Despite the hard-line nature of his leadership, Bonar Law was not in fact an irreconcilable Unionist. In 1910 he had been associated with a federalist stand, and indeed for this reason he was not immediately acclaimed by Ulster Unionists when elected leader in November 1911 (Jackson 1989: 320). Moreover, between 1912 and 1914 neither he nor Carson could afford to appear unreasonable before the British electorate when the stability of the kingdom was at stake; neither could afford – given the combustible nature of loyalist paramilitary activity – to maintain indefinitely a warlike stand. In any event, Bonar Law could push his diehard rhetoric only to certain limits, for British Unionists like Lord Hugh Cecil would not automatically accept a leadership bent on civil war. Each leader, therefore, was interested in the possibility of compromise, and – given the Liberal government's unbending attitude towards a dissolution – the only possibility of compromise lay in some form of exclusion from the Home Rule Bill.

Bonar Law and Carson each looked forward to the possibility of civil war, but impelled by temperament, by training, and by political advantage, each was anxious for a pacific settlement (Jackson 1993: 29–41). Bonar Law met Asquith twice for secret talks – on 14 October 1913 and on 6 November 1913, although this caused some anxiety and suspicion among his front-bench colleagues. After these meetings Bonar Law understood that Asquith would propose to the cabinet that 'Ulster' (either four or six counties) would be excluded from the operation of the Home Rule Bill with the promise of a plebiscite within the excluded area: he thought that this expedient would rob the Unionist party of 'our best card for the Election', but argued that 'I don't see that we could possibly take the responsibility of refusing' (Blake 1955: 165). In the event he had either misinterpreted Asquith, or the prime minister reneged on the proposal. A third meeting between the two leaders, held on 9 December, was frosty and brief.

These negotiations indicate that Bonar Law (contrary to a recent argument) was willing to subordinate party advantage to what he perceived as an unsatisfactory, but still tolerable, proposal for settlement (*pace* Smith 1993: 177–8). His treatment of a further episode in the home rule controversy underlines the hesitation in his approach. Between January and March 1914 Unionist politicians and soldiers debated the possibility of amending the Army Act in order to prevent the government offering a military threat to Ulster before a general election. This was an unprecedented, but nonetheless a constitutionally viable strategem: it was rendered obsolete by the Curragh Incident, which occurred on 20 March 1914. Nevertheless, even before the 'mutiny' of General Gough and his fifty-seven officers, and even though many Unionist leaders favoured amendment, Bonar Law hesitated. Despite fiery rhetoric, Bonar Law still shied away from any scheme which threatened to bring disunity and controversy onto the Unionist party. In these qualms lay the measure of Bonar Law's militancy (Blake 1955: 181).

A final attempt to reconcile the parties was held at Buckingham Palace between 21 and 23 July 1914, where the ultimately abortive discussions focused on a variety of exclusion options. None of those won cross-party acceptance. Within a week, however, in the context of mounting international tension, Bonar Law and Carson had agreed to postpone the debate on Ulster exclusion. Six weeks after the outbreak of war, on 15 September, this party truce was temporarily disrupted. Asquith simultaneously placed the third Home Rule Bill on the statutes, and introduced a measure suspending the new Act until the end of the war. Bonar Law responded with a bitter speech, and by leading his party out of the Commons chamber. An angry address and a histrionic gesture were a fitting conclusion to a period of Unionist resistance which was characterized by bluster and theatricals and by a persistent hesitation.

The fate of the home rule question only serves to underline Bonar Law's essential caution. The Lloyd George negotiations, conducted in the wake of the Easter rising, produced what proved to be a highly fragile agreement between Carson and Redmond on the basis of a poorly defined exclusion proposal. Bonar Law, backed by Carson, Balfour and other Unionist elders, supported the Lloyd George initiative, but at a party meeting held on 7 July 1916 he faced considerable diehard opposition, and found himself in what Robert Blake has assessed as a 'dangerously isolated position' (Blake 1955: 288). However, the initiative failed, and Bonar Law was spared the likelihood of a diehard revolt against his leadership. But the episode throws his apparent fanaticism into a useful comparative perspective, and underlines the strategic dimension to his leadership in 1912–14. Bonar Law by this time had accepted that home rule was on the statute books and was therefore an inevitability: his principal concern in 1916 and after, as in 1913–14, was to secure a settlement acceptable to Ulster Unionist opinion. Thus the Unionist stalwart of 1914 had become, by March 1920, one of the most eloquent defenders of the fourth home rule measure – the Government of Ireland Bill: Bonar Law's speech in favour of the second reading of this measure was widely regarded as being among his finest parliamentary performances (Blake 1955: 418). He was out of office in December 1921, when the Anglo-Irish Treaty was under debate in the Commons. But, once he was assured that there would be no coercion of northern Unionists as a result of the Treaty, he offered his, admittedly reluctant, support. Had this not been forthcoming – had Bonar Law chosen to cultivate and exploit diehard loyalism – the coalition government might well have fallen, and with it the immediate possibility of an Irish settlement.

The third, and last, dominant issue within Bonar Law's political career was the First World War. This had a profound personal as well as political impact. Bonar Law, whose wife had died in 1909, had two sons in the armed forces, and concern for them, as well as the eventual burden of their loss (both were killed in action in 1917), seems to have fostered his naturally melancholy and lugubrious temperament: Lloyd George contrasted the Bonar Law of 1909, 'childishly optimistic' about the political outlook, and bumptious about the Tories' electoral prospects, with the much more sombre and diffident figure of the war years (Lloyd George 1933: 1029). Certainly the ambitious tariff reformer, the bullish leader of the Unionist cause, had lost both energy and confidence by 1915. Throughout the war Bonar Law deferred to the superior energy and talents of Liberal rivals, and especially Lloyd George.

Between August 1914 and May 1915 Bonar Law led the Unionist party in a policy of patriotic opposition, a policy which became increasingly untenable as the months passed and as a series of embarrassing setbacks – particularly at sea – were sustained by the British forces. With the failure of the expedition to the Dardanelles, and the resignation of the First Sea Lord, Lord Fisher, on 15 May 1915, Unionist frustration came to a head, and (to Bonar Law's relief) Asquith made the offer of a coalition government (Pugh 1982: 167). He was content to take the Colonial Office for himself, a decision which reflected on Asquith's guile (the prime minister, who had no faith in Bonar Law's intellectual strength, was determined to keep him out of senior office) and indeed on his own modest assessment of his abilities: Bonar Law's choice of appointment also recalled that of Joseph Chamberlain, who – faced with a similar decision in 1895 – took the

Colonial Office, and it may have been that Bonar Law was still, in 1915, struggling for his hero's mantle. The demands of his department were also comparatively light, and this freed him for the war council, or Dardanelles Committee, an inner cabinet of which he was a member, and which was dedicated to the supervision of British military strategy. Within this body he was an influential advocate of evacuation from the Dardanelles (this was carried out in December 1915), and a strong supporter of conscription (partial conscription was enacted in May 1916). But the War Council was only a consultative body, with no power to bind the rest of the cabinet, and with all too many opportunities for a wasteful duplication of business. A perception of executive confusion and inefficiency took hold of many Unionist backbenchers, and some influential Liberals, and created pressure for a better defined and more powerful war council within the cabinet: the disastrous losses sustained in the Somme offensive after July 1916 only served to intensify this pressure. The Unionist malcontents were led by Carson, who at this time was threatening Bonar Law's leadership of the party: a division forced by Carson on 8 November over a minor colonial matter (which came within Bonar Law's province) divided the Unionist party, and revealed widespread dissatisfaction with the government and with the Conservative leadership. This division brought matters to a head. Max Aitken (later Lord Beaverbrook), a convinced opponent of Asquith, was able to bring his friend Bonar Law into contact with the two other most influential critics of the existing management of the war: Lloyd George, the frustrated War Minister, and Carson, the leading backbench Tory malcontent. The triumvirate (the label was Aitken's), allied to supportive opinion in the press, manoeuvred Asquith into resignation on 5 December 1916. Bonar Law, who might have become prime minister, deferred once again to Lloyd George, and was content to serve as Chancellor of the Exchequer and as a deputy leader of the new coalition government: as Robert Blake has argued, 'Bonar Law had neither the desire nor the energy to emulate Lloyd George. He was content to be an auxiliary, an invaluable ally, but always a junior partner in the firm' (Blake 1955: 343).

Bonar Law served as Chancellor until January 1919 and as Leader of the Commons until March 1921. He was, in addition, a member of the new War cabinet, but because of his particular departmental responsibilities was not expected to assume a leading role. The chancellorship was ideally suited to his experience and strengths, for he could bring to play his very considerable abilities as a banker and trader. His particular achievement was in financing the British war effort, which he did through reversing the earlier policy of short-term loans at high rates of interest. Instead, he devised a series of War Loans, which were issued over long terms at low rates of interest: the first of these loans, launched in January 1917, was highly successful, and brought over £2 billion into the Treasury by 31 March 1917. In October 1917 he announced a new issue of national war bonds for an unlimited amount, which was a similar success, and ensured a sustained supply of money until the end of the conflict. Thomas Jones (a former Professor of Economics at Queen's University, Belfast, and Lloyd

George's assistant cabinet secretary) described these loans as 'among the greatest achievements in the history of British finance' (Jones 1937: 487). In his budget of 2 May 1917 Bonar Law pointed out with understandable pride that the United Kingdom was unique in being able to raise 26 per cent of its wartime expenditure out of revenue.

However, he had little direct influence over the running of the war. He had no military experience, and no firm convictions on strategy. He was inclined (like Carson) to be over-deferential to the opinions of the generals, and – along with his colleagues on the War cabinet – allowed himself to be persuaded into supporting Douglas Haig's disastrous Passchendaele campaign in July 1917. His particular field of action was the Commons, which he managed during Lloyd George's frequent, enforced absences. Here again, he exhibited particular strengths as a mediator and as a diplomat, qualities which had been hard won in the iron market of Glasgow. Like his successor, Stanley Baldwin, he was an accessible manager, with the gift of defusing individual tensions. He was at his weakest in formal debate when his personal honour, or the integrity of his government, was under suspicion. On such occasions – such as the Maurice debate of 9 May 1918 – it required Lloyd George's particular blend of courage, eloquence and insensitivity to rescue the government.

'The most perfect partnership in political history' was in office at the time of the armistice, in November 1918, and was sustained at the general election of December 1918. The Unionists might well have fought the election on their own, and won (some diehards would have preferred this), but Bonar Law chose to sustain the life of the coalition. The reasons for this apparently wilful lack of ambition are in fact not hard to disentangle. Lloyd George and the coalition had won the war, and could not lightly be abandoned. Moreover, by binding Lloyd George to the coalition, Bonar Law (like Baldwin with Ramsay MacDonald and Labour) was granting him pre-eminence at a high price – the continued disruption of the Liberal party. The Unionists also remained uncertain about the prospect of dealing with militant labour unrest, and the presence of progressive elements in the government helped to postpone a direct confrontation between the party and the unions. Finally, and linked with this, was the mass electorate created by the Representation of the People Act 1918: as Martin Pugh has argued, 'for the Conservatives alliance with Lloyd George clearly provided the safest means of effecting the transition from war to peace on the basis of a vast new electorate' (Pugh 1982: 175).

The coalition government triumphed, winning 474 seats and a majority of 252: Bonar Law was himself returned for the Glasgow Central constituency. In January 1919 he moved from the Exchequer to the less demanding office of Lord Privy Seal: however, he remained Leader of the House. It was a comparatively easy tenure of office. Bonar Law was only marginally involved with the great international questions which dominated the first years, indeed the entire duration of the coalition: he had little to do with the negotiation of the Treaty of Versailles, which was left to Lloyd George and Balfour, although he was one of the

British signatories on 28 June 1919. Nor did he have much to do with the ongoing question of German reparations, except that he had the task of dampening the demands of some Unionists in the Commons for a punitive settlement. Bonar Law remained in office through the post-war boom, and resigned within three months of the onset of the great slump: he had, therefore, few great economic questions to address. The most serious industrial problem which came his way was the threatened strike of the Triple Alliance (the coalition of railwaymen, miners and transport workers) in March 1919: but this threat was successfully averted. The other potential area of controversy for which he had a responsibility was Ireland, but there were few effective critics of the government's Government of Ireland Bill at the end of 1920, and his speech in defence of the measure was a great success. He was spared the great controversies which rocked the last months of the coalition government. For, in March 1921, demoralized by personal tragedy, and exhausted by ten years as leader of the Unionist party, he announced his retirement. The decision had been forced upon him by his doctors: but there is little evidence that he chose to resist.

The brief, final coda to Bonar Law's career came between October 1922 and May 1923. Out of office, Bonar Law was able to serve as a focus for backbench discontent with the increasingly highhanded actions of the coalition government and with the remote, intellectually austere Unionist leadership. At the end of 1921, when he felt restored to health, he offered a highly cautious support for the Anglo-Irish Treaty. He retreated from this position after the assassination of Sir Henry Wilson, admitting that while he did not favour the scrapping of the Treaty, he doubted whether he would have voted for it had he suspected the outcome: in addition he warned that unless the government adopted a firmer stand on Ireland then they should forfeit his future support. Bonar Law was therefore avoiding any crude or overt revolt against his former partners in the coalition, but he was expressing sufficient doubts to encourage other, more thoroughgoing malcontents within the Unionist party. He sustained this combination of formal support and subtle query in October 1922, at the time of the Chanak crisis, when war with the Kemalist forces in Turkey seemed likely. He endorsed the government's handling of the crisis in a celebrated public letter, while warning that Britain 'cannot alone act as policemen of the world': that is, he supported the government's tactics while condemning its strategy (Blake 1955: 448). It was, however, the Unionist ministers in the coalition who, by calling a party meeting in the Carlton Club on 19 May 1922, brought matters to a head. They sought the party's approval for the survival of the coalition, but were opposed by Bonar Law and 187 of the 275 present at the meeting. Isolated from the bulk of their party, the Unionist ministers, supported by their Liberal colleagues, decided to compel Bonar Law to undertake what they imagined would be the impossible task of forming a ministry. Lloyd George tendered the resignation of the government, and George V sent in turn for Bonar Law. He demurred until he had been confirmed as leader of the Unionist party. A party meeting on 23 October 1922 unanimously supported his candidature, and he was immediately appointed as prime minister. The keynote of the new government was 'tranquillity and stability', and aided by this unpromising manifesto (and by the confusion in the Liberal ranks) he secured a majority of 75 at the general election held in November 1922.

Bonar Law's premiership lasted 209 days, and already in the last weeks he was clearly suffering from the throat cancer which would kill him. Three key issues dominated his last parliament, in February–March 1923: the international debt question, unemployment, and housing. None of these was addressed comprehensively or satisfactorily. Bonar Law did not think that it was within the capacity of government to deal adequately with unemployment. The problem created by the shortage of housing was too overwhelming to permit any easy solution – but a tentative start was made through the replacement of the limited Minister of Housing, Arthur Griffith-Boscawen, by the more energetic and efficient Neville Chamberlain. The international debt problem had two dimensions, neither of which was adequately settled within Bonar Law's tenure of office. German reparations remained a divisive issue, and British and French opinion diverged: the French sought punitive reparations, and in January 1923 occupied the Ruhr. The question of reparations was indirectly tied to the problem of American debt. The debt owed by the British government to the United States was renegotiated by the inexperienced Chancellor of the Exchequer, Stanley Baldwin, with what Bonar Law regarded as a highly unsatisfactory result. Here again, however, the issue was only finally settled long after Bonar Law's death.

Bonar Law resigned from office on 19 May 1923, and died on 30 October. His premiership was too brief to permit any great legislative achievement, yet there were party dividends: Bonar Law located a popular thirst for caution and tranquillity which Baldwin inherited, and put to good electoral use in the inter-war years. In ending the coalition, in freeing his party from the Lloyd George cavalcade, he also spared the Conservatives from dangerous ideological tensions and potential internal division. He had come to the leadership of the party in 1911 as a unifying figure, and he remained conscious of this role throughout his subsequent career. Like those Tories who lived under the shadow of the Peelite schism, Bonar Law was most effectively energized by the clear-cut issue of party unity.

He was a great Chancellor of the Exchequer, and a formidable Leader of the Commons. He served loyally and effectively as Colonial Secretary in 1915–16, condemned to relatively junior office by the 'mildness' of his ambition, by Asquith's genial contempt, and by the jealousy of senior Tory colleagues. Yet this gentle widower was as adept at breaking governments as serving within them. He destroyed two coalitions, and applied a dangerous pressure to the pre-war Liberal administration. Without his wholehearted endorsement, Ulster Unionism would have had a much slighter impact on British politics. Equally, however, this endorsement meant that Irish loyalist expectations were raised in ways which almost certainly he was not prepared to satisfy.

Despite his reputation as a firebrand, he was essentially a pragmatic politician. Even with the two issues which fired him – tariff reform and Ulster – he displayed more rhetorical truculence than conviction. He was a skilled party leader, offering simple, hard-hitting leadership after the philosophical ambiguities and remoteness of Balfour. His leadership of Unionism in 1912–14 was as much as an essay in party revival as in loyalist conviction (Smith 1993: 177–8). Through his trenchant loyalism he also consolidated his own, hitherto somewhat limp, control over the Conservative party. He was ambitious, but not in any overweening sense (as his actions in May 1915 and again in December 1918 illustrate): instead he carried a painful combination of ambition and diffidence. He tended to defer to those whose abilities he respected (such as Lloyd George); he also tended to choose those offices which matched his experience or inclination rather than his lust for power.

It is easy to depict Bonar Law in stereotypical Calvinist or Scots terms. He was capable of ferocious industry, was rigidly teetotal and served as a Presbyterian elder. But, although a son of the manse, he had little personal faith. A confirmed milk-drinker, he enjoyed the company of riotous Tories such as F.E. Smith. He smoked incessantly (Beaverbrook 1956: xix). A streak-worker, he loved tranquillity: Lloyd George complained that 'he had no constant urge towards action of any kind'. He could be blunt, but this was 'all manner' (Lloyd George 1933: 1031). Bonar Law survived because he was an intermittently brilliant speaker, an accessible party leader and a competent, sometimes excellent, administrator. But his contemporaries also attributed his success to the basic features of his personality: 'elusive and wistful' in the verdict of Stanley Baldwin (Chamberlain 1935: 220). A more telling paean came from Austen Chamberlain, whose political career Bonar Law had done much to thwart: 'he was indeed a most lovable man' (Chamberlain 1935: 221).

References and further reading
Beaverbrook, Lord (1956) *Men and Power, 1917–1918*, London: Hutchinson.
Blake, R. (1955) *The Unknown Prime Minister: The Life and Times of Andrew Bonar Law, 1858–1923*, London: Eyre & Spottiswoode. (Although written to Lord Beaverbrook's commission, this was a judicious and exhaustive biography, based on a range of contemporary archives. It remains an indispensable starting-point for Bonar Law's career.)
—— (1985) *The Conservative Party from Peel to Thatcher*, London: Macmillan.
Chamberlain, A. (1935) *Down the Years*, London: Cassell. (Highly cautious, even defensive, autobiographical jottings which include a memoir of Bonar Law.)
Green, E. (1995) *The Crisis of Conservatism: The Politics, Economics and Ideology of the British Conservative Party, 1880–1914*, London: Routledge.
Jackson, A. (1989) *The Ulster Party: Irish Unionists in the House of Commons, 1884–1911*, Oxford: Clarendon Press.
—— (1993) *Sir Edward Carson*, Dublin: Historical Association of Ireland.
Jones, T. (1937) 'Andrew Bonar Law', in J. Weaver (ed.) *Dictionary of National Biography (1922–30)*, London: Oxford University Press.
Lloyd George, D. (1933) *War Memoirs*, vol. 2, London: Ivor Nicholson & Watson. (Contains a series of perceptive (if tendentious) memoirs on leading politicians, including Bonar Law.)
Pugh, M. (1982) *The Making of Modern British Politics, 1867–1939*, Oxford:

Blackwell. (A brilliant overview of British high and low politics. Contains a number of intricate deconstructions of Bonar Law's tactical problems.)

Ramsden, J. (1978) *The History of the Conservative Party: The Age of Balfour and Baldwin*, London: Longman.

Riddell, Lord (1934) *More Pages from my Diary, 1908–1914*, London: Country Life. (Excellent, though much underrated, political comment from the proprietor of the *News of the World*.)

Ridley, J. (1985) 'Leadership and management in the Conservative Party in Parliament, 1906–14', DPhil thesis, University of Oxford.

Smith, J. (1993) 'Bluff, bluster and brinkmanship: Andrew Bonar Law and the third Home Rule Bill', *Historical Journal* 36: 161–78. (Emphasizes the integrity of purpose behind Bonar Law's strategy 1912–14.)

Stewart, A. (1967) *The Ulster Crisis: Resistance to Home Rule, 1912–14*, London: Faber.

Sykes, A. (1979) *Tariff Reform in British Politics 1903–1913*, Oxford: Clarendon Press. (A detailed analysis of the triumph of the 'Conservative' over the 'radical' elements of Edwardian Unionism.)

Taylor, H. (1932) *The Strange Case of Andrew Bonar Law*, London: Chapman & Hall. (The first full-length biography, useful for biograpical detail – especially on Bonar Law's early life.)

Alvin Jackson

Stanley Baldwin, First Earl Baldwin of Bewdley

Born 3 August 1867, only child of Alfred Baldwin and Louisa MacDonald. Educated at Harrow and Trinity College, Cambridge. Married 1892 Lucy Ridsdale. MP for Bewdley 1908–37. Joint Financial Secretary to the Treasury 1917–21; President of the Board of Trade 1921–2; Chancellor of the Exchequer 1922–3; Prime Minister 1923–4, 1924–9 and 1935–7; Lord President of the Council 1931–5; Lord Privy Seal 1932–3. Left Commons 1937, ennobled the same year. Died 14 December 1947.

Baldwin has long provided fuel for historical debate, and not surprisingly. Inheriting a divided party uncertain of its future in 1923, he proved surprisingly resilient and when he finally retired, in 1937, he had set it firmly as the main party of resistance to Labour in Britain. Despite losing two of the first three general elections he fought as Conservative leader, he was in office for all but three years of his tenure as party leader. He was prime minister for a total of six years and ten months in three separate stints, and effective deputy prime minister of the Conservative-dominated National government under the former Labour leader Ramsay MacDonald. This record was all the more remarkable given his relative lack of experience before succeeding to the premiership, the heavy criticism he had to endure from his party and sections of the press for much of the period, and his commitment to leading the party on centrist lines at a time when many were calling for a more robust approach.

Baldwin was head of his party at a time when Britain and the world were struggling to cope with the aftermath of the First World War. In Europe, 1917 marked the start of a period of revolutions and civil wars. Fascism had begun its ascent by 1922. Problems of war debts and reparations held back European recovery, and a period of pacification in the later 1920s was brought to an end in 1929 with the effects of the slump which hit most of Europe and the United States. Many liberal democracies collapsed, and with the rise of Hitler in 1933, Germany began once again to pose problems to European stability.

Although Britain did not suffer such economic and social instability as some other countries, these were nevertheless years of challenge for British governments. Unemployment was never to fall below 1 million in the years that Baldwin was leader of the Conservative party. In the early 1930s it approached 3 million and the nation appeared to be in severe crisis. The strength of organized labour was demonstrated in 1926, at the time of the General Strike. The pace of foreign policy quickened after the rise of Hitler and the threats of Italy and Japan became increasingly apparent in the 1930s. And even the monarchy was to cause problems, with the abdication of Edward VIII providing a serious challenge in 1936.

Baldwin's succession to the leadership in the wake of the dying Bonar Law's resignation in 1923 was somewhat fortuitous. Before the war, Baldwin had been an inconspicuous figure, succeeding his father as MP for Bewdley in 1908 and appearing as a fairly typical backwoods Tory MP with little distinctive to say. He had been a minister in the Lloyd George coalitions from 1917, and in 1921 had entered the cabinet as President of the Board of Trade. However, he had soon become dispirited with the immoral atmosphere of the coalition, and when it was proposed that it should be perpetuated by the calling of a general election in October 1922, Baldwin rebelled. At the meeting of Conservative MPs and peers called to discuss the proposal, Bonar Law (who had retired as leader the year before) and Baldwin both made strong speeches in favour of dropping Lloyd George and fighting the election as an independent party. Baldwin in particular attacked Lloyd George as 'a dynamic force . . . a very terrible thing', continued association with whom would see the Conservative party 'smashed to atoms and lost in ruins' (Middlemas and Barnes 1969: 123). The meeting voted to leave the coalition, and Chamberlain resigned as party leader and was replaced by Law. Because most of the coalitionists refused to serve in a Law government, Baldwin was appointed Chancellor of the Exchequer. At the subsequent general election, the government won a substantial majority. However, in May 1923 Law was forced to retire through ill-health. The field of potential successors was thin: ultimately the choice was between Baldwin and Lord Curzon, the Foreign Secretary. For largely negative reasons, not least – but not only – the fact that Curzon was a member of the Lords, where the main party of opposition (Labour) had only a handful of representatives, Baldwin was the choice of those advising the King. Luck always plays a part in politics, but few would dispute that Baldwin had more than his share of good fortune in succeeding to the premiership.

However, the notion that Baldwin was then excessively fortunate in retaining the leadership of his party is one which should be dismissed. It was once the norm to argue that Baldwin was an indolent figure of no great importance, whose ascendancy was the product of a combination of accidents and conspiracies like the 'Red Scare' election of 1924 or the 'Bankers' Ramp' poll in 1931. George Orwell described him as 'a hole in the air' (Orwell 1941: 37); C.L. Mowat talked of 'the rule of the pygmies', of whom Baldwin was clearly among the more vertically challenged (Mowat 1955: 142); while his official biography was almost unremittingly hostile (Young 1952). However, starting in the late 1960s, as passions cooled, archives were opened and government once again became a matter of crisis management, historians began to re-evaluate Baldwin, so much so that recent work has cautioned against going too far in seeing him as 'the inspired puppet-master of British politics' (Self 1992: 270). Even now, half a century after his death, there is very little consensus on this enigmatic figure.

Baldwin had two basic commitments: to capitalism and to the parliamentary system. The former was unremarkable, for Baldwin was the son of an ironmaster, and had followed his father as head of the family firm. He was always to retain a firm belief that capitalism was the natural order of things: it was only through productive private enterprise, uninhibited, so far as possible, by high levels of taxation and government interference, that wealth could be created and standards of living rise. But his commitment to parliamentarism clearly marked Baldwin out from his ideological counterparts on the continent, in so far as, in many cases, they would eventually be prepared to sacrifice parliamentary institutions in the cause of capitalism. It could be argued that Baldwin was never presented with such a stark choice as some of them, but, even so, he was firmly committed to the parliamentary system. Baldwin was nevertheless always somewhat nervous about 'democracy', which was understandable given the vast increase in the electorate which began in 1918 and culminated in universal adult suffrage in 1928.

The instrument which Baldwin saw as the key to preserving the capitalist system and parliamentary government was the Conservative party. His 'strategy' as a political leader, therefore, can be summed up as follows: to simplify politics into a straight choice between Labour and Conservative. This in turn involved crushing out the Liberals by appealing to the political middle ground, reuniting and reorganizing the Conservative party after the divisions and dissensions of the post-war period, and, after 1923 at any rate, avoiding an auction with the Labour party on policy. Implicit in all this was a rejection of the Lloyd George Coalition and all its works, and of Lloyd George himself.

The party Baldwin took over in 1923, though possessing a decent parliamentary majority, was still divided and lacking in direction. That October, in an attempt to provide a sense of direction and possibly to try to outbid Labour on unemployment, Baldwin came out for protection, and despite his original intention of carrying out a lengthy campaign of education on the subject, was forced by the pace of events to call an election in December 1923. But while emerging as the largest party, the Conservatives lost their majority and, in January 1924, were defeated in the House on a protectionist King's Speech. They left office and the first Labour government, dependent on Liberal support, was formed.

This setback seems to have had a salutary effect on Baldwin, convincing him that attempts to outbid Labour (and later the Liberals under Lloyd George) on policy were misguided. In that sense, the final strand of Baldwin's strategy was now in place.

In another sense, the events of 1924 eventually worked in his favour: the party was reunited. Forcing the Liberals to support a free-trade Labour government hastened their demise, since voters were forced to see the Liberals as surrogate socialists, while a number of leading politicians, subjected to the same pressures, now came over to or back into the Conservative fold, very much on Baldwin's terms. Thus when he formed his new government after his party's smashing electoral victory in October 1924, Baldwin was able to include all the leading coalitionists who mattered, such as Austen Chamberlain, Winston Churchill and Lord Birkenhead. Buoyed by a great electoral victory, Baldwin seemed well set to survive as head of a united party.

This is not to say that his authority was never shaken again. In the latter stages of the 1924–9 government there were concerns that he seemed lethargic and unwilling to think seriously about future policy. This can be seen as a conscious decision, informed by the débâcle of 1923, not to be drawn into an auction with Labour and the Liberals under Lloyd George over policy to deal with unemployment. However, once the election of 1929 was lost, it became part of a longer charge sheet against his leadership of the party. The election had left the parliamentary party more right wing than previously, which made Baldwin's centrism more difficult to sustain: and, as economic crisis mounted under Labour, moderation began to seem increasingly inappropriate. These feelings against Baldwin were exploited by the press barons, Beaverbrook and Rothermere, who launched a strong campaign in favour of protectionism and against Baldwin's leadership. For much of the period between 1929 and 1931 it seemed unlikely that Baldwin could survive: indeed, in March 1931 he was on the verge of resignation. However, he was saved by the lack of a credible agreed alternative, by the inherent strengths of a Conservative party leader in an era before leadership elections, by the nature of his opponents, who were widely distrusted within the party, and by the fact that he was finally persuaded, in October 1930, to shift party policy towards full protectionism with imperial preference. By mid-1931 the party was substantially reunited, and on course for victory at the next general election (Ball 1988).

By the time that election came, Baldwin and his party were part of a National government under the leadership of the erstwhile Labour leader, MacDonald. Baldwin had been initially cautious about participation in such an administration, but was persuaded by colleagues that the financial crisis was so grave that there was no alternative. In fact, he soon found that he liked working with MacDonald, that the idea of a National government was popular, and that the government would be able to do all the things he wanted a Conservative government to do, such as balance the budget and introduce protection. He also believed that Labour had acted irresponsibly during the financial crisis by preferring to resign than to cut public expenditure, and that it should be roundly beaten at the polls to teach it a lesson. The result of that October's general election, with 554 National MPs (including 470 Conservatives) to Labour's 46 achieved this last aim spectacularly. It also had the effect of finally restoring Baldwin's authority within the party. The new MPs were, on the whole, grateful to him as the leader who had shepherded them in to parliament: they also tilted the balance of the parliamentary party away from the right wing once more. The perpetuation of the National government also ensured that Baldwin could pursue a more centrist line. Despite diehard attacks on government policy, most notably over plans to liberalize British rule in India, Baldwin's position was now secure, and he continued to lead a reasonably united party until he chose to retire (having succeeded MacDonald as premier in 1935) in 1937.

The centrism that Baldwin had pursued so ardently, and often at some discomfort to himself, had by that time had the desired effect of squeezing the Liberals, and ensuring that politics was restored to a virtual two-party system. While it would be facile to argue that Baldwin was the principal agent of the Liberals' problems, he did make a significant impact on their fortunes. He did so, first, by refusing to treat the Liberal party seriously. Following the 1923 election, he pressed ahead with a protectionist King's Speech, rather than seeking any kind of arrangement with them. In that way, he forced the Liberals into the unwilling arms of Labour, which then allowed the Conservatives to portray the Liberals as socialists in disguise. Similarly, in 1929 he refused to negotiate with Lloyd George, preferring instead to resign the premiership as soon as the results were known, and once more forcing the Liberals to support – and be tainted by the failure of – another minority Labour government. In the 1929–31 period he supported moves to split the Liberals, which eventually bore fruit with the formation of the Liberal National party in September 1931. He made no effort to keep the free trade ('Samuelite') Liberals in the government when they were considering resignation before the general election of that year, and in September 1932 made few efforts to keep them in when they did eventually resign.

Second, Baldwin tried to play down the 'Tory' aspects of the Conservative party in order to make a broad appeal to erstwhile Liberals. This could be seen in trade policy. Here, he appointed the free trader, Churchill, to the Exchequer in 1924 and, more generally, refused to shift to greater protectionism during the 1924–9 government. One reason for his eventual acceptance of a fully protectionist programme in 1930 was the realization that many leading Liberals were now, under the pressure of severe economic crisis, coming to accept the need for a move away from free trade. Linked to this was his attempt to soft-pedal on the empire, with the marginalization of ardent imperialists like Leo Amery. Similarly, realizing the damage that Ireland had done to the Conservative party in the 1910s, he was determined not to allow India to become a similar political football, and largely succeeded. He also tried to ensure that the Conservatives did not make gratuitous attacks on the trade unions: hence in 1925 he opposed a back-bench proposal to replace 'contracting out' of the political levy with 'contracting in'. However, once the unions had 'let themselves down' in the 1926 General Strike, he was prepared to see such legislation enacted. Finally, he tried to avoid a close identification of the Conservative party with the Church of England, which would have been offputting to many nonconformist erstwhile Liberals. He did this by stressing Christianity in an ecumenical manner: his rhetoric was godly but unsectarian. It seems that the controversy over the *Revised Prayer Book* in 1928, which despite his best efforts heightened awareness of the continuing links between the party and the Church, was a significant factor in the Liberal revival and Conservative collapse in many nonconformist parts of the country in 1929.

Baldwin's rhetoric might have been 'found out' by the *Prayer Book* controversy, but on the whole it was one of his strongest suits. Baldwin was a keen speech-maker, and five collections of his orations were published. At one level, they were rather anodyne, even bland: the first collection included speeches entitled 'Stour-port', 'The Church Army' and 'Harrow', hardly, it might be thought, the most fascinating subjects of the day (Baldwin 1926: 14–16, 198–201, 265–8). Yet this was not the point. Baldwin's speeches aimed to create an image of himself and of the country. Hence his stress on peace in industry, with frequent references to a golden age of paternalism and close relations between workers and employers, his emphasis on the importance of service and duty, his concern with democracy as a system which brought obligations as well as rights, and his concern to evoke a notion of 'Englishness' which was replete with rural imagery. The aim was 'to appeal not for some impossible reversal of entrepreneurial progress, but for the preservation through changing conditions of a spirit of co-operation which pro-moted economic efficiency and enterprise because it was humane' (Williamson 1993: 193). In other words, Baldwin's speeches were designed for wide public consumption and to underscore his commitment to parliamentary democracy and capitalism. He claimed 'Englishness' for the Conservative party, implicitly – and sometimes explicitly – demonizing 'cleverness' (as represented by Lloyd George) and 'intellectuals' (as represented by sections of the Labour party).

Baldwin's evocative rhetoric paid especial dividends when it came to the mod-ern media. Indeed, Baldwin can be seen as the first 'media prime minister'. In a sense, this is surprising. His relations with the press were never easy. He could almost invariably rely on the support of the editor of *The Times*, Geoffrey Dawson, but the mass-circulation Conservative papers, Rothermere's *Daily Mail* and Beaverbrook's *Daily Express*, were never very enthusiastic about him, turned ferociously against him in 1929–31, and never really forgave him subsequently for his survival in the party leadership. That this did not matter more than it did was due, in large part, to the fact that Baldwin adapted rapidly and effectively to the opportunities presented by radio and, from 1930 onwards, sound newsreels. Taking advice from professionals, he did not orate to the viewer or listener, but spoke in calm, confidential tones, seeking above all to seem ordinary, decent and trustworthy.

Baldwin himself was not over-concerned with matters of party organization, but this did not mean that he did not recognize the importance of the issue: far from it. The party he took over in 1923 was in something of a shambles, the machine having rusted in the coalition years, and finance was a problem. Baldwin gradually brought in his own people, most notably J.C.C. Davidson as party chairman in 1926. Davidson began a major reconstruction of the machine, including its financing, and it was in this period that corporate donations, rather than contributions from wealthy individuals, began to figure largely in the party's funding. Under Davidson the party also developed new propaganda techniques, adding cinema (and espionage at the Labour party's printers) to older methods. Davidson had to be sacrificed to save Baldwin from attack by the press barons and the wider party in 1930, but was succeeded by Neville Chamberlain, who continued the party's hardheaded approach to organization. However, Chamberlain's successors were less able and there was some decay after 1931. On the whole, though, the Baldwin era can be seen as the one in which the Conservative party came to terms organizationally with the needs of a mass electorate rather more quickly than its rivals (Ramsden 1978).

What of Baldwin as premier? He was not a great dynamic reformer: he 'could be moved to tears by social deprivation; [but not] moved to the point of legislation' (Jones and Bentley 1978: 34). Certainly after 1923, he was resolved so far as possible to avoid extensive intervention, not least as a reaction against, and to mark a clear distinction with, both Lloyd George and the Labour party. However, he was prepared to let ministers like Neville Chamberlain pursue moderate administrative reform, as in 1924–9, and he was ready to be persuaded – as over derating in the 1928–9 and protection in 1930. His relations with colleagues were usually amiable, but when they mistook listening for agreement they were frequently disappointed and left to rue what they saw as his insincerity. He had a streak of ruthlessness, as his sacrifice of Davidson in 1930 made clear. His closest political confidantes were generally second-rank figures, like Davidson and Bridgeman – his relations with Chamberlain, on the other hand, were never as close as their long association might be taken to suggest. Essentially, Baldwin was a much more neurotic and insecure character than his public persona would have suggested, a fact testified to by his nervous breakdown in the summer of 1936, when he spent three months out of politics, and by the fact that every year he needed to disappear for a month to Aix-les-Bains for rest and recuperation, isolated from politics except for the Davidsons. Baldwin was in many ways an effective co-ordinator of colleagues: he was prepared to allow them to get on with reform, but rarely initiated legislation. His interest in foreign policy was minimal. This has been criticized, but on the other hand the record of his successor, Chamberlain, in intervening in foreign affairs was not an altogether happy one. Baldwin did at least preside over the beginnings of rearmament, and the long-standing charge that he should have pursued a more assertive foreign policy in the 1930s, especially against Hitler, is one that many present-day historians would question.

On the whole, Baldwin was at his best when the constitution seemed to be under threat. His handling of the 1926 General Strike was firm and uncompromising, although the Trade Disputes Act which followed it was a blow to his attempts to appeal to the political middle ground. In 1931, he was clear in his own mind that Labour had imperilled the nation's future for party advantage, and stressed that the election of that year really was 'the acid test of democracy'. And in 1936, faced with Edward VIII's determination to marry a twice-divorced American, and despite his own recent nervous breakdown, he acted with great aplomb, securing the abdication of the King and his succession by George VI.

Baldwin's career at the apex of politics was a tangled one. He frequently attracted severe criticism, and at times it seemed impossible that he could survive the onslaught. Yet his retirement, in May 1937, was unusual among prime ministerial departures in that he went when he wanted to go and in a blaze of glory. In the years that followed his stock fell very low indeed, as he came to be seen as one of the men who had failed to stop Hitler early enough, and as the solid achievements of inter-war governments paled against the full employment of wartime and post-war Britain. Yet as passions cooled, archives opened, and realization increased of how difficult a job government is, historians softened their criticisms and, in some cases, became positively glowing in their tributes to his performance.

Baldwin certainly had his failings. He often lacked drive and easily became depressed. He was arguably too pessimistic about the ability of government to improve the lives of its citizens. His neglect of foreign affairs was obvious and, in some ways, damaging. Yet at the same time he was a politician of considerable ability. His aims, to preserve capitalism and the parliamentary system, were achieved, through the instrument of his choosing, the Conservative party. Indeed, it was in no small part due to his leadership that the Conservatives became the party of resistance to socialism. By so adeptly identifying himself as above party and the opposition as somehow 'un-English', he was able to help establish the electoral supremacy of the Conservative party in the inter-war period and lay a basis for it in the longer term as well. He may have been, as Lord Birkenhead said, a 'second-class brain', but he was without doubt a political operator of the highest order.

References and further reading

Baldwin, S. (1926) *On England*, London: Philip Allan.

—— (1928) *Our Inheritance*, London: Hodder & Stoughton.

—— (1935) *This Torch of Freedom*, London: Hodder & Stoughton.

—— (1937) *Service of our Lives*, London: Hodder & Stoughton.

—— (1939) *An Interpreter of England*, London: Hodder & Stoughton. (All the above are collections of speeches, invaluable for an understanding of Baldwin's ideas and style.)

Ball, S. (1988) *Baldwin and the Conservative Party: The Crisis of 1929–1931*, London: Yale University Press. (A challenging and well-researched account of the challenge to Baldwin's leadership.)

Cowling, M. (1971) *The Impact of Labour 1920–24: The Beginning of Modern British Politics*, Cambridge: Cambridge University Press.

Hyde, H. (1973) *Baldwin: The Unexpected Prime Minister*, London: Hart-Davis, MacGibbon.

Jones, A. and Bentley, M. (1978) 'Salisbury and Baldwin', in M. Cowling (ed.) *Conservative Essays*, London: Cassell.

Jones, T. (1969) *Whitehall Diary*, ed. K. Middlemas, 3 vols, London: Oxford University Press. (The assistant secretary to the cabinet provides an intimate account of Baldwin in the 1920s.)

Middlemas, K. and Barnes, J. (1969) *Baldwin: A Biography*, London: Weidenfeld & Nicolson. (The standard 'Life'.)

Mowat, C. (1955) *Britain between the Wars 1918–1940*, London: Methuen.

Orwell, G. (1941) *The Lion and the Unicorn: Socialism and the English Genius*, London: Secker & Warburg.

Ramsden, J. (1978) *The Age of Balfour and Baldwin 1902–1940*, London: Longman. (The standard work on the party in this period.)

Rhodes James, R. (1969) *Memoirs of a Conservative: J.C.C. Davidson's Memoirs and Papers, 1910–37*, London: Weidenfeld & Nicolson. (Revealing insights from Baldwin's *éminence grise*.)

Self, R. (1992) 'Conservative reunion and the general election of 1923', *Twentieth Century British History* 3: 249–73.

Thorpe, A. (1991) *The British General Election of 1931*, Oxford: Clarendon Press.

Williamson, P. (1992) *National Crisis and National Government: British Politics, the Economy and Empire, 1926–1932*, Cambridge: Cambridge University Press.

—— (1993) 'The doctrinal politics of Stanley Baldwin', in M. Bentley (ed.) *Public and Private Doctrine: Essays in British History Presented to Maurice Cowling*, Cambridge: Cambridge University Press. (A superbly illuminating study of Baldwin's rhetoric and aims.)

Young, G. (1952) *Stanley Baldwin*, London: Rupert Hart-Davis.

Andrew Thorpe

(James) Ramsay MacDonald

Born 12 October 1866, Lossiemouth, Morayshire, to Anne Ramsay, farmworker, and John MacDonald, ploughman. Educated Drainie Board School. Married 1896 to Margaret Ethel Gladstone, daughter of Dr J.H. Gladstone (died following childbirth 1911). MP for Leicester 1906–18, Aberavon 1922–35, Scottish Universities 1936–7. Secretary of the Labour Party 1900–12, Treasurer 1912–24; Leader of the Parliamentary Labour Party 1911–14, Chairman of the Parliamentary Labour Party and Leader of the Opposition 1922–3 and 1925–9; Prime Minister, First Lord of the Treasury and Secretary of State for Foreign Affairs 1924; Prime Minister and First Lord of the Treasury 1929–31 (Labour government) and 1931–5 (National government); Lord President of the Council 1935–7. Died 9 November 1937.

MacDonald's political life was exciting, unprecedented, dramatic and tragic. The illegitimate son of Scottish farmworkers, he was brought up by a doting, respectable but poor mother and grandmother. He devoted his life to Labour politics, becoming the party's leading intellectual, contributing massively to its early development, and eventually becoming its first prime minister. Yet in 1931, against the wishes of most members of the party, he left the Labour ministry to form a National government committed to substantial cuts in unemployment benefit. He was subsequently reviled and abused by former colleagues, and harshly judged in many early historical accounts (Mowat 1955; Miliband 1961). He remains an almost demonic figure in Labour party mythology. Not all early accounts were so critical (Basset 1958; Lyman 1962) but a more favourable 'revisionist' interpretation did not become widespread until the 1970s (Barker 1972; Marquand 1977). More recent accounts (especially Tanner 1991, 1994; Thane 1991; Stewart 1993) have contributed still further to MacDonald's historical rehabilitation.

MacDonald was one of many Scottish Labour figures to make a pronounced impact on British Labour politics. He was born and educated in Lossiemouth, a small fishing port some forty miles from Inverness. This background was an important influence on MacDonald. The family lived in London, but returned to Lossiemouth for comfort and holidays. The moralism of the Kirk and the love of rural tranquillity were central to his character, despite his reputation as an upwardly mobile politician with a penchant for the high life. MacDonald's wife and eldest son were buried near Lossiemouth, and though cremated in London his ashes were appropriately buried in his wife's grave.

Like a number of Labour leaders from a working-class background, MacDonald had limited direct experience of unskilled labour or unemployment. A pupil-teacher in the village school, he subsequently found work as a clerk in Bristol and London. By the age of 20 he was involved with the 'Marxist' Social Democratic Federation, writing articles, giving lectures, reading hard and contemplating a career as a chemist (he remained interested in both science and natural history). Two years later he was secretary to a London Radical MP and Home Ruler, although his closest political contacts were already with the Fabians and the Labour Electoral Association. He was an unsuccessful parliamentary candidate at Southampton in 1895, receiving the endorsement of the Independent Labour party (ILP) but little public support. An active participant in radical liberal/socialist intellectual circles throughout the 1890s, he joined the Progressive 'Rainbow Circle' and gained election to the ILP's National Administrative Council. As secretary of the Labour party after 1900, he worked at the most mundane activities – establishing local branches, arranging delegations, dealing with the selection procedures for parliamentary candidates.

MacDonald had less to do with trade unionism than many Labour leaders. His roots were in the struggle for dignity, independence and advancement, not the struggle for survival. Nonetheless, MacDonald helped build the alliance between trade unionism and socialists which became the Labour party. He cautiously avoided offending the trade unions, and through his tacit electoral pact with the Liberals delivered what they wanted – a voice in parliament. MacDonald was one of twenty-nine Labour MPs elected at the 1906 election, almost all of them without Liberal opposition.

By 1906 MacDonald was a leading figure within the ILP, and soon became one of the most prominent Labour MPs. He was striking in appearance, an excellent speaker and a tireless worker. He tried to prod the Liberals into passing reforming legislation, while working to replace them as the main party of the left. This sometimes dictated a cautious approach. By 1914 MacDonald was finding it harder to cope with those who vehemently criticized his stance and questioned his commitment to socialism. He had already given so much that these doubts seemed irrational and bitter. He was a complex and sensitive man. After the death of his mother, eldest son and wife in close succession he became more prone to bouts of depression and increasingly isolated from colleagues. A section of the ILP – MacDonald's spiritual home – had turned against him, and he was already estranged from the Fabians following personal and ideological disagreements.

MacDonald resigned as chairman of the parliamentary Labour party in 1914 when Labour supported British intervention in the war. Although no pacifist, he felt that war was a preventable mistake. Secret alliances created by unaccountable diplomats and officials were at fault. The xenophobic newspaper *John Bull* resorted to a simpler analysis of his views, suggesting he was a traitor who should be 'taken to the Tower and shot at dawn'. It also publicly revealed his illegitimacy. He lost his parliamentary seat in the 1918 'khaki' election.

While MacDonald's views on the war cut him off from many former colleagues, his principled opposition and suffering restored his credentials with members of the ILP – especially those from a radical Liberal background. He used the period from 1918 to 1922 constructively (Lyman 1962), engaging in international socialist work and writing political philosophy. These activities, his wartime repu-tation, and Labour's failure to make an impact in parliament ensured his election to the party leadership on his return to the Commons in 1922. But his desire to move gradually soon exposed him to attack from the left. Following a cautious first ministry in 1924, a dissident section moved onto the offensive. MacDonald, who repeatedly referred to the 'pettifogging' mentality and egotism of self-advancing cliques within the ILP, retreated from its circles, thereby reinforcing his isolation within the party. Pre-war allies, such as Stephen Walsh and Ben Spoor, were already in political or personal decline, and MacDonald had few friends among the trade union leaders and MPs. He had a low opinion of their abilities and motives, although he treated trade union barons like Citrine and Bevin (and even lesser lights) with respect. He believed in new and challenging ideas, but had few friends among the party's intellectuals and felt that the Advisory Committee system established in 1918 had failed him. Although a dour man, whose views were drenched in the Victorian enthusiasm for duty and service, his respect for formal learning, wit and beauty led him increasingly into more socially elevated circles. His isolation from party members became more evident still during the 1929–31 Labour government, as did his bouts of depression and his private doubts about the aims and abilities of his Labour and trade union colleagues.

MacDonald wanted Labour to be better equipped with ideas and policies, and with the organizational ability to develop its independent message. As editor of the *Socialist Review* he wished to create a forum for intellectual discussion, to make Labour part of a broader and more cosmopolitan socialist movement. Before 1914 he worked to expand the party's independent financial and organizational position. He strove to make the parliamentary party a disciplined force, dedicated to the achievement of agreed democratic socialist ends. He supported the extension of central party control over MPs and the expulsion of communists from the party. His desire to foster intellectual analysis and a sharp political edge was matched by intolerance of those who disagreed with his views. He lacked the ability to 'manage' dissent through tact and diplomacy. He spent more effort complaining about the left between 1925 and 1929 than he did devising concrete policies for office.

MacDonald and the Labour party were unprepared for the crisis which struck the country in 1931. MacDonald was not a modest man, but he lacked confidence in his own views when faced with formally educated 'experts'. He consulted widely, but found it difficult to side with one authority over another. Conflicts over the appropriate response to the slump divided the Labour cabinet. In the face of a threatened economic collapse, MacDonald sought support for the emergency measures proposed by the Chancellor and advanced by most economic experts outside the party. He formed a National government, hoping this to be a temporary measure. Former colleagues attacked him to cover their own role in the party's 'failure' between 1929 and 1931. To MacDonald, the policies and the values which he stood for had been sacrificed. The party he had built had betrayed him. He remained within the National government until his death. An important figure initially, he gradually declined in health and in political influence.

Despite the shadow over the end of his political career, MacDonald led a significant and largely successful political life. In addition to being at the heart of Labour's political development over a thirty year period, he made three particular contributions. First, he was an important democratic socialist writer. Second, he was an important democratic socialist leader, emphasizing the ways in which reforming policies could contribute to the construction of a new social and economic system: at a time when democratic socialism was an embryonic ideology which few European Socialist parties would fully embrace, MacDonald enthusiastically supported its development and application as an alternative to capitalism, Bolshevism or inertia. Third, at a time when Labour had no experience of office, he helped establish its credibility as a governing party, not least through his contributions in foreign and imperial policy.

MacDonald wrote a series of books, many of which attempted to supply Labour with its own democratic socialist philosophy. Few of his ideas were original. He admired the continental revisionists and his works were a blend of radical Liberal and socialist ideas. His emphasis on evolutionary change and on the notion of progress without class conflict – like his ideas on imperialism, reform and the nature of the state – were similar to the more philosophically sophisticated views of the 'New Liberals'. Yet he also saw socialism as a higher creed, which would follow from and extend the steps taken by Liberals. Socialism meant a changed society, an ethically better Britain, a revolution in human relationships which liberalism could not deliver.

MacDonald's works were often hastily assembled and written in response to criticism of Labour's moderate approach. Some were designed to give the party a sense of identity. Until recently they have been devalued even by those sympathetic to MacDonald (Marquand 1977). This is partly because historians often see democratic socialism as an intellectually weak creed, wavering between liberalism and socialism. Yet the best of MacDonald's works – like *Socialism and Government* (1908) – deserve to be taken far more seriously (Thane 1991: 263–9).

Unlike many political leaders, MacDonald did not perceive policies simply as pragmatic responses to problems. He was concerned that they should contribute to the construction of a new social and economic order. An opponent of Marxism, Bolshevism and the Communist party, MacDonald was not simply an unthinking 'Labourite' or a quasi-Liberal. He did not believe that an unregulated capitalist system would produce a fair distribution of wealth and a decent standard of life; on the contrary, he wrote that excess competition would naturally drive living standards down and force companies into bankruptcy. However, he also thought that capitalism was evolving towards a new economic structure. Large companies had erected a system of trusts and price-fixing arrangements to limit competition or had established semi-monopolies by other means. They were quite capable of exploiting the consumer. It might thus be necessary for Labour to regulate or take into public ownership sectors of the economy where competition was limited. Economic organizations could not be allowed to dictate to the public and to the government: 'economic power ought to be developed as the handmaiden of democratic liberty and of human freedom' ('The general case for nationalisation', unpublished memo, no date, MacDonald MS; Tanner 1994).

MacDonald had similar ideas on the broad direction of social policy. He wanted to destroy the class conflict, selfishness, individual degradation, pettiness and greed which were the perceived consequences of a capitalist system. Social reforms were not to be palliatives, but the underpinning of a new set of social relations. MacDonald wanted a partnership between the public and private sector as a means to reconstruct the economy; he wanted a partnership between the state and the individual to reconstruct society. Welfare benefits were not a substitute for personal responsibility, but a means of enabling individuals to enjoy security and make progress. The public had rights, but also duties. Legislation should aim to advance human character and communal efficiency, to increase opportunity, liberty and participation.

MacDonald attacked Labour dissidents whose policy 'ideals' were unrealistic slogans. But he himself paid little attention to the means by which his broad aims and ideals might be realized through legislative arrangements. Successful Labour social policies – such as the Wheatley Housing Act 1924 – owed little to MacDonald, and in education and other areas he was disinclined to be radical.

In office, unusually for an early Labour politician, MacDonald was more involved with foreign and imperial matters than with domestic policy. His first book, published in 1902, was an examination of South African labour conditions, and this was followed in 1907 by *Labour and the Empire*. He imported ideas gleaned from discussions with European revisionists such as Bernstein and from examination of conditions in Germany, Australia and elsewhere.

MacDonald was an active campaigner against 'secret diplomacy', and perceived the outbreak of war in 1914 as a vindication of his views. He retained a belief in settling matters through international agreements and arbitration. Much of the period from 1918 to 1922 was taken up with international socialist affairs, especially the construction of a 'middle way' between Bolshevism and capitalism. In office he added a sharp diplomatic realism to his public support for arbitration, the resumption of international trade, restoration of financial systems, international disarmament and the League of Nations. His diplomatic successes included the Washington Hours conference on hours of work, the Hague conference on reparations, the London naval conference of 1930 and the Geneva tariff conference held in the same year. MacDonald also committed Labour to the recognition of the Soviet Union and the restoration of Anglo-Soviet trade; moreover the Colonial Development Act, the formation of the Simon Commission on India and the promise of Dominion status for India enhanced his own and party's reputation as advocates of 'sane' reform and progress within the empire. Although not responsible for some of these initiatives, MacDonald handled matters well – even if he did not satisfy radical critics (Williams 1992: 169–70; Howe 1993: 52–3). He intervened in matters being addressed by the Foreign Secretary, Arthur Henderson, and the Chancellor, Philip Snowden, but characteristically backed down from confrontations over key policy decisions, especially on tariffs. After the collapse of the second Labour government he retained an informed interest in international affairs and initially played an important role.

MacDonald's important contributions to the Labour party, and his unusual attributes as a politician, have been overshadowed by his role in the crisis of 1931, which dominates assessments of his career. Yet his 'failure' needs to be placed in a more objective perspective. There were no obviously 'better' policy alternatives which MacDonald simply ignored (McKibbin 1975). There were few countries where the left fared better. Across Europe the left floundered during the slump while the fascist or neo-fascist right gained influence. MacDonald was faced with both a Chancellor of the Exchequer and opposition leaders who insisted on major economic cuts. There was a run on the pound which threatened to become disastrous, and the spectre of Germany's immediate post-war economic collapse loomed in the background. Given the information available to him, MacDonald took an unavoidable decision and the inevitable blame. He had not planned the situation, and he did not commit the action without a heavy heart. If he had led the opposition rather than the government in 1931, his historical reputation would now be substantially better. MacDonald was unlucky.

Nonetheless, the crisis did reveal some of MacDonald's weaknesses. By 1931 he was isolated within the Labour party and dissatisfied. He felt that his political beliefs were being fundamentally challenged by the party's intransigence. There were certainly some who would not face realities. To MacDonald, the cabinet's reluctance to make cuts in expenditure confirmed his belief that trade union opinion and sentimentality were dominating good sense. But MacDonald had *allowed* the position to deteriorate and polarize, permitting himself to be backed into a corner from which there was no easy escape. He insisted on seeing every disagreement as a conflict of principle. A better and braver political leader would have avoided the crisis. He would have insisted that his Chancellor adopt less economically orthodox policies in 1930, even if this then led to his resignation and a general election. During the crisis of August 1931 itself MacDonald did not consult those in his party who could have suggested 'moderate' alternatives to massive cuts in expenditure (Thorpe 1991: 75–6). The crisis confirmed his inability to understand and influence even those who were partially sympathetic to his views. It emphasized his reluctance to compromise. In forming the National government rather than resigning he committed a major political error, allowing himself to believe the King's view that his leadership was indispensable. He fell into a trap laid by opposition leaders who did not want the responsibility for making cuts to fall solely on their own shoulders (Williams 1992: 299–303). MacDonald did not react with deft political skill but – as accounts of the crisis now recognize – Labour's own failures, the depth of the problem, and the actions of the other parties, all contributed to the dilemma. The 1931 split is a dramatic but overemphasized part of MacDonald's career. It was not the final episode in a history of error and betrayal.

MacDonald merits a central role in the history of democratic socialism. He took a new ideology, fitted it to British circumstances, and tried to show how reforms could lead to real changes in the social and economic system. Unlike many European socialists of the period, he did not avoid the challenge of forcing a capitalist economy in a socialist direction by avoiding office. He was thoughtful, principled and committed. He was also an oversensitive and depressive man who was ill equipped to lead a party in which fraternal understanding was less evident than ingrained scepticism. He failed to develop the policies needed to turn ideas into purposeful legislation or to cultivate those who might have done this for him. He was an arrogant man whose isolation from the views of others in his party allowed difficulties to develop and grow. He lacked resolve in times of crisis and shrank from difficult decisions which would arouse controversy. MacDonald played a vital part in the creation of a mature Labour party; but by the late 1920s the party was mature enough for a more assertive stance. It was ready for a new leader.

References and further reading

Barker, B. (1972) *Ramsay MacDonald's Political Writings*, London: Allen Lane. (Extracts from MacDonald's books, but not his journalism or pamphlets.)

Bassett, R. (1958) *Nineteen Thirty-One: Political Crisis*, London: Macmillan.

Howe, S. (1993) *Anticolonialism in British Politics: The Left and the End of Empire 1918–1964*, Oxford: Clarendon Press.

Lyman, R. (1962) 'James Ramsay MacDonald and the leadership of the Labour party', *Journal of British Studies* 2: 132–60.

MacDonald, J.R. (n.d. but 1920s) 'The general case for nationalisation'. (One of many surprising items in MacDonald's private papers, which includes his personally revealing diary as well as personal and political correspondence and papers. The papers are the main source for this entry and a still unexhausted source for studies of MacDonald and his party.)

McKibbin, R.I. (1975) 'The economic policy of the second Labour government', *Past and Present* 68: 95–123.

Marquand, D. (1977) *Ramsay MacDonald*, London: Jonathan Cape. (The standard, most substantial and best biography. Ungenerous to MacDonald the intellectual, kind to MacDonald the man and politician. Sympathetic to his critical views on the trade unions' role in Labour politics.)

Miliband, R. (1961) *Parliamentary Socialism: A Study in the Politics of Labour*, London: Allen & Unwin.

Mowat, C. (1955) *Britain between the Wars 1918–1940*, London: Methuen.

Skidelsky, R. (1967) *Politicians and the Slump: The Labour Government of 1929–31*, London: Macmillan. (Classic, flawed study of alleged missed opportunities.)

Stewart, J. (1993) 'Ramsay MacDonald, the Labour party and child welfare, 1900–14', *Twentieth Century British History* 4: 105–25. (A broader analysis than the title suggests, revealing MacDonald's ideas on people's rights and obligations under a system of state welfare provision.)

Tanner, D. (1991) 'Ideological debate in Edwardian labour politics: Radicalism, Revisionism and Socialism', in E. Biagini and A. Reid (eds) *Currents of Radicalism*, Cambridge: Cambridge University Press. (Sees MacDonald's writings as part of a pan-European intellectual process by which radical and socialist traditions were integrated.)

—— (1994) 'Travail, salaires et chômage: l'économie politique du Labour à l'époque edouardienne 1900–14', in M. Mansfield *et al.* (eds) *Aux sources du chômage 1880–1914*, Paris: Belin. (Identifies MacDonald's pre-war economic views and sets them within the framework of Edwardian Labour politics.)

Thane, P. (1991) 'Labour and local politics: radicalism, democracy and social reform, 1880–1914', in E. Biagini and A. Reid (eds) *Currents of Radicalism*, Cambridge: Cambridge University Press. (Identifies the sophistication of MacDonald's pre-war views on social and constitutional matters, emphasizing his links to a British radical tradition.)

Thorpe, A. (1991) *The British General Election of 1931*, Oxford: Clarendon Press. (Provides a useful summary account of the political crisis and informative detail on MacDonald's significant role in the 1931 election.)

Ward, S. (1990) *James Ramsay MacDonald: Low Born among the High Brows*, New York: Peter Lang. (Stronger on the family background and the man than the politics.)

Williams, P. (1992) *National Crisis and National Government: British Politics, the Economy and Empire, 1926–1932*, Cambridge: Cambridge University Press. (Detailed study of the National government's origins, though stronger on the involvement of the Liberals and Tories.)

Duncan Tanner

(Arthur) Neville Chamberlain

Born 18 March 1869, first child of Joseph Chamberlain and his second wife, Florence Kenrick. Educated at Rugby and Mason College, Birmingham. Married 1911 Anne Vere Cole. Lord Mayor of Birmingham 1915–16. Director-General of National Service 1916–17. MP for Birmingham Ladywood 1918–29, Edgbaston 1929–40. Postmaster-General 1922–3; Paymaster-General 1923; Minister of Health 1923, 1924–9 and 1931; Chancellor of the Exchequer 1923–4 and 1931–7; Prime Minister 1937–40; Lord President 1940; Chairman of Conservative Party 1930–1 and Leader 1937–40. Died 9 November 1940.

Chamberlain remains one of the most controversial of modern prime ministers. He dominated his cabinet, yet was prime minister for only three years; he had overwhelming support from his party, yet fell from office due to a backbench revolt. He is the only twentieth-century premier who never led his followers in a general election. His personal quest for European peace through the 'appeasement' of the dictators culminated in the Munich conference of 1938. After the failure of his policy and the wartime reverses of 1940, Chamberlain shouldered most of the blame for Britain's lack of preparedness and success. His reputation remained low for most of the post-war era, but in recent years admiration for his vigour and clarity of vision have encouraged attempts at rehabilitation.

The first essential point about Chamberlain is his parentage. His father Joseph was a prominent late-Victorian politician who 'made the political weather' and threw both of the main parties into turmoil. Neville Chamberlain's social background was in prosperous, middle-class, provincial industry; his political roots were in Liberalism and radical Unionism, and not in orthodox Conservatism. His father's influence and prestige were crucial in giving resonance to the family name, but it was Neville's elder half-brother Austen who was groomed for a glittering political career. Neville was not expected to go into politics; he did not attend university, but was looked to as guardian of the family business interests. The formative experience of his early life was seven years of lonely isolation from 1890 to 1897 on a remote island in the Bahamas overseeing a speculative scheme of his father to grow sisal. Despite his stubborn efforts, the venture was a failure. Neville held himself responsible, and returned home physically and mentally toughened but with wounded pride. Thereafter he involved himself in business and followed his father's footsteps in Birmingham local government, becoming a councillor in 1911 and serving with success as Lord Mayor in 1915–16. Two episodes in the First World War shaped Chamberlain's outlook. He was profoundly affected by the death in action of his younger cousin and closest friend, Norman Chamberlain, while a bruising encounter with Lloyd George resulted in lasting personal antagonism. In December 1916 Chamberlain was appointed to the new post of Director-General of National Service, overseeing the vital resource of manpower. However, his powers and responsibilities were undefined, he lacked resources and assistance, and had no seat in parliament from which to defend himself. Lloyd George considered him to be too rigid and stubborn, lost patience, and effectively forced his resignation after only seven months in office. Chamberlain retired to Birmingham, embittered at this further personal failure.

In 1918 he entered the Commons as a supporter of the Lloyd George coalition, but with no affection for its leader. Chamberlain was 49 years old, but the combination of his ability, his family connections and the unexpected turn of events were to lead to rapid advancement. Neville's half-brother Austen became the Conservative leader in 1921, but fell in October 1922 when his proposal to continue the coalition under Lloyd George was rejected by a party meeting at the Carlton Club. Neville did not play a major part in the revolt, although he shared the anti-coalition view. The new Conservative ministry under Bonar Law was in need of capable administrators, and so Neville was appointed first to junior ministerial posts before entering the cabinet in March 1923 as Minister of Health. After Bonar Law's retirement and replacement by Baldwin, Chamberlain was moved in August 1923 to fill the vacancy at the Treasury. His first spell there was extremely brief, for only a few weeks later the new leader called the general election of 1923 which resulted in defeat and the installation in January 1924 of the first Labour government. In 1922–4 Neville acted as a bridge with Austen, and helped to heal the dangerous rift which the fall of the coalition had created in the Conservative leadership.

When the Conservatives returned to office in November 1924 Chamberlain surprised many by declining Baldwin's offer of the Exchequer, opting instead for the Ministry of Health. In fact Chamberlain was playing to his strengths, and was able to draw on his own municipal experience in England's second city. He established his reputation by coming into office with an ambitious legislative programme already mapped out, and further impressed by carrying nearly all of his measures by the end of the parliament. Chamberlain's dynamism and constructive purpose stood out among the cabinet; his only rival was the imaginative but erratic and distrusted figure who had been given the Chancellorship after he had turned it down – Winston Churchill. Chamberlain's endeavours at the Ministry of Health were worthy but rather dull, consisting mainly of overdue rationalization and reforms. However, his proposals for local government, poor law and factory reform later in the parliament aroused vocal opposition. The derating policy which he devised jointly with Churchill as the platform for the 1929 election proved to be a damp squib. By the end of the 1920s Chamberlain had established a formidable reputation, but more as a bureaucrat than a politician. His poor relations with the Labour opposition were shaped in this period. Chamberlain had a low opinion of the quality of their arguments, which his command of his subjects enabled him easily to demolish in debate. He disliked the emotionalism and impracticality of the outbursts from the Labour backbenches which were a common feature of the 1924–9 parliament. Chamberlain had no empathy for the experience of working-class life, and had to be warned by Baldwin of the dangers of showing his contempt so openly. Although a sincere social reformer who was willing to tackle vested interests within his own party, he became a detested figure on the left long before he became prime minister.

Chamberlain played three significant roles during the Conservatives' troubled period in opposition from 1929 to 1931, all of which were tributes to his drive, methodical thoroughness and loyalty. First was his assumption in March 1930 of the chairmanship of the party's newly created 'think tank', the Conservative Research Department. This was a task after Chamberlain's heart, for it put him at the centre of policy-making. With typical pragmatism, he focused its work on immediate planning rather than long-term investigation and debate. He made the department his personal fiefdom and remained its head until his death. Chamberlain's second role was his tenure of the party chairmanship from June 1930 to March 1931, where he completed the reorganization set in train by his predecessor, J.C.C. Davidson. He also played a major part in resolving the crisis within the party over economic policy. In October 1930 his forcefulness and tactical grasp propelled Baldwin into seizing a vital chance to defeat his critics, and in March 1931 Chamberlain was responsible for ending the remaining strife by concluding a deal with the press baron Lord Beaverbrook. Shortly before this Chamberlain had passed on to Baldwin a memo by the party's senior official, Robert Topping, which implied that the leader should quit. This caused a short period of tension between Chamberlain and Baldwin, but within the month their effective working relationship had been restored. In August 1931 Chamberlain represented his party during key stages of the meetings which shaped the fall of the Labour government and its replacement by an all-party National ministry, and it has been suggested that he did more than any other figure to bring this about. Chamberlain was now the recognized heir apparent who would succeed Baldwin, although not until the latter chose to depart.

After the 1931 election Chamberlain was appointed Chancellor of the Exchequer. This move not only confirmed his authority within the cabinet and the Conservative party, but also symbolized the latter's final victory in the long battle over free trade. His first task as Chancellor was to oversee the introduction of protective duties and imperial preference. Achieving his father's grand design gave Neville emotional satisfaction, but in a very different world economy the imperial aspect of the policy bore little fruit. Chamberlain's record as Chancellor has been criticized for caution, negativism and the slowness first of the recovery and later of rearmament. Although lacking a deep understanding of economics, he had the confidence of a practical background in business. He moved with the economic orthodoxy of the day, which emphasized the need for balanced budgets and for reducing the tax burden during a depression. In fact, the domestic policy of the National government was more pragmatic and inter-ventionist than has often been allowed. By 1934 economic prospects were improving and Chamberlain scored a particular success with his budget, using the surplus to outflank the Labour party by restoring the 1931 unemployment benefit cuts in full.

The combination of his influence as Chancellor and his practical command of policy extended Chamberlain's influence throughout the government, initially in domestic matters but later and increasingly in foreign policy. Developing tensions in international affairs exposed weaknesses in British defence provision, especially against air attack, and from 1934 the government wrestled with the problems of financing increasingly larger programmes of rearmament. The policy of 'appeasement' was intended to tackle these tensions at their root, and so avoid the need for costly military preparations and the instability and danger of war which went with them. With his customary logic and clarity of vision, Chamberlain was one of the first to make this connection, and so became the most determined to avoid the horrors of needless conflict. As Baldwin passed through a period of lethargy and collapse in 1936, Chamberlain began to assume the mantle of acting prime minister and this gave his personal initiatives all the more force. However, his final weeks as Chancellor saw a rare reversal when his proposed National Defence Contribution, a tax on business profits to pay for rearmament, had to be withdrawn due to heavy opposition.

Chamberlain finally succeeded Baldwin on 28 May 1937. He was 68 years old, but although he had been the workhorse of the government since 1931 he was seen as being the most vigorous figure in it. Physical health is vital to any occupant of the premiership: apart from occasional discomfort due to gout, Chamberlain's health and mental resilience remained robust until after his fall from power. Far from buckling under the immense strains of this period, he was tireless and throve on responsibility. He was an effective debater but not an inspirational orator, being plain, sober, direct and factual. His financial position and the support of his family gave him a secure foundation which was modestly middle class in style. He enjoyed music, but his principal relaxation was the solitary pursuit of fly-fishing. In personal contacts Chamberlain was shy and awkward, and many considered him to be cold, narrow and humourless. He was convinced of his ability to solve the problems facing Britain, especially in Europe, and of the rightness of his policy. However, Chamberlain's pride, stubborn perseverance and self-confidence led him into over-confidence, vanity and complacency. He employed unofficial channels and intermediaries to speed his diplomacy, and relied upon the senior domestic civil servant Sir Horace Wilson for advice which was more supportive than that of the Foreign Office. He dominated his cabinet, chairing all the important committees, and closely monitored the work of every department. Decision-making was centralized, and in the Chamberlain cabinet collective responsibility ran in only one direction – upwards. The prime minister was not dictatorial in manner, but his views and leadership were authoritative, and his colleagues acquiesced even when they had doubts. This was partly due to the support given to the prime minister by his 'inner cabinet', the informal but powerful group of Sir John Simon, Sir Samuel Hoare and Lord Halifax with whom the key decisions were taken. Below this, party discipline was maintained by the powerful and autocratic chief whip, David Margesson, while the director of the Conservative Research Department, Joseph Ball, massaged a favourable press and manoeuvred against the handful of dissident MPs.

Any British government would have been constrained by the economic and political climate of the 1930s, but the foreign policy of the Chamberlain government was deliberately chosen. It was a logical path, but not the only possible one – a fact underlined by the rift between Chamberlain and the Foreign Secretary whom he had inherited, Anthony Eden, which led to the latter's resignation in February 1938. He was replaced by Lord Halifax, and from this point the prime minister spoke on foreign policy for the government in the Commons. Chamberlain's policy was not one of feeble surrender, but of active intervention in Europe in order to restrain the unstable powers and prevent developments which might threaten British interests. It has been categorized as 'a bold, venturesome policy' by which Chamberlain 'struggled to impose his system of orderly conduct' on the recalcitrant leaders and problems of central Europe (Parker 1993: 345). Realism and appeasement were not polar opposites in Chamberlain's mind, but one and the same. Appeasement was also an idealistic, even Christian, policy – a magnanimous redress of just grievances, willing to acknowledge the flaws of the Versailles settlement in order to bring lasting peace and harmony between nations.

Chamberlain's moment of triumph was the settlement of the crisis over the Sudeten German population within Czechoslovakia. In an unprecedented and dramatic initiative, aimed largely at German public opinion, he made two flights to southern Germany to negotiate with Hitler face to face. The plan was entirely his own conception, and these unaccompanied missions underlined his position as the sole author and executor of British policy; they also had a tremendous impact on the British public, deeply anxious over the imminence of another terrible war. Just at the point where conflict seemed unavoidable, Chamberlain flew again to the four-power conference at Munich brokered by Mussolini. Here the crisis was resolved on 29 September 1938, essentially on Hitler's terms, but without war and with a promise of future goodwill. Chamberlain returned to an atmosphere of euphoric relief. At this point appeasement was hugely popular, and its critics few and beleaguered. The optimism of Munich soon soured, but Chamberlain pursued his vision more fervently after every setback. The critical blow came with the German occupation of Prague in March 1939. This demolished the Munich agreement and incorporated into the *Reich* non-German lands for the first time, indicating that there were no limits to Nazi expansionism. While at the outset there had been a broad consensus for appeasement, after this it ebbed away. The prime minister's response was the system of unilateral guarantees to the threatened small states of Eastern Europe. However, he was still determined to find peace by negotiation, and thus postponed too long the necessary but distasteful step of underpinning the guarantees with an agreement with Soviet Russia. Instead, the Nazi–Soviet Pact of 23 August 1939 left Poland isolated and exposed to German attack.

The German invasion of Poland on 1 September 1939 resulted in an ultimatum and then the declaration of war, but not until Chamberlain's apparent reluctance to give up negotiation had led to angry scenes in the Commons and to a cabinet revolt. Chamberlain was shattered, declaring in the House on 3 September that 'everything that I have worked for, everything that I have hoped for, everything that I have believed in during my public life, has crashed into ruins'. However, his toughness and resilience ensured his determination to carry on, and he regarded himself as indispensable. Churchill and Eden were brought into the cabinet, but Chamberlain considered it small loss when the Labour opposition refused to join him. In fact, the coming of war undermined Chamberlain's position, for it denoted the absolute failure of the policies upon which he had staked his credibility. Doubts about the competence and commitment of the government grew during the 'phoney war' of September 1939 to April 1940. Chamberlain increasingly appeared to be narrow, unimaginative, inflexible and impervious to criticism. His position was affected by the widespread lack of confidence in key members of his cabinet, but he would not remove them. Cabinet changes in January and April 1940 were poorly handled and inadequate, and support began to slip away. This became apparent in the debate of 7–8 May 1940 on the disastrous Norwegian campaign, in which the government suffered a massive drop in its normal majority. This was effectively a vote of no confidence in Chamberlain, and it was clear that he would have to step down in favour of a Conservative under whom Labour would serve. Chamberlain was repudiated not because of any rebel intrigue, but as the cumulative result of his own actions. The real causes were the failure of his policy, the erosion of his prestige, his stubborn refusal to alter either the policy or the personnel of his ministry, and his alarming complacency.

Chamberlain surrendered the premiership in May 1940, but remained leader of the Conservative party. In recognition of his executive abilities and the support which he still commanded in the House and in the country, he became Lord President of the Council with a seat in the War cabinet. At first Chamberlain retained a powerful role in the government, but his influence declined with the revolution in public feeling after Dunkirk. The rapid deterioration of his health forced him to resign at the end of September; he died from cancer on 9 November.

References and further reading

Aster, S. (1989) ' "Guilty men": the case of Neville Chamberlain', in R. Boyce and E. Robertson (eds) *Paths to War*, London: Macmillan.

Ball, S. (1988) *Baldwin and the Conservative Party: The Crisis of 1929–31*, New Haven, CT and London: Yale University Press. (Analyses his tenure of the party chairmanship and role in the formation of the National government, and argues that this period was crucial in establishing Chamberlain as the certain successor to Baldwin.)

Beattie, A. (1977) 'Neville Chamberlain', in J. Mackintosh (ed.) *British Prime Ministers in the Twentieth Century*, vol. 1, London: Weidenfeld & Nicolson.

Charmley, J. (1989) *Chamberlain and the Lost Peace*, London: Hodder & Stoughton. (Controversial revisionist account which argues that Chamberlain's policy was an accurate reflection of Britain's world interests.)

Dilks, D. (1984) *Neville Chamberlain: Volume 1, Pioneering and Reform 1869–1929*, Cambridge: Cambridge University Press. (The massive first instalment of a new official biography, including a detailed account of his work at the Ministry of Health in the 1920s; the second volume is still awaited.)

Feiling, K. (1946) *The Life of Neville Chamberlain*, London: Macmillan. (The original official biography is remarkably balanced given the political atmosphere in which it was completed, and remains the only substantial complete life.)

Fuchser, L.W. (1982) *Neville Chamberlain and Appeasement*, London: Norton.

Jefferys, K. (1991) 'May 1940: the downfall of Neville Chamberlain', *Parliamentary History* 10: 363–78.

Macleod, I. (1961) *Neville Chamberlain*, London: Muller. (Bearing the name of the 1960s cabinet minister but mainly ghost-written, this is unsatisfactory and uneven but includes useful extracts from his diary and family letters.)

Parker, R.A.C. (1993) *Chamberlain and Appeasement: British Policy and the Coming of the Second World War*, London: Macmillan. (The authoritative account which places the responsibility for the outbreak of war upon Chamberlain's decisions and determination.)

Stuart Ball

Winston Leonard Spencer Churchill

Born 30 November 1874, son of Lord Randolph Churchill and Jennie Jerome, grandson of the seventh Duke of Marlborough. Educated at Harrow and Sandhurst. Commissioned in the 4th Queen's Own Hussars 1895. Married 1908 Clementine Hozier. MP (Conservative) for Oldham 1895–1906, (Liberal) Manchester North-West 1906–8, (Liberal) Dundee 1908–18, (Coalition) Dundee 1918–22, (Constitutionalist) Epping 1924–31, (Conservative) Epping 1931–45, (Conservative) Woodford 1945–64. Parliamentary Under-Secretary for the Colonies 1905–7; President of the Board of Trade 1908–10; Home Secretary 1910–11; First Lord of the Admiralty 1911–15; Chancellor of the Duchy of Lancaster 1915; Minister of Munitions 1917–19; Secretary for War 1918–21; Secretary of State for the Colonies 1921–2; Chancellor of the Exchequer 1924–9; First Lord of the Admiralty 1939–40; Prime Minister and Minister of Defence 1940–5; Prime Minister 1951–5. Knight of the Garter 1953; Nobel Prize for Literature 1953. Died 24 January 1965.

Of prime ministers who might fall into the category of 'Great Men', Churchill is certainly the most likely candidate. He steered Britain through its 'finest hour', galvanizing the country with emotional speeches. He was the symbol of British unity when Britain was most united. Since the war he has become a central symbol for the greatness, internal and international, that Britain no longer possesses. He has become a legend in a way that no other Briton has during the twentieth century. Yet his popular image is often at odds with assessments by contemporaries and historians. To many of his contemporaries he was a dangerous maverick, operating outside party discipline. And since the war, historians have continued to debate his merits as a politician and as a war leader. It is the coincidence of Churchill's life beginning at the height of Britain's strength and then, in a sense, keeping pace with its decline as a great power that gives this contest over Churchill's stature a special irony – an irony that is highlighted by the beguiling romanticism of Churchill's extensive prose.

He was born into the aristocracy at Blenheim, the son of one of the most important Tory politicians of the late nineteenth century. His mother was a wealthy American. Churchill might have either built upon his father's reputation to become a prominent figure or receded into the obscurity that surrounded many of the sons of public figures. For much of his life it appeared that he would do neither. All through his career he was a public figure who drew intense criticism; yet despite a series of disasters that might have stopped many a lesser man, he did rise to the greatest heights.

From his childhood Churchill appeared to be a failure. In his earliest years, he was a lacklustre student, initially with his governesses at home, then at St George's School, Ascot (where he was beaten by a sadistic headmaster) from which he was withdrawn by his parents and placed at a more congenial school in Hove, and then at Harrow. He also had a nose for trouble. One altercation in a drawing class when he was 12 years old resulted in a minor knife wound. He showed little respect for authority when on another occasion he demolished the headmaster's straw hat after being caned for stealing sugar. While he appeared to be even less popular with his fellow students than he was with his teachers, he remained confident and precocious.

As he entered adolescence and became aware of his father's, and consequently his own, celebrity status, he grew increasingly self-possessed. But it was his relationship with his father that also proved to be the least satisfying aspect of his early life. Though Churchill was sheltered within the confines of the family during his early years, it was with servants and governesses, most particularly Mrs Everest, his nanny, that he had the most contact. His mother pursued a very active social life while his father was absorbed with politics. Churchill's childhood letters have a pathos that foreshadow the regret with which he later viewed his lonely childhood. He was ever conscious of his failure to live up his father's expectations and many, contemporaries and historians alike, have attributed his political drive to his ambition to do so.

Churchill's performance at Harrow fell short of what was needed to gain admission to university, which was not necessarily the goal of many public school boys (although of almost all who became politicians); instead, he decided to pursue a military career. It was only on the third attempt, in 1893, that he passed the exam to enter Sandhurst to begin his training as an officer. As early as 1895 he observed war first hand in Cuba. His career in the military was brief but eventful. He was stationed in India in 1896, the only time in his life that he visited the great sub-continent which he would later attempt to keep within the empire. He spent much time there playing polo and reading Gibbon's *Decline and Fall of the Roman Empire*, Macaulay's *History of England* and copies of the *Annual Register* in order to learn about politics. He wrote his first book, one of many, *The Story of the Malakand Field Force*, in 1898. That same year in Africa he made a name for himself. Churchill once again sought out trouble and, as part of Kitchener's army at the battle of Omdurman in 1898, participated in one of the last successful cavalry charges in British military history. He left the army to run unsuccessfully for parliament as a Conservative for the constituency of Oldham in 1899. When he lost, his attention returned to the empire and to military affairs. As a journalist during the Boer War, Churchill rose to national fame, initially for his adventures. His greatest exploit was his capture and daring escape from the Boers – though there always remained a question of whether he had behaved badly towards those who were supposed to have escaped with him in the episode. The adulation he received after this venture made him famous in his own right, helped by the two books he wrote about the campaign and his one novel, *Savrola*, all in 1900. Most importantly, these events enhanced his ability to operate in politics on a national level. Primarily through his own accounts of his adventures, Churchill entered the public imagination in a powerful way.

The popularity Churchill enjoyed in his twenties allowed him to operate apart from the institutions that structured politics at the turn of the century. He was unable and unwilling to conform to strict party discipline. Soon after he was elected as member for Oldham in 1900, he became part of a group of young Tory MPs who were dissatisfied with the Conservative front bench, led in the Commons by Balfour with his uncle, the Marquess of Salisbury, the prime minister in the Lords. Churchill was always uncomfortable in the party system. His own convictions were too passionate, his personality too strong for compromise. He approached issues impulsively, even obsessively. His interest in social issues and his belief in free trade first led him to the more progressive part of the Conservative party and then, in 1904, to the Liberal party, a move prompted by his opposition to the Tory position on tariff reform. He rose quickly in his new party hierarchy, perhaps helped more there than among the Tories by his distinguished lineage. He rapidly ascended to the cabinet, serving as President of the Board of Trade in 1908, Home Secretary in 1910 and then in 1911 at the Admiralty. (In 1908 he married Clementine Hozier for a supremely happy marriage which lasted until his death, although his relations with some of his children were, from time to time, more troubled.) Alongside Lloyd George, he became a chief proponent of social reform, constructing a minimal 'safety net' for the poorest members of the nation. It was at this time that he was closely associated with social reform; later in his life he was much more involved with military and international questions. The great wars of the century would move him away from a social agenda.

It was during these early years in parliament that he cultivated another source of power, his ability to speak. He did his best to render his colourful prose into the spoken word, but to do so he had to overcome an impediment that always affected his speech. As a result, Churchill talked with deliberation; his speeches were finely crafted and, early in his career, often memorized. From his first appearance in the Commons, the power of his oratory gained him notice and also the enmity of Conservatives, who were deeply irritated by his first speech attacking measures for expanding the number of army corps earmarked for service abroad. His power as an orator inspired audiences, but it also bred antagonism among fellow politicians. His heated rhetoric contributed to his image as passionate and dangerous.

By the time Churchill was 35 it appeared that he had proven himself. But his switch from Conservative to Liberal in 1904 and his subsequent meteoric rise did have its costs. Churchill's power rested on a sympathetic public that admired him as an adventurer, inside and outside of politics. His political wanderings contributed to this reputation and gave critics and friends alike cause to consider him eccentric and, even worse, unstable. The journalist A.G. Gardiner described him in 1926 as an 'uneducated' man who 'threw himself into life with the uncalculating vehemence and passion of the boy in the school playground' (Stansky 1973: 51). The problem with Churchill was that he was formidable as both an advocate and opponent, and even his allies were aware that his allegiances could shift unexpectedly. He remained in high office as the First Lord of the Admiralty, having done splendid work in preparing the navy for war, when the First World War broke out. He was forced to resign in May 1915, being with some justification held responsible for the disaster at Gallipoli. He was demoted to Chancellor of the Duchy of Lancaster, a position he resigned in November. Once again when he suffered a political setback he sought solace in action, serving at the front for a brief period before Lloyd George, now prime minister, called him back to the cabinet in 1917 as Minister of Munitions. Churchill moved to the War Office in 1919 where he directed the British effort in Russia against the Bolsheviks, and then finally he became Colonial Secretary in 1921.

Churchill had survived a political fall that might have crippled him permanently to return to the ranks of the government. But the turbulence of his political life continued as the peace pulled the Liberal party apart. He enjoyed the favour of Lloyd George, but after the fall of the latter's coalition, Churchill's strained relationship with Asquith began to make his political position untenable. In 1924 he ran as a 'Constitutionalist' with Conservative support and was immediately brought into the Conservative cabinet in Baldwin's government, this time as the Chancellor of the Exchequer. Once again, despite his broad experience and political abilities, he pursued policies that, although they received much support at the time, made many, in retrospect, question his judgement. His determination to restore Britain to the gold standard proved to be so ill conceived that even Churchill's most ardent supporters subsequently considered it to have been a mistake. The grandstanding of Churchill against the strikers at the time of the General Strike in 1926 brought back memories on the left of his actions against unions as Home Secretary in 1911, confirming the picture of him as an enemy of labour.

When the Tory government fell in 1929, Churchill retained his seat, but receded into relative obscurity. He had held an impressive array of cabinet posts, but had also been involved in several disasters. In 1929 he was 55 years old and appeared to have passed the peak of his political career. The 1930s were Churchill's 'wilderness years'. The reputation that he had earned for unconventional opinions, unreliability and hare-brained schemes precluded his participation even in the coalition National governments under MacDonald and Baldwin. As the country focused increasingly on the domestic problems of unemployment and poverty, Churchill put international and imperial issues first. Churchill seemed to be completely out of step with the national mood. In 1930 he denounced concessions made to the Indian National Congress and the influence exercised by Mahatma Gandhi, whom he described as

> a seditious Middle Temple lawyer, now posing as a fakir of a type well-known in the East, striding half-naked up the steps of the Vice-regal palace, while he is still organising and conducting a defiant campaign of civil disobedience, to parley with the representative of the King-Emperor.
>
> (Rhodes James 1974: 485)

His opposition to self-government for India in the early part of the decade and to the slow rearmament and appeasement in the latter part – all policies supported by the Conservative leadership as well as a wide range of public opinion – ensured Churchill's isolation. He took the threat of the rise of Nazism very seriously.

Churchill became a political outcast. Apart from championing unpopular causes, he continued to suffer from the perception of inconsistency. He had been the originator of some of the most important social legislation in the years leading up to the First World War but remained a firm enemy of the labour unions, most notably during the General Strike in 1926. This apparent change in attitude toward social legislation may actually have been a shift in emphasis. While Churchill may have lost interest in broad social reform after the First World War, his anti-union feeling was constant both before and after. Even when he was in charge of setting up the national insurance scheme and of establishing labour exchanges, he was a staunch and even militant opponent of the unions. One explanation for his ability to mix apparently contradictory positions is that his values were more in tune with the eighteenth century than the twentieth. *Noblesse oblige* does not fully describe his position, but there were strong elements of this ethos in his thinking on social matters. Churchill was from an aristocratic family and remained loyal to this heritage in his thinking. His employment of Gibbon's writing style was paralleled in a patrician approach to politics and social issues.

The impression of changing convictions and even disloyalty was reinforced by his extraordinary shifts of party affiliation – his 're-rating', to use his own term. Few politicians could survive even one such change. But during the period following the First World War, a time when the political system was redefining itself, Churchill's beliefs may have appeared to be inconsistent only relative to changing party ideologies. It is difficult to assess Churchill's constancy in political matters or the meaning of his shift back to the Conservative party during the period of turbulence that accompanied the collapse of the Liberal party. His anti-Bolshevism and the rise to prominence of the Labour party also played a role in his diminished interest in social legislation. Churchill was firmly and con-sciously rooted in the past: the past of Britain, of the British empire and of his own family, whom he immortalized in his life of his great ancestor, the first Duke of Marlborough, in four volumes. Churchill himself always felt that he had remained true to his own principles despite two shifts in party affiliation.

Yet his isolation during the 1930s contributed to his suitability as coalition leader in May 1940. Even though he had alienated the left by his anti-union and anti-Bolshevik policies and antagonized his own party leadership with his maverick behaviour, he was still recognized as a man of extraordinary strength, experience and vision. Labour was willing to serve in a coalition under a limited number of Conservatives; Churchill had distanced himself from Neville Chamberlain's policies of appeasement sufficiently to satisfy the government's critics on both the left and the right. At the beginning of the Second World War he was brought back into the government and, after serving under Chamberlain at the Admiralty for half a year, he was summoned to Buckingham Palace to receive the offer to lead the government. (It was the campaign in Norway for which Churchill was primarily responsible that had brought the govern-ment down.) The choice for prime minister had been between Lord Halifax, Chamberlain's Foreign Minister, and Churchill. By the time Chamberlain left office his government had sunk in popularity to such an extent that Halifax proved to be unacceptable. But not everyone was happy to see Churchill at Number 10. John Colville, personal secretary to both Chamberlain and Churchill, had serious reservations about Churchill when he assumed power. Colville spent the first day of Churchill's premiership 'in a bright blue new suit from the Fifty-Shilling Tailors, cheap and sensational looking, which I felt was appropriate to the new Government' (Colville 1985: 129). But Churchill certainly enjoyed widespread national support. The British were looking for relief from the depressing series of mistakes and defeats that had led up to war and had con-tinued to the fall of France and the evacuation at Dunkirk. Hopes that the worst was behind them were invested in the new government and above all in its leader. The public perception of Churchill's as the lone voice of realism in the midst of a bankrupt policy of appeasement, and also a sense of him as a visionary who could guide Britain through a protracted struggle, resurrected his political career and placed him in the highest office. In 1940 Churchill the adventurer seemed to be the only one who could take the risks needed to win, a man of strong convictions who would put an end to the weakness and indecisiveness of his predecessors. Even his critics could see that his impulses and obsessions might serve the country well if directed to winning the war. His moment had come.

Churchill's contemporaries did not know what to make of him, but almost all seemed convinced that he was in some way remarkable. Colville, discussing his own inability to predict Churchill's opinions, attributed to him 'some strange intuitive power' that operated 'contrary to the normal mental workings of everybody else' (Colville 1985: 125). Though Colville wrote glowingly of him later, his scathing attitude to Churchill during the early days of the coalition government was indicative of the problems that surrounded his personal and idiosyncratic style. Isaiah Berlin explained Churchill's unpredictability and unconventional world-view in similarly ambivalent terms.

> Churchill is preoccupied with his own vivid world, and it is doubtful how far he has ever been aware of what actually goes on in the heads and hearts of others. He does not react, he acts; he does not mirror, he affects others and alters them to his own powerful measure.
>
> (Stansky 1973: 80)

Perceptions of the separateness and special quality of the world that Churchill inhabited certainly are at odds with the popular image of the man who saw through Hitler and appeasement. During most of his career Churchill was out of touch with the larger society in which he lived, except for one very important period. During the early years of the Second World War Churchill's vision seemed to be as much in touch with the times as it had been out of touch a decade earlier. As prime minister, Churchill behaved as he had always done. He was impulsive, even obsessive, in his approach to policy matters. This style did not always transfer well to military matters. A quick decision to defend Greece from German invasion caused Churchill to dispatch forces from North Africa in 1941, halting an offensive that could have denied the Axis a base to conduct operations against Egypt. His insistence on invading Italy in 1943, the 'soft underbelly' of Europe, despite American misgivings, showed the tenacity with which he pursued policies that he thought to be right. These impulsive actions had mixed results, and are examples of how Churchill allowed his romantic vision of the world and an inflated sense of British power to interfere with effective and sensible conduct of the war. Churchill believed deeply that his decisions were for the best but the campaigns in the Mediterranean were costly and only indirectly contributed to the final defeat of Germany. The loss of the battleships *Repulse* and the *Prince of Wales* in 1941, and the surrender of over 70,000 British and imperial troops to the Japanese at Singapore the same year, were even more clearly the result of Churchill's direct intervention in military affairs.

In diplomacy his handling of the American alliance was also not entirely successful. Since ultimately the United States rather than Germany eclipsed Britain, Churchill's willingness to sacrifice all to defeat Germany did not necessarily serve the best interests of Britain as a world power. But the strategic realities of Britain's position were out of Churchill's control. The depletion of gold reserves that preceded lend-lease, an event that ensured Britain's poverty after the war, was not the doing of either Churchill or Roosevelt. The unwillingness of the US Congress in 1939–41 to commit the United States to full support of Britain could only fade when the situation became truly desperate. If the financial bankruptcy of Britain was an essential component of that desperation, there was little that Churchill or anyone in Britain could do to change it. Ultimately it was to Churchill's credit that he was willing to pay any price for victory.

Churchill made many decisions, good and bad, but above all he knew how to inspire the people who worked for him. During the war he assumed the mantle of both prime minister and Minister of Defence, and as such was undisputed leader of the war effort. He brought an intensity and impatience, along with a quick intelligence, to complicated problems. He employed all of his powers to exhort his staff to perform to the utmost. This style reflected much of his approach to morale in general. He gave his staff, as he did to the public, a sense of common cause. They had to struggle to meet his expectations as well as win the war.

Though much has been made of his role in promoting solidarity, Churchill faced dissent and opposition during the war. The Labour party leaders had become part of the coalition and were placated with extensive domestic responsibilities. The appointment of Ernest Bevin, a former union leader, to the Ministry of Labour and National Service helped to convince rank-and-file labour that the coalition represented their interests. In parliament, the Independent Labour party and the new Commonwealth party, established by Sir Richard Acland explicitly to oppose the coalition, provided at least the semblance of a debate within the Commons. Labour party ambitions continued, however, and in 1942 Churchill was seriously challenged and won a vote of confidence by a surprisingly close vote.

Despite his mixed record as a military leader and a diplomat, Churchill emerged as the greatest British war leader of the twentieth century. He made his contribution to the war effort above all by providing the British public with a rallying point. Britain had its 'finest hour', a phrase he coined, in large part because Churchill told the British public so over the radio. And if it was Britain's finest hour, it was also Churchill's. All of the belligerence and romanticism, bluster and vivid rhetoric came together in his radio speeches during the Battle of Britain and the Blitz. The historian, Robert Rhodes James, observed that 'it was Churchill's outstanding quality as a war leader that he made the struggle seem not merely essential for national survival, but worthwhile and noble' (Rhodes James 1974: 122). The speaking skills that made him such a fearsome adversary in parliament were from 1940 to 1942 employed to give people hope; ultimately this was his greatest achievement.

The challenge to Churchill's leadership in 1942 was not simply reflective of the passing of a moment of crisis. Stafford Cripps, the man who was proffered as an alternative in 1942, was a central figure in Labour's post-war planning for Britain and the empire. As victory became more assured and public attention focused on the post-war world, tensions within the coalition grew. Churchill retained his conservative view of Britain as an imperial power with a domestic social order that would remain essentially unchanged. Labour's more radical vision of reconstruction appealed to the electorate as something worthier of the struggle they had just endured and won. Churchill was dramatically uninterested in the Beveridge plan of social reform that so captured the public imagination in 1942.

Churchill marked the extent to which the spirit of commonality had disappeared when, during the election of 1945, he compared Labour rule to 'totalitarianism', asserting that they would employ 'some sort of Gestapo'. Once again Churchill's vision seemed to be out of touch with that of the public. The Labour party was returned in a landslide in 1945 after the war in Europe had ended. Churchill was consigned to be leader of the opposition.

During the period of Labour government from 1945 to 1951 Churchill saw the Labour party dismantle institutions that he loved and create several that he despised. Independence for India and the creation of the welfare state put the country on a new course that deviated greatly from Churchill's own vision of post-war Britain. As the leader of a small minority in the Commons, Churchill took refuge in his writing and during this period he composed most of his six-volume *The Second World War*. (He received the Nobel Prize for literature in 1953.) But though he was now out of power and ageing, he was still a major influence on world politics. His 'iron curtain' speech, given in Fulton, Missouri, in 1946 with the full approval of Attlee and senior officials from the Truman administration, provided a powerful description of the Cold War world. The iron curtain that he saw stretching 'from Stettin in the Baltic to Trieste in the Adriatic' became a dominant image of the Cold War and symbolized the transformation of the wartime alliance to post-war antagonism.

Churchill's second tenure as prime minister began in 1951 when he was nearly 77 years old. (He was determined not to take any proffered title of nobility but in 1953 he became a Knight of the Garter.) By this time he was clearly past his prime. He was still an effective manager and hard taskmaster, and his staff seemed even more loyal and in awe of him than they had been during the war. But he was losing his edge in parliament. His increasing deafness contributed to variable performance in debates in the House. And he more and more relied on Colville to write his speeches. The second Churchill government lacked the energy of the wartime coalition. The acceptance of the structure of social welfare that it inherited from the Attlee government showed that Churchill realized the limitations placed upon him to reshape Britain domestically. His primary interest remained with the military and foreign policy. But here, too, he could do little to alter Britain's secondary role in the Cold War. Even in imperial matters, Churchill had to pin his hopes to the Commonwealth as a means of preserving a semblance of the empire.

Ultimately, Churchill found it impossible to live up to his wartime achievements and throughout his tenure there was dissension from within the Conservative ranks that made his leadership uncomfortable. He resigned the premiership in 1955, to be succeeded by his protégé, Anthony Eden. He had finally retired at the age of 81.

When Churchill died early in 1965, Britain was treated to a spectacular funeral in the style of the war heroes of the previous century, most notably those of Nelson and Wellington. He was hailed as 'The Greatest Englishman'. No longer was he dogged by criticism even from within his own party. The nation let loose a flurry of encomiums; Churchill became the symbol of a greatness that many nostalgically felt had ceased to be. The war had become a touchstone for the unity, apparent conformity and social order that was being challenged in the mid-1960s. Churchill was the hero who embodied the values that were threatened. Perceptions of a continued breakdown of social consensus continued over the next two decades, fuelled by the success of the anti-establishment youth culture, increased union militancy and growing racial diversity. In the midst of these changes the Britain of Churchill seemed to offer security. The power of Churchill as a symbol persisted. Thatcher, in her attempts to assert British power abroad and to crush the unions at home, echoed Churchill's politics and much of his rhetoric, even if she did not share his reluctant acceptance of the welfare state that he had done much to found in his earliest political activities.

Just as Churchill's greatest contribution to the war effort was to unify the public through his speeches, he is now remembered as the chief symbol of a time when the nation united to save Britain and its allies from Nazi conquest – notwithstanding that during his long career he held controversial opinions and took actions of which many had disapproved.

References and further reading

Addison, P. (1992) *Churchill on the Home Front 1900–1955*, London: Jonathan Cape.

Blake, R. and Louis, W. (eds) (1993) *Churchill*, Oxford: Oxford University Press.

Bonham-Carter, V. (1965) *Winston Churchill: An Intimate Portrait*, New York: Harcourt, Brace & World.

Charmley, J. (1993) *Churchill: The End of Glory*, London: Hodder & Stoughton. (A challenging but unconvincing questioning of Churchill's wartime leadership.)

Churchill, R. (1966) *Winston S. Churchill: Youth 1874–1900*, London: Heinemann.

—— (1967) *Winston S. Churchill: Young Statesman 1901–1914*, London: Heinemann.

Colville, J. (1985) *The Fringes of Power: 10 Downing Street Diaries 1939–1955*, London: Hodder & Stoughton.

Gilbert, M. (1971–88) *Winston S. Churchill*, London: Heinemann. (Longest biography in the English language, covering Churchill's life from 1914 to 1965. Essential chronicle.)

Moran, Lord (1966) *Churchill: The Struggle for Survival*, New York: Houghton Mifflin.

Rhodes James, R. (ed.) (1974) *Winston S. Churchill: His Complete Speeches 1897–1963*, New York: Chelsea House.

Sandys, C. (1994) *From Winston with Love and Kisses*, London: Sinclair-Stevenson.

Stansky, P. (ed.) (1973) *Churchill: A Profile*, London: Macmillan. (A collection of assessments.)

Taylor, A.J.P. *et al.* (1969) *Churchill: Four Faces and the Man*, London: Allen Lane. (An important collection, including the cited piece by Robert Rhodes James.)

Woods, F. (ed.) (1979) *A Bibliography of the Works of Sir Winston Churchill*, Godalming: St Paul's Bibliographies.

Peter Stansky and Philip Wainwright

Clement Richard Attlee, First Earl of Prestwood

Born 4 January 1883, son of Henry Attlee and Ellen Watson. Educated at Haileybury and University College, Oxford. Married 1922 Violet Millar. MP for Limehouse 1922–50, West Walthamstow 1950–5. Deputy Leader of the Parliamentary Labour Party 1931–5; Leader of the Parliamentary Labour Party 1935–55. Mayor of Stepney 1919; Under-Secretary of State for War 1924; Chancellor, Duchy of Lancaster 1930; Postmaster-General 1931; Lord Privy Seal 1940–2; Deputy Prime Minister 1942–5; Secretary of State for Dominion Affairs 1942–3; Lord President of the Council 1943–5; Minister of Defence 1945–6; Prime Minister 1945–51; Leader of the Opposition 1951–5. Left Commons 1955, ennobled the same year. Died 8 October 1967.

'His limitations are obvious. His virtues and his powers are hidden and unexpected' (Durbin 1945). Attlee stole upon greatness quietly. As *The Times* suggested in its obituary, there was an obvious contrast between the scale of the 1945–50 Labour government's achievements and the diminutive character of its leader: 'one of the least colourful and most effective of the British Prime Ministers of this century' (*The Times* 1967). Attlee's tenure in Downing Street saw the structure of British domestic and foreign policy transformed, whether through the independence of India, the formation of the North Atlantic Treaty Organization (NATO), or domestic achievements such as the maintenance of full employment and the establishment of the National Health Service (NHS). In the Labour party – which he led for a record twenty years – there was a similar discrepancy between contemporary impact and retrospective judgement. Some, like Richard Crossman, complained that 'the cult of personality was replaced by the cult of anonymity' (Crossman 1961). In an unlikely fashion, however, Attlee became the Keir Hardie of the late-twentieth-century Labour party, the centre of what has been called the 'deeply-entrenched Attlee myth' (Morgan 1988: 773). In the 1970s and 1980s, with the party floundering in a morass of electoral impotence and infighting, Attlee became an icon to figures at polar opposites of Labour's wide spectrum. The mantra 'if Clem Attlee was alive today' may not have echoed round the conference hall with the same emotional force as references to the cloth-capped Hardie, but the stooped figure of Attlee still lurked in the shadows as the 'sensible socialist' who had held the party together, when its warring factions were bent on destroying one another. It is an ironic comment indeed upon the nature of the Labour party that its most effective leader was the reticent, unassuming Attlee, who throughout his career was assailed by jibes about his strength and personality.

The late-Victorian era into which Attlee was born at Putney left an enduring mark of service and sensibility on his character and outlook. He was the seventh child in a family which presented a picture of upper-middle-class domesticity and moral conscience. Haileybury, a public school founded by the East India Company, shaped the young Attlee's imagination with cricket, literature and schoolboy imperialism. In 1901, he went up to University College, Oxford, emerging with a second-class degree in History. At this point, he was an apathetic Conservative. With no inclination to do much else, he drifted into a career in law, the profession of his father. The gentle rut along which his life was moving was rudely disturbed in October 1905, when he paid a visit to Haileybury House, a boys' club in Stepney, deep in the East End of London. As he reflected fifty years later, the visit awakened his sense of social conscience and public service (*The Haileyburian* 1955). By 1907, he had taken over as manager of the club. Political commitment followed. That same year, eschewing the middle-class Fabian Society, he plunged into the heart of working-class politics in the East End by joining the Stepney Independent Labour party.

Between 1907 and the outbreak of the First World War, Attlee was an active member of the ILP, making speeches on street corners, helping to convert the local unions, participating in the dock strike of 1911, and running unsuccessfully for local office. He also served as campaign secretary and speakers' organizer for Sidney and Beatrice Webb's Poor Law Minority Report Campaign, was an 'official explainer' for the National Insurance Act 1911, and lectured on trade unionism for Ruskin College.

The First World War interrupted this burgeoning career. Against the grain of many in the ILP, Attlee joined up, serving in Gallipoli, Mesopotamia and France, ending the war with the rank of major. In 1918, he returned to Stepney and obtained a position at the London School of Economics as a lecturer on social work. The end of the war also marked the beginning of Attlee's development as a serious Labour politician.

Within a year, he had become the first Labour mayor of Stepney and was prospective parliamentary candidate for Limehouse. Labour made substantial gains in the borough elections of 1919 and Attlee was appointed mayor in Stepney, giving him his first taste of political power. This tenure was an early demonstration of his characteristic style of leadership:

Decisions on any statement not in order are given in intensely concentrated, firm – almost curt – precise and unmistakeable sentences, like the slamming of a railway carriage door, so that a person on the wrong side is nonplussed, and before he can recover mental balance the opportunity has passed and he is left, the Mayor hurrying on with the next item on the agenda . . . as a rapidly restarting train.

(*East London Observer* 1919)

Substitute 'leader' or 'prime minister' for 'mayor' and this style – with its military curtness, disdain for unnecessary temporizing, and overriding emphasis on efficiency and consensus – could well describe his chairmanship of parliamentary Labour party meetings or cabinets some thirty years later. The mayoralty also underlined Attlee's lifelong role as an outsider. He had to cope with the warring Jewish and Irish factions on the Stepney council, sidestepping destructive disputes while steering the council towards action. The theme of maintaining order over anarchy became a dominant one in Attlee's life. He proved a quiet but forceful mediator, disguising his surprising and often disconcerting strength behind an inscrutable exterior and an unwavering commitment not only to what he considered to be right, but also to what he thought to be the possible or practical course.

In the 1922 general election he was elected for Limehouse and was immediately taken on by Ramsay MacDonald as parliamentary private secretary. If his mayoralty had reflected his developing style of leadership, his maiden speech to the Commons revealed the simplicity of his perception of socialist strategy: 'As the nation was organised for war and death, so it can be organised for peace and life if we have the will for it' (*Parliamentary Debates* 1922: 159). It was an unsophisticated but effective theme, grounded in compassion and practicality, and one to which he persistently returned in later life. In the 1920s, Attlee enjoyed, if not a meteoric rise, then steady progress towards the first or second rank of the parliamentary Labour party. After the formation of the first Labour government in 1924, he was made Under-Secretary of State for War. Three years later, he served as a member on the Simon Commission on Indian self-government. Politically, this was not a comfortable position for Attlee, as Labour was very critical of the Commission, but he threw himself into its deliberations, gaining an education in an issue which demonstrated his greatest personal contribution to post-war Britain.

Attlee was fortunate that his role in the ill-fated second Labour government was relatively minor. In May 1930, Attlee replaced the departed Oswald Mosley as Chancellor for the Duchy of Lancaster. He had even less power than Mosley but used the position to ground himself in economic policy, producing a memorandum on 'The Problems of British Industry'. In 1931, he was, briefly, Postmaster-General, the only administrative department he held before becoming prime minister. Both positions gave Attlee the opportunity to reflect seriously on the organization of government, a theme to which he returned in the 1940s and which informed his own premiership.

In the Labour collapse in the election of October 1931 Attlee held on to his seat, if only barely. But his talent was always for stoic survival. It was the survivor's path which eventually led to the leadership of the Labour party in 1935. This route did not wind through constituency politics or the corridors of Transport House. Like his friend Stafford Cripps, Attlee flirted with the radical left after the election, telling his brother, for instance, that he was tired of 'blooming gradualism and palliatives' (Golant 1970: 321). Such left-leaning instincts were never quite abandoned, but, in sharp contrast to Cripps's career in the 1930s, they did not distort the essential pragmatism of Attlee's political acumen. Unlike Herbert Morrison and Hugh Dalton, Attlee made no significant contribution to the reformulation of economic and foreign policy which characterized the recasting of Labour's identity in the 1930s. He was willing to follow at a respectful distance, but not to offer a lead in policy. This reticence encouraged Dalton to denigrate him caustically as 'a small person, with no personality, nor real standing in the Movement' (Pimlott 1986: 168). Dalton was wrong. As deputy leader between 1931 and 1935, first to Arthur Henderson and then to George Lansbury, Attlee worked tirelessly to invigorate the depleted parliamentary Labour party. By 1935, he had built up a skeleton power base at Westminster, particularly among mining MPs, gaining a reputation for solid, if colourless reliability. Happy accident, hard work and, to no small degree, lack of controversy, left him well placed to contest the leadership.

Henderson retired in 1934, succeeded by the idealistic if ineffectual George Lansbury. Lansbury's leadership was destroyed by the hulking Ernest Bevin just before the election of November 1935. In this vacuum, Attlee was chosen as interim leader. Labour returned to parliament with an increased parliamentary force of 154, including such casualties of the 1931 election as Morrison and Dalton, and a leadership vote was called. Morrison and Arthur Greenwood were the best known and most senior figures in the party and joined the fray. After a first ballot eliminated Greenwood, Attlee conclusively defeated Morrison, earning the latter's lifelong emnity. He was to remain leader for two decades.

It would be wrong to suggest that Attlee distinguished himself as a forceful leader between 1935 and the formation of the Churchill coalition in 1940. He offered no initiatives on policy, unlike Dalton and Ernest Bevin. He was not a particularly good speaker, and was unable to work the constituency circuit. This lack of obvious strength led to continual mutterings within the party. In 1939, after a prolonged absence through illness, there was an abortive attempt to replace Attlee with Arthur Greenwood, and even after the 1945 election Morrison attempted to usurp the throne. Attlee's strength in the late 1930s, however, may well have been that he recognized his own limitations: he was willing to act as part of an informally collective leadership made up of Dalton, Morrison, Greenwood, Cripps and – from outside the parliamentary Labour party – Bevin. Amid these mercurial personalities, Attlee played the role of chair to an often unruly committee rather than insisting upon a dynamic style of leadership in the manner of his predecessor Ramsay MacDonald or his immediate successor, Hugh Gaitskell. Flair and cleverness were left to others. Attlee's strength lay in his unflappability, which both calmed and confused. His steely will was shown on occasion, as in 1939 when he acceded to the expulsion of his friend Stafford Cripps.

The Second World War demonstrated many of the strengths of this role, as well as some of its weaknesses. One early achievement for Attlee was the definition of Labour's distinctive position, focused on the attainment of commitments to reconstruction along lines sympathetic to the party's ideals. This he pursued from 1939 until the end of the war (Brooke 1992). When he told the pivotal Labour conference of 1940, which brought the party into coalition under Churchill, that 'the world that must emerge from this war must be a world attuned to our ideals', he meant that Labour would be an active agent in this change (*Labour Party Conference Report* 1940: 125). Coalition was a commitment not only to national unity, in Attlee's perception, but also to the aim of social change.

Attlee occupied four positions within the Coalition government between 1940 and 1945: Lord Privy Seal, Secretary of State for Dominion Affairs, deputy prime minister and Lord President of the Council. He and Bevin were key members of the War cabinet between 1940 and the end of the war. As deputy prime minister, Attlee filled in for Churchill as chair of the cabinet when the latter was on one of his many foreign trips. Without a strong administrative portfolio, Attlee may not have enjoyed the status or public esteem of Bevin at the Ministry of Labour or Morrison as Home Secretary; nor did he catch the public fancy as Cripps did in 1942. But he did gain further experience in manoeuvring between personalities more superficially flashy or talented than himself. His handling of Churchill during the war is instructive in this regard. Though always supportive of the prime minister, he was never Churchill's poodle. Attlee was always determined to challenge or rein in the prime minister when he felt Churchill had gone too far or not far enough. In 1943 and 1944, for instance, he criticized Churchill over reconstruction and for his often meandering handling of cabinet. On the latter point, Attlee's own tenure at the head of the cabinet table was noticeably efficient and effective. Attlee also took great initiative on two matters, India and the establishment of the United Nations.

His relationship with his own party through the war was less happy. The strain of being in the unenviable position as leader of a party occupying the simultaneous roles of government and opposition sometimes showed. As the Chuter Ede diaries have shown, Attlee often vacillated in his handling of a sometimes unruly group of parliamentary rebels, including, for instance, Aneurin Bevan. Harold Laski, Labour's leading and most prominent intellectual, also made life difficult for him; Laski publicly criticized the worth of Attlee's leadership numerous times and privately caballed with other members of the top rank to replace him. Attlee made great efforts in 1944 to assure the party that it would regain independence once victory had been achieved.

If the election of July 1945 was Labour's finest hour, it also saw Attlee's reticent sensibility at its most politically effective. His calm puncturing of Churchill's infamous 'Gestapo' broadcast during the campaign underlined the reasonableness and responsibility of Labour's stance, while continuing to press its distinctive message of economic planning and state welfare. When the results came in and Labour formed its first majority government, the triumph was Attlee's as well as the party's, as Chuter Ede remarked after the first meeting of the new parliamentary party:

> Attlee had come into his own . . . the country desiring to give power to the Left had followed the precedent of 1906 when it installed the steady, faithful but uninspiring Campbell-Bannerman . . . Attlee's speech was typical. Without a trace of emotion he alluded to the tremendous nature of our victory. . . . We were not going to postpone bringing in our measures. This session we should submit our programme. This determination moved the gathering to great enthusiasm.
>
> (Jefferys 1987: 227–9)

Assessing Attlee's relationship as premier to the work of his governments between 1945 and 1951, one is struck by an unlikely comparison: Margaret Thatcher. Both were heads of governments with immense programmatic commitments strongly informed by ideology. The tenures of Attlee and Thatcher both resulted in the restructuring of domestic British politics, the first towards the post-war consensus of the managed economy and the welfare state, the second towards the dismantling of that consensus and the promotion of market-orientated 'enterprise culture'. Both could claim the title of most important post-war premier, one modestly, the other stridently. There the comparison ends. Attlee's premiership was largely that of a conciliator and co-ordinator within his government; Thatcher's was characterized by a tone of restless and often abrasive initiative and confrontation, more presidential than prime ministerial. The toll can be counted both in cabinet casualties – under Attlee there was only one major cabinet resignation, that of Aneurin Bevan in 1951, while Thatcher's list resembled that of Balaclava – and political survival; despite numerous challenges, Attlee held on to the leadership until he decided to retire in 1955. Again, one can point to the steadiness which Attlee offered at the heart of an enormous legislative programme and an often tumultuous government. At points this stillness seemed comatose, rather than calm. Attlee's lack of decisiveness amid the crises of 1947 and the cabinet divisions of 1951 cost both his political reputation and the unity of his party dearly. And he should share some of the blame for the failure to make Labour's reforms exciting to the public (Fielding 1991). Generally, however, Attlee's chosen role as a chair of cabinet seeking consensus, rather than as a presidential prime minister, aided the effectiveness of his government.

Attlee's astuteness can be seen in the structuring of his cabinet in 1945. Giving Morrison the responsibility for the realization of the legislative programme as Lord President of the Council and Bevin the post of Foreign Secretary not only reduced the possibility of conflict between two men who loathed one another, but also played to the strengths of each: Morrison as a political manager, Bevin as a tough-minded negotiator. In a similar way, he assuaged Dalton's chagrin at losing the Foreign Secretaryship by making the former economist Chancellor of the Exchequer. Attlee was skilled in inducting the left rather than marginalizing it, always a problem within the Labour party. Former poachers – Stafford Cripps, Aneurin Bevan and Emanuel Shinwell – were made gamekeepers with important grounds to protect: the first as President of the Board of Trade, the second at the Ministry of Health (with responsibility for the establishment of the National Health Service), the last as Minister of Fuel and Power. He was careful to encourage the wealth of younger talent within the new parliamentary party, bringing Harold Wilson, Hugh Gaitskell and Douglas Jay into the corridors of power relatively quickly. To anchor the government, Attlee relied upon old hands such as Chuter Ede at the Home Office, George Isaacs as Ministry of Labour, and Christopher Addison at the Dominions Office.

Premiership underlined Attlee's talent for administration and management. Following the pattern of his time as mayor of Stepney and as Churchill's wartime deputy, he made sure that cabinet sessions sought consensus and moved on quickly with the least amount of controversy. This was, of course, central to the success of the programme. One need only look at the political cost of the prevarications over the nationalization of iron and steel in 1947 and 1948, and the budget debates of 1951, to understand how the programme could have been derailed without such single-mindedness. As it was, most of Labour's commitments had been put in place within three years of taking office. Generally, as well, there was a clear demarcation of responsibilities within the government and relatively little confusion or rivalry about power. Expenditure was one predictable and unavoidable exception, particularly over the cost of defence commitments. Economic planning was less excusable, and Attlee did little to clear up the mystery of who was responsible for its direction, whether the Treasury, the Lord President's Committee, or the Ministerial Committee on Economic Planning. The coal and convertibility crises of 1947 cruelly exposed this lacuna. The accession of Stafford Cripps to the chancellorship later that year did much to centralize responsibility, but through circumstance rather than design.

Attlee's position within the government did not go unquestioned through the life of the Labour administrations between 1945 and 1951. He could not rely upon personal charisma or even popularity to aid him against potential rivals. The year 1947 was a particularly difficult time and Attlee did not come out of it unscathed. In the autumn a palace plot to replace him was hatched by Morrison and Dalton. It failed primarily because of Bevin's refusal to join the cabal and unseat whom he called his 'little man'. Attlee later remarked that his relationship with Bevin was 'the deepest of my political life' (Williams 1961: 293). This friendship proved a bulwark in low moments in his premiership. But Attlee was not totally dependent upon the Foreign Secretary. As at many moments, he showed his political acumen. Particularly delicious was opening the office door to Stafford Cripps as a messenger of doom and sending him through it with a promotion, a moment of real genius.

Where one can chip away at the Attlee myth is in his failure to offer a lead in domestic politics, particularly after the realization of much of the initial programme by 1948. The prime minister had little to contribute to the growing disarray within the party over the question 'what next'. His sentiments tended towards the left, but he seemed unwilling or unable to nip the debate between 'consolidationists' and 'expansionists' in the bud, before it became more destructive or associated with other divisive tendencies. Nor could he do much to popularize the work of the Labour government or soften the blows of its necessary policy of austerity – as a Churchill, Macmillan or Wilson might have done through a charismatic appeal to the nation – beyond calling for further sacrifices in consumer demand.

Attlee's quiet competence did much, however, to complement the pursuit of the 'special relationship' with the United States, the cornerstone of Labour's foreign policy, reassuring the United States that Britain was not running amok with either Bolshevism or imperialism after the war. The sober and comforting explanation of democratic socialism which Attlee made to the US Congress in 1945 may not have ensured the opening of that nation's coffers or led to its unconditional support of Britain's strategic aims, but it did convince the Americans that Britain had not veered to the far left. '[T]here is not much danger that [Labour] will attempt to transform Britain into a thoroughgoing Marxian state', the *New York Times* commented after the election of 1945, 'Mr Attlee is certainly not the model of a revolutionist' (*New York Times* 1945). Attlee's successful efforts to disengage Britain from India and the more reluctant withdrawal from Palestine were further steps in convincing the Americans of Britain's good faith in decolonization.

Managing a dignified and effective withdrawal from South-East Asia might be seen as Attlee's greatest personal achievement in power (Moore 1983). By 1949, he had played the major role in crafting the transition from empire to Commonwealth in this sphere, with the independence of India (1947), Pakistan (1947), Burma (1948) and Ceylon (1948), and the maintenance of India within the Commonwealth as a republic. As already indicated, the Simon Commission first instructed Attlee in the Indian question and he kept up a keen interest, particularly during the war years when Stafford Cripps had been sent to negotiate independence, based upon an offer of a single central government. Attlee hoped that the aim of independence and a single government for India might be effected during the Labour government. He was successful with the first, but the second foundered on sectarian divisions within India itself. After some months of negotiation, Attlee's impatience began to show; he told the cabinet in 1946 that 'it was impossible to be confident that the main political Parties in India had any real will to reach agreement between themselves' (Public Record Office 1946). In two bold moves in early 1947, he replaced Viceroy Wavell with Lord Mountbatten and laid down a definite timetable for British withdrawal by 31 March 1948, in order to shock Indian politicians into agreement. This worked, though it did result in the formation of two nations, India and Pakistan, and continuing sectarian violence between Hindus and Muslims. Independence was granted on 15 August 1947. Attlee also played a central role in keeping India as a republic within the Commonwealth in 1949, thus laying down a sure principle for the developing family of nations and the maintenance of British relevance.

If his touch was sure in imperial affairs, particularly in South-East Asia, the efforts he made in other foreign spheres was less obviously effective. Acutely conscious of Britain's limited resources, he fought a losing battle within the government against Bevin's desire to expand British interests in the Middle East (Louis 1984). His contribution to the development of nuclear weapons also brought mixed results. From the time of Hiroshima, Attlee was determined that there be international or at least mutual control of nuclear weapons between the Americans and Britain. He was unsuccessful in his attempts to convince Harry Truman that Britain should not be frozen out of the development of nuclear weapons, thus leading to the decision to construct a British nuclear deterrent in January 1947. On the other hand, he did intervene successfully in 1950 with the US President to prevent the possible use of nuclear weapons in Korea.

Attlee's management of his own often fractious party was generally strong. Despite occasional rumblings over foreign policy, few serious divisions emerged until the late 1940s. After the election of 1950, however, when Labour was returned with a much reduced minority, splits developed which Attlee seemed unable to solve. The most serious emerged within his own cabinet between Cripps's successor as Chancellor, Gaitskell and Bevan, now Minister of Labour, over expenditure on health and defence in the wake of the Korean conflict. Though personally favouring Bevan as a possible heir, Attlee did not or was unable (being in hospital at a critical juncture in the controversy) to dampen the increasingly bitter rivalry. Nor was he willing to sacrifice the American relationship for the sake of domestic policy. With his old ally Bevin failing in health, Attlee hesitated. Eventually, following the lead of cabinet, he came down on Gaitskell's side and asked Bevan for a commitment to cabinet consensus, which the latter refused. Bevan resigned over the budget in April 1951, taking with him Wilson and John Freeman, a junior minister. The resignation shattered the drive of an already enervated government and furnished a powerful and destructive focus for growing opposition within the party itself. Attlee may also have committed a political blunder in calling the election of October 1951 when he did, out of a perceived obligation to the King. Labour lost to a Conservative majority of seventeen, while polling more votes.

The period as Leader of the Opposition between 1951 and his retirement in December 1955 was not a happy one for Attlee. Power focused Attlee's virtues; opposition brought out his weaknesses. A querulous mood dominated the party at Westminster and in the constituencies, particularly with the open rebellion of the Bevanites on issues of foreign policy. Once again, Attlee may not have been the party leader to have best dealt with such internecine warfare. He offered few leads beyond loyalty and no initiatives in policy or strategy. He did succeed once again, however, in frustrating the leadership ambitions of Morrison. Hanging on as long as he did meant that the torch had to be passed to a younger generation. Though Attlee had once favoured Bevan, the clear choice by the autumn of 1955 was Gaitskell. Attlee resigned from the leadership on 7 December 1955.

Between 1955 and his death in 1967, Attlee was an active member of the

Lords, while gaining a reputation as a book reviewer for the press. The last sphere afforded him the opportunity to give vent to an ego he had apparently suppressed during his political career, offering arch reviews of the work of such former political rivals as Churchill. He lived to see the Labour victories of 1964 and 1966, dying the following year from pneumonia. His ashes were interred at Westminster Abbey.

References and further reading

Attlee, C. (1935) *The Will and the Way to Socialism*, London: Methuen. (The best exposition of Attlee's political outlook.)

—— (1954) *As It Happened*, London: Heinemann. (More an unintentional ode to Attlee's reticence than an informative account of his career, but still amusing.)

Brooke, S. (1992) *Labour's War*, Oxford: Oxford University Press.

Burridge, T. (1985) *Clement Attlee*, London: Jonathan Cape. (Less compelling than Harris's (1982) biography, but stronger on the context of party development and foreign policy.)

Crossman, R. (1961) 'The voice of the tortoise', *New Statesman and Nation* 14 April.

Durbin, E. (1945) 'Clem Attlee', British Library of Political and Economic Science, Evan Durbin Papers, 3/9.

East London Observer (1919) London, 6 December.

Fielding, S. (1991) ' "Don't know and don't care": popular political attitudes in Labour's Britain 1945–51', in N. Tiratsoo (ed.) *The Attlee Years*, London: Pinter.

Golant, W. (1970) 'The emergence of C.R. Attlee as leader of the Parliamentary Labour Party', *Historical Journal* 13: 318–32.

The Haileyburian and Imperial Service College Chronicle (1955) December.

Harris, K. (1982) *Attlee*, London: Weidenfeld & Nicolson. (Still the best life of Attlee, based upon interviews and primary research, though stronger on the person than on the historical context.)

Jay, D. (1980) *Change and Fortune*, London: Hutchinson. (Jay was Attlee's personal assistant after the war and his autobiography provides many illuminating anecdotes and insights.)

Jefferys, K. (1987) *Labour and the Wartime Coalition: From the Diary of James Chuter Ede 1941–45*, London: Historian's Press.

Labour Party Conference Report (1940).

Louis, W. (1984) *The British Empire in the Middle East 1945–51*, Oxford: Oxford University Press.

Moore, R. (1983) *Escape from Empire*, Oxford: Oxford University Press. (The strongest account of Attlee's involvement with India.)

Morgan, K. (1984) *Labour in Power*, Oxford: Oxford University Press. (The best general survey of the post-war Labour governments.)

—— (1987) 'Attlee', in *Labour People*, Oxford: Oxford University Press. (A concise and sharp assessment.)

—— (1988) 'Review of R. Ovendale, *The English-Speaking Alliance*', *English Historical Review* 103: 773.

New York Times (1945) New York, 28 July.

Parliamentary Debates (1922) 159: 23 November 1922, cs. 92–6.

Pimlott, B. (1986) *The Political Diary of Hugh Dalton 1918–40, 1945–60*, London: Jonathan Cape.

Public Record Office (1946) CAB 128/8, CM (46) 104, Cabinet Minutes, 10 December 1946, Confidential Annex.

The Times (1967) London, 9 October.

Williams, F. (1961) *A Prime Minister Remembers*, London: Heinemann. (Made up of a series of interviews with Attlee, with many flashes of Attlee's laconic wit.)

Stephen Brooke

(Robert) Anthony Eden, First Earl of Avon

Born 12 June 1897, third son of Sir William Eden and Sybil Grey. Educated at Eton and Christ Church College, Oxford. Married (1) 1923 Beatrice Beckett (divorced 1950); (2) 1952 Clarissa Churchill, niece of Winston Churchill. MP for Warwick and Leamington 1923–57. Parliamentary Private Secretary to Parliamentary Under-Secretary at Home Office 1924–6; Parliamentary Private Secretary to Parliamentary Under-Secretary at Foreign Office 1926; Parliamentary Private Secretary to Foreign Secretary 1926–9; Parliamentary Under-Secretary at Foreign Office 1931–3; Lord Privy Seal 1933–5; Minister without Portfolio for League of Nations Affairs 1935; Foreign Secretary 1935–8; Secretary of State at Dominions Office 1939–40; Secretary of State for War 1940; Foreign Secretary 1940–5 and 1951–5; Prime Minister 1955–7. Left Commons 1957, ennobled 1961. Died 14 January 1977.

Eden was the last prime minister to believe that Britain was an independent world power, and he will always be associated with the Suez crisis, which proved that it was not. Despite his unrivalled experience of foreign affairs, he miscalculated American reaction to the Anglo-French invasion of Egypt, in collusion with Israel, following Colonel Nasser's nationalization of the Suez Canal Company in 1956. President Eisenhower publicly humiliated Britain by insisting on the unconditional withdrawal of the Anglo-French forces, and Eden resigned on grounds of ill-health shortly afterwards. His inability to delegate detailed matters to departmental ministers, and his tendency to be indecisive, had already cost him the confidence of some senior colleagues. He was very sensitive to criticism, from the press and elsewhere, and even a sympathetic biographer has referred to his 'temperamental inaptitude for the supreme office' (Rothwell 1992: 165).

Eden was very much an establishment figure. The baronetcy held by his father dated from 1672, and his mother was a great-niece of Lord Grey, the prime minister who brought in the 1832 Reform Bill. Eden was brought up on an 800-acre estate in County Durham. However, his home background was unstable. There is some evidence that his real father may have been the politician George Wyndham. Be that as it may, family life was marred by Sir William Eden's rages and by the apparent inability of Eden's mother to express affection for her children. He was unhappy at Eton but found fulfilment as an officer on active service on the Western Front in the First World War. His physical courage was recognized by the award of the Military Cross, and he became the youngest brigade major in the army. He was highly intelligent – he graduated from Oxford after the war with a first-class honours degree in oriental languages – but his single-minded devotion to a career in politics contributed to the breakdown of his first marriage.

Eden rose to be prime minister on the basis of his reputation as Foreign Secretary, a post he held on three occasions for a total of over ten years. He resigned from Neville Chamberlain's government in 1938 over the latter's interference in Eden's conduct of Anglo-Italian relations, and subsequently acquired a reputation as an opponent of the policy of 'appeasement'. Although not wholly deserved, Eden's reputation stood him in good stead when Chamberlain's principal critic in the Conservative party, Churchill, took over as prime minister in May 1940. In December that year Eden was restored as Foreign Secretary, and given a place in the War cabinet, and thereafter he took a prominent role in wartime diplomacy. His final period as Foreign Secretary was marked by diplomatic success at the Geneva Conference in 1954, which ended the war between the French and Communist guerrillas in Indo-China, albeit at the cost of a major disagreement with the US Secretary of State, John Foster Dulles, who had hoped for Britain's participation in an anti-communist coalition in the Far East. Eden also negotiated the 1954 agreement with Egypt whereby all British forces were to be withdrawn from the Suez Canal Zone by 1956, thereby unwittingly preparing the way for Nasser's nationalization of the Canal Company in the latter year.

In the 1950s Eden was dogged by ill-health, which seems to have increased a natural tendency to impatience and irritability. He had had a minor heart attack in 1935 and an ulcer in 1951, but really serious problems arose from an unsuccessful bile-duct operation in 1953; two further operations were required, with the result that he was absent from the Foreign Office for six months. Although he gained relief from pain and recurrent fevers, he was regarded by at least one cabinet colleague as 'fragile'. The symptoms were to return in October 1956, forcing him to have recourse to drugs, and possibly affecting his judgement during the crucial phase of the Suez crisis (Carlton 1981: 298–9, 327–8, 330; Lamb 1987: 242), although his official biographer denies that Eden's decision to attack Egypt was influenced by his health (Rhodes James 1986: 533).

Eden also suffered from frustration in his last period as Foreign Secretary, in that, as Churchill's heir apparent, he was anxious that the ageing prime minister should make way for him, but Churchill engaged in prolonged prevarication before retiring in April 1955. Eden decided on a general election in the following month, when the Conservatives increased their majority. This success probably owed much to a 'feel good' factor on account of rising prosperity since 1951, a feeling that the Chancellor of the Exchequer, R.A. Butler, did nothing to dispel in his budget immediately before the election. In the budget there were tax cuts, even although the level of demand in the economy pointed to deflationary measures. Subsequently pressure on sterling forced Butler to deflate in an emergency budget in the autumn, and Eden has been accused of starting a cycle of 'stop-go' policies, whereby the government's powers to manage the economy were used for political ends, regardless of the destabilizing effect on investment (Pinto-Duschinsky 1970: 67–9).

In fact, Eden had only modest comprehension of economics, although he worried constantly about the economic situation, and concerned himself with inessential details of the second 1955 budget. He replaced Butler with Harold Macmillan who, on the advice of Treasury officials, insisted on further measures to curb demand in the economy early in 1956. According to one of Eden's biographers, David Carlton, Macmillan won a significant victory by threatening to resign if the Treasury's requirements were not met; but other writers have suggested that Eden was the victor, in that Macmillan's proposals for tax increases and a withdrawal of state subsidies on bread and milk prices were much diluted in his budget, which was broadly neutral rather than deflationary (Carlton 1981: 396; Lamb 1987: 54–8; Rothwell 1992: 191). Eden worried that a rise in bread and milk prices would stimulate wage demands, and he hoped that his diplomatic skills could persuade trade union leaders to exercise restraint. In the event, despite the publication of a prophetic white paper on *The Economic Implications of Full Employment*, which warned that a vicious circle of rising wages and prices could lead to a loss of exports and employment, his government achieved nothing substantial in wages and employment policy.

Eden had no real experience of domestic policy and even as prime minister his chief interest lay in foreign policy. He attempted, without any notable success, to act as a mediator between the United States and the Soviet Union at the Geneva 'summit' conference in 1955. Then he invited the Soviet leaders, Nikolai Bulganin and Nikita Khrushchev, to make a state visit Britain in 1956, but any benefits to East–West relations were cancelled by the effects of the Soviet invasion of Hungary later in the year. As was common in political circles at the time, Eden attached great importance to the cohesion of the Commonwealth, and for that reason he was unwilling even to contemplate any curb on immigration from Commonwealth countries. Likewise he shared Whitehall's scepticism of the movement towards European unity, and he resisted American pressure for Britain to join the European Common Market, which was being negotiated by France, West Germany, Italy and the Benelux countries in 1955–7.

Eden had been concerned to maintain Britain's position in the Middle East against American encroachment as early as 1944, and he was certainly not prepared to play the part of the United States' junior partner there in the 1950s. Dulles, for his part, was determined that the United States should not be implicated in any act of 'imperialism' by Britain or France. Thus, although Britain and the United States agreed in 1956 not to support Nasser by providing him with finance for his grandiose Aswan Dam project, they did so for different reasons. Eden and the Foreign Office objected to Nasser's propaganda against British interests in the Middle East; the Americans were influenced by doubts about Egypt's credit-worthiness. When Nasser nationalized the Suez Canal Company on 26 July, with a view to securing the canal revenues for the Aswan Dam project, Dulles was willing to take part in diplomatic action to preserve the interests of nations whose ships used the canal. However, he did not fully share British concern about the strategic importance of the canal, which, in an age before supertankers that made the Cape of Good Hope the preferred route for oil, seemed to many in London to place the British economy at the mercy of the Egyptian dictator. Eden was not alone in seeing acquiescence to nationalization of the Canal Company as being comparable to Chamberlain's policy of 'appeasement'; even Hugh Gaitskell, the leader of the Labour opposition, who opposed armed action against Egypt, compared Nasser's approach to that of Mussolini and Hitler. If Eden had not 'stood up' to Nasser, he would have faced a major rebellion in the cabinet and the Conservative party.

The fact that Eden's response to nationalization of the Canal Company was in part also a response to domestic political pressure may account for his lack of clear objectives in relation to Nasser or Egypt. Despite public statements that Nasser had acted illegally, it was admitted within the British cabinet that the legal case against him was weak, and there was no suggestion that the company, which was registered as Egyptian and which was subject to Egyptian law, should simply be restored to private ownership. Instead, the Egypt Committee of the cabinet was told on 30 July that Britain's 'ultimate purpose' was to bring the canal under international control, and its 'immediate purpose' was to bring down Nasser. General Gruenther, the US Supreme Allied Commander in Europe, noted early in August that there was no doubt the British Chiefs of Staff would recommend military action, but he wondered how they could be confident that they could finish it quickly, when the presence of 80,000 troops in the Canal Zone in the early 1950s had not enabled Britain to control events in Egypt. In fact as late as 25 October the Chiefs of Staff drew Eden's attention to the problems of imposing order in Egypt after a successful operation, without receiving any political guidance from him (Kyle 1991: 138, 148, 181, 335).

Eden was aware that the use of force would divide the Commonwealth. More important, despite Eden's claims to the contrary, the United States made its opposition to a military adventure absolutely clear. Carlton attributes Eden's acquiescence in collusion with Israel – whereby the latter would invade Egypt, and Britain and France would intervene to protect the canal by occupying the Canal Zone – to the 'desperate nature of his domestic political problem': the need to maintain support within his own cabinet and party (Carlton 1981: 412–14, 419–20, 426, 432). On the other hand, Eden's official biographer draws attention to the prime minister's concern about Nasser's increasing links with the Soviet Union, and the need for an early *casus belli*, as the forces which Britain and France had gathered in the Mediterranean could not be held in readiness indefinitely (Rhodes James 1986: 532). Accounts vary on the extent, if any, to which Eden lied to the cabinet on 25 October about collusion with Israel: Richard Lamb, who admires Eden, nevertheless accuses him of being 'specifically untruthful'; whereas the normally hostile Carlton prefers a less severe judgement. He notes that ministers avoided asking penetrating questions, while Rhodes James has no doubt that no minister could claim that he had been deceived (Rhodes James 1986: 537; Lamb 1987: 243; Carlton 1988: 68).

Under the terms of their secret understanding with Britain and France, the Israelis invaded Egypt on 29 October, and Britain and France sent an ultimatum to both Egypt and Israel on the following day, calling upon both to withdraw their forces from the Canal Zone, which was to be occupied by an Anglo-French task force. British and French aircraft put the Egyptian air force out of action in a series of raids from 31 October, and, ignoring United Nations' calls for a cease-fire, the task force landed at Port Said on 5 November. Eden quickly discovered that he had overestimated the extent to which Britain could act without the approval of the United States. Whereas the Soviet Union supported Egypt only with bluff, in the form of an implied threat of a rocket attack on Britain and France, the Americans enforced their will by withholding support from sterling, which had come under heavy speculative pressure, until the British and French agreed first to a cease-fire on 6 November and then to withdraw their forces (Kunz 1991).

There is still some mystery over Eden's decision to resign on 9 January 1957. His health had deteriorated and, following a period of rest in Jamaica, he had decided that he was unfit to continue. His decision may also have been influenced by the silence with which he was received by Conservative MPs on his first appearance in the Commons on his return from Jamaica. Moreover, he was aware that he had misled the House on 20 December by denying collusion with Israel – something that was bound to have been exposed sooner or later, with serious implications for his reputation. However, his continuing poor health after retirement suggests that the official reason for his resignation was a sufficient one.

References and further reading
Carlton, D. (1981) *Anthony Eden: A Biography*, London: Allen Lane. (Written before the British public records for the 1950s were made available to researchers, but makes good use of American sources. Generally critical of Eden.)
—— (1988) *Britain and the Suez Crisis*, Oxford: Blackwell.
The Economic Implications of Full Employment, Cmd 9725, BPP 1955–6, XXXVI: 565–77.
Eden, A. (1960) *Full Circle*, London: Cassell. (Memoirs that are particularly lacking in frankness regarding the Suez episode.)
—— (1976) *Another World, 1897–1917*, London: Allen Lane. (Eden's account of his early years.)
Kunz, D. (1991) *The Economic Diplomacy of the Suez Crisis*, Chapel Hill, NC and London: University of North Carolina Press.
Kyle, K. (1991) *Suez*, New York: St Martin's Press.
Lamb, R. (1987) *The Failure of the Eden Government*, London: Sidgwick & Jackson. (First account to make extensive use of the British public records for 1955–6.)
Pinto-Duschinsky, M. (1970) 'Bread and circuses? The Conservatives in office, 1951–1964', in V. Bogdanor and R. Skidelsky (eds) *The Age of Affluence, 1951–1964*, London: Macmillan.

Rhodes James, R. (1986) *Anthony Eden*, London: Weidenfeld & Nicolson. (Markedly less critical than Carlton (1981), as might be expected of an official biography.)

Rothwell, V. (1992) *Anthony Eden: A Political Biography 1931–57*, Manchester: Manchester University Press. (Attempts to steer a course between Carlton and Rhodes James.)

George Peden

(Maurice) Harold Macmillan, First Earl of Stockton

Born 10 February 1894, third child of Maurice Macmillan and Helen Belles. Educated at Eton and Balliol College, Oxford. Married 1920 Lady Dorothy Cavendish, daughter of the Duke of Devonshire. MP for Stockton-on-Tees 1924–9 and 1931–45, Bromley 1945–64. Parliamentary Secretary at the Ministry of Supply 1940–2; Under-Secretary of State for the Colonies 1942; Resident Minister in North Africa 1942–5; Secretary of State for Air 1945; Minister of Housing and Local Government 1951–4; Minister of Defence 1954–5; Foreign Secretary 1955; Chancellor of the Exchequer 1955–7; Prime Minister 1957–63. Left Commons 1964, ennobled 1984. Died 29 December 1986.

If we judge Macmillan's premiership by what he tried to achieve, then his record in foreign policy, which was what he himself prized most, is a good one; the trouble is that, though he garnered a fair amount of sometimes spectacular publicity, his achievements were pretty hollow given the decline in Britain's position as a world power. In the area which really mattered, Britain's relationship with Europe, he failed. He did appreciate that Britain's days as an imperial power were over, and one could credit him with some symbolic achievements in this sphere and in educating the British public. But he continued to believe it proper for Britain to spend far more on defence than any of the continental European countries. In social policy and economic policy, he represented, respectively, the best and worst of consensus politics: he safeguarded the welfare state, but did nothing about Britain's fundamental economic problems.

Macmillan's paternal grandfather was a Scottish crofter made good. The family into which Harold was born had become prosperously upper class, engaged in the prestigious trade of publishing books, with a town-house in Cadogan Place, and a country residence, Birch Grove, the sort of family whose sons, should they so choose, were destined to rule. Macmillan did so choose, and was helped both in choice and fulfilment by his proud and strong-willed American mother. When war broke out, he immediately volunteered, his mother using her influence to get him into the Grenadier Guards. At the front he demonstrated conspicuous bravery, and was seriously wounded. His mother rescued him from military hospital, where he might well not have survived, to place him in a private hospital. Without the war experience, Macmillan would undoubtedly have had a top career in a top job; the war both instilled a sense of responsibility towards the ordinary men alongside whom he served, and yet at the same time brought to the surface the kind of ruthlessness which can be handy in the political jungle. Such characteristics are not incompatible with a deep shyness and occasional self-doubt.

Maternal influence was again behind Macmillan's first post-war career move: he went to Canada as aide to the Duke of Devonshire, whose daughter, Dorothy, he shortly married. The marriage was a social triumph, but a personal disaster. Public appearances were kept up, but from 1929 Macmillan had to live with the knowledge that he had been, and was continuing to be, cuckolded by someone he considered a friend, fellow Conservative MP Robert Boothby. Macmillan's political bonus from the marriage was the opportunity to win the former Liberal seat of Stockton-on-Tees. Unquestionably, Macmillan was affected by the plight of the unemployed in this depressed industrial town, though it would be wrong to suggest that he felt any strong sense of identification with them; rather he was fortified in his Disraelian conservatism which he believed should be directed to the industrial regeneration of Britain. His biggest problem was that he associated himself closely with Churchill: as Churchill was denied office, so too was Macmillan. Macmillan's awkwardness, earnestness and somewhat clumsy speechmaking were more obviously in evidence than the intense hard work he constantly put in to make himself an authority on Britain's economic problems (Macmillan 1933). The real inspiration behind the 'Middle Opinion' groups, which worked out blueprints for the kind of state planning that became fashionable in Britain after 1945, was the frail, pacifist, National Labour peer, Lord Allen of Hurtwood (Marwick 1964); Macmillan was in fact quite ruthless in elbowing Allen aside and himself assuming the leadership of the Next Five Years Group.

'I enjoy wars', Macmillan once said (Clarke 1991: 216–17). A failure up to 1939, he found his fortunes transformed by war. Little changed for him while Chamberlain was still prime minister, but with the formation of the Churchill government in May 1940 Macmillan at least got his start – even if he was no more than parliamentary secretary to the Minister of Supply, Labour's Herbert Morrison. When Lord Beaverbrook was brought in to Supply in June 1941, Macmillan became the spokesman for that department in the Commons, continuing as a main Commons' spokesman after his promotion to the post of Under-Secretary at the Colonial Office. A particularly delicate question facing the Churchill government was that of relationships with those French groups which had escaped from Occupied France. One base from which the French could fight Hitler was the French colony of Algeria, where General Giraud was in command. An intense rivalry existed between Giraud and General de Gaulle, based in Britain. Macmillan had seized the opportunities offered by junior office to demonstrate his qualities of energy, initiative and application, as well as his loyalty to Churchill. In December 1942 he was given the unique new post of Minister Resident at the Allied Force Headquarters, Algiers. The responsibilities of the job constantly expanded, for, as the Allies advanced along North Africa, across to Italy, and up through that country into northern frontiers, Macmillan advanced with them as the cabinet minister responsible for all the many political and economic issues involved. Initially, his work was mainly diplomatic, and he rightly received the highest praise for the way in which he sorted matters out with the extremely touchy de Gaulle. Macmillan was a central figure in setting out the terms for the Italian surrender, subsequently taking on responsibility as UK High Commissioner to the Advisory Council for Italy. Then he had a period in Greece, still with the portmanteau title of Resident Minister of State, then he was back again in Italy in the final year of the war as Acting President of the Allied Council for Italy. He did, indeed, have 'a good year'.

There was but one fly in the ointment, but a fly which was not to start buzzing till long after Macmillan had retired as prime minister. The accusation against Macmillan was that he, in the 'Klagenfurt Conspiracy', had been personally responsible for bringing about the repatriation (and thus persecution and death) of anti-Soviet Russians, without regard to whether or not they still were Russian citizens, or indeed were truly fascist. Later, Macmillan was ready to admit: 'I may have said "We'd better send them all back"' (Horne 1988: 261). His overriding concern was to get British prisoners out of the camps, which were now controlled by the Russians and Yugoslavs. The actual decision was taken during a half-hour meeting with General Keightley, the local commander, at the V Corps head-quarters at Klagenfurt. The action taken was in accordance with the strict letter (and indeed spirit) of the Yalta Agreement. There is absolutely no reason to believe that it went against the views of Field Marshal Alexander, Commander in the entire Mediterranean theatre. Cruel, yes, as war is cruel; conspiratorial – rubbish! (Bethell 1977; Knight 1986; Tolstoy 1986).

Macmillan (very much a hero) returned to Britain to be rewarded with the odd job of Secretary of State for Air in the Churchill 'caretaker' government. If he had changed he had been changed by office, and, above all, by success in office. The magic potion of power smoothed away the blemishes, nurtured self-confidence into a patrician air of easy assurance and unflappability (assisted by Macmillan's very genuine courage). The upward gradient was firmly set, only the Conservatives lost the general election, and Macmillan lost Stockton. Within months, aged 51, he was back in parliament as MP for the London suburban seat of Bromley, Beckenham and Penge.

To most historians the period after 1945 is a period of 'political consensus', till that consensus was explicitly repudiated by Thatcher from 1979 onwards. Pimlott has led the academic challenge to this notion (Pimlott 1989: 12–14). The debate is a rather sterile one. In standard usage the term 'consensus' is a comparative one, intended to distinguish the period 1945 to 1979 from earlier periods and from the subsequent Thatcherite period. It is not usually intended to suggest that political animosities and the forms of adversarial politics disappeared. Macmillan was now an outspoken critic of socialism, for all his reformist rhetoric of previous years; he fought his election campaigns vigorously and he was a sharp and witty critic of Labour MPs in the Commons. At the same time, in the years of opposition after the war, he was active among those Conservatives who succeeded in adjusting Conservative policies to take account of the changed Britain of the welfare state. He had long been something of a Keynesian, and a Keynesian he remained.

With the Conservatives in office after 1951, Macmillan managed to attract considerable attention and prestige to himself as Minister of Housing and Local Government. Beset by shortages, committed to the principle of public housing built by local authorities, and determined that such housing should be to high standards, Labour had failed to respond adequately to people's desperate need for housing in the post-war years. At the 1952 Conservative party conference Macmillan promised that houses would be built at an annual rate of 300,000. That he succeeded, with full publicity, in meeting this target partly through cuts in defence expenditure and industrial investment mattered little beside the fact of the achievement itself. As Churchill gave place to Eden in 1954, Macmillan began to be clearly perceived as number three in the party hierarchy, somewhat behind R.A. Butler. Prior to the general election of 1955 which confirmed Eden as prime minister, Macmillan had moved from Housing to Defence; after the election he received the Foreign Office, and then in December he went, reluctantly, to the Chancellorship of the Exchequer in order to enable Butler to move from that post to where he was happiest, the Home Office. A former Minister of State at the Foreign Office, Selwyn Lloyd – who at the time of his initial Foreign Office appointment had protested, 'I've never been to a foreign country, I don't speak any foreign languages, I don't like foreigners' (Clarke 1991: 220) – became Foreign Secretary. Eden, as prime minister, saw himself as *the* expert on foreign affairs, and fully intended to operate as such. The principal roles had been filled for the truly shabby episode, for which it is hard to find any excuses for Macmillan, the Suez crisis of 1956.

The British and French governments felt they had to react to Nasser's nationalization of the Suez Canal. What turned a problem into a crisis was the over-reaction of the British, in particular Eden and Macmillan. Both had been beneficiaries of their opposition to the Munich settlement, and of their important roles in the war against Nazism. Both made an entirely false equation between the current situation and Munich, and between the small-time dictator of a small country trying to cast off the last influences of colonialism, and Adolf Hitler. Both thought, again quite mistakenly, that the rest of the developed world would share their sense of outrage. When, next day, Eden set up a special committee of the cabinet, the Suez Committee, Macmillan was a member of it, as he remained right through to the end. Shortly, the full cabinet resolved to act together with the French in regaining the canal by force, and overthrowing the Nasser regime (Carlton 1989; Scott Lucas 1991).

As a combined military operation – following the initial Israeli invasion – the whole venture was not unsuccessful, but as a costly and unpopular one it pro-voked a severe financial crisis. There was a disastrous run on the pound with the Americans refusing to offer any support. Macmillan, as Chancellor of the Exchequer, had earlier ignored the risks on the unfounded basis that he could always get American support; now he knew that the losses were unsustainable.

Macmillan was thus the first to argue that Britain must accede to American demands, withdrawing unconditionally and giving place to a United Nations force.

Anthony Nutting, Under-Secretary at the Foreign Office, resigned rather than support the invasion. Neither Macmillan, nor any other member of the government, ever admitted that collusion had taken place with France and Israel. The relevant parts of Macmillan's own diary were destroyed at the time, and the official government papers are either heavily weeded or unavailable. Government statements at the time, inevitably, were clumsy and contorted; the condemnations of the government were powerful enough, though made without knowledge of the full extent of its wrong-doing. But also there were storms within the Conservative party over the sudden bringing of the operation to an end. In one of the most explosive Commons debates in modern times, on 12 November, Macmillan passionately expounded his opposition to 'appeasement': 'It is because I have seen it all happen before'. Macmillan's version was that the cease-fire had been declared, not because of American pressure and the run on the pound, but because 'the job was finished' (Macmillan 1971: 480).

Macmillan was principal aider and abettor in the Suez folly, but the fundamental responsibility lay with Eden, who had overruled his Foreign Secretary (who would have preferred action through the United Nations) and his Foreign Office advisers. Eden was a sick man and the stresses of covering up collusion, and then collapsing in ignominy, were too much for him. He went into hospital, and Butler was left in charge of explaining an episode he had always been unenthusiastic about and on which he had never been fully informed (he had not been a member of the Suez Committee). Macmillan was very aware that a successor to Eden was going to be needed sooner than later: during this 'interregnum' he made a point of staying away from the Commons, speaking only once and then on purely economic matters. Commentators have generally mingled admiration for the brilliance with which Macmillan maintained an air of enthusiastic conviction and calm confidence, and the brutality with which he demeaned Butler as his principal rival for the succession. The fact is that, though Macmillan never admitted to the collusion, he genuinely believed it and the British action to have been fully justified. He saw himself as a better man for the prime ministership than Butler. His leading role in the Suez operation can reasonably be termed 'criminal', and his initial assumption of American support and subsequent failure to spot that the manifest lack of that support would be financially disastrous, must be accounted crass incompetence brought on by serious wishful thinking. But his besting of Butler was merely part of the political game.

A crucial date is 22 November when both Butler and Macmillan addressed the 1922 Committee. Butler made a feeble and boring speech on Conservative party propaganda (Macmillan could hardly be blamed for that), while Macmillan made a rousing speech, again playing the old Munich card (Turner 1994: 123). Eden, a broken man, returned briefly. At 3.00 p.m. on 9 January 1957 Macmillan was called to 10 Downing Street: Eden told him that he had already informed the

Queen of his intention to resign on the grounds of ill-health. The cabinet met two hours later. Lord Salisbury, a senior cabinet minister, announced that he would summon the remaining cabinet ministers one by one to his room in the nearby Privy Council Offices, to get their views on the succession. Salisbury was assisted by Lord Kilmuir. As the famous story has it, Salisbury, with a grandee's disrespect for the letter 'r', asked each minister in turn: 'Well, who is it, Wab or Hawold?' Salisbury also interviewed the Chief Whip, Edward Heath, and the Chairman of the Party, Oliver Poole. Kilmuir took a telephone call from John Morrison, Chairman of the 1922 Committee. It seems that there was practical unanimity in favour of Macmillan; Eden was not consulted (Kilmuir 1964: 285; Howard 1987: 247). Macmillan was summoned to the Palace for 2.00 p.m. the next day; his sixty-fourth birthday was only days away.

Macmillan's phlegmatic comment in his memoirs (not actually written all that much later) is illuminating in several respects:

> I have often been reproached for having been at the same time one of the most keen supporters of strong action in the Middle East and one of the most rapid to withdraw when that policy met a serious check. 'First in, first out' was to be the elegant criticism of one of my chief Labour critics on many occasions.
>
> (Macmillan 1971: 163)

The unnamed 'critic' was Harold Wilson, whom Macmillan admired (he detested Gaitskell). The Suez crisis had seemed at the time to mark a cataclysmic polarization in British society, but actually the turmoil subsided extremely quickly. Macmillan not only survived a very shabby episode, but also prospered, and went on to win the 1959 general election by over one hundred seats. Hence the labels pinned on him: 'Supermac' (even if intended ironically, actually pregnant with genuine admiration) and 'The Actor Manager' (less flattering, but still containing a strong element of admiration).

'Appeasement' (hostility to) had been the talisman explaining the major events to date; now the talisman was the oft-expressed notion that Britain should be playing Greece, the brains and the culture, to America's Rome, the military power and economic strength (Evans 1981: 112). Whatever the scars left by Suez, there can be no doubt that Eisenhower and Dulles were far happier with Macmillan than they would have been with Butler, and Macmillan did indeed succeed in quickly re-establishing cordial relations with the Eisenhower administration; perhaps his biggest success was getting the US President to visit Britain, and appear on television with him, as two world statesmen together. From Eisenhower Macmillan obtained the Blue Streak nuclear missile (which, however, was quickly obsolete). At the beginning of 1958 he set out on a tour of the Commonwealth. Macmillan was no radical upholder of black African rights, nor campaigner against apartheid, but a famous speech signalled that he recognized that white supremacists would have to yield to changing circumstances: in Africa, he said, he detected 'a wind of change' (Macmillan 1972: 473–82). As well as his speech, the tour yielded a useful television appearance, an interview with Robin Day on 23 February 1958. Nevertheless, there was no significant running down in overseas commitments. Macmillan continued to maintain a good relationship with Kennedy, who came into office in 1961. On his own terms, his outstanding achievement came in the Nassau Agreement of December 1962 when Macmillan's pertinacious lobbying persuaded Kennedy that it was politically expedient to grant Britain Polaris submarines, though, in Kennedy's view, 'a piece of military foolishness' (Clarke 1991: 229). In February 1959 Macmillan had presented himself as someone who could speak to the Russians, going on a famous (though also much jeered at) trip to Moscow. At the end of the same year he took part in something very close to his heart, his summit conference in Paris. Macmillan's pertinacity paid off in another apparently striking event: neither Kennedy nor the rest of the British government were particularly enthusiastic about the signing of a treaty banning the testing of nuclear weapons. Yet Macmillan succeeded in bringing this about in July 1963. But Macmillan's vaunting of his ties (real and imagined) with America was the last thing to endear his bid (launched in August 1961) to join the Common Market to General de Gaulle: Macmillan was genuine in his belief in Europe, but his lack of total commitment merited the decisive veto of January 1963.

There is no fundamental incompatibility between steady economic growth and a generous welfare system. The Attlee government had demonstrated this, though admittedly in the favourable circumstances of high post-war demand; but the Attlee government had failed to renovate Britain's ageing infrastructure. By the end of the 1950s Britain's structural problems were very serious: inadequate communications, low investment, incompetent management (most notably in what should have been the fulcrum of the economy, the motor industry) and restrictive trade union practices. As Chancellor of the Exchequer, Macmillan had addressed none of these problems; he showed no more inclination to do so as prime minister. Conservative politicians were sensitive to the most obvious symptom of economic weakness, inflation, and Macmillan's first Chancellor of the Exchequer, Peter Thorneycroft, wanted to combat inflation through cuts in the welfare state. Macmillan opposed Thorneycroft's proposals, leading to the latter's resignation in January 1958, together with Nigel Birch and Enoch Powell. In a carefully prepared phrase, which was part of the assiduously cultivated (though far from bogus) 'unflappability', Macmillan spoke of 'little local difficulties'. Thorneycroft was replaced by Derrick Heathcoat Amory, who, after the election, was replaced by the docile, and broadly expansionist, Selwyn Lloyd. Under Amory the economy was expanded far too rapidly, good for the subsequent election, but not for Britain's economic health. Macmillan, of course, is associated with the arrival of affluence – and endlessly misquoted as mindlessly exulting in this. His worries about inflation come through strongly in his most famous speech of all, actually made in a football stadium in Bedford, as early as 20 July 1957 (*not* during the 1959 election campaign, though the famous phrase extracted from the speech was much quoted in that campaign):

Let's be frank about it; most of our people have never had it so good. Go around the country, go to the industrial towns, go to the farms, and you will see a state of prosperity, such as we have never had in my lifetime – nor indeed ever in the history of this country. What is beginning to worry some of us is 'Is it too good to be true?' or perhaps I should say 'Is it too good to last?'. For, amidst all this prosperity, there is one problem that has troubled us – in one way or another – ever since the war. It's the problem of rising prices. Our constant concern today is – can prices be steadied while at the same time we maintain full employment in an expanding economy? Can we control inflation? This is the problem of our time.

(Turner 1994: 228)

However, though it is important to be accurate about what Macmillan actually said, he did not in practice do anything about his concern over inflation, and did very much rejoice in, and was very ready to cash in on, rising living standards. The (pre-election) 1959 budget was later to be stigmatized as 'over-generous' and lying at the root of subsequent economic problems. What Macmillan governments undoubtedly did do was to follow a stop-go economic policy – no help to the steady investment which was so desperately needed. Inflation failed even to bring expansion: the phenomenon of 'stagflation' had arrived. By March 1962 failures to address fundamental economic problems really were coming home to roost. Macmillan sacked one-third of his cabinet, including Selwyn Lloyd, in the 'Night of Long Knives'. This may have been a tribute to Macmillan's continuing streak of ruthlessness, but it did no credit to his reputation for 'unflappability'. The quip from the Liberal leader, Jeremy Thorpe, was: 'Greater love hath no man than he lay down his friend for his life'. Harold Wilson, now leader of the Labour opposition, joked, with understandable exaggeration, that half the cabinet had been sacked – 'the wrong half, as it happened'.

By 1963 there was something of a boom in critical analyses of the weaknesses of British society, and also the more famous 'satire boom' – for which, in many ways, Macmillan was a perfect target. Macmillan was getting old, and worse was feeling old. He actually behaved with decency, as well as with the fastidiousness and fear of sexuality which had been a characteristic throughout his life, in dealing with the 'Profumo case'. Profumo, a junior minister at the War Office, had consorted sexually with a high-class prostitute, Christine Keeler, who also had a liaison with Captain Ivanov of the Russian Embassy. Security risk was joined to sexual truancy. When Profumo denied what was called 'impropriety', Macmillan believed him. When the full scandal came out, Macmillan was placed in a cruelly embarrassing position. He was in fact suffering from cancer of the prostate, and would soon need an operation. As it transpired, he triumphantly survived the operation, which had to be suddenly carried out on 10 October 1963. Yet one more ruthless act lay within his power. On 9 October he wrote to the Queen that he would have to resign – but he did not formally do so till, from his hospital bed, he had successfully done his damnedest to ensure that Douglas-Home, not Butler, should inherit the prime ministership (Turner 1994: 228).

Macmillan in 1983 memorably defined Thatcher's privatization programme as 'selling off the family silver'. Though he was very far from keeping up a profile as a critic of Thatcherism, this was enough to lead to many Thatcherites to denigrate him as a spendthrift, overly consensual prime minister. However, Richard Lamb's riposte in identifying him as 'by far the best of Britain's post-war prime ministers' cannot be sustained (Lamb 1995: 15). There have been some rather feeble cases – Eden, Douglas-Home, Callaghan and Major. The two big names (however severe the criticisms one might make of them) are Attlee and Thatcher. Macmillan falls into the middle range, alongside his wittiest critic, Wilson. The upper-class background, the ruthless determination triumphing over the shyness as the luck steadily ran his way, the application, the intellectual power and the bravery: these explain him better than the once fashionable nonsense about his being, in the words of the *Financial Times*, 'the most puzzling and enigmatic of all Britain's prime ministers'.

References and further reading
Bethell, N. (1977) *The Last Secret*, London: Deutsch. (An example of the 'conspiracy' case regarding the repatriation of anti-Soviet Russians during the Second World War.)
Carlton, D. (1981) *Anthony Eden: A Biography*, London: Allen Lane.
—— (1989) *Britain and the Suez Crisis*, Oxford: Blackwell. (A good introduction to the subject.)
Clarke, P. (1991) *A Question of Leadership*, Harmondsworth: Penguin. (A short but scintillating discussion of Macmillan's premiership.)
Evans, H. (1981) *Downing Street Diary: The Macmillan Years 1957–1963*, London: Hodder & Stoughton.
Horne, A. (1988) *Macmillan 1894–1956*, London: Macmillan.
—— (1989) *Macmillan 1957–1986*, London: Macmillan. (Lengthy two-volume official biography.)
Howard, A. (1987) *RAB: The Life of R.A. Butler*, London: Cape. (Excellent biography of one of Macmillan's main rivals.)
Kilmuir, David Patrick Maxwell Fyfe, first Earl of (1964) *Political Adventure*, London: Weidenfeld & Nicolson.
Knight, R. (1986) 'Harold Macmillan and the Cossachs: was there a Klagenfurt Conspiracy?', *Intelligence and National Security* 1: 234–54. (A thorough rebuttal of the 'conspiracy' case.)
Lamb, R. (1995) *The Macmillan Years 1957–1963: The Emerging Truth*, London: John Murray. (Lengthy analysis of Macmillan's premiership drawing on recently released documentation.)
Macmillan, H. (1933) *Reconstruction: A Plea for National Unity*, London: Macmillan. (A substantial volume on the contemporary economic situation in Britain.)
—— (1966) *Winds of Change 1914–1939*, London: Macmillan.

—— (1967) *The Beast of War 1939–1945*, London: Macmillan.

—— (1969) *Tides of Fortune 1945–1955*, London: Macmillan.

—— (1971) *Riding the Storm 1956–1959*, London: Macmillan.

—— (1972) *Pointing the Way 1959–1961*, London: Macmillan.

—— (1973) *At the End of the Day 1961–1963*, London: Macmillan. (Multi-volume series of memoirs drawing copiously on Macmillan's diaries.)

—— (1984) *War Diaries*, London: Macmillan. (An edited version.)

Marwick, A. (1964) 'Middle opinion in the 1930s: planning, progress and political "agreement"', *English Historical Review*, 79: 285–99.

Pimlott, B. (1989) 'Is the postwar consensus a myth?', *Contemporary Record* 2 (summer): 12–14.

Sampson, A. (1967) *Macmillan: A Study in Ambiguity*, London: Allen Lane.

Scott Lucas, W. (1991) *Divided We Stand: Britain, the US and the Suez Crisis*, London: Hodder & Stoughton.

Tolstoy, N. (1986) *The Minister and the Massacres*, London: Hutchinson. (Another example of the 'conspiracy' case.)

Turner, J. (1994) *Macmillan*, London: Longman. (Accessible biography of marvellous wit and cynicism.)

Arthur Marwick

Alexander Frederick Douglas-Home, Lord Home of the Hirsel

Born 2 July 1903, eldest son of the thirteenth Earl of Home and Lady Lilian Lambton. Educated at Ludgrove, Eton and Christ Church, Oxford. Became Lord Dunglass in 1918, fourteenth Earl of Home in 1951, and Sir Alec Douglas-Home on disclaiming his peerage in 1963. Married 1936 Elizabeth Alington, daughter of the headmaster of Eton and later Dean of Durham. MP for South Lanark 1931–51. Minister of State, Scottish Office 1951–5; Commonwealth Secretary 1955–61; Foreign Secretary 1961–3; Prime Minister 1963–4. Left Commons 1974, made a life peer the same year. Died 9 October 1995.

The rise of the fourteenth Earl of Home to the leadership of the Conservative party on 18 October 1963 was one of the more baffling phenomena of an era of transition in British politics. The last time anyone drawn from the Lords had led the party had been the third Marquess of Salisbury, between 1895 and 1902. Yet Home's opportunity was made possible by legislation promoted for radical reasons by a left-wing Labour MP, Anthony Wedgwood Benn. The Peerage Act became law only on 30 July 1963. Home became premier when the beleaguered Harold Macmillan fell ill, after a year of financial pressure and government scandals, notably the Profumo affair. In a secret memo, Macmillan wrote on 15 October 1963:

> Lord Home is clearly a man who represents the old, governing class at its best and those who take a reasonably impartial view of English history know how

good that can be. He is not ambitious in the sense of wanting to scheme for power, although not foolish enough to resist honour when it comes to him.

(*The Independent*, 1 January 1995)

Although the apparent decency and ingenuousness of 'Sir Alec' (he had been created a Knight of the Thistle in 1962) helped repair his party's reputation in the year before the general election on 11 October 1964, his 'evolution' was seen as reflecting the 'grouse-moor image' against which more radical elements – notably Iain Macleod and Enoch Powell – rebelled. Moreover, his lack of economic expertise contributed to the increase in the balance of payments deficit, to a record £800 million for 1964. Home left his own *mortmain*: under him the Conservative parliamentary party adopted a procedure for the annual election of the leader which in 1990 was to bring down Margaret Thatcher.

The Earls of Home (pronounced Hume) had substantial estates (over 120,000 acres in 1900 and still 96,000 in 1964) centred on the mansion of the Hirsel near Coldstream on the Anglo-Scottish border. Lord Dunglass's mother was a whiggish Lambton who voted Labour. Two of his four younger brothers were talented: Henry was an ornithologist, the 'BBC Birdman' of the 1950s, and William was a playwright, pacifist-inclined soldier (jailed for disobeying an order which he believed would endanger civilian lives) and Liberal candidate. The Coldstreamers reckoned Alec the most calculating of the family, which rather contradicted his usual air of *noblesse oblige*.

Dunglass was an Eton contemporary of Eric Blair (George Orwell), Cyril Connolly and Anthony Powell. They do not figure in his memoirs and he was similarly oblivious at Oxford to the 'Brideshead generation' of John Betjeman, Evelyn Waugh and Maurice Bowra, although he knew Harold Acton, and Connolly said of him in *Enemies of Promise* (1938) that in 'the eighteenth century, he would have become Prime Minister before he was twenty'. He took no part in the Union nor, it seems, in strike-breaking in 1926, and graduated with a third-class degree in History. As a cricketer he toured South Africa and Argentina, and then in 1927 spent two years on the family estates, shooting and fishing. These, along with a gift for tipping racehorse winners, remained interests throughout his life.

Dunglass won South Lanark in the 'National' landslide. On the protectionist wing of the Tory party, successful after the Ottawa Agreements of 1932, he was influenced by the reforming Scots Tory MP, Noel Skelton, who coined the phrase 'property-owning democracy' but died in 1935. Dunglass called himself 'as much a Clydesider' as James Maxton, David Kirkwood and company (who were friendly to him) but his tactless suggestion that miners and their families ought to migrate south to enter domestic service was mocked by Labour MPs.

In 1938, as parliamentary private secretary, Dunglass accompanied the new prime minister, Neville Chamberlain, to Munich and the negotiations which led to Hitler's takeover of Czechoslovakia. He shared Chamberlain's assessment of European power politics, regarding the Soviets as constitutionally predatory, and Germany as a possible check on them. Frustrated by the 'insanity' of Hitler, the failure of appeasement brought about a breakdown. He was diagnosed in 1940 with tuberculosis of the spine, which meant two years of near-total immobility and isolation from wartime administration and service life, although he corresponded with his former Oxford tutor (Sir) J.C. Masterman, a head of British intelligence, and educated himself, politically and religiously, reinforcing the strong anti-communism he had acquired from Chamberlain. Later, his evangelical Christianity was much influenced by Dr Billy Graham. In 1945, on returning to the House, he strongly criticized the Yalta treaties and the extension of the Soviet sphere of influence.

Dunglass lost South Lanarkshire in 1945 but won it again in 1950, only to succeed his father in 1951. He had intended to return to his estates but Churchill's response to the Scottish Covenant movement for home rule was to appoint a minister resident in Scotland. The post, under the former Chief Whip James Stuart as Secretary of State, was offered to the new Earl, who held it until 1955. Home had limited interests, and backbench life was not among them – 'I had learned early in my political life never to accept political office detached from a busy Department of State' (Home 1976: 84). He concentrated on his major interests, agriculture and foreign affairs, and ascended in the Eden and Macmillan ministries: as Commonwealth Secretary his expertise as a landowner was useful in his relations with the white dominions but his conservatism made him suspicious of the new African liberation movements, and quick to brand their leaders as irrational and immature (Home 1976: 119). As Foreign Secretary under a theatrical and innovative premier, he made little mark and was identified with none of the major currents in the party. Macmillan seems to have used him as a makeweight to more radical ministers such as Iain Macleod – 'As Colonial Secretary I had always thought him to be the wrong man in the wrong place' (Home 1976: 186) – while taking the main initiatives himself, such as the attempted entry to the Common Market in 1961, and the 'wind of change' speech which led to the secession of South Africa from the Commonwealth in the same year. Uninterested in domestic politics, the Earl caused a minor crisis in 1962, when he criticized the 'third world' members of the UN, and called for the wealthier nations to be granted commensurate power – a view not unacceptable to the Conservative rank-and-file.

On the illness of Macmillan in 1963 the Conservatives split into two camps, centrist MPs supporting Butler and the constituencies Hailsham. The ailing premier, no friend to either contender, settled on Home after 'soundings' indicated he would get general backing, although the cabinet was divided. Home disclaimed his peerage and was elected handsomely for Kinross and West Perthshire. He enjoyed a popularity with the party rank-and-file which only Thatcher would subsequently overtake, and his very amateurishness – he hated television and was an indifferent public speaker – helped him against the somewhat bogus scientism of the Labour party's Harold Wilson. The Tories made a remarkable recovery in the polls and proceeded with Macmillan's modernizing agenda, Dr Beeching's rationalization of the railways and the expansion of the universities following the Robbins report. The Minister of Power, Frederick Errol, was allowed to gift much of the North Sea 'oil province' to the multinational oil companies, in an allocation of 960 licences which later governments were to regret. Most fateful for Sir Alec was the abolition of Resale Price Maintenance in March 1964 by the President of the Board of Trade, Edward Heath. This alienated many small business people, and Home's confession that he worked out economic problems with a box of matches did not help when his Chancellor, Reginald Maudling, who saw 'no sign of any lack of confidence in sterling', bequeathed a record balance-of-payments crisis to his successor. He was lucky to lose the general election by only seven seats. In July 1965 he announced his intention to step down, and Heath was elected leader by a ballot of the Conservative parliamentary party on 2 August.

Heath had a marked 'Europeanizing' effect on the course of party policy. While in opposition Home acted as Heath's foreign affairs spokesman but in 1968, because of his popularity in Scotland, he became the Chair of a Committee on the Constitution, which reported in 1970. Its recommendation for an Assembly as a Scottish third chamber was not acted on when Heath came to office in June 1970. Home served Heath as Foreign Secretary until his ministry fell in February 1974. While Heath made Geoffrey Rippon responsible for the successful negotiations with the European Economic Community, Home (also pro-Market) tried to secure a settlement in Rhodesia with the rebel regime under Ian Smith (an agreement acceptable to Tory party opinion seemed possible). An assessment of the views of the native Zimbabweans through their tribal chiefs indicated that an agreement acceptable to Tory opinion was possible, but this failed after a campaign by Bishop Abel Muzorewa, when control slipped out of the hands of the chiefs.

Home's major initiative was to expel 108 Soviet spies in 1973, but he did not seem to realize how oil politics, fostered by growing world scarcity, was imposing a new balance of its own. Heath had wanted to retain an East-of-Suez presence, but in mid-1971 the Foreign Office, Ministry of Defence and Treasury reversed this line, though he distanced himself from the American–Israeli alliance in the Yom Kippur War. Retiring from politics and returning to the Lords in November 1974, as Lord Home of the Hirsel, he intervened effectively in February 1979, when he advised Scots to reject Labour's devolution measure for a Conservative offer of 'something better'. After the return of Thatcher in May no more was heard of this.

In his 1963 memo Macmillan contrasted the values of Lord Home's generation with those of the younger men, claiming that the former 'think about the question under discussion and not about themselves'. This might seem to distance Home from the obsessive economic individualism of the Thatcher years, but the continuity was there, both in his somewhat ruthless manoeuvrability and in his anti-communism – and in the gap between flattering image and a less successful reality.

References and further reading

Cannadine, D. (1990) *The Decline and Fall of the British Aristocracy*, New Haven, CT and London: Yale University Press. (Sees Lord Home as 'the very end of the thin purple line'.)

Dickie, J. (1964) *The Uncommon Commoner*, London: Pall Mall. (Partisan biography by *Daily Mail*, but informative on foreign policy.)

Home, Lord (1976) *The Way the Wind Blows*, London: Collins. (Somewhat laconic autobiography.)

—— (1983) *Letters to a Grandson*, London: Collins. (Interesting on his political principles.)

Home, W.D. (1991) *Old Men Remember*, London: Collins. (Amusing family memoir.)

Margach, J. (1984) *The Anatomy of Power*, London: W.H. Allen. (Shrewd and on the whole complimentary.)

Young, K. (1970) *Sir Alec Douglas-Home*, London: Dent. (Partisan but pretty comprehensive.)

Christopher Harvie

(James) Harold Wilson, Lord Wilson of Rievaulx

Born 11 March 1916, son of James Herbert and Ethel Wilson. Educated at Royds Hall Secondary School, Huddersfield, and Jesus College, Oxford. Married 1939 Gladys Mary Baldwin, daughter of Revd D. Baldwin. MP for Ormskirk 1945–50, Huyton 1950–76. Director of Economics and Statistics, Ministry of Fuel and Power 1943–4; Parliamentary Secretary to Minister of Works 1945–7; Secretary for Overseas Trade 1947; President of the Board of Trade October 1947–51; Leader of the Labour Party 1963–76; Prime Minister 1964–70 and 1974–6; Leader of the Opposition 1963–4 and 1970–4. Resigned 1976. Left Commons 1979; made a life peer 1983. Died 24 May 1995.

Harold Wilson has secured a prominent place in British history as Labour's longest serving prime minister and one of the leading political figures of the post-war period. Yet the nature and significance of his political contribution remain widely contested. Two radically different images recurred in the tributes and assessments which followed his death: according to the first, he was a machiavellian and untrustworthy opportunist; according to the second he was a benign, pragmatic and quintessentially provincial English figure. Both pictures have informed judgements of his political career: while some commentators stress the expediency and disillusionment which characterized government under his stewardship, others celebrate his ability to ride successive political crises and bring stability and good sense to British government.

Ever since the crises and disillusionment which accompanied his first spells in office from 1964 to 1970, Wilson has been demonized by sections of the British left who regard his lack of vision and excessive pragmatism as the causes of the betrayal of the radical hopes of his generation (Williams 1968). But in the wake of his death, several commentators and politicians, including the Labour leader Tony Blair, portrayed Wilson as well attuned to the *zeitgeist* of the 1960s – socially aspirant, modern and egalitarian in outlook (Blair 1995). Three major biographical studies published in the years preceding his death provide a welter of information and fresh reflection on many episodes within his career, contributing in two cases to a qualified rehabilitation of his reputation (A. Morgan 1992; Pimlott 1992; Ziegler 1993). In political terms, the limitations of the Thatcher governments' attempts to provide remedies for many of the problems which beset Labour in power under Wilson have stimulated calls for a more balanced reappraisal of his years in office (McKibbin 1991).

All of his recent biographers illustrate the politically formative nature of some of his earliest experiences, not least the nonconformist radicalism he inherited from his grandfather, the unemployment of his father (an industrial chemist by trade) in the 1930s, and his self-discipline, classroom popularity and academic success. These attributes were abundantly evident throughout his student days and proved useful in his first post-university occupation as a research assistant for the remorseless William Beveridge. His political journey into Labour circles was neither predetermined nor conventional. At Oxford he joined the Liberal Club, switching to Labour at the end of the 1930s. He became the successful candidate for Ormskirk in Lancashire, an industrious civil servant, and then a junior minister in the post-war Labour government – despite his lack of experience within labour movement politics. These early administrative experiences shaped his political outlook considerably, bequeathing a firm commitment to the socially progressive benefits of rationally designed, statistically grounded policy initiatives; his undoubted desire for change within British society was inseparable from the belief that reform could be administered only from above, by a trained bureaucratic elite.

In other respects, though, the significance of his eclectic political and cultural inheritance, and the absence of an apprenticeship within party or union circles, remain under-explored in academic and biographical work on him. His unusual journey into Labour's ranks resulted in a lack of understanding of the world of the movement's grassroots, especially the intricate workings of trade union politics. This unfamiliarity was in many ways remedied by the experiences he gained as chairman of a committee on party organization in 1955. And some of his most salient characteristics – 'the zeal for self-improvement, the pursuit of social mobility and security, the insistence on the central place of morality in politics, the participation in a variety of high-minded cultural activities' (Howell 1993: 180) – struck chords with the movement.

Equally important within his political make-up were his experiences and relationships within the Labour party. Wilson never sat easily within the highly factionalized world of Labour politics in the 1940s and 1950s. He confounded many of his contemporaries by joining Aneurin Bevan and John Freeman in resigning from the cabinet over the issue of national health charges in 1951. While this move won him the admiration of some on the left of the party, he was regarded with suspicion by many others – as a career-orientated schemer whose behaviour was unpredictable and deeply self-interested. This feeling deepened when in 1954, formally aligned with the left-wing Bevanite faction, he accepted the offer of a seat in the shadow cabinet as Bevan's replacement following the latter's resignation on foreign and defence policy. Both right and left remained uneasy about his political trajectory and motives, though many respected his obvious talents. This distance from the factional politics of the 1950s was also the product of his social alienation from the grouping around Hugh Gaitskell, which was emerging as the dominant force on the party's right. The Gaitskellite 'set', with its Hampstead base, was imbued with a particular mixture of intellectual and social cosmopolitanism which was far removed from Wilson's own cultural background. Gaitskell's appointment to the post of Shadow Chancellor in 1951 laid the seeds for a generally strained relationship between the two. Alienated from the Gaitskellites, and suspected by Gaitskell himself, Wilson felt his place within the party's elite to be precarious.

His ambiguous position in relation to the dominant groups in the party became a source of strength following Gaitskell's unexpected death in 1963. Presenting himself as a candidate with a left pedigree who could also appeal to other sections of the party, he defeated George Brown and James Callaghan for the leadership. In the following months he oversaw one of the most impressive periods which Labour in opposition has ever experienced, and one of the most dynamic of his own career. Launching a fierce campaign against the outdated and class-ridden culture pervading British society under Tory rule, Wilson developed an alternative picture of Britain's future development. This centred around his belief in the state's capacity to construct a new macro-economic framework and to oversee the expansion of science and technological innovation within a more modern and dynamic economy. These ideas underpinned the programme which he outlined during the 1964 election campaign. They stemmed from his acute sense of the relative disadvantages facing the British economy in the 1960s, a position he put down to the absence of a political culture of enterprise and modernity within key industrial sectors. While it is easy to exaggerate the impact of Wilson's rhetoric on a cautious and sceptical public, this amounted to a distinctive and appealing vision which simultaneously allowed him to sidestep the most divisive doctrinal questions within the labour movement coalition.

The first eighteen months of the new government are generally regarded as one of Wilson's most successful spells in office. Despite a tiny overall majority, his management of both the party and the Commons was sufficiently effective to engineer working majorities for the administration. In 1966 he went to the polls and was rewarded with a small overall majority. The conditions seemed set for a new era of social and economic reform to rival the achievements of the Attlee administration; instead many within the party and movement became profoundly disillusioned with, and alienated from, the government (Foot 1968; Lapping 1970).

With the increased majority which Wilson possessed after the 1966 election, the excuse for caution provided by the government's previously precarious parliamentary position was no longer available. Almost immediately problems arose in the form of the seamen's strike, a renewed sterling crisis, cuts in public expenditure and the effective abandonment of the Wilsonite planning strategy. The sterling crisis of 1966 provided a dramatic indication that Labour's economic strategy was in ruins. Together with Callaghan and Brown, he had already taken the highly significant decision, in 1964, to avoid devaluation and defend sterling. This set the Labour administrations of the 1960s on a deflationary road that culminated in confrontation with the unions as government sought first to freeze and then control wages, and also to restrict the growth of public expenditure. In 1964, and again more controversially in 1966, Wilson clung to the strategy of shoring up sterling. Hindsight suggests that both decisions were damaging to the British economy, but his own experience of the political trauma associated with devaluation (in 1949) convinced him that it represented too great a political risk.

The government was continuously on the defensive after 1966. As inflation drove the cost of living upwards, and disillusionment set in, Wilson was faced by a spate of militant union actions. In response he sponsored one of the most radical and controversial legislative moves of his career: *In Place of Strife*, a White Paper drawn up by Barbara Castle, was designed to regulate the rising tide of unofficial industrial actions. His defeat on these issues in 1969, as the majority of the cabinet came out in open opposition, symbolized his increasing estrangement from many in the labour movement. The government's failure to maintain previous levels of economic growth – the prerequisite for the industrial peace of the 1940s and 1950s – placed the economy under even greater pressure, and called into question the political and social relationships which the post-war 'settlement' of the 1940s and 1950s had stabilized.

Placed in the context of a longer term series of socio-economic developments, Wilson's period in office appears in a slightly different light. By the mid-1960s, the British economy was struggling to cope with new international economic trends and was reaping the dividend of a pattern of economic development which had been laid down in the nineteenth century. In this context, some commentators have argued that Wilson's attempts to bolster sterling, hold the party together and avoid the ravages of either excessive inflation or the increasingly pronounced stop-go tendencies in the economy, represented the only realistic course available (McKibbin 1991). But Wilson's optimistic rhetoric in the mid-1960s encouraged the view that remedies to these problems were relatively painless and required little in the way of wider political and institutional transformation. In particular, the belief that the state, through an enhanced and dynamic planning strategy, could provide a more suitable framework for improving the competitiveness of British industry, was accompanied by a staunch conservatism about fiscal and monetary policy. On the latter Wilson conducted a sophisticated, though short-sighted, holding operation, convinced that reform in these areas was politically dangerous and economically unnecessary. Yet his belief that fluctuations in the financial markets and monetary policy more generally could be separated from Labour's wider macro-economic goals foundered on the harsh realities of the British economy, especially as the growth rates of the previous decade began to tail off.

His particular style of political management tended to produce a 'bunker mentality' within his administrations as they dealt with economic crises. Policy was inseparable, as with most politicians, from calculations of party advantage and sensitivity to the balance of power within the cabinet, but Wilson took awareness of these considerations further than any of his political contemporaries. His intense political insecurity, extensively chronicled by his recent biographers, led him to surround himself with a coterie of non-parliamentary lieutenants (notably his long-serving secretary Marcia Williams). This group was often impenetrable to others, and from 1974 to 1976 was seriously divided: throughout these years Wilson and his 'kitchen cabinet' were endlessly fascinated by political intrigue. This atmosphere merely encouraged the short-termism prevalent within his administrations, to the detriment of clear and coherent policy development.

This aspect of his leadership was often most visible in his handling of foreign affairs. As with economic matters, Wilson's periods in office coincided with some profound dislocations and the emergence of harsh new realities for Britain. The fall-out from the end of empire exerted a slow and destabilizing effect on British foreign policy and self-perception, as well as generating immediate problems for the government. These included the need to oversee the transition to a post-colonial regime in former British colonies such as Rhodesia, as well as the impact of the emergence of national liberation struggles around the world. These threatened protracted conflicts in the context of an intensifying Cold War between the superpowers. The United States' involvement in Vietnam provided the most troubling foreign policy issue for Wilson in this period. To his critics, his behaviour on this issue was shrouded in calculations of political advantage rather than obvious doctrinal principle. The support he declared for President Johnson's policies horrified many within the party and beyond, for whom Wilson's stance came to symbolize the government's lack of principle in its dealings with other nations (its unsympathetic treatment of Kenya's Asian community in 1968 also enraged many). Yet his stance on Vietnam can be interpreted more benevolently: his room for manoeuvre in dealing with Johnson was greatly limited by British dependence on American financial support. He therefore adopted a course between these competing imperatives, offering only moral, not military, support to the United States.

The most important principle which governed his foreign policy decisions concerned his perception of British interests in its new post-imperial role. He proved reluctant to wind down Britain's military presence 'East of Suez', though he was compelled by economic considerations to do so. By 1966–7 membership of the Common Market was seen by some of the cabinet as an important arena for the assertion of British influence. Yet, like many others in the political establishment, Wilson was generally unwilling to consider the longer term implications of the abandonment of Britain's imperial possessions. At times this bordered on a refusal to face the geopolitical realities of the post-war world, leading him to overestimate Britain's (and his own) influence in world affairs. In Rhodesia, his (over)confidence in his own ability to negotiate a settlement foundered on his underestimation of the obduracy of the constituencies represented by Ian Smith, the white Rhodesian leader. In Northern Ireland, Labour had little choice but to send in troops to protect the minority Catholic population; yet a clear sense of strategic goals was generally absent in its dealings here.

Despite the adverse atmosphere in which policy was conducted throughout these years, the 1966–70 adminstration was responsible for some pathbreaking legislation in the fields of social policy and educational provision. During Roy Jenkins's tenure as Home Secretary a raft of progressive legislation concerning homosexual, sexual and racial equality was placed on the statute book, though Wilson himself was uneasy about some of this. He played a more active role in a programme of educational reform and expansion, founding the Open University and supporting the establishment of a number of new universities.

In June 1970, as the country's economic position was beginning to stabilize, Wilson called an election which, on balance, he thought he would win. In the event, he narrowly lost to the Conservatives under Heath. Wilson's tenure in opposition was at first marked by a surprising indifference, spending his time writing a lengthy, self-justificatory account of his time in office (Wilson 1971). As a new set of economic problems coincided with a series of social and moral 'panics' 1971–3, he returned to his energetic best, denouncing the Heath government's inability to manage the economy and its increasingly antagonistic relationship with the unions, especially after the bitter dispute with the miners which began in 1972.

Within the Labour party, however, important changes to the prevailing balance of forces were taking shape. Chastened by the disappointments of 1964–70, the mood of much of the grassroots in the party and unions began to shift leftwards. From inside the shadow cabinet Tony Benn emerged as the champion of this defiant new mood. Some of the radical commitments contained within 'Labour's Programme 1973' – including major extensions of public ownership and greater state intervention in the economy – reflected this shift of opinion. Despite his lack of sympathy for these goals, Wilson fought an effective campaign in the election of February 1974, focusing upon the government's inability to cope with rising inflation and unemployment, and blaming it for the hardships associated with the three-day week. Labour's slender victory, however, ensured that he took office in economic conditions that were even less propitious: as inflation spiralled out of control in the aftermath of the 1973 oil crisis, prices and unemployment rose alarmingly.

These problems provided the backdrop to the years of the next Labour administrations. At first the government responded with a mildly expansionist budgetary policy, borrowing heavily to subsidize food prices and funding increases in state pensions. Wilson's intention was to keep inflation to a reasonable level and send the country to the polls again as soon as possible. This strategy secured a small swing to the party in the election of October 1974 and an overall parliamentary majority of three. In the following months the government was beset by two particular difficulties. First, on the question of the Common Market Labour was committed to renegotiating Britain's terms of entry. But the only conditions that Wilson and his Foreign Secretary Callaghan could secure fell short of those demanded by many Labour activists. In this divisive and potentially damaging situation, Wilson responded by calling for a referendum in which he allowed party members to campaign on different sides. The overwhelming majority for entry in the final vote vindicated his strategy, though some of the fundamental questions about the nation's identity and role in Europe were displaced rather than resolved by this move. More immediately, the divisions which this issue unleashed during 1974–5 revealed that Wilson had, for the first time, lost control of the party. For all his political skills as a reconciling leader, he was finding Labour's increasingly disparate and divided coalition almost impossible to manage.

Domestic economic policy was the second, equally troublesome policy area facing the government. Scrapping the incomes policy of his previous administration, Wilson negotiated a 'social contract' with the unions, seeking to regulate the process of wage bargaining in return for the extension of welfare benefits which would be paid for by a more redistributive taxation policy and large-scale borrowing. This strategy was severely undermined by the deepening of the world recession in 1975, and the consequent drop in British exports and decline in economic growth. Inflation was now running at unprecedented levels. Increasingly fearful of the country's economic position, the Chancellor, Denis Healey, forced the reversal of Labour's economic strategy: in his April budget he raised income tax dramatically and pushed through swingeing defence cuts and reductions in subsidies for prices and nationalized industries. Despite reservations Wilson went along with this change of tack, and supported Healey's overtures to the International Monetary Fund (IMF) in 1975. This alienated the left of the party still further. In June he removed Benn from the key post of Industry Secretary. Though Healey's remedies appeared to be reaping dividends towards the end of the year, as wage increases and inflation began to slow down, Labour's ratings in the polls had plummeted.

In March 1976, following two embarrassing government defeats in the Commons, Wilson pulled off his most impressive political coup of all – a shock announcement of his resignation, which took nearly everyone by surprise. This has elicited a number of conspiratorial interpretations, ranging from impending revelations about his pro-Soviet links from Secret Service sources, to his recognition of the onset of a debilitating illness. The truth, as with much of his career, probably involves a more mundane mixture of personal and political calculation.

Perhaps the most distinctive aspect of his management of the party throughout these years stemmed from his detachment from its predominant factions – he was 'Mr-facing-two-ways' according to one of his critics (Hall 1989: 30). As he rose within the party in the late 1950s, and then as leader, he proved a highly successful establishment figure – wary of the left, instinctively cautious in policy terms and willing to draw upon different aspects of Labour's traditions and culture. But in other respects he maintained a rapport with the politics of Labour's left, often deploying a radical-sounding rhetoric on economic issues and a highly ethical tone on policy questions. Figures from across the party came to resent Wilson's politics bitterly, but he was familiar with the mind-set of Labour's different groupings and highly skilful at holding this coalition together in the most trying of circumstances. In this sense, he remained closer to the 'soul' of the party than many of his senior colleagues (Marquand 1991). But as several of their memoirs reveal, Wilson inspired an unusual degree of suspicion and hostility during his time as prime minister (J. Morgan 1981; Benn 1987; 1989). More generally, the depth and degree of disillusionment which the 1966–70 administration aroused within the party and beyond is almost unrivalled. Recent scholarship has tended to present a more favourable and balanced account of his years in office (Coopey et al. 1993), but a full explanation of how and why such hostile reactions to Wilson emerged remains more elusive.

A large part of this explanation stems from the collapse of the project – of a confidently expansionist, modernist and technocratic social democracy – which he laid before the British public from 1963 to 1964. This vision was highly influential in governing circles in the mid-1960s and became the focus for a wide array of social and political aspirations, many of which were encouraged by Wilson's optimistic and confident rhetoric. His public discourse astutely captured the spirit of the age, presenting a dynamic and attractive vision of a national future in which both security and enterprise would be secured. But in practice this project proved surprisingly brittle. It unravelled as economic crises and political pressure sapped the will of the party's elite to carry forward the programme of expansion in social expenditure and state-led reorganization of the economy. Much of the debate about how and why this project failed has centred around fetishistic accounts of Wilson's betrayal or incompetence (Tiratsoo in Coopey et al. 1993), or has encouraged overgeneralized accounts of the inherent conservatism of Labour's ethos and ideology. But explanation should be sought in other areas too: the impact of some profound structural problems within the British economy; the paucity of realistic and considered policy alternatives from other sections of the party in these years; and the increasingly difficult task of party management in the late 1960s (Coates 1980; Marquand 1991; Howell 1993).

The failures of this period have had some momentous consequences, providing a legacy which continues to affect recollections of Wilson's period as prime minister. Within the party, the demise of his project as well as the absence of his authority after 1976 allowed full rein to right and left to advance their very different causes. The divisiveness which characterized Labour's subsequent internal politics had disastrous electoral consequences for the party after 1979. In terms of Labour's subsequent approach to the management and reform of Britain's political economy, the disappointments of the Wilson era contributed to the marked scepticism about the benefits of state intervention on many economic questions under Neil Kinnock's leadership of the party. Equally Margaret Thatcher and her New Right allies were undoubtedly able to legitimize their radical programme for rolling back the state and unleashing the forces of the market by conflating the relative decline of the British economy of the late 1960s and early 1970s with Labour policy under Wilson.

Yet Wilson's political legacy can be presented more positively. His recognition of the need to construct an alternative macro-economic framework for the British economy, based on new kinds of relationships between the public and private sectors, anticipated aspects of Labour's economic rethinking in the 1980s. Indeed, Wilson was one of the first post-war Labour thinkers to consider the relationship between markets, state and society outside the often sterile orthodoxies of the party's left and right. In this respect, his ideas were premised on a relatively hardheaded assessment of the long-term weaknesses of the British economy. The inability of his administrations to develop the framework he desired was as much the product of fierce opposition and institutional conservatism as his own weaknesses. Likewise, his desperate attempts to hold the party together in government around a broadly Keynesian commitment to increased social expenditure and reductions in unemployment, foundered on circumstances which were mainly beyond his control, not least the downturn in the economy's rate of growth and the oil crisis of the early 1970s. It remains unclear whether Labour could have feasibly pursued an alternative strategy with any success in these circumstances.

But in other respects the implications and legacy of the Wilson era remain troubling for the left. At a time when profound social and cultural change opened up a set of new issues and themes within British political life, and produced a more diversified and differentiated civil society, Wilson refused to think beyond Labour's traditional approaches to politics and mobilization. By the 1970s these left Labour increasingly out of kilter with changes taking place both in the party and society at large. The party's administrative machinery and constitutional mechanisms were increasingly unable to deliver support for the leadership on all issues; while the emergence of a substantially new political mood and the propagation of different social and cultural values passed unnoticed. Wilson's unchanging belief that social and economic progress could be delivered by the party once it had captured power within the state was increasingly at odds with popular scepticism about Labour's economic management and disenchantment with the kinds of bureaucratic provision which Labour had traditionally delivered. Though most accounts of Wilson's demise stress the importance of his inability to manage and understand the party after 1970, of even greater significance was his lack of comprehension of the changing public mood of the late 1960s and early 1970s. The tough decisions facing any social democratic politician in a period of economic decline and retrenchment necessitated the orchestration of the loyalty of different social groups. This Wilson failed to achieve after 1966, finding that his support melted away as each crisis arose. Despite his continual anxieties about opinion polls and obsessive electoral calculations, his vision of a more modern and dynamic society overseen by a benign, corporate state, failed to take root in the political imagination of the British public after the 'honeymoon' years of 1963–4.

Towards the end of the 1970s, Labour was singularly vulnerable to the arguments mounted by the Thatcherite right which allied itself with the new mood of popular disenchantment and disaffection.

For the contemporary left, coming to terms with the legacy of Wilson means not just a re-evaluation of the minutiae of the policy decisions and choices which he made during his time in office, but also involves the critical reappraisal of some of the most fundamental and deeply buried assumptions about politics, the economy and social reform which sustained Labour in government in these years.

References and further reading

Benn, A. (1987) *Out of the Wilderness: Diaries, 1963–67*, London: Hutchinson.
—— (1989) *Against the Tide: Diaries, 1973–76*, London: Hutchinson.
Blair, T. (1995) 'Lessons of the Wilson years', *The Independent* 25 May.
Coates, D. (1980) *Labour in Power? A Study of the Labour Government, 1974–1979*, London: Longman.
Coopey, R., Fielding, S. and Tiratsoo, N. (eds) (1993) *The Wilson Governments 1964–1970*, London and New York: Pinter. (Includes a number of perceptive essays which seek to debunk overly critical accounts of these administrations.)
Foot, P. (1968) *The Politics of Harold Wilson*, Harmondsworth: Penguin. (Influential left-wing critique of Wilsonism, which places the failings of his government firmly in the context of the limitations of labourism.)
Haines, J. (1977) *The Politics of Power*, London: Cape. (An insider's account of Wilson's administrations, which shows a high regard for his political skills and illustrates the troubled atmosphere of the 'kitchen cabinet'.)
Hall, S. (1989) 'The first new left: life and times', in R. Archer *et al.* (eds) *Out of Apathy: Voices of the New Left Thirty Years On*, Verso: London.
Howell, D. (1993) '1966 and all that', *Twentieth Century British History* 4: 174–87. (A stimulating review essay which examines the merits and weaknesses of Wilson's historiography.)
Lapping, B. (1970) *The Labour Government 1964–70*, Harmondsworth: Penguin. (A largely defensive account of the government's policy, stressing the constraints imposed by international economic forces.)
McKibbin, R. (1991) 'Homage to Wilson and Callaghan', *London Review of Books* 24 October.
Marquand, D. (1991) 'Harold Wilson: alibi for a party?', in *The Progressive Dilemma*, London: Heinemann. (Thoughtful and perceptive reappraisal which challenges some of the most common assumptions about Wilson's politics and career.)
Morgan, A. (1992) *Harold Wilson*, London: Pluto. (Generally lively biography which is peppered with harsh judgements of its subject.)
Morgan, J. (ed.) (1981) *The Backbench Diaries of Richard Crossman*, London: Hamilton, Cape.
Morgan, K. (1987) 'Harold Wilson', in *Labour People: Leaders and Lieutenants, Hardie to Kinnock*, Oxford: Oxford University Press.
Pimlott, B. (1992) *Harold Wilson*, London: HarperCollins. (Lengthy and impressive biography based upon extensive archival research and numerous interviews. Sheds light on some of the most controversial episodes of his career.)
Roth, A. (1977) *Sir Harold Wilson: Yorkshire's Walter Mitty*, London: Macdonald &

Jane's. (Famous because Wilson took out an injunction against the author, this biography provides a critical overview of Wilson's personality and achievements.)

Williams, R. (ed.) (1968) *May Day Manifesto, 1968*, Harmondsworth: Penguin. (Highly influential critique of Labour's policies penned by some of Britain's leading radical intellectuals.)

Wilson, H. (1971) *The Labour Government 1964–70*, Harmondsworth: Penguin.

—— (1979) *Final Term: The Labour Government 1974–1976*, London: Weidenfeld & Nicolson.

Ziegler, P. (1993) *The Political Life of Lord Wilson of Rievaulx*, London: Weidenfeld & Nicolson. (The authorized biography of Wilson, which offers a perceptive account of his political career, stressing his involvement in foreign affairs and relations with international statesmen.)

Michael Kenny

Edward Richard George Heath

Born 9 July 1916, first child of William Heath and Edith Pantony. Educated at Chatham House School, Ramsgate, and Balliol College, Oxford. Unmarried. MP for Bexley 1950–74, Sidcup 1974–83, Old Bexley and Sidcup 1983–. Conservative Whip 1951–5; Chief Whip 1955–9; Minister of Labour 1959–60; Lord Privy Seal 1960–3; Secretary for Trade and Industry 1963–4; Shadow Chancellor of the Exchequer 1964–5; Leader of the Opposition 1965–70; Prime Minister 1970–4; Leader of the Opposition 1974–5. Father of the House 1992–. Knight of the Garter 1992.

Edward Heath was leader of the Conservatives for almost ten years from 1965 to 1975, but for most of this time he was Leader of the Opposition. He served as prime minister for only three years eight months from June 1970 to February 1974. As Conservative leader he fought four general elections but lost three of them. His period in office was relatively brief, and ended in spectacular disarray and high drama created by the oil crisis, the miners' strike, the imposition of a three-day week on industry, and the decision to call an election on the issue of who governs Britain, which the government lost. In 1975 Heath lost the leadership of the Conservative party to Thatcher. Partisans of the new leader regarded the Heath government as having betrayed Conservative principles, and specifically the manifesto pledges on which it was elected. During Thatcher's leadership Heath became an increasingly isolated figure, often critical of the direction of policy, particularly on the economy, social policy and Europe. Heath and Thatcher represent different strands in twentieth-century Conservatism, and the battle between their visions of what the Conservative party should stand for is still unresolved. Yet the polarization between them should not be exaggerated. Heath's premiership can be plausibly seen both as the last attempt to govern within the constraints of the post-war settlement and as anticipating the programme which the Thatcher governments attempted to carry out in the 1980s.

Douglas Hurd has described Heath as a Tory reformer in the tradition of Peel and William Pitt: the aim of Tory reform was not to enlarge the power of the state, but to 'sweep away whatever was antiquated and inefficient in our public institutions and create a new framework within which the individual could take his own responsibilities and create his own prosperity' (Hurd 1979: 13). Heath wanted to lead a great reforming administration which would modernize British institutions and government, reverse the relative decline of the British economy, and define a new role for Britain in the world. His success was limited. His single most important achievement was the successful negotiation of entry into the European Community. But few of his legislative changes and administrative reforms have endured, and Britain's economic and political problems worsened. His government was overwhelmed by a combination of domestic conflicts and external pressures, and ended prematurely.

Heath did not have the traditional attributes of either birth or wealth normally required for a Conservative political career. He was born and brought up in Broadstairs. His father was a carpenter, who later became the owner and manager of a small building firm. His mother was in service before she married. Given this background he relied heavily upon educational opportunities. He won a scholarship to Chatham House School, Ramsgate, a fee-paying grammar school, and from there he went to Balliol College, Oxford, to read Politics, Philosophy and Economics. He became President of the Union and President of the Oxford University Conservative Association, and showed early political independence by working for the anti-Munich candidate, A.D. Lindsay, in the 1938 Oxford by-election. He served with distinction in the Royal Artillery during the war, rising to the rank of colonel. After the war he came top in the civil service examination. He entered the Commons as MP for Bexley with a majority of 133 in 1950.

His rise was not at first as spectacular as some of the other stars of the 1950 cohort, such as Iain Macleod, Reginald Maudling and Enoch Powell. He was recruited to the Whips' office, and became Chief Whip in 1955, playing an important role in holding the party together during the Suez crisis. In 1959 he entered the cabinet as Minister of Labour, but his real breakthrough came the following year when he was made Lord Privy Seal and entrusted with the negotiations for entry to the European Community. Although the negotiations were ultimately unsuccessful because of the French veto, Heath became established as a rising star, and a strong pro-European.

In 1963 Douglas-Home made him Minister of Trade, Industry and Regional Development. He carried through legislation which partially abolished Resale Price Maintenance, against the opposition of the small business lobby. It further identified Heath with the reforming modernizing wing of the party, which wanted to increase economic efficiency and competition.

After the Conservatives' election defeat in 1964 Heath became Shadow Chancellor, a role in which he was able to demonstrate his potential as a future leader during the 1965 Finance Bill. When Home resigned in 1965, Heath, Maudling and Powell contested the first Conservative leadership election. Although

Maudling was initially the favourite and the more experienced, Heath narrowly won the first round (Heath had 150 votes, Maudling 133, Powell 15) after which Maudling conceded. Heath was chosen because he represented the meritocratic, modernizing wing of the party, and likely to be an effective opponent for Harold Wilson.

Defeat in the 1966 general election, eight months after Heath was elected leader, ensured that the Conservatives could expect no early return to office. The years of opposition were spent preparing for government. Heath set up a detailed policy review which at its height involved thirty separate study groups. Heath was determined to ensure that he had a full legislative programme worked out and ready to implement, although critics of this approach to opposition argued that it committed the party to a set of specific policies which might not be appropriate in the altered circumstances of government.

The Conservatives fought the 1970 election on a programme of modernization. Like the earlier modernization programmes of the Macmillan government 1960–2 and the Labour government 1964–6, it aimed to reverse the relative decline of the British economy and the political overload of British government. But at the same time it struck some new notes. In their recoil from the failed interventionist measures of the Wilson government, the Conservatives under Heath put much more emphasis on the need to limit government and release private initiative and enterprise. In this sense the Heath programme of 1970–2, set out at the Selsdon Park meeting in early 1970, anticipated in important respects the Thatcher programme of the 1980s. Both emphasized the importance of reducing rates of direct taxation, limiting government intervention, cutting back public expenditure, introducing greater selectivity in welfare, and reforming industrial relations. The key difference between the two was that Heath wanted a small reduction in government as a means to improve the performance of the economy which would then release greater funds for welfare and the public sector. The Thatcherites sought to roll back the state as a matter of principle.

The four core policies of the 1970 programme were reform of taxation, reform of industrial relations, reform of welfare, and reform of central and local government administration. Underpinning all these, however, was the commitment to negotiate entry into the European Community. Europe was important in two ways. It signalled a new global role for a post-imperial Britain. Heath was the first British prime minister to give Britain's European role greater priority than its Atlanticist or Commonwealth role. He did not regard the other roles as unimportant, but he was opposed to fostering illusions about Britain's global power and influence or where Britain's real interests now lay. He believed that building a successful European partnership was vital to Britain's future prosperity and security.

Britain's membership of the European Community was important in a second sense. It was the indispensable framework within which domestic reform could be pursued. Britain needed to be modernized and its institutions reformed to compete effectively with the other member states in the European Community.

Heath's political objectives in Europe could be realized only if the British economy became stronger. More open competition and the example of best practice elsewhere in the Community were seen as the spurs to raise efficiency in Britain.

Heath strongly supported the pooling of sovereignty and the creation of supranational European institutions where appropriate. He believed that a Britain wholeheartedly committed to Europe, and with the new energy and improved performance which Community membership would inspire, would be in a strong position to shape the future direction of the Community.

Heath did not perform well as Leader of the Opposition and always trailed his party in poll ratings, but the Conservatives won the 1970 general election convincingly with a 4.8 per cent swing and a majority of thirty. Since he had been widely expected to lose, his victory gave him a new confidence and authority. His personality and talents were much better suited to government than opposition. He was at his best working with small teams to achieve clearly defined objectives. He attracted enormous loyalty from those who worked closely with him. No one resigned from his cabinet on policy grounds and only two of the shadow cabinet are known to have voted against him in 1975. He was often a poor communicator on television and in parliament, or in front of large audiences. He had a reputation for rudeness and insensitivity in dealing with those, especially backbenchers, who were not directly working for him.

As prime minister he developed a close understanding and sympathy with top civil servants, particularly William Armstrong, which often exceeded that achieved with ministers. He appreciated civil servants' grasp of detail and commitment to the public interest. His absorption in the detail of government administration may at times have insulated him from political advice. He had few senior colleagues who could give him such advice. The death of Iain Macleod a few weeks after the election was a serious loss.

Heath was often intolerant of opposition and preferred, like Peel, to lead from the front. He dominated his cabinet and his party, but he could also be flexible, even over something as important as Europe. In the crucial division on 28 October 1971 Heath was reluctantly persuaded by his Chief Whip, Francis Pym, to allow a free vote, to enable the pro-European wing of the Labour party to vote for entry. Thirty-nine Conservatives voted against but they were more than outweighed by the sixty-nine Labour MPs who defied their party and voted with the government. Heath's style of leadership did increase the level of dissent in the parliamentary party, although it never approached the levels that were to be experienced under Thatcher and Major.

One of the most notable features of the Heath government was its concerted attempt to reform the machinery of the state to make government more efficient. The changes included the establishment of Programme Analysis Review (PAR) to identify savings in public expenditure, and the Central Policy Review Staff (CPRS) to advise on policy options; the creation of new super departments such as Environment, and Trade and Industry; task forces of ministers and civil servants; new independent functional agencies such as the Procurement Executive;

and a complete reorganization of both local government and the National Health Service. PAR, CPRS and the task forces were designed to enable the cabinet to take strategic decisions. The problem for the government was that the pressure of events rarely allowed it to think beyond crisis management.

The Heath government came into office at a time of growing problems in the world economy. The international monetary system established at Bretton Woods was no longer viable – it finally collapsed in 1971 – and the conditions for full employment, low inflation and rapid growth, which had existed for twenty years, were rapidly disappearing. Inflationary pressures were being transmitted through demands for bigger profits, increased public expenditure, and higher pay claims.

The priority of the Heath government was to find a way to maintain and if possible increase the rate of economic growth in order to fund the public sector and rising living standards while keeping control over inflation. The accumulation of pressures, particularly in the labour and the financial markets, made economic management increasingly difficult.

Opinion was beginning to polarize over how to respond to this new economic problem. Heath repudiated the solutions of the Labour government, but he also rejected the free-market solutions offered by Enoch Powell, who had been sacked as Shadow Defence spokesman by Heath after his 1968 speech on immigration. Powell became Heath's severest internal party critic on a wide range of issues, including economic management, entry to the European Community, and the Union with Northern Ireland, as well as immigration. He managed to vote against the party whip on 113 occasions during the 1970–4 parliament.

One of Powell's specific charges was that the Heath government betrayed the party and its own manifesto by reversing several key policies, particularly on immigration, incomes policy and industrial intervention. On immigration the manifesto had pledged, 'There will be no further large-scale permanent immigration'. The government introduced a new Immigration Act in 1971 to fulfil that pledge, but then to the fury of the Conservative right accepted that it had a legal and moral obligation to admit 60,000 Ugandan Asians holding British passports who were under threat of expulsion from Uganda.

The other alleged U-turns went to the heart of the government's economic strategy. The manifesto had stated, 'We utterly reject the philosophy of compulsory wage control'; in his 1970 speech to the party conference Heath promised radical policies to encourage individuals and businesses to take their own decisions, stand on their own feet, and take responsibility for themselves and their families. The Labour government's interventionist agencies, such as the Prices and Incomes Board and the Industrial Reorganization Corporation, were abolished, and the government made plain that it would fight excessive pay claims in the public sector.

The abrasive style of the new government, and its determination to shake up attitudes throughout British society and to get on top of inflation, created a climate of confrontation, fuelled by the bitter battle which erupted over the Industrial Relations Act 1971, and a series of major public sector strikes, some of which like the 1971–2 miners' strike ended in defeat for the government. There was also considerable conflict over attempts to make private companies more self-reliant, expressed through the withdrawal of subsidies for 'lame-duck' companies. But the government was forced to rescue one 'lame-duck' company – Rolls-Royce – by nationalizing it when it suddenly went bankrupt in 1971; it also became embroiled in a long struggle over the future of Upper Clyde Shipbuilders, eventually conceding the workers' case for a further subsidy to keep the yard open.

Occasional reverses and tactical retreats would not have mattered if the government had stuck to its original policies, but in 1972 it decided on a major shift in policy, prompted by the rise in unemployment to over 1 million (the first time since the war). A very large reflation of the economy (the Barber boom) was the result. At the time it received strong support from the media, business and the financial markets. To handle the inflationary dangers of this monetary expansion the government attempted to negotiate a voluntary prices and incomes policy, but when this failed it made the policy compulsory. The underlying objective had not changed – the creation of an efficient, competitive, expanding economy which could hold its own within the European Community – and in this sense there was no U-turn. What did change was the government's assessment of the best means to achieve it. The Industry Act 1972 gave very wide-ranging powers to ministers to intervene in industry to promote investment and reorganization.

The direction of industrial policy and economic management in the last eighteen months of the Heath government were certainly different from the earlier policy of disengagement. Many other areas of government policy, however, including the Industrial Relations Bill, administrative reform, the introduction of Value Added Tax (VAT), and entry to the European Community showed no hint of any U-turn. In its first phase the Heath government gave the impression that it was seeking to achieve a different political balance, particularly between the interests of capital and labour, than the one which had prevailed since the 1940s. In its second phase it sought to involve labour and capital once again in partnership. The mistrust which the earlier phase had generated, however, was difficult to dispel.

The main cause of the mistrust was the Industrial Relations Act. Far from creating a new framework for industrial relations and reducing industrial unrest, it produced a series of damaging confrontations between organized labour and the courts. By the end of the parliament it was clear that the legislation had failed; the unions had refused to accept it, although it conferred many advantages on them, and the employers had refused to operate it. It was repealed by the new Labour government.

The aim of the legislation was to modernize the trade unions, making them more reliable and responsible partners for both employers and the government. The failure of this reform and the previous proposals of the Wilson government opened the way for the more radical reforms of the Thatcher years aimed at weakening the bargaining strength of the unions and excluding them from influence over national economic policy.

The Heath government also failed to control inflation through its compulsory incomes policy. It nearly worked. Stage one and two of the policy were implemented without difficulty, and almost all groups of workers settled within the limits of Stage three. The exception was the miners, who exploited the situation created by the quadrupling of oil prices by the Organization of Petroleum Exporting Countries (OPEC) to demand a settlement outside the limits of the pay policy. The energy crisis in the winter of 1973–4 foreshadowed the deep recession in the world economy in 1974–5 which brought the final end of the long postwar boom, the acceleration of inflation, a return to mass unemployment and a long and painful period of economic restructuring.

By calling a crisis election in February 1974 once the miners had voted for a strike, Heath raised the stakes very high. The result of the election was inconclusive, but Heath lost his majority and with it the premiership and the ability to shape events. The Conservatives were no longer the largest party in the Commons and lost their right to continue in government because the Ulster Unionists elected in 1974 refused to take the Conservative whip. In seeking to deal with the escalation of terrorism in Northern Ireland the Heath government had abolished Stormont, imposed direct rule, and then tried through the Sunningdale Agreement to establish a power-sharing executive between the constitutional parties.

Edward Heath was an extremely dominant and forceful prime minister, who might have achieved much more had he not had the misfortune to be premier at a time of fundamental structural shifts in the global economy. His period in office was a turning-point in British politics, as a consequence of both his successes and his failures. His great achievement was to negotiate entry into the European Community. His greatest failure was his inability to create the kind of partnership between capital and labour which had delivered economic success in other European economies. The failure of the modernization project of the Heath government opened the way for a much deeper polarization within British politics.

References and further reading

Blake, R. (1985) *The Conservative Party from Peel to Thatcher*, London: Methuen. (The best short historical survey of the Conservative party which puts Heath's premiership in the context of Conservative party history.)

Campbell, J. (1993) *Edward Heath*, London: Cape. (The best and most comprehensive biography which abounds with information and insights.)

Cosgrave, P. (1978) *Margaret Thatcher: A Tory and her Party*, London: Hutchinson. (Written by a Thatcherite insider, it gives insight into the ideological and political rift between Thatcher and Heath.)

Harris, R. and Sewill, B. (1975) *British Economic Policy 1970–74: Two Views*, London: Institute of Economic Affairs. (Contrasting assessments of the economic policy of the Heath government from a leading critic and an insider.)

Hennessy, P. (1986) *Cabinet*, Oxford: Blackwell. (Provides useful detail on how the cabinet was organized under Heath.)

Holmes, M. (1982) *Political Pressure and Economic Policy: British Government 1970–74*, London: Butterworth. (Detailed account of the policies and events of the Heath government, written from a Thatcherite perspective.)

Hurd, D. (1979) *An End to Promises*, London: Collins. (Insider's account of the 1970–4 government. Particularly good on the pressures of Downing Street.)

Kavanagh, D. (1987) 'The Heath government, 1970–74', in P. Hennessy and A. Seldon (eds) *Ruling Performance: British Governments Attlee to Thatcher*, Oxford: Blackwell. (Summarizes main events and assesses achievements and failures.)

Norton, P. (1978) *Conservative Dissidents: Dissent within the Parliamentary Conservative Party 1970–74*, London: Temple Smith. (Lists and analyses the scale of dissent in the parliamentary party.)

Ramsden, J. (1980) *The Making of Conservative Party Policy: The Conservative Research Department since 1929*, London: Longman. (Comprehensive account of the policy review conducted under Heath.)

Andrew Gamble

(Leonard) James Callaghan, Lord Callaghan of Cardiff

Born 27 March 1912, younger child of James Callaghan and Charlotte Cundy. Educated at Portsmouth Northern Secondary School. Married 1938 Audrey Moulton. MP for South Cardiff 1945–50, South East Cardiff 1950–83, Cardiff South and Penarth 1983–7. Parliamentary and Financial Secretary, Admiralty 1950–1; Chancellor of the Exchequer 1964–7; Home Secretary 1967–70; Secretary of State for Foreign Affairs 1974–6; Prime Minister 1976–9; Leader of the Opposition 1979–80; Father of the House 1983–7. Left Commons 1987, ennobled the same year.

Callaghan was prime minister from 5 April 1976 until 5 May 1979 – three of the most politically tumultuous years of the post-war period. Lacking an overall majority the government was defeated on devolution and incomes policy, and fell after a winter of confrontation with the trade unions. The combination of a minority government and an increasingly polarized political scene made the task of holding together the government and Labour party immensely difficult. However, these years saw some successes, and when Callaghan left office both unemployment and inflation were falling (Artis *et al.* 1992; Morgan 1997: 557–84, 698–9). Simply keeping the government in office for as long as he did must be counted as a remarkable political achievement.

For a decade after 1979 there was a clear consensus among political commentators that Callaghan's premiership had been a disaster. The left charged that there had been a retreat from the radical commitments of the 1974 general election manifesto, resulting in an unnecessary confrontation with the trade unions in the 'Winter of Discontent' (Coates 1980). The allegation of the Labour right, by contrast, is that Callaghan's inability to grasp the nature of the crisis engulfing his government enabled the left to capture the party apparatus, forcing Labour into the political wilderness for a generation. They also maintain that he was dissuaded from legislating against the excesses of trade union power by the belief he could do a deal with the Trades Union Congress (Jenkins 1991; Owen 1991). Britain's decline was accelerated by the 'beer and sandwiches approach' of dealing with trade unions, according to the Tory right, coupled with a more general complacency (Holmes 1985). For a decade afterwards, the Wilson and Callaghan governments of 1974–9 were a central part of political discourse and their legacy dominated the internal politics of the Labour party – leading indeed to its split.

Callaghan was well qualified for the job. He was the only prime minister in the twentieth century to have held all the major offices of state – Home Secretary, Chancellor of the Exchequer and Foreign Secretary – and had been elected with the landslide victory in 1945, serving in the Attlee government and sitting on the National Executive Committee for the first time in 1957. Most importantly for the fate of his premiership, he had been Chancellor from 1964 to 1967 and had backed Wilson in his determination not to devalue. He was not a trained economist, however, and his period as Chancellor was not an unqualified success, ending as it did with devaluation (Morgan 1997: 203–89). The other defining experience was his implacable opposition to the trade union reforms proposed by Barbara Castle in her 1969 document *In Place of Strife*. Although failure to regulate the trade unions came back to haunt him in the 'Winter of Discontent', he never seems to have given up the idea that, as leader of the political wing of the Labour movement, he could do a deal with its industrial wing, a faith retained as late as 1996 when reflecting on the future of the trade union link (Morgan 1997: 745).

Callaghan's experience in domestic politics was matched by an international reputation acquired after twenty-five years at the centre of British politics. Another strength was his ability as a broadcaster. Callaghan had ascended the political ladder at a time when the ability to communicate effectively through television was becoming essential. When Michael Foot and A.J.P. Taylor were dropped from *In the News*, the BBC's top current affairs programme in the 1950s, Callaghan was brought in. He developed an effectively ebullient and jocular style, and insisted on strict conditions for interviews, stopping those he was not happy with and ensuring that the tapes were suppressed (Cockerell 1988). This private petulance was a sign of someone not intimidated by the medium, and Robin Day has described the most difficult interviews he had to do as ones in which Jim Callaghan decided 'to mix it'. Despite this early skill with television, he was to be resoundingly outflanked by the Thatcher team in the 1979 general election when they took the use of the medium to new heights.

The media form one of the many pressures on the modern premier and it is important to understand the separate and competing constraints that Callaghan was under when he succeeded Wilson (Drucker 1976). It is arguable that such a combination of economic, political and social pressures will not be repeated with the same intensity again because of the ending of the Cold War, the evolution of the European Union and the trade union legislation of the Thatcher administrations. But in 1976 the European Community was still relatively marginal to economic management; the autumn of Callaghan's first year as prime minister was dominated by the British tradition of a sterling crisis; the Cold War was still dominating international politics, and nuclear defence was therefore a central concern of domestic politics; trade unions were still unregulated and capable of paralysing the country in opposition to an incomes policy, which in turn was a response to the highest inflation in British history. On top of this was the over-arching political constraint of the lack of a parliamentary majority. In such a circumstance, cabinet government itself was placed under enormous pressure. Callaghan was also constrained by the difficulties of managing an internally protean Labour party.

Callaghan's main strengths were his conduct of cabinet business and his stand-ing internationally. His principal weaknesses were his inability to grasp the chan-ging nature of the Labour party and his preference for a short political fix over a lasting political solution. The sterling crisis, which was Callaghan's first real test as prime minister, resulted from an international loss of confidence in the pound, caused in part by the deposit and then gradual withdrawal of £2,500 million by petroleum producing states (Cairncross 1992). Inflation was running at 25 per cent when Callaghan took over; despite a package of public expenditure cuts adopted in July 1976 the pound continued to spiral downwards. It became increasingly likely that the International Monetary Fund (IMF) would have to be approached to restore international confidence.

The decision to ask for a loan from the IMF, which entailed a review of the government's fiscal policy and recommendations for change, forms the first major source of criticism of Callaghan's premiership. Despite the fact that the July pack-age of public expenditure cuts was already in place, the left accuse Callaghan of abandoning the 1974 manifesto in response to the demands of international capitalism. In turn, the right charge that the bankruptcy of the Keynesians is revealed by the humiliation of Britain being the first developed country to apply for aid of this kind, and that in so accepting the need to reduce public expenditure the Labour government accepted the monetarist arguments.

The main evidence for both kinds of criticism is Callaghan's speech to the Labour party conference in 1976. The key passage in the speech was drafted by Peter Jay, Callaghan's son-in-law and 'one of the few converts to monetarism who did not embrace Thatcherism or Conservatism' (Cockett 1995; Morgan 1997: 535). The speech was a manifesto for good housekeeping. 'For too long', Callaghan said,

> perhaps, ever since the war, we postponed facing up to fundamental choices and fundamental changes in our society and in our economy. That is what I mean when I say we have been living on borrowed time. For too long this country . . . has been ready to settle for borrowing money abroad to maintain our standards of life. . . . The cosy world we were told would go on forever, where full employment would be guaranteed at the stroke of the Chancellor's pen. . . . I tell you in all candour that that option no longer exists, and that, insofar as it ever did exist, it only worked on each occasion by injecting a bigger dose of inflation into the economy.

Edmund Dell maintains that this had been the message of governments for years (Dell 1991: 236–7). But in the context of the cuts in public expenditure, the radical content of the 1974 manifesto and the increasingly right-wing tone of the Conservative opposition under Margaret Thatcher, the impact of the speech was politically profound and lasting – even if its long-term impact on the economic policy of the government was limited (Morgan 1997: 537).

Despite the proposed cuts and Callaghan's speech, the pound continued to fall. The IMF seemed the last chance of saving the pound and the government. Callaghan claims in his memoirs that he had no doubts from the outset about the best course but had to manage the cabinet in such a way that he could carry the government united behind the decision.

> It would have been best if we had reached a quick decision, but I knew this would not be possible if we were to remain together, so by instinct more than rational judgement I decided not to bring the matters to a head but to allow time to work and Ministers to become familiar with the problems.
>
> (Callaghan 1987: 434)

While this has been judged to have been a masterful strategy (Hennessy 1986: 91; Whitehead 1987: 258), the actual course it took left the government stranded for over a month. The cabinet divided into various factions: the Crosland group felt that the package of cuts that would be needed to accompany the IMF loan were unnecessary and that the existing government policy should be given time to work; the supporters of the Chancellor, Denis Healey, argued for the modified package of cuts as presented to the cabinet in November; and the left, led by Michael Foot and Tony Benn, argued for the alternative policy of import controls and a siege economy.

In allowing all the members of the cabinet to have their say, Callaghan held the Labour party together and kept the government in office. To achieve the result he had wanted from the outset to mobilize international support from the German Chancellor, Schmidt, and the US President, Ford – an important political asset, even though their ability to deliver the aid that they promised has been questioned (Morgan 1997: 544–8). Finally, Anthony Crosland agreed to support Callaghan, not because he was convinced of the arguments but for the political reason that the prime minister should not be defeated on so substantial an issue. The loan was agreed, as was the package of cuts, and 'confidence was restored in the markets, the pound shot up in the spring of 1977 and Britain needed to borrow less than half of the total loan of $3.9 billion. All in all Callaghan and Healey could deem the whole episode a success' (Burk 1994: 366). His political aide, Tom MacNally, 'felt it was a great single-handed achievement' (Morgan 1997: 552).

The small majority the Labour party had gained at the general election of October 1974 was slowly eroded by by-elections, the resignation of the political heavyweight Roy Jenkins and the defection of left-wing MPs on issues of nationalism or in opposition to public expenditure cuts. At the beginning of the 1976–7 session Callaghan had pinned his hopes on the Nationalists' support for the devolution bills to maintain a majority. But in February 1977 the motion for a guillotine was defeated by a backbench revolt. Without the limitation of the time for debate, the Leader of the House, Michael Foot, judged that the Bills would not be passed in reasonable time and they were therefore postponed until the next session. (The Bills were finally passed in February 1978.) The Nationalists thereafter opposed the government. The government just averted a defeat over the white paper on public expenditure in the spring of 1977, and this forced Callaghan to seek an accommodation with the Liberal leader, David Steel. The Lib–Lab pact survived until July 1978 – according to Bernard Donoughue's account, Callaghan suggested to Steel that the Liberals should disengage because of the likelihood of a general election (Donoughue 1987: 158) – and was on balance a political success for Callaghan. He used the Liberals to moderate his programme, ensuring that the government survived long enough to begin to see the benefits flowing from the IMF deal and the anti-inflationary cuts in public expenditure as well as increases in employers' national insurance contributions.

The other main element in the anti-inflation package was the incomes policy. Callaghan was personally committed to the incomes policy and the social contract as an alternative to legislating on trade union reform. The basis of the policy was that trade unions accepted voluntary limits to pay increases. This held increases down until the autumn of 1978, when all decisions were influenced by the expectation of an autumn election.

In the budget of April 1978, Healey produced £2,400 million in tax cuts, scrapped a rise in the price of school meals and promised an increase in child benefit. The pay norm for the year was set at 5 per cent and the aim was to hold inflation down through the election year. From being neck and neck in the opinion polls through the spring, Labour pulled ahead in the summer (Butler and Butler 1994: 255). It was at this point in Callaghan's premiership that his usually sure domestic political acumen seemed to desert him as he became increasingly preoccupied with international affairs.

Callaghan ended the Lib–Lab pact – but not the alliance with the Ulster Unionists – in the expectation of an early election. The week before the Trades Union Congress conference, six leading trade unionists lunched with him and came away with the distinct impression that there would be an autumn election, though Callaghan's own notes suggest the opposite (Morgan 1997: 691). He then teased the Trades Union Congress conference with the prospect of an election, singing the old music hall song, 'There was I waiting at the church', which was meant to imply that Thatcher would have to wait for the election – but was not understood like that at all. Callaghan then arranged a ministerial broadcast which raised expectations of a general election even higher, only to announce that he would not be calling one until the spring of 1979. Donoughue believes that Callaghan enjoyed teasing the press but had decided that although Labour might have won in the autumn they would not have secured an overall majority (Donoughue 1987: 164–6). The argument either way, as Peter Shore makes plain, was evenly balanced, and the decision, in the end, was Callaghan's (Shore 1993: 119).

The postponement of the election and its manner, coupled with the adoption of the 5 per cent norm, resulted in a winter of bitter industrial action. However, the signs of a tide of increasing militancy in the Labour movement had been there at least since the late 1960s. Callaghan was aware of the debates on entryism, the widespread feeling that the manifesto of 1974 had been abandoned, and the takeover of constituency Labour parties, the Labour Youth section and the student organization by the left and in some cases by entryist Trotskyist groups like Militant (Crick 1986: 50–70, 95–113). Thus when the trade unions in the public sector began to make demands well in excess of the pay norm, there was a fertile political ground within and on the fringes of the Labour party to press the point home.

The road haulage and oil-tank drivers came out and demanded a pay rise of 25–30 per cent, and the Transport and General Workers Union made the strike official. Shop stewards organized secondary picketing and there were violent confrontations. As Callaghan records in his memoirs:

> The contagion spread to other industries and services, and during January 1979 unofficial strikes erupted every week, with workers in one industry inflicting hardship on their fellows in other industries. Even with the passage of time I find it painful to write about some of the excesses that took place. One of the most notorious was the refusal of Liverpool grave diggers to bury the dead, accounts of which appalled the country when they saw pictures of mourners being turned away from the cemetery.
>
> (Callaghan 1987: 537)

Against this background Callaghan made what has been described as the 'greatest publicity mistake of his political life' by attending the security summit in Guadaloupe (Cockerell 1988). In fact, while the pictures of him sunning himself on the beach and swimming were indeed disastrous, so too would have been his failure to attend the meeting. The decision over the replacement for Polaris in the face of Russian deployment of SS-20s transcended the immediate political concerns of that autumn. The decision on Polaris was actually deferred at Guadaloupe but it seems clear that Callaghan favoured the modernization of the deterrent if a deal could be worked out. On his return, at the suggestion of Tom MacNally, he gave a calamitous news conference at the airport, when he tried to defuse the air of crisis by smoothing over the difficulties (Morgan 1997: 661). Just as it was Larry Lamb of the *Sun* who coined the 'Winter of Discontent' label for the strikes of January to February 1979, so it was the same newspaper that ran the headline, 'Crisis, what crisis?' The general thrust of the press coverage of Guadaloupe infuriated Callaghan and this mood characterized his general election campaign.

The general election was finally precipitated by the failure of the devolution policy in the referenda of March 1979. Callaghan used the electioneering methods that he had previously employed and lent heavily on the dignity of office (Morgan 1997: 687–700). But a new campaigning style was developed by Margaret Thatcher, using photo-opportunities, advertising agencies and a heavy emphasis on slogans and images. The 1979 general election was not, of course, devoid of political issues, and areas of substantial difference over the role of trade unions, the management of the economy and the role of the state – and the combination of the new campaigning style of Thatcher and the anti-trade union vote in the election – were indicative of the fact that the Callaghan premiership marked the end of an era.

On the level of political management Callaghan was a successful prime minister. The critiques of his time in office cannot detract from the fact that simply in terms of keeping the government together and managing the crises in parliament, in the economy and with the trade unions, Callaghan did a remarkable job and for a critical period in the middle of the administration the country was well run and the government popular (Morgan 1997: 485–8). His style of leadership was based on team work, especially with Denis Healey, his Chancellor, and Michael Foot, the Leader of the Commons, and his approach collective and consensual. The political deals with the Liberals, Nationalists and Ulster Unionists were shrewd, his handling of the IMF crisis impressive and his international reputation high. If one applies criteria other than simply political management, however, his premiership shows a less sure touch, and if one includes the decision to postpone the general election and the failure to grasp the impact of the 'Winter of Discontent', then the balance sheet is perhaps less positive. In the final analysis, Callaghan and his cabinet seemed to lose sight of the overall objective of the government: it became unclear quite what they were in power to achieve other than re-election. If Callaghan had called the election in October 1978 and lost he would have gone down as a competent premier who weathered a difficult time. In clinging to power through the winter of 1979, he lost much of his credibility and the Labour party much of its political coherence.

References and further reading

Artis, M., Cobham, D. and Wickham-Jones, M. (1992) 'Social democracy in hard times: the economic record of the Labour government 1974–79', *Twentieth Century British History* 3: 32–58. (A well argued defence of the Labour government's record, concluding that it left the country in better condition than when elected.)

Benn, T. (1989) *Against the Tide: Diaries 1973–76*, London: Hutchinson.

—— (1990) *Conflicts of Interest: Diaries 1977–80*, London: Hutchinson.

Burk, K. (1994) 'The Americans, the Germans and the British: the 1976 IMF crisis', *Twentieth Century British History* 5: 350–69. (A full summary of the international context of the International Monetary Fund crisis derived from her book, *Goodbye Great Britain*.)

Burk, K. and Cairncross, A. (1992) *Goodbye Great Britain: The 1976 IMF Crisis*, London and New Haven, CT: Yale University Press.

Butler, D. and Butler, G. (1994) *British Political Facts*, 7th edn, London: Macmillan.

Cairncross, A. (1992) 'Economic policy after 1974', *Twentieth Century British History* 3: 199–208.

Callaghan, J. (1987) *Time and Chance*, London: Collins. (Rather dry and unrevealing memoirs but packed with narrative detail.)

Coates, D. (1980) *Labour in Power? A Study of the Labour Government 1974–79*, London: Longman. (A readable left-wing attack on the Labour government.)

Cockerell, M. (1988) *Live from Number 10*, London: Faber & Faber.

Cockett, R. (1995) *Thinking the Unthinkable: Think-tanks and the Economic Counter-revolution, 1931–1983*, London: Fontana.

Crick, M. (1986) *The March of Militant*, London: Faber & Faber.

Dell, E. (1991) *A Hard Pounding: Politics and Economic Crisis, 1974–76*, Oxford: Oxford University Press. (An eyewitness account that challenges many of the views in existing memoirs on the IMF and other issues.)

Donoughue, B. (1987) *Prime Minister: The Conduct of Policy under Harold Wilson and James Callaghan*, London: Cape. (A frank portrait of life inside Number 10 policy unit in these years.)

Drucker, H. (1976) 'Leadership selection in the Labour Party', *Parliamentary Affairs*, 29: 378–95.

Healey, D. (1990) *The Time of My Life*, Harmondsworth: Penguin.

Hennessy, P. (1986) *Cabinet*, Oxford: Blackwell.

—— (1990) *Whitehall*, London: Fontana.

Holmes, M. (1985) *The Labour Government 1974–79, Political Aims and Economic Reality*, London: Macmillan. (The standard Thatcherite account of Callaghan's government.)

Jenkins, R. (1991) *Life at the Centre*, London: Macmillan. (Useful for the background of Callaghan on the way up but Jenkins was in Europe for most of the premiership.)

Mackintosh, J. (1978) 'Has social democracy failed in Britain?', *Political Quarterly* 48: 259–70.

Mitchell, A. (1983) *Four Years in the Death of the Labour Party*, London: Methuen.

Morgan, K. (1997) *Callaghan: A Life*, Oxford: Oxford University Press. (A definitive political biography which will remain the main source on Callaghan for generations. As much a life and times as an effective account of an individual politician's impact on his party and country.)

Owen, D. (1991) *Time to Declare*, London: Michael Joseph. (Good narrative detail of the Foreign Office in the last years of the government.)

Shore, P. (1993) *Leading the Left*, London: Weidenfeld & Nicolson. (Good discussion of the internal politics of the Labour party and generous portrait of Callaghan as prime minister.)

Whitehead, P. (1987) 'The Labour government, 1974–79', in P. Hennessy and A. Seldon (eds) *Ruling Performance: British Governments Attlee to Thatcher*, Oxford: Blackwell.

Brian Brivati

Margaret Hilda Thatcher (née Roberts), Baroness Thatcher of Kesteven

Born 13 October 1925, younger daughter of Alfred Roberts and Beatrice Stephenson. Educated at Kesteven and Grantham Girls Grammar School and Somerville College, Oxford. Married 1951 Denis Thatcher. MP for Finchley 1959– 92. Joint Parliamentary Secretary, Ministry of Pensions and National Insurance 1960–4; Secretary of State for Education and Science 1970–4; Leader of the Opposition 1975–9; Prime Minister 1979–90. Left Commons 1992, ennobled (hereditary peerage) the same year.

Thatcher's premiership was remarkable by any standards. She was the first female prime minister in Britain, holding office without interruption for longer than anyone since Liverpool. She was the first serving prime minister to be removed by a ballot of her MPs. She was the only twentieth-century party leader to give her name to what was an ideology – affirming the virtues of limited but firm government – and also a project to rescue Britain from post-war collectivism. According to conventional wisdom Conservative prime ministers travel unencumbered by excessive ideological baggage and without a strong sense of direction: their task is to keep the ship of state bobbing along rather than navigating it – as socialists purportedly wish to do – towards beguiling horizons. But in pursuit of her mission to unravel the corporate state Thatcher displayed an evangelical fervour not seen since Gladstone's time. With the possible exception of Lloyd George – another formidable outsider who reached the top unaided by a charmed circle of party elders – she was the most combative premier of the twentieth century, despising the 'fudge and mudge' of consensus and compromise, believing that a leader's objectives can best be secured, inside and outside the cabinet, by robust argument and by the ruthless treatment of those enemies, within and without the country, liable to obstruct the march to national recovery. Her natural element appeared to be the politics of warfare, and in the struggle to make Britain great again she was often accused of being humourless, dogmatic and imperious: an impatient workaholic who was sometimes fractious and irritable, and unfailingly fussy, brisk and emphatic. Attlee, the only other twentieth-century prime minister to preside over the installation of a mighty political project – the planned, welfare economy which she was so determined to dismantle – was reserved and conciliatory. She was unflinching in her convictions, apparently relishing skirmishes with those she considered to be either spineless or not clearly 'one of us' in the task of restoring to Britain the riches and splendour of a glorious past, and conveying the impression that she wanted to manage everybody and everything.

Ironically, however, she did not invariably rush to embrace policies which others considered necessary to renew the enterprise culture and buccaneering spirit of what she liked to call 'this island race'. There is some plausibility in the view that the Thatcherite agenda was a set of transparent policy initiatives driven for eleven years by a consistent strategy that had been largely set in place during the years in opposition following her election as party leader. Yet Thatcher, who was not without a sense of statecraft, was sometimes more cautious than other free-marketeers eager to proceed with the permanent revolution; ministers such as Nigel Lawson later complained that the Thatcherite project hit the rocks because of her willingness to dilute sound measures in a misguided calculation of expediency. Some who remained loyal to her, by contrast, intimated that she was less than courageous in retaining in cabinet those such as Lawson whose eventual departure from the project contributed to her downfall.

Caution and timidity were not characteristics associated with Thatcher in the public perception, however, and her dominant personality and ideological zeal provoked passionate responses. People tended to adore or loathe her. For her admirers she fulfilled Callaghan's prediction, made during the 1979 general election campaign, of an impending 'sea-change in politics' by turning the tide of national decline; and they acclaimed her as a heroine whose stance as the 'iron lady', battling against East European communism and the federalist drift of the European Community, had given the country a place on the world stage not enjoyed since the Second World War. Indeed the 'warrior-queen' liked to think of herself as the heir to Churchill, with whom she shared a romantic view of Britain as a mighty nation which in stirring historical moments had been rescued from nemesis by the sturdiness of its people and the determination of its leaders. Many on the right, among them academics, reckoned that she had outpaced even Churchill to become 'the greatest British leader of the twentieth century' (Charmley 1996: 197). For her detractors, within the Conservative party and beyond, she was a heartless virago whose blinkered adherence to free-enterprise nostrums split the country into the two nations of rich and poor lamented by Disraeli in his novel *Sybil*, and whose strident pursuit of a misconceived national interest left Britain isolated and derided abroad.

Thatcher's legacy is ambiguous. Her counter-revolutionary project to restore to Britain the competitive spirit and international influence of the Victorian age revived a sense that the nation could be steered in a purposive direction instead of being buffeted by the storms of economic vicissitude and the demands of sectional interests. Political scientists no longer lamented, as they were prone to do during the Heath and Callaghan administrations, that the country had become ungovernable, and Thatcher won sneaking admiration from some on the left who by no means shared her distaste for collectivism. Yet her libertarian impulse to create 'the first post-socialist society' by curtailing the functions of government resulted, paradoxically, in a state that was more centralized and bureaucratic, and less tolerant of certain individual liberties, than the regime she inherited. And her confrontational demeanour, fundamentalist rhetoric and ultimate inability to reconcile the various groups within the broad church of Conservatism, left the party more divided than at any time since the repeal of the Corn Laws.

Not that it immediately collapsed after her political demise. Major's unexpected victory in the general election of 1992 obscured the situation that Thatcher had brought about. But Major's premiership, during which he presided over the fag-end of the Thatcherite agenda, revealed lingering wounds which some claimed – perhaps with a touch of hyperbole – signalled the party's terminal decline. Peel was less ideologically vociferous than Thatcher. Yet for whatever reasons – stubborn refusal to compromise over matters of principle, increasing remoteness from many of the parliamentary party, lack of diplomacy – two commanding prime ministers bequeathed to their successors bickering, dispirited factions. It remains to be seen whether post-Thatcher Conservatives are quicker to re-form themselves into a strong organization with a unity of purpose than were their predecessors after the débâcle of 1846.

Thatcher was the younger daughter of a lower-middle-class family in the small Lincolnshire town of Grantham. Her father was a self-made grocer who owned the shop above which the family lived. Her mother was a former seamstress who helped in the business. From their disciplined, sabbatarian home the two girls were expected to walk to chapel four times on a Sunday, and Margaret was encouraged to eschew trivial pursuits in favour of self-improvement through, for instance, piano lessons and attendance at lectures on current affairs. Her mother imparted the skills of running an efficient household and managing a hectic schedule. From her father she learned much more. Alfred Roberts, a local Independent councillor who became mayor of Grantham, was self-taught and a lay preacher steeped in the Methodist ethic of self-help and hard work, a man of simple but steadfast convictions, committed to public service, and staunchly patriotic. He introduced Margaret to the necessity of financial rectitude by teaching her to balance the shop's accounts, and widened her horizons by bringing home library books about politics. Alderman Roberts, whom Margaret idolized, may not have been quite the pillar of civic respectability depicted in her speeches and memoirs. In 1937 Grantham residents were scandalized when they seemed to recognize some of their burghers in a farcical novel, written by a young journalist using the pseudonym Julian Pine, which exposed the corruption of small-town politics through regular character assassinations in the *Weekly Probe*. According to one story a local councillor, who happened to be a grocer, used his position as a committee chairman to ensure that the contract for floodlights in the town's main street was given not to a firm making electric lamps, but to a gas company in which he owned shares. One evening, having neglected to draw the blinds, he induced a young female assistant to 'serve behind the Counter in a rather Unusual Way and she Served readily because otherwise she feared she might lose her Job and then her widowed Mother who was dying of Consumption might Starve!'. The floodlight outside the shop went on, and

several House-Wives of the Lower Classes, whose faces were pressed against the Window coveting the Pork Pies they could not afford to Buy, saw Everything. So the Naughty Councillor was in more Senses than one Undone and he had to resign from the Town Council and go out of Business and finally he Hanged Himself with a pair of Woolworth's braces in a Public Convenience.

(Anderson 1989: 142).

There is no certainty that Alfred Roberts, who died in bed attended by his second wife, indulged in such naughtiness, though in the 1990s Grantham pensioners who had known him were still insisting that he was 'a mean old bugger' who exploited his employees, economically and sexually (Creasy 1997; Crick 1997; Nuthall 1997).

From the constellation of values acquired in this earnest household of thrifty endeavour Thatcher never wavered, though the moral absolutes of childhood were later fortified by the intellectual certainties of free-market economics. There, as she often announced when party leader, she learned about the sin of idleness, the need to pay your way and not get into debt, the importance of adhering to principle, and the imperative to love one's country and respect the forces of law and order. These homespun verities were to underpin her affirmation of an enterprise society of low taxation which rewards individual achievement, where personal responsibility replaces dependence upon a morally enervating 'nanny state' of extensive welfare provision, and in which government acts firmly against social indiscipline while ensuring the nation's prominence in the councils of the world. As prime minister she was not unhappy to be cast as a busy housewife operating on a grand scale, Britannia who in her struggle against collectivism was recovering the vanishing values of middle England.

Thatcher's background gave her the ambition to succeed against the odds, and also immunized her against the *noblesse oblige* ethos of patrician Tories for whom high public expenditure is a legitimate means of safeguarding the lower classes from unemployment and indigence. From Kesteven and Grantham Girls Grammar School, a grant-aided institution where her father was a governor and she was known as 'Snobby Roberts', she went to Somerville College, Oxford, immediately joining the Conservative Association and eventually graduating with a second-class degree in Chemistry – which was to make her the first British prime minister with a university education in the physical sciences. She worked for a while in industrial and commercial chemistry, and in 1949 became the parliamentary candidate for Dartford, failing to win the seat in the general elections of 1950 and 1951. By now she was reading for the Bar, a more conventional route into politics than chemistry, and after passing her exams in 1953 was to practise for a few years as a tax lawyer.

The other boost to her political career was her marriage in 1951 to a man of substance whom she had met two years earlier on her adoption night at Dartford. Denis Thatcher, still bearing the scars of a failed wartime marriage, was ten years her senior and the managing director of a family business which manufactured paints and chemicals. During Thatcher's premiership her consort, whose retirement coincided with her election as party leader, was lampooned in the press as an old buffer, cowering before the Boss, and made stupid by a concoction of gin and the racial and other prejudices of the English middle classes. Denis certainly startled guests at official functions by his blunt expression of antediluvian political opinions. But, as the affectionate memoir by his journalist daughter reveals, he provided an oasis of calm for his frenetic partner as well as having better insight into character (C. Thatcher 1996). Margaret was a poor judge of men – she tended to avoid the company of women and did little to promote their political careers – and often, having succumbed to the charms of her male colleagues, subsequently became disenchanted and withdrew her patronage. During her long reign many ministers were to leave the cabinet, a few because they could no longer tolerate her but most because they were dismissed, sometimes brutally. An early victim of her habit of continuously tinkering with her team – who was downgraded in her first shadow cabinet shift to make way for a more ardent free-marketeer, but was rehabilitated and held cabinet posts for much of the Thatcher decade – noted that no prime minister in 'recent years used the reshuffle more regularly and methodically than Margaret Thatcher' (Fowler 1991: 84). One reason she failed to win enough votes in the leadership contest which brought about her downfall as prime minister was the number of disgruntled former courtiers eager to settle old scores. Denis, unimpressed by sycophants but loyal to his friends, was a constant source of succour and sound advice. The Thatchers' son – the twins Carol and Mark, who were born in 1953, were their only children – inherited few of his father's qualities. In 1982 he was to terrify his doting mother and infuriate his father by disappearing for a week in a desert during a car rally. Later he embarrassed the whole family by involving himself in shady financial deals.

After four unsuccessful bids for a safer seat than Dartford, Thatcher was chosen in 1958 for the prized constituency of Finchley, entering parliament in the general election of the following year. Two years later she became parliamentary secretary at the Ministry of Pensions, and during the years of Conservative opposition moved through several junior posts until her promotion to the shadow cabinet, where eventually she had responsibility for education. As Secretary of State at the Department of Education and Science (DES) in the Heath administration from 1970 to 1974 she hectored obstructive civil servants, particularly as she considered the ethos of the DES to be 'self-righteously socialist' (M. Thatcher 1995: 166), campaigned for an extension of nursery education, fought – ironically, given her distaste for high public expenditure – with cabinet colleagues to increase her budget and, in a foretaste of the hostility she was to endure as prime minister, was demonized in the popular imagination as Mrs Thatcher, milk snatcher for abolishing free milk for primary schoolchildren above the age of 7. Through these thirteen years she assiduously attended to the details of her various portfolios, only rarely raising her head above the parapet to make the odd speech attacking what were to become the *bête-noire* of Thatcherism, the evils of big government and consensus politics. She was a competent, diligent, reliable and loyal – if sometimes infuriating – politician of the middle rank. There was nothing to indicate that she would soon be pushed up the greasy pole by a 'peasants' revolt'.

The revolt consisted in the decision of Conservative backbenchers in 1975 to abandon Heath, partly because of his curmudgeonly and unclubbable style but largely as revenge for him losing the two general elections of the previous year. Two years into office the Heath administration, which had pledged to trim the state, abandoned its 'quiet revolution' by supporting ailing industries and implementing a comprehensive prices and incomes policy. A few weeks after the first general election defeat of 1974, Sir Keith Joseph who – like Thatcher – had been a loyal and high-spending minister in Heath's government, announced his conversion to 'authentic' conservatism, and established the Centre for Policy Studies with the intention of reformulating the party's strategy and changing the 'climate of public opinion'. Joseph, a tormented intellectual prone to recant past errors, had begun to devour the writings of free-market gurus such as Milton Friedman and F.A. Hayek, and was struck by the latter's claim, in a book published in 1944, that there could be no sanctuary between unbridled capitalism and communist regimentation: for Hayek Keynesian-style techniques of economic demand-management were irretrievable steps along *The Road to Serfdom*. The Heath administration had been compelled to make its ignominious U-turn down this road, Joseph concluded, because of the 'ratchet effect' of post-war collectivism which burdened successive governments with increasingly impossible demands. Consensus politics placed upon government the intolerable responsibility of guaranteeing full employment and rising living standards by means of economic fine-tuning and redistributive taxation. In consequence Britain had become a 'totalitarian slum' of excessive bureaucracy and economic and moral stagnation (Joseph 1976: 79). Entrepreneurial endeavour had been stifled by misguided attempts to regulate competition as well as by crippling levels of direct taxation; trade unions had become so powerful that at the end of the Heath administration the miners had made the nation ungovernable; and the poor were trapped in a stranglehold of welfare dependency that sapped any incentive to self-improvement. The solution lay in reducing the state to its proper functions of maintaining the rule of law and a stable currency, leaving the distribution and generation of wealth to the spontaneous interaction of private individuals in pursuit of their varied interests. All this was Thatcherism in the making.

Thatcher signalled, albeit faintly, her disenchantment with consensus politics and approval of minimal statism by becoming vice-chairman of the Centre for Policy Studies in June 1974. It was Joseph, however, who strode into controversy with a series of speeches promulgating the new political creed, and his faithful lieutenant hoped that the mantle of party leadership would eventually pass to him. But the agonizing Joseph, to whom she was to dedicate her memoirs, was temperamentally unsuited for the post, and in an October speech crassly suggested that the 'human stock' was threatened by high birth-rates among those 'least fitted to bring children into the world': working-class mothers. Having been vilified in the press as a deranged eugenicist intent on solving the world's problems with an ample supply of contraceptives, Joseph realized that he was unfit to challenge Heath. The following month Thatcher announced that she would do so, and having been recently switched from Environment to the post of deputy Shadow Chancellor she enhanced her reputation among Conservative MPs by some sinewy parliamentary performances. In the leadership election she campaigned on the need to rescue Britain from socialist mediocrity by recovering the values of her provincial childhood, and in the first ballot secured 130 votes as against 119 for Heath, who then withdrew from the contest. In the second ballot, held a week later on 11 February 1975, she was challenged by latecomers such as the bluff and amiable Heathite, William Whitelaw – who as deputy leader and then deputy prime minister was to give her the kind of candid advice she also received from her husband, and whose retirement in 1988 she was to mark with the encomium 'Every prime minister needs a Willie' – but she won comfortably with 146 votes. Few Conservative MPs had been bewitched by Thatcherism in the making. She had beaten Heath because of mass defection from him on personal and political grounds, the organizational skills of her campaign manager, Airey Neave, and the unanticipated momentum she had gained from the first ballot. She had won by default, and many did not expect her to last the course.

During the years when Thatcher led the opposition much was done to seize the intellectual high ground for her political credo. Numerous think-tanks, complementing the call of the Centre of Policy Studies for a shift from the middle ground to a hard-right agenda, emerged with detailed policies to reduce taxation, dismantle the welfare state, deregulate industry, and prevent workers from using restrictive practices and frequent strikes to disrupt the laws of supply and demand. Thatcher surrounded herself with like-minded advisers, and in 1975 academics founded a Conservative philosophy group, whose seminars she sometimes attended, to make a principled case against creeping collectivism (Harrison 1994).

There were also efforts to make Thatcherism the common sense of the age by connecting the precepts of political economy with the anxieties and aspirations of ordinary people. Joseph, with responsibility in the shadow cabinet for policy and research, continued to make speeches linking the failures of corporatism to the irresponsibility of individuals corrupted by the egalitarian ethos of welfare dependency. The tax burdens imposed on decent folk by the 'loungers and scroungers' of social welfare who were too feckless or cunning to seek employment; the inconvenience endured by the public because of frequent strikes; the increase in vandalism, hooliganism and other forms of crime; the spread of pornography as well as the displays of lewd behaviour and foul language on television; the stampede of rebellious youth into drug-taking and other exotic activities: all were the fault of a bloated, indulgent state which had presided over an outbreak of morally flabby, permissive behaviour. The message conveyed was that the state had to be rolled forward and backward, simultaneously removing the shackles on private enterprise and assembling the corner-shop values of Grantham into a new regime of social order. The postlapsarian human condition, Thatcher told her listeners at a London church in the year before becoming prime minister, required government to become stronger to tackle the forces of social dislocation (M. Thatcher 1989b: 69). Even after a decade in power she persisted in attributing trade union militancy and other forms of loutish behaviour to the legacy of the permissive age whose motto was 'Never say no':

> That's why we've toughened the law on the muggers and marauders. That's why we've increased penalties on drink-driving, on drugs, on rape. That's why we've increased the police and strengthened their powers. That's why we've set up the Broadcasting Standards Council. . . . For there can be no freedom without order. There can be no order without authority; and authority that is impotent or hesitant in the face of intimidation, crime and violence, can not endure.
>
> (M. Thatcher 1989a: 10–11)

Academics of the right rejoiced in this affirmation of what one was to characterize as the 'vigorous virtues' of self-sufficiency, robustness, respect for the rule of the law, and loyalty to country (Letwin 1992: 33), while those on the left were quick to identify in the rhetoric of modernization a hegemonic project to enable the rich to become wealthier by persuading the many of the need to batten down the hatches on those inclined to be unruly: a form of 'authoritarian populism' which aligned the crusade for an enterprise culture with a widespread demand to restore the discipline of an organic community (Hall 1988: 7).

There were also attempts in these years to cultivate a softer image of Thatcher as a woman of the people. Gordon Reece – whom she appointed to her staff when elected leader and who was to become Director of Publicity at Conservative Central Office – established closer links with the press, gave advice on her appearance and sent her to an elocutionist to learn how to be less piercing in her public delivery. But many of Thatcher's parliamentary colleagues were unattracted by her brand of authoritarian individualism, even when expressed *sotto voce*. Some were repelled by her union-bashing rhetoric and what they regarded as her narrowly provincial hostility to working-class values, and despite several reshuffles only a minority in the shadow cabinet were committed to Friedmanite monetarism, the doctrine that tight control of the money supply is a cure for inflation and every other economic ailment. Her Treasury team did consist of monetarist converts, but with responsibility for employment the unrepentant corporatist James Prior was unimpressed by her wish to emasculate the unions and abandon a prices and incomes policy (Prior 1986: 111). Although he was eventually persuaded of the need to clip the wings of truculent workers by the public-sector strikes in the 'Winter of Discontent' of 1978–9, the Conservative manifesto was a no more than moderate endorsement of entrepreneurial endeavour and of the desirability of enacting legislation against picketing and the closed shop. The general election was won by a combination of Labour failures and a diluted Thatcherism which promised modest steps towards national recovery.

In government Thatcher was less disposed to permit her instincts to be moderated by irresolute colleagues (Prior 1986: 118). Shortly before the general election she told an interviewer that as a conviction politician shunning consensus she would exclude from her government anyone uncommitted to the anti-collectivist crusade. Her first cabinet nevertheless contained many unbelievers – patrician, One Nation Tories who from 1980 she was to designate as 'wet' – and as a consequence Thatcher soon promulgated the idea, peculiar for a prime minister, that she led an opposition against those who did not share her enthusiasms. As a roundhead surrounded by those she thought were effete cavaliers, she tended to rely on her own determination and the advice of her monetarist Treasury team. The intellectually distinguished Sir Ian Gilmour, an ultra-wet Foreign Office minister, later complained that she made cabinet debate superfluous by governing through 'clique and committee' in a bid to secure a 'one-woman consensus' (Gilmour 1992: 5, 6). After he was sacked from the cabinet another wet grumbled that, being a busybody who believed she could do everything better than anyone else, she 'would ideally like to run the major Departments herself and tries her best to do so – not just in terms of overall policy, but in strategic detail. This is neither practical nor desirable' (Pym 1984: 34). One cabinet colleague, who though not sharing many of Thatcher's convictions was shrewd enough to survive until the end of her reign, commented that she 'categorised her ministers into those she could put down, those she could break down, and those she could wear down' (Baker 1993: 256).

She also tended to bypass Whitehall mandarins, many of them sceptical of the proposed assault upon consensus politics, by turning her private office into an entourage of trusted counsellors. Bernard Ingham, a former *Guardian* journalist and apostate from socialism who shared her bullying predilections, became her press secretary in 1979, and each day for eleven years fed her censored synopses of newspaper stories (she was disinclined to read the papers herself) intended to rekindle her Thatcherite instincts in moments of doubt. Within a couple of years he had begun what was to become a habit of leaking to the press her displeasure with any minister who was not firmly 'one of us', and so became a conduit for ditching the doctrine of collective cabinet responsibility:

> In the past, the rule which Prime Ministers had insisted upon was that the Cabinet could argue strenuously in private, but that in public a united front must be presented. Mrs Thatcher used the lobby system in precisely the opposite way: Cabinet discussions were kept to a minimum, whilst she reserved the right to make public her disagreements with her own ministers.
> (Harris 1990: 150)

In such ways a combative prime minister indicated her resolve not to be deflected from her mission.

Yet in her first administration the Thatcherite project was still rudimentary. The 1979 manifesto had not committed the party to widespread deregulation of industry and there was little privatization beyond the sale of council houses; and as Employment Secretary Prior continued his tiptoe approach to reform of the trade unions. In one respect, however, Thatcher did signal her fidelity to the strategy devised by the Centre for Policy Studies. For two years Treasury ministers were given licence to test the Friedmanite proposition that the economy was best left to its own devices, apart from policies to beat inflation through 'monetary continence'. Public spending and direct taxation were reduced, price controls were abolished, and value added tax was virtually doubled; as a consequence of these measures interest rates rose, inflation soared, unemployment reached 3 million, and the fall in industrial output was sharper in 1981 than at any time for sixty years. On 23 July, at what 'was unquestionably the worst Cabinet meeting that took place in our first period of office' (Fowler 1991: 148), ministers revolted against another Treasury proposal to axe public expenditure, and urban riots by black youths during the summer – which Thatcher characteristically attributed to a 'decline in authority', to be dealt with by more effective policing, rather than to deprivation or racial discrimination – aroused some ministers to denounce monetarism as a formula threatening imminent social collapse. But the dissidents lacked a clear alternative economic strategy and were reluctant to cabal; in a September reshuffle Thatcher brought more of the faithful into key cabinet posts by dispatching Prior to Northern Ireland and sacking Gilmour and others. By the end of the year the party was trailing badly in the opinion polls, and she scored the lowest rating of any prime minister since polling began. The impression was of a woman of messianic delusions, commanding a band of partisans, and fortified by the veneration of her stalwarts – Thatcher, unlike Heath, went out of her way to cultivate the party's rank-and-file – but despised by the Tory old guard and detested in the country at large.

What transfigured her was the battle of the South Atlantic. On 2 April 1982 the Falkland Islands, a British territory of 1,800 inhabitants near the tip of South America, were invaded on the orders of the Argentine military junta. Outraged Conservative backbenchers blamed the occupation on cuts in defence spending and the duplicity of the Foreign Office, which since 1977 had been negotiating a proposal, abandoned because of the islanders' hostility, to transfer sovereignty to Argentina on leaseback terms to Britain. The Foreign Secretary, Lord Carrington, and two other ministers resigned in a bid to appease the right of the party, and in consultation with the military establishment Thatcher gambled on recovering the islands, establishing a War cabinet of a handful of ministers and the Chief of Defence Staff to superintend the venture. During the voyage of the armada assembled for the task, she resisted overtures to make concessions to Argentina from both the USA, which was attempting to broker an accommodation, and her new Foreign Secretary, the morose Francis Pym: it was Pym who in 1982 had been an early victim of her custom of publicly castigating errant ministers when Bernard Ingham told the Lobby of her annoyance with the then Leader of the House for making a speech predicting rising unemployment and falling living standards. The islands were eventually recaptured on 14 June with the loss of 650 Argentine and 255 British lives.

Had the war been lost Thatcher would have been derided as a megalomaniac, impelled by an obstinate belief in her own infallibility and by nostalgia for imperial grandeur to send men to their deaths on the other side of the world in the last colonial battle of an enfeebled nation. Victory transformed her perceived vices into virtues, and at home and abroad her esteem rose as a woman of courage and resolution, who from fidelity to principle rather than strategic calculation had swept aside diplomatic waverers to liberate the inhabitants of some politically insignificant islands from dictatorship. Military triumph also reinforced her conviction that she personified the values of 'this island race', and an invincible Thatcher proclaimed that what had been done in combat must now be achieved on the home front. In Churchillian mood she told a euphoric crowd that the 'spirit of the South Atlantic' marked the renaissance of a nation no longer in thrall to the corporate state. It was time to use this renewed confidence in the values of old Britain, 'born in the economic battles at home and tested and found true 8,000 miles away', to deal with the remaining enemies within – a rail strike was threatened – who clung to the illusions of post-war collectivism; and the task force – a disciplined social order in microcosm – was an 'object lesson' in how the Thatcherite project should be carried forward (M. Thatcher 1989b: 160–4). The Falklands war was a dramatic juncture in Thatcher's fortunes. In the ascendant in her cabinet and party, and assisted by some economic recovery as well as a weak and divided opposition – part of the Labour party had defected to form a third force, the Social Democrats, and what remained was led by the decent but ineffective Michael Foot – she returned to power in the general election of June 1983 with a majority of 144, larger than any party had secured since the Labour landslide of 1945.

'There was a revolution still to be made, but too few revolutionaries,' Thatcher reflected in her memoirs about her first term in office, and a new cabinet gave her 'a chance to recruit some' by sacking among others her detested Foreign Secretary, Francis Pym, who during the election campaign had unwisely suggested that large parliamentary majorities were undesirable (M. Thatcher 1993: 306). An early indication of the resolve to carry forward the Thatcherite agenda was accelerated confrontation with organized labour. In January 1984 the new Foreign Secretary, Sir Geoffrey Howe, banned trade union membership at Government Communications Headquarters (GCHQ), which as part of the national intelligence agencies used electronic surveillance to eavesdrop on Eastern Europe. After a public outcry against this encroachment upon democratic rights, Howe and others negotiated a 'card in the pocket' solution whereby GCHQ workers would retain union membership in return for a pledge not to strike. But Thatcher, advised by her press secretary Bernard Ingham not to be perceived as engaging in a U-turn, rejected the compromise on the ground that belonging to a trade union in a high-security organization was incompatible with loyalty to the state. This equation of union membership with treason, according to Howe,

> was a case where she was at the end driven by her 'all or nothing' absolutist instinct. She could not find room in her thinking for acceptance of the parallel legitimacy of someone else's loyalty. It was probably the clearest example I

had seen so far of one of Margaret's most tragic failings: an inability to appreciate, still less accommodate, somebody else's patriotism.

(Howe 1994: 347–8)

Later in the year measures were enacted to outlaw strikes and subscriptions to political funds unless approved by union members in secret ballots.

Little use was made of the accumulated legislation, however, to discipline the workforce in what became the most protracted act of collective defiance in the history of the British labour movement: the strike of coal-workers in opposition to pit closures, which began in March 1984. During the strike Arthur Scargill, president of the National Union of Miners (NUM), conveyed the impression that he was leading a revolutionary vanguard to cleanse Britain of the entire Thatcher-ite project. Thatcher's impulse was to use 'the civil remedies which our trade union laws had provided' to sequestrate the funds of the NUM and other unions engaged in secondary action (M. Thatcher 1993: 353), but having been per-suaded not to antagonize moderate opinion by such draconian measures she pretended that the dispute was a local matter between the miners and the Coal Board. The government was nevertheless set on defeating the miners, and Thatcher revealed that she was no less manichean than Scargill by letting slip her conviction that the strikers had to be taught as firm a lesson as the Argentines in the Falklands war. Among measures that had been taken to counteract social indiscipline since the urban riots of 1981, and a coal strike in the same year, was the refurbishment of the police, which promoted more effective control of crowds and mass picketing. Denis Thatcher's remarks disarmingly belie his wife's fiction that the government was not involved in the dispute:

I had no doubt that Margaret would eventually see off the miners but the strike dragged on for a year – a long time. She was totally determined. The general view is 'We'll beat the buggers', and so she did. The miners brought down Heath's government and she wasn't going to have it happen twice. . . .

Margaret saw the strike coming and we put coal stocks everywhere – an enormous quantity stockpiling. She also had to make sure that the electric generating union didn't go on strike, and, thankfully, they didn't.

(C. Thatcher 1996: 216–17)

By eventually beating 'the buggers' Thatcher won admiration for vanquishing the strategically inept though oratorically persuasive Scargill, but her inflexibility when confronted by an industry that was a bastion of working-class values con-firmed a perception of her as an intransigent politician unsympathetic to those who did not view events from her confined perspective.

Another sign of the government's determination to dismantle corporatism was the decision to sell off state-owned industries and utilities – taken several years after think-tanks had urged converts to the new conservatism to make it the flagship of their policy. The government embarked on a programme of privatization only after the sale of public housing to tenants at a discount price had proved to be electorally attractive in Thatcher's first administration. Many people were induced to buy shares by the flotation of nationalized industries on the stock exchange for less than they were worth, enabling the government to claim that it was engaging in an exercise of popular capitalism by increasing the number of share-holders and, through council house sales, extending home-ownership. Privatization had the additional advantage of providing the Treasury with revenue that could be used for tax cuts and other electoral bribes. British Telecom was disposed of in 1984, British Gas two years later, and by the time Thatcher left office about half of the public-sector industries had been sold.

There was also an assault upon local government, which Thatcher reviled as left wing and prodigal. In the attempt to destroy the heartlands of municipal social-ism, a move which was opposed by all the cabinet apart from Thatcher and her Treasury ministers, the Greater London Council was abolished, as were the met-ropolitan authorities. Treasury controls were imposed on remaining councils by a form of rate-capping which curtailed their power to adjust local levels of taxation. In such ways a government committed to trim the state arrogated more powers to itself in a bid to remove obstacles to the Thatcherite agenda.

On a wider front Thatcher had some notable successes in her second term. She helped to unfreeze the Cold War by establishing a rapport with Mikhail Gorbachev whom she met when he visited London in December 1984, a few months before he became leader of the Soviet Union. Already close to the US President, Ronald Reagan, she persuaded him that what he called the 'evil empire' was on the brink of economic and political reformation, and achieved global prominence by interceding between the two superpowers. When she was deposed by her party Thatcher was more esteemed in the USA and Eastern Europe than at home. Between 1984 and 1986 she won concessions from the European Com-munity. By haranguing the European heads of government, whom she treated as though they were members of her own cabinet, she managed to reduce the dis-proportionate amount which Britain paid to the Community, and also obstructed what she considered to be a drive towards a federal Europe by insisting that the Community provided an opportunity, not for monetary and political integration, but for greater economic competition as its member states opened their markets to one another. In the Commonwealth, for which she had no more affection than for the European Community, Thatcher also had her way by stubbornly resisting the determination of the other heads to impose mandatory sanctions on the apartheid regime in South Africa.

Perhaps Thatcher's greatest achievement in her second term was the one of which she was least proud, the signing in November 1985 of the Anglo-Irish Agreement which gave the Republic of Ireland a formal role in Northern Irish affairs. The Conservatives, though overwhelmingly instinctive Unionists, were on the whole remarkably ignorant about the politics and geography of Northern Ireland. A visit to Belfast as Minister of Defence confirmed the opinion of one of

Thatcher's more exotic admirers 'that it is hopeless here. All we can do is arm the Orangemen – to the teeth – and get out' (Clark 1993: 395), while Carol Thatcher, extolling her parents' concern for the place, wrote of how they met the troops and loyal inhabitants on 'regular morale-raising trips to the Republic'! (C. Thatcher 1996: 221). Thatcher's own unionist impulses were reinforced by the death of Airey Neave, her campaign manager in the leadership contest of 1975, who had been murdered at Westminster by the Irish National Liberation Army (INLA) shortly before the 1979 general election; and also by the Irish Republican Army (IRA) bombing in 1984 of the Grand Hotel, Brighton, when she and most of the cabinet were in residence for the annual party conference, which killed five people and injured many more. For her, terrorism was a law-and-order issue requiring a resolute stance by the British government. In 1981 Thatcher, whose initial preference was to restore to Northern Ireland a system of majority rule similar to that prevailing under the former Stormont regime (M. Thatcher 1993: 385–6), was prepared to let IRA hunger-strikers become martyrs rather than concede to their demand for political status. She was sceptical of James Prior's proposal in the same year for a scheme of 'rolling devolution' to establish a Northern Irish Assembly, initially to be a forum for debate but eventually to possess legislative powers in matters where there was cross-community consensus, fearing that it would rekindle devolutionary aspirations in Scotland and Wales. Convinced that Northern Ireland should be governed from Westminster, she diluted the aspect of Prior's plan which would have given the Republic a role in Northern politics, and encouraged by the party's hard right she announced in cabinet that it was 'a rotten Bill, and that in any case she herself would not be voting for it because she was off to the USA' (Prior 1986: 199). In 1984 she even contemplated redrawing the boundary between the two parts of Ireland as a means of strengthening security in the north by removing from it a proportion of nationalists (M. Thatcher 1993: 398).

Thatcher was instinctively repelled by the Anglo-Irish Agreement's inclusion of Dublin in the management of Northern Ireland through a joint secretariat and structures for enhancing cross-border co-operation. She was induced to sign the international treaty by the immensely able Douglas Hurd, who had replaced Prior at the Northern Ireland Office, and the shrewd Irish taoiseach, Garret FitzGerald, who told her that political stalemate would drive an increasing number of Northern catholics from the constitutional nationalist Social and Democratic Labour party (SDLP) into the clutches of republican Sinn Fein:

> It took a gigantic struggle by many far-sighted people to persuade her; but though her head was persuaded, her heart was not. Her respect for Garret's integrity was tempered by misgiving at his success in persuading her to compromise with an Irish nationalism for which she had neither sympathy nor understanding.
>
> (Howe 1994: 427)

In her memoirs, which minimize FitzGerald's influence upon her, Thatcher regretted that she had been propelled by a desire to defeat terrorism to concur with a measure which antagonized Ulster Unionists without securing a cessation of violence, announcing that 'it is surely time to consider an alternative approach' (M. Thatcher 1993: 415). The decision to sign the Agreement is one she preferred to forget, and is given scant attention in the annals of the Thatcher era. By consenting to formalize inter-state co-operation in Northern Irish affairs, however, she unleashed a process that in the long term nudged Unionists, who exceeded even her in their obduracy, towards some form of accommodation with nationalists as well as persuading republicans of the prospect of a non-violent settlement. Although the IRA cease-fire of 1994 is often attributed to the tenacity of John Major, it was achieved largely through the energy of the SDLP leader, John Hume, and the Irish taoiseach, Albert Reynolds, as well as by American brokerage. Increasingly dependent upon Ulster Unionist votes in the Commons because of a dwindling parliamentary majority, Major was instrumental in triggering the breakdown of the cease-fire by continually tightening the conditions upon which Sinn Fein could enter all-party talks. It was left to the Blair government, again with Irish and American involvement, to renew the search for a peaceful outcome to the Northern Irish conflict. The Anglo-Irish Agreement, by internationalizing the situation and thereby raising the sights of successive British governments above issues of security, may have set in place a framework for eventually resolving an apparently intractable problem. If so, though she would have vehemently dissented, the Agreement will be among Thatcher's most enduring legacies.

The strangest episode in Thatcher's second term, one which almost brought about her downfall, was the Westland affair, an intra-cabinet dispute of such byzantine complexity as to prompt Denis Thatcher to confess a decade later that he still did not have 'a clue what it was all about' (C. Thatcher 1996: 233). As Secretary of State for Trade and Industry the capable but insecure Leon Brittan, who in his previous incarnation as Home Secretary had demonstrated an extraordinary capacity of putting his brain on hold to indulge the whims of his political mistress, urged the cabinet in late 1985 to approve a proposal to rescue Westland, Britain's only helicopter manufacturer, from bankruptcy by selling it to the American company Sikorski. As Defence Secretary the immensely ambitious Michael Heseltine, an unreconstructed corporatist who opposed the American takeover of an important defence industry, spent the Christmas recess assembling a European consortium willing to purchase Westland. On 3 January 1986 he sanctioned the publication of a letter he had sent to the consortium, and as Solicitor-General Sir Patrick Mayhew was prevailed upon by Downing Street to write to Heseltine highlighting some 'material inaccuracies' in his letter. After disclosure by Collette Bowe, chief information officer at the Department of Trade and Industry, to the Press Association of the part of Mayhew's letter intimating that Heseltine had been telling fibs, the Attorney-General Sir Michael Havers threatened to invoke the assistance of the police unless the government instigated an inquiry into the leak. Bowe, who had phoned Bernard Ingham for advice, insisted that he told her to place Mayhew's letter in the public domain, though Ingham pointed the finger of blame at the hapless Brittan by persisting in his claim that he neither bullied Bowe to break the Official Secrets Act nor involved the prime minister in a campaign to smear Heseltine (Ingham 1991: 335).

When Thatcher tried to muzzle her Defence Secretary by declaring to her ministers on 9 January that any statements about Westland must be cleared by the cabinet secretary, Sir Robert Armstrong, Heseltine strode out of the meeting to announce his resignation from the government to startled journalists who happened to be in Downing Street. On the night of 13 January Brittan, who earlier in the day had made a disastrous speech about the affair to the Commons, apologized to the House for misleading it. Following an inconclusive inquiry by Armstrong into the leaking of Mayhew's letter, Thatcher gave a turgid performance in the Commons, and to appease furious Conservative backbenchers Brittan – still protesting his innocence – resigned on 24 January. Before an emergency debate on the affair some days later Thatcher confided that she might not survive as premier, but Brittan's martyrdom and a lame speech by Neil Kinnock as leader of the Labour opposition were enough to rally her party behind her.

Although Thatcher narrowly escaped nemesis in the Westland affair, whose murky waters remain to be fathomed, she did not emerge unscathed. An impression was left of a prime minister who, though boasting of her steadfast adherence to principle, was no less inclined than her predecessors to save her political skin by indulging in machinations and being economical with the truth. And in bringing to the surface her vulnerable political style the affair revealed, not the invincible Britannia of the Falklands war, but a person like the rest of us with feet of clay. The frailties that were to contribute to her demise in 1990 were apparent in two ways: her inability – despite and possibly because of an overbearing personality – to preclude tribal warfare between her ministers, especially over European issues; and her tendency to retreat into the bunker, leaving the management of issues to her entourage, particularly Ingham and her private secretary, Charles Powell.

There were other indications of discontent with her style of government. There was less than enthusiastic support for the Thatcherite project among the 'chattering classes'. In 1985 Oxford dons had provoked a rumpus by voting not to award their alumnus an honorary doctorate, partly in response to her socially divisive policies but also in protest against savage cuts imposed upon universities by a government determined to make higher education subservient to economic needs as well as to align its structures with those of business. The revolt of the intelligentsia was matched by that of the established church which, declining to become the spiritual appendage of Thatcherism, finally erased its reputation as the Conservative party at prayer by continuing to articulate the values of consensus politics. Its primate Robert Runcie, always willing to discern subtleties where Thatcher preferred simplicity, was vilified in the Tory press, and a Church of England report on the plight of the urban poor was denounced by government ministers as a Marxist document. There were also rumours that the Queen was unimpressed by Thatcher's distaste for the Commonwealth, her apparent lack of concern for the underprivileged, and by her confrontational attitude to the 'enemies within'. The monarch was probably not enamoured of her prime minister's cultivation of a grand manner, and the royal household was irritated by the tendency of Thatcherites to deride it as an epitome of patrician 'wetness' (Pimlott 1996: 459–69, 494–518).

Nor was there much affection for the Thatcherite agenda in the country at large. Following Westland the Conservative party trailed in the opinion polls, and Thatcher's own rating was as low as it had been before the Falklands war. The economy, however, was improving, privatization provided revenue for reducing direct taxation, monetary targets were surreptitiously abandoned to increase spending on education, housing and health, popular capitalism had enabled a growing number of people to acquire shares and buy their own homes, and although unemployment remained above 3 million those in work enjoyed rising living standards. In the general election of 11 May 1987 the government won a third term with a majority of 102.

Electoral victory gave Thatcher the confidence to purge the cabinet of more of those who were unreliable or incompetent, and also to surge ahead with her agenda. In 1986 Keith Joseph, certain in his convictions but an indecisive minister, had been replaced at Education by the less doctrinally charged but hyperactive Kenneth Baker who initiated a laborious process that was to culminate in the Education Reform Act 1988. Parents and governors were given the option of making their schools centrally funded government-maintained institutions if they wished to remove them from local control for whatever reason – the most plausible, for Thatcher, being a desire 'to escape from the clutches of some left-wing local authority keen to impose its own ideological priorities' (M. Thatcher 1993: 592). By introducing a core curriculum, with regular testing of children, the Act also eroded the discretion of teachers and examination boards to decide what should be taught. Much energy was expended in cabinet discussing what constituted an appropriate syllabus, particularly in history, which Thatcher wanted to transform into a comfortable story of 'this island race' told through cardinal political events. In 1989 the National Health Service, though not – as some think-tanks advocated – privatized, was restructured as an internal market: hospitals, like schools, were permitted to opt out of local government control to become self-governing trusts funded by Whitehall; and general practitioners were encouraged to become budget-holders able to shop around among hospitals in search of the most economical treatment for their patients. There were further trade union reforms, and the legal profession was incensed by an offensive against its restrictive practices, as well as by a reduction of judicial discretion, in the Criminal Justice Act 1988, which authorized ministers to override the courts by increasing lengths of imprisonment for serious crimes. These attempts to standardize sentencing and also what was taught in schools were further evidence of how a government pledged to decentralize power was engaged in a programme of nationalization by other means. There was also an accelerated effort to strengthen the social fabric against indiscipline: the pay of the police was again increased and its resources improved; and a Broadcasting Standards Council – eventually given statutory authority in 1989 – was established to counteract the effects of permissiveness by monitoring the amount of sex and violence displayed on television.

What she described as the flagship of her third term, the community charge, turned out to be Thatcher's 'greatest blunder throughout her eleven years' as premier (Lawson 1992: 584; see also Crick and van Klaveren 1991). The poll tax, as nearly everyone except Thatcher called the charge, originated in a promise to abolish domestic rates which Heath had prompted her to make in 1974 when she had opposition responsibility for Environment. There was an impeccable Thatcherite logic for replacing the rating system, which levied local taxation on those who owned homes and businesses, by a flat charge on all resident adults: local government would become accountable to all the voters who benefited from its services; as a consequence local authority spending would be curbed by the installation of a regime which, as the minister presiding at Environment when the poll tax was conceived put it, was designed to 'reward the thrifty and punish the extravagant' (Baker 1993: 123).

The tax was intended to be the final solution to the problem of municipal socialism. The practical difficulties of abolishing rates were nevertheless immense, and since the failure of the Heath administration to fulfil its electoral pledge there had been numerous inconclusive inquiries into the matter. A team assembled at Environment in 1984 gradually formulated the idea of a new tax, and what persuaded Thatcher and others to embrace the scheme in the following year was a rate re-evaluation in Scotland (where the number of Conservative seats was already small) which provoked a middle-class outcry against increases – in some cases dramatic – of their rates bills. In early 1986 the poll tax was approved by the cabinet with hardly a murmur of dissent, perhaps because those present at the meeting were dumbfounded by the departure during the previous item of Heseltine over the Westland issue. Baker – who though later claimed to have been sceptical about the proposal was probably instrumental in helping to devise a scheme he thought would appeal to Thatcher (Cole 1995: 317) – wanted the charge to be phased in over ten years with pump-priming revenue from the Treasury to mitigate its effects. But Nicholas Ridley, his replacement at Environment, was an ardent Thatcherite who favoured a 'big-bang' approach, and in 1987 the decision was taken to introduce the tax in one go, initially in Scotland in 1989, and the next year in England and Wales. Despite measures in 1989 to moderate the charge many people faced enormous increases in local taxation, there were protests and demonstrations throughout the country, vast numbers refused to pay their bills, the cost of collecting the tax was immense, local authorities spent more while blaming the government for the rises, and the government slumped in the opinion polls. After Thatcher's demise, Heseltine – rehabilitated as Environment Secretary in the first Major administration – replaced the community charge with a council tax based upon the capital value of property.

Perhaps because the poll tax was such an exemplar of the Thatcherite project, the disastrous decision to abolish the rates is often attributed to the prime minister's obduracy. For once the finger of blame is somewhat misdirected. If Thatcher showed some remorse for having failed to fulfil the election pledge of 1974, she was initially disinclined by her instinctive statecraft to embrace the scheme hatched at the Department of the Environment. In the cabinet only Nigel Lawson, who as Chancellor of the Exchequer produced a paper in 1985 indicating the impracticalities and political dangers of the tax, remained staunchly opposed to its introduction. Lawson, though claiming that Thatcher eventually became obsessed with the merits of the proposal (Lawson 1992: 577), readily acknowledged that she did not have to deploy her usual tactics of bullying her ministers into submission. Her problem was her 'political longevity . . . : she had almost run out of ministers who were prepared to be openly critical even when she would have benefited from a restraining hand' (Cole 1995: 314). Qualities heralded as her virtues during the Falklands war were nevertheless perceived again as vices as a result of the charge. The regressive nature of the tax, by which the widow in her council flat was required to pay the same flat charge as the laird in his castle, confirmed a widespread impression of an intractable, dictatorial and uncompromising woman who had been propelled by her ideological fixations to widen the gap between rich and poor.

The poll tax débâcle convinced many outside parliament of the prime minister's wayward judgement, but what persuaded a growing number of Conservative MPs that she had become an electoral liability was an anti-Thatcher alliance of two of her three chief ministers: Nigel Lawson and Sir Geoffrey Howe, who since 1981 had between them been responsible for implementing the government's economic policy. The clever but arrogant and undiplomatic Lawson, who succeeded Howe as Chancellor of the Exchequer in 1983, had engineered the economic recovery which helped to secure Thatcher's third term. Lawson, having discarded monetarism, believed that the solution to fiscal indiscipline lay in Britain's entry into the Exchange-Rate Mechanism (ERM) of the European Union, and from March 1987 he began to shadow the German mark in a covert operation to make sterling part of the European Monetary System. For Thatcher, who was unaware of what Lawson was doing until told by journalists in November, settled exchange rates were a bid to sidestep the disciplines of the market as well as a move towards European integration, and shortly before the 1988 budget she instructed Lawson to cease his surreptitious activities. In a September address to the College of Europe at Bruges she further antagonized Lawson and other pro-Europeans by condemning the emergence of a European super-state at a time when Britain was rolling back the frontiers of government, thereby intimating that entry into the Exchange Rate Mechanism would reverse the Thatcherite project. Her message appeared to be that there could be no comfortable middle way between national sovereignty and European federalism, just as she had discovered from Hayek's *The Road to Serfdom* that there was no haven for the state somewhere between the free market and socialist regimentation. At a European summit in June 1989 Thatcher nevertheless committed Britain to enter the ERM, having been told by

Lawson and Howe on the eve of the Madrid meeting that they would resign unless she complied with their wishes. Four months later Lawson did resign because she refused to dismiss her personal economic adviser Alan Walters – an unpolluted monetarist who had returned to the post after an absence of five years – after he had derided the ERM as 'half-baked' and suggested that shadowing the Deutschmark had jeopardized Britain's economic miracle. In his resignation speech to the Commons Lawson insinuated that Thatcher was an incessant meddler who used her entourage of advisers to undermine ministers:

> for our system of Cabinet government to work effectively, the Prime Minister of the day must appoint Ministers whom he or she trusts and then leave them to carry out the policy. When differences of view emerge, as they are bound to do from time to time, they should be resolved privately and, whenever appropriate, collectively.
>
> (Lawson 1992: 1063)

Here was additional ammunition for those who charged the prime minister with turning the doctrine of collective cabinet responsibility upside down.

Meanwhile, in a July cabinet reshuffle, Thatcher had punished the other partner in the alliance for his disloyalty by removing him from the Foreign Office on the pretext that 'something had happened to Geoffrey. His enormous capacity for work remained, but his clarity of purpose and analysis had dimmed' (M. Thatcher 1993: 756). Howe had been a safe pair of hands through the Thatcher decade: 'a quiet zealot' who, though less ideologically vociferous than the prime minister, had stubbornly adhered to her agenda (Cole 1995: 296), and so unexciting in his dogged attention to detail that Denis Healey, his Labour shadow at the Treasury, was prompted to tell the Commons that debating with him was akin to being 'savaged by a dead sheep'. Thatcher, though assisted in her project by the docile competence of the only member of her team who had served without interruption in her shadow cabinet and every administration, was continuously infuriated by his plodding rehearsal of every side of an issue, and probably intimidated by the burning ambition which his somnolent tenacity barely concealed. Thatcher's often brutal treatment of Howe exceeded her normal standards of brusqueness in dealing with irritating ministers, and she frequently humiliated him in cabinet.

In the reshuffle she annoyed Douglas Hurd, who with Howe and Lawson formed the trio of her top ministers, by offering Howe his post as Home Secretary. After some wrangling Howe agreed to become Leader of the Commons on condition that he was given a government house in the country and made deputy prime minister. The next day Bernard Ingham, always ready to be the prime minister's mouthpiece, informed the press that the latter was a courtesy title without political significance, and Howe's resentment was aggravated by his exclusion from some cabinet committees. On returning from a European summit in late October 1990, at which Britain was the only member state to vote against further economic and monetary union, Thatcher indulged in a spectacular parliamentary display of Euro-bashing from a perspective of what Howe described as 'nationalist crudity' (Howe 1994: 645). Howe left the government after she had used a trivial issue to ridicule him yet again in cabinet, and in his resignation speech on 13 November 'the dead sheep' startled the Commons by giving one of its most accomplished and devastating performances in the twentieth century. With Lawson sitting beside him Howe said that Thatcher's hostility to the European Union was making Britain isolated and ineffective, and intimated that her increasingly reckless behaviour had undermined cabinet responsibility because any effort to formulate a common policy 'risked being subverted by some casual comment or impulsive answer'. Announcing that he could no longer reconcile loyalty to the prime minister with his perception of the national interest, Howe concluded with an injunction to 'others to consider their own response to the tragic conflict of loyalties with which I have myself wrestled for perhaps too long' (Howe 1994: 697–703).

Some of the party's unease with Thatcher's style had already been revealed in December 1989 when Sir Anthony Meyer, an obscure patrician Tory, challenged her in a leadership contest, and one-fifth of Conservative MPs either voted for him or abstained. The day after Howe's resignation Michael Heseltine, who since he left the government over the Westland affair had contrived to give the impression that he was leader in waiting, announced that he would challenge Thatcher, and following an inept campaign on her behalf she secured 204 votes as against his 152, which under the party's electoral rules left her four short of the 15 per cent margin she required for victory. She immediately declared her intention of standing in the second ballot but in private conversation most of her ministers predicted her defeat; on 22 November, overcome with emotion, she informed the cabinet of her withdrawal from the contest.

Throughout her premiership Thatcher had been a reluctant parliamentarian. She expended enormous energy preparing for the set-piece prime minister's question time, but made fewer speeches, statements and impromptu interventions in the Commons than any of her predecessors in the twentieth century (Dunleavy *et al.* 1990). Perhaps there were too many contingent factors at work in the volatile atmosphere of the House for someone who preferred to control any situation in which she found herself. In her final mandatory appearance in the Commons after she had announced her resignation, however, Thatcher's unscripted performance was sufficiently cathartic to send pangs of remorse and doubt through some MPs who had voted for Heseltine in the leadership contest. Her resignation enabled Douglas Hurd and John Major to enter the campaign, and Thatcher was quick to anoint the latter as the man most likely to defeat the detested Heseltine as well as to carry forward her agenda.

There were various explanations for her demise. Some of Thatcher's more fervent admirers suggested that the 'iron lady' had become somewhat brittle in her last years because of her failure to surround herself with enough of her own kind (Ridley 1992: 17, 258), which had a ring of truth because by the time of her downfall there were few true believers left in the cabinet. Alan Clark, commenting upon her unpopularity in the aftermath of the poll tax, noted that she had no 'Praetorian Guard' to protect her in hard times:

> There's been a lot of talk about 'one of us', all that, but most of them are still left to moulder at the '92 dinner table. When's the Revolution? In the meantime, all the Wets and Blue Chips and general Heathite wankers, who seem ineradicable in this bloody party, stew around and pine for her to drop dead.
>
> (Clark 1993: 289)

Those from whom she had already parted company attributed Thatcher's increasingly erratic judgement and excessive authoritarianism to her dependence upon private advisers, reinforcing her belief that key members of the cabinet were dispensable and allowing the 'coherent' ideology of earlier years 'to take second place to a cult of personality and personal infallibility' (Lawson 1992: 975). Shortly before his wife's downfall, Denis Thatcher commented that after more than a decade in power there were inevitably numerous disgruntled Conservative MPs: the 'usual combination of the "ambitious coupled with the disaffected" and "disappointed" is nothing new – indeed when we passed ten years I have long foretold it' (C. Thatcher 1996: 260).

In her parliamentary party Thatcher's treatment of Lawson and Howe 'confirmed what errors about policy had already suggested: she had replaced the political savvy which is needed to hold a government together with a stubborn omniscience' (Cole 1995: 324). There was nothing inevitable about Thatcher's undoing, however, and a better campaign team would probably have secured more than the additional four votes she needed in the first ballot. In the absence of an effective campaign those of her faults identified by Howe in his resignation speech were magnified in the minds of MPs because of the party's poor rating in the opinion polls – a consequence of the poll tax, high inflation and a faltering economy. Too many Conservative backbenchers thought that she had become an electoral liability.

Thatcher was shell-shocked by the party's failure to rally to her support, and for a long time was overwhelmed by a sense of betrayal (C. Thatcher 1996: 278). After suffering from dreadful withdrawal symptoms, however, she renewed her fearsome schedule. She collaborated on her memoirs, superintended a foundation bearing her name which awarded generous grants to causes that promoted understanding of free-enterprise institutions, and gave lucrative lectures to huge audiences in America, Japan and those other parts of the world where she was more honoured than at home. The ennobled Thatcher appeared rarely in the Lords, but in occasional interviews and speeches she reminded people of her achievements in 'rolling forward the frontiers of freedom' in Britain and on a larger stage, pronouncing that Thatcherism would long survive her because 'we had the courage to restore the great principles and put them into practice', and continuing to blame the stalling of her economic agenda on Lawson's decision to shadow the Deutschmark. Sometimes she tried to intervene in the political process, revealing by 1995 that she had become disillusioned with Major because of his lack of vigour in pursuing the free-market crusade, and adding to his problems with Conservative Euro-sceptics by calling for a firmer stance against the perceived drift towards a federal Europe. In the leadership contest following Major's resignation in 1997 she announced before television cameras that William Hague was the candidate most likely to recharge the Thatcherite project. Later in the year she joined him in the campaign against the Labour government's plan for Scottish and Welsh devolution, prophesying that the creation of regional assemblies would prompt the disintegration of the Union. By now, however, her shrill and imperious demeanour verged on self-parody, and her minders seemed anxious to shield the battling baroness from derision by curtailing her exposure to the public.

Thatcher had become leader of the Conservative party at a time when the country lacked self-confidence. Her achievement was to persuade a sizeable section of the nation, by force of personality and unwavering conviction, that economic and political decline was not irreversible. Largely through her iron resolve a more-or-less coherent strategy unfolded through the 1980s, though often tempered by expediency and sometimes blown off course by her increasingly wayward behaviour. During the Thatcher era, however, many of the electorate would have preferred to inhabit a society that was more irenic and magnanimous, less ranting and intolerant, than the brutopia of competitive individualism which she strove to accomplish. Some suspected that the 'great principles' of free enterprise she claimed to have rediscovered were little else than a licence for the rich to become wealthier while permitting others to slip into an underclass of the unemployed and socially deprived on the pretext that poverty was primarily a consequence of individual irresponsibility. Many remained committed to the collective provision of health and welfare, and persisted in their belief that the ethos of service prevailing among those who worked in the public sector was a clearer index of a civilized society than the bureaucratic structures of an internal market imposed by a government that seemed to prize the calculation of rational self-interest as the mainspring of human endeavour. Nor was there much evidence that the beneficiaries of a consumer spree were eager to constrain their personal preferences by joining a crusade to retrieve the values of a less permissive, more austere and deferential age.

Thatcher commanded the political agenda less through her advocacy – however persuasive for some – of a free economy framed by a strong state than because her administrations, particularly in the middle period, managed to reduce personal taxation, extend home-ownership, and secure a measure of consumer prosperity for those in work. Her 'authoritarian populism' may have achieved a programme of what the left called regressive modernization: regressive because it tilted the balance even more in favour of the rich; modernizing because, though not arresting Britain's relative decline in the global economy, it made descent more controllable. But it did so without creating a moral hegemony. A sufficient proportion of the electorate was prepared to collude with her radical agenda, though often lamenting its socially divisive effects, so long as they benefited economically. The catastrophic scale of the Major government's defeat in the general election of

1997 revealed not only the damage she had done to her party in fracturing it, particularly over Europe, by her combative style, but also the fragility of her credo.

The Thatcherite project nevertheless achieved a kind of hegemony, though not by precipitating a national stampede towards the self-help, anti-permissive values extolled by its principal architect in her endorsement of Victorian Britain. The exposure to the imperative of the market of so many established institutions, including the professions, altered the cultural landscape, perhaps irreversibly, by eroding those traditional attitudes of deference and respect which had conserved patrician Toryism. If the Thatcherite agenda failed to forge a new consensus around the themes of free enterprise and a disciplinary state, it did undermine the comfortable image of an intricate, beneficent and secure social hierarchy which the bulk of Conservatives since Disraeli had made the basis of their One Nation electoral appeal by promising to improve 'the condition of the people'. The two rudiments that had supported Conservative doctrine since Peel – meritocratic individualism and benevolent paternalism – were both damaged, perhaps irreparably, by the Thatcherite programme, leaving the party to seek fresh ideological foundations.

In a sense, too, Thatcher's claim to have made Britain a post-socialist society is not implausible. By harnessing widespread discontent with incessant strikes to emasculate the power of organized labour, and also in capitalizing on the popularity of share-ownership to reduce public ownership, the Thatcherite project tackled – in a way a Labour government would not have dared to do – two of the cardinal obstacles to the formulation of a credible left-of-centre political creed for a post-Keynesian age. Thatcher's prolonged ascendancy prompted an incompetent Labour Opposition – undisciplined, still mesmerized by the shibboleths of statism, and apparently destined for oblivion – to reorganize and design market-orientated policies that were more socially cohesive than those devised by the devotees of unfettered capitalism. By enabling the Labour party to embrace market communitarianism she assisted the left to relocate to a position where it could convey the values of a majority which, though largely silent in the 1980s, had rarely been enamoured of Thatcherism. If the Anglo-Irish Agreement which she came to detest was one of Thatcher's more enduring legacies, another was a Labour party re-equipped to articulate the aspirations of consensus politics. Her feat had been to restore to a nation contemplating nemesis in the 1970s a sense of purpose and a belief in its governability. It was left to more emollient politicians to demonstrate that Britain could be directed along a course that was less rugged than the terrain mapped out by Thatcher.

References and further reading

Anderson, O. (1989) *Rotten Borough*, London: Fourth Estate. (Hilarious novel about the corruption of small-town politics which features a local councillor who owns a corner grocer's shop. The book was withdrawn three weeks after it was first published in 1937 because of writs issued by Grantham dignitaries.)

Baker, K. (1993) *The Turbulent Years: My Life in Politics*, London: Faber & Faber.

(Lucid if somewhat self-serving account of many of Thatcher's reforms by a minister who was successively at Trade, the Environment, and Education, before becoming party chairman in 1989.)

Charmley, J. (1996) *A History of Conservative Politics, 1900–1996*, London: Macmillan.

Clark, A. (1993) *Diaries*, London: Weidenfeld & Nicolson. (Entertaining glimpse into the Conservative political world by a robustly Thatcherite junior minister.)

Cole, J. (1995) *As It Seemed to Me: Political Memoirs*, London: Weidenfeld & Nicolson. (Chronicle of the period by the political editor of the BBC which is packed with tittle-tattle gleaned from numerous conversations with ministers.)

Creasy, R. (1997) 'Was it grocer's misconduct?', *Punch* 21 June: 20–3. (On the Grantham gossip about Thatcher's father.)

Crick, B. (1997) 'Dishing the dirt – all for the greater common good', *Punch* 21 June: 21–2. (On how he failed to persuade the press during the 1987 general election to publish the rumours about Alderman Roberts.)

Crick, M. and van Klaveren, A. (1991) 'Mrs Thatcher's greatest blunder', *Contemporary Record* 5: 397–416. (The story of the poll tax débâcle.)

Dunleavy, P., Jones, G. and O'Leary, B. (1990) 'Prime ministers and the Commons: patterns of behaviour, 1868–1987', *Public Administration* 68: 123–40.

FitzGerald, G. (1991) *All in a Life: An Autobiography*, Dublin: Gill & Macmillan. (Intricate account of the making of the Anglo-Irish Agreement which reveals, though not uncharitably, both how hard he had to work to persuade Thatcher of its merits and her incomprehension of the political complexities of Northern Ireland.)

Fowler, N. (1991) *Ministers Decide: A Personal Memoir of the Thatcher Years*, London: Chapmans. (A rather sanitized, though occasionally revealing, version of events from the perspective of a minister who, though not a pure Thatcherite, was always a safe pair of hands.)

Gamble, A. (1988) *The Free Economy and the Strong State*, London: Macmillan. (One of the best accounts of Thatcherism as a hegemonic project.)

Gilmour, I. (1992) *Dancing with Dogma: Britain under Thatcherism*, London: Simon & Schuster. (Penetrating critique of Thatcher's style and policies by a former minister on the left of the Conservative party.)

Hall, S. (1988) *The Hard Road to Renewal: Thatcherism and the Crisis of the Left*, London: Verso. (Includes the essays from the late 1970s and early 1980s in which Hall was the first writer to characterize Thatcherism as a form of authoritarian populism.)

Harris, R. (1990) *Good and Faithful Servant: The Unauthorized Biography of Bernard Ingham*, London: Faber & Faber. (Blistering account of how Thatcher's press secretary used the Lobby to undermine ministers who had fallen out of favour.)

Harrison, B. (1994) 'Mrs Thatcher and the intellectuals', *Twentieth Century British History* 5: 206–45.

Howe, G. (1994) *Conflict of Loyalty*, London: Macmillan. (Invaluable chronology by someone who was at the centre of government through the Thatcher era until his resignation precipitated the prime minister's downfall.)

Ingham, B. (1991) *Kill the Messenger*, London: HarperCollins. (The story of the era from the perspective of Thatcher's notorious press secretary.)

Jenkins, S. (1995) *Accountable to None: The Tory Nationalization of Britain*,

Harmondsworth: Penguin. (An elegant critique of the Thatcher administrations for centralizing power by stealth.)

Joseph, K. (1976) *Stranded on the Middle Ground? Reflections on Circumstances and Policies*, London: Centre for Policy Studies.

Lawson, N. (1992) *The View from No. 11: Memoirs of a Tory Radical*, London: Bantam Press. (Formidable account of how economic policies were formulated during the Thatcher decade as well as an assault upon what he perceived as the weaknesses of her style of governing.)

Letwin, S. (1992) *The Anatomy of Thatcherism*, London: HarperCollins. (An intelligent endorsement from an academic of the right of Thatcher's moral agenda to retrieve the 'vigorous virtues' of a market economy.)

Nuthall, K. (1997) 'Thatcher's dad: mayor, preacher, groper', *Independent on Sunday* 22 June: 3.

Pimlott, B. (1996) *The Queen: A Biography of Elizabeth II*, London: HarperCollins. (Discusses the courteous though cool relations between the monarch and the prime minister as well as the widespread assumption that the Queen would have preferred a more consensual style of governing.)

Prior, J. (1986) *A Balance of Power*, London: Hamish Hamilton. (Engaging story of the problems which a minister who believed in consensus politics had with Thatcher during the first half of her decade in power.)

Pym, F. (1984) *The Politics of Consent*, London: Hamish Hamilton. (A trenchant defence of patrician conservatism by another minister whose 'wetness' infuriated Thatcher.)

Ridley, N. (1992) *'My Style of Government': The Thatcher Years*, London: HarperCollins. (A heavyweight vindication of Thatcherism, as well as a valuable insight into policy-making, by the minister who was responsible for implementing the poll tax.)

Sharp, P. (1997) *Thatcher's Diplomacy: The Revival of British Foreign Policy*. London: Macmillan. (Sympathetic account of how, ironically, the intensely nationalist Falklands warrior and arch Euro-sceptic helped to create a post-Cold War international order.)

Thatcher, C. (1996) *Below the Parapet: The Biography of Denis Thatcher*, London: HarperCollins. (Fascinating portrait of her father by his journalist daughter which also reveals much about the thinking and personal habits of her mother.)

Thatcher, M. (1989a) *Speech . . . to the Central Council at Scarborough on Saturday 18 March 1989*, London: Conservative Central Office. (On the need to roll forward the frontiers of the state against the permissive society.)

—— (1989b) *The Revival of Britain: Speeches on Home and European Affairs 1975–1988*, compl. A. Cooke, London: Aurum Press.

—— (1993) *The Downing Street Years*, London: HarperCollins. (Described in a review by Nigel Lawson as 'setting standards of self-regard hitherto unknown', these memoirs of the years in power nevertheless provide valuable insight into her perspective on every issue.)

—— (1995) *The Path to Power*, London: HarperCollins. (The detailed story of how she eventually climbed the greasy pole from her humble origins in Grantham.)

Young, H. (1991) *One of Us: A Biography of Margaret Thatcher*, London: Macmillan. (By far the best biography from her childhood to her political demise.)

Robert Eccleshall

John Major

Born 29 March 1943, younger son of Thomas Major and Gwendolyn Minny Coates. Educated at Rutlish Grammar School. Married 1970 Norma Johnson. MP for Huntingdonshire 1979–83, Huntingdon 1983–. Parliamentary Private Secretary to the Ministers of State, Home Office, 1981–3; Government Whip 1983–5; Parliamentary Under-Secretary of State for Social Security 1985–6; Minister of State for Social Security and the Disabled 1986–7; Chief Secretary to the Treasury 1987–9; Secretary of State for Foreign and Commonwealth Affairs 1989; Chancellor of the Exchequer 1989–90; Prime Minister 1990–7.

Major emerged as a candidate for the leadership of the Conservative party in 1990, largely unknown in terms of his political philosophy and his capacity for leadership. Seven years later, after a prime ministerial career longer than that of many of his predecessors, commentators still had difficulty in knowing what to make of him. Young in both age and cabinet experience when he succeeded to the premiership, he proved to be a political enigma. Not overtly ambitious, he reached the top of the 'greasy pole' at the age of 47. As a candidate for the Conservative leadership, he was claimed as 'one of us' by both wings of the parliamentary party. Assailed by the press and many of his own party from 1992 onwards for poor leadership, and leading a party which in 1995 trailed in the opinion polls by unprecedented margins, he forced and won re-election as party leader and remained more firmly ensconced in Downing Street than his predecessor when she was faced with electoral unpopularity and doubts about her leadership. By the summer of 1995 he had been in office longer than six of his ten twentieth-century Conservative predecessors, and was emerging as the great survivor of British politics. Two years later he led his party to its worst defeat since 1906 and promptly resigned the leadership.

In terms of background Major was the most remarkable person to become leader of the Conservative party since Disraeli. Although his two predecessors had come from modest backgrounds, they nevertheless made their way in the world by a conventional route from unremarkable lower-middle-class homes through Oxford University. Major had neither a conventional social background nor the experience of a university education. His father was Abraham Thomas Ball, who was later to take the stage name of Major and at times appeared to mix both surnames. Tom Major spent his early life as a master bricklayer, the bulk of his working life in the theatre (juggler, acrobat, comedian) and his later years as a small businessman, producing garden ornaments, before eventually having to sell up to meet a debt. John's mother was his father's second wife, his first having been killed in a freak stage accident. Both wives worked in the theatre. John's childhood was spent initially in Worcester Park, Surrey, but at the age of 12 his father's indebtedness resulted in a move to Brixton, in south London. At school his interests veered toward sport rather than scholarship and at 16 he left, influenced apparently by a desire not to burden his ageing – and ailing – parents. He got a job as a clerk, but later endured a spell of unemployment while helping care for his dying father and ill mother. When he managed to return to employed work, it was in banking. One of his jobs was with the Standard Bank of West Africa and involved a posting to Nigeria. While there, he was involved in a car accident that was to cost him his kneecap and leave him unable to walk long distances. The accident resulted in his return to England for a series of operations, and at one point the possibility of having to amputate his leg was discussed.

Major stayed in banking, working in development finance and serving briefly as an assistant to the bank's chairman, and future Chancellor of the Exchequer, Anthony Barber. At the same time, he began his political career, serving as an active Young Conservative – he formed the Brixton branch in 1965 – and then getting elected in 1968, at the age of 25, to the Lambeth borough council. In the three years that he served on the council, he was a member of the housing committee, becoming vice-chairman and then chairman, in which role he presided over a liberal housing policy (Pearce 1991: 23–4). It was during this period as a councillor that he met and married Norma Johnson, a teacher and dressmaker. In 1971 Major was selected as prospective Conservative candidate for the Labour seat of Camden, St Pancras North, unsuccessfully contesting it in both general elections of 1974. In 1978 he was adopted as candidate for the safe seat of Huntingdonshire, entering parliament in the general election of 1979.

Major's rise to office was speedy, though the period between entering the Commons and sitting on the Treasury bench was not quite as short as that of his two predecessors. Within two years of his election, he was appointed as parliamentary private secretary to the ministers of state at the Home Office. Two years later he began his rapid ascent of the ministerial ladder, spending four years in junior positions – assistant whip, whip, under-secretary, minister of state – before being elevated to the cabinet as Chief Secretary to the Treasury. Of twentieth-century prime ministers, he had the shortest parliamentary experience before entering the cabinet. His rise within the cabinet was as rapid as it had been outside it. In 1989, two years after Major first sat at the cabinet table, Geoffrey Howe was removed unwillingly from the Foreign Office, and Major was appointed as his replacement. Four months later Nigel Lawson resigned as Chancellor of the Exchequer, and Major was shifted to the post. The following year Thatcher lost her grasp of the party leadership, and Major emerged as her favoured successor in the second ballot for the leadership. So he entered Downing Street after seven years' ministerial experience, only three of which had been spent in the cabinet. The premiership was the only ministerial post that he held for a period of more than two years.

The conclusion to be drawn is that in becoming prime minister he was very lucky or very able, or both. There was clearly an element of *fortuna* involved in the timing of the departures of Howe, Lawson and Thatcher, and in the fact that John Wakeham did not want the post of Chief Secretary to the Treasury in 1987 (Lawson 1992: 711). Major's appointment as Foreign Secretary, as he admitted to a cabinet colleague, took him completely by surprise (Baker 1993: 287; see also

Wyn Ellis 1991: 94). There may also have been an element of luck in Major's short tenures of office because there was little time for things to go wrong – though some regard his stint at the Foreign Office as a troubled one. Yet Major's apparently effortless rise also appears to be the consequence of an ability that encompassed character, beliefs and administrative capacity. There is little evidence that it extended to advancement by ingratiation – if anything, the reverse. In his first significant encounter with Thatcher after he had been appointed to government, he got into an argument with her. She did not see him as 'one of us'. 'I did not treat him or his argument kindly', she recalled (Thatcher 1993: 422–3). He had further battles with her when he became Chancellor (Wyn Ellis 1991: 120). He appeared to have had no particular sponsor. His promotion within the Department of Social Security was recommended by the Secretary of State, Norman Fowler (Fowler 1991: 272), and his appointment as Chief Secretary was on the urging of Chancellor of the Exchequer, Nigel Lawson (Lawson 1992: 710–11) at a time when Major was being considered for the post of Chief Whip. His appointment as Foreign Secretary appears to have been the consequence of personal choice by Thatcher, who was determined to appoint anyone other than Douglas Hurd.

Major had a personality that made him popular with those he met. He clearly enjoyed meeting people, took trouble over attending to their needs and focused on the individual to whom he was talking. He was extremely calm in temperament. He mixed easily, including with political opponents. He was unpretentious. As Alan Clark recorded, 'he's not at all *flash* . . . and he's not classy . . . he doesn't even *aspire* to be classy' (Clark 1993: 349–50). Nor was he prone to push his own ideological commitments. When he was Chancellor of the Exchequer, one senior treasury official was asked by this writer what the Chancellor's views were on economic policy. 'We don't know', came the reply, 'all we know is that he likes meeting people'. Major was not devoid of distinctive political views, but his stance was one which was difficult for others to gauge and his short period on the backbenches had given him little time to acquire a reputation for pursuing a particular line within Conservative debate. He was thus able to avoid opposition from particular sections of the party. He also benefited from a good memory. Once in office he was able to master a brief very quickly. That, coupled with his personality, meant that he was generally effective in negotiations, be it with ministers, representatives of particular groups, or – later – heads of government in meetings of the European Council.

In his character and stance towards politics Major resembled the aristocrat Douglas-Home rather than his two immediate predecessors. Like Sir Alec, too, his ambitions for occupying Downing Street were present but not obvious. Major was essentially a fiscal conservative but a social liberal. He had a belief in financial prudence and shared with Thatcher the determination to combat inflation. 'First and foremost', he declared in 1990, 'I loathe inflation' (Anderson 1991: 294). He also shared his predecessor's belief in rolling back the frontiers of the state and putting public utilities in the private sector. He established his position as a liberal on the issue of race relations while serving as a Brixton councillor. In the Commons he voted consistently against the reintroduction of capital punishment, and in 1991 he had a much publicized meeting with gay rights activist, Sir Ian McKellen.

He nonetheless adopted a pragmatic approach, avoiding a rigid stance and being willing to modify his position if persuaded intellectually or by the force of political necessity. For him mobilizing a consensus was important. It was this stance that helps explain his election as party leader. He could be claimed as 'one of us' by supporters of Thatcher (fiscal conservative) and equally by the wets and damps (social liberal). His two opponents were drawn from, and appealed to, the same constituency of 'wets and damps' (see Norton 1990a; 1990b). One, Michael Heseltine, was a self-made millionaire; the other, Douglas Hurd, was a party grandee. Both also carried a lot of political baggage. Major was new, with no ideological or political history to count against him. Like most Conservative MPs, he was middle class. As soon as his candidature was announced, he built up an immediate body of support which, with effective management, soon grew and overtook that being garnered by Heseltine (Anderson 1991; Norton 1993). Opinion polls suggested that he could be as effective as Heseltine in leading the party to victory in the next election, thus undermining the latter's strongest appeal to Conservative MPs. Major achieved a plurality of votes in the second ballot, Heseltine and Hurd withdrew, and Major was declared the victor.

Major had a relatively successful first two years as premier. Despite economic recession, he was praised as an effective leader during the Gulf war and for supporting Boris Yeltsin in Russia in 1991, and led his party to a narrow but unexpected victory in the 1992 general election. He was largely credited with the success, adopting a personal campaign style that was much criticized before the election (he took to campaigning in the streets, standing on an upturned box), but not after it. He was aided considerably by the fact that electors looked upon his government as a new one rather than a continuation of that of Thatcher.

Major's political pragmatism was an asset in the short term in that he was able to modify or jettison those policies to which Thatcher had been committed but which were electorally unpopular. The poll tax was the most notable casualty. He also modified the government's stance on Europe, adopting a less confrontational position. On the issue of greater European integration, Major was a Euro-agnostic (Norton 1993: 41–2), adapting his position to whatever appeared to be in Britain's interest at the time. In the Maastricht treaty of December 1991 he negotiated a successful outcome for Britain. In the long term, however, his pragmatism was a disadvantage (Norton 1994). He had no future goal to pursue. He was concerned with the here and now of politics. The result was that his government appeared increasingly responsive to events. Others were able to set, or disrupt, the agenda, particularly with regard to the issue that was to provide the fault-line of British politics: European integration. Conservatives opposed to greater European integration (dubbed Euro-sceptics) became more vocal and disruptive following the 'no' vote in the first Danish referendum in 1992. The government was knocked off course by the sterling crisis of September 1992 resulting in Britain's withdrawal from the European Exchange Rate Mechanism, further fuelling criticisms of the government's European policy. The recession lasted longer than expected.

The bill to ratify the Maastricht treaty took a year longer than expected to reach the statute book, being achieved only after a final Commons vote had been made a vote of confidence. In November 1994 a bill following the Maastricht negotiations – to give effect to a British commitment to increase the nation's budget contribution to the European Community – was opposed by several Euro-sceptics within the parliamentary party. Major, supported by the cabinet, made the passage of the bill a matter of confidence. Eight Conservative MPs who failed to support the bill at second reading had the whip withdrawn from them and a ninth then resigned the whip in protest. The action was unprecedented (Norton 1995: 10–11) and exacerbated tensions within the party. It rid the government formally of an overall majority and created a body of semi-independent Euro-sceptics on the backbenches. In December, most of the whipless MPs failed to support the government in a vote on an increase in value added tax on domestic fuel: the result was an embarrassing defeat for the government, which then abandoned the increase. The whip was restored to the MPs in April 1995 but the move did little to still tensions within the party. The party suffered huge losses in the May local elections. The Labour party, under a new, young and moderate leader, Tony Blair, achieved unprecedented leads in the opinion polls. Conservative MPs – including some members of the cabinet – took opposing stances on the desirability of a single European currency. Major's leadership came under public attack from a number of disaffected backbenchers. Talk of a leadership challenge in the autumn became more frequent, adding to the uncertainty and disarray within the party.

Also adding to Major's problems were scandals affecting ministers and backbench MPs. Some were personal (allegations of extra-marital or gay affairs) and were used by the media to belittle Major's call at the 1993 party conference for a return to basic values. Others concerned parliamentary activity. In the summer of 1994 two Conservative MPs were accused of accepting cash in return for tabling parliamentary questions, and by the autumn other MPs were caught up in the scandal. Major responded by setting up a Committee on Standards in Public Life headed by a judge, Lord Nolan, and following publication of its report the Commons voted to ban paid advocacy by MPs and to require disclosure of income earned from services offered as an MP. The proposals divided Conservative MPs, some criticizing Major for establishing the committee. Further scandals added to the perception of 'sleaze' in British politics. The publication in 1996 of a critical report by Sir Richard Scott into the actions of junior ministers in deciding guidelines for the export of arms-related equipment to Iraq put further pressure on government. Major was portrayed as presiding over a scandal-ridden administration, offering no leadership while his ministers and backbenchers variously got into trouble.

Divisions within the party over Europe, and Major's failure to give a lead in government, overshadowed the one critical policy area where he was decisive. The willingness of Major to address the Northern Irish problem won him praise but little increase in support in the opinion polls. The Downing Street

Declaration – an attempt to persuade those who supported violence in the province to enter the democratic process – was agreed by Major and Irish premier Albert Reynolds in December 1993. It provided the basis for a cease-fire by the IRA and loyalist paramilitary groups in the province in 1994, and the publication in February 1995 of a consultative framework document for the future government of the province. In March 1995, regular army patrols in the province ceased. Major's stance on the issue was a politically high-risk one, involving no guarantee of success and provoking in March 1995 a sharp exchange between Major and US President Bill Clinton, over the latter's decision to allow Sinn Fein President Gerry Adams to raise funds for Sinn Fein – the political wing of the IRA – in the USA. It also demonstrated some of the qualities that Major had shown during his first two years of office, but rarely since. Major appeared able to move towards achieving in Northern Ireland what he was unable to achieve within his own parliamentary party at home: an agreement between competing factions.

These factions became more vocal during 1995. Major attended a meeting of a group of more than fifty Euro-sceptic MPs – the 'Fresh Start Group' – in June and faced sharp criticism, the MPs showing little respect for his position (Seldon 1997: 562–6). The experience unsettled him and acted as a spur to challenge his critics. He announced his resignation as party leader in order to force a leadership election in which he would be a candidate. He told his critics in the party to 'put up or shut up'. The move proved popular with local parties. Major was expecting – and was expected – to win by a decisive margin. However, when his Welsh Secretary, John Redwood, resigned from the cabinet in order to stand, it was widely predicted that he would draw the support of the Euro-sceptic right. In the first ballot, Major won by a margin that cleared both hurdles necessary for election. He got 218 votes against 89 for Redwood. Twelve MPs spoilt their ballot papers, eight abstained, and two failed to vote. More than one hundred MPs had declined to support the prime minister. However, Redwood failed to poll the full strength of the right in the parliamentary party, and the result was presented as a good, if not overwhelming, win for Major. In the immediate wake of the contest, support for Major – and the Conservative Party – increased in the opinion polls, but then receded.

Although Major's re-election served to confirm that he would lead the Conservative party into the next election, it also showed the fragility of his support in the parliamentary party. His support had moderate breadth but no depth. In 1990 he relied on the votes of those on the right, and in 1995 the votes of those on the left (Cowley 1996; Norton 1997). His re-election failed to still the conflict within the party over the issue of Europe. Euro-sceptics continued to press for a tougher policy on European integration. Pressure for a more sceptical stance was opposed by pro-Europeans within the cabinet, notably Michael Heseltine (made deputy prime minister following the 1995 contest) and Chancellor Kenneth Clarke. When Major looked set to take a more critical line on a single currency, Clarke blocked the move (threatening resignation according to some accounts) and forced Major to reaffirm existing policy. Sceptics pressed for a referendum on Europe and were increasingly vocal in calling for a commitment by government to rule out British participation in a single European currency.

Major appeared unable to bring the party together. The splits attracted continuing and unwelcome headlines. Despite an improvement in economic indicators (inflation fell to its lowest level since 1964), the government's fortunes seemed to go from bad to worse. In Northern Ireland, the government refused to allow Sinn Fein to participate in peace talks until the IRA decommissioned arms. An international commission under a former US Senator (the Mitchell Commission) was set up to try to resolve the deadlock. At the beginning of 1996 the IRA cease-fire ended and bombings resumed on mainland Britain. Also at the beginning of 1996 an announcement of a possible link between bovine spongiform encephalopathy (BSE: 'mad cow disease') and the human consumption of beef, caused a public panic, the imposition by the European Union of a ban on the export of British beef and a subsequent clash between the government and the EU – Britain for a time adopting an 'empty chair' policy at meetings of the Council of Ministers.

By 1997 Major was heading a government that was trailing badly in the opinion polls and, by virtue of by-election losses and the defection of three of its own MPs, had lost its parliamentary majority. It was widely assumed that little progress was likely on the issue of Northern Ireland because of the government's presumed dependence on the support of Ulster Unionist MPs. The government managed to struggle through to March, when Major announced that a general election would take place on 1 May. In the election campaign – the longest in recent history – the Conservatives suffered from a recrudescence of the 'sleaze' issue and from continuing splits over Europe, with an ever-growing number of Conservative candidates (the number eventually exceeded 200) announcing their personal opposition to a single currency. Major toured the country, trying to re-create the success of his 1992 campaign. He failed. The Conservatives suffered their biggest loss in seats since 1906 and their lowest share of the vote in the history of the party. As soon as the defeat was apparent, Major announced that he was resigning the leadership of the party. 'When the curtain comes down', he said, 'it is time to leave the stage'.

For almost seven years, John Major played the politics of survival. His skills were those of persuasion and reaching consensus, not of decisive leadership. He did his best in a situation not faced by any previous Conservative prime minister of the twentieth century: he led a party that was bitterly divided and one that enjoyed a small – and then non-existent – parliamentary majority. Julian Amery once said that a good jockey rides a difficult horse. Major did well to stay astride his horse for as long as he did.

References and further reading

Anderson, B. (1991) *John Major: The Making of the Prime Minister*, London: Fourth Estate. (A detailed, and generally accurate, account of the 1990 Conservative leadership contest, told from the perspective of an insider in the Major campaign.)

Baker, K. (1993) *The Turbulent Years: My Life in Politics*, London: Faber & Faber.

Clark, A. (1993) *Diaries*, London: Weidenfeld & Nicolson.

Cowley, P. (1996) 'How did he do that? The second round of the 1990 Conservative leadership contest', in D. Farrell, B. Broughton, D. Denver and J. Fisher (eds) *British Elections and Parties Yearbook 1996*, London: Frank Cass.

Fowler, N. (1991) *Ministers Decide*, London: Chapmans.

Hogg, S. and Hill, J. (1995) *Too Close to Call*, London: Little, Brown. (A narrative of life from the inside of Downing Street by the head of the Number 10 Policy Unit and Major's political secretary.)

Jenkin, J. (ed.) (1990) *John Major: Prime Minister*, London: Bloomsbury. (A series of press clippings, put together by the Press Association, and useful at least in saving the time of the researcher.)

Junor, P. (1993) *The Major Enigma*, London: Michael Joseph. (More up to date than the other biographies and without the tabloid psychology and padding of Wyn Ellis (1991), though – for the period up to the premiership – not adding a great deal to that already written. Despite numerous quotations from other sources, it is devoid of footnotes.)

Kavanagh, D. and Seldon, A. (1994) (eds) *The Major Effect*, London: Macmillan. (A series of analyses of the effect of the Major government on British politics, economy and society. Each chapter is essentially a short essay, the length limiting the capacity to convey much useful insight and information.)

Lawson, N. (1992) *The View from No. 11: Memoirs of a Tory Radical*, London: Bantam Press.

Norton, P. (1990a) ' "The lady's not for turning": but what about the rest of the party? Margaret Thatcher and the Conservative party 1979–89', *Parliamentary Affairs* 43 (1): 41–58.

—— (1990b) 'Choosing a leader: Margaret Thatcher and the Parliamentary Conservative Party', *Parliamentary Affairs* 43 (3): 249–59.

—— (1993) 'The Conservative Party from Thatcher to Major', in A. King (ed.) *Britain at the Polls*, Chatham, NJ: Chatham House.

—— (1994) 'Factions and tendencies in the Conservative party', in H. Margetts and G. Smyth (eds) *Turning Japanese? Britain with a Permanent Party of Government*, London: Lawrence & Wishart.

—— (1995) 'Whipless MPs: working without the whip', *The House Magazine* 20 (659): 10–11.

—— (1997) 'The Conservative Party: "in office but not in power" ', in A. King (ed.) *New Labour Triumph: Britain at the Polls*, Chatham, NJ: Chatham House. (A review of the party under Major's leadership in the one full parliament of his premiership.)

Pearce, E. (1991) *The Quiet Rise of John Major*, London: Weidenfeld & Nicolson. (A relatively short and sympathetic biography of John Major, focusing on his rise from the terraces of south London to the pinnacle of political power.)

Seldon, A. (1997) *Major: A Political Life*, London: Weidenfeld & Nicolson. (A substantial biography, based on extensive interviewing and focusing primarily on Major's time as prime minister. The work draws together a mass of material, serving largely to confirm much of what had already seeped into the public domain. An assessment of Major's premiership is confined to a short epilogue.)

Thatcher, M. (1993) *Margaret Thatcher: The Downing Street Years*, London: HarperCollins.

Wyn Ellis, N. (1991) *John Major*, London: Macdonald. (Useful for quotations from Major and those close to him, but essentially a 'tabloid' biography, full of padding and low-level analysis.)

Philip Norton

Anthony Charles Lynton Blair

Born 6 May 1953, second child of Leo Blair and Hazel Corscaden. Educated at Durham Choristers School, Fettes College, Edinburgh, and St John's College, Oxford. Married 1980 Cherie Booth. MP for Sedgefield 1983–. Leader of the Opposition 1994–7; Prime Minister 1997–.

In 1997 Tony Blair became Labour's first prime minister for eighteen years. As Leader of the Opposition he had redefined party ideology and policy as well as advancing party presentation and media campaigning techniques. Blair shifted the party away from the social democracy of nationalization, Keynesianism and state welfare towards a more neo-liberal and conservative programme. He also introduced a communitarian one-nation tone to his government against the economic individualism of previous Tory administrations. Under Blair, *new* Labour retained social democratic concerns – for community and the excluded – but with a more conservative emphasis on responsibilities and moral values. As prime minister Blair reached out beyond party and class to an inclusive politics appealing to the broadest public concerns. He sought to combine a sensitivity to the public mood and to a pluralist view of society with strong centralized leadership and an attempt to set a moral tone in society.

Blair was born into a Conservative family. His father, Leo, was a law lecturer and Tory activist in the north-east of England. A stroke in 1963 ended Leo's political ambitions and resulted in a significant drop in the income of the Blair family. Tony Blair went to the top Scottish public school, Fettes College, on a scholarship, and was by all accounts a bright but rebellious pupil. Blair junior was not born into the Labour party – he *chose* to join it, as he later said. Neither was he a political animal in a party sense at school or later at Oxford: he preferred acting and rock music, playing in a band *Ugly Rumours*. At Oxford Blair threw himself into religious, philosophical and political discussions with a regular group of friends. He read the works of the philosopher John Macmurray whose idea of community involved a radical critique of liberal individualism – and also of Christian ethical socialists such as R.H. Tawney, who saw socialism as a 'remoralization' of capitalist society. At St John's College Blair was confirmed in the Church of England.

Blair graduated in 1975 and moved to London to train as a barrister, joining the Labour party the following year. He became a pupil at the chambers of Alexander Irvine, later to be Lord Chancellor in Blair's first cabinet. The other pupil in Irvine's chambers was Cherie Booth who, unlike Blair, *was* born into the

Labour party – her left-wing father, the actor Tony Booth, had played the socialist son-in-law to the bigoted working-class Alf Garnett in the long-running BBC television serial, *Till Death Us Do Part*. Blair and Booth married in 1980. Both were seeking parliamentary seats and in the early 1980s it was Cherie Booth more than Tony Blair who looked set for the political career. As a barrister Blair specialized in employment law. In public Blair was an assiduous supporter of party policy. Behind the scenes, however, he was a modernizer in the making. His politics in the early 1980s were characterized by an attempt to steer a middle course between the old social democratic right, exemplified by the former prime minister James Callaghan, and the 'hard' left led by Tony Benn who wished to see Labour take up much more radical socialist policies. Blair's first attempt to enter parliament was at a 1982 by-election for the safe Conservative seat of Beaconsfield. At the 1983 general election he was elected to parliament for Sedgefield in the north-east of England.

The 1983 election was Labour's nadir. But under a new leader, Neil Kinnock, the modernization of the party began. Kinnock believed that the hard left inside the party had to be marginalized; and in the case of the Marxist 'Militant Tendency', expelled. Under Kinnock policies of the 1983 election manifesto, such as nationalization and withdrawal from the European Community, slowly disappeared. As a new MP Blair was a Kinnock supporter and a member of the 'soft' left Tribune group which was willing to work with a reforming party leadership. In his 1983 maiden speech to the Commons, he defined socialism as community; he argued for equality not of outcomes but as the basis for the fulfilment of individual potential. Inside parliament Blair assisted John Smith, then Labour's employment spokesman and a leading figure on the right of the party, on trade union issues. Blair shared a Commons room with another of the new 1983 intake of MPs, Gordon Brown, who was to become Chancellor of the Exchequer in the 1997 government. Brown was already a formidable party figure. Within a year Blair, the youngest Labour MP, joined the shadow Treasury team under Roy Hattersley. But over the next few years, of the 'two bright boys' as Tory diarist Alan Clark dubbed them, it was Brown not Blair who seemed destined for the highest political honours.

Although by 1987 the presentation of the Labour message had been transformed, the party nevertheless lost the general election. In defeat Kinnock established a formal policy review which lasted until the next election in 1992 (Smith and Speer 1992; Shaw 1996). Blair became deputy to the shadow Trade and Industry Secretary Bryan Gould, with special responsibility for the City and consumer affairs, and following his election to the shadow cabinet in 1988 was appointed shadow Energy Secretary with the job of fighting electricity privatization. His promotion in 1989 to shadow Employment Secretary enabled Blair, the fully fledged modernizer, to shift Labour policy to acceptance of Conservative trade union reforms on the closed shop and mass picketing – reforms which he had opposed vigorously in the early 1980s.

Kinnock's policy review led to significant shifts in policy on the economy, industrial relations, Europe and defence; at the 1992 election the party supported the market economy, membership of the European Economic Exchange Rate Mechanism, and multilateral rather than unilateral nuclear disarmament. The Tory government's privatizations and trade union laws would stay. As a leading member of Kinnock's shadow team, Blair had been at the heart of these policy changes. The party's defeat at the 1992 election was widely blamed on what Conservatives had called Labour's 'tax bombshell': higher rates of tax and national insurance to fund increases in pensions and child benefit. The policy review had failed to rid the Labour party of these last vestiges of tax-and-spend – a point not lost on Blair in the run-up to the 1997 election as he promised to stick to the Conservative government's spending plans and not to raise income tax rates.

Defeated for a second time Kinnock resigned, and John Smith was elected Labour leader. Blair became shadow Home Secretary. Across the Atlantic self-styled 'New Democrat' Bill Clinton had become US President in 1992 by distancing himself from the New Deal and Great Society traditions in the Democratic party. Clinton had campaigned on a platform of free trade, tax cuts, deficit reduction, supply-side economics and value-for-money welfare reform, projecting a populist communitarianism of rights and responsibilities, civic duties and family values. Clinton also promised to be tough on crime. In a visit to the USA in January 1993 Blair absorbed the Clinton message, and soon after his return he uttered in a BBC Radio interview what was to become a classic soundbite: a Labour government would be 'tough on crime and tough on the causes of crime'. The novelty was in the first part of the sentence. During the 1992 election campaign, Conservatives had accused the Labour party of being 'soft on crime' – and the voters agreed. As shadow Home Secretary Blair began to outflank the Tories on law-and-order issues, a process continued by Jack Straw, his successor after Blair became leader. Blair, and then Straw, shifted Labour's traditional focus on the causes of crime – unemployment and poverty – to a far greater emphasis on the personal responsibility of criminals for their actions and for the need for toughness on crime in terms of policing and the criminal justice system. As shadow Home Secretary and then as party leader, Blair injected a conservative moral communitarianism into Labour party thinking. He argued that rights (to social security, for example) were conditional on fulfilling responsibilities; and that greater attention should be paid to the duties and obligations (of parents, for example) which provided the basis for communal life. Blair offered a distinctive message in the 1990s. The get-what-you-can individualism of the Conservatives and the rights-claiming permissiveness of the left were as bad as each other: both had undermined the ethical basis of society which Blair suggested new Labour would help to rebuild by supporting the family and by being tough on law and order. In taking up such a position Blair drew accusations of social conservativism, even authoritarianism. Yet he remained a liberal on many issues such as the death penalty, race, sexuality and abortion.

As a member of the Labour party's National Executive Committee (NEC), Blair supported greater democracy inside the party. Since the early 1980s he had advocated 'one person one vote', and in the following decade he campaigned to reduce the role of the trade union block vote. In a compromise typical of John Smith's leadership of the party, the block vote was retained for deciding policy at the annual party conference, but 'one member one vote' was adopted for choosing parliamentary candidates and the party leader.

In May 1994 Smith died of a heart attack. It was immediately clear that the chief contenders for his job were Brown and Blair. At first Brown had achieved higher votes than Blair in NEC contests and was widely considered to be more likely leadership material. After 1993 Blair drew ahead of Brown, impressing in his job as shadow Home Secretary while Brown faced a rougher ride as shadow Chancellor of the Exchequer. After Smith's death Brown stood aside for Blair, and in the election which followed Blair decisively beat John Prescott and Margaret Beckett, both from the left of the party. Blair was the first Labour leader to be elected by a voting procedure which bestowed upon him a personal mandate from individual party members, freeing him from attachment to any particular sectional interest within the party.

The party Blair inherited was one already in the throes of modernization, and what he would later label 'old' Labour had been beaten by the time he became leader. Blair moved to consolidate the modernization of the party and to accelerate the pace of policy reform. In doing so he proved a more radical modernizer than Smith, more willing to take on and outvote opponents rather than aim for compromise and consensus. In his first speech to the annual party conference as leader, Blair argued that as *new* Labour they should 'say what they mean and mean what they say'. This, it quickly transpired, was Blair's code for rewriting Clause Four of the party's constitution, which committed Labour to the common ownership of property.

Blair's argument for a modernized Clause Four was that 'new times' required new policies to achieve old socialist values such as community and social justice. To Blair the old Clause Four committed Labour to an outdated policy – the nationalization of private property. It was a means not an end in itself; and a means moreover that no Labour government had any intention of putting into practice. After a ballot of individual party members, a new statement of aims and values was adopted. Common ownership was removed and replaced by a commitment to the 'dynamic market economy' and to greater individual opportunities. The new Clause Four consolidated an important shift in official party thinking away from opposition to support for market capitalism, and from an egalitarian to a meritocratic understanding of social justice.

This early test of Blair's leadership was achieved without a return to the disunity which had marked Labour politics in the 1980s. In the face of an increasingly divided Conservative government and an apparently weak prime minister, John Major, the rewriting of Clause Four strengthened Blair's position within the Labour party, enabling him to project the image of a strong and decisive leader willing to distance himself from the ideas of old Labour and from the record of past Labour governments.

Under Blair new Labour became a party committed to free markets, low taxes, sound money and welfare reform. Blair nailed the Labour party's colours to low inflation as the central macro-economic objective. Keynesian demand management to create full employment – the heart of Labour's post-war social democracy – was, Blair argued, impossible in a global economy. Instead, he and his shadow Chancellor, Gordon Brown, shifted Labour's emphasis to supply-side micro-economics: in particular, to policies for enhancing the skills of labour which, they argued, would attract investment and equip workers to respond to the insecurities of flexible labour markets. Protection for workers needed to be kept to a minimum to allow for greater flexibility, but would include a minimum wage and the European Union social chapter. This shift in the Labour party's economic policy reflected debates on the centre-left about the relative merits of different models of capitalism. Britain, according to Blair, needed to follow the flexible, free-market route of the Anglo-American tradition rather than the more heavily regulated model of continental Europe. Blair also projected Labour as the party of the post-industrial generation (the 'young country') committed to the new information technologies and supportive of the British cultural and design industries.

With regard to the welfare state, which Labour had done so much to build, Blair urged new Labour to 'think the unthinkable', arguing that welfare should give a 'hand up, not a hand out' and that high social security bills were a sign of policy failure rather than success. Under Blair, the party adopted a welfare-to-work programme to help the unemployed and single parents find work. Welfare-to-work broke new ground for the party: the young unemployed had the right to a job or training opportunity but they also had a responsibility to accept what was offered them. This, some claimed, amounted to a coercive 'workfare' scheme: working for benefits. Labour also proposed a reform of the tax-and-benefit system to 'make work pay' for the unemployed. In Blair's 'stakeholder' philosophy, the labour market is the principal means for giving the excluded a route back into participation in society. Under Blair the party also began to advocate greater individual responsibility for pension provision. With regard to education Blair and David Blunkett, who became Secretary of State for Education in the 1997 government, largely accepted the Conservative government's structural reforms of the 1980s and shifted attention to standards in teaching and learning.

New Labour also advocated modernization of the British constitution including devolution for Scotland and Wales; a greater role for English regional government and enhanced powers for local government (including elected mayors); abolition of hereditary peers in the Lords; and incorporation of the European Convention on Human Rights. Blair promised to restore the 'trust' in government by making politics cleaner, more open and more accountable. On Europe he promised that a Labour government would be a constructive partner without conceding the British national interest; a position continued in office with the announcement that the country would not join the single currency until after the next general election.

The party's political communications, reformed by Peter Mandelson in the 1980s, were further modernized under Blair. The selling of new Labour to the voters focused on Blair as the young, attractive and dynamic leader, a tactic which reinforced a trend towards the 'personalization' of British campaign politics and to the increasingly presidential character of British general elections (Foley 1993). In opposition the Labour party went on to a permanent campaign footing, using the latest media techniques such as focus groups to test the party's 'message' with voters and an 'instant rebuttal unit' to counter the Conservative message. (Later, when in government, this campaigning culture would cause friction between ministers' policy advisers and civil servants because of the blurring of the distinction between government and party communications.) Blair appointed the former political editor of the *Daily Mirror* and *Today*, Alastair Campbell, as his press secretary to help the Labour party set the news agenda and he courted the largely Tory-supporting press; as the 1997 campaign officially started, the *Sun*, which had vilified Kinnock in 1992, came out for Blair.

Following the Labour party's defeat in 1992, political scientists debated whether the election had been its last chance to form a government (Heath *et al.* 1994). After four straight election wins, the Conservatives looked like the natural party of government. The political sociology of Britain appeared to some to be loading the electoral dice against the Labour party: the working class was shrinking in absolute terms; and 'class dealignment' meant that working-class voters were less likely to vote on class lines for the Labour party (Crewe 1993). Labour modernizers such as Giles Radice urged Blair to win over 'middle England': the middle-class and skilled working-class voters, particularly in southern Britain, who had voted for Thatcher in the 1980s (Radice and Pollard 1994). Blair responded by rewriting Clause Four and by drawing a line under the Thatcherite reforms of successive Conservative governments. Blair's intention was that new Labour would set a 'post-Thatcherite agenda' rather than reverse Tory reforms by returning to a pre-1979 form of politics. Blair reached beyond class and party, projecting new Labour as the party of individual opportunity and 'One Nation', an 'inclusive' politics which crossed the boundaries of left and right. New Labour, Blair suggested, was a party of the 'radical centre'. In opposition he offered an olive branch to former social democrats who had left the party in the early 1980s, and also wooed disaffected Tories, such as the MP Alan Howarth, who eventually crossed the floor of the Commons. Blair supported a less adversarial, even pluralistic, form of politics. He established a working relationship with the Liberal Democrat party which continued in government when he offered its leader, Paddy Ashdown, seats on a cabinet committee to consider constitutional reform. And just as Blair distanced new Labour from the trade unions, so he forged links with the business world which were maintained in government as ministerial and policy review appointments were made. Yet for all this, Blair remained hostile to proportional representation for general elections on the ground that it would undermine 'strong government' by a single party.

The Labour party's sweeping victory on 1 May 1997 – the 'first past the post' electoral system delivered a 179 seat Commons majority on a minority vote – was testament to Blair's ability to reassure voters in a mood for a change that the party could be trusted to govern. Blair successfully projected the modernization of the Labour party as a precursor for the modernization of Britain: 'New Labour, New Britain'. The party's share of the vote was up by 10.8 per cent on 1992. Crucially, the Labour party increased its share of the middle-class vote, from 24 to 40 per cent, though it is worth noting that more people voted for John Major in the 1992 election than did for Blair in 1997. In bringing to an end eighteen years of Conservative government, the result showed that the competitive party system was back in business; and that government and opposition still had a meaningful place in the British political system.

In his first months as prime minister Blair displayed two characteristic sides to his political personality: commanding leadership and sensitivity to the people's mood. He moved quickly to reorganize and consolidate the powers of the 'core executive': in particular, the Downing Street press and policy units, and the cabinet office. Blair's view was that the centre of government was too weak under the Major administration. Peter Mandelson was appointed Minister without Portfolio inside the cabinet office to co-ordinate the work of government departments; and a strategy committee of the cabinet was established under Blair's chairmanship. The government also published a new ministerial code. Aside from notes on the personal conduct of ministers, the code required all media contacts and policy initiatives by ministers to be cleared in advance by Downing Street. Political commentators were divided on the significance of the innovation. Some viewed it as marking a shift to a 'presidential' form of government which undermined collective responsibility, cabinet government and ministerial responsibility for departments and policy-making: a move marking a return to the style of leadership – admired by Blair – practised by Thatcher. Others argued that strong leadership from the centre was already common practice in British government; and also that, once Labour's plans to devolve power away from Westminster and Whitehall were taken into consideration, Blair's style of leadership reflected not a return to 'elective dictatorship' but a more effective use of those powers retained by central government post-devolution (Mandelson 1997).

The death of Diana, Princess of Wales, on 31 August 1997 cast Blair as populist leader. As the news broke of her death Blair spoke with apparent emotion, prefiguring widespread displays of public grief. Blair called her the 'people's princess', showing awareness of her popular appeal, and negotiated a public funeral with the royal household that incorporated representatives of charities she represented and ordinary people she had met. Blair's own 'compassionate' agenda, and concern 'for the many and not just the few', seemed in tune with a public mood which responded to the Princess's perceived like-minded humanitarianism and popular touch. At his first conference speech as prime minister, which came weeks after her death, he claimed that the government expressed a 'giving age' of increased compassion.

Assessments of Blair broadly fall into two camps (Kenny and Smith 1997). One view is that he modernized the Labour party within the social democratic tradition by taking account of the changing social and economic context of the late twentieth century, especially 'globalization'. On this reading, new Labour retained old left values such as community and social justice while finding fresh policies to express them. Another view is that Blair abandoned socialist values in the pursuit of power: for some Blair became the 'son of Thatcher' by embracing neo-liberal economics and neo-conservative social policies; while for others new Labour stole the mantle of One Nation Toryism. It is perhaps more plausible to characterize Blair as a 'post-Thatcherite'. While radically breaking with the Labour party's past (and with social democracy) and nudging the party on to Thatcherite economic and social territory, he remained deeply critical of neo-liberal economic individualism. Blair was both attracted to Thatcherism and repelled by its neo-liberal aspects which, according to him, engendered social division and exclusion as well as moral decay. It remains to be seen whether Blair's market communitarianism can be distilled into hard policies.

References and further reading

Anderson, P. and Mann, N. (1997) *Safety First: The Making of New Labour*, London: Granta.

Blair, T. (1996) *New Britain: My Vision of a Young Country*, London: Fourth Estate. (A collection of Blair's articles and speeches.)

Crewe, I. (1993) 'Voting and the electorate', in P. Dunleavy, A. Gamble, I. Holliday and G. Peele (eds) *Developments in British Politics 4*, London: Macmillan. (Provides an accessible survey of British electoral politics and the problems faced by the Labour party after 1992.)

Driver, S. and Martell, L. (1998) *New Labour: Politics after Thatcherism*, Cambridge: Polity Press.

Foley, M. (1993) *The Rise of the British Presidency*, Manchester: Manchester University Press.

Heath, A., Jowell, R. and Curtice, J. (eds) (1994) *Labour's Last Chance? The 1992 Election and Beyond*, Aldershot: Dartmouth.

Jones, T. (1996) *Remaking the Labour Party: From Gaitskell to Blair*, London: Routledge.

Kenny, M. and Smith, M. (1997) '(Mis)understanding Blair', *Political Quarterly* 68: 220–30.

McSmith, A. (1996) *Faces of Labour: The Inside Story*, London: Verso. (Especially Chapter 7, 'Calling Tony Blair'.)

Mandelson, P. (1997) *Labour's Next Steps: Tackling Social Exclusion*, London: Fabian Society.

Radice, G. and Pollard, S. (1994) *Any Southern Comfort?* London: Fabian Society.

Rentoul, J. (1995) *Tony Blair*, London: Little, Brown.

Shaw, E. (1996) *The Labour Party since 1945*, Oxford: Blackwell.

Smith, M. and Speer, J. (eds) (1992) *The Changing Labour Party*, London: Routledge.

Sopel, J. (1995) *Tony Blair, The Moderniser*, London: Michael Joseph.

Stephen Driver and Luke Martell

INDEX

Note: Major entries for prime ministers are **emboldened**

Elgin, Thomas Bruce, 7th Earl of 168, 243
Elizabeth II, Queen 325, 327, 373–4
Elliott, A. 181
Ellman, R. 223
Emancipation Bill 92
Empire *see* imperialism
employment 200, 305; *see also* unemployment
EMS *see* European Monetary System
Emy, H. 250
English, Richard ix; on Wellington 123–8
entente cordiale 170–1, 178, 234
ERM *see* Exchange Rate Mechanism
Errol, Frederick 330
Esher, Lord 255
Establishment Bill 53
Europe *see* Central and Eastern Europe; Western Europe
European Common Market/European Economic Community and later European Union: and Blair 394, 396; and Callaghan 351; and Douglas-Home 331, 332; and Eden 317; and Heath 344–9 *passim*; and Macmillan 326; and Major 387–8, 389–90; and Thatcher 359, 370, 376–8; and Wilson 337, 339
European Convention on Human Rights 396
European Monetary System 376
Evangelicalism 101, 103, 105, 197, 331
Evans, Eric ix; on Liverpool 106–16; on Melbourne 136–42
Evans, H. 325
Everest, Mrs 296
Exchange Rate Mechanism 376–7, 387–8, 394
excise *see* duties/excise
Exeter, Lord *see* Gascoyne-Cecil
expenditure, public: and Attlee 313; and Callaghan 353, 354; and Campbell-Bannerman 240; and Heath 346; and Liverpool 110; and Macmillan 320, 323; and North 68, 69; and Russell 157; and Thatcher 367; and Wilson 339; *see also* economic and financial policy

Fabians 225, 229, 237, 282, 283, 306
Factory Acts 128, 135, 180, 245
Falklands War 367–8, 376

famine in Ireland 149, 156, 164, 178
fascism 274, 307; *see also* Hitler
Feuchtwanger, E. 201
Fielding, Henry 12
Fielding, S. 310
finance *see* economic and financial policy
Finance Bill (1965) 344
Finland 181
First Lord of the Treasury: Addington as 96; Bute as 36, 39; Devonshire as 35; Grenville, George as 44; Grenville, William as 99; Newcastle as 29, 30, 39, 55; North as 66, 68; Pelham as 19–20, 29; Pitt the Younger as 96; Portland as 77, 82; Shelburne as 79; Sunderland as 4; Walpole as 2, 3, 4, 6, 8–9; Wilmington as 16
First World War: and Asquith 244, 247–9, 250; and Attlee 306; and Balfour 234, 235, 238; and Bonar Law 266, 267–9; and Chamberlain 289; and Churchill 298; and Eden 315–16; and Lloyd George 234, 253, 254–6, 260; and MacDonald 283, 286
Fisher, John Arbuthnot, 1st Baron 267
FitzGerald, Garret 371–2
Fitzgerald, Vesey 125
Fitzmaurice, Lord E. 160
Fitzroy, Anne (née Liddell, wife of Grafton) 61
Fitzroy, Augustus Henry *see* Grafton
Fitzroy, Elizabeth (née Wrottesley, wife of Grafton) 61
Fitzwilliam, William, 2nd Earl 81, 82, 92, 100
Foley, M. xiii 397
food tax suggested 264
Foot, Michael 351, 353, 354, 356, 368
Foot, P. 335
Ford, Gerald 353
foreign policy: and Aberdeen 169–71; and Attlee 305; and Balfour 232–3; and Blair 394, 396; and Bonar Law 267–8, 270–1; and Bute 37–9, 40; and Callaghan 351, 353; and Canning 118–19; and Churchill 297, 299; and Disraeli 192–4; and Douglas-Home 330–1; and Eden 315–19; and Gladstone 196–7, 203–8; and Goderich 121; and Grafton 62, 63; and Grenville, George 43–5; and Grenville, William 100; and Heath 344–9 *passim*; and